Hands-On ATM

ATM Professional Reference Series

To order or receive additional information on these or any other McGraw-Hill titles, in the United States please call 1-800-722-4726. In other countries, contact your local McGraw-Hill representative.

Hands-On ATM

David E. McDysan

Darren L. Spohn

McGraw-Hill

New York   San Francisco   Washington, D.C.   Auckland   Bogotá
Caracas   Lisbon   London   Madrid   Mexico City   Milan
Montreal   New Delhi   San Juan   Singapore
Sydney   Tokyo   Toronto

Library of Congress Cataloging-in-Publication Data

McDysan, David E.
     Hands-on ATM / David E. McDysan, Darren L. Spohn.
          p.   cm.—(The McGraw-Hill series on computer communications)
     Includes index.
     ISBN 0-07-045047-1
     1. Asynchronous transfer mode.   2. Internetworking
(Telecommunication)   3. Local area networks (Computer networks)
4. Wide area networks (Computer networks)   I. Spohn, Darren L.
II. Title.   III. Series.
TK5105.35.M34   1998
004.6′6—dc21   97-46059
                                                                CIP

McGraw-Hill

A Division of The McGraw·Hill Companies

1 2 3 4 5 6 7 8 9 0   FGR/FGR   9 0 2 1 0 9 8 7

ISBN 0-07-045047-1

*The sponsoring editor for this book was Steven M. Elliot, the editing supervisor
was Stephen M. Smith, and the production supervisor was Tina Cameron.*

Printed and bound by Quebecor / Fairfield.

McGraw-Hill books are available at special quantity discounts to use as pre-
miums and sales promotions, or for use in corporate training programs. For
more information, please write to the Director of Special Sales, McGraw-Hill,
11 West 19th Street, New York, NY 10011. Or contact your local bookstore.

This book is printed on recycled, acid-free paper containing a
minimum of 50% recycled, de-inked fiber.

Contents

Preface

PURPOSE OF THIS BOOK

Why did we decide to write this book? A lot has happened since the publication of our first book, *ATM: Theory and Application,* in the fall of 1994. The content-driven surge of the World Wide Web is taking data networking into the next millennium beyond the previous benchmarks set by the ubiquitous voice networks that encircle our planet. Internet service providers have turned to Asynchronous Transfer Mode (ATM) backbones to handle the intense load as traffic volumes double of quadruple each year. Simultaneously, many government and research networks continue to deploy ATM networks. Concurrently, convinced of ATM's inherently lower life-cycle costs, corporations are installing high-performance ATM local area networks, private networks, and WANs based on private ATM networks and public ATM services. The range of products and services being offered are now nearly a multibillion-dollar business. As further evidence of ATM's move towards ubiquity, every major carrier around the globe now offers ATM service.

With all of this going on, we just couldn't fit it all into one book. Therefore, we decided to split the material into two volumes: this one — *Hands-On ATM* — and an update to our best-selling book, *ATM: Theory and Application.* *Hands-On ATM* takes a higher-level, less technically detailed look at the broad range of technologies that now intersect with ATM. We've also moved all of the ATM device vendor, service provider, and market information into *Hands-On ATM* to make space for additional technical coverage of advanced topics in the expanded *ATM: Theory and Application.* Detailed comparison tables obtained from our survey of vendors and carriers highlight Parts 3 and 4 of this *Hands-On ATM.* This book also summarizes all of the key ATM-related protocols, but ties each back to its business roots and drivers, leaving the more detailed technical exposition to the forthcoming second edition of *ATM: Theory and Application.*

Great strides have been made in the area of ATM protocol standardization. Therefore, Part 2 of *Hands-On ATM* provides an up-to-date overview of the ATM protocol landscape. Several activities and close cooperation between standards bodies made this happen. Inevitably, the NATO treaty–initiated International Telecommunications Union and the upstart ATM Forum are cooperating. Also, the de facto standards body for the Internet, the Internet Engineering Task Force, has been busy in concert with the ATM Forum crafting methods for internetworking over ATM. Highlights from the standards arena include LAN emulation, multiprotocol support, and a cornucopia of methods for supporting the Internet Protocol (IP) over ATM.

Meanwhile, major changes have occurred elsewhere in the networking world, as we summarize in Parts 5 and 6. The local area networking market has entered a commodity phase where price is king. Gigabit Ethernet claims to offer local area networking price benefits over ATM once it is standardized. And although SMDS and SNA seem to be setting with the sunset, technologies that postdate ATM continue to enter the scene, sporting new paradigms for transferring IP over ATM. The efficiency of packet transfer over ATM has also come under criticism from those requiring only best-effort datagram services. Now that router manufacturers have learned to make devices that go real fast, they can do so for ATM without requiring the use of advanced hardware. No matter which technology wins out in the marketplace, the concepts of guaranteed bandwidth and quality of service tailored to specific voice, video, and data application needs are certain to remain. At the same time, ATM continues to expand into new frontiers: wireless, satellite, and high-performance access into the home. We invite you to join us in sharing this fast-paced, exciting glimpse into the future, and welcome your feedback!

INTENDED AUDIENCE

This book provides a high-level summary of ATM protocols, operation, standards, technology, and services for use by the data communications manager, network design engineer, and student of data networking. The book has been written to appeal to professionals, with the structure designed to first educate the reader on the business drivers, then give the principles of how ATM meets these needs, and conclude with real-life hands-on networking experience. Specific details are provided for key points in understanding the technology, with technical references identified for the reader who wishes to pursue a particular subject further.

The reader should have some prior knowledge of telecommunications principles, although some of the basics of data transmission are briefly covered. Many principles set forth in the book *Data Network Design, Second Edition,* by Darren Spohn (McGraw-Hill, 1997) are not reiterated; instead references are given to that text and other books for readers who want to study or refresh their knowledge in certain background areas. Specific interest groups include telecommunication and computer professionals, IS staff, LAN/WAN designers, network administrators, capacity planners, programmers, and program managers. This book is written at a higher level with less technical detail than our first book in a sincere attempt to communicate to a broader audience the hands-on application of ATM to solve real-world business problems. Therefore, groups other than the technical professional will also benefit, including sales and marketing, end users of the technology, and corporate executives who want an overview of how ATM technology and services might be used to make an impact on their business. Both LAN managers/administrators and data design engineers must be well versed in the principles presented and be able to communicate these principles effectively to their management. Computing and engineering professionals must have a good understanding of current technology to make wise corporate decisions on their data communication needs, which may certainly involve ATM for many years to come. Thus, the book seeks to address the issues and needs of the local area network, wide area network, and end-user application communities, highlighting commonalties as well as differences in these diverse environments.

The book is written in a light, easy reading style in order to retain the reader's interest during the dry topics while making the learning process more enjoyable. Befitting its higher-level approach, this book contains no equations or formulas. A word of caution: Readers may find inconsistencies in descriptions of protocols and the ever-evolving ATM standards because of the changing state of affairs found in standardization processes. We attempt to address this by providing in an appendix detailed references as well as information on how to obtain the latest standards. While we attempted to keep the text accurate up to the time of publication, the reader is urged to use the sources provided to confirm information and obtain the latest published standards.

OVERVIEW OF THIS BOOK

This book begins by considering key business needs and market trends, followed by definitions of basic technical terminology as an introduction to readers unfamiliar with ATM. The text then summarizes the current state of ATM technical standards' support for video, voice, local area networks and the IP. A companion book, *ATM: Theory and Application, Second Edition*, covers the suite of ATM-based protocols in detail. The text features a 1997 view of available ATM devices and carrier services through a set of comparison tables and narratives provided by the vendors and carriers. Devices reviewed include workgroup switches, Network Interface Cards (NICs), and carrier switches. We also review some basic design principles for private and public networks, and give case studies across a broad range of applications to illustrate how ATM meets real business and government needs. Finally, we compare ATM with competing technologies, such as IP and gigabit Ethernet, concluding with our opinion on the prognosis for ATM in the major business networking environments — the home, the workgroup, the local backbone, and the carrier edge and core switching networks.

Although this book provides a summary of current standards, it brings the concepts up a level through illustrations, examples, and real-world applications to make the transition from theory and application to-hands on practicality. In this book we strive to teach the reader not only what the ATM-based technologies involve, but why each subject is important.

In some ways, the book presents an unconventional point of view. Taking the same tack as our first book, we don't assume that the paradigm of a voice-oriented telephony structure will be the future of data communications. Narrowband ISDN (N-ISDN) will not make the transition to extensive hands-on application, despite a resurgence as the only technology to provide high-performance access to the Web, while Ethernet and the Internet have taken the world by storm. The promise of even higher performance Asymmetric Digital Subscriber Line (ADSL) technologies will eclipse ISDN's brief renaissance. Since the Internet has become the de facto networking protocol standard, we focus a great deal of material on how ATM applies to real-world internets, intranets, and extranets.

Like other books in this series, this text covers the three critical aspects of: business drivers, technology, and practical, hands-on application. This is a very action-oriented text, interleaving descriptive material with application notes and the results of actual networking experience. You will also see a slant toward designing networks, citing references to complementary texts and sources for further detail for the reader interested in more depth.

Hands-On ATM covers the subject of applied ATM networking in six parts.

Part 1 covers networking basics, including a discussion of the business drivers for ATM, explores computer and information networking directions, and introduces the basic concepts of ATM.

Chapter 1 introduces ATM and summarizes its business drivers. These include the real business benefits of reduced cost and higher performance. The needs of user applications as business drivers are then explored, ending with the accelerating bandwidth principle.

Chapter 2 covers the role of ATM technology in the marketplace. The material covers technological advances which enable ATM and lower networking costs. A market forecast for ATM products and services indicates that ATM has achieved critical mass in the wide area network, yet certain critical factors are still needed for ATM to play a key role in the LAN. It concludes with a summary of ATM benefits and risks.

Chapter 3 sets ATM in the context of the rapidly changing computer and information networking environment. It begins with a review of the evolving corporate communications environment, ranging from the desktop to the local area network and client-server networking domains to the rapidly growing world of intranets and extranets. This chapter presents a brief analysis of outsourcing and the status of the battle for the desktop, the LAN, and the WAN.

Chapter 4 reviews the basics of transmission systems, network topologies and connection types as background. Here, we also introduce basic protocol layering concepts used throughout the book. The chapter also presents an overview of bridging and routing, along with a discussion of connectionless and connection-oriented data services. It concludes with a review of private, public, and virtual private data networking.

Chapter 5 provides an introduction to ATM, beginning with a view of its many facets: an interface, a protocol, a technology, an access method, an infrastructure, and a service. We then introduce ATM terminology through high-level illustrations and analogies. The chapter concludes with some illustrations of ATM's key attribute: multiple service qualities.

Part 2 covers the basics of the ATM protocol landscape, providing a structured introduction and reference to all ATM-related terminology, protocols, and standards.

Chapter 6 presents the overall broadband ISDN protocol reference model, which defines the concepts of the user, control, and management planes. This chapter then summarizes the physical-layer and ATM-layer protocols. It continues with a practitioner-level guide to the ATM traffic contract and quality of service. We conclude with an overview of the available bit rate closed-loop congestion control technique.

Chapter 7 covers the ATM Adaptation Layer (AAL), which provides support for all higher-layer services, such as signaling, circuit emulation, frame relay, and IP. It concludes by introducing the remaining chapters of the book, which cover control plane signaling; the higher layers in the user plane in the WAN, LAN and the internetwork; and the management plane.

Chapter 8 summarizes the concepts and standards of the ATM control plane, focusing on the signaling protocol itself and how it establishes connections of various types. This chapter also introduces the important Private Network-to-Network Interface (PNNI) protocol defined by the ATM Forum.

Chapter 9 moves on to the support of higher-layer protocols in the user plane. Specifically, the chapter covers the emulation of Time-Division Multiplexed (TDM) circuits and interworking with narrowband ISDN. It also covers video on demand, along with interworking with frame relay and SMDS. Also, the business implications of frame-based ATM interfaces are discussed.

Chapter 10 moves into the local area network, beginning with a tutorial on key concepts of LAN protocols, bridging, and routing. It concludes with a review of the LAN emulation protocol and its advantages over traditional LAN bridging.

Chapter 11 is a lengthy chapter covering ATM's internetworking role. It begins with a brief introduction to the Internet Protocol, routing, and addressing. The coverage moves on to standards support for carrying multiple protocols over ATM, negotiating maximum packet sizes, and classical IP over ATM for a single logical IP subnetwork. We then introduce the newer subjects of multiprotocol over ATM, IP multicast over ATM, and the set of new capabilities being developed in the IETF's MultiProtocol Label Switching group.

Chapter 12 concludes Part 2 by covering the often-slighted subjects of network management and testing. We cover not only the standards, but some real-world network management and testing systems.

Part 3 presents a categorization of vendor devices, the questions used in our survey, and the vendor and carrier responses.

Chapter 13 begins with a categorization of ATM devices as either carrier edge or backbone switches, enterprise edge or LAN backbone switches, or workgroup switches and desktop interfaces. It also presents the survey questions given out to the vendors.

Chapter 14 defines the characteristics of carrier edge and backbone ATM switches. It then summarizes the results of the vendor survey for carrier edge and backbone switches in tabular format.

Chapter 15 defines the characteristics of enterprise ATM devices. These include many device types that have ATM interfaces, including routers, switches, hubs, LAN/campus backbones, and private WAN networks. It then summarizes the results of the vendor survey for enterprise switches in tabular format.

Chapter 16 covers ATM workgroup switches and desktop adapters. A tabular summary compares the switches, and a detailed narrative gives an example of an ATM NIC.

Chapter 17 collects vendor-specific responses to our survey and reports on some general observations we made from analyzing the survey results.

Part 4 moves into the domain of ATM services and the carriers that provide them.

Chapter 18 introduces ATM service access methods ranging from 64 kbps to hundreds of Mbps. The chapter highlights the emerging ATM over Digital Subscriber Loop (xDSL) technology, which promises to extend high-performance, guaranteed quality service to the home office and residence. It also summarizes cable modems, telecommuting support, and voice over ATM.

Chapter 19 summarizes the status of ATM in the North American market, providing the results of a survey in tabular format.

Chapter 20 covers the status of ATM service provider activities for the rest of the world. It also covers the emerging ATM over satellite service.

Part 5 provides the reader with some generic ATM network design guidelines, applies these to private and hybrid public-private networks, and concludes with an analysis of some real-world case studies.

Chapter 21 walks the reader through the generic network design process of collecting user requirements and traffic forecasts. This chapter then considers migration strategies for getting applications to ATM, using videoconferencing as an example. We also present some design considerations that could affect application performance. The chapter concludes with some guidelines for migrating from frame relay to ATM.

Chapter 22 addresses the issues and considerations involved in designing private local area and wide area networks. It also discusses considerations involved in hybrid public-private networking, important criteria in selecting vendors and service providers, and further design considerations.

Chapter 23 presents a range of case studies from production and trial networks. The studies cover commercial, government, and research applications.

Part 6 provides the reader a comparison of technologies that compete with ATM and concludes with a look at the future of ATM.

Chapter 24 first covers technologies that compete with ATM in the local area network, including Fast Ethernet, LAN switching, and gigabit Ethernet. It then moves into the wide area network, focusing on the more efficient transfer using frame-based protocols when compared with ATM and AAL5. It concludes with a comparison of alternative and complementary means to deliver end-to-end quality of service (QoS), namely the IETF's Reservation Protocol and the Cells In Frames proposal.

Chapter 25 concludes the book with a view of the future, beginning with a review of how ATM continues to expand into new frontiers: satellite, ADSL, and wireless. Next, it considers the continual emergence of new applications and the need for increased performance. The chapter also discusses the contention and cooperation going on between IP and ATM, highlighting some of the challenges envisioned in achieving QoS with frame-based protocols. Finally, it concludes with some key challenges for ATM technology and service providers.

This book also contains two Appendixes. *Appendix A* lists the major acronyms and abbreviations used in the book. *Appendix B* provides a reference of national and international standards sources. A glossary of commonly used terms associated with the technologies, architectures, services, and protocols encountered throughout the book is provided at the end of the book, along with a detailed index.

INTRODUCTION

This book takes a new perspective on ATM, focusing on a hands-on, practical point of view. After an initial wave of media hype, ATM has made the transition from theory to application, and is in full production in Internet service provider networks, carrier services, and private corporate and government networks. The coincidence of the exponentially increasing power of computers, the increasing information transfer needs in the reengineering of business, and the vast content of the World Wide Web continues to drive a revolution in transmission, switching, and routing technologies. These trends combined create an accelerating need for bandwidth. Furthermore, the issue of different service qualities has now come to the forefront. Technology, applications, and businesses now need the power of ATM, which provides the only technique that simultaneously delivers high performance and differentiated qualities of service.

With books, timing is everything. The same is true with technology. ATM technology, standards, applications, and implementations have finally come of age. Many standards for ATM signaling, addressing, traffic management, network management, the physical layer, the ATM layer, and the AAL (where the true protocol intelligence resides in ATM) have been finalized for some time. Furthermore, a large degree of interoperability has been achieved between various ATM devices. The standards for higher-layer protocols targeted at the local area network and the Internet are now complete. We therefore believe that *now* is a good time for a higher-level book on ATM, summarizing the technology and standards, but focusing on the business drivers, user applications, and practical design guidelines.

This book provides all the information you need in order to determine if and how ATM will become part of your network. You will find that we do not present ATM from a myopic or biased view, but instead offer you a look at competing and complementing technologies such as Fast Ethernet, frame relay, and IP. In fact, ATM offers the capability to integrate these protocols and services into a single architecture that is scalable, flexible, and capable of handling bandwidths from several to hundreds of megabits per second, and even gigabits per second in the near future.

Many ATM books on the market today are either too technical (tied up in explaining every detail of the standard without relating to the reader what each aspect means to the user or provider) or too telephony-based, with the reader dragged through the older telephony point of view without the benefit of viewing the technology through the eyes of the data and computer communications user. This book attempts to show the many aspects of ATM through the eyes of the network manager focused on business objectives and the data communications user focused on productivity, as well as the ATM-based service designer or provider.

The demand for flexible, on-demand bandwidth for multimedia applications is growing. One technology for voice, data, and video integration, offering single access to a virtual data service, is a must. Data transfer bandwidths for text, video, voice, and imaging traffic are increasing exponentially, with data communications networks based on technologies such as ATM providing the intelligent network. We live in a distributed data world where everyone needs access to everyone else's data. Private lines are quickly becoming the exception as switched public and private data networks span the globe. Computers need to talk to one another the same way people pick up the phone and dial anyone else in the world. Because of this need, the market for high-speed data transport is exploding. The dawning of the age of gigabit-per-second data communication is upon us — witness the explosive growth of the Internet. LANs, MANs, and WANs have already crossed the 100-Mbps barrier and are moving toward gigabit-per-second, intelligent virtual data services.

LANs and the Internet have become an integral element of almost every major corporation. The move toward visually oriented end-user interfaces in computer software packages through the use of Graphical User Interfaces (GUIs) creates a tremendous need for flexible networking capabilities — witness the rapid adoption by business and residential users of the World Wide Web browser user interface. As the number of LANs and Web traffic continue to grow, so does the requirement to interconnect these LANs at native LAN speeds, and thus there is an emerging need for technologies like ATM. The low-speed private line bridge solutions are reaching their limits, further driving the need for higher-speed, cost-effective, flexible data networking.

Frame relay provides users with high-speed bandwidth-on-demand services which have displaced many private line networks. IP is the de facto networking standard to the desktop. ATM is poised to integrate aspects of multiple services over a single intelligent architecture and technology.

Many business bandwidth requirements are exploding: For example, medical institutions are transferring multimegabit imaging files, and filmmakers are transferring digitized video images, which are then stored and manipulated directly on a high-performance computer. An important aspect of these new-age networks is their ability to store and retrieve large image files. In the search for new technology to provide data communications on this scale, packet switching technology has seen a series of refinements that result in higher performance at lower costs. To wit, frame relay supplants X.25 for higher speeds, efficient IP implementations support sophisticated internetworking, and cell-based multiplexing and switching are positioned to replace time-division multiplexing and switching. As ATM-based services gain increasing support from equipment vendors, local exchange carriers, and interexchange carriers, user acceptance will be a key factor in determining the degree to which the technology succeeds.

After reviewing the available technologies and services, many users ask the classical questions: "Which service do I use?" and "Do I need ATM or just want ATM?" This book shows that the answers to these questions are based on many factors, and there may be multiple answers depending upon the specific user application. There is rarely a single solution, and the decision as to technology and service generally comes down to what is best for the application and what is affordable — price versus performance, as well as migration and future expansion considerations. The decision to use ATM, or an ATM-based public network service, is also a complicated one. This book presents the business and technological cases for the use of ATM, explains its use, and offers methods of implementation.

HOW TO USE THIS BOOK FOR COURSES

This book can be used to teach a single-semester course focused on a high-level view of ATM or a course surveying data communications technologies. It is not an introductory text in data communications, but it can stand alone for some readers with some technical background. Readers are also referred to *Data Network Design, Second Edition,* by Darren Spohn (McGraw-Hill, 1997) as an introductory text on the techniques and principles needed as background to this book.

The book can be used as a stand-alone text for a course intended to survey ATM networking with a focus on business implications and practical application. The vendor- and carrier-specific details of Parts 3 and 4 could be skipped in such a course.

A single-semester course surveying a broader range of data communications services (e.g., circuit switching, frame relay, SMDS, IP, and ATM) could use material from Parts 1, 2, and 6.

Labs should contain ATM design problems based on the cumulative knowledge gained from the class readings and outside reading assignments (recent technology updates). The exercises should involve multiple end-system and intermediate-system design problems. Because of the fluid nature of emerging ATM standards, students should be encouraged to use the text as a working document, noting any changes as the standards from the sources listed in the appendices are revised and updated. This is your book — write in it! The authors plan to publish updated editions as changes in technology and standards warrant. Supplemental documentation and instructional tools can be obtained from the authors at extra charge.

AUTHORS' DISCLAIMER

Accurate and timely information as of the date of publication was provided. Some standards used were drafts at the time of writing, and it was assumed that they would become approved standards by the time of publication. At times, the authors present material which is practical for a large-scale design, but must be scaled down for a smaller business communications environment. Many data communications networks will operate, and continue to run, quite well on a dedicated private line network, but eventually the economics of switched technologies and services, even on the smallest scale, are worth investigating. Please excuse the blatant assumption that the user is ready for these advanced technologies — in some cases it may take some time before these technologies can be implemented. Also, please excuse any personal biases which may have crept into the text.

ACKNOWLEDGMENTS

Many people have helped prepare this book. They have provided comments on various drafts, information on products and services, and other value-added services. In particular, we would like to thank our manuscript reviewers — Mr. Sudhir Gupta of DSC Communications; Mr. Herb Frizzell, Sr., Mr. Boris Gamarnik, Mr. Edsel Garciamendez-Budar, Mr. Wedge Greene, Ms. Claire Lewis, and Mr. James Liou of MCI Communications; and Mr. Craig Tysdal and Mr. Mike Powers of NetSolve. We would like to thank the following people for vendor- and product-specific contributions — Sultan Dawood of ADC Kentrox; Juan M. Calderon of Cabletron; Chris Baldwin and Joe Whitehouse of Cascade Communications; Mohammed Azhar Sayeed of DEC; Portia Switzer, Jim Critzer, Jack Reinhart, Seth Redmore, Mihir Mohanty, Robert Schiff, and Joe Skorupa of FORE Systems; Gary Lee at General DataComm, Inc.; Haissam Alaiwan, Michael Taddei, Bill Caldwell, and Tom Belz of IBM; David Boone of NEC America; Alex Horwitz and Vivian Kelly of

NewBridge Networks; Timothy J. Kraskey of Sahara Networks; Volker Tegt-meyer of Siemens Stromberg-Carlson; Neal Hartsell of Telematics International; and Liz Hervatic and Kevin Walsh of Xylan. We also thank our other colleagues who over the last several years have shared their knowledge and expertise. They have helped us develop a greater understanding and appreciation for ATM and data communications.

This book does not reflect any policy, position, or posture of MCI Communications or NetSolve. This work was not funded or supported financially by MCI Communications or NetSolve or by MCI Communications or NetSolve resources. Ideas and concepts expressed are strictly those of the authors. Information pertaining to specific vendor or service provider products is based upon open literature or submissions freely provided and adapted as required.

Also, special thanks to Mr. Herb Frizzell for the English style and syntax review, and to Debbie McDysan for the review and editing of the graphics.

Finally, we would like to thank Debbie McDysan and Becky Spohn for their support, encouragement, and sacrifice of time with their husbands while we were writing this book.

The combined support and assistance of these people has made this book possible.

David E. McDysan
Darren L. Spohn

1

NETWORKING BASICS

Why is everyone interested in Asynchronous Transfer Mode (ATM)? Is it an overhyped technology, or the catalyst for an impending explosion of multimedia applications? Will ATM penetrate the domain of the cost-competitive LAN? Or will it reside mainly in the WAN? Will it achieve the promised goal of end-to-end voice, video, and data communications? Part 1 answers these questions and more. ATM products and services have matured to the point that ATM can offer viable business benefits to almost any corporation. Basic ATM capabilities have already made the transition from the realm of theory to area of practical application. This book shows specifically how ATM can benefit you.

Before delving into the many facets of ATM applied to real-world business problems, Part 1 introduces the basics — the precursors to understanding ATM. These include the business drivers and enablers (Chapter 1), the move of many corporations away from centralized computing to distributed client-server processing (Chapter 2), the drastic increase in local, campus, metropolitan, and wide area network bandwidth requirements as well as the reengineering of the corporation (Chapter 3).

The next chapters introduce the reader to the unique terminology employed within ATM and the higher-layer protocols that employ ATM. Chapter 4 presents the basic building blocks of ATM, followed by a brief introduction to ATM terminology and examples in Chapter 5. Part 2 delves into more specifics of ATM, including quality of service, traffic management, adaptation layers, signaling and network management, as well as signaling, support for WAN and LAN protocols, internetworking and network management.

1

Business Drivers for ATM

Many business requirements drive the need for an Asynchronous Transfer Mode (ATM) network. Various factors make networks change and evolve, requiring continual redesign. Increasingly, data and computer communications are an integral part of any major business. As businesses continually reengineer themselves, they must also evolve their voice, video, and data networks to emerging requirements.

The adoption of multimedia, client-server applications, and intranet and Internet communications — along with broadband technologies such as frame relay and ATM — has intensified. The effect of the emerging broadband data networks and the Internet upon corporate data networking is nothing short of phenomenal. Sound business benefits warrant using ATM. This chapter explores the many changes and enablers affecting the data communications landscape, including:

- End-user applications requiring multimedia and real-time, high-speed data transfer
- Application demand for increased bandwidth in the Local Area Network (LAN) extended across the Wide Area Network (WAN), caused by the client-server architecture inherent in intranets
- Paradigm shifts in the computing environment that modify traffic types, patterns, and distribution
- Evolving changes in corporate infrastructure

The following analysis extrapolates the principles and trends of the late 20th century forward into the 21st century. Shifts in network paradigms occur because corporations and enterprises continually create innovative applications, technologies, and infrastructures to compete in their own market segments. This chapter introduces the business reasons that make ATM a viable, attractive alternative to competing networking technologies. The technical advances of ATM, buttressed by business reasons, establishes its merit as a network infrastructure and public service.

1.1 WHAT IS ATM — AND WHY SHOULD I CARE?

What is ATM, and why should you be interested in it? If someone sitting next to you on a plane were to ask you what you do and you answered ATM, what else would you say? How would you answer if the person wanted help getting back the $20 an ATM machine had shortchanged him or her? This section answers this question and more by briefly defining ATM from the 30,000-foot view. As the golden age of ATM was ushered in at about the same time as the reemergence of the David Letterman show, we will do a Letterman take-off and a humorous look at the top 10 reasons why ATM has not made it big right off, and why it will succeed in the end. Then we use the concepts of market acceptance and technology adoption to introduce the key enablers required if ATM is to move from the pioneering world of early innovators and adopters, across the chasm of product acceptance, and into the mass market and ubiquity of profitable products and services.

1.1.1 What Is ATM? The 30,000-Foot View

First, let's take a look at ATM from the window of our plane soaring high over the data communications landscape. Fundamentally, ATM is a technology that simultaneously transmits data, voice, and video traffic over high-bandwidth circuits, typically at hundreds of megabits per second (Mbps) in 1997 and even gigabits per second (Gbps) before the year 2000. ATM hardware and software platforms form a communications architecture based on the switching and relaying of small units of data, called *cells*. The primary differentiation between ATM-based services and other existing data communications services is that ATM is the first technology and protocol structure to effectively *integrate* voice, data, and video over the same communications channel at any speed.

Let's use an everyday example of planes, trains, and automobiles to illustrate ATM's support for multiple service categories. Just as airlines have different service categories (first class, business class, coach class); and trains have sleeper cars, freight cars, and box cars; and highways have high-occupancy vehicle (HOV) lanes, emergency lanes, and passing lanes; so too does ATM have varying methods of handling different types of users, or more accurately, application traffic. Just as different people have varied class requirements (first class, business class, coach class), applications also need different class requirements (voice, video, data). Applying the notion of service categories to communication networks, think of how corporations should assign a higher priority to their executive videoconferences, while consumers want to make sure voice conversations are not interrupted when files are being transferred across the Internet.

1.1.2 Top 10 Reasons Why ATM Has Not Made It Big

This section present a David Letterman–style list of the top 10 reasons why ATM has *not* made it big, but *will* succeed in the end.

10. ATM is high speed, and high speeds are too expensive in the WAN.
9. ATM is much more complex than originally envisioned.
8. Fast Ethernet exploded onto the scene.
7. Switched Virtual Circuits (SVCs) aren't available yet.
6. People confuse it with Automated Teller Machines.
5. Not enough people have read our books yet.
4. There is no bottom-up demand from users who demand multimedia applications, which in turn require ATM.
3. Incumbent players aren't interested in cannibalizing their own product install base with lower-cost alternatives.
2. Why not wait until next year? Many customers feel that needs will then be clearer, and ATM technology will be better, and prices will be lower if they wait.

And the number one reason why ATM has not made it big . . .

1. All great ideas begin as heresy!

Not to be outdone, Jay Leno might also add:

- Did someone call it irrational exuberance?
- Look how long it took ISDN to catch on.
- No one ever gave it away for free — like Microsoft's Web browser.

1.1.3 Top 10 Reasons Why ATM Will Succeed in the End

And now the top 10 reasons why ATM *will* eventually succeed:

10. Hardware (firmware) is always faster than software.
9. 900 members in the ATM Forum can't all be wrong.
8. A new generation of multimedia PCs is coming with the MMX Pentium, IEEE 1394, and WIN NT 4.0 — all ATM-capable!
7. Microsoft's next operating system will use Winsock 2.0, which can use ATM networks.
6. The Internet itself may crash if it isn't upgraded to ATM. Most leading Internet Service Providers currently use ATM switches in their backbones.
5. All of the smart people will eventually read our books.
4. The Asymmetric Digital Subscriber Line (ADSL) standard for providing megabit-per-second service to the residence over existing copper wire now utilizes ATM.
3. Every phone company and public operator is implementing ATM.
2. A network can never be too fast, too ubiquitous, or too flexible.

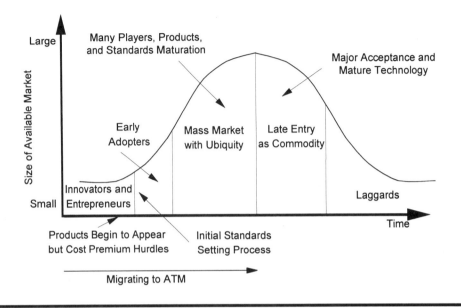

Figure 1.1 Technology Adoption Life Cycle

And the number one reason why ATM will succeed in the end . . .

1.   Great ideas, like great books, eventually succeed.

If these aren't enough reasons to convince you, consider the following.

- Almost half of existing Internet traffic runs over ATM.
- Doom runs great on 155-Mbps ATM!
- If Bill Clinton can get reelected, there is hope for ATM in the LAN!
- Tell the truth, now: If an ATM machine gave you extra money, would you return it?

1.1.4 Market Acceptance and Technology Adoption

One measure of a technology's success is how fast it moves through the phases of market acceptance or catches the wave of technological innovation. Figure 1.1 shows the standard product or technology adoption life cycle, with the arrow at the bottom of the figure illustrating how ATM is migrating from the innovation and early adopter phases into the mass market. When technologies initially appear on the scene, they are usually expensive; appealing primarily to innovators and entrepreneurs. This customer class enjoys working with bleeding-edge technology and can afford to do so. Next, as a technology becomes standardized and matures, its price begins to drop, often drastically. This is called the early adopters phase, and at this point standards setting begins to move at full steam. As more players become involved and prices continue dropping, products and services become ubiquitous in the mass market. Then, the product or service reaches commodity status once it reaches maturity and achieves major market acceptance. Players in this phase are called late entrants. These two stages at the top of the curve are where products and services make the most money. Finally, a technology passes its maturity and lags behind newer, improved mass market or commodity products and services.

Another way to view networking technology is through the history of innovations. Figure 1.2 illustrates a 30-year view of networking protocol waves. Here we see the mass adoption of private lines, ISDN, and frame relay before that of ATM. The model also predicts that technologies like Wave Division Multiplexing (WDM) and ADSL will follow ATM in mass adoption.

1.1.5 What Will Make ATM "Cross the Chasm"?

Over time, a technology can meet the needs of only a portion of the overall market. Based on current market indicators, it appears that ATM technology is currently poised between the early adopters and the mass market phases, at the point commonly called the "chasm".

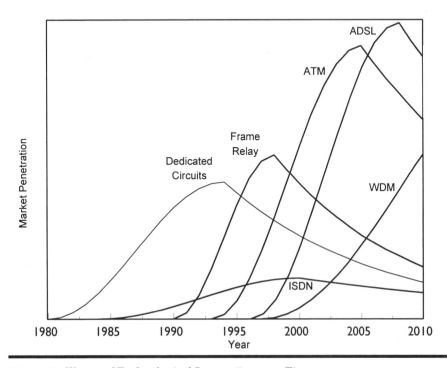

Figure 1.2 Waves of Technological Innovation over Time

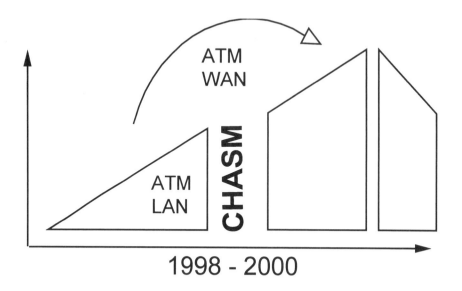

Figure 1.3 ATM Enablers for "Crossing the Chasm"

According to Geoffrey Moore's *Crossing the Chasm* model [1], there is a large chasm that exists between the early adoption and mass market phases. Enablers must make the technology or service "leap the chasm" to meet the needs of a much larger market and customer base. Figure 1.3 shows where WAN and LAN ATM fit in the chasm model. ATM in the WAN is already bridging the gap, while the market acceptance and economics of ATM in the LAN are still undecided — it stands at the edge of the precipice.

What will enable ATM to leap this chasm into the mass market? Some pundits argue that ATM WAN has already leapt the chasm and ATM LAN never will. To answer this question, we must understand the enablers affecting ATM and their ability to leap the chasm.

Timing is as key as the enablers, if not more so. What are the enablers for ATM to cross the chasm? What enablers will make this leap more likely to happen? The following sections address these questions with answers:

- ATM drives business benefits.
- Multimedia applications enable ATM.
- Technological advances enable ATM.
- ATM has lower cost in parallel with lowering network cost.
- ATM is becoming standardized.

1.2 ATM DRIVES BUSINESS BENEFITS

ATM technology provides the following four key business benefits:

- Integration savings
- Economies of scale
- Flexibility
- Single enterprise-wide solutions

1.2.1 ATM as the Single Network Technology Integrator

Users are spending much more on service and support budgets than on hardware and software budgets. This statistic shows the decreasing cost of the equipment, as opposed to the increasing cost of the support systems required to run networks. As further evidence of this trend, the use of high-bandwidth circuits and services to support these networks *doubles* each year.

ATM is the first technology that offers a corporation the capability to use a common enterprise-wide protocol and infrastructure for all voice, data, and video communications – desktop-to-desktop. ATM excels when applications require multiple qualities of service. While most corporate enterprise networks will remain a blend of public network services and private leased lines, many corporations more and more are turning to hybrid outsourced or outtasked solutions. ATM offers combined switching and routing within the WAN, as well as a backbone "technology of choice" for high-performance campus backbones, coexisting with IP and LAN switching. These are key steps for ATM to become the common platform for enterprise-wide communications.

Prior to ATM, users required multiple legacy technologies for communication, as shown in Figure 1.4. Often, enterprises implemented separate networks for voice, videoconferencing, and data communications. ATM changes the situation to that depicted in Figure 1.5, where a user can employ multiple protocols to send voice and data from the workstation on her LAN to peer workstations anywhere across the WAN. ATM provides the infrastructure of a seamless, single protocol for all traffic types that provides logical access to all services (e.g., SMDS, IP) and interworks with those that have similar characteristics (e.g., frame relay and N-ISDN). These concepts are described in Chapters 9, 10, and 11.

The demand for bandwidth has never been greater, and it shows no signs of decreasing. Users' applications are constantly requiring more bandwidth and speed, but only when they truly need it — usually referred to as "bandwidth-on-demand." But the network and the end station have to make a joint call for true end-to-end bandwidth allocation.

Dedicated bandwidth provides no advantage if it isn't used efficiently. ATM users dynamically share bandwidth resources, because ATM allocates bandwidth fairly based on requested quality of service and traffic levels. Users can harness bandwidth as required without worrying about controlling the amount and variability of delay through careful traffic engineering of their communication networks, as network designers must do in LANs supporting integrated services.

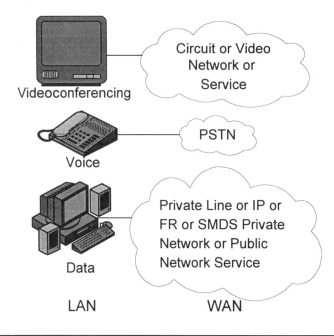

Figure 1.4 Legacy Multiservice Environments

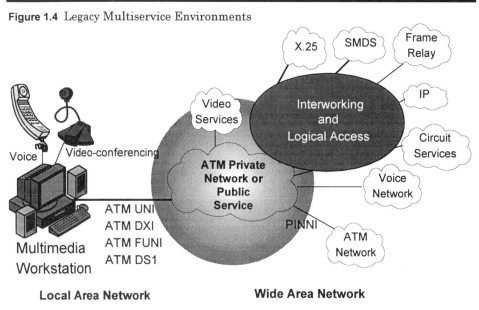

Figure 1.5 ATM Multiservice Environments

1.2.2 ATM Offers Economies of Scale

Through integration of multiple traffic types, ATM achieves economies of scale in network infrastructure because it is more efficient than multiple separate networks, and because the laws of large numbers often make larger networks with larger traffic loads easier to engineer. Furthermore, ATM is well positioned to be the dominant corporate and service-provider for the WAN infrastructure of the near future. ATM offers a single, multiservice architecture and universal backbone that integrates narrowband and broadband access technologies, while simultaneously offering a smooth transition path from legacy networks. Thereby, ATM lowers the unit cost of bandwidth, simplifies operations, reduces maintenance support costs, and optimizes overall bandwidth and resource utilization efficiency. Many network designers have learned over the past two decades that throwing large amounts of bandwidth at the problem is not always the most cost-effective answer. For example, large private line–based networks are moving to more cost-effective public network services, such as frame relay. Also, running parallel voice and data networks is extremely inefficient and costly. But most companies run standalone networks today because there is no viable alternative — or was not until very recently.

Even though the percentage of nonvoice traffic continues to increase, the requirement for integration of voice with data over a single access technology remains a constant conundrum. A key role for ATM is to eliminate the cost of running and managing duplicate infrastructures. Although enterprise ATM networks use ATM for scalable infrastructures, ATM has been most widely adopted by service providers. It is clear that traditional carriers (RBOCs, LECs, and CAPs), as well as many Internet Service Providers (ISPs), are increasingly relying on ATM technology in their backbone infrastructure. These service providers now have the opportunity to offer a single, common platform technology rather than operating separate networks for voice and various data services.

1.2.3 Flexibility of ATM

ATM is a multiplexing and switching technology designed for flexibility, versatility, and scalability at the expense of somewhat decreased efficiency. For any *single* application it is usually possible to find a better data communications technique, but ATM excels where it is desirable for applications with different performance, quality of service, and business requirements to be performed on the same computer, multiplexer, router, switch, and/or network. For these applications, the flexibility of ATM can result in a solution that is more cost-effective than several separate, individually optimized technologies. Furthermore, the flexibility of ATM can "future-proof" network investments, since as yet unenvisioned future applications may also be supported by ATM. Also, ATM enables network managers to flexibly adapt to changing enterprise communication requirements, evolving business environments, and fluctuating traffic patterns.

1.2.4 ATM as an Enterprise-wide Solution

Clearly, the deciding factor for ATM's success in the LAN will be the widespread use of ATM-friendly applications that rely on standards like Microsoft's Winsock 2.0. The cost per user or per LAN workstation port is, in many studies, less for ATM than for 10-Mbps switched Ethernet — ATM's major competitor in the LAN — when measured on the basis of cost per megabit per second. In the WAN, no technology beats the flexibility and multiple Quality of Service (QoS) levels provided by ATM technology. But ATM's penetration in the LAN has been limited, since the new 100BASET switched Ethernet technologies can undercut ATM's costs. In the LAN the requirement that users purchase Network Interface Cards (NICs) for workstations and forklift upgrades to existing LAN switches and routers makes for a harder sale for ATM.

Visualize an enterprise-wide ATM network. Applications on a workstation run using an ATM-aware Application Programming Interface (API) that interfaces to a local ATM network via a high-performance ATM NIC. From that point out through the LAN and over the WAN, the network protocol and technology remains ATM. Standards are evolving in the Internet in parallel with ATM's deployment that will extend QoS capabilities through IP using protocols such as the Reservation Protocol (RSVP). However, a single enterprise-wide, end-to-end ATM network ensures quality of service for multiple traffic types (voice, data, and video), while LAN segments must be engineered to low utilization in order to achieve equivalent performance. The ATM WAN could be either a private ATM network or a public ATM service.

ATM offers a tighter coupling between the user application and the networking protocol. Protocols like IP across the WAN effectively turn the network into a dumb pipe. ATM places intelligence back into the WAN, making the network smarter and allowing the network to become more like a computer and less like a dumb transport medium.

1.3 APPLICATIONS ENABLE ATM, WHICH IN TURN ENABLES APPLICATIONS

Consumer and commercial applications are changing, creating a need for more bandwidth-on-demand, or, more appropriately, "bandwidth-on-call." New applications require new network capabilities. Simultaneously, new network capabilities enable new applications. Multimedia is one example of this chicken-and-egg situation. Multimedia requires a high-speed, QoS-aware communications network. When such networks did not exist, multi-media applications were few and far between, and largely incapable of interoperation.

The combination of the exponential growth in computing power and the nonlinear growth in personal communication over the Web and corporate communication through intranets creates an overall growth trend for data communications that is greater than exponential. These factors, referred to as the *accelerating bandwidth principle,* are further accelerated by the ever-increasing power of the desktop computer. The change in traffic composition from text-based applications to network-based multimedia successors drives the use of ATM as the network technology of choice for LAN and WAN communications.

1.3.1 Consumer and Commercial Applications

Consumer service applications requiring high bandwidth flexibility and performance include:

- Home-shopping services employing multimedia voice, data, image, and video using on-line databases and catalogs
- Interactive multimedia applications and gaming
- Medical imaging
- Video-on-demand
- Shared-whiteboard applications
- Telecommuting applications
- Electronic commerce
- Multimedia applications to the home desktop (i.e., ADSL)
- E-mail and multimedia messaging systems

Some applications require not only broadband service but also the capability of a broadcast public service. These include:

- Distance learning and training
- Desktop Video Collaboration (DVC)
- On-line video libraries for home study
- Video desktop training courses
- Video-on-demand

Further processing of video programming at the server yields exciting consumer applications, such as DVC, where users share applications through videoconferencing. DVC reduces the amount of travel to meetings and decreases the time to market for many corporations. For example, DVC replaces the situation where three people in different parts of the world discuss blurry faxes of a new automobile blueprint on a conference call with full-motion videoconferencing and computer renditions of the proposed automobile on a shared whiteboard. Much as in the business arena, the rallying cry for consumers is for more bandwidth-on-demand (or on call); the hope is that consumers will exclaim, "I want my ATM TV!"

Meanwhile, there are many commercial public service applications that are pushing the envelope for high and flexible bandwidths, such as:

- Seamless LAN/MAN/WAN interconnectivity
- Graphic-intensive industrial engineering applications (e.g., CAD, CAM, CAE, CIM) on-line
- Video on demand
- Collaborative and cooperative computing, such as groupware
- Real-time computer simulations (i.e., aeronautics)
- Integrated voice, video, data multiplexing, and switching
- Videoconferencing
- Remote access to shared server farms
- Multimedia applications on the desktop
- Desktop publishing (DTP), electronic publishing, and large file document management
- Remote distributed database access
- Financial modeling and industry reports
- Collapsed backbone campus networks
- Seamless interworking with legacy systems

Many of these applications are just now beginning to be widely deployed, driving the need for greater and more flexible bandwidth. A key potential application driver for consumer ATM is the support requirements for consumer services, most notably *video-on-demand*. Several cable companies and telecommunications service providers are providing broadcast-quality video-on-demand delivery using ATM switches at the headend of cable distribution networks with sophisticated video servers. ATM is well suited to the ever-changing marketplace of video coding in providing a flexible, multiple-rate, integrated switching vehicle that can handle today's fixed video coding rates (such as MPEG and JPEG carrying a 60-Mbps standard video NTSC signal at a compression ratio of up to 100:1!), as well as future variable video coding rates.

1.3.2 Application Demand for Bandwidth

The above applications range from providing cost-consolidation efficiencies and productivity improvements to fundamental changes in people's lives and the way businesses or enterprises operate. Many applications demonstrate that people increasingly rely on visual or image information, rather than audio or text information, as predicted by the old, but accurate, adage that "a picture is worth a thousand words". The increase in telecommuting and conducting business from the home also illustrates the trend toward relying on visual or image information. The partnering and buyout of cable firms by information transport and telecommunications providers, as well as the advent of cable modems and technologies such as the digital subscriber line family of technologies (e.g., HDSL, ADSL, VDSL, etc.) using ATM, also portend major changes in the infrastructure for providing interactive multimedia networking to the home. Indeed, the ADSL Forum predicts that

ATM will be the access method from concentrators to various services. Some early ADSL equipment and trials support end-to-end ATM services.

As new technologies emerge, their proponents often look for a single "killer application" for success. It is more often the case that many applications or implementations working together make a technology successful on the desktop or the local, campus, metropolitan, and wide area network. This is true of ATM.

Typically, applications utilize one of two generic types of information: an object of fixed size that must be transferred, or a stream of information characterized by a fixed data rate. Multimedia involves combinations of these basic information transfers. The tradeoffs in response time, throughput, and the number of simultaneous applications that can be supported by technologies such as ATM are illustrated through several simple examples.

Figure 1.6 shows the time required to transfer an object of a certain size at a particular transfer rate. Along the horizontal axis a number of common information objects are listed as an illustration of object size in millions of bytes (megabytes or Mbytes). In general, the transfer time decreases as the transfer rate is increased. A real-time service requires transfer in the blink of an eye, which is on the order of one-twentieth of a second (i.e., fifty milliseconds). The utility of the service in an interactive, near-real-time mode is usually perceived as requiring a transfer time of no more than a few seconds. A non-real-time or batch application may require many seconds or even minutes for transfer of a large object.

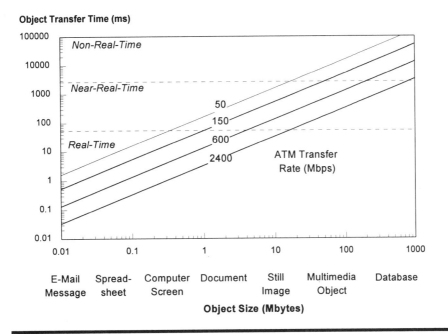

Figure 1.6 Object Transfer Time as a Function of Bandwidth

Number of Sessions

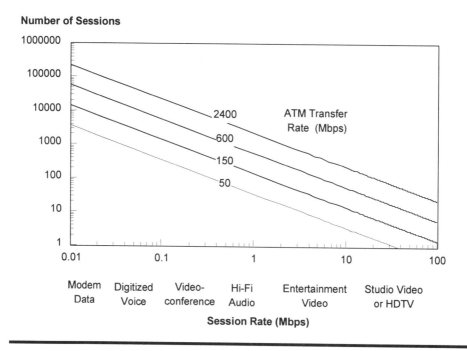

Figure 1.7 Number of Fixed-Rate Application Sessions Supported

Now let's look at applications such as audio and video that use a specified amount of bandwidth. The bandwidth may be a fixed, continuous amount or an average amount if the network statistically multiplexes the input sources. Figure 1.7 illustrates the simplest case, a fixed bandwidth per application source.

Figure 1.7 plots the number of application sessions requiring a certain fixed rate supportable by bandwidths standardized in WAN fiber-optic transmission equipment. In general, as the bandwidth required by each application session increases, the number of simultaneous sessions supported decreases. Of course, allocating more overall bandwidth increases the maximum number of fixed-rate application sessions. Current network technologies support transmitting these applications separately. ATM offers the flexibility to combine a variety of sources in arbitrary proportions. This is a key advantage of ATM.

This acceleration toward sessions demanding greater bandwidth, combined with ATM as an enabler, points toward a move toward virtual reality — a dynamic, interactive visual and audio representation of information rather than just textual or simple, static graphical representation. *Multimedia* is a term often used to represent the combination of multiple forms of data and their simultaneous presentation to an end user. The current generation of children, accustomed to sophisticated electronic gaming systems running on

200-MHz Pentium MMX machines, will expect even more sophisticated capabilities in the workplace and their homes in the twenty-first century.

Figure 1.8 illustrates the bandwidth requirements and response time requirements of multimedia by showing how much time is required to transfer a high-resolution graphical image in the presence of a number of high-quality video sessions. This example illustrates ATM's flexibility by allowing an application to trade off the number of active fixed-rate 10-Mbps high-quality video windows against the required time to transfer a 1-Mbyte file for representative ATM network bandwidths. Observe how the transfer time for the large file increases as the number of active video sessions increases. The fixed-rate application must have continuous bandwidth in order for the video to appear continuous, while the object transfer application can simply take more time to transfer the object as the available bandwidth is decreased because another, higher-priority session is activated.

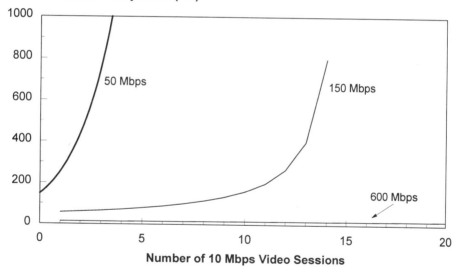

Figure 1.8 Bandwidth Rate Required for Multimedia in Mbps

1.3.3 Enabling New Multimedia Applications

Multimedia applications are steadily penetrating the user community. Sound cards, microphones, and cameras are now commonplace in many home and business computers. Internet Web pages using Java sport full-motion multimedia. Multimedia has also found its way into the commercial market, driven by applications listed in the previous section. ATM is being deployed to offer the capability to support time-sensitive traffic, typically voice or video, and offers enhanced delivery options such as point-to-multipoint and broadcast.   High-speed ATM point-to-multipoint applications include broadcast-quality video and videoconferencing applications involving simultaneous transmission of text, data, and video. Applications such as telemedicine and distance learning that take advantage of the attributes of ATM broadband data technologies are now appearing, to support true voice, data, and video traffic integration with guaranteed QoS for each traffic type. ATM supports these applications by flexibly and dynamically allocating bandwidth and connectivity.

Figure 1.9 shows an example of a person with a multimedia desktop workstation in Chicago participating in a video and audio conference with four other individuals in New York, London, Paris, and Washington, D.C. Users share a virtual whiteboard and exchange electronic mail (E-mail) interactively, while simultaneously running a Web browser to research information on the World Wide Web (WWW). Users can insert movie clips into the clipboard so that their peers can play them back on demand. In this example, an automatic translation server (not shown in the figure) could be connected to facilitate communication between the parties speaking different languages.

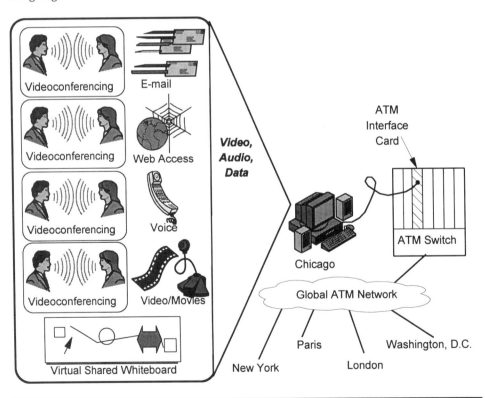

Figure 1.9 Multipoint, Multimedia ATM Application of the Future

Using ATM technology, an ATM interface card in the Chicago workstation combines the video of the built-in monitor camera, the telephone, and text data into a single 25- or 155-Mbps ATM transmission stream to a local ATM switch.   The ATM switch then broadcasts the voice, data, and video to switches at all four locations through intervening ATM WANs in the global ATM network.   Each of the other sites does the same in return.   Each of the attendees has four individual pop-up screens on the workstations so that he or she can see the other participants, and can share a common whiteboard or database.   The conference leader dynamically controls videoconferencing connections.   Alternatively, the participants may use a "meet me" or CU-SeeMe–type conference.   Although this may sound futuristic, applications such as these are emerging in corporations today.

1.3.4 The Accelerating Bandwidth Principle

The processing speed of the CPU sitting on the average desktop is often measured in millions of instructions per second (MIPS). A desktop machine of today would have filled a medium office building 20 years ago.   In fact, desktop workstations are now available that offer more than a billion instructions per second (BIPS).   Not only are the MIPS of yesteryear distributed to the computing power on the desktop today, but the need to interconnect them is growing as well.   Rather than having all the computing power of the network residing in one computer (i.e., in the mainframe in legacy systems), personal computers and servers distribute the total computing power among many remote devices. Thus, the interconnection of many of these devices becomes the common bus or back-plane of old — causing the network to become the computer.   New distributed processing applications, like groupware, shared databases, desktop video conferencing, shared workspaces, multimedia, and electronic mail, accelerate the need to communicate data between desktops and servers. Furthermore, the comput-ing pathways are any-to-any, as opposed to the old many-to-one mainframe paradigm. The increased desktop computing power and bandwidth combined with the need for any-to-any communications results in the *accelerating bandwidth principle*. Let's now look at each of these megatrends in detail to reinforce these key principles.

Applications have become much more processor-intensive. Additionally, as users learn how to apply these applications to increase communications and productivity, bottlenecks can form in both the LAN and the WAN.   Legacy LAN and WAN bandwidths simply cannot handle this accelerating need for bandwidth. Witness Ethernet, where 10 Mbps, even if utilized at only a 40 percent efficiency, initially offered a tremendous amount of bandwidth to local area users. As workstation power and application bandwidth demands increased, however, Ethernet LANs "ran out of gas."   LAN administrators segmented and resegmented LANs to increase the bandwidth allocated to each computer, until in some cases there was only one server or workstation per Ethernet segment!   LAN switching then emerged to more efficiently interconnect such highly loaded LAN segments. Next, 100-Mbps Ethernet came on the scene, but some high-end servers still required dedicated 100-Mbps segments to handle all their traffic. FDDI and Fast Ethernet were invented to provide 10 times more bandwidth (100 Mbps) than 10-Mbps Ethernet, but on the leading edge of workstation technology these speeds have already become a bandwidth constraint. Furthermore, FDDI was initially designed to support only data applications.

The unit cost of WAN bandwidth constantly decreases over time, as evidenced by continually declining tariffs from every major carrier and private-line bandwidth provider. Although there are occasional price increases, the overall trend is driven by the decreasing cost of transmission technology and operations. So your WAN bill should be less over time. The move to public data services, such as frame relay, only increases these cost savings. But not so fast — show users that there is available bandwidth, and they will always find ways to use it. Client-server applications' hunger for more bandwidth is increasing just as rapidly as bandwidth is increasing across the WAN. Applications like shared database applications, desktop videoconferencing, Lotus Notes, and even Internet browsing have caused LAN and WAN bandwidth requirements to skyrocket! Thus, the lower cost of WAN bandwidth per megabit per second is counterbalanced by the need for higher WAN speeds. Figure 1.10 illustrates the declining cost per megabit per second per port over time [2] for bandwidth in the LAN. Note that this comparison is based upon the cost per Mbps. This means that the absolute cost for 155 Mbps ATM is much greater than the cost for a 10-Mbps Ethernet connection.

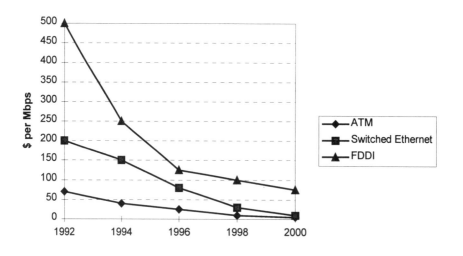

Figure 1.10 Cost Trends per Mbps for ATM, FDDI, and Switched Ethernet

As a further illustration of the explosive growth caused by open interconnection and multimedia applications, observe the tremendous growth rate of traffic on the Internet and the World Wide Web (WWW) — by some estimates over 20 percent per month! Furthermore, with the advent of audio and video multicast, the demand outstrips Internet capacity during periods of peak usage.

Business methodology, the flow of information, and the nature of the organizational structure drive required connectivity. In a flatter, empowered organization, each individual sends, or provides access to, information that was sent upward in the hierarchical organization. As a witness to this trend, most office workers lament the ever-increasing number of E-mail messages they receive and must process every day.

The following analysis shows how the combined exponential growth in computing power and the nonlinear growth in intercommunications creates an overall demand for data communications with a greater than exponential growth rate, called hyperexponential by mathematicians. We refer to these phenomena collectively as the *accelerating bandwidth principle*. Before exploring this concept, let's first review Amdahl's law, which states that the average application requires processing cycles, storage, and data communication speeds in roughly equal proportion. For example, an application requiring 1 MIPS also needs 1 megabyte of storage along with 1 Mbps of communications bandwidth. The accelerating bandwidth principle shows that Amdahl's rule no longer holds true.

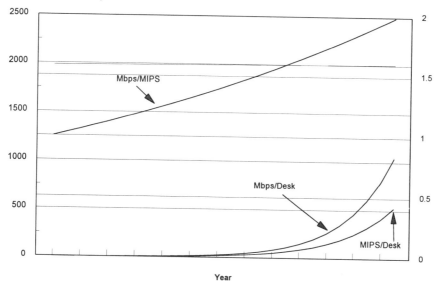

Figure 1.11 Accelerating Bandwidth Principle

Figure 1.11 illustrates the accelerating bandwidth principle. The curve labeled MIPS/Desk represents the exponential growth in computing power at the desktop —a growth rate of approximately 175 percent every two years. The curve labeled Mbps/MIPS represents the nonlinear growth of the required data communication of approximately 3 percent per year, resulting in a doubling of Amdahl's law for the relation of bandwidth to processing power over 25 years. The curve labeled Mbps/Desk, the product of MIPS/Desk and Mbps/MIPS, represents the data communications bandwidth predicted by the accelerating bandwidth principle. The growth rate for the Mbps/MIPS curve is hyperexponential because the exponent grows at a faster than linear rate because of the nonlinear increase in interconnection and desktop communications bandwidth.

The accelerating bandwidth principle shows the inadequacy of Ethernet and FDDI and identifies the need for true gigabit-per-second (Gbps) networking in the near future. ATM-based LANs already serving high-end workgroups and the gigabit Ethernet effort stand as evidence in support of this principle. Another way to offset the increasing need for communications bandwidth is the use of improved compression, which reduces the amount of data requiring transmission. However, compression yields improvement only up to the information theoretic limits.

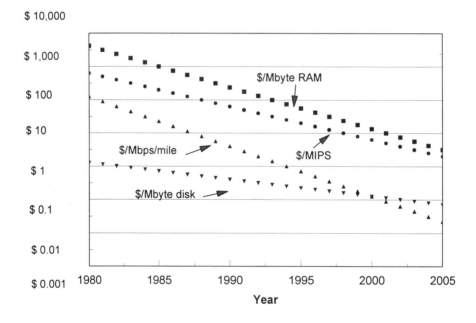

Figure 1.12 Technology Cost Trends over Time

Figure 1.12 plots over time the costs of processing, storage, and communications [3]. The $/MIPS, $/Mbyte of RAM, $/Mbyte of disk, and $/Mbps/mile over time shown in this figure all decrease at exponential rates, since they form nearly straight lines on the semilog scale. The $/MIPS and $/Mbyte curves are derived for microprocessor technology and the semiconductor memory. The exponential increase in computing speed and accessible memory is a well-established trend, driven by integrated circuit technology, that will extend well into the next century. Recent trends in processor and memory technology may even exceed exponential decline! The $/Mbps/mile curve is for fiber-optic transmission. Note that the cost of transmission is decreasing slightly faster than the cost of computer processing. The cost of mechanical disk storage is decreasing at the slowest rate.

1.3.5 The Network Is the Computer

The fact that transmission costs are decreasing more rapidly than mass memory and processing costs provides the economic environment for the accelerating bandwidth principle. It is becoming less expensive to have information transmitted over a data network than to store it locally or perform calculations to generate it. If you believe in this principle, you may subscribe to each user's having less *intelligent* personal computing devices and accessing intelligent services within the network, as network computers access the Internet today or corporations do with intranets. The concept of the network computer is to provide minimal local storage and rely on loading programs from the network when needed, rather than retrieving them from a local hard drive. Why pay the license fees to store programs on a local hard drive or CD-ROM, when the network allows many more users to have on demand, infrequent access to expensive programs? Similar logic applies to database and information storage. Instead of distributing data to many local disks, many networks now utilize servers which clients access on demand. This is the paradigm employed by many intranets today.

Is networking moving backwards? After all, computing users spent the last 15 years moving from the dumb VT100 terminal to the powerful desktop workstation. Or is the network becoming the computer, storing, processing, and sending all the needed information? When the cost or value of copyrighted or licensed information content required by applications, such as distance learning, information on demand, and other interactive services, is taken into account, the justification for the accelerating bandwidth principle becomes even greater. Indeed, the need to access an even greater volume of content drives the need for computing back into the network. The exponentially increasing growth of World Wide Web (WWW) traffic on the Internet and intranets is largely due to the increased need for information predicted by the accelerating bandwidth principle. Another advantage of network computing is that you always run the latest version of the application. An example of this paradigm shift is the use of Java applets on the World Wide Web.

1.4 REVIEW

This chapter introduced key business drivers for ATM: business benefits, applications, technological advances, and lower costs. Corporate and consumer applications demand high-speed, multimedia bandwidth for multiple traffic types to the desktop. Worldwide industry support ensures ubiquity, while ATM provides the intelligence to transform the network into the computer. The next chapter moves on to a review of technological advances that stimulate the adoption of ATM, along with a presentation of several market studies.

1.5 REFERENCES

[1]   Geoffrey Moore, *Crossing the Chasm*, Harper Business, 1991.
[2]   U. Black, *ATM: Foundation for Broadband Networks*, Prentice-Hall, 1995.
[3]   D. McDysan and D. Spohn, *ATM: Theory and Application*, McGraw-Hill, 1995.

2

ATM Technology
and the Marketplace

Networking technologies follow predictable trends: they emerge, move through trial phases, and then either prosper or falter. Asynchronous Transfer Mode (ATM) in the WAN has moved into the prosperous stage, while ATM in the LAN stands at the crossroads of these two outcomes. This chapter explores the technology and marketplace factors affecting the data communications landscape, including:

- Protocol simplification and higher performance expectations
- Fundamental changes in network infrastructure
- Increasing public network service availability at attractive prices
- Technology and business market directions

In support of the claim that ATM is entering a stage of rapidly growing user acceptance, ATM market statistics and forecasts will be presented. This chapter concludes with a summary of ATM benefits, counterbalanced with a listing of risks involved with ATM and challenges ahead.

2.1 TECHNOLOGICAL ADVANCES ENABLE ATM

Now that we have explored the applications drivers for ATM, we move on to recent technological changes and paradigm shifts that are enablers for ATM. Technology enablers take many forms, ranging from the need for higher speeds, increased flexibility, and improved efficiency, to support for multiple traffic types and entirely new applications. ATM provides a technology upgrade from older, less flexible Time-Division Multiplexing (TDM) technology and is also more efficient than even regular statistical multiplexing that applies to data but not voice. Protocol and processor enhancements allow greater throughput and flexibility, while cheaper, higher-performance, modern digital transmission facilities feed the need for speed demanded by the accelerating bandwidth principle. We use the S-curve model to describe the phases of user acceptance of technological evolution and to illustrate the short- and long-term benefits to the user.

2.1.1 S Curves of Technological Evolution

The evolution of a technology can be viewed as an S curve in a market technology maturity versus time plot. In Figure 2.1, the horizontal axis is time and the vertical axis is the maturity or market presence of the technology. The curves depict the maturation of SMDS, ISDN, frame relay, Asymmetric Digital Subscriber Line (ADSL), and ATM, with focus on both LAN and WAN ATM. Notice that frame relay was first deployed in 1990, picked up steam with a phenomenal growth rate of greater than 200 percent per year in 1993, but has decreased to a more modest 100 percent annual growth rate. Frame relay leads the charge in flexible bandwidth-on-demand services, with worldwide service and equipment revenues going from less than $50 million in 1992 to $2 billion as of 1996, representing more than 10,000 customers and 200,000 ports. Predictions for ATM service growth outstrip even these figures, as covered later in this chapter. ATM, while still picking up steam, has tremendous growth potential — even more than frame relay, because it serves more traffic types and services (including frame relay itself). Note that ATM market presence in the WAN precedes wide-scale adoption in the LAN in the figure. Sometimes a technology never reaches critical mass and dies out, as was the case with SMDS; to a large extent, a similar fate faced ISDN in the United States until recently. The ISDN curve was flat for many years, indicating a slowly maturing service, but it has recently picked up due to the need for residential and small business access to the Web.

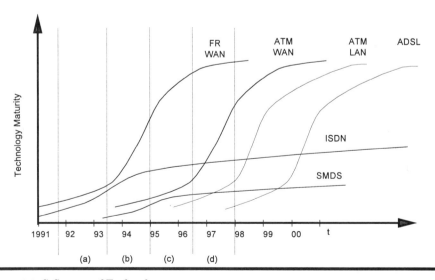

Figure 2.1 S Curves of Technology

One example of a possible next technology wave after ATM is the use of ADSL modems with existing copper pairs. ADSL promises megabit-per-second speeds from the network downstream to the user, along a slower-speed upstream channel. This technology is ideally suited for client access to the World Wide Web, for which annual growth rates are predicted to be on the order of 200 percent. ADSL will likely limit the penetration of the older ISDN technology. Again, we see the accelerating bandwidth principle at work in the innovation phase of a product life cycle. At lower speeds, ATM has competition from improved compression, modems, and IP technologies. The relative values and timing of each of these technologies are not intended to be precise, but merely illustrate possible future scenarios. Note that no technology lasts forever, although legacy technologies generally take a long time to disappear from the scene.

2.1.2 Protocol and Processor Enhancements

A major technology enabler for ATM is the greater than exponential growth in desktop processing power, fueled by the continuing decentralization of computing power from the centralized host to the desktop, with its associated requirement for more peer-to-peer and client-server networking. Desktop machines not only have the processing power the centralized host once had, but also control information passage, employing a wider and more sophisticated range of controlling network and transport protocols, such as TCP/IP and Novell's IPX.

Increased storage in the end stations allows larger retransmission windows to be maintained. Accordingly, RFC 1323 [1] increases TCP window size from 64k to over 1 Gbyte for this very reason. Increased processing power enables the implementation of more sophisticated flow control and windowing mechanisms. One example of protocol complexity is demonstrated by comparing the sophisticated TCP flow control algorithms in the end station with the relatively simple Internet Protocol (IP) used in routers.

2.1.3 Transmission Protocol Simplification and Cost Reduction

Older network protocols such as X.25 implemented complex procedures just to ensure that a packet could be reliably sent from node to node; this sometimes required multiple retransmissions over noisy analog links. The simplification of network switching protocols is primarily a result of essentially error-free physical-layer communications over digital facilities replacing the older error-prone analog facilities. The infrequent occurrence of errors and less frequent retransmission is thus achieved cost-effectively in end systems. Simpler network protocols, such as frame relay, SMDS, and ATM, rely on the high-performance of digital fiber-optic transmission, which provides very low error rates, typically less than 10^{-12}. The cost-effective availability of plesiochronous digital transmission rates such as DS1, DS3, and synchronous SONET at rates of 150 Mbps, 600 Mbps and 2.4 Gbps is a key enabler for ATM services.

2.1.4 Modernization of Transmission Infrastructures

Fiber optics replaced digital microwave transmission in industrialized nations even more rapidly than digital transmission systems had earlier replaced analog systems. Satellite communications has evolved as a high-quality digital transmission medium for connectivity to remote areas or as backup to terrestrial facilities, and there are even satellites designed specifically to handle ATM traffic, such as those designed by COMSAT. Most carrier national networks and all major metropolitan areas are served almost exclusively by fiber, and most main routes rely on linear SONET automatic restoration facilities. Bandwidth between cities across optical fibers with 44 pairs operating at 10 Gbps will reach into the terabits per second by the year 2000. The prefix "tera" means 10 raised to the 12th power, or a thousand billion. Get used to it; the prefix "giga," the Greek word meaning 10 raised to the 9th power, will become passé early in the next millennium.

Many carriers are deploying significant amounts of fiber to the curb (FTTC), and even fiber to the home (FTTH). Modern digital and fiber-optic transmission communications establish a new baseline for the performance of digital data communications, just as digital transmission made the sound quality of long-distance calls comparable to local calls "next door" only 15 short years ago. The impact and benefits of high-performance digital transmission over fiber optics are recurring themes throughout this book. These changes in the modernization of the fiber infrastructure have all accelerated. This will enable a rapid move toward broadband networking.

2.1.5 TDM's Inflexibility Compared to ATM

Let's compare the technology revolution of the 1980's T1 multiplexer technology to ATM technology of the late 1990s. The widespread use of "T1" multiplexers in the 1980s was predicted to be a precursor to a wave of "T3" multiplexer deployment, a development that never occurred. Understanding the reasons for the success of the T1 multiplexer and the lack of adoption of T3 multiplexers is central to placing the potential benefits of ATM in perspective. T1 multiplexers allowed high-performance, relatively low-cost DS1 (colloquially called T1) facilities to be shared among a variety of applications on a quasi-static basis using TDM. TDM bandwidth allocation is not well suited to high-performance, bursty data communications because it limits the peak transmission rate, and wastes bandwidth during the frequent idle periods typical of data communications. While data communications demand increased dramatically, the demand for TDM-based private line service did not keep pace with the overall demand for bandwidth. The speed of a DS3 is 28 times that of a DS1, but a DS3 costs only 5 to 10 times more. Most users couldn't justify the economics and restrictions of TDM inherent in the T3 multiplexer paradigm. Instead, network designers saw better choices for public services within the planning horizon, such as frame relay, SMDS, and ATM.

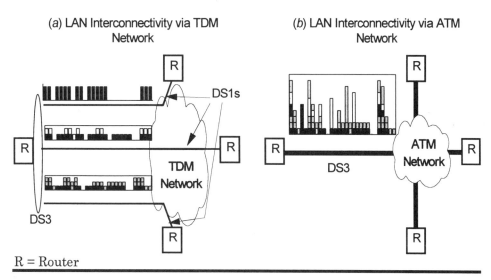

Figure 2.2 ATM Provides More Usable Bandwidth to Data for Less Cost than TDM

ATM offers the capability to extend the LAN or MAN across the WAN at speeds comparable to the LAN or MAN (currently 10 to 100 Mbps) at a lower cost than dedicated private line or TDM circuits, because the bandwidth and switches are economically shared across many users. Instead of having to funnel the bandwidth of interconnected LANs down to the lower bandwidth provided by the static allocation of TDM connecting sites via DS1s in the DS3 access line, as shown in Figure 2.2a, ATM provides each LAN with the capability to burst at the full LAN access speed across the WAN on the DS3 access line, as shown in Figure 2.2b. This figure shows how TDM LAN interconnection takes much longer to transfer data, as shown by the time plots of actual usage on the access lines. Since users cannot all burst simultaneously, ATM accommodates access to peak bandwidth on demand virtually all of the time. And, in addition, ATM achieves significant economies of scale by integrating multiple applications on the same physical network.

2.2 LOWER-COST ATM LOWERS NETWORKING COSTS

ATM provides the best price/performance per megabit per second of any public network technology. Better yet, the cost to implement ATM continues to decline. The advent of ATM Switched Virtual Connections (SVCs) providing "bandwidth-on-call" makes the economics of ATM even more attractive. Decreasing transmission facility costs also drive down the actual cost of high-speed circuits, if not the price — making ATM even more attractive for large meshed networks. Implementing ATM across the entire enterprise can lower overall network cost by lowering capital and support costs through more efficient use of a single ATM infrastructure, as well as a variety of other benefits described later in this chapter. Public service providers now offer WAN ATM services at rates lower than those for dedicated private lines and comparable to those of hot-selling services like frame relay. ATM also includes the efficiencies of handling multiple types of traffic — voice, data, and video. Thus, ATM is a low-risk WAN investment.

2.2.1 Transmission Cost Reduction

Two complementary and competing phenomena are occurring simultaneously. LAN and WAN speeds are converging to provide LAN extension speed connectivity across the WAN. And WAN and LAN bandwidth is becoming less expensive per bps. Let's explore both.

Bandwidth in the WAN and LAN, when viewed on a cost per megabit per second basis, has decreased in cost over time (years). Wave Division Multiplexing (WDM) provides terabit speeds across a single fiber-optic strand, whereas the highest commercial-grade fibers carried 40 gigabits per second in 1997. And look at fiber to the desktop and home at a few cents per foot. Putting fiber in the ground, or through the building to the desktop, dominates cost considerations now.

Bandwidth in the WAN is not yet "free," as many pundits projected, but it is becoming less expensive all the time. However, these cost decreases are less pronounced than they should be because the transmission and service providers must pass along to the end user the cost to upgrade transmission and switching facilities and equipment. Either way, however, transmission technology decreases the real cost for transport of high-bandwidth services such as ATM.

2.2.2 Lower Network Life-cycle Costs and Future-Proof Investment

Corporations and consumers look for a technology or service that maximizes their investment. A key consideration is the lifetime of a technology. While ATM seems to be the technology leader for the rest of this decade, standards continue to evolve, and intervals of only a few years now separate generations of equipment. Some public service providers plan to deploy ATM as a core part of their backbone and service offerings, hoping to realize the benefits of cost-effective flexibility and scalability. Flexibility and scalability take many forms. Being able to increase the number and size of switches, users, and circuits are key measures of scalability. Support for a distributed architecture for high reliability is another benefit. The capability to upgrade network elements to faster processors, and to upgrade routers, switches, hubs and workstations to the same standards-based architecture, is also a potential benefit. No technology remains efficient and cost-effective forever, but the flexibility and scalability of ATM hardware and software potentially provide a longer life cycle than other MAN and WAN technologies, which thus "future-proofs" the ATM investment.

Purchasing ATM equipment across the enterprise achieves purchasing discounts, since purchasing large volumes of capital equipment decreases unit costs. The overall cost per Mbps is greatly reduced, along with the cost of spares, maintenance, and training of support staff. A long-term technology like ATM also future-proofs your network, providing a solution that will last many years into the future and lowering the overall cost of life-cycle management.

2.2.3 Lower Public Service Cost

The demand for public network ATM service is growing as users discover the sobering capital cost of building a private line or even a private ATM WAN, compared with the cost of a shared public network service. The cost of multiple point-to-point DS3 circuits can be greatly reduced by using a public data service. This benefit is accelerated by the advent of protocol interworking over ATM service (i.e., frame relay to ATM) and SVCs, which allow multiple types of services at different speeds (DS0, DS1, Fractional DS1, DS3, Fractional DS3, and DS3) to interwork with one another.

Fiscal interests also play a role here, since companies pay tax deductible expense dollars for public services versus depreciable capital dollars for private equipment. Many corporations can justify the expense-oriented approach of using a public network service more readily than the capital-oriented approach of purchasing and building a private network. It is interesting to note that over half of the Internet traffic is transported over ATM. Internet service providers have embraced ATM as the transport technology of choice for solving bandwidth bottlenecks in their backbone infrastructure: Routers simply can't run fast enough.

2.3 MARKET FORECAST FOR ATM

So, you ask — what data and documentation back up these claims and promises for ATM? This section provides a compilation of marketing data as of publishing time that paints a rosy future for ATM. The real measure of ATM's success, of course, will be determined by the end user's purchasing decision. There are contrarian scenarios in which no one buys ATM Network Interface Cards (NICs) because they do not come down in price, or the price of switched gigabit Ethernet drops to the current level of 100-Mbps Ethernet prices. The market crystal ball readers could be wrong. Predicting is a very dangerous business without a few years of history. Therefore, each of our marketing forecasts starts with at least two years of factual trends.

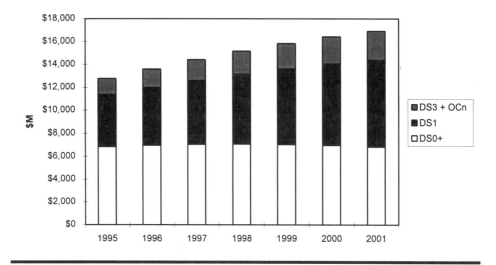

Figure 2.3 U.S. Private Line Market Revenues by Speed

2.3.1 The Demand for New Technologies

It may surprise you, but despite all the hype about technologies like frame relay and ATM, most of the bandwidth in use in corporate networks is still at the DS1 rate and below. In fact, most forecasts say that this will be true at least through 1999, as shown in Figure 2.3! Remember, there are still a huge number of SNA devices on analog multidrop circuits that are working just fine! In fact, not until 1995 did U.S. West finally upgrade its last party line — a technology that has been in place for over 50 years! Thus, history shows that incumbent technologies hang on for longer periods than expected, but that eventually great ideas succeed and replace them.   But ATM is well positioned to provide its benefits at rates of DS3 and above, as well as multiple Quality of Service (QoS) features down to nxDS1 and DS1 speeds. Furthermore, cycle times for migration to new technologies continue to shorten. This has caused businesses to realize that the cost of upgrading to newer technologies like ATM is usually justified by the benefits. One such case is LAN switching, which ushered in a wholesale replacement of hubs. These new LAN switches operate at gigabit switching speeds and also sport enhanced network manageability through a Remote Monitoring (RMON) capability. Of course, many users often overlook the cost of supporting these technologies, which is one reason why outsourcing and outtasking of design, installation, and management of these networks is such a growing market.

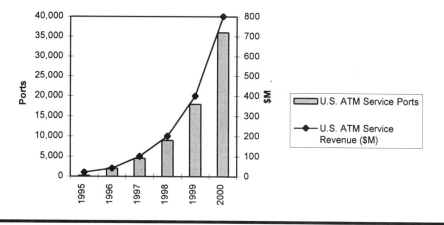

Figure 2.4 U.S. ATM Service Ports and Revenue by Year

2.3.2 The ATM Services and Equipment Market

What does the market for ATM services and equipment look like? The following tables and charts represent market data available at the date of publication. Figure 2.4 compares the number of U.S. carrier ATM service ports to ATM service revenue, showing dramatic growth by the end of this century. The Cumulative Annual Growth Rate (CAGR) for service ports is 150 percent, while the CAGR for revenue is 110 percent. This means that the price per port is projected to decrease over time.

Figure 2.5 compares the number of ATM equipment ports to total ATM equipment revenue. The CAGR for ports is 133 percent, while the CAGR for port revenue is only 69 percent; this means that ATM equipment, like most network hardware, decreases in average cost per port over time. Dataquest estimates that the ATM WAN switch market will be $3 billion by the year 2000. Vertical Systems Group estimates a $2 billion product and services market by the end of 1998. Note that these revenue forecasts exclude switches that are ATM-capable or ATM-ready, approximately halving the total.

Figure 2.6 forecasts the total number of ATM LAN ports and ATM LAN nodes. As you can see, the growth of both LAN ports and LAN nodes accelerates into the next century. Worldwide revenue for integrated circuits used in ATM technology is forecast to hit $144 million by 1997. Dataquest forecasts a billion-dollar ATM LAN backbone market in 1998. In addition, it predicts that nearly 854,000 ports — wide area network access and trunk ports, adapter card access ports, and internetworking connection ports — will be installed around the world by year-end 1997. The projected CAGR of ATM LAN ports is 130 percent, while the CAGR for ATM nodes is 45 percent.

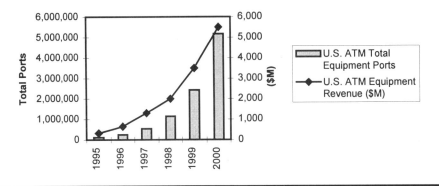

Figure 2.5 U.S. ATM Equipment Ports and Revenue Sold by Year

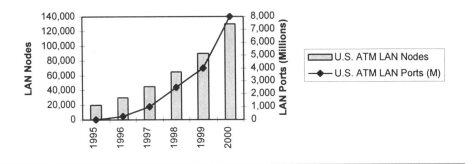

Figure 2.6 U.S. ATM LAN Ports and Nodes Sold by Year

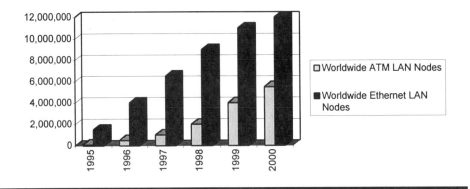

Figure 2.7 Worldwide LAN Ports Sold – ATM and Switched Ethernet by Year

Figure 2.7 shows the number of ATM LAN ports in the United States compared to the number of switched Ethernet ports. Observe that switched Ethernet LAN new installs continue to outpace ATM, but ATM gains on Ethernet, possibly overtaking it in 2001 as the LAN technology of choice. This is because the CAGR for Ethernet is only 50 percent as compared with 130 percent for ATM LAN ports. In fact, some forecasts (Dataquest) have ATM switch revenues exceeding Ethernet revenues by the end of the century. *Data Communications's* report of September 1996 showed users' interest in 155 Mbps almost equal to that in switched Ethernet, with FDDI and 25-Mbps ATM farther behind by a factor of one-half. A survey of desktops revealed that four times as many users employ switched Ethernet as employ 155-Mbps ATM. The study revealed the same level of preference for 100BASET and 155-Mbps ATM. Some studies show the number of ATM desktop ports reaching 3 million by the year 2000. This number represents 17 percent of total desktop ports [2]. Sales of LAN switches, the hottest segment of networking equipment, will quadruple between 1994 and 2000, reaching a $24 billion market [3].

Figure 2.8 shows Ethernet clearly beating ATM as the international LAN technology of choice, although Ethernet clearly levels off and ATM is still rapidly gaining into the next century. The growth rates are almost identical with U.S. growth rates, but there are far fewer ATM LAN nodes installed internationally.

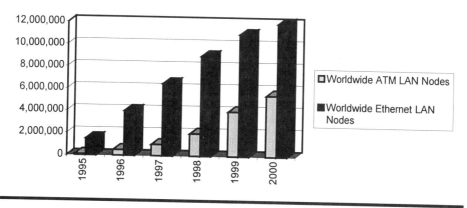

Figure 2.8 Worldwide ATM LAN Nodes Sold by Year

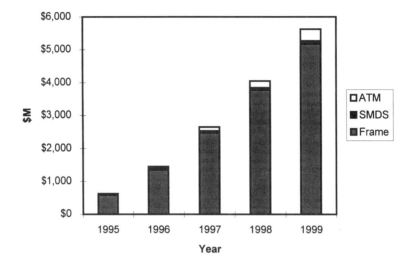

Figure 2.9 U.S. Public Data Service Revenue

From these reports, it seems that ATM mass deployment in both the LAN and the WAN, offering enterprise-wide ATM networking, is due around the turn of the century. This was evident from the previous discussion about the S curves of technology, as ATM in the WAN has just reached mass markets and ATM in the LAN remains in the early innovators stage. Frame relay has already reached mass market, becoming the first widely successful carrier public data service, whereas X.25 and ISDN never reached this status. It remains to be seen if ATM can. Figure 2.9 shows evidence of public data service revenue supporting these claims of frame relay success and small penetration of SMDS and ATM.

ATM switch forecasts are mixed. Most switch ports sold to date (by most estimates greater then 60 percent as of 1996) are edge switches, with the balance being split between enterprise and backbone, or core, switches. The total switch ports are split almost evenly between LAN or campus and WAN, with LAN growing more rapidly. Most of this revenue is from U.S. sales (again greater than 60 percent as of 1996), with Western Europe as the major secondary market.

Newbridge, Cascade, and Cisco (from the Stratacom acquisition) appear to be leading in WAN equipment sales, with almost half the market between them (Dataquest, 1995). However, as more players enter the arena, this dominance may change. Table 2.1 [4] shows the U.S. ATM LAN/WAN market potential for ATM equipment as of mid-1995.

Table 2.1 US ATM LAN/WAN Market Potential Entering 1996

Size of Site	Number of Employees	Number of Sites
Single office	<10	4.3 million
Branch office	<50	1.3 million
Headquarters	>50	700,000

2.3.3 Industry Watch — Market Segment Adoption of ATM

Table 2.2 shows the key applications, adoption period, and market size for major industry segments. Note that each segment can be an early, mass market, or late adopter.

To date, ATM products and services have largely focused on the research and development (R&D) and technical community — typically the early adopter community — but they will focus on the mass market by the year 2000. While the retail market seems to be a late adopter, a recent 3Com survey of the top 100 retailers in the United States showed a large retail network market for ATM emerging. This is primarily due to lower WAN costs and a new generation of Web-based GUI distributed client-server applications that enable multimedia collaboration, along with an increase in capital budget allocations to the network [5].   These trends of increased WAN budgets and decreased WAN costs have enabled many industry segments to consider using technologies like ATM.

Table 2.2 ATM Market Adoption by Segment

Segment	Applications	Adoption Period	Market Size
Medical	Telemedicine	Early	Small
Education	Distance learning	Early	Medium
Manufacturing	Applications that decrease time to market, CAD/CAM/CAE, remote video processing	Early	Large
Wholesale/retail	High-end videoconferencing, multimedia sales kiosks	Late	Small
Financial services/ insurance	Transactions, record verification, transport	Mass	Small
Service providers	Public network service platform	Early	Large
Government	Intelligence, research, command and control	Late	Medium
Transportation/ utilities	Process control	Late	Small
Agriculture/ construction	CAD/CAM/CAE	Late	Small

2.3.4 Future of the ATM Market

Many industry pundits believe that based on ATM's intrinsic value and the
market projections presented so far, the ATM equipment and services
markets are getting ready to explode [6]. This has not yet been the pattern of
ATM growth, especially in the LAN, but it is not inconceivable. Similar
growth curves occurred with the personal computer in the 1980s and with
Ethernet, and to a lesser extent with frame relay, in the 1990s. Only time
will tell.

2.4 BENEFITS AND RISKS OF ATM SUMMARIZED

What benefits do you derive from ATM? We will first summarize ATM
benefits from a macro-level view for service providers, consumers, and
corporations. While there are many potential benefits of ATM, realistically,
we must also identify risks as well as threats from competing technologies.

2.4.1 ATM Benefits Summarized

ATM handles a mix of delay-insensitive, loss-insensitive, delay-sensitive,
and/or loss-sensitive traffic over the same ATM interface and network
infrastructure. In other words, it handles *everything*! From ATM APIs that
talk directly to NICs, which in turn talk to LAN and WAN ATM switches,
ATM offers a true edge-to-edge single platform for all these types of traffic.
Furthermore, standards such as LAN emulation (LANE) and multiprotocol
over ATM (MPOA) enable native ATM devices to interwork seamlessly with
legacy LAN devices. ATM combines the high speeds of *circuit* switching with
the flexibility of *packet* switching over a single simplified network infrastructure. ATM is also highly flexible and scalable, allowing support of systems
ranging from small private networks to very large public networks. ATM
offers the following benefits:

- ☺ Seamless integration of multiple traffic types through QoS class sup-
  port
- ☺ Efficient bandwidth utilization by statistical multiplexing for bursty
  traffic
- ☺ Guaranteed bandwidth and resource allocation
- ☺ Dynamic bandwidth management
- ☺ Suitability for both delay/loss-sensitive and delay/loss-insensitive traffic
- ☺ Seamless private and public network technology
- ☺ Seamless LAN-to-WAN technology, enterprise-wide
- ☺ Automatic configuration and failure recovery
- ☺ Cost-effective, hardware-based fixed-length cell processing
- ☺ Improved transmission utilization versus multiple separate networks
- ☺ Future-proof investment resulting in lower life-cycle cost

ATM will allow companies and users to build networks based on the future vision of uniting voice, data, and video communications on ATM-based equipment. The potential of ATM to improve application and network performance and lower overall network, equipment, and operating costs in the long term, and in many cases in the short term, is the theme and reason for this book.

2.4.1.1 Service, Corporation, and Customer Benefits

The greatest benefits to ATM that are immediately recognizable to the service provider, corporation, and customer are:

Service Provider
- Consolidation into a single common network protocol infrastructure
- Increased interoperability and service functionality
- Single, integrated access circuit used for voice, data, and video
- Reductions in support cost and capital cost
- Future-proof network services architecture

Consumer
- Lower cost
- Single, integrated access circuit used for voice, data, and video
- Definable quality of service
- Single public communication infrastructure

Corporation
- Same benefits as service provider if building private network
- Same benefits as consumer, but on a larger scale
- Single, cost-effective technology for seamlessly handling both multimedia LAN and WAN communications requirements

Let's look at each of these benefits in more detail.

2.4.1.2 Service Provider Benefits

ATM offers service providers the ability to install and manage a single, common protocol infrastructure over which they can trunk integrated access of voice and data services such as ATM, frame relay, SMDS, X.25, private line, videoconferencing, and voice. ATM offers a mature, international standard–based public communications infrastructure for combining voice and data, guaranteeing compatibility and interoperability among various vendors and service providers.

Significant capital and operations/support cost savings can be achieved through the statistical multiplexing features of ATM. Public shared networks serve corporate customers which would otherwise build large networks based on dedicated private lines. A combined network avoids inefficient and costly parallel voice and data networks. This future-proofs the service provider's network, while supplying an infrastructure that provides maximum protocol and service interoperability.

2.4.1.3 Consumer Benefits

ATM lowers the cost of voice, video, and data services delivery to the residential consumer by combining these into a single access facility. ATM to the home lowers the cost per megabit per second for multimedia services while maintaining a definable quality of service for each type of media traffic through a single, integrated access circuit used for voice, data, and video. A single public communication infrastructure and provider can be used. Instead of having separate phone, cable TV, and Internet bills, ATM would offer the potential for a single service.

2.4.1.4 Corporate Benefits

Corporations can gain the same benefits of shared access and trunking that a service provider or residential consumer would. They could also enjoy the same lower cost per megabit per second and integrated access benefits as other consumers. In addition, corporations could deploy ATM as the single, cost-effective technology for handling their multimedia LAN and WAN communications requirements.

2.4.2 ATM Barriers and Risks

What are some of the predicted barriers and risks to ATM's success? Already, ATM has blown past many of these barriers and reduced the risk with its rapid deployment in both WAN and LAN implementations. Table 2.3 shows the risks and barriers as well as the reality of ATM today [7].

While we paint a somewhat rosier picture than some industry sages foresee, we are cognizant that ATM still has barriers to overcome. The lack of applications development has discouraged some early adopters of ATM. Cost is now much less of an issue than in the past, since the prices for equipment and communications lines continue to decrease. Operational costs remain high, however, because the cost of managing the network may exceed the hardware and software costs — and usually does.

ATM also has some competitive risks from technologies such as 100-Mbps FDDI, 100-Mbps Ethernet, switched Ethernet, and fast Ethernet, although these technologies handle only data, while ATM allows for multimedia — voice, data, and video. After the main body of the book defines ATM and its applications and implementations, Part 6 will provide an in-depth analysis of these competing technologies. Only time will tell which technology or service will succeed the most — in fact, combinations of them will probably be used for many years to come. Learning to mix and match these technologies is a part of the art of networking for the future.

Table 2.3 ATM Risks versus Reality

Predicted Risk or Barrier	Reality
Cost of switching equipment	Total workstation cost per Mbps is less than half of Ethernet and switched Ethernet.
Forklift upgrade	True in workgroups, but interworking over public service can lower costs, and switched Ethernet often requires a LAN switch forklift upgrade.
Cost of new NIC cards	155-Mbps NIC costs are less than double the price of 100BASET NICs, and the gap is narrowing.
Lack of standards	All important standards are now available, some still include LANE, PNNI and MPOA.
Interoperability issues	Service interworking is available with FR now, ATM interoperability labs (e.g., UNH) opening up.
Higher operations costs	ATM Forum and IETF standards promise multivendor management
High communications costs: DS1 or DS3	Cost-effective nxDS1 and DS1 services, standard inverse multiplexing over ATM (ATM) are available.
Performance issues	Many switch performance benchmarks prove ATM achieves near wire speed switching.
Lack of product choice	100+ ATM vendors from NICs to backbone switches. All major LAN and telco manufacturers have ATM products.
Network management	This is a real issue to explore — consider outtasking.
Security	This is a real issue with few solutions today. High-speed encryption (DS3) over ATM is available.

2.5 REVIEW

ATM now interworks seamlessly with other WAN and LAN networking technologies. ATM offers protocol and transmission enhancements over today's communications superhighways by providing cost-effective transport of these new applications. Marketing data has been reviewed that predicts that ATM will dominate older technologies by the year 2000. ATM has emerged to interwork with other broadband technologies to offer protocol and transmission enhancements over today's communications superhighways and also enable cost-effective transport of these new applications. The landscape of data networking into the next century (and millennium) is one of constant change and ever-increasing virtualization of networking resources. It will be a continuing war on technological obsolescence. It is to that environment that we turn our study. The next chapter reviews the major changes shaping the corporate and residential network computing environment.

2.6 REFERENCES

[1]   V. Jacobson, R. Braden, and D. Borman, IETF RFC 1323, "TCP Extensions for High Performance," May 1992.

[2]   A. Gerard, Issue 908, *Electronic Engineering Times*, July 1, 1996.

[3]   Dell'Oro Group, Menlo Park, California.

[4]   Dynatech Communications, *LAN Times* article, April 10, 1995.

[5]   www.3Com.com/nsc/industry.

[6]   *Communications Week*, November 13, 1995.

[7]   *Data Communications*, September 1996, www.data.com.

3

Major Changes in the Network Computing Environment

This chapter describes the major changes in today's computing environment that serve as additional drivers for ATM. Battles rage for the desktop, LAN, and WAN while old empires and paradigms topple and new ones gain in magnitude and power. ATM has the opportunity to play a lead role as the key technology in these corporate and communication architecture shifts that offer enterprise-wide multiprotocol interworking. Outsourcing and outtasking play a key role in many corporations' migration to new technologies like ATM.

3.1 CHANGING CORPORATE AND COMMUNICATION INFRASTRUCTURES

Corporate infrastructures on the business side continue to change and evolve with the times at an ever-increasing pace. One example is the flattening of the corporate organization and the empowerment of the professional and general worker with workstations and/or PCs. So too must network and transmission communications infrastructures change. Organizations streamline processes and communications through automation, increasing their speed and productivity—this is progress in the information age. In parallel, the advent of technologies like ATM running over high-performance digital transmission facilities fundamentally changes networking and communications. ATM, as a network technology, improves the way business is done and provides strong business benefits that parallel advances in organizational development. Networks have slowly evolved, for example, from centralized to distributed processing, fueled by the move toward distributed computing, client-server, and Web server intranetworking. This shift has caused traditional SNA legacy protocols to merge with inter-networking protocols like TCP/IP, and legacy IP to merge with ATM. The communications traffic patterns between what were traditionally local, metropolitan, and wide area networks are changing. The old 80/20 rule, that 80 percent of the traffic is local and 20 percent long distance, is no longer true in many enterprises. Indeed, in some organizations that make heavy use of intranets, only 20 percent of the traffic is local and the remaining 80 percent remote. Its the 80/20 rule all right, but in reverse. Merging and meshing in the evolutionary networking process, LANs demand native transfer speeds across the WAN, and applications now require multiple quality of service (QoS) standards to handle the mix of voice, data, and video over a single shared medium.

Many technology changes are occurring in parallel with organizational and infrastructure changes. Faster protocols are replacing 10-Mbps Ethernet and 4- to 16-Mbps Token Ring LANs as multiuser LANs run out of bandwidth. Many users require far-reaching solutions beyond segmenting LANs and LAN switching. Technologies like 100-Mbps Ethernet and ATM in the LAN, combined with LAN and ATM switching, are displacing older technologies like Token Ring and FDDI.

Distributed routing with IP and ATM technology moves to the periphery of the network, where it is more cost-effective, connecting families of LAN switches together which offers lower cost per port alternatives. The cost of bandwidth in the LAN and WAN decreases rapidly, and advances in fiber-optic transmission technology such as Wave-Division Multiplexing (WDM) will make WAN bandwidth in the future relatively inexpensive. Gigabit Ethernet and ATM will have the same effect in the LAN. These trends have enabled new methods of creating LAN work-groups that share multiple servers spanning multiple physical locations – and hence the growth of virtual LANs (VLANs). The Internet has not escaped these trends either; witness the creation of intranets and extranets within the Internet and the creation of client-server and Web server intranetworks. Now, it is time for a rhetorical question: Will IP and ATM be the technologies that will provide the infrastructures to support these trends? Let's look first at the evolution in transmission infrastructures that will help answer this question.

3.1.1 Change Started at the Desktop

Applications and business needs expand to fill the opportunities that technology provides cost-effectively. Cost drives the usage of computing and communications by applications. Although basic computing and communications costs have declined dramatically over the last 20 years, applications have offset these gains by requiring more and more bandwidth in the LAN, as well as the WAN. User expectations have risen.

The workstation provided the user with the device for desktop access to the world of data. Mass storage of information shrank to a fraction of its original size and cost. Now the most expensive and dynamic element is no longer hardware, but software. Indeed, the cost of software on a modern PC easily exceeds the hardware investment.

Initially, corporate data processing looked upon personal computers (PCs), such as the first Apple computer born in a "garage shop", as mere toys for games and other amusements. That all changed as the PC matured and then bore a more powerful offspring, the workstation. Large computer manufacturers noticed PCs on the desks of users who had previously had only a "dumb" terminal connected to the host. IBM legitimized the personal computer through the announcement of its personal computer in 1983. Since then, the PC has been the industry standard for corporate and government computing. Today, a PC occupies virtually every information worker's desktop. Workstations and their close cousin the network computer now hold the premier position in the computing industry. In the 1990s, mobile personal computing devices pack mainframe power in packages decreasing in size to the laptop and even the palmtop.

The battle for the desktop over the next few years will be between the power workstation with Pentium processor and mass gigabyte storage, running Windows and many other memory-intensive programs locally, and the network computer that accesses programs from the network and stores data within the intelligent network. ATM is well positioned to play a dominant role to connect either of these devices in new and interesting ways.

3.1.2 Distributed Computing and Client-Server Networking

Corporate infrastructures require communications networking flexibility to respond to ever-changing business needs. Reorganizations, mergers, and layoffs frequently place information workers in different physical locations, accessing different network resources. These changes have caused a move toward the distribution of the processing of data, along with the geographic distribution of clients and the servers supporting groups of these clients. Today, more and more computing is accomplished through distributed processing and client-server relationships. *Distributed processing* is the distribution of network intelligence and processing to many network sites, where each site communicates on a peer-to-peer level, rather than through a centralized hierarchy.

Client-server architectures, where client workstations communicate with distributed servers for their core information, have become a major trend in distributed processing. These servers provide the means for multiple clients to share applications within a logical, or virtual, workgroup. Client-server computing distributes the actual storage and processing of information among many sites, as opposed to storing and processing all information at a single, centralized location. This model reflects the increasingly flatter organizational structure and the need for increased connectivity and communications. Figure 3.1 illustrates a computer communications network supporting the distributed client-server architecture. A server may be locally attached to a router or LAN switch, part of a VLAN but within the same logical local network, or else remotely accessed across the WAN.

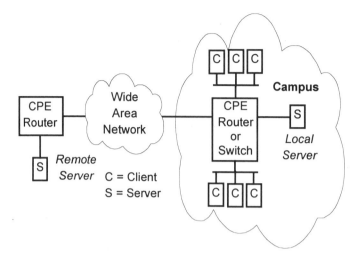

Figure 3.1 Distributed Client-Server Processing Network

3.1.3 IBM SNA and Internetwork Protocol Convergence

The architectural differences between IBM's hierarchical SNA protocol structure and the newer Internet Protocol (IP)–based routed networks are significant, but the ability exists for the two to converge. Many devices explored in the following chapters allow SNA traffic to be combined with true "routable" traffic in a routed or switched architectural environment. This is creating a groundswell of traditional SNA legacy users moving to technologies like frame relay and ATM.

IBM has cautiously embraced ATM as its next-generation technology, and has featured a new line of ATM switches called the Nways product line. Details on these products can be found in the hardware summary in Part 3.

3.1.4 The Need for LAN/MAN/WAN Connectivity

Most major corporate locations have one or more LANs. LAN traffic, once confined to significantly lower speeds across the WAN, is now being transported over broadband private lines and services like ATM to provide communication at full LAN speeds across the WAN. The limiting factor now becomes delay, which is affected only by the speed of light propagation. Typically, two scenarios found in corporations and growing businesses drive the need for greater LAN connectivity across the wide area. The first is an increased need for interconnection between distributed computing devices on remote LANs. The second is the logical extension of LAN-speed communications across wider geographic areas, for example, access to intranet servers. Geographically dispersed LANs now have a range of connectivity choices — from dedicated circuits to switched wide area and metropolitan area networks to public multimegabit broadband data services. The choice of technology and services is based upon many factors other than cost. In fact, the technology drivers of internetworking LANs lead to the hybrid use of private data networks in conjunction with public WAN services in many large corporations.

Computer networking has been defined in many ways. The following six definitions are commonly used in the industry:

Local Area Network (LAN): Distance on the order of 0.1 km (350 ft); provides local connectivity, typically within a building, floor, or room. Some environments can dedicate LAN segments to single users through LAN switching.

Campus Area Network (CAN): Distance on the order of 1 km (0.6 mi); provides connectivity between buildings in the same general area. FDDI and ATM backbones often serve this need.

Metropolitan Area Network (MAN): Distance on the order of 10 km (6.0 mi.); provides regional connectivity, typically between campuses over the geographic area associated with a major population center.

Wide Area Network (WAN): Distance on the order of 100 to 10,000 km (60 to 6000 mi); provides national connectivity.

Global Area Network (GAN): Distance on the order of 1000 to 20,000 km (600 to 12,000 mi) or more; provides connectivity between nations.

Virtual Local Area Network (VLAN): Distance varies from a few feet to thousands of kilometers; provides virtual LAN connectivity to geographically diverse users. A VLAN appears as a single shared LAN to its users.

3.1.5 Increasing Inter-LAN Traffic

Typical LAN interconnect speeds across the WAN, which were once limited to thousands of bits per second (kbps), are now typically tens or hundreds of millions of bits per second (Mbps), and up to billions of bits per second (Gbps) in leading-edge networks. Recently, IP switching has promised to increase routed LAN interconnect speeds across the WAN using ATM as the backbone switching fabric. Once an enterprise establishes a LAN, many factors drive the LAN to expand in physical and logical size. The amount of data traffic continues to grow at rates averaging 30 percent per year, or more. The capacity of the bridges, routers, hubs, gateways, and switches required to transport, switch, and route that data must increase in the same proportion. Many international corporations have already implemented worldwide LAN interconnection using a mix of private and public data services, including the Internet. The business drivers for expanding local area networking usually fall into one or more of the following categories:

- Increased inter- and intra-LAN traffic
- Remote and mobile access to LAN resources
- Higher-speed transmission rates
- Increased application function and performance
- Cross-domain routing or cross-mainframe access capabilities
- Need for additional intra- and intercompany user connectivity
- Expansion of the business through growth or acquisition
- Changing organizational structures and right sizing

3.1.6 Bandwidth-on-Demand

One interpretation of bandwidth-on-demand originally arose in the LAN environment, where many users shared a single high-bandwidth medium. At any instant only a few users statistically speaking were likely to be active — thus a large portion of the shared-medium bandwidth was available for their use. Hence, bandwidth was not dedicated and was available to users more or less "on demand." Another interpretation of bandwidth-on-demand comes from the telephone network, where a call (demand) is placed for bandwidth. The call attempt usually succeeds, failing only with a small blocking probability, and hence can also be interpreted as bandwidth-on-demand. One advantage ATM adds to bandwidth-on-demand is the fair allocation of bandwidth among multiple users based on a set of service classes (assigning different priorities), unlike the contention-based bandwidth allocation of Ethernet.

Another opposite, but lesser, trend is the actual decrease in the need for bandwidth due to more efficient coding and compression schemes. The most common evidence is the fact that with availability of modems using compression for communication, voice-grade lines now approach the capacity of basic ISDN service. Also noteworthy is the continual decrease in the coding rates for videoconferencing, North American Television Standard Coding (NTSC), and High-Definition Television (HDTV) over time. Acceptable videoconferencing for business can be achieved at DS0 (64 kbps) rates today. NTSC coding was achieved at DS3 (45 Mbps) rates in the late 1980s, and is now approaching the DS1 (1.5 Mbps) rate for noninteractive programming. The need for 150 Mbps for HDTV transmission has also evaporated due to similar increases in coding efficiencies. Of course, the improvements in coding efficiencies are limited by the actual information content of the signal. In general, these schemes for efficient coding and compression arise when bandwidth is inordinately expensive, or when there is a competitive niche that justifies the expense of such coding or compression. The maturation of these compression schemes in standards-based forms will likely enable cost-effective video distribution and applications.

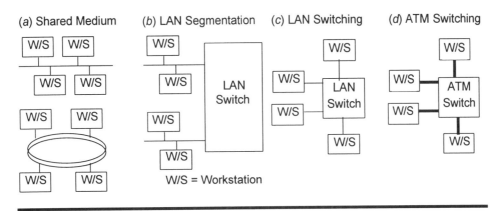

Figure 3.2 Evolution from Shared Medium to High-Performance Switching

3.1.7 The Death of Shared Media, the Middle-Age Crisis of Routing, and the Birth of Switching

A fundamental technology change is a shift from routers and hubs to LAN and ATM switching. The 1990s saw LAN segmentation, along with LAN or MAC-layer switching, move into the LAN to resolve bottlenecks and overcome broadcast storms. Historically, LAN and MAN technologies — Ethernet (IEEE 802.3), 100BASET Fast Ethernet, Token Ring (IEEE 802.5), FDDI (ANSI X3.139 or ISO 9314), and the Distributed Queue Dual Bus (DQDB) (IEEE 802.6) — all connected to network devices through a shared medium, as shown in Figure 3.2a. Users on the shared medium potentially have access to the entire shared-medium bandwidth. A problem occurs when more than a few users are active on a 10-Mbps Ethernet, resulting in a usable throughput of less than 4 Mbps. Capacity then becomes the limiting factor. The same phenomenon occurs with 100-Mbps Ethernet, Token Ring, FDDI, and DQDB, although some of these protocols achieve network throughputs approaching media speed through more sophisticated resource allocation methods. However, when the users' desktop rate approaches the shared-medium speed, there is no choice but to move to the next higher-speed shared-medium LAN solution or to segment the LANs into several LANs with fewer users per segment. As application demand for more bandwidth increases, LAN administrators must decrease the number of users per LAN segment. The need to manage this environment and enable greater throughput between heavily loaded LAN segments created the market for LAN switches, as shown in Figure 3.2b. The shared bus speed inside the LAN switch limits the maximum network throughput. As workstation power increases, this example reduces to a single user per LAN segment connected to a LAN switch, as shown in Figure 3.2c. Typically, LAN switches operate at higher speeds than hubs; hence network throughput increases further. ATM Network Interface Cards (NICs) in workstations and servers, working in conjunction with ATM workgroup switches, act as a common logical interface technology that can scale each interface from 25 Mbps to 155 Mbps without requiring changes in software to support a new shared-medium solution, as shown in Figure 3.2d. Because the ATM network switches work coopera-tively, network throughput grows as the number of ATM switches increases — readily achieving gigabit virtual LAN performance.

As users move from 10-Mbps to 100-Mbps Ethernet as their LAN technol-ogy of choice, each user also typically requires more bandwidth to the desktop, which has the net effect of reducing the number of users on each Ethernet segment (sometimes down to a single user) despite the higher bandwidth available per segment. A requirement emerges for a device that can provide simple switching of LAN traffic within the LAN at the MAC layer without complicated routing schemes. Thus, LAN switches begin to dominate the LAN intra- and interconnectivity market, solving the problems of graceful LAN segmentation and growing capacity constraints with a scalable switched LAN solution.

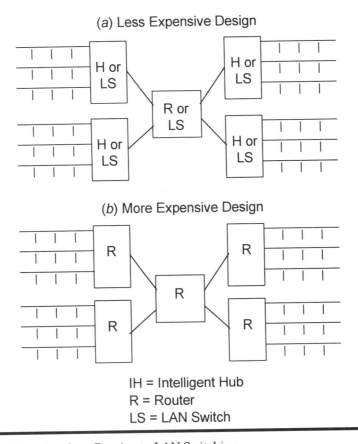

Figure 3.3 Migration from Routing to LAN Switching

Another way to look at this move to LAN switching is from a cost perspective. Hubs, intelligent hubs, and LAN switches are often simpler and thus less expensive than routers. Routers historically have handled the more complex routing functions, while hubs handled the less complex aggregation and bridging functions. In IP networks, end systems in the same IP subnet can communicate at the MAC layer without more complex IP routing. One example, bridging, works at the MAC layer. Figure 3.3 shows two examples. In the first (Figure 3.3a), a router is used to aggregate LAN switches to the WAN; this is the least expensive way of performing this function. Figure 3.3b illustrates the older and more expensive method of aggregating multiple LAN segments with routers and then using a single router to access the WAN. In these configurations, each router can become the bottleneck. The solution is to install bigger, more expensive routers, or to move to alternative higher-performance technologies, many of which involve ATM.

3.1.8 Virtual Networking and Virtual LANs (VLANs)

The LANs we have grown to love (or hate) over the last 20 years were designed so that all users of specific resources were grouped and assigned on a single physical LAN. First repeaters extended a LAN segment, and then bridges connected multiple physical LAN segments. As internetworks grew, LAN administrators employed routers to interconnect them and address the limited scalability of bridged networks. A trend in this evolution is that each new technology overcame the bottlenecks and limitations of its predecessor. As distributed LAN-based server and application resources proliferate at multiple diverse physical locations, the requirement that users not *physically* colocated be able to share resources increases. VLANs enable users to transcend their physical bodies for the greater nirvana of the *logical* workgroup. VLANs create communities of interest between users on different physical LAN media, giving the appearance that they are physically attached to the same physical LAN. VLAN resources still appear local to each user, regardless of whether they share the same physical LAN segment or are half a world away. Connectivity is readily achieved over the WAN; however, performance may suffer unless the VLAN is carefully designed. Multiple MAC and network protocols can be supported within the same VLAN, rather than requiring the conformation of all users within a VLAN to use the same MAC protocol (such as Ethernet over IP).

VLANs can greatly reduce the administrative burden involved in adds, moves, and changes — the greatest cause of increased cost, complexity, and downtime for a LAN administrator. Client workstations operate only a shell of the original application retrieved from the server. A similar environment is emerging in the Internet, where users with network computers access multiple servers across the Internet, downloading Java programs only when they are required to run, and then releasing them from taking up memory when the user is finished with the program. This paradigm also has the side benefit that the user always runs the latest version of the program. Servers typically enable users to share expensive resources such as printers, CD-ROM jukeboxes, mass storage, and large databases — now they can share application and networking software as well.

Figure 3.4 shows an example of a virtual LAN connecting user devices in three geographic locations. Note that users A, B, and C have access to the server in location 2 as if it was on a local Ethernet or FDDI LAN, since they are bridged. Many VLAN designs are being built with switching hubs that use some proprietary method of switching between VLAN user groups. The most common methods of implementing VLANs as of press time included the proprietary Inter-Switch Link (ISL), IEEE 802.10, and ATM LAN Emulation (LANE) standards. More information on ATM LANE will be provided in Chapter 10.

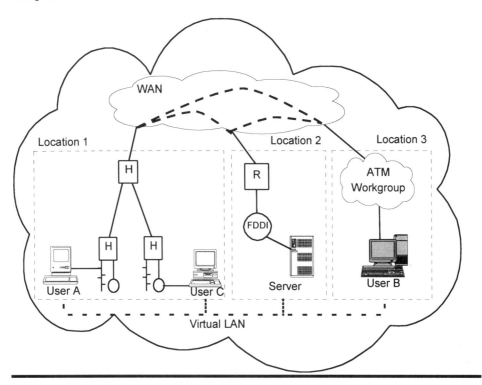

Figure 3.4 Virtual LAN Example

3.1.9 Intranets and Extranets

The Internet has grown phenomenally in the mid 1990s, and shows no signs of slowing down. The Internet continues to be the most commonly used medium for computer communications. The Internet services market was estimated at $4 billion in 1997. The number of Internet users is estimated to be over 50 million, with a double-digit growth rate each month. The Internet continues to be *the* information superhighway — the Infobahn. No speed limits are defined (once you get past the on-ramp), but congestion can occur — and often does.

Data traffic often represents the most private and sensitive information of an enterprise. Therefore, the majority of data traffic is typically intra-enterprise. In contrast, enterprises communicate a large amount of voice traffic over public telephone lines, both on network (intranet) and off the network (extranet). Enterprises are now forming intranetworks and extranetworks using the Internet as the transport medium, rather than purchasing more expensive dedicated transport facilities. Labeled "intranet within Internet", these communities of users communicate with each other within their company by means of the public Internet. The concept is similar to Virtual Private Data Networks (VPDNs), but uses the Internet as the transport utility. An "extranet" is created when a corporate intranet is extended to external entities, as when a corporation has a distribution partner with whom it shares computing resources. Figure 3.5 illustrates these concepts. In this example location 1 is an intranet for Company ABC, which is part of an extranet with Company XYZ's server at location 2 and high-end Web page design group at location 3. The tremendous growth in Internet traffic is an example of the burgeoning demand for data communication over public shared facilities.

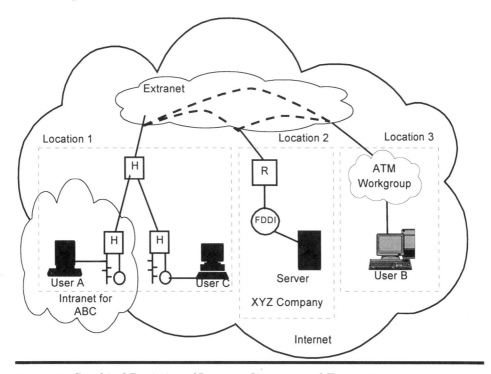

Figure 3.5 Graphical Depiction of Internet, Intranet, and Extranet

Companies are designing enterprise and interenterprise (or intercorporate) intranets, partitioned by firewalls, guaranteeing bandwidth and delivery using ATM technology. Traffic requirements in the LAN and across the WAN will explode as intranet and extranet users access information via their browsers from multimedia Web servers over switched LAN and ATM infrastructures. The challenge for ATM will be to gain market share by enabling Internet providers to offer a QoS-enabled solution (versus IP's RSVP) and bring low-cost competition to bear.

3.1.10 Intranet and Extranet Security

When the corporate network of company A is tied to the corporate network of company B, via either private lines or switched services, internetworking takes place across a secure extranet, as shown in Figure 3.6. This is often the case when two companies need to share vital information such as engineering CAD/CAM files, databases, groupware, and other applications. This connectivity between two or more corporate, government, or university private networks usually occurs through the use of public network services.

If public data services provide good security and partitioning, then the portion of interenterprise traffic carried by carrier services should increase. An enterprise, however, needs to control what communication can occur both within and outside its boundaries. Security screening, filtering, and blocking can be done in a connection-oriented environment through signaling, or in a connectionless environment through the use of screening tables or filters in routers. However, implementing too much filtering on a router interface can dramatically reduce routed throughput, since the security rules must be applied to every packet. Internetworking works well as long as security precautions are taken by both the service provider and the end-user networks. It is a common practice today for users to install separate "fire-wall" routers that filter the context and content of packets, circuits, and application protocols to prevent intrusion from the "outside" and "inside," but the key is to keep constant vigilance on these firewalls to make sure the security policy is well enforced. Some management service providers offer a service of this type. Another trend is to install security servers within the LAN and WAN infrastructure and use physical key-coded security devices on the remote and dial access ports to the network, but placing these "bars on the windows" is just the first step in network perimeter security. Monitoring all security policies 24 hours a day, 7 days a week is a must. An experienced hacker can always find a way in, no matter how good the security precautions, and someone must be watching round the clock and repel the break-in attempts.

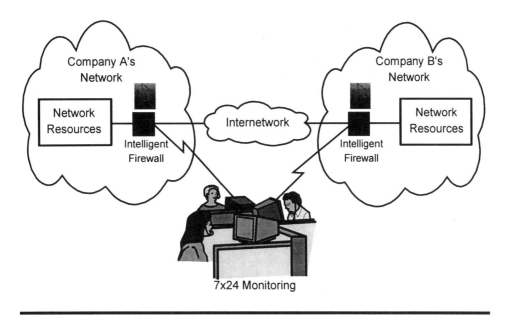

Figure 3.6 Intercorporate Internetworking

3.1.11 Supporting the Mobile Workforce

The need for seamless interworking also extends to mobile computing and access. Mobile communications and phone links that extend the LAN to the automobile, commuter train, meeting room, or hotel room are becoming commonplace as business travelers carry mobile-communications-equipped computers and computing devices. Lower-speed access will perform sophisticated data compression and protocol conversion for interconnection into the seamless internetwork. The development of the wireless ATM standards described later in this book targets this environment.

The percentage of mobile workers and telecommuters in many businesses is drastically increasing. Mobility ranges from taking a laptop home at night or over the weekend, to complete home offices, to being a traveling salesperson with continual remote access from wherever (i.e., airports, hotel rooms, customer facilities), to the user located in a remote area requiring alternative access like cellular or wireless, to customers and partners remote from the business yet needing access to information resources, and vice versa. Thus, PC and workstation mobility with ubiquitous access to mainframe, server, and LAN corporate resources is key to the success of any technology. This is also a key requirement for ATM.

3.2 THE OUTSOURCING AND OUTTASKING PHENOMENON

The many complexities of ATM networking may require a decision to outsource, or outtask, the design, installation, and management of an ATM network. This is a business decision that users must carefully investigate. Interworking ATM with non-ATM protocols creates a complex environment. In fact, the complexity of networking increases at a rate that exceeds the capability of even large firms to hire and train people. Thus enterprise network managers turn to outtasking providers, such as NetSolve, to provide the outtasking functions.

The outtasking decision will be one of the most important decisions made by the network manager. Internally designing and developing a network involves the stages of planning, building, and maintaining a network for the business. Outsourcing network support involves a third party's taking over *some* (outtasking) or *all* (outsourcing) aspects of the corporation's data network. Elements of outtasking range from simple monitoring and reporting to life-cycle design, installation, and management of the entire network. Outtasking runs the gamut from mundane tasks to mission-critical functions, and ranges from augmenting to replacing internal resources (i.e., tools and talent). Furthermore, outtasking and outsourcing are competitive tools, not just means to achieve cost savings.

The decision to outsource or outtask key business and network functions is often one of business policy based on many factors, such as

* Ease of transition to new technologies or architectures
* Allowing company to focus on its core competencies
* Corporate resource limitations
* Return on investment (ROI) analysis within financial constraints
* Skill set and reliability of the outtasking vendor
* Cost factors of either owning the network business elements or leasing them from the outsource partner (make vs. buy)
* Retention of network control
* Resource or financial constraints
* Deductible expense versus capital investment
* Sensitivity and security of network data

Other factors also play a major role in the outsourcing decision such as how much support is required for how long, contract stipulations between user and vendor, and loyalty to existing company employees. The decision to outsource or outtask may have many potential business impacts, including

⇒ Resources (staff and existing investments in tools)
⇒ Questions on skill sets and reliability of the vendors performing the outsourcing function
⇒ Cost savings or eventual loss (insufficient ROI)

⇒ Control of the network hardware and software

⇒ Network management or monitoring

⇒ Ability of the company to either continue outsourcing or outtasking or bring the network business back in-house

A business considering outsourcing should perform the following process:

- Identify candidate network and application elements for outsourcing and/or outtasking
- Define expectations of the implementation
- Compare current employee skill sets with those of outtasking/ outsourcing company
- Plan what to do with current resources (if there are any)
- Fully understand the vendor-user relationship
- Fully understand when you "break even" on ROI
- Define the outsourcing demarcations — for example, which protocols, interfaces, and locations are covered and which are not
- Determine the duration of the outsourcing contract, ideally three to five years depending on the amount of effort required to regain control of the network should the outsourcing deal not work out
- Plan for future capability and expansion
- Choose a reliable outsourcing company, preferably one with experience and a track record — be sure to ask for references
- Maintain the loyalty of the retained staff and ensure the loyalty of the new staff by providing a retraining plan
- Do not announce your intentions prematurely to your staff

Outsourcing, or outtasking, should be a partnership between the user and the vendor. Define the vendor's plan for updating its technology and workforce. Make sure the outsourcing vendor is able to adapt to your company's business needs as well as its own, to maintain your future growth and competitiveness. This is a key element of the ideal partnership. However, wise network managers should always keep alternative outsourcing vendors available as an option since any partnership can falter over time.

The primary benefits of outsourcing are the following:

- + Uses vendor experience and specialists.
- + Allows the company to focus on its core business rather than designing, installing, and managing networks.
- + Reduces costs (improves ROI) and resources required.
- + Augments your existing workforce with skilled workers.
- + Enables fault tolerance in your staff through outtasking.
- + Frees up your time to be more strategic and proactive — to make your core business grow faster and further.

The potential drawbacks of outsourcing include:

- − Loss of control
- − Possible loss of in-house expertise and resources
- − Possible sacrifice of technology flexibility
- − Risk of impact to critical systems if vendor fails

These potential drawbacks can be countered with good planning, smart management, and the proper choice of a partner/vendor. The requirement for ATM outsourcing and outtasking will continue to grow rapidly. As a final recommendation, ask yourself the following questions: Is designing, installing, and managing a network a part of our core competencies? If not, will outsourcing *all* or outtasking *part* of it be the best decision?

3.3 THE DESKTOP, LAN, AND WAN PROTOCOL WARS — MONOPOLIES ABOUND!

Multiple players and technologies have networked the desktop, LAN, and WAN over the last 20 years. Who are the new kings of these domains? Who is the "king of the hill?" This section provides an overview of the battles raging across desktops, LANs, and WANs worldwide by identifying the dominant players and how they may affect the future of ATM. Table 3.1 shows the vendors and products that are losing in market presence (Out) and those that are increasing in market presence or leading their field (In).

Table 3.1 Who's Hot and Who's Not

Domain	Out	In
Operating system	Macintosh	Windows 9X and NT
LAN media protocol	10BASET, Token Ring, FDDI	100BASET, 100BASEFX, ATM
LAN and WAN networking protocol	DECnet, NetBEUI/NetBIOS, AppleTalk, SNA, IPX	IP, ATM

3.3.1 The Battle for the Desktop

Many bodies litter the battlefield for the space in front of the information worker's seat. Most of them wear the color red or smell of decaying fruit. DEC's, IBM's, and Macintosh's decrease in desktop market share made room for new players such as Compaq, Hewlett-Packard, and Sun. The winning side is clearly the Intel-based personal computer, originally running Microsoft's DOS but now, after yearly reinforcements, running the new and improved Windows 9X operating system. Intel, with an installed base of 180 million personal computers using its chip design, is by far the lead supplier, with few sizable competitors. In the high-powered workstation market, the winner is clearly the Sun and HP workstation, with the UNIX operating system fighting a rear-guard action against Java. In the server market, Novell once held over 70 percent of the network operating system market, but market dominance is quickly passing to Microsoft's Windows NT. Workstation and server hardware is still a close race between Compaq, Dell, and IBM.

Who will challenge Microsoft's dominance in the next century? The leading consortium, and the only currently viable option, appears to be the unlikely union of Sun Microsystems with its wildly popular Java language, IBM, and HP, all combined with the network computer (manufactured by most leading PC hardware vendors).

So how does this affect ATM? If Microsoft Windows is indeed the clear operating system winner, then ATM will require an interface into that operating system. This will enable support for ATM's key features, namely quality of service (QoS) and bandwidth allocation. The application programming interface (API) for ATM is Winsock 2.0, which both Windows NT and Windows 95 support. An API provides a software interface for applications to open connections and specify QoS requirements to an ATM network as described in Part 2.

3.3.2 The Battle for the Network Protocol — IP vs. "IPX and Everyone Else"

The battlefield is also littered with the flags of fallen nations who once ruled large internetworking kingdoms. Their names are chiseled like Gettysburg memorials in computer rooms across the world: MAP TOP, XNS, DNA, DECnet, NetBEUI/NetBIOS, AppleTalk, IPX, and even OSI. There are a few battles still raging, but the war has clearly been won — IP is the internetworking protocol of choice on desktops, servers, and network devices around the world. Who can win against a protocol that holds sway over 30 million Internet users alone? The last few Novell IPX fortresses have been surrounded and are under constant siege, and most companies that want to travel outside their IPX fortresses are doing so under the guise of IP. This upstart Internet protocol now dominates the networking world. By most studies, IP holds at least 70 percent of the internetworking market, with Novell's IPX now holding less than 18 percent.

How does ATM compete with IP in the WAN? It doesn't compete — it complements. A discussion of the comparisons of IP and its Reservation Protocol (RSVP) are found in Part 6.

3.4 REVIEW

With ATM options ranging from DS1/E1 through inverse multiplexed fractional (nxDS1/E1) speeds, to the 155-Mbps OC3 speed and higher, most industry pundits forecast that ATM will be the winning metropolitan, campus, and wide area network technology of choice by the end of the decade. The debate still rages, however, over control of the LAN. In this chapter we introduced the key application, technology, and infrastructure changes that are the shaping forces of networking for the beginning of the 21st century. ATM is at the forefront of this change in both the LAN and WAN. Having discussed the business and technological drivers for ATM, and weighed the risks and benefits of ATM, let's now explain the underlying principles of ATM.

4

Building Blocks of ATM

This chapter introduces basic network topologies and the terminology of layered communication networks. ATM utilizes an asynchronous approach to transferring data streams, as opposed to the synchronous schemes used widely today. Additionally, ATM supports both connectionless and connection-oriented services. ATM also implements most topologies, connection types, and circuit modes implemented in other technologies. Finally, the principles of private, public, and Virtual Private Networks (VPNs) will come into play. These concepts provide a firm foundation upon which to build the house of ATM in the next chapter.

4.1 TRANSMISSION BASICS REVIEW

This section provides the basics of the network topologies, connection and circuit types and services, and protocol layering concepts used in ATM.

4.1.1 Network Topologies

Physical network topology defines the interconnection of physical *nodes* by physical transmission *links*. *Nodes* are a network element, such as an ATM switch. This text also refers to nodes as *devices*, and to links as transmission *paths*.

Logical topology defines connections between logical nodes (or simply interfaces), which may be either *point-to-point* or *point-to-multipoint* configurations in ATM. Furthermore, each connection may be either *unidirectional* or *bidirectional*. A spatial point-to-multipoint connection has at the most one leaf per physical port, while a logical point-to-multipoint connection may have multiple leaves per physical port.

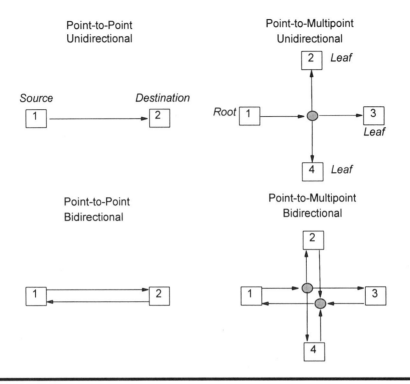

Figure 4.1 Conceptual Illustration of Logical Topologies

Figure 4.1 illustrates each of these logical topologies. Other technologies, such as Ethernet, support as a broadcast medium where any one station's transmission is received by all other stations. Additional protocols and configurations are required to support the broadcast logical topology. Part 2 describes the means by which ATM standards support broadcast through LAN Emulation (LANE) and IP multicast over ATM.

Links represent connections between nodes, either physical or logical. Therefore, a link may be either a logical, or virtual, connection, or it may be a physical connection such as a dedicated private line [1].

Figure 4.2 depicts the relationship between the physical transmission path, Virtual Path (VP), and Virtual Channel (VC). A transmission path contains one or more virtual paths, and each virtual path contains one or more virtual channels. ATM multiplexing and switching devices operate on the Virtual Path Identifier and Virtual Channel Identifier (VPI and VCI, respectively) to switch ATM cells. VP switching operates on the VPI field alone, while VC switching operates on both the VPI and VCI fields. This means that a virtual path carries multiple virtual channels between the endpoints of a logical connection.

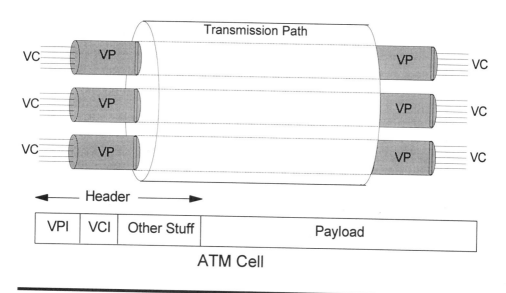

Figure 4.2 Relationship of VP, VC, and Transmission Path

4.1.2 Connection and Circuit Types and Services

A *private line*, or *leased line*, physically connects two devices, for example, a CPE-based LAN backbone switch and a carrier edge switch. Carriers lease private lines for a predetermined period of time, usually in increments of months or years. Thus, a dedicated, private portion of an actual, physical facility, such as copper or fiber, as well as bandwidth, is allocated between devices — hence the term *private line*. The only users of the circuit are the ports at the two ends of the circuit. In the United States, most private lines now utilize fiber-optic facilities. Leased lines used to access public services, like ATM, are frequently called *access lines* or *local loops*. These circuits provide the physical medium for the ATM User-to-Network Interface (UNI).

Switched services range from simple circuit switching, in which users dynamically select from a pool of multiple public service lines with fixed bandwidths, to intelligent ubiquitous switched access networks, where bandwidth is allocated and used only when needed, such as frame relay and ATM. Users signal the network with the addresses of the endpoints they desire to connect, similar to making a voice phone call to someone (point-to-point) or joining a conference call (multipoint-to-multipoint). This is how ATM provides bandwidth-on-demand, or, literally, bandwidth-on-call. Thus, switched networks offer an additional level of network flexibility and intelligence not found with private line networks.

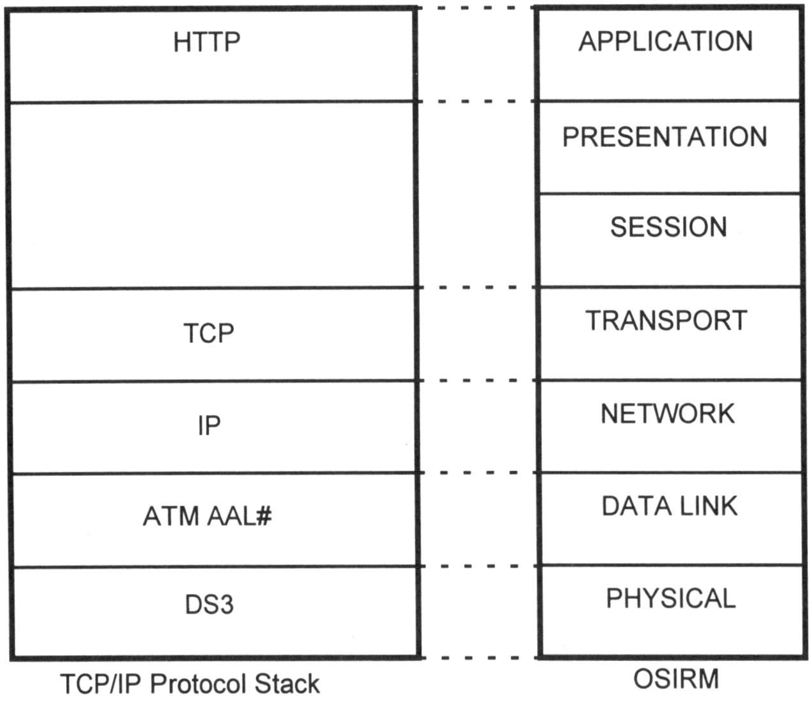

TCP/IP Protocol Stack	OSIRM
HTTP	APPLICATION
	PRESENTATION
	SESSION
TCP	TRANSPORT
IP	NETWORK
ATM AAL#	DATA LINK
DS3	PHYSICAL

Figure 4.3 TCP/IP Protocol Stack Compared to the OSIRM

4.1.3 Basic Protocol Layering Concepts

Figure 4.3 shows a simple IP over ATM mapped to the generic layered Internet protocol model. Although the International Standards Organization (ISO) created the concept of protocol layering with its infamous Open Systems Interconnection (OSI) protocol reference model (OSIRM), only X.25 and DECnet remain as major implementations of the protocols actually specified in this model. However, the concept of "layering" is an extremely useful one, as evidenced by its wide use within the industry and this text. Therefore, this key concept of layering is covered since the remainder of the book employs it extensively.

Interfaces provide boundaries between different types of hardware, and *protocols* provide rules, conventions, and the intelligence to pass data over these interfaces. Interfaces and physical media provide the path for data flow, while the protocols "manage" that data flow across the path and interfaces. Both interfaces and protocols must be compatible for accurate and efficient data transport. Often, interfaces are referred to only in the physical layer of the OSIRM. Protocols can also act as interfaces, being defined as interface protocols. Such protocols define the "interface" between the Data Termination Equipment–to–Data Communications Equipment (DTE-to-DCE) signaling and that information is transferred to higher-layer protocols for user presentation. Many network designs now incorporate multiple levels of protocols and interfaces, from the physical layer to the application layer of the seven-layer OSIRM.

Physical-layer protocol standards define electrical, optical, and mechanical interfaces to the transmission medium, as well as procedures and functions for their operation. The physical layer is concerned only with assuring the transmission and reception of a digital data stream between two devices. The intelligence managing the data stream and the protocols residing above the physical layer are unknown to the physical layer. Physical cable-connector characteristics, voltages and currents, and timing and signaling are examples of physical-layer specifications. Detailed specifications define data, control, timing, and grounding pin assignments on connectors. Procedural specifications define the procedures that govern the activation, use, and interpretation of these interface characteristics. Examples of the physical layer covered in this book include private lines, serial connectors, and local building wiring.

The terms *data termination equipment* and *data communication equipment* refer to the hardware on each side of the communications channel interface. A DTE is a computer or terminal which acts as an endpoint for transmitted and received data. The DTE communicates with the DCE via a physical interface. Typically, the DCE is a modem. Normally, the terms DTE and DCE are used only at the edge of the network, where end users connect. The DTE and DCE terminology also identifies standard cable configurations. Figure 4.4 shows a common end-to-end network configuration in which DTE 1 talks to DCE 1, which in turn formats the transmission for transfer over the network to DCE 2, which interfaces to DTE 2.

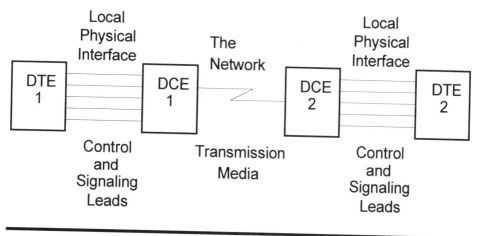

Figure 4.4 DTE-to-DTE Communication via DCE Physical Interfaces

The *data link layer* operates as layer 2 in both the TCP/IP and seven-layer OSI protocol models. The data link layer interfaces to the physical layer below it and the network layer above it, converting the bit stream on the physical media into information usable by the network-layer protocols. The primary functions of the data link layer are to establish a logical connection across the physical medium, manage reliable data flow, and terminate the logical connection if requested to do so. This layer may also provide functions and services such as error control, detection, and correction; flow control; framing and character formatting; synchronization; sequencing for proper delivery; connection control; and management functions.

Data link protocols use many circuit topologies including point-to-point, point-to-multipoint, and broadcast. Local area networks further divide the data link layer into the Media Access Control (MAC) and Logical Link Control (LLC) sublayers, as we describe in Part 2 as an introduction to ATM-based LAN Emulation (LANE). Once the data link layer builds frames and places them onto the physical medium, the network- and transport-layer protocols take over. Examples of data-link-layer protocols covered in this book are frame relay, ATM virtual path/channels, and LAN protocols.

The *network layer* is also common to both the TCP/IP and OSI layered models. The principal function of the network layer is to provide reliable, in-sequence delivery of protocol data between transport-layer entities. In order to do this, the network layer has an end-to-end addressing capability, where a unique network-layer address is assigned to each network-layer protocol entity. A network-layer protocol may communicate with its peer over a route of intermediate machines which process packets at the physical, data link, and network layers. The determination of this route is called the *routing function*. Network-layer protocol data units (PDUs) are often called *packets*.

The network layer may also perform end-to-end flow control and the segmentation and reassembly of data. Usually, the network layer is the most protocol-intensive portion of packet networks. Some examples of network-layer protocols covered in this book are the Internet Protocol, ATM signaling, and N-ISDN signaling. The network layer defines connection establishment procedures for Switched Virtual Connections (SVCs) in ATM, as covered in Chapter 9. SMDS also employs a layer 3 protocol to provide a connectionless datagram service using E.164 telephone-style addressing [2, 3].

The fourth layer encountered is the *transport layer*. The principal function of the transport layer is to interconnect session- (OSI) or application- (TCP/IP) layer entities. Historically, some also call this the host-host layer. Principal functions that it performs are segmentation, reassembly, and multiplexing of multiple transport connections over a single network-layer interface. The transport layer allows a session-layer entity to request a class of service, which must be mapped onto appropriate network-layer capabilities. The Internet's Transmission Control Protocol (TCP) is the dominant transport protocol in use today. TCP performs error detection and manages end-to-end flow control, sequencing, and multiplexing between multiple logical ports on a single computer. The transport layer provides error correction and retransmission for frame relay, SMDS, and ATM.

4.2 INTRODUCTION TO BRIDGING AND ROUTING

This section provides an introduction to the bridging and routing features embodied in ATM implementations.

4.2.1 Bridges

Initially, bridges provided connectivity between LANs of the same type — for example, Ethernet to Ethernet or Token Ring to Token Ring. Enterprises first employed bridges to link LANs with the same physical- and link-layer protocols, first across the hallway and then, in the 1980s, across entire continents. Bridges have more function than LAN repeaters, which simply extend the LAN physical media to greater distances. Translation bridges interconnect dissimilar media, such as Ethernet and Token Ring. Although this may seem trivial, it's not; for example, even the bit order differs on these media!

As depicted in Figure 4.5, bridges operate only at the physical and data link layers, and hence use less processing than a router, which must process both the data link layer and the network layer. Bridges are network-layer-protocol transparent; therefore, they support any higher-layer protocols. Bridges support both the LLC and the MAC sublayers within the data link layer.

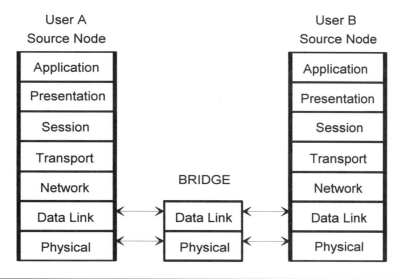

Figure 4.5 Bridge Communications Relationship in the OSIRM

Bridges pass traffic from one LAN segment to another based solely upon the destination MAC address. If the destination address of the frame received by the bridge is not local to the LAN segment, the frame is obviously destined for another LAN. Different types of bridges use different methods to determine the segment on which to send the frame. There are four major types of bridges: transparent, encapsulating, translating, and source-routed. The key attributes of each type of bridge are briefly summarized. Most modern bridges learn about the network through the spanning tree method standardized by the IEEE 802 committee. Some bridges implement more sophisticated, proprietary bridging protocols which perform some network-layer functions.

When operating in *transparent* mode, bridges at both ends of a transmission support the same physical media and link-layer (MAC-level) protocols from the IEEE 802.X suite; however, the transmission speeds may differ. Figure 4.6*a* and *b* shows examples of transparent bridging between two local Ethernet LANs and two local Token Ring LANs. Figure 4.6*c* shows encapsulation bridging between two Token Ring LANs using Channel Service Units (CSUs) or Data Service Units (DSUs). In encapsulation bridging, the LAN frame is placed in a data-link-layer frame [e.g., High-level Data Link Control (HDLC) or Point-to-Point Protocol (PPP)] over the point-to-point circuit, then deencapsulated without modification at the other bridge.

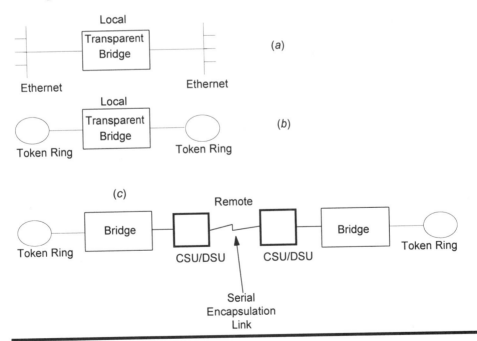

Figure 4.6 Transparent Mode Bridging

Figure 4.7 Translation Bridging

Sometimes network designers require bridges to interconnect dissimilar LANs, for example, Ethernet and Token Ring, as shown in Figure 4.7. Bridges must support a *translation* mode to interconnect different physical LAN media and link-layer protocols. Translation bridges, however, convert between the different MAC-layer frame structures of different LAN standards. A number of issues must be resolved for conversion between LAN protocols, including changing bit transmission ordering, reformatting, checksum recalculation, and control field interpretation [5]. Translation bridges cannot overcome different maximum frame sizes on different LAN types. Instead, the network administrator must ensure that users employ a maximum network-layer packet size that isn't too large for the most constraining LAN. For example, the maximum Ethernet frame size is 1500 bytes, while a token ring could have a maximum frame size of up to 4000 bytes. In this case, the hosts should use maximum packet sizes less than 1500 bytes since the Ethernet frame size is the most constraining.

When operating in *encapsulation* mode, bridges at both ends of the transmission use the same physical- and link-layer (MAC-level) LAN protocols, but the network between the bridges may be a different physical medium and/or link-layer MAC-level protocol. Encapsulating bridges place MAC frames from the originator within a media- and link-layer-specific envelope and forward the encapsulated frame to another bridge, which deencapsulates the MAC frame for delivery to the destination. Users frequently employ encapsulation bridges when multiple Ethernet segments are served by a high-speed Token Ring or FDDI backbone.

Figure 4.8 shows two examples of encapsulation bridging. The first example illustrates two local 10-Mbps Ethernet LANs bridged via a campus area 100-Mbps FDDI network. The second example shows the same two Ethernet LANs, this time bridged over a 4- or 16-Mbps Token Ring network. Beware of higher-layer network time-out problems when interconnecting higher-speed LANs over lower-speed LANs.

Figure 4.9 illustrates the *source route bridging* scheme between source and destination Token Ring LANs through three intermediate source route bridges. Source route bridging automatically distributes network topology information so that the source can determine the hop-by-hop path through specific intermediate bridges to the destination. These discovery packets add additional traffic to the network, but bridges and hosts cache the topology information for subsequent reference and use. The name *source route bridging* derives from the fact that the source determines the entire route. Interestingly, the ATM Forum's Private Network-Network Interface (PNNI) protocol uses source routing.

Source route bridging utilizes bandwidth more efficiently than spanning tree bridging; however, such systems are not truly plug-and-play, since some configuration must be performed before they will operate. We cover bridging protocols in more depth in Chapter 10.

4.2.2 Bridge Network Design

Bridges are best used in small networks which have a small number of end stations. Bridging device capacities and speeds vary, supporting subrate DS0 up through DS1 or DS3 across the WAN, and 100-Mbps FDDI or 155-Mbps ATM in the LAN. Higher speeds are needed to support the high-speed LANs connected to the bridge, such as 10-Mbps Ethernet and 16-Mbps Token Ring. Bridges provide local, remote, or both local and remote support.

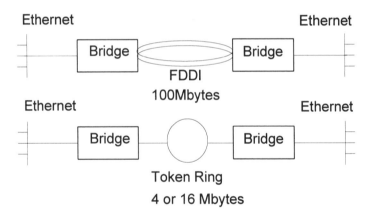

Figure 4.8 Encapsulation Bridging

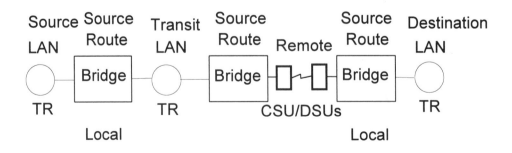

Figure 4.9 Source Route Bridging

Careful future planning is required when deploying a bridged network solution. The manager or engineer who employs a bridge solution may find that very soon his or her bridge solution will resemble a wood and stone bridge built in 1850 and designed to accommodate a horse and carriage. Soon there will be a need to drive not only a car but trucks over the bridge — only a few years later, rather than 100 years later. Also, remember that bridges support only a single network protocol.

Although simplicity and true plug-and-play operation are major advantages of bridging, some major disadvantages are also associated with bridging. Until a transparent bridge learns the destination LAN, it broadcasts packets on all outgoing LAN ports. When destinations are unreachable or have problems, applications resend data. Also, the spanning tree bridge uses LAN bandwidth inefficiently by sending all traffic up a tree to a root node and back out to destinations. Source route bridges add additional traffic through the use of discovery packets. Discovery packets are aptly named, as they are sent out to discover the best routing. Higher-layer protocols, such as NetBEUI, also generate significant amounts of broadcast traffic, which the bridges forward to every host. These phenomena and others create broadcast storms, a problem which increases with the size of the network and the number of users attached.

To minimize the problem, smart bridging techniques provide some level of traffic isolation by segmenting the bridged network into domains that restrict broadcast storms to a limited area. This containment method, coupled with a multicast traffic ceiling, provides some control over broadcast storms. Limited MAC address memory also limits the size.

Because of these disadvantages and limited capabilities, designers should avoid bridges in networks requiring multiple protocol support networks of greater than 50 nodes. Networks with one or more of the aforementioned requirements are better served by routers, for reasons explained in the next section.

4.2.3 Routers

Unlike most bridges, routers provide connectivity between like and unlike devices attached to local and wide area networks. Routers operate at the network-layer protocol, but usually also support link-layer bridging. Routers have a view of the entire network, not just locally connected devices, and determine the next hop to forward a packet based on many factors. The first generation of routers appeared at MIT, Stanford, and CMU in 1983, three years after their ARPANET predecessors. Over the last two decades routers have become the hottest thing in the marketplace since multiplexers, with much more intelligence than bridges or multiplexers.

Routers operate at the physical, data link, and network layers to provide a connectionless service between systems, as shown in Figure 4.10. In contrast to bridges, systems connected via routers may utilize different physical-, data-link-, and network-layer protocols. Of course, systems must employ the

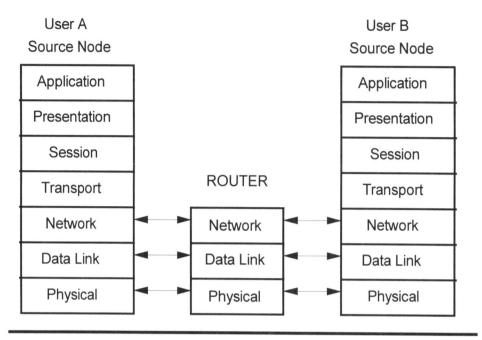

Figure 4.10 Router Communications via the OSIRM

same transport and application layers when communicating via routers, as they would with bridges.

Routers basically implement several key interrelated functions, as illustrated in Figure 4.11. Starting from the left-hand side, routers interface to a variety of LAN media, encapsulating and converting to a common network-layer protocol. Thus, routers naturally interconnect Ethernet, Token Ring, FDDI, and even ATM networks. Routers usually employ a packet forwarding engine which often resides in hardware or firmware. The packet forwarding function contains a lookup table which identifies the physical interface of the next hop toward the destination based upon the high-order bits of the packet address.

Routers employ routing protocol engines to dynamically obtain knowledge of the location of packet address prefixes across the entire routed internetwork. The routing protocol engine fills in the next-hop forwarding table in the packet forwarding function. Routing protocols discover network topology changes and provide rerouting by updating the forwarding tables. Routers employ routing protocols to continually monitor the state of the links that interconnect routers in a network, or the links with other networks. Routers can also limit the number of hops by the use of intelligent routing protocols and packets that keep track of the number of hops through use of a time-to-live algorithm. Routers employ large addressing schemes, typically 4 bytes worth in IP and even more with Novell IPX or OSI CLNP. Routers also support large packet sizes. Internal router bus speeds are also much higher than those of bridges, typically in excess of a gigabit per second. The other major advantage of routers is their ability to perform these functions primarily through the use of software, which makes future revision and support for upgrades much easier. A corresponding disadvantage is that the more complex software implementations of routers may have less throughput than simpler implementations of bridges.

Multiprotocol routers support multiple protocols simultaneously. Figure 4.12 illustrates the range of interfaces and scope of routing. Routers may be connected by real or virtual circuits. Routers use routing protocols to determine the next best hop based upon specific criteria, such as least cost, minimum delay, minimum distance, or least congestion conditions. Routers employ an interior routing protocol with a single autonomous system, for example, the Routing Information Protocol (RIP) or the Open Shortest Path First (OSPF). In a network of networks they use an exterior routing protocol, such as the Border Gateway Protocol (BGP). Static routing, where the router is manually configured, is also possible but should be used with great care since the routing protocol can propagate errors throughout the network. The same term, *network,* may refer to a piece of Ethernet cable or to a collection of many devices internetworked across a large geographic area sharing a coordinated addressing scheme. Packets are routed based upon the destination address and sometimes the source address as well, or even an end-to-end route specification. Routers interwork dissimilar protocols by transforming packet headers, and interconnect dissimilar media via conversions as well.

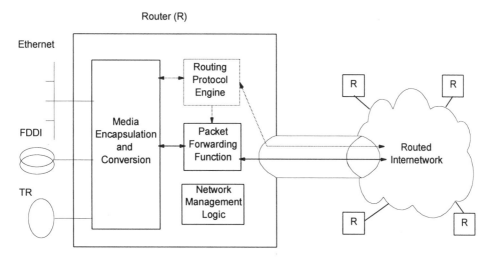

Figure 4.11 Router Functions

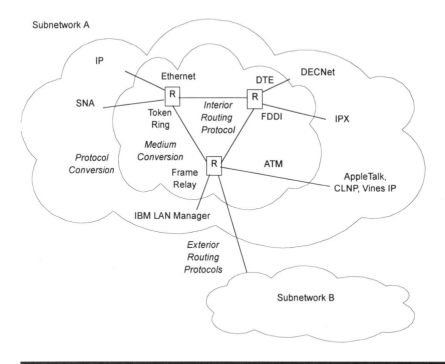

Subnetwork A

IP

Ethernet

DECNet

DTE

SNA

Interior Routing Protocol

Token Ring

FDDI

IPX

Medium Conversion

ATM

Protocol Conversion

Frame Relay

AppleTalk, CLNP, Vines IP

IBM LAN Manager

Exterior Routing Protocols

Subnetwork B

Figure 4.12 Routing Interfaces, Functions, and Architecture

When routers support multiple protocols, they route them to another port on the router, which converts them to the corresponding link and/or network protocol for that port. For example, a router encapsulates IP traffic into frame relay frames, SMDS, or ATM cells for transmission over a public network service. Routers also convert between protocols such as IPX and IP. Most routers must reassemble ATM cells into packets before processing them.

4.2.4 Routing Compared with Bridging

A great sage once wrote, "Bridge when you can, but route when you must." Bridges offer true plug-and-play operation, but don't scale to very large networks and have other problems. While routing is much more complex than bridging, it also provides more features and advantages — but at a price. Routers *dynamically* reroute traffic over, for example, the least-cost path.   Routers reduce the danger of broadcast storms by terminating broadcast sources, such as NetBEUI or Banyan Vines.   Routers allow a network designer to build a hierarchical addressing scheme that scales to very large networks, as the construction of the global Internet proves. Routers also provide filtering capabilities similar to those in bridges to restrict access only to known users, and can also be programmed through filters to block out specific higher-layer protocols.   Routers have the additional flexibility to define virtual networks within a larger network definition. Routers using IP solve packet-size incompatibility problems by fragmenting larger packets into smaller ones and reassembling them. However, this solution should be used with care, since it significantly affects performance.

Routers do have a few disadvantages. Routing algorithms typically require more system memory resources than bridges and are very complex to design and manage. Modern routing algorithms and implementations [i.e., Intermediate System-to-Intermediate System (IS-IS), Open Shortest Path First (OSPF), and Border Gateway Protocol (BGP)] are comparable to bridging [such as Spanning Tree Protocol (STP)] in the amount of bandwidth overhead required for topology updates.

Many router vendors have implemented multiple processors within the network interface card and faster platforms and processors (such as RISC machines) to eliminate throughput problems caused by increased traffic loads of routing protocols. Table 4.1 shows a comparison of bridge and router uses and capabilities.

Table 4.1 Comparison of Bridging with Routing

Function	Bridging	Routing
Data source connectivity	One source and destination	Multiple sources and destinations
Network addressing	No	Yes
Packet handling	Pass packet transparently (except translation bridges)	Interpret packet at link and network layers
Packet forwarding efficiency	Poor for spanning tree, good for source routing	Good for least cost (OSPF), poor for least hop (RIP)
Configuration required	None, except for source routing	Some always required
Priority schemes	No	Yes
Security	Based on hardware isolation of LAN segments	Based on processor-intensive filtering of each packet

It is a good idea to *bridge* when you desire simplicity, use the same LAN media type across the entire network, have a small centralized LAN with a simple topology, or need to transport protocols that cannot be routed, such as NetBIOS and DEC LAT.

Select *routing* when you want to route traffic based upon network parameters like least-cost route, use multiple MAC protocol environments, have large, dynamic networks with complex topologies, want optimized dynamic routing around failed links over paths that run in parallel, or have network and subnetwork requirements.

Many bridging and routing functions have been built into workstations, PCs, and servers. While this offers the cost and management advantages of using only a single device, users should be aware of product support, scale, upgrade, and manageability limitations. Choosing the right device that will grow with your network pays back in benefits, such as low cost to upgrade with minimal operational impact. One option is to purchase a full router rather than a bridge—you may not need routing today, but as your network grows, you can upgrade without having to replace the device. Avoiding the operational impact of downtime and addressing changes may be well worth the additional cost of upgrade, even if you lose one revision of the technology. It may be less expensive in the long run to purchase a router with port expansion, rather than taking the network down and installing a larger or more feature-rich router later. Port sizing and traffic growth patterns typically dictate the size of the router required. A good book on network design can help you make the right hardware design decisions.

4.3 CONNECTIONLESS VS. CONNECTION-ORIENTED NETWORK SERVICES

The OSI reference model categorizes data network services as being either connection-oriented or connectionless. Connection-oriented network services (CONS) involve establishing a connection between physical or logical endpoints prior to the transfer of data. Examples of CONS are frame relay, TCP, and ATM.

Connectionless network services (CLNS), on the other hand, provide end-to-end logical connectivity without establishing any connection before data transfer. Examples of CLNS are IP and SMDS. Historically, wide area networks have employed connection-oriented services, while local area networks used connectionless services. As we show later, ATM, along with its supporting cast of adaptation layers, supports *both* connection-oriented and connectionless services.

4.3.1 Connection-Oriented Network Services

Connection-oriented services require establishment of a connection between the origin and destination *before* transferring data. The connection is established as a path of links through intermediate nodes in a network. Once the connection is established, all data travels through the network over the same preestablished path. The fact that data arrives at the destination in the same order as it was sent by the origin is fundamental to connection-oriented services.

If the connection is established by network management or provisioning actions ahead of time and is left up indefinitely, then it is called a Permanent Virtual Channel (PVC). If control signaling of any type is used to establish and take down the connection dynamically, then the connection is called a Switched Virtual Channel (SVC). Each of these types of CONS will be covered in turn, with examples for each.

Provisioning a PVC connection may be established by physical wiring, equipment configuration commands, service provider provisioning procedures, or combinations of these actions. These actions may take several minutes to several weeks, depending upon exactly what is required. Once the PVC is established, data may be transferred over it. Usually PVCs are established for long periods of time. Examples of PVCs are the X.25 PVC, frame relay PVC, and ATM PVC.

In the case of an SVC service, only the access line and address for the origin and each destination point are provided beforehand. The use of a control signaling protocol plays a central role in SVC services. The origin requests, via the signaling protocol, that the network make a connection to a destination. The network determines the physical (and logical) location of the destination and attempts to establish a connection through intermediate node(s) to the destination. The success or failure of the attempt is indicated to the originator. There may also be a progress indication to the originator, alerting for the destination, or other handshaking elements of the signaling protocol as well. Often the destination also utilizes signaling to either accept or reject the call. In the case of a failed attempt, the signaling protocol usually informs the originator of the reason the attempt failed. Once the connection is established, data can be transferred over the connection. Networks employ SVCs to efficiently share resources by providing dynamic connections and disconnections in response to signaling protocol instructions generated by end users.

Probably, the simplest way to explain an SVC is to compare it to a phone call — the communications device "picks up the phone" and "requests" a destination address; the call is then established, data is sent, and then the call is taken down or disconnected. The above description may sound complicated, but it isn't. There is a direct analog of each of the above terms in the steps of establishing and taking down an SVC connection-oriented service and a normal telephone call, as illustrated in Table 4.2. In fact, much of the complexity of ISDN is introduced by having a more complicated signaling protocol with new names as summarized below. ISDN supports voice calls since the required signaling primitives are part of the signaling protocol.

Table 4.2 General Signaling Comparison to Voice Call

General Signaling Protocol Terminology	Voice Telephone Call Example
Provision access/address	Order service from phone company
Handshaking	Dial tone
Origin request	Dialing the number
Successful attempt indication	Ringing tone
Unsuccessful attempt indication	Busy tone
Destination acceptance	Answering the phone
Data transfer	Talking on the phone
Disconnect request	Hanging up the phone

4.3.2 Connectionless Network Services

As the name implies, connectionless services never establish connections of any kind. Network nodes provide connectionless services by transferring packets, also called datagrams, toward the destination on a link determined by a routing protocol to be the next hop on the best path to the destination. The origin node initiates this next-hop forwarding process and each intermediate node repeats it until the packet reaches the destination node, which delivers the packet to its local interface. Pretty simple, right?

Yes and no. The magic in the above simple description is the routing protocol. It determines the next hop at the origin and then each intermediate node. Part 2 gives more details about different types of routing protocols, but they all achieve the same end stated in the previous sentence — that is, they determine the contents of the next-hop forwarding table. A bad routing protocol could create next-hop entries that created endless loops, where a packet never arrives at the destination, but loops around the network indefinitely. On the other hand, a good routing protocol chooses an optimized path through the network. But routers are not as plug-and-play as their vendors would have you believe. Addresses need to be configured, along with many variances and complexities like subnet masks and the routing protocol areas.

Connectionless services do not guarantee packet delivery; therefore applications rely on higher-level protocols (e.g., TCP) to perform the end-to-end error detection/correction. Additionally, higher-layer protocols must also perform flow control (e.g., TCP or RSVP), since connectionless services typically operate on a best-efforts basis without any notion of bandwidth allocation.

4.3.3 Connection-Oriented vs. Connectionless Services Analogy

One simple analogy for understanding the difference between CONS and CLNS is that of placing a telephone call compared with sending a telegraph. To make a CONS phone call, you pick up the phone and dial the number of the destination telephone. The network makes a connection from your house through one or more telephone switches to the destination address's switch and rings the phone. Once the called party answers, the telephone network keeps the connection active until either party hangs up.

For a CLNS example, consider sending a telegram in the nineteenth century. A person visits the telegraph office and recites a message, giving the destination address as a city and country. The telegraph operator picks a next-hop telegraph station, and keys in the entire message to that telegraph office. Since the originating telegraph operator does not know the status of telegraph lines (up or down) other than those lines connected to his station, he must rely on the other operators to forward the message toward the destination. If there is a path to the destination, then the persistent telegraph operators in our example would eventually relay the message to the destination, even if some telegraph lines on the most direct path are down.

4.4 PRIVATE, PUBLIC, AND VIRTUAL PRIVATE NETWORK SERVICES

A VPN is defined as a partition of shared public network resources between multiple users to form a network that *appears private to the users* but is still part of a larger public network. VPN services have the benefits of a private network, but also provide the economies and cost savings of switched services. Carriers implement many VPNs within a single physical network. A corporate-wide ATM WAN provided over a public ATM service network is one example of a VPN. Shared network resources are assigned in fair proportion to the bandwidth required by customers, and users receive specific quality of service (QoS) guarantees. Part 4 provides a complete study of public ATM service features.

In a virtual private network, a single access circuit from the site to the network is usually sufficient, because multiple virtual circuits and paths can be provided from multiple users from a site to their destination. For example, each virtual circuit or path can be allocated a peak rate equal to the access circuit, but have a sum of average rates that is less than the access circuit. Figure 4.13 demonstrates this concept by showing how users A, B, C, and D at site 1 all have a single physical circuit into their premises ATM device which converts these inputs to four ATM virtual circuits (as indicated by the different line styles) and then transmits them over a *single* physical link between network ATM switches to the destination-based ATM switch. These individual user virtual circuits are logically switched across the ATM network to the destination premises device, where they are delivered to the physical access circuit of the end user, as illustrated in the figure. Note that while this single circuit provides good aggregation, it can also be a single point of failure for all users accessing the network, so alternative facilities may be desirable for backup.

The availability of a public switched ATM service, with its bandwidth-on-demand sharing capabilities, will likely lure users away from private point-to-point networks and onto public networks. Thus, they attain the increased reliability of very large public network platforms and cost savings vis-à-vis private line operations as a result of the economies of scale of the larger backbone infrastructure with its high availability and resiliency to failure through built-in alternative routing.

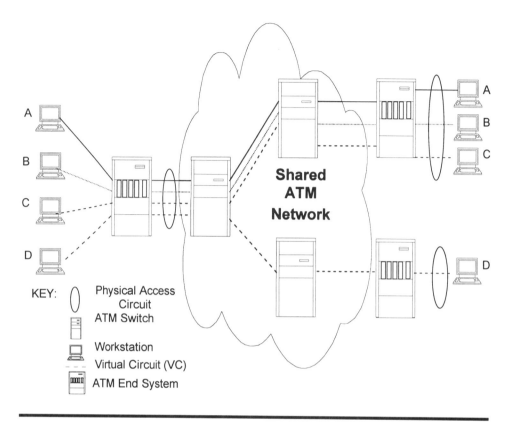

Figure 4.13 Detailed Example of a VPN

An added advantage to public network services now being used quite often is that the user can tap the knowledge of the public network engineers and managers. Customers of public network services gain access to public network assets, such as engineering personnel, experience, resources, and network management. With proper vendor management, and sometimes with the addition of a small management fee, it can be like having an in-house consulting or management service.

As you can see, by using a public network service to transport your voice, data, and video services with customized network management, billing, and support systems to back these services, many data service providers offer a form of outsourcing. This outsourcing takes the form of resource reduction for systems and services which otherwise would have to be provided in house. Other benefits of VPNs which parallel those of outsourcing include service-provider network management, bandwidth management, fault tolerance, intelligent bridging and routing, security, order entry and order processing, and integration and standardization. VPNs can also be used as an overflow technique or as a complete replacement for existing networks. The network manager needs to decide what portion of the network resources to retain or replace, keeping in mind the costs of access to the public network, not just end-to-end transmission and switching facilities as in a private network. These advantages are additional bonuses of public network services.

There are many challenges facing VPN providers. Users require an increased level of control over network resources, like the ability to modify network resources —VPs and VCs — on the fly without long lead times, along with the capability to change parameters like QoS.

In summary, the advantages of the public (VPN) ATM network services are:

- Reduced access-line charges
- Capability to satisfy high peak bandwidth demands (particularly during low activity intervals for other services)
- Cost impacts proportional to usage (versus cost proportional to peak rate in the dedicated network alternative)
- Enhanced availability and reliability

Disadvantages include:

- Less predictable peak capacity
- Less user control

4.4.1 ATM Interworking

Large enterprise networks typically have a few large locations that serve as headquarters locations and major traffic sources and sinks. Typical locations are large computer centers, large office complexes with many information workers, campuses requiring high-tech communication, server farms, data or image repositories, and large-volume data or image sources. These large locations have a significant community of interest among them; however, the enterprise usually also has a relatively large number of smaller locations needing at least partial, lower-performance access to this same information. The smaller locations have fewer users, and generally cannot justify the higher cost of equipment or networking facilities. Cost generally increases as performance, number of features, and flexibility needs increase.

Many users have turned to hybrid networking, using high-speed ATM at the larger sites interworking with lower-speed frame relay at the many smaller locations. These lower-speed access sites require more efficient access rather than high performance, and thus frame relay access through low-end routing and bridging products is often more cost-effective than ATM. This is because the cost per bit per second generally decreases as the public network access speed increases. For example, the approximate cost ratio of DS1/DS0 and DS3/DS1 tariffs is approximately 10:1, while the speed difference is approximately 25:1. This means that a higher-speed interface can be operated at 40 percent efficiency at the same cost per bit per second.

Conversely, the lower-speed interface costs 3.5 times as much per bit per second, and therefore efficiency can be important.

What does the virtual enterprise network look like for the beginning of the next century? Figure 4.14 illustrates an ATM-based interworking network cloud connecting a few large ATM sites to many smaller frame relay sites. Such a network is composed of many smaller sites and few larger sites, which is typical of large enterprises, such as corporations, governments, and other organizations. Principal needs are multiple levels of service characterized by parameters such as throughput, quality, and billing.

4.5 REVIEW

Logical topology protocol layering is a fundamental concept. This chapter defines a shorthand notation, used throughout the remainder of the book, that maps protocol layers to messages that traverse interfaces between nodes, both logical and physical. This chapter lays the foundation for the next chapter, in which we peel back the layers of the ATM onion.

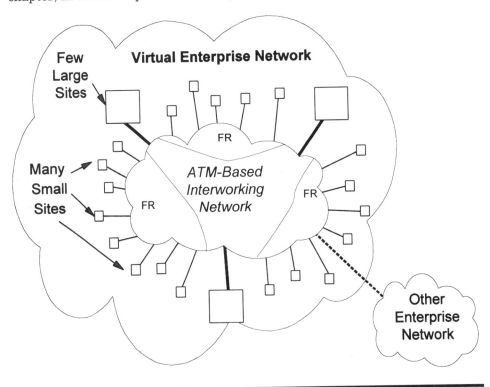

Figure 4.14 Typical Enterprise Network

4.6 REFERENCES

[1]   D. Spohn, *Data Network Design*, 2d ed., McGraw-Hill, 1997.
[2]   D. McDysan and D. Spohn, *ATM: Theory and Application*, McGraw-Hill, 1995.
[3]   D. Minoli, *Enterprise Networking — Fractional T1 to SONET, Frame Relay to BISDN*, McGraw-Hill, 1993.
[4]   R. Perlman, *Interconnections*, Addison-Wesley, 1992.
[5]   A. Tannenbaum, *Computer Communications*, 3d ed., Prentice-Hall, 1996.

Introduction to ATM

This chapter introduces the reader to the basic building blocks of ATM. Asynchronous Transfer Mode (ATM) is a technology defined by protocols implemented according to standards and specifications defined by the ITU-T, ANSI, ETSI, the ATM Forum, and the IETF. Users experience ATM technology through use of both ATM equipment and services. This chapter introduces the reader to the basic principles and concepts on which ATM equipment and services are predicated. The exposition starts with the technical and service visions of ATM. Next, we look at ATM through many different glasses — as an interface, a protocol, a technology, integrated access, a scalable infrastructure, and a service. The exposition continues by giving a chef's menu of ATM terminology, then taking one order at a time, starting with the user-network interface.

5.1 STANDARDIZATION FOR ATM

Most industry sectors at least support ATM, and some, such as the ATM Forum, embrace it. ATM standards began with the International Telecommunications Union selecting ATM as the basis for Broadband Integrated Services Digital Networks (B-ISDN) in 1988. The late 1980s ushered in the development of early prototype Central Office (CO) ATM switches. The traditional customer premises multiplexer and switch vendors then adopted ATM in the early 1990s. The mid-1990s ushered in the next generation of CO switches, some derived from expertise arrived at in Customer Premises Equipment (CPE) designs. CO switches continued to evolve rapidly in the mid-1990s, becoming larger, faster, and more capable than preceding generations. Next, router and hub manufacturers began building ATM interfaces for their existing models, as well as including ATM capabilities in their latest designs.

Computer vendors soon started building ATM Network Interface Cards (NICs) for workstations and personal computers, and the loaded per port or per workstation cost of ATM to the NIC has fallen to within $100 of that of

100-Mbps Ethernet. The final piece of the puzzle is falling in place with the initiation of operating system and Application Program Interface (API) software development for ATM-based systems, offering the capability for a true end-to-end homogeneous ATM network. These efforts point toward a strong commitment to the success of ATM because they address the users' need for consistent and predictable quality of service on an end-to-end basis. Many of these efforts are being stimulated and facilitated by the ATM Forum, founded in 1992. ATM user and network standards are now mature, and a large degree of interoperability has already been achieved. The ATM Forum now works more closely than ever with the ITU-T standards bodies and related industry forums to advance ATM.

5.2 ATM'S MANY FACES

ATM technology takes on many forms and means many different things to different people, from providing a User-to-Network Interface (UNI) protocol, a signaling protocol, and a basis for interworking; to software and hardware multiplexing, switching, and cross-connect functions and platforms; to an integration technology for multiple switched and packet services; to serving as an economical, integrated network access method; to becoming the core of a network infrastructure; to acting as a common multiprotocol platform for a public network service. ATM can be looked at as a(n):

- Interface
- Protocol
- Technology
- Economical, integrated access
- Scalable infrastructure
- Service

Figure 5.1 illustrates these concepts. Let's now explore each.

5.2.1 As an Interface

ATM is an interface defined between the user and a network, as well as an interface between networks. The user-network interface, commonly abbreviated UNI, defines physical characteristics, ATM cell format, and management signaling. Interfaces provide the boundary between different types of hardware, while protocols provide rules, conventions, and the intelligence to pass data over these interfaces. The network-node interface, commonly called NNI, is essentially a superset of the UNI, addressing aspects unique to interconnection between nodes and connections between networks. ITU-T defined B-ISDN standards, and ATM Forum specifications define a number of variants of UNI and NNI interfaces covered in subsequent chapters.

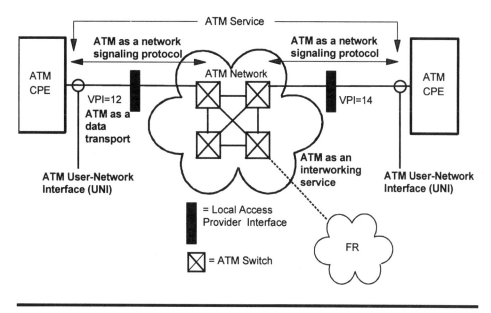

Figure 5.1 ATM as an Interface/Access, Protocol, Infrastructure, and Network Service

5.2.2 As a Protocol

ATM is defined as a protocol designed to switch constant, variable, unspecified, and available bit rate traffic over a common transmission medium. The ITU-T–defined B-ISDN protocol stack defines a telephone company administration–oriented set of standards for simultaneously supporting video, voice, and data on a network that is an evolutionary follow-on to Narrowband ISDN (N-ISDN). Extensions to this protocol structure by the ATM Forum enable users to utilize existing protocols and networks, such as LANs and internetworking protocols (e.g., IP), in a more cost-effective and efficient manner than separate networks can. Furthermore, ATM can interwork with legacy protocols such as frame relay and SMDS. ATM is a cell-based switching and multiplexing technology designed to be a general-purpose, connection-oriented transfer mode for a wide range of services. The ATM Forum has defined additional protocols over ATM in its LAN Emulation (LANE) specification to enable ATM to work seamlessly with legacy LANs employing Token Ring, Ethernet, and FDDI. Additionally, the ATM Forum has specified a sophisticated private ATM network NNI in the Private Network-to-Network Interface (PNNI) specification that supports automatic configuration, optimized routing, bandwidth allocation, hierarchical scalability, and multiple qualities of service.

5.2.3 As a Technology

ATM is often referred to as a technology, comprising hardware and software conforming to ATM protocol standards, which provides multiplexing, cross-connect, and switching functions in a network. ATM technology takes the form of a network interface card, multiplexer, cross-connect, or intelligent switch. Today, ATM prevails in the switch market and as a WAN interface on traditional data communications products like routers and hubs, and ATM end systems (NICs) and applications (APIs) are beginning to appear in significant quantities. ATM also provides an insurance policy of sorts against technological discontinuity.

5.2.4 As Economical, Integrated Access

Virtually all carriers provide some form of public ATM service, enabling users to capitalize on a basic advantage of ATM — integrated physical and service access which reduces cost. The development of ATM nxDS1/E1 inverse multiplexers and access products ranging from DS1 rates into OC-N bandwidths has extended many of ATM's benefits to users who have a TDM network today or require low-speed access to ATM public services. Integrated access and transport of voice, data, and video over a single infrastructure is one of ATM's key benefits. ATM offers equipment and bandwidth savings by providing all data, voice, and video requirements over a *single* infrastructure. Multiple services share a single physical access circuit, allowing tremendous savings in network interface equipment, optimizing local loops, and reducing wide area network bandwidth costs.

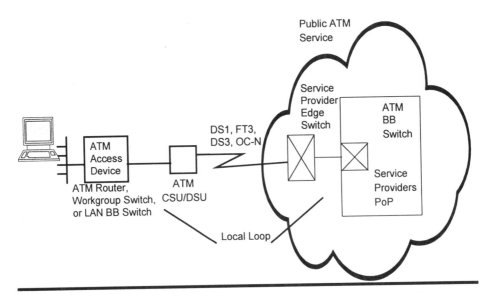

Figure 5.2 ATM Public Service Access Connectivity

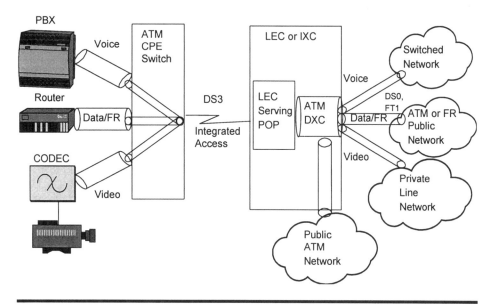

Figure 5.3 ATM Integrated Access

The standard ATM access configuration to a public service is shown in Figure 5.2. Using a typical LAN-attached workstation, the LAN interfaces in turn to the WAN-attached router with an ATM WAN interface, ATM workgroup, LAN backbone, or edge ATM switch. This device in turn communicates directly with the network, or occasionally through an ATM CSU/DSU. A local loop at the same speed as the UNI is required.

Another alternative is integrated access, as shown in Figure 5.3. When ATM is used for integrated access, the provider performs a Digital Cross-Connect (DXC) function at the serving PoP to split off traffic destined for other public or private networks, such as voice for the public switched phone network, frame relay for remote interworked sites, or IP for Internet access.

5.2.5 As a Scalable Infrastructure

ATM technology has a chief advantage over legacy technologies at the core of a network infrastructure. ATM hardware and associated software together provide an efficient backbone technology for an advanced communications network. In fact, ATM-based architectures offer the best future integrated platform for data, voice, and video. ATM also provides a highly scalable infrastructure, from the campus environment to the central office. It serves small and large efficiently. Scalability occurs along the dimensions of interface speed, port density, switch size, network size, multiple application support, and addressing.

ATM also provides greater bandwidth granularity and flexibility in designing network topologies. As an illustration of this, consider the network shown in Figure 5.4. In Figure 5.4*a*, the headquarters (HQ) site communicates with each of sites A, B, C, and D over dedicated DS3 private lines. Each private line has an average utilization of 25 percent. With this private line solution, the HQ site requires four DS3 network (router) access ports, four local loops, and four interLATA circuits. Alternatively, in the ATM network scenario shown in Figure 5.4*b*, the HQ site has only a single DS3 physical access (ATM switch) port and provides a logical VP to each user: A, B, C, and D. Thus, the HQ site saves the cost of three WAN ports, three local loops, and three interLATA dedicated DS3 circuits.

Even greater savings accrue if all users communicate peer-to-peer instead of in a hierarchical manner through a central site. In this scenario, if each user communicates directly with the others, *each* user requires four DS3 access ports in the private line example, as shown in Figure 5.5. The shared network ATM design shown in Figure 5.6 requires only a single DS3 access port to the public ATM switch for each user, thus reducing the number of WAN ports, CSUs, and local loops by 15! This design also has the by-product of reducing processing power and memory requirements in the network access devices by focusing them on a single WAN port.

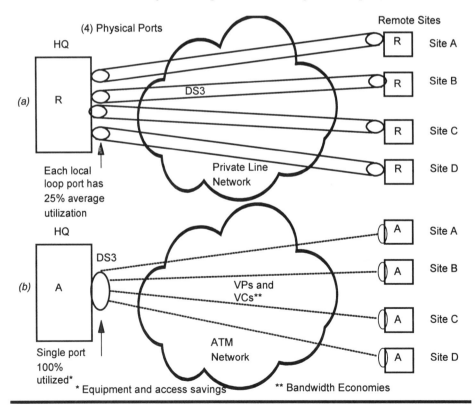

Figure 5.4 ATM Equipment and Bandwidth Savings

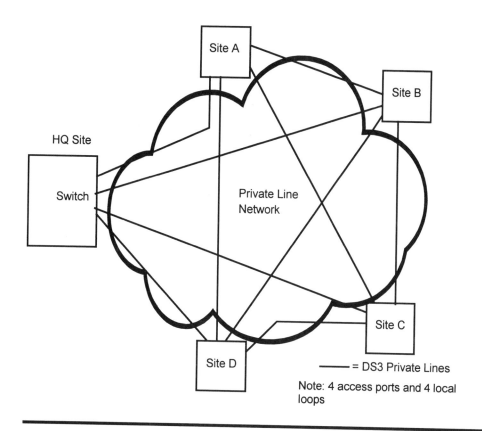

Figure 5.5 Meshed Peer-to-Peer Communications Private Line Access

Figure 5.7 shows the ATM versus private line access circuit requirements for networks with up to 10 sites. The formula for a private line (PL) meshed network is the number of nodes times the number of nodes less one, all divided by 2, or $[(n)(n-1)]/2$, where n equals the number of nodes. In comparison, the number of ATM access circuits required is just n. It is easy to see from this graph the advantages of ATM port aggregation as the number of sites requiring meshed connectivity increases. And because of the statistical multiplexing properties inherent in ATM, backbone link bandwidth utilization also improves. This quality drives up the price/performance ratio of ATM favorably as the size of the network increases.

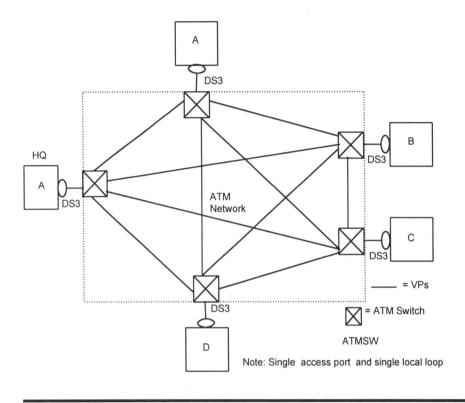

Figure 5.6 Peer-to-Peer Communications with Shared ATM Access

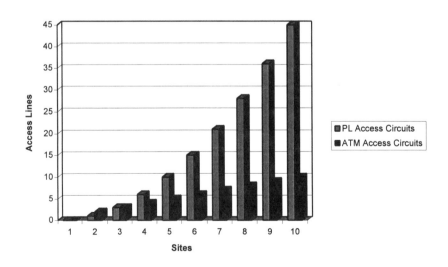

Figure 5.7 ATM vs. Private Line Meshing Efficiencies

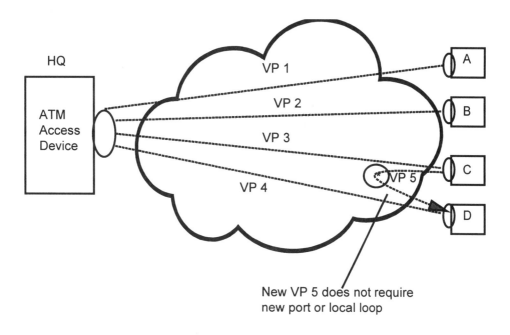

Figure 5.8 Ease of Provisioning ATM

The ATM architecture also offers dynamic and flexible adds, moves, and changes. Once a site has established a port to the ATM network, it is much easier to provide additional virtual paths (VPs) and virtual channels (VCs) to new remote sites than to order and install a new dedicated circuit from every existing site requiring connectivity to every new site on the network. This concept is illustrated in Figure 5.8, where the addition of a new VP 5 between users C and D does not require any additional ports or circuits, and so it can typically be provided in no more than a few days.

5.2.6 ATM as a Service

ATM handles both connection-oriented traffic, either directly (cell-based) or through adaptation layers, and connectionless traffic, through the use of adaptation layers. ATM virtual connections may operate according to the following service categories:

- Constant Bit Rate (CBR)
- Variable Bit Rate (VBR) in real-time (rt) and non-real-time (nrt)
- Unspecified Bit Rate (UBR)
- Available Bit Rate (ABR)

Each ATM cell sent into the network contains addressing information that the network utilizes to sequentially forward cells on a virtual connection from origination to one or more destinations in a connection mode. ATM provides two modes for the establishment of virtual connections, permanent and switched, commonly referred to as PVCs and SVCs, respectively. ATM is asynchronous because the transmitted cells need not be periodic, as time slots are defined in Synchronous Transfer Mode (STM). However, ATM supports synchronous traffic through a specific adaptation layer, proving how multifaceted it is!

ATM offers the potential to standardize on a single end-to-end or edge-to-edge network architecture for multiplexing and switching voice, data, and video. The key to ATM is support for multiple Quality of Service (QoS) classes for differing applications' delay and loss performance requirements. Thus, the vision of ATM is that an entire network can be constructed using ATM and ATM Adaptation Layer (AAL) switching and multiplexing principles to support a wide range of services involving AALs. These AALs include circuit emulation services that provide for the transport and interworking of circuit and packet services, such as:

- ★ Voice
- ★ Packet data (SMDS, IP, FR)
- ★ Video
- ★ Imaging
- ★ Circuit emulation
- ★ LAN extension and emulation

The ATM equipment and service market is already a multibillion-dollar market, with services alone soon to exceed a billion dollars. Figure 5.9 shows competing services, and how ATM offers many of the benefits of private lines, frame relay, and SMDS for all traffic types. The chart plots burstiness, defined as the ratio of peak-to-average traffic rate, on the vertical axis versus the supportable peak rate of the service, or throughput, on the horizontal axis. The term *PL circuits* encompasses both circuit switching and private lines, the choice being based upon tariff economics. The enclosed region for a particular service indicates that the service is applicable to that combination of burstiness and throughput. Note that a number of the services overlap in their range of applicability. Note that the time frame in which peak rate throughput has been available progresses from left to right.

5.3 ATM TERMINOLOGY — A HIGH-LEVEL INTRODUCTION

This section introduces some key concepts and terminology of ATM through simple analogies and examples. The chapters in Part 2 then build upon this foundation by providing more detail and references for further reading.

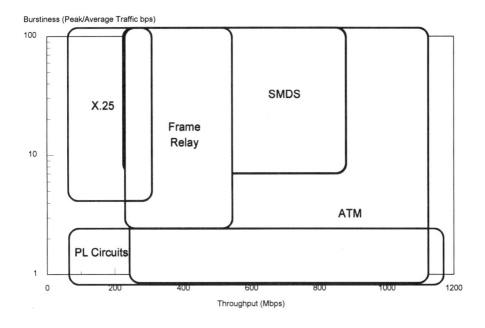

Figure 5.9 ATM Applicability Compared to Competing Services

5.3.1 The ATM Menu

A user defines an ATM connection by selecting from a set of options, just as when ordering from a menu. Here are the menu and service options from the chefs at the ATM Forum and the ITU-T that you can order. The following dialogue takes you through a somewhat whimsical conversation with a waiter in ordering an ATM service as a means of introducing a number of new terms. If you don't understand the terms from this little story, don't worry. Each of them will be covered in more detail and summarized in a proper order later.

> ⇒ UNI access port speed: over 30 entrees to choose from!
> ⇒ Virtual Path or Virtual Channel Connection (VPC or VCC): Choose a set selection or meal, or order a la carte.
> ⇒ PVC or SVC: Do you want a guaranteed reservation at Chez Nois or just an on demand meal at McDonald's? With PVCs you'll work with a tuxedoed waiter (a network management system) or else order at the window (i.e., use signaling messages).
>> ⇒ Specify your source and destination addresses: Who are the host and guest of honor?
>> ⇒ If you're ordering an SVC, please select from the options on the menu; that is, fill out your sushi order and give it to me.

⇒ Select point-to-point or point-to-multipoint: How many people are in your party?

⇒ Unidirectional or bidirectional: Do you know and want to tell me what you want, or would you like to discuss your options?

⇒ For each direction of service, please select one service class:

⇒ Constant Bit Rate (CBR): Dedicated, most expensive service

⇒ Variable Bit Rate (VBR), real-time and non-real-time: Bring me my food when it is ready! Or bring the entrees when you see me finish my appetizer.

⇒ Available Bit Rate (ABR): Shared waiters, and you get your food and drink delivered to your table when a waiter is available.

⇒ Unspecified Bit Rate (UBR): You get whatever service is available, possibly no service at all. I'll give you the lowest price for this service.

⇒ Would you care for tagging (i.e., cell loss priority)?

⇒ For all services, please select your:

⇒ Peak Cell Rate (PCR)

⇒ For the VBR services, also please choose:

⇒ Sustainable Cell Rate (SCR)

⇒ Maximum Burst Size (MBS)

⇒ For ABR, the choices are:

⇒ Minimum Cell Rate (MCR)

⇒ Initial Cell Rate (ICR)

⇒ Your closed-loop congestion control parameters? If you don't know this, would you like me to suggest a predefined set?

⇒ And finally, would you like to select from a number of other options, such as no pickles, hold the lettuce, etc.?

As you can see from the above list, there are a number of selections and choices that must be made to order up an ATM SVC or PVC. Let's start delving into the physical components of an ATM connection and make some other analogies to further explain some of the above terms.

5.3.2 A Simple Transportation Analogy

Let's begin with the simple example in Figure 5.10. Imagine each user node as a city surrounded by mountains and the ocean. From the mountain passes leaving the cities, freeways lead out to the other cities. In this analogy, the mountain passes are the physical access circuits, the freeways are virtual paths, and the highway lanes are virtual channels. Two VPs of different quality connect cities A and C. VP 1 takes the seaside route, while VP 2 takes the overland route through the mountains. VPs 3 and 4 take another overland route and pass through City B. This analogy isn't perfect, since the counterpart of ATM cells would actually be the vehicles traveling on the highway. On real highways, vehicles come in all shapes and sizes, while ATM cells are always the same size of 53 bytes. Hopefully, this simple example gives a mental picture to act as an aid in remembering the new terminology.

5.3.3 VP and VC Post Office Analogy

Let's take, for example, a post office that delivers packages of various sizes and weights. A large package weighing several pounds, in which a company includes many smaller letters (each individually addressed), is analogous to a VP. Individually addressed and stamped letters are analogous to VCs. VPs make sense only when the two locations (origination and destination) have a large volume of mail (information) to exchange. VCs make sense when small, ad hoc, intermittent correspondence is required, such as for remote offices.

5.3.4 Analogy to TDM Switches and Digital Cross-Connects

This capability to switch down to a virtual channel level is similar to the operation of a Private or Public Branch Exchange (PBX) or telephone switch in the world of telephony. In the PBX/switch, each channel within a trunk group (path) can be switched. Figure 5.11 illustrates this analogy. ATM devices which perform VC connections are commonly called VC switches because of this analogy with telephone switches. Transmission networks use a cross-connect, which is basically a space division switch, or effectively an electronic patch panel. ATM devices which connect VPs are often called VP cross-connects in the literature because of their analogy with the transmission network.

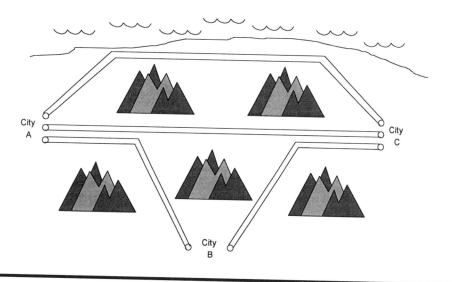

Figure 5.10 Simple Physical Interface, ATM Virtual Path and Channel Analogy

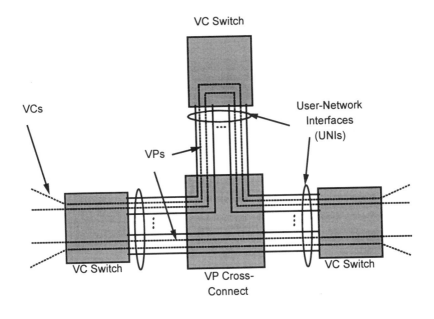

Figure 5.11 TDM Switch and Cross-Connect Analogy

These analogies are useful in helping those familiar with TDM/STM and telephony to understand ATM, but should not be taken literally. There is little reason for an ATM cell switching machine to restrict switching to only VCs and cross-connection to only VPs, although some manufacturers do so.

5.4 ATM PHYSICAL AND LOGICAL CONNECTIONS

This section defines the concepts of physical connections between ATM devices and the logical connection capabilities of ATM at a basic level. Several examples then will extend these definitions to a network context.

5.4.1 ATM User-Access Ports and Circuits

Figure 5.12 shows the ATM user access port as a physical port on the CPE, such as a workgroup, LAN backbone, edge switch, ATM multiplexer, ATM access device, or router with an ATM WAN interface. A single physical access circuit, typically at DS1, DS3, or OC-3 or higher transmission rate, connects the customer's access port to an ATM switch port in the ATM service provider's network. Standards call this collection of two ports interconnected by physical transmission, along with the format, protocols, and procedures operating over the physical media, a user-to-network interface (UNI).

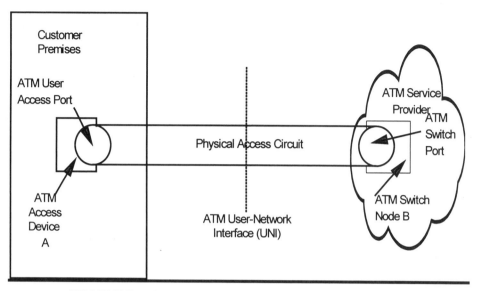

Figure 5.12 ATM UNI Equals Two Ports and a "Wire"

5.4.2 Transmission Paths, Virtual Paths, and Virtual Channels

Each UNI supports one or more VPs, which in turn support one or multiple VCs. ATM users view VPs (or VCs) as an end-to-end logical connection from the source endpoint (node A) to the exit endpoint (node B) as shown in Figure 5.13*a*. Standards call this an end-to-end VP (or VC). Think of a PVC VP (or VC) as a static logical highway from one location (user access port) to another. SVCs are dynamically established by signaling, similar to telephone calls, as detailed in Chapter 6. A VP (or VC) PVC has characteristics similar to those of a dedicated private line: The destination never changes, and a certain bandwidth and quality is always allocated. Any data transmitted over an ATM VP (or VC) arrives in exactly the same sequence as it was sent.

From the network's point of view, the end-to-end VP (or VC) actually involves switching based upon the VPI (and for VCs the VCI value as well) at each connecting point within the network, as shown in Figure 5.13*b*. This set of connecting points and switching within the network is done transparently to the end users. The physical interfaces between network switches are called network-node interfaces. Standards utilize the term *VP (or VC) link* for the smaller segments between connecting points that make up the overall end-to-end connection, as identified in the figure.

(a) At the end points a VP (or VC) appears as a single pipe to users A and B

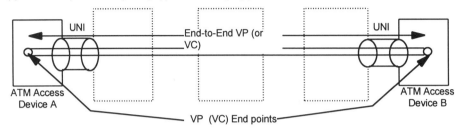

(b) To the network, a VP (or VC) appears as a set of links linked together at connecting points

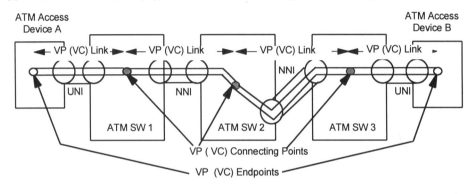

Figure 5.13 Basic VP and VC Terminology

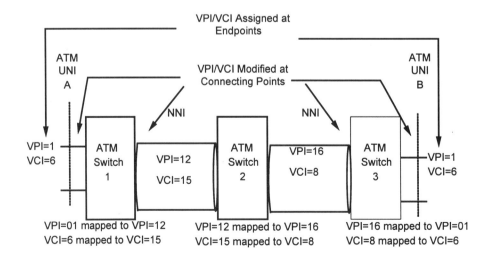

Figure 5.14 VPI/VCI Switching in a Link and End-to-End Context

5.4.3 ATM Cell Switching Using VPI and VCI Values

Intermediate ATM switches may modify both the Virtual Path Identifier (VPI) and Virtual Channel Identifier (VCI) values at connecting points to forward cells along the VC links that make up an end-to-end VC. Note that VPI and VCI values must be unique on any particular physical transmission facility used as an NNI. Thus, ATM switches use VPIs and VCIs independently on each NNI. Figure 5.14 illustrates this concept through a simple example in which each switch maps VPIs and VCIs to different VPIs and VCIs at each connecting point. In this example, all three switches have a single transmission path between them. At ATM UNI A, the input device to switch 1 provides a video channel over virtual path 1 (VPI 1) and virtual channel 6 (VCI 6). Switch 1 then maps VCI 6 on the UNI to VCI 15 on the NNI connecting to switch 2, and VPI 1 on the UNI to VPI 12 on the NNI. This mapping is performed symmetrically in both directions in this example, although it can be done independently in each direction. Usually, it's a good idea to keep the mapping identical in each direction for point-to-point, bidirectional connections. Switch 2 then maps the VPI and VCI values on the NNI to switch 3 to different virtual path and channel identifiers (i.e., VPI 16 and VCI 8). Thus, VPIs and VCIs are tied onto each individual link across the network. This is similar to frame relay, where Data Link Connection Identifiers (DLCIs) address a virtual channel at each end of a link. Finally, switch 3 translates VCI 8 on VPI 16 on its NNI from switch 2 to VCI 6 on VPI 1 on the ATM UNI B. This example illustrates how the destination VPI and VCI need not be the same at the endpoints of a connection because of intermediate switching.

Each ATM access circuit can contain a combination of up to 255 VPCs and 65,535 VCCs per VP in theory, but service providers and CPE typically support less. VCIs 0 to 31 are typically reserved as specified by ITU-T and ATM Forum standards. Generally, higher-speed circuits support more VPCs and VCCs than lower-speed ones do.

5.4.4 ATM Virtual Connection Networking

A user connects to an ATM network through the use of an ATM UNI access port and circuit. Standards also refer to the UNI as a Transmission Path (TP). The logical connection between user ports is called a VP and VC, where one or multiple VCs reside within each VP. Each VP and VC can be unidirectional or bidirectional, point-to-point or point-to-multipoint, and carries a service category and traffic parameters from the service menu assigned to it. At each VP endpoint a VPI acts as a locally significant address. At VC endpoints a combination of a VPI and a VCI acts as a locally significant, link-level address.

One concept used consistently throughout the book is that of the network "cloud," which represents a variety of network environments. Cases generically represented by a cloud include, but are not limited to, service provider networks, the local exchange environment, and even multiple intervening networks that interconnect end users. Typically, we employ the cloud symbol when the network transparently interconnects end users. Figure 5.15 illustrates a sample ATM network environment, with three users, A, B and C, accessing the ATM network cloud via a single UNI. This network illustrates the ATM terminology details of the simple analogy employed at the beginning of this chapter of cities interconnected by freeways, with the highway lanes representing channels. In the figure, each VP connects with another site. VCCs within each of these VPs are identified by VPIs and VCIs as indicated in the figure. Note that the VPI and VCI values can be different on each end of the connection, since the intermediate switches can change the values. In general, it's wise to keep the VPI/VCI values identical on each end; however, in some operational situations, such as those resulting from network migrations or changes, this isn't always possible. But don't worry; ATM has the flexibility to support these cases. This is what is meant by saying that the VPI and VCI are the local link-level address.

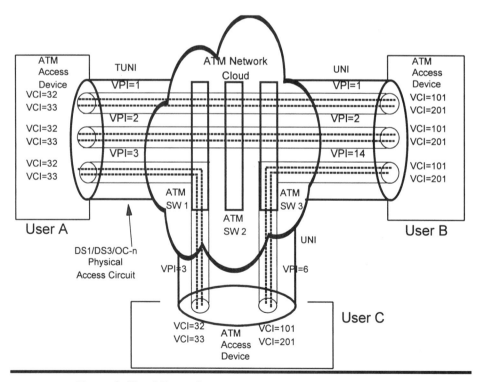

Figure 5.15 Network Cloud Example

5.5 INTRODUCTION TO ATM SERVICE CATEGORIES

Now that we've covered the three major building blocks of ATM — the physical interfaces, the VP, and the VC — let's move on to an example of how an end user would employ these in a multimedia application. The coverage then provides several analogies illustrating the need for multiple service categories, as well as basic mechanisms for implementing them.

5.5.1 Multimedia Application Example

ATM switches take a user's data, voice, and video, then chop it up into fixed-length cells and multiplex it into a single stream of cells transmitted across the UNI physical medium. An example of a multimedia application is that of a person needing to send an important manuscript for a book to his or her publisher. Along with the letter, this person wishes to communicate enthusiasm and gratitude at receiving a contract to publish the book.

Figure 5.16 illustrates the role of ATM in this real-life example, with Jeanne sitting at her ATM workstation equipped with an ATM interface card, sound board with microphone, and video camera. A cost-effective 25-Mbps ATM connection over existing building wiring connects her workstation to a local ATM switch, which in turn attaches to a public ATM-based wide area network via a 45-Mbps ATM UNI to a network service provider, to which the publisher is also connected.

Jeanne first places a multimedia call to the publisher, begins transmitting the data for her manuscript, and begins a conversation with the publisher. The call involves three connections: one for voice, one for video, and a third for data interchange. Jeanne and the publisher interact through separate text, voice, and video connections, all integrated by their workstations in real time. The publisher looks through the manuscript at her workstation, and interactively questions Jeanne about certain negotiating points in her proposal. Let's break down this scenario into its working ATM components.

Video and voice are delay-sensitive; that is, the information cannot be delayed for more than a blink of the eye. Furthermore, delay cannot have significant variations for voice and video traffic, either. Disruption in the video image of Jeanne's face or distortion of the voice destroys the interactive, near-real-life quality of this multimedia application. Voice traffic may be sent at a constant rate, while newer video coding schemes send at a variable rate in proportion to the amount of image movement. Transferring a video segment from a high-action motion picture, such as dogfights between jet fighters in the movie *Top Gun*, requires a much higher transmission rate than the session where Jeanne and her publisher make eye contact and exchange simple gestures.

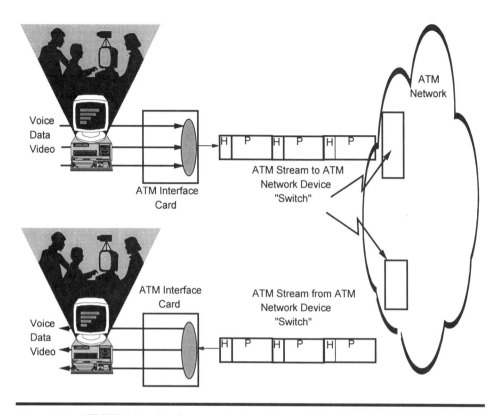

Figure 5.16 ATM Multimedia Communications Example

Data, such as a file transfer using TCP/IP, on the other hand, isn't nearly as delay-sensitive as voice or video traffic. Data traffic, however, is very sensitive to loss. Therefore, ATM must discriminate among voice, video, and data traffic, giving voice and video traffic priority with guaranteed, bounded delay, while simultaneously assuring that data traffic has very low loss.

When using ATM, longer packets cannot delay shorter packets as in other packet-switched implementations because long packets are chopped up into many cells. This enables ATM to carry CBR traffic such as voice and rt-VBR video in conjunction with nrt-VBR data traffic, potentially having very long packets within the same network.

Examining this example in further detail, the software in Jeanne's and her publisher's workstations establishes three separate virtual connections for data, voice, and video, each with a different service category. The workstation software assigns nrt-VBR to data, CBR to voice, and rt-VBR to video. Figure 5.17 shows how all three types of traffic are combined over a single ATM UNI, with VCs being assigned to the data (VCI = 51), voice (VCI = 52), and video (VCI = 53). These all utilize VPI = 0, which is reserved for VC connections in ATM standards. VP connections can be made only on nonzero VPI values.

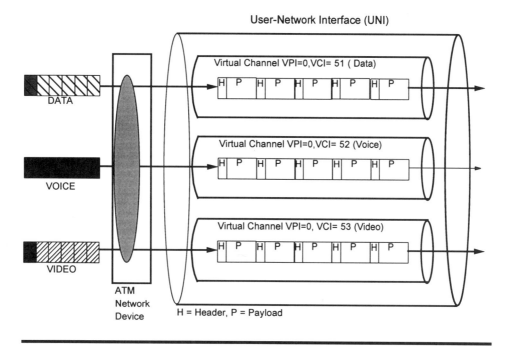

User-Network Interface (UNI)

Figure 5.17 Illustration of Virtual Channels Supporting Multimedia Application

Let's look further into Jeanne's workstation as it simultaneously transmits data, voice, and video data traffic. The ATM interface card inside her workstation contains a segmentation, or "chopper," function which slices and dices the separate streams into 48-octet pieces, as shown in Figure 5.18. In the next step, the "postman" addresses the payload by prefixing it with the VPI, the VCI, and the remaining fields of the 5-octet cell header. The result is a stream of 53-octet ATM cells from each source: voice, video, and data. These cells are generated independently by each source, and so there may be contention for cell slot times on the interface connected to the workstation. The data, voice, and video are each assigned a virtual channel connection (VCC): VCI 51 for data, VCI 52 for voice, and VCI 53 for video, all on VPI = 0.

The bottom half of Figure 5.18 shows an example of how Jeanne's terminal sends the combined voice, video, and text data over the UNI toward the local switch. A gatekeeper in her terminal shapes the transmitted data using a shaping interval of eight cells (about 80 μs at the DS3 rate), normally allowing one voice cell, then five video cells, and finally what is left — two data cells — to be transmitted. On a DS3 interface this would correspond to about 4 Mbps worth of bandwidth for high-fidelity audio, 24 Mbps for video, and 9 Mbps for text data. On a 25 Mbps interface the available bandwidth is halved. All data sources (data, voice, and video) contend for the bandwidth in each shaping interval of eight cell times, with the voice, video, and then text data being sent in the above proportion. Furthermore, the gatekeeper gives priority to slot times among the various streams. Voice cells have the highest priority, video cells have the second priority, and data cells the lowest priority. The gatekeeper sends the highest-priority cells first in the shaping interval. Cells are retained in the buffer by the gatekeeper in case all of the cell slot times in the shaping interval are full. A much larger shaping interval is used in practice to provide greater granularity in bandwidth allocation.

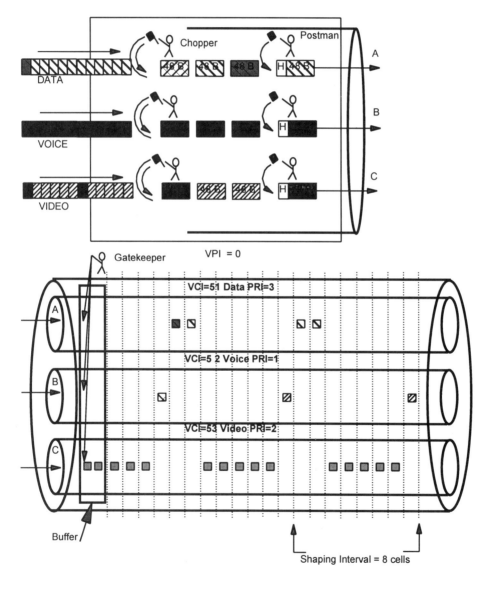

Figure 5.18 Asynchronous Transfer Mode Example

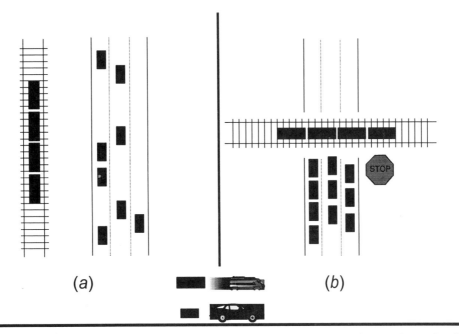

Figure 5.19 Mixing Voice and Data. (*a*) Separate "Channels"; (*b*) "Unchannelized" Voice and Data

5.5.2 ATM   Prioritization   Compared   with   Prioritized   Packet Switching

Why are long, variable-length packets detrimental to short, fixed-length pulse-code modulation (PCM)-type voice samples on a packet-switched network? Why are cells important? We use a simple example based upon an analogy suggested by Goralski [1] to illustrate these points.

In the United States today, railroads are still used for moving large, bulky loads of freight. Railroad engines pull variable-length trains of boxcars, up to 200 or so, on special "networks" of railroad tracks. Highways were built as another special kind of network, but this time optimal for variable-length and variable-speed cars that are optimized for carrying people. As long as the networks are separate — and the trains stay on the tracks and the cars stay on the roads — the networks both work fine, as shown in Figure 5.19*a*.

The problem arises when the highway (cars) must cross the railroad tracks. At a railroad crossing, the train clearly takes priority, and once the train starts across the highway, the cars must all queue until the entire train clears the intersection. This delays the cars, possibly for a long time if the train has a large number of boxcars. Only after the train clears the crossing may the queued-up cars cross the intersection. The number of queued-up cars may be quite large, further exacerbating the delay.

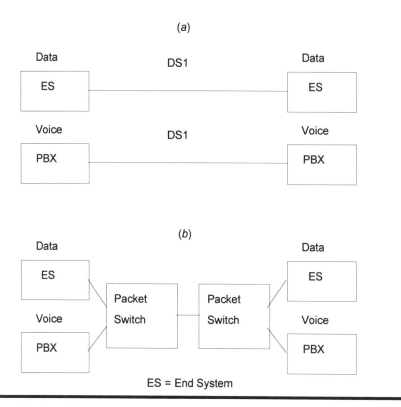

Figure 5.20 Analogy Carried to Voice and Data Network Integration

In this analogy, the train is the large, variable-length data frame, and the cars are the smaller, but more numerous, fixed-length voice PCM samples. The entirely separate railroad tracks and highways are the separate voice and data Time-Division Multiplexed (TDM) networks commonly in use today. The crossing situation represents an attempt to mix the data and delay-sensitive voice samples on a single packet network. Figure 5.20*a* and *b* illustrates the TDM and packet data networks corresponding to Figure 5.19.

Clearly, scenario *b* causes a problem. The backup of voice traffic will cause the receiver to think that something is wrong if the absence of "cars" arriving persists too long. Exactly how long it persists, however, depends on the length of the train.

There are actually two potential solutions to this problem. First, if the engine pulling the train runs very much *faster* than usual, the delay for the cars waiting for the train to pass will be correspondingly *shorter*. That is, if the train runs twice as fast, the wait is half as long. If it runs ten times as fast, the wait is one tenth as long, and so on. The point is that if the train runs fast enough, the time that the cars have to wait, and the number built up at the crossing, can be made to seem almost insignificant relatively speaking. The solution, then, is to make a packet network that runs much faster than ever before, and the trains to run on it. Figure 5.21*a* illustrates this solution.

There is a drawback to this approach, however. Data requirements have grown by leaps and bounds in the past, and the trend is upward. Files today are larger than the entire DOS partition (32-megabyte limit with DOS 3.2) not long ago. It is not unusual to have 16 Meg of RAM on a PC today — larger than the most common hard drive size of 10 years ago (10 Meg). In other words, the data packet trains keep getting longer and longer! Rebuilding the railroad to stay ahead of the trend may be a self-defeating proposition in the long run. Faster railroads may actually encourage longer trains.

Maybe there is another solution. What if each boxcar were a self-propelled unit about the same size as a car? Now if a "train" starts across the intersection and a car arrives, there is only a very short delay before the boxcar is through the crossing and the car may pass. This is much simpler than the previous solution and requires no reengineering of the railroad or the highway. This is illustrated in Figure 5.21*b*. This is the ATM solution, with the boxcars and cars becoming cells (ATM switches replace the packet switches of the last example) with the capability to be prioritized.

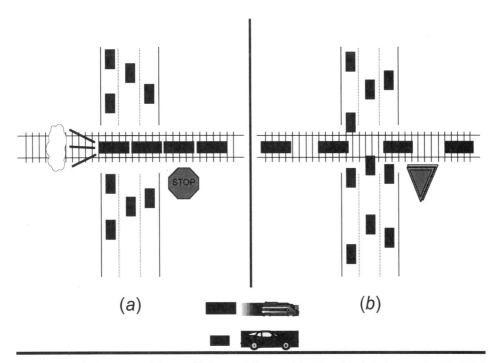

Figure 5.21 Solutions to Mixing Voice and Data. (*a*) "Fast Train" Approach; (*b*) ATM Approach

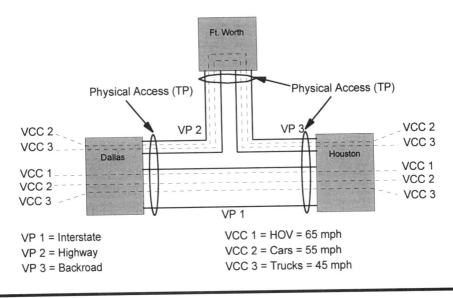

Figure 5.22 Transportation Example of ATM Principles

5.5.3 Transportation Analogy

Let us look at a simple analogy between service category concepts and vehicle traffic patterns. Remember that analogies are never exact; instead, they illustrate a concept through a familiar experience or comparison. Think of cells as vehicles, transmission paths as roads, virtual paths as a set of directions, and virtual channels as a lane discipline (or protocol) on the route defined by the virtual path.

Figure 5.22 illustrates our example employing three transmission paths that form the set of roads between three cities: Dallas, Fort Worth, and Houston. There are many interstates, highways, and back roads between any two cities, which creates many possibilities for different routes; but the primary routes, or virtual paths, are the interstate (VP 1) from Dallas to Houston, the highway from Dallas to Fort Worth (VP 2), and a back road (VP 3) from Fort Worth to Houston. Thus, to travel from Dallas to Houston, a car (cell) can either take the highway to Fort Worth and then the back road to Houston or take the direct interstate. If the car chooses the interstate (VP 1), it has the choice of three lanes: car pool or High-Occupancy Vehicle (HOV) (VCC 1), car lane (VCC 2), or truck lane (VCC 3). These three lanes have speed limits of 65 mph, 55 mph, and 45 mph, respectively, which will cause different amounts of delay in reaching the destination. In our analogy, the drivers in these vehicles strictly obey this lane discipline — unlike the rules that prevail on real highways, especially in rush hour traffic!

In our example, the interstate carries high-speed traffic: tractor-trailers, buses, tourists, and business commuters. The highway can carry car and truck traffic, but at a lower speed. The back roads carry locals and traffic avoiding backups on the interstate (spillover traffic), but at an even slower speed.

Note that our example of automotive traffic (cells) has many opportunities for missequencing. Vehicles may decide to pass each other, there can be detours, and road hazards (like stalled cars with hot radiators in August in Texas!) may cause some vehicles (cells) to arrive out of sequence or vary in their delay. This is evident in normal transportation: You always seem to leave on time, but traffic causes you to be delayed. Automotive traffic must employ an Orwellian discipline where everyone follows the traffic routes exactly (unlike any real traffic) in order for the analogy to apply.

The routes also have different quality. When you get a route map from the American Automobile Association (AAA), you have a route selected based on many criteria: least driving (routing) time, most scenic route, least cost (avoids most toll roads), and avoiding known busy hours. The same principles apply to ATM.

Now, let's give each of the road types (VPs) and lanes (VCCs) a route choice. A commuter from Dallas to Houston who was in a hurry would choose the VP 1, the interstate. A sightseer would choose the highway to Fort Worth (VP 2) to see the old "cow town", and then the back road to Houston (VP 3) to take in Waxahachie and the Davidian cult memorial in Waco along the way. When commuters enter the interstate toward Houston, they immediately enter the HOV lane (VCC 1) and speed toward their destination.

Figure 5.23 adds a railroad (VCC 4) running from Dallas to Houston along the same interstate route (VP 1) as in the previous example. Assuming no stops between Dallas and Houston, the railroad maintains the same speed from start to finish, with one railroad train running after another according to a fixed schedule. This is like the STM or TDM discussed in Chapter 6. Imagine that there are passengers and cargo going between Dallas and Houston, each having to catch scheduled trains. The arriving passengers and cargo shipments originating at Dallas must wait for the next train. Trains travel regardless of whether there are any passengers or cargo present. If there are too many passengers or cargo for the train's capacity, the excess must wait for the next train. If you were a commuter, would you want to rely on the trains always having capacity, or would you prefer to have a car and statistically have a better chance of making it to Houston in an even shorter time period using ATM?

Studying this analogy, observe that the private vehicles (and their passengers) traveling over VCC 1, VCC 2, or VCC 3 have much more flexibility (ATM) than trains (STM) in handling the spontaneous needs of travel. The trains are efficient only when the demand is accurately scheduled and very directed, such as during the rush hour between suburbs and the inner city.

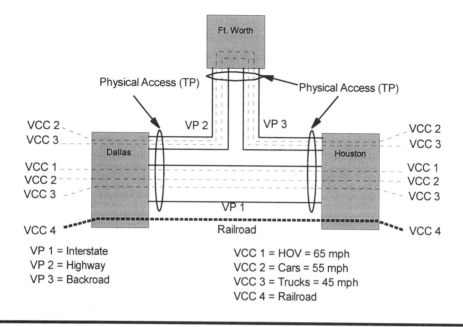

Figure 5.23 Transportation Example — STM versus ATM

Note that the priorities, or choice, of each VCC can vary throughout the day, as can priorities between VPs in ATM. An additional VCC can be configured on a moment's notice and assigned a higher priority, as in the case of an ambulance attempting to travel down the median during a traffic jam to get to and from the scene of an accident. As a final word of caution, we again remind the reader that no analogy is perfect, and therefore extensions or comparison of other aspects of transportation with ATM may not always be valid.

5.6 REVIEW

This chapter introduced the reader to the foundational elements of ATM. These include ATM's multifaceted nature, the notion of logical topology, protocol layering, and private versus shared networking. ATM presents many faces: an interface, a protocol, a technology, economical integrated access, a scalable infrastructure, and a service. This chapter introduced the reader to the basic building blocks of ATM: the physical transmission interfaces, the virtual path (VP), and the virtual channel (VC). The presentation then moved on to a multimedia example as motivation for multiple service categories for voice, video and data. We then presented several analogies to illustrate the importance of priority and different quality of service requirements for voice, video and data. This gives us a good start.

5.7 REFERENCES

[1]   W. Goralski, *Introduction to ATM Networking*, McGraw-Hill, 1995.
[2]   D. McDysan and D. Spohn, *ATM: Theory and Application*, McGraw-Hill, 1995.
[3]   D. Spohn, *Data Network Design*, 2d ed., McGraw-Hill, 1997.

2

ATM BASICS

This part covers what you really need to know about Asynchronous Transfer Mode and its supporting cast of higher-layer protocols. After reading this chapter, you will have the necessary expertise to select the appropriate ATM equipment and/or services for your network design. Our approach starts at the bottom layers of the ATM protocol stack, beginning with the physical and ATM layers in Chapter 6 and proceeding upwards into higher layers in subsequent chapters. The treatment in Chapter 6 includes the fundamental concepts of Quality of Service (QoS), traffic parameters, congestion control, and service categories. Next, Chapter 7 proceed upwards into the ATM Adaptation Layer (AAL) and surveys the user, control, and management planes. Chapter 8 then proceeds to a review of key standards and ideas involved in signaling and routing. The text covers protocols and standards used in private as well as public networks, such as the Private Network-Network Interface (PNNI) and the Broadband Intercarrier Interface (B-ICI). Continuing up the protocol stack, Chapter 9 moves on to ATM support for voice, video, and wide area networking data protocols, such as frame relay and SMDS. The topics covered include video on demand, circuit emulation, and interworking with narrowband ISDN. Chapter 10 addresses the important topic of ATM's expanding role in Local Area Network (LAN) designs. This chapter surveys LAN standards and bridging as an introduction to LAN Emulation (LANE). Chapter 11 then moves up into the network layer, focusing on the Internet Protocol (IP) suite. Subjects addressed include Multiprotocol over ATM (MPOA) and a survey of all the IP standards related to ATM. This chapter also covers leading-edge proprietary implementations of IP over ATM. Last, but certainly not least, Chapter 12 describes how to manage and test ATM devices and networks using ATM Forum and ITU standards and architectures.

6

ATM Foundations

This chapter covers the physical layer and the basic ATM layer. The ATM layer encompasses a range of topics, including the many features of the ATM cell header, traffic management, congestion control, and interfaces to the physical layer below it, as well as the adaptation layers above it. This chapter also covers the ATM layer notions of guaranteed bandwidth and quality of service. The next chapter moves on to protocols above the ATM layer, detailing the ATM Adaptation Layer (AAL) along with an introduction to signaling and management.

6.1 B-ISDN/ATM PROTOCOL REFERENCE MODEL

This section describes the protocol model for the ITU-T's Broadband Integrated Services Digital Network (B-ISDN) built upon the foundation of ATM. Figure 6.1 depicts the B-ISDN protocol reference model from ITU-T Recommendation I.321, which provides a structure the remaining recommendations. Subsequent sections will be introduced by a shaded version of the model in Figure 6.1, illustrating the topic covered.

The top of the cube labels the planes, which are defined on the front and side of the cube. The user plane and control plane span all the layers, from the higher layers, down through the AALs (which can be null), to the ATM layer and the physical layer. Therefore the physical layer, ATM layer, and AALs are the foundation for B-ISDN. The user and control planes make use of common ATM and physical-layer protocols, and even utilize some of the same AAL protocols, however, service-specific components of the AALs and the higher layers differ according to function. Therefore, ATM provides a common foundation over a variety of physical media for a range of higher-layer protocols serving voice, video, and data.

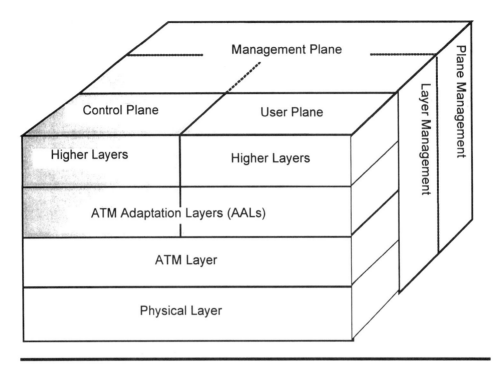

Figure 6.1 B-ISDN Protocol Model

The management plane is further broken down into layer management and plane management. As shown in the figure, layer management interfaces with each layer in the control and user planes. Plane management has no layered structure and is currently only an abstract concept with little standardization at this point. It can be viewed as a catchall for the things that do not fit into the other portions of this model, such as the role of overall system management.

6.2 THE PLANE-LAYER TRUTH — AN OVERVIEW

Unfolding the front and right sides of the B-ISDN protocol cube yields the two-dimensional layered model shown in Figure 6.2, which lists the functions of the four B-ISDN/ATM layers along with the sublayer structure of the AAL and Physical (PHY) layer, as defined in ITU-T Recommendation I.321. Starting from the bottom, the physical layer has two sublayers: Transmission Convergence (TC) and Physical Medium (PM). The PM sublayer interfaces with the actual physical medium and passes the recovered bit stream to the TC sublayer. The TC sublayer extracts and inserts ATM cells within the Plesiochronous or Synchronous (PDH or SDH) Time-Division Multiplexed (TDM) frame and passes these to and from the ATM layer, respectively. The

ATM layer performs multiplexing, switching, and control actions based upon information in the ATM cell header and passes cells to, and accepts cells from, the AAL. The AAL has two sublayers: Segmentation and Reassembly (SAR) and Convergence Sublayer (CS). The CS is further broken down into Common Part (CP) and Service-Specific (SS) components. The AAL passes Protocol Data Units (PDUs) to and accepts PDUs from higher layers. PDUs may be of variable length, or may be of fixed length different from the ATM cell length.

The physical layer corresponds to layer 1 in the OSI model. Most experts concede that the ATM layer and AAL correspond to parts of OSI layer 2, but others assert that the Virtual Path Identifier (VPI) and Virtual Channel Identifier (VCI) fields of the ATM cell header have a network-wide connotation similar to OSI layer 3. A precise alignment with the OSI layers is not necessary, however, because the OSI layers are only a conceptual model. Use any model that best suits your networking point of view. As we shall see, B-ISDN and ATM protocols and interfaces make extensive use of the OSI concepts of layering and sublayering.

Layer Name		Functions Performed	
Higher Layers		Higher-Layer Functions	L a y e r M a n a g e m e n t
A A L	Convergence Sublayer (CS)	Service-Specific (SS)	
		Common Part (CP)	
	SAR Sublayer	Segmentation and Reassembly	
ATM		Generic Flow Control Call Header Generation/Extraction Cell VCI/VPI Translation Cell Multiplexing/Demultiplexing Cell Rate Decoupling (Unassigned Cells)	
P h y s i c a l	Transmission Convergence (TC) Sublayer	Cell Rate Decoupling (Idle Cells) Cell Delineation Transmission Frame Adaptation Transmission Frame Generation/ Recovery	
	Physical Medium (PM)	Bit Timing Physical Medium	

Figure 6.2 B-ISDN/ATM Layer and Sublayer Model

B-ISDN Sublayers

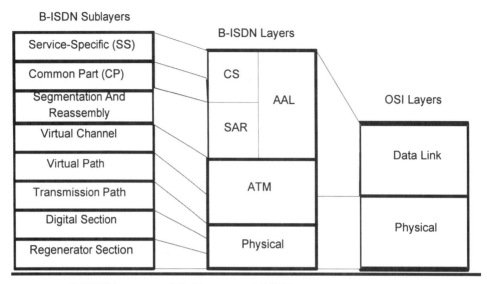

Figure 6.3 B-ISDN Layers and Sublayers and OSI Layers

Figure 6.3 illustrates the mapping of the B-ISDN layers to the OSI layers and the sublayers of the PHY, ATM, and AALs used in this text.

Now our journey up through the layers of the B-ISDN/ATM protocol model begins, starting at the bottom with the physical layer. You may want to return to this layered model for reference as we progress through each of the higher layers in subsequent chapters.

6.3 PHYSICAL LAYER

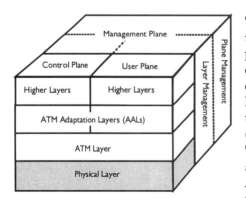

This section covers the key aspects of the PHY layer. The PHY layer provides for transmission of ATM cells over a physical medium connecting ATM devices. The PHY layer is divided into two sublayers: the Physical Medium Dependent (PMD) sublayer and the TC sublayer. The PMD sublayer provides for the actual transmission of the bits in the ATM cells. The TC sublayer transforms the flow of cells into a steady flow of bits and bytes for transmission over the physical medium, such as a DS1/E1 or DS3/E3 private line access circuit into the WAN, or twisted-pair cabling within an office or residence.

6.3.1 Physical Medium Dependent Sublayer

The PMD sublayer provides for the actual clocking of bit transmission over the physical medium. Multiple standards bodies define the physical layer in support of ATM: ANSI, ITU-T, ETSI, and the ATM Forum.

Table 6.1 Physical Layer Interfaces, Media, and Bit Rates

Interface Name/ Description	Physical Media	Line Rate (Mbps)	User Bit Rate (Mbps)	Standardizing Group(s)
DS1	Twisted pair	1.544	1.536	ITU, ANSI, ATMF
E1	Coaxial cable	2.048	1.920	ITU, ETSI, ATMF
nxDS1 IMA	Unshielded twisted pair	$n \times 1.544$	$n \times 1.488^*$	ATMF
nxE1 IMA	Coaxial cable	$n \times 2.048$	$n \times 1.860^*$	ATMF
J2	Coaxial cable	6.312	6.144	ITU, ATMF
Token Ring–based	(Un)shielded twisted pair	32	25.6	ATMF
E3	Coaxial cable	34.368	33.92	ITU, ETSI, ATMF
DS3	Coaxial cable	44.736	40.704, 44.21[†]	ITU, ANSI, ATMF
Midrange PHY	Unshielded twisted pair	51.84, 25.92, 12.96	49.536, 24.768, 12.384[‡]	ATMF
STS-1	Single/multimode fiber	51.84	49.536	ANSI
FDDI-based	Multimode fiber	125	98.15	ATMF
E4	Fiber, coaxial cable	139.264	138.24	ITU, ETSI
STS-3c	Single/multimode fiber	155.52	148.608	ITU, ANSI, ATMF
STM-1	Fiber, coaxial cable	155.52	148.608	ITU, ETSI, ATMF
155.52 Mbps	Unshielded twisted pair	155.52	148.608	ATMF
Fiber channel–based	Multimode fiber, Shielded twisted pair	194.4	155.52	ATMF
STS-12c	Single-mode fiber	622.08	594.432	ITU, ANSI, ATMF
STM-4	Fiber, coax	155.52	594.432	ITU, ETSI
STS-48c	Single-mode fiber	2,488.32	2,377.728	ATMF

[*]The user bit rate for nxDS1 and nxE1 inverse multiplexing over ATM (IMA) physical interfaces specified by the ATM Forum assumes the default value of one overhead cell for every 32 cells at the DS1 or El level. The IMA standard is limited to eight DS1s.

[†]The two user bit rates for DS3 are for the older method called Physical Layer Convergence Protocol (PLCP), taken from the 802.6 Distributed Queue Dual Bus (DQDB) standard, and the new method that employs cell delineation.

[‡]The lower bit-rate values for the midrange PHY are for longer cable runs.

Table 6.1 summarizes each of the standardized interfaces in terms of its name, physical medium, interface speed, user bit rate, and standardizing group(s). The user bit rate is the cell rate times the cell size of 424 bits (53 bytes). The difference between the interface speed and the usable bit rate is due to physical-layer overhead.

6.3.2 Transmission Convergence Sublayer

The TC sublayer maps between the TDM bit stream of the physical interface and ATM cells. On transmit, TC maps the cells into the TDM frame format. On reception, it delineates ATM cells in the received bit stream.

Figure 6.4 gives an example of direct cell delineation mapping by the TC sublayer of the physical layer for a DS1 physical interface. Note that the cell boundaries do not align with octet boundaries defined for DS1, for example, as defined in ISDN. Most TC layer specifications are similar in form to this standard.

6.3.3 TC Header Error Check Functions

The Header Error Check (HEC) is a 1-byte code applied to the 5-byte ATM cell header that is capable of correcting any single-bit error in the header. It is also capable of detecting many patterns of multiple-bit errors. The TC sublayer generates the HEC on transmit and uses the received HEC field to determine if the received header has any errors. If errors are detected in the header, then the receiver must either correct the cell if a single bit error is detected, or discard the cell if more than one error is detected. Most equipment also allows the user to discard any cells with detected errors. Since the header tells the ATM layer what to do with the cell, it is very important that it not have errors; if it did, the cell might be delivered to the wrong user or a function in the ATM layer may be inadvertently invoked.

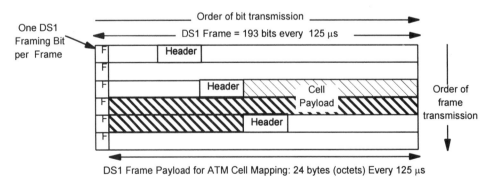

Figure 6.4 DS1 Transmission Convergence Sublayer Mapping

The TC also uses the HEC to locate cells when they are directly mapped into a TDM payload, for example, as in the DS1 mapping in the previous section. The HEC infrequently matches random data in the cell payloads when the 5 bytes that are being checked are not part of the header. Thus, almost all ATM standards employ the HEC to locate cell boundaries in the received bit stream. One notable exception is the North American standard for DS3, which uses a separate Physical Layer Convergence Protocol (PLCP) for cell delineation [1]. Once several cell headers have been located through the use of the HEC, then TC knows to expect the next cell 53 bytes later. Standards call this process *HEC-based cell delineation*.

6.3.4 TC Cell-Rate Decoupling

The TC sublayer performs a cell-rate decoupling, or speed-matching, function as well. Special codings of the ATM cell header indicate whether a cell is either *idle* or *unassigned*. All other cells are *assigned* and correspond to the cells generated by the ATM layer. Figure 6.5 illustrates an example of cell-rate decoupling between two ATM devices. The transmitting ATM device multiplexes multiple cell streams, queuing them if a time slot is not immediately available on the physical media as illustrated in the figure. If the queue is empty when the time to fill the next cell time slot arrives, then the TC sublayer in the transmitter inserts either an unassigned cell or an idle cell, indicated by the solid black filled cells in the figure. The receiving device extracts unassigned or idle cells and distributes the other, assigned cells to the destinations as determined from the VPI and VCI values. Also, note how the act of multiplexing and switching changes the intercell spacing in the output cell streams, as the reader can see from the example. Here is one caveat. Since the ITU-T standardized on idle cells, while the ATM Forum chose unassigned cells for cell-rate decoupling, these methods are incompatible. Look for ATM systems that either support the same method or allow the method to be selected by software to ensure interoperability.

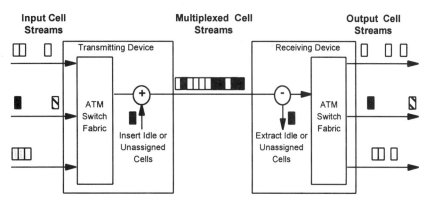

Figure 6.5 Cell-Rate Decoupling Using Either Idle or Unassigned Cells

6.4 ATM LAYER — PROTOCOL MODEL

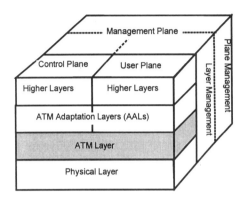

The remainder of this section moves to the focal point of B-ISDN, the ATM layer. First, we cover the relationship of the ATM layer to the physical layer and its division into a Virtual Path (VP) and Virtual Channel (VC) level. This is a key concept, which is the reason the previous part presented several analogies.

It is interesting to look at the number of instances of defined standardized protocols or interfaces that exist for each layer, and whether their target implementation is in hardware or software. Figure 6.6 depicts the number of instances at each layer by boxes in the center of the figure. The arrows on the right-hand side illustrate the fact that ATM implementations move from being hardware-intensive at the lower layers (PHY and ATM layers) to software-intensive at the higher layers (AALs and higher layers). The figure shows the ATM layer instance at the center as the pivotal protocol, shown as the tip of the inverse pyramid in the illustration. There is only one instance of the ATM cell structure which a large number of physical media listed carry as described in the previous section. Atop the ATM layer, only three AALs support an ever-expanding set of higher-layer functions as described in Chapter 7. In summary, ATM allows machines with different physical interfaces to transport data, independently of the higher-layer protocols, using a common, well-defined protocol amenable to a high performance and cost-effective hardware implementation. This flexibility of a single, multipurpose protocol is a key advantage of ATM-based equipment and service architectures.

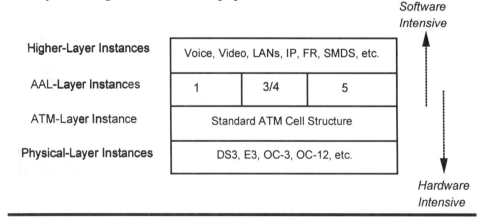

Figure 6.6 ATM Protocol Model Hardware-to-Software Progression

6.5 THE ATM CELL EXPOSED

The primary unit of operation in ATM is the fixed-length *cell*. Standards bodies chose a constant-length ATM cell to simplify the design of electronics in ATM switches and multiplexers. Hardware processing of variable-length packets is more complex than processing fixed-length packets. Indeed, many packet-switching devices allocate hardware buffers for each packet equal to the size of the maximum packet to simplify the hardware design. This section defines the basic fields and meanings of the ATM cell.

6.5.1 ATM Cell

ATM standards define a fixed-size cell with a length of 53 octets (or bytes), made up of a 5-octet header (H) and a 48-octet payload (P), as shown in Figure 6.7. The standard cell format is shown at the bottom of the figure. The bits in the cells are transmitted over the transmission path from left to right in a continuous stream. Cells are mapped into a physical transmission path by the physical layer as described in the previous section.

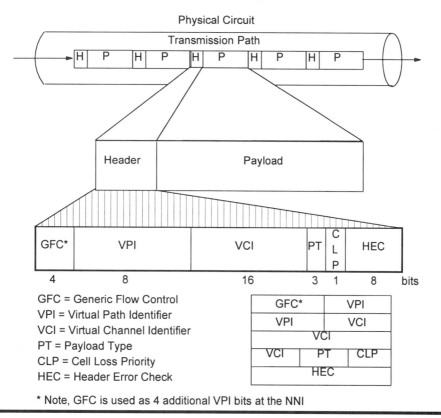

Figure 6.7 ATM Cell Format — Header and Payload

All information is switched and multiplexed in an ATM network using these fixed-length cells. The cell header identifies the destination, cell type, and priority. The VPI and VCI have significance only on a single interface. Each switch translates the VPI/VCI values from input port to output port along the path of an end-to-end connection. Therefore, in general, the VPI/VCI values differ on the input and output ports of the same switch which is part of an end-to-end connection. The sequence of VPI/VCI mappings in the switches along the path makes up the end-to-end connection, as described in Chapter 5. The Generic Flow Control (GFC) field allows a multiplexer to control the rate of an ATM terminal. While the GFC has been defined in B-ISDN standards, there have been no ATM Forum implementation standards or agreements produced on how to actually use or implement it. The format of the ATM cell at the Network-Node Interface (NNI) eliminates the GFC field and instead uses the 4 bits to increase the VPI field to 12 bits as compared to 8 bits at the User-Network Interface (UNI).

The number of bits allocated in the ATM cell header to the VPI limits each physical UNI to no more than $2^8 = 256$ virtual paths and each physical NNI to no more than $2^{12} = 4096$ virtual paths. Each virtual path can support no more than $2^{16} = 65,536$ virtual channels on the UNI or the NNI. Although the UNI and NNI cell formats specify 8 and 12 bits for the VPI, respectively, and 16 bits for the VCI on both interfaces, systems typically support a smaller number of the lower-order bits in the VPI and VCI. Ranges of VPI/VCI bits supported by interconnected devices must be compatible. One way to handle this is to use the ATM Forum's Integrated Local Management Interface (ILMI), which allows each system to query the other about the number of bits that is supported, and thus guarantees interoperability.

The ITU-T reserves the first 16 VCI values (0–15) on every VPI to indicate that cells are one of the following types:

- Idle/unassigned
- Reserved for physical layer
- VP-level Operations Administration and Maintenance (OAM)
- Signaling or metasignaling channel

The ATM Forum assigns the next 16 VCI values (16–31) on every VPI to indicate that cells are one of the following types :

- Integrated local management interface
- Private Network-Network Interface (PNNI) routing channel

The Payload Type (PT) indicates whether the cell contains:

- User data
- VCC-level OAM information
- Explicit Forward Congestion Indication (EFCI)

- AAL information
- Resource management information

The Cell Loss Priority (CLP) bit indicates the relative priority of the cell, similar to Discard Eligible (DE) bits in frame relay service. Lower-priority cells may be discarded before higher-priority cells by the Usage Parameter Control (UPC) at the ingress to the ATM network, if cells violate the predetermined user contract, or within the network if congestion is experienced.

6.5.2 ATM UNI and NNI Defined

Figure 6.8 defines the ATM reference configurations at the UNI and the NNI. The ATM UNI occurs between the user equipment or End System (ES) and switches, also called Intermediate Systems (IS). The figure illustrates the ATM Forum terminology and context for private and public UNIs. Chapter 9 covers the NNI for private networks as defined in the ATM Forum's PNNI specification, as well as the interface between carrier networks, called the Broadband Intercarrier Interface (B-ICI).

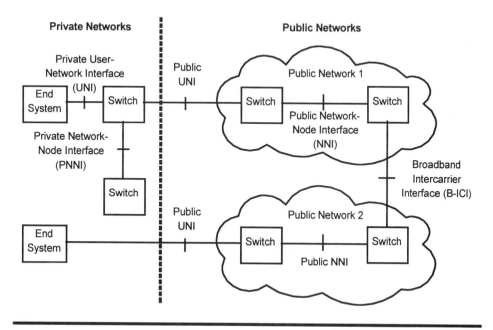

Figure 6.8 ATM User to Network Interface (UNI) and Network Node Interface (NNI)

6.6 ATM-LAYER QUALITY OF SERVICE

As you read anything about ATM, you will encounter the claim that ATM is the best communications networking technology to guarantee Quality of Service (QoS). The next few sections define QoS and how to measure it. We then describe how ATM guarantees QoS only when user traffic conforms to a traffic contract. The most commonly used ATM QoS parameters are:

* Average Cell Transfer Delay (CTD)
* Cell Delay Variation (CDV)
* Cell Loss Ratio (CLR) (defined for CLP = 0 and CLP = 1 cells)
* Cell Error Ratio (CER)
* Cell Misinsertion Rate (CMR)

For all applications, the CER and the CMR must be extremely small, on the order of one in a billion or less. Therefore, the principal QoS parameters are average delay, variation in delay, and loss ratio. To a large extent, human sensory perceptions determine the acceptable values of these major QoS parameters, while data communication protocol dynamics define the rest. Let's explore these QoS drivers in more detail.

Characteristics of the human body's nervous system and sensory perceptions drive many QoS requirements for delay, loss, and delay variation. The blink of an eye is approximately one-fiftieth of a second, or 20 milliseconds. Video broadcast and recording systems utilize frame rates of between 25 and 30 video frames per second. When frames are played back at this rate, in conjunction with the image persistence provided by television displays, the human eye-brain perceives this as continuous motion. When loss or errors cause a few frames in succession to be lost, the human eye-brain detects the discontinuities in motion, which are subjectively objectionable. The human ear is also sensitive to differences in delay on a slightly finer time scale. This shows up in telephony, where the reception of a speaker's echo becomes objectionable within less than the blink of an eye; indeed, 12 milliseconds is the standard delay where echo cancellation is required. Delay variation also affects the perception of audio and video. Audio is the most sensitive, since the human ear perceives even small delay variations. The human ear-brain combination is less sensitive to short dropouts in received speech, being able to accept loss rates on the order of 0.5 percent.

Data applications determine other aspects of QoS. Many data protocols respond to delay and loss through retransmission strategies to provide guaranteed delivery. One example is the Internet's Transmission Control Protocol (TCP), widely used to distribute World Wide Web text, image, sound, and video files. Data applications are extremely sensitive to loss because they respond by retransmitting information. A user perceives this as increased delay if, for example, retransmissions due to loss extend the time required to transfer a large file carrying a video or audio image to a user surfing the Web. Most data communication protocols remain relatively insensitive to delay variations, unless the delay varies by values on the order of a large fraction of a second which causes a retransmission time-out.

Table 6.2 lists the major causes of these QoS impairments [3]. Note that the offered traffic load and functions performed by the switch primarily determine the delay, variation in delay, and loss parameters. Error statistics largely involve cell errors, but they also include misinsertion events when a cell header is corrupted by several errors so that the cell erroneously appears as valid. Of course, the more switching nodes a cell traverses, the more the quality degrades. All QoS parameters accrue in approximately a linear fashion except for delay variation, which grows at a rate no less than the square root of the number of nodes traversed.

Table 6.2 Mapping of Network Impairments to ATM QoS Parameters

Impairment	CTD	CDV	CLR	CER	CMR
Propagation delay	✓				
Switch queuing architecture	✓	✓	✓		
Switch buffer capacity	✓	✓	✓		
Switch resource allocation/admission control	✓	✓	✓		
Variations in traffic load	✓	✓	✓		✓
Switch and link failures			✓		
Media bit error rate and error burst statistics			✓	✓	✓
Number of switching nodes traversed	✓	✓	✓	✓	✓

6.7 THE ATM TRAFFIC CONTRACT

The ATM traffic contract is an agreement between a user and a network, where the network guarantees a specified QoS — *if and only if* the user's cell flow conforms to a certain predesignated set of traffic parameters. The traffic descriptor is a list of parameters which captures intrinsic source traffic characteristics. It must be understandable and enforceable. ATM traffic descriptors include [3]:

- A mandatory Peak Cell Rate (PCR) in cells per second in conjunction with a CDV Tolerance (CDVT) expressed in seconds
- An optional Sustainable Cell Rate (SCR) in cells per second (always less than or equal to PCR) in conjunction with a Maximum Burst Size (MBS) in cells

Figure 6.9 illustrates these traffic contract parameters in a worst-case, bursty traffic scenario.

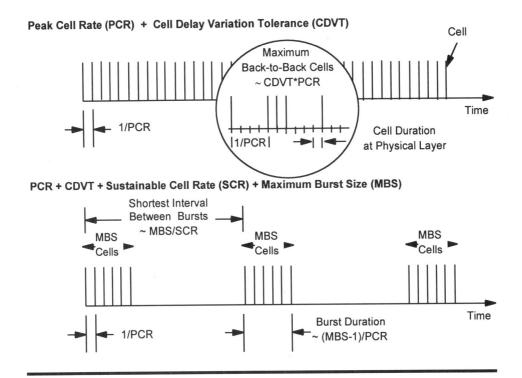

Figure 6.9 Illustration of Principal ATM Traffic Parameters

- ◎ PCR, expressed in units of cells per second, defines the fastest rate at which a user can send cells to the network.
- ◎ CDVT, expressed in units of seconds, constrains the number of cells the user can send at the physical medium rate as indicated in the figure.
- ◎ SCR, expressed in units of cells per second, defines maximum sustainable, average rate that a user can send cells to the network.
- ◎ MBS is the maximum number of cells that the user can send at the peak rate in a burst, within the sustainable rate.

ATM standards utilize a *leaky bucket* algorithm to determine conformance of an arriving cell stream to the above traffic parameters in an action called Usage Parameter Control (UPC) [1]. Standards also refer to this technique as policing. A leaky bucket algorithm in the network checks conformance of a cell flow from the user by conceptually pouring a cup of fluid for each cell into two buckets, one leaking at a rate corresponding to the PCR, and the second leaking at a rate corresponding to the SCR. If the addition of any cup of cell fluid would cause a bucket to overflow, then the cell arrival is considered *nonconforming*, and its fluid is not added to the bucket. The ATM Forum gives a formal definition of the leaky bucket algorithm, called the Generic Cell Rate Algorithm (GCRA), in [3].

An increasing amount of user equipment and switches also implement traffic shaping according to the above parameters. Traffic shaping ensures that the cell stream for a particular connection conforms to the traffic descriptor. Traffic shaping implementations may operate at the peak rate only or at the combined peak and sustainable rates, subject to a maximum burst size. Shaping is essential for user equipment in a network which does not support tagging using the CLP bit. Also, shaping is very useful when interconnecting networks to ensure that traffic exiting one network conforms to the traffic contract with the next network down the line.

6.8 ATM-LAYER SERVICE CATEGORIES DEFINED

We've used the term ATM service category several times so far, but now we define what all the darn acronyms mean. They are hard to keep straight, so this section explains each in lay terms, with later sections providing the detail behind the transport and traffic contract, or parameters, of each. Each service category definition includes terms that define the traffic characteristics which this section details next.

The ATM Forum Traffic Management 4.0 specification [3] (usually abbreviated TM 4.0) defines the following ATM-layer service categories:

- **CBR**   Constant Bit Rate

- **rt-VBR**   Real-time Variable Bit Rate

- **nrt-VBR**   Non-real-time Variable Bit Rate

- **UBR**   Unspecified Bit Rate

- **ABR**   Available Bit Rate

The TM 4.0 specification advanced the concept of QoS (begun in UNI 3.1) by adding a new category ABR, splitting the VBR category into real-time and non-real-time components, and better defining the UBR (also known as best effort) service. Video service requirements largely drove the distinction between rt-VBR and nrt-VBR. The ATM Forum defines some application characteristics for each of these service categories [4] as follows:

- The CBR service category supports real-time applications requiring a fixed amount of bandwidth defined by the PCR. CBR supports tightly constrained CTD and CDV for applications that will not tolerate variations in delay. Example applications are voice, constant-bit-rate video, and Circuit Emulation Services (CES).

- The rt-VBR service category supports time-sensitive applications, which also require constrained delay and delay variation requirements, but which transmit at a time varying rate constrained to a PCR and an "average" rate defined by the SCR and MBS. The three parameters PCR, SCR, and MBS define a traffic contract in terms of the worst-case source traffic pattern for which the network guarantees a specified QoS. Such bursty, delay-variation-sensitive sources, conforming to the traffic contract, such as voice and variable-bit-rate video, may be statistically multiplexed.

- The nrt-VBR service category supports applications that have no constraints on delay and delay variation, but which still have variable-rate, bursty traffic characteristics. The traffic contract is the same as that for rt-VBR. Applications include packet data transfers, terminal sessions, and file transfers. Networks may statistically multiplex these VBR sources effectively.

- The ABR service category works in cooperation with sources that can change their transmission rate in response to rate-based network feedback used in the context of closed-loop congestion control. The aim of ABR service is to dynamically provide access to bandwidth currently not in use by other service categories to those users who can adjust their transmission rate. In exchange for this cooperation by the user, the network provides a service with very low loss. Applications specify a maximum transmit-rate bandwidth (PCR) and minimum required rate [Minimum Cell Rate (MCR)]. ABR service does not provide bounded delay variation; hence real-time applications are not good candidates for ABR. Example applications for ABR are LAN interconnection, high-performance file transfers, database archival, non-time-sensitive traffic and Web browsing. The next section covers ABR in detail.

- The ATM Forum also calls the UBR service category a "best effort" service, which does not require tightly constrained delay and delay variation and provides no specific quality of service or guaranteed throughput. This traffic is therefore "at risk," since there are no performance guarantees. Most LANs and IP implementations provide a "best effort" service today. Example applications are LAN emulation, IP over ATM, and non-mission-critical traffic.

Table 6.3 summarizes the attributes of these ATM-layer service categories from the ATM Forum's Traffic 4.0 specification.

Table 6.4 shows the suitability of the above service categories for a number of commonly used applications [4].

Table 6.3 Service Category Attributes and Guarantees

| Service Category | Traffic Descriptor | Guarantees | | | |
		Loss (CLR)	Delay Variance (CDV)	Bandwidth	Feedback Control
CBR	PCR	Yes	Yes	Yes	No
rt-VBR	PCR, SCR, MBS	Yes	Yes	Yes	No
nrt-VBR	PCR ,SCR, MBS	Yes	No	Yes	No
ABR	PCR, MCR, and behavior parameters	Yes	No	Yes	Yes
UBR	PCR	No	No	No	No

Table 6.4 Suitability of ATM Forum Service Categories for Various Applications

Applications	CBR	rt-VBR	nrt-VBR	ABR	UBR
Critical data	Good	Fair	Best	Fair	No
LAN interconnect	Fair	Fair	Good	Best	Good
WAN transport	Fair	Fair	Good	Best	Good
Circuit emulation	Best	Good	No	No	No
Telephony, videoconferencing	Best	TBD	TBD	No	No
Compressed audio	Fair	Best	Good	Good	Fair
Video distribution	Best	Good	Fair	No	No
Interactive multimedia	Best	Best	Good	Good	Fair

Note: TBD = to be determined.

6.9 ATM CONGESTION CONTROL AND RECOVERY

ATM congestion control methods are categorized according to the type of response (namely, management, avoidance, and recovery) and the time scale over which the response operates. These time scales are the cell level, the burst level, and the call level, as illustrated in Table 6.5.

Table 6.5 Congestion Control Categories and Levels

Category	Cell Level	Burst or Packet Level	Call Level
Management	UPC discard	Resource allocation	Network engineering
Avoidance	EFCI, UPC tagging	Flow control via ABR	Overbooked CAC, call blocking
Recovery	Selective cell discard, dynamic UPC	Loss feedback or packet-level discard	Call disconnection, operations, and procedures

Congestion management works to ensure that a condition of congestion is never reached. ATM uses the following congestion management methods:

- Switch resource allocation
- UPC discard
- Fully booked Connection Admission Control (CAC)

Congestion management attempts to avoid congestion in the first place through more conservative methods, which include proper network engineering.

Congestion avoidance reacts to unforeseen situations, or more aggressively designed networks, using the following methods:

- EFCI
- UPC tagging using the CLP bit
- CAC overbooking
- Blocking new connection attempts
- ABR Explicit Rate (ER) flow control

Finally, in extreme situations, congestion recovery procedures prevent severe degradations in QoS delivered by the network. These procedures are typically initiated when the network has begun to experience loss or markedly increased delay as a result of congestion. Congestion recovery methods include:

- Early/Partial Packet Discard (EPD/PPD)
- Selective cell discard using the CLP bit
- Dynamic alteration of UPC parameters
- Disconnection of active connections
- Operational procedures to reroute connections
- Resource management cell feedback (e.g., ABR congestion indication)

A common, simple method for ATM congestion recovery is selective cell discard based upon the CLP bit in the cell header. When the network becomes congested, it simply discards lower-priority cells. The next section describes a new, much more sophisticated method — the ABR closed-loop congestion control scheme jointly developed by the ATM Forum and the ITU-T.

The ATM Forum TM 4.0 specification also specifies an intelligent frame discard function, since many studies indicate that a more effective reaction to congestion is to discard at the frame level rather than at the cell level. This occurs because a network element that discards at the cell level discards pieces of many packets, causing congestion collapse in the packet-layer retransmission protocols, such as the Internet's TCP/IP. Commonly used industry terminology defines the following cases for the predominant packet-level AAL, AAL5:

- PPD occurs when a device discards all remaining cells, except the last one, when it discards a cell in the middle (i.e., not the first or last cell) of an AAL5 packet.
- EPD occurs when a device in a congested state discards all cells of an AAL5 packet.

If you plan on sending traffic between a number of LANs or internetworks over your ATM network, look for equipment and services that support packet discard or available bit rate congestion control methods to maximize higher-layer application throughput.

6.10 AVAILABLE BIT-RATE CLOSED-LOOP CONGESTION CONTROL

The ABR specification from the ATM Forum [3] and the ITU-T share a common goal: to make unused bandwidth available to cooperating end users in a fair, timely manner. As such, this objective goes well beyond that of today's best-effort LANs, where a single selfish, or "highly motivated", user can paralyze a LAN. If sources conform to the rules of ABR, then the network guarantees a fair level of data loss in exchange for conforming sources. The network may penalize nonconforming sources.

On the other hand, TCP congestion control assumes everyone follows the same rules. For example, policing of TCP/IP conformance is limited to a professor's failing the graduate student who hacks the OS kernel to eliminate TCP's adaptive flow control and achieves markedly improved throughput at the expense of other TCP users sharing the same IP network. ABR's congestion control overcomes this problem by providing the means for an ATM network switch to police users that do not conform to the mandated source behaviors. Hence, a rogue user who sends at a greater rate than that determined by the ABR protocol receives poorer performance than those ABR users that followed the rules. In the TCP scenario, the single rogue user achieves good performance while all the other honest users suffer.

Although TCP sounds more like our daily lives and ABR seems to strive for a lofty, utopian goal, we now describe how ABR achieves fairly arbitrated congestion control. Let's begin by considering some simple analogies from everyday life that involve congestion control.

ABR's binary mode is like the green/red lights at the entrance to congested freeways. The light turns green and another car (cell) enters the freeway (interface). Downstream sensors detect congestion and meter cars entering the freeway so that reasonable progress occurs. A police officer tickets vehicles that do not conform to this rule. By analogy, ATM switches indicate congestion using the EFCI bit in the ATM cell header in the forward direction. The destination end system employs a Congestion Indication (CI) field in a Resource Management (RM) cell to communicate the presence of congestion back to the source, which makes green-light/red-light type decisions regarding the source's current rate.

The ER mode of ABR operation adds another degree of complexity. Similar to the manner in which air traffic controllers control the speed of multiple airplanes (cells) converging on a crowded airport, ATM switches along the path of the end-to-end connection communicate an explicit rate for each source, using RM cells to throttle back fast planes (cells) during periods of congestion to yield a regular arrival pattern at the congested airport (interface).

The Virtual Source/Virtual Destination (VS/VD) mode is analogous to air traffic controllers and airline carriers coordinating the speed and route of aircraft (cells) as they approach airports (interfaces), making connections that maximize the number of seats filled — as well as customer satisfaction. Each airport-to-airport (virtual source-destination pair) route makes decisions with an awareness of congestion at other airports (other VS/VD pairs).

Of course the details of ABR are more complex than these simple analogies; however, keeping these insights in mind may help the reader to grasp the essence of ABR as the following treatment proceeds through more abstract details. In a WAN environment, a key issue that a network ABR switch addresses is how to set the explicit rates to control the sources. This is accomplished such that each switch receives a fair allocation of available bandwidth and buffer resources in a responsive manner, so that high utilization with negligible loss is also achieved.

6.10.1 Three Flavors of ABR

ABR specifies a rate-based, closed-loop, congestion-control mechanism. A key objective of ABR is to fairly distribute the unused, or available, bandwidth to subscribing users at a very low loss rate. Users must conform to feedback provided via RM cells according to particular rules detailed in the ATM Forum's TM 4.0 specification [8]. ABR flow control occurs between a sending end system, called a source, and a receiving end system, called the destination. Sources and destinations must be connected via a bidirectional, point-to-point connection. For a bidirectional ABR connection, each of the terminals is both a source and a destination for each direction of the connection.

TM 4.0 describes the information flow from the source to the destination and its associated RM flows for a single direction. The forward direction is the flow from the source to the destination, and the backward direction is the flow from the destination to the source. Figure 6.10 illustrates the information flow from the source to the destination, which is composed of two RM flows, one in the forward direction and one in the backward, that make up a closed control loop.

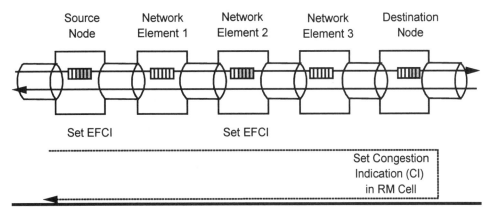

Figure 6.10 Binary-Mode ABR

Two basic modes of end-to-end ABR are the binary mode and the ER mode. The binary mode, shown in Figure 6.10, involves ATM switching nodes setting EFCI in the forward direction so that the destination end station can set the CI field in a returned RM to control the flow of the sending end station. The binary mode ensures interoperability with older ATM switches which set the EFCI bit in the forward direction only in response to congestion. This mode is the simplest mode; however, it experiences loss in certain situations, such as those where congestion occurs at multiple points in the network.

Figure 6.11 illustrates the ER mode where each Network Element (NE) sets the allowed rate in RM cells looped back by the destination as they progress backward along the path to the source. The ATM Forum specification gives examples of how switches may set the explicit rate in the feedback path, leaving the implementation as a vendor-specific decision.

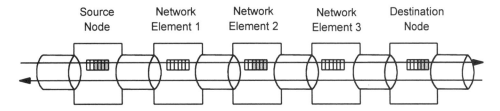

Figure 6.11 Explicit Rate ABR

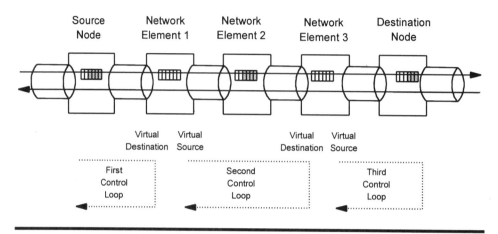

Figure 6.12 VS/VD ABR

Figure 6.12 illustrates an ABR virtual connection that incorporates segmentation using the concept of mated pairs of VS and VD points within the network. A configuration where every switch on the path is a virtual source/destination on is also called hop-by-hop flow control. The VS/VD scheme also provides a means for one network to isolate itself from noncon-forming ABR behavior occurring in another network. The virtual destination terminates the ABR control network for its source, and the same switch originates the traffic using a new virtual source, where the ABR compliance is understood by that switch.

6.10.2 ABR Parameters and Resource Management Cells

Upon connection establishment, ABR sources request and/or negotiate a number of operating parameters via information elements in signaling messages for SVCs, or network management interfaces for PVCs. These parameters include:

☞ A MCR guaranteed by the network
☞ The Initial Cell Rate (ICR) used by the source prior to any feedback
☞ The number of user cells between forward RM cells
☞ The maximum interval between forward RM cells
☞ Factors that control the dynamics of the ABR congestion control loop

In order for the ABR algorithms to operate responsively, feedback must occur. Figure 6.13 shows how RM cells sent periodically by the source probe the forward path, while the destination assumes the responsibility for turning around these RM cells and changing the DIRection bit in the RM cell. The final ABR specification allows the destination to return fewer RM cells than it receives, in case the MCR of the backward connection cannot sustain such feedback. This occurs in practice in ATM over ADSL applications where the bandwidth differs by an order of magnitude in the forward and backward directions. *In-rate* RM cells count towards the Actual Cell Rate (ACR) of an ABR connection in each direction. End systems may optionally send *out-of-rate* RM cells at a lower priority by setting CLP = 1 to make the ABR algorithm more responsive.

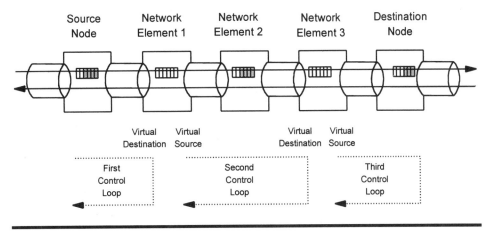

Figure 6.13 ABR RM Cells Insertion and Feedback

ATM Forum 4.0 ABR RM cells contain the following fields, aligned with the ITU-T ABR specification:

- Direction Indication (Forward = 0 and Backward = 1)
- Backward Explicit Congestion Notification for use in LAN environments
- Congestion Indication and No Increase bits
- Explicit Rate
- Current Cell Rate
- Minimum Cell Rate
- Queue Length and Sequence Number from ITU-T I.371

6.11 REVIEW

This chapter introduced the foundations of ATM: the physical layer and the ATM layer. There are a large number of physical media and bit rates supported by ATM, ranging from a few million bits per second to billions of bits per second. The physical layer's transmission convergence sublayer maps a single common ATM layer to this broad range of physical transport layers. Next, we looked at the details of the ATM cell header and how it supports the basic building blocks of ATM networking introduced in the previous part, namely the virtual path and the virtual channel. The QoS and traffic parameters were then defined as components used in defining ATM-layer service categories in support of constant, variable, unspecified, and available bit rate applications. Finally, the coverage moved on to congestion control, highlighting the ABR closed-loop congestion control capability developed to provide high-performance, fairly allocated service to data applications.

6.12 REFERENCES

[1]   D. McDysan and D. Spohn, *ATM: Theory and Application*, McGraw-Hill, 1995.

[2]   ATM Forum, *User-Network Interface Specification*, Version 3.1, September 1994.

[3]   ATM Forum, *ATM Forum Traffic Management Specification*, Version 4.0, af-tm-0056.000, April 1996.

[4]   L. Lambarelli, "ATM Service Categories: The Benefits to the User," http://www.atmforum.com/atmforum/service_categories.html.

[5]   ATM Forum, *Integrated Local Management Interface (ILMI) Specification*, Version 4.0, af-ilmi-0065.000, September 1996.

[6]   R. Jeffries, "Three Roads to Quality of Service: ATM, RSVP, and CIF," *Telecommunications*, April 1996.

[7]   K. Fendick, "Evolution of Controls for the Available Bit Rate Service," *IEEE Communications*, November 1996.

[8]   R. Jain et al., "Source Behavior for ATM ABR Traffic Management: An Explanation," *IEEE Communications*, November 1996.

[9]   M. Gaddis and W. Kelt (eds.), *Quantum Flow Control*, Version 2.0, July 25, 1995, Ascom Nexion.

[10] E. English, "25Mbps vs. 51Mbps: The Great ATM Debate," *LAN Times*, January 23, 1995.

[11] P. Bernier, "Bridging ATM Gap with Inverse Muxing," *Inter@ctive Week*, August 7, 1996.

7

The ATM Protocol Landscape

This chapter moves up to the next layer in the protocol stack, the ATM Adaptation Layer (AAL), which converts ATM cell streams into formats that a broad range of different applications can use. We then introduce the critical role that B-ISDN's control plane plays in signaling, addressing, and routing. The principal purpose of the control plane is to support the services provided by the user plane, such as LAN emulation and voice over ATM. The coverage then moves on to an overview of the higher layers above AAL in the user plane in support of voice, video, and data. Finally, we cover the essential functions of the management plane. This chapter then introduces the remaining chapters in this part using a brief narrative and layered protocol diagrams:

- ☞ Chapter 8, "Signaling and Routing in the Control Plane"
- ☞ Chapter 9, "ATM Support for Voice, Video, and WAN Data"
- ☞ Chapter 10, "ATM in Local Area Networks"
- ☞ Chapter 11, "Internetworking using ATM"
- ☞ Chapter 12, "Managing and Testing It All"

7.1 ATM ADAPTATION LAYER — PROTOCOL MODEL

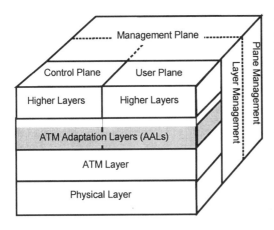

ITU-T Recommendations I.362 and I.363 define the next higher layer of the ATM/B-ISDN protocol stack, the AAL. First, we cover AAL service class attributes and example applications, followed by the generic AAL protocol model. The chapter then describes the Common Part (CP) AAL format and protocol, along with examples of applications.

7.1.1 AAL Service Attributes Classified

ITU-T Recommendation I.362 defines the basic principles and classification of AAL functions. The attributes of the service class are the timing relationship required between the source and destination, whether the bit rate is constant or variable, and whether the connection mode is connection-oriented or connectionless. The service class is a separate concept from the ATM layer's service category and Quality of Service (QoS) described in Chapter 6. In the next chapter, the service class (or bearer capability), service category, and QoS class (or optionally, explicit parameters) can all be signaled separately in a SVC call setup message. Figure 7.1 depicts these key attributes four currently defined AAL service classes, labeled A through D, summarized as follows:

- Class A — Constant Bit Rate (CBR) service with end-to-end timing, connection-oriented
- Class B — Variable Bit Rate (VBR) service with end-to-end timing, connection-oriented
- Class C —VBR service with no timing required, connection-oriented
- Class D —VBR service with no timing required, connectionless

Attribute	Service Class			
	Class A	Class B	Class C	Class D
Timing relation between source and destination	Required		Not required	
Bit rate	Constant	Variable		
Connection mode	Connection-oriented			Connection-less
AAL(s)	AAL1	AAL2	AAL3/4 or AAL5	AAL3/4 or AAL5
Example applications	DS1, E1, nx64 kbps emulation	Packet video, audio	Frame relay, X.25	IP, SMDS

Figure 7.1 ATM ITU ATM/B-ISDN Service Classes

Some standards — for example, classical IP over ATM — specify in detail how to the higher-layer protocol sets the closely related, yet different parameters of service class, service category, and AAL in signaling messages.

The mapping of service classes to AALs is only partially complete in the standards. The next section indicates the AAL(s) that can support the attributes of the defined AAL service class and also gives several application examples for each service class and AAL.

Table 7.1 identifies applications that utilize particular combinations of AALs and the ATM-layer service category (from Chapter 5). As seen from the table, not all combinations of AAL and ATM-layer service category are relevant. We introduce many of the protocols listed in this table later in this chapter. AAL1 is used to interwork with Time Division Multiplexing (TDM) protocols. AAL2 is intended to support video when it is standardized. AAL3/4 is currently standardized only for ATM access to Switched Multi-megabit Data Service (SMDS). Early LAN and internetworking protocols [i.e., LAN Emulation (LANE) and classical IP over ATM] utilized only the Unspecified Bit Rate (UBR), also known as the best effort, service category. The ATM Forum's LANE specification version 2.0 and the Private Network-Network Interface (PNNI) specification provide access to all ATM service categories. Most data-oriented applications utilize AAL5, as can be seen from the table, including an early specification for video on demand defined by the ATM Forum in advance of AAL2 standardization. A native ATM Application Programming Interface (API) and basic signaling procedures provide access to any combination of AAL and ATM service category. However, most users will use the standard combinations listed in Table 7.1.

Table 7.1 Applications of AAL and ATM-Layer Service Category

| AAL | ATM-Layer Service Category | | | | |
	CBR	rt-VBR	nrt-VBR	ABR	UBR
AAL1	Circuit emulation, N-ISDN, voice over ATM				
AAL2		Variable bit rate video			
AAL3/4			ATM/SMDS		
AAL5	LANE 2.0, PNNI 1.0	Video on demand, LANE 2.0, PNNI 1.0	Frame relay, ATM/SMDS, LANE 2.0, PNNI 1.0	LANE 2.0, PNNI 1.0	Classical IP over ATM, LANE 1.0/2,0, PNNI 1.0, MPOA
Null	PNNI 1.0	PNNI 1.0	PNNI 1.0	PNNI 1.0	PNNI 1.0

7.1.2 AAL Protocol Structure Defined

The B-ISDN protocol model adapts the services provided by the ATM layer to those required by the higher layers through the AAL. Figure 7.2 depicts the structure and logical interfaces of the AAL. An AAL Service Access Point (SAP) provides services to higher layers by passing primitives (e.g., request, indicate, response, and confirm) concerning the AAL Protocol Data Units (AAL-PDUs) as shown at the top of the figure. See the referenced standards for details on the protocol primitives. We summarize the resulting transfer of PDUs between sublayers or across an SAP from a functional point of view in the subsequent sections.

Standards further subdivide the AAL into the Convergence Sublayer (CS) and the Segmentation and Reassembly (SAR) sublayer as shown in the figure. The CS is further subdivided into Service-Specific (SS) and Common Part (CP) components. The SSCS may be null, which means it does nothing. The CPCS must always be implemented along with the SAR sublayer. These layers pass primitives regarding their respective PDUs among themselves as labeled in the figure, resulting in the passing of SAR-PDU primitives (which is the ATM cell payload) to and from the ATM layer via the ATM-SAP.

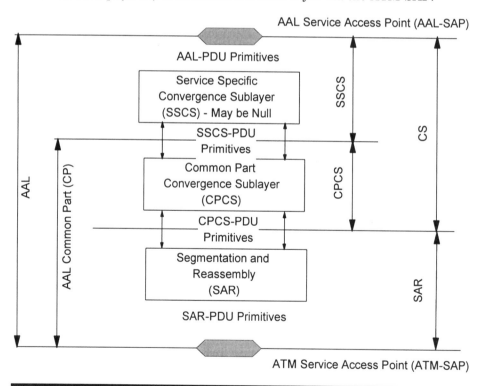

Figure 7.2 Generic AAL Protocol Sublayer Model

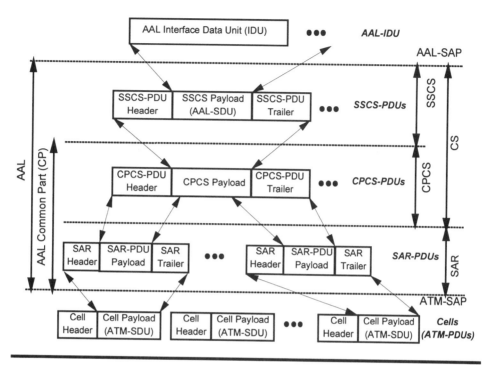

Figure 7.3 AAL PDU Model

The layered AAL protocol model is rather abstract, so let's look at it from another point of view, down at the PDU level. Figure 7.3 depicts the ATM layer at the bottom and moves up to the AAL SAR sublayer, and up through the AAL CS sublayers to the higher-layer protocol. This model follows the general layered methodology first defined in the OSI reference model. The PDU at each layer has a header, and optionally a trailer, that conveys information for use at the particular sublayer. Starting at the bottom of the figure, the ATM layer passes cell payloads from cells with valid headers up to the AAL SAR sublayer for a particular VCC. The SAR sublayer interprets the header (and optional trailer) for SAR-PDUs constructed from the cell payloads. The SAR-PDU and cell payload boundaries need not be aligned. If the SAR layer successfully reassembles an entire AAL CPCS-PDU, then it passes it up to the CPCS layer, which has its own header and optional trailer. The CPCS layer extracts the AAL SDU. If the AAL-SSCS layer is null, then the AAL-SDU is passed directly to the AAL user across the AAL SAP.

If the SSCS sublayer is nonnull, then the CPCS sublayer passes its payload up to the SSCS sublayer. The SSCS sublayer finally extracts the AAL-SDU using its header and optional trailer. In some AAL definitions, the SSCS layer may derive multiple AAL Interface Data Unit (IDUs) from a single SSCS-PDU to the higher-layer protocol. If the SSCS is null, then the IDU is exactly the same as the CPCS payload. The process of receiving AAL-IDUs from the higher-layer protocol and processing them down through the AAL convergence sublayer and segmentation is the reverse of the above.

The IDU provides the all-important interface to the AAL that makes the cell level accessible to voice, video, and packet data applications, as shown in the chapters in the remainder of this part. The IDU, for example, is the API in the Windows operating system for packet-layer transmission. In the case of AAL1 emulating a TDM circuit, the IDU is a sequence of bits. The following sections summarize the CPCS and SAR sublayer for each of the currently standardized CP AALs:

* AAL1 — constant bit rate traffic
* AAL3/4 — variable bit rate traffic
* AAL5 — lightweight variable bit rate traffic

7.2 ATM ADAPTATION LAYER — DEFINITION

The CCITT initially defined AAL1 through AAL4 to directly map to the AAL service classes A through D. The history of AAL development for VBR services changed this simple concept. Initially, AAL3 was targeted for connection-oriented services, while AAL4 would support connectionless services. However, as the experts defined the details, they realized that AAL3 and AAL4 were common enough in structure and function to be combined into one, called AAL3/4. More recently, AAL5 was conceived by the computer industry in response to perceived complexity and implementation difficulties in AAL3/4, which the IEEE 802.6 standard adopted and applied to SMDS. Initially, AAL5 was named the Simple Efficient Adaptation Layer (SEAL) for this reason [1]. AAL5 was adopted by the ATM Forum, ANSI, and the CCITT in a relatively short time compared to the usual standards process and has become the predominant AAL of choice in a great deal of data communications equipment. AAL5 is also employed for the transport of signaling messages and frame relay. AAL1 was defined by the ITU-T and further clarified in the ANSI T1.630 and ATM Forum circuit emulation standards for CBR applications. The standards bodies have not yet competed AAL2, intended to support variable bit rate voice and video.

7.2.1 AAL1

The AAL1 protocols specify the means to:

☞ Transfer service data units received from a source at a constant source bit rate and deliver them at the same bit rate to the destination
☞ Optionally transfer timing information between source and destination
☞ Optionally transfer of structure information between source and destination

☞ Optionally perform Forward Error Correction (FEC) on the transferred data

☞ Optionally indicate the status of lost or erroneous information

The AAL1 SAR sublayer provides the following services:

☞ Map between the 47-octet CS-PDU and the 48-octet SAR-PDU using a 1-octet SAR-PDU header

☞ Indicate the existence of CS function using a bit in the SAR-PDU header

☞ Generate sequence numbering for SAR-PDUs at the source and validate received sequence numbers at the destination before passing them to the CS sublayer

☞ Perform error detection and correction on the Sequence Number (SN) field

The AAL1 CS defines various functions needed for the transport of TDM circuits, video signals, voiceband signals, and high-quality audio signals. The AAL1 CS protocols provide a menu that these higher-layer applications use to provide required service features (e.g., timing recovery), deliver end-to-end performance (e.g., loss and delay), and account for anticipated network impairments (e.g., cell loss and delay variation). Table 7.2 illustrates some examples of this selection of AAL1 CS menu items by higher-layer services [3].

AAL1 supports transfer of constant bit rate data in one of two modes: the unstructured method or the Structured Data Transfer (SDT) method. First, we cover the unstructured method, which takes data from the AAL1 source, performs CS functions (e.g., asynchronous clocking information or FEC) and passes these data units to the SAR sublayer as illustrated in Figure 7.4. The SAR sublayer segments CS-PDUs into 47-octet segments, prefixes these segments with a 1-octet SAR header, and passes them to the ATM layer on transmit. At the destination, the receiver's SAR sublayer takes the 48-octet ATM cell payloads and examines the SAR-PDU header for errors. If the SAR-PDU header contains errors, the SAR sublayer then passes an indication to the CS, which may indicate this to the end application. The SAR sublayer passes correctly received SAR-PDU payloads to the CS, if present. The CS then reclocks the received bit stream up to the destination AAL user, transparently passing any framing information in the original source signal as indicated in the figure by the fields marked "F" in the AAL1 user bit stream.

Table 7.2 Application of AAL1 CS Functions to Transport of Specific Services

AAL1 CS Function	Structured TDM	Unstructured TDM	Video Signals	Voiceband Signals
CBR rate	nx64 kbps	PDH rate *	MPEG2 rate	64 kbps
Clock recovery	Synch	Synch, asynch	Asynch	Synch
Error correction	Not used	Not used	Used	Not used
Error status	Not used	Not used	Used	Not used
SDT pointer	Used†	Not used	Not used	Not used
Partial cell fill	Not Used	Not used	Not used	Not used

* For example, 1.544, 2.048, 6.312, 8.448, 34.368, or 44.736 Mbps.

† Pointer not necessary for $n = 1$ (64 kbps).

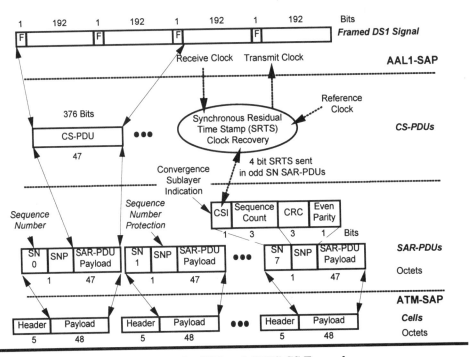

Figure 7.4 Unstructured-Mode AAL1 SAR and SRTS CS Example

A key CS function in unstructured mode is the transfer of the source clock frequency to the destination in the asynchronous clock recovery method. This function is essential to the support of legacy TDM networks, for example T1 multiplexers, over an ATM network. The standards define two methods for this function: Synchronous Residual Time Stamp (SRTS) and adaptive clock recovery. SRTS measures the difference between the source data rate and an accurate clock reference and transmits the difference to the destination in odd-numbered sequence number fields. The destination uses this information to compute the clock rate at the destination prior to clocking out the received bit stream to the destination AAL1 user. The SRTS method requires that both the source and the destination have access to the same extremely accurate reference clock. This works well in a single carrier network, but may suffer from degraded performance in private networks without an accurate time reference at all sites. On the other hand, the adaptive clock recovery method does not require a reference clock at all, and hence offers a plug-and-play approach to circuit emulation. Since detailed standards are not defined for adaptive clock recovery, many implementations offer a range of tuning parameters. In adaptive clock recovery, the destination recovers an estimate of the source clock frequency from the inter-cell spacing of the received cell stream. Although the SRTS method delivers less jitter and receive frequency wander than the adaptive method, it can be used only when an accurate reference clock can be guaranteed. Carefully investigate the timing source capabilities of your application to select the method best for your application.

The Structured Data Transfer (SDT) method supports transfer of nx64 kbps signals using a CS pointer field passed up by the SAR layer, as illustrated in Figure 7.5. The CS accepts specific 64-kbps time slots — for example, those used in an N-ISDN video teleconference — from the AAL1 user as indicated in the figure. Note that the TDM framing information, indicated by the fields labeled "F," is not conveyed from the source to the destination; only the user payload is transferred, as indicated by shading in the figure. The CS utilizes a pointer field in an even-numbered SAR-PDU once every eight SAR-PDUs to communicate the beginning of the structure boundary. According to standards, the pointer field should be used at the first opportunity, that is, sequence number zero, as shown in the figure. This means that CS-PDUs carry only 46 octets of user data when the pointer is present, as compared with the 47 octets always used in the unstructured mode. The pointer field is necessary to reconstruct the precise 64-kbps time slot alignment at the destination, since the time slot octets will in general not coincide with the CS-PDU boundaries. The 7-bit offset within the pointer field in the CS performs this function by pointing to the first octet of the structure, as illustrated in the figure. The octets prior to this octet are filled with data from the structure, from the previous sequence of eight CS-PDUs. Furthermore, the source and destination must have access to the same accurate reference clock, which is required for N-ISDN and is usually available in most modern private and public digital telephone systems. The destination utilizes the structure pointer along with the structure parameters and its accurate clock to place the received 64-kbps time slots in the framed TDM structure for delivery to the end AAL1 user. The SDT mode is best suited to network designs that do not require an entire DS1/E1 between sites. For example, SDT works well in designs requiring the interconnection of PBXes in a corporate network. Accurate timing can be obtained from carrier interface circuits connected to the PBXes, from a SONET ATM UNI, or from the DS3 PLCP layer.

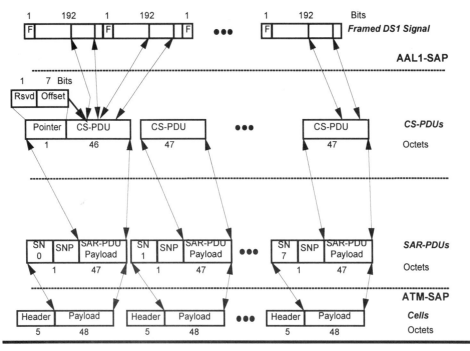

Figure 7.5 Structured Mode AAL1 SAR and CS Example

7.2.2 AAL2

The intent of AAL2 is to provide support for ATM transport of connection-oriented circuit and VBR high-bit-rate packetized audio and video. The current standard [3] identifies most specifics as topics for further study; however, we present an overview of the preliminary standard to illustrate some key methods that the protocol employs to minimize delay and delay variation for real-time voice and video. Services provided by AAL2 include transfer of service data units at a variable bit rate, transfer of timing information between source and destination, and indication of lost or erroneous information. Some standards currently use either AAL5 or AAL1 in advance of a formal AAL2 standard.

Figure 7.6 illustrates an example where AAL2 multiplexes four real-time, variable-bit-rate sources (labeled A, B, C, and D) into a single ATM virtual channel connection. In this example, each source generates 16 octet samples, which are passed across the AAL2 Service Access Point to the Common Part Sublayer (CPS), which forms CPS packets by prefixing each sample with a 3-octet header. The CPS Packet Header (CPS-PH) contains an 8-bit Channel ID (CID), a 6-bit Length Indicator (LI), and a 5-bit User-to-User Indication (UUI) field. A 5-bit Header Error Control (HEC) field provides error detection and correction for the important CPS-PH. The CPS packet header payload may be up to 64 octets in length. The CPS sublayer collects CPS packets over a specified interval of time and forms CPS-PDUs comprised of 48 octets worth of CPS packets using a 1-octet Start Field (STF), as shown in Figure 7.6. The 6-bit Offset Field (OSF) identifies the starting point of the next CPS packet header within the cell. A 1-bit Sequence Number (SN) and Parity (P) field help in providing error recovery for the start field. If the sources have been inactive, then the STF offset points to the next octet in the CPS-PDU, as shown by the arrow in the leftmost CPS-PDU. In general, the STF offset points to some other position, as shown in the second and third CPS-PDUs. In order to maintain real-time delivery, the AAL2 protocol times out if no data has been received and inserts a PAD field to fill out the 48-octet ATM cell payload, as shown in the third CPS-PDU in Figure 7.6. Finally, the AAL2 CPS-PDUs are mapped to ATM cell payloads for a Virtual Channel Connection. Thus, AAL2 reduces packetization delay by multiplexing multiple sources together, and controls delay variation by inserting the PAD field if the period of source inactivity exceeds a specific timer threshold. As we shall see in later chapters, minimal packetization delay is critical for voice over ATM due to echo control problems. Furthermore, control of delay variation is critical for both voice and video over ATM.

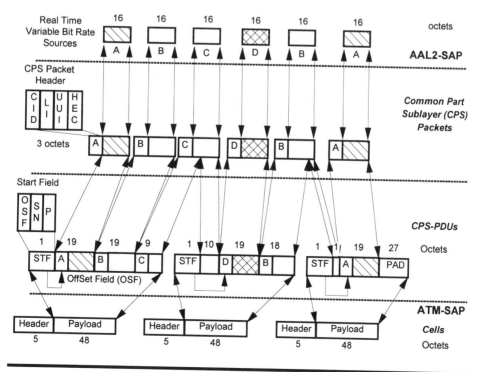

Figure 7.6 AAL2 Operation

7.2.3 AAL3/4

AAL3 and AAL4 are combined into a single CP, AAL3/4, in support of VBR traffic, both connection-oriented and connectionless. Figure 7.7 depicts the SAR and CS sublayers for AAL3/4. Starting from the bottom of the figure, the 48-octet payload of a sequence of cells on the same Virtual Channel Connection (VCC) [i.e., cells having the same Virtual Path Identifier (VPI) and Virtual Channel Identifier (VCI) values] are passed up to the AAL3/4 SAR sublayer. The AAL3/4 SAR-PDU encoding and protocol function and format are nearly identical to the Layer 2 PDU defined in the IEEE 802.6 Distributed Queue Dual Bus (DQDB) standard. A 2-bit Segment Type (ST) field indicates whether the SAR-PDU is a Beginning Of Message (BOM), a Continuation Of Message (COM), or an End Of Message (EOM), as shown in the example. The protocol also defines a Single Segment Message (SSM). The 2-bit SN is incremented by the sender and checked by the receiver. Numbering and checking begins when an ST=BOM is received. The 10-bit Multiplex Identification (MID) field allows up to 1024 different CPCS-PDUs to be multiplexed over a single ATM VCC, allowing multiple logical connections to be multiplexed over a single VCC. This is important when a carrier charges per VCC, which motivates users to do their own multiplexing to minimize cost. The SAR-PDU trailer has two fields: a 6-bit Length Indicator (LI) that specifies how many of the octets in the SAR-PDU contain CPCS-PDU data and a Cyclic Redundancy Check (CRC).

If all SAR-PDUs are received in sequence and with correct CRC values, then the reassembled packet is passed up to the CPCS layer. The Common Part Indicator (CPI) indicates the number of counting units (bits or octets) for the Buffer Allocation Size (BASize) field. The sender inserts the same value for the 2-octet Beginning Tag (BTag) and Ending Tag (ETag) so that the receiver can match them as an additional error check. The 2-octet BASize indicates to the receiver how much buffer space should be reserved to reassemble the CPCS-PDU. A variable-length padding field (PAD) of between 0 and 3 octets is inserted in order to make the CPCS-PDU an integral multiple of 32 bits to make end-system processing simpler. The trailer has three fields, as shown in the figure. The 1-octet Alignment field (AL) makes the trailer a full 32 bits to simplify the receiver design. The length field encodes the length of the CPCS-PDU field so that the pad portion may be subtracted before the payload is delivered to the CPCS user. In message mode, AAL3/4 accepts one AAL-IDU at a time and optionally sends multiple AAL-IDUs in a single SSCS-PDU. In streaming mode, the higher-layer protocol may send multiple AAL-IDUs separated in time; the SSCS may deliver these in multiple AAL-IDUs, or reassemble the pieces and deliver only one AAL-IDU [4]. The principal advantages of AAL3/4 are multiplexing of multiple logical connections over a single ATM VCC, additional error checking fields, and the indication of message length in the first cell that can be used for efficient buffer allocation in intermediate switches.

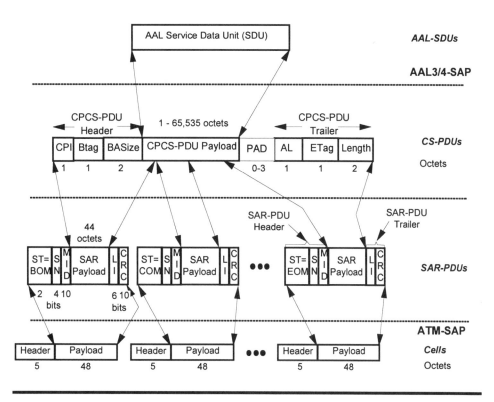

Figure 7.7 Example of AAL3/4 SAR and CS Sublayers

7.2.4 AAL5

If AAL1, AAL2 and AAL3/4 appear complicated, you can now appreciate the motivation for developing a SEAL. Standards assigned the next available number to this lightweight protocol, which made it AAL5. As of publication time, it was still the last word in AAL supporting packet data, a number of proposals for AAL6 never having achieved sufficient backing for standardization. The CP AAL5 protocol supports VBR traffic, both connection-oriented and connectionless. However, despite its simplicity, it is now coming under criticism for relatively inefficient operation, especially for the mix of packet sizes typically used on the Internet. This important subject will be covered in more detail when we consider the future of ATM in Chapter 25.

Figure 7.8 depicts the SAR and CPCS layers for AAL5. The relative simplicity of AAL5 should be readily apparent by comparing this figure with Figure 7.7. Starting from the ATM cell stream on a single VCC at the bottom of the figure, note that the only overhead the SAR sublayer uses is the payload type field in the last cell of a sequence of cells corresponding to a single PDU (i.e., packet). A nonzero value of the AAL_Indicate field identifies the last cell of the sequence of cells, indicating that reassembly should begin.

This was intended to make the reassembly design simpler and make more efficient use of ATM bandwidth than AAL3/4, which was the root of the name for the original AAL5 proposal, SEAL. The CPCS payload may be any integer number of octets in the range of 1 to $2^{16} - 1$ (i.e., 65,535). The PAD is of a variable length chosen such that the entire CPCS-PDU is an exact multiple of 48, so that it can be directly segmented into cell payloads. The User-to-User (UU) information is conveyed between AAL users transparently. The only current function of the CPI is to align the trailer to a 64-bit boundary, with other functions being the subject of further study. The length field identifies the length of the CPCS-PDU payload so that the PAD can be removed. Since 16 bits are allocated to the length field, the maximum payload length is $2^{16} - 1 = 65,535$ octets. The CRC-32 detects errors in the CPCS-PDU. The CRC-32 is the same one used in IEEE 802.3, IEEE 802.5, FDDI, and Fiber Channel.

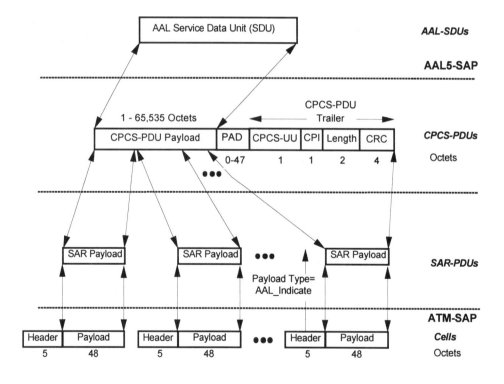

Figure 7.8 AAL5 Common Part SAR and CS Example

7.3 CONTROL PLANE AAL

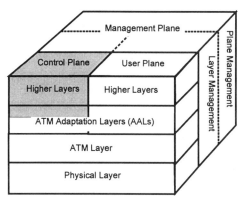

The control plane handles all virtual connection–related functions, most importantly the switched virtual circuit capability. The control plane also performs the critical functions of addressing and routing. The higher-layer, service-specific AAL portions of the signaling protocol are now well standardized. This section covers the shaded portions of the B-ISDN cube as shown in the figure on the left.

7.3.1 Control Plane Functions

The control plane provides the means to support the following types of connections on behalf of the user plane:

* Switched Virtual Connections (SVCs)
* Semipermanent Virtual Connections (SPVCs)

SVCs and SPVCs can be either point-to-point or point-to-multipoint Virtual Path Connections (VPCs) or VCCs. A VPC or VCC of a particular service category provides a specified QoS for specified traffic parameters in an ATM-layer traffic contract, as defined in Chapter 6. SVCs allow users or applications to set up connections on demand, as we shall see for LAN Emulation and Multiprotocol over ATM later in this part. SPVCs provide a standard means for automatically provisioning permanent connections across multivendor networks using the PNNI protocol as described in Chapter 8.

7.3.2 Control Plane Overview

Figure 7.9 illustrates an overview of the ATM control plane protocols detailed in Chapter 8. The specifications for the Service-Specific Connection-Oriented Protocol (SSCOP) provide a guaranteed, reliable packet delivery service to all signaling protocols, as indicated in the figure. First, we cover the signaling protocols at the User-to-Network Interface (UNI). The ATM Forum has produced three versions of UNI signaling protocols, numbered 3.0, 3.1, and 4.0. ITU-T Recommendation Q.2931 specifies B-ISDN signaling on the ATM UNI. The ATM Forum UNI 4.0 and Q.2931 specifications are closely aligned as described in Chapter 8. The ITU-T's formal name for the ATM UNI signaling protocol is the Digital Subscriber Signaling System 2

(DSS2), a natural evolution from the DSS1 name employed for ISDN UNI signaling.

Next, Chapter 8 covers the Network-Node Interface (NNI) signaling protocols used between switches and between networks. B-ISDN adapts the ISDN User Part (ISUP) at the NNI in a manner similar to narrowband ISDN, resulting in a protocol called B-ISUP. The ATM Forum's adaptation of B-ISUP at the NNI for a Broadband Intercarrier Interface (B-ICI) has two versions, 2.0 and 2.1, aligned with UNI 3.1. The ATM Forum defined an Interim Interswitch Signaling Protocol (IISP) as a simple, multivendor interoperable NNI protocol. Finally, the ATM Forum's PNNI protocol defines not only signaling at the NNI, but a scalable, hierarchical topology distribution and routing protocol.

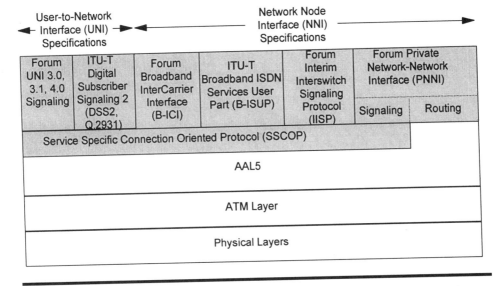

Figure 7.9 Overview of Control Plane Protocol Stack

7.4 USER PLANE OVERVIEW

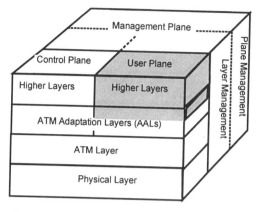

As shown in the shaded portion of the figure to the left, this section covers the general purpose and function of the service-specific and higher-layer protocols of the user plane. The control and management planes exist to support the user plane. The state of standardization in the Service-Specific Convergence Sublayer (SSCS) and higher layers of the user plane is also summarized.

7.4.1 User Plane — SSCS Protocols

To date, the following SSCS protocols have been developed specifically for the user plane:

❋ SSCOP
❋ Frame relay SSCS (FR-SSCS)

These protocols are covered in Chapters 8 and 9, respectively. Although SSCOP was originally developed for signaling, some proprietary user plane higher-layer implementations use it to provide an assured data transfer service in the user plane, such as ATM over satellite networks as described in Chapter 20. More SSCS protocols will likely be defined in the future as standards work on the B-ISDN protocol suite progresses.

7.4.2 User Plane — Higher Layers

Standards bodies have defined a significant number of higher-layer protocols in the user plane to support voice, video, TDM circuits, LAN protocols, and internetworking protocols over ATM. In fact, Chapter 9 covers ATM support for voice, video, and WAN data in depth, while Chapters 10 and 11 cover ATM support for LANs and internetworking. Many of these higher-layer user plane applications work hand in hand with control plane protocols. Therefore, we introduce the control plane and routing first in more detail in Chapter 8. As a prelude, this section provides an overview of the higher-layer protocols defined to date operating over ATM.

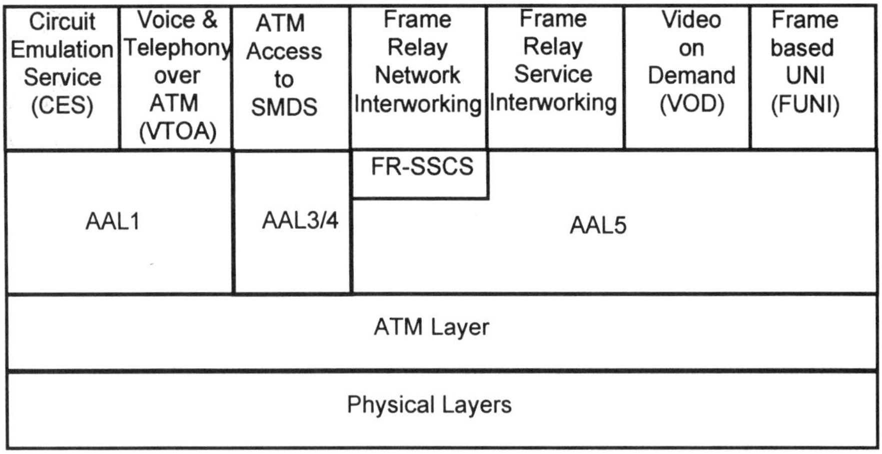

Circuit Emulation Service (CES)	Voice & Telephony over ATM (VTOA)	ATM Access to SMDS	Frame Relay Network Interworking	Frame Relay Service Interworking	Video on Demand (VOD)	Frame based UNI (FUNI)
AAL1		AAL3/4	FR-SSCS	AAL5		
ATM Layer						
Physical Layers						

Figure 7.10 User Plane Higher-Layer Protocols for Voice, Video, and WAN Data

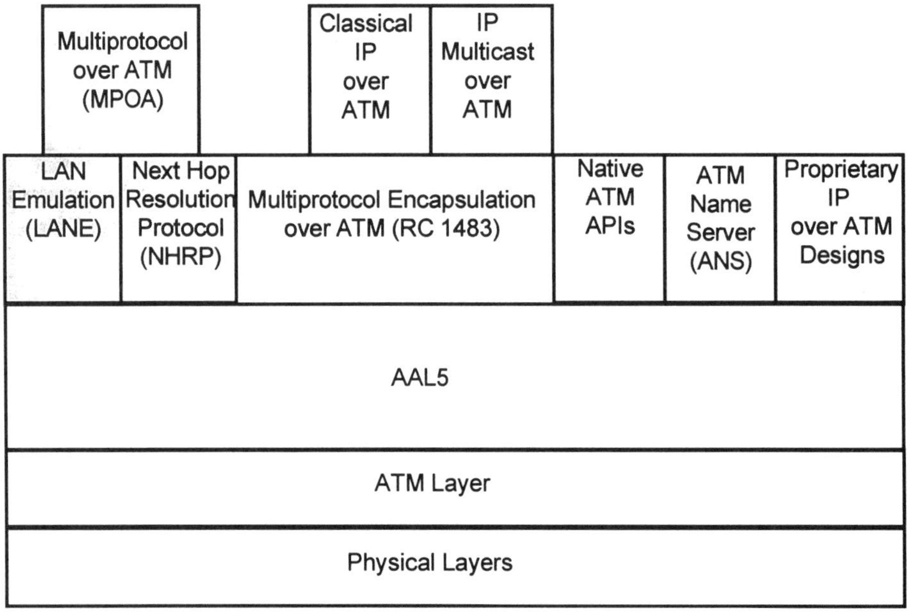

Multiprotocol over ATM (MPOA)		Classical IP over ATM	IP Multicast over ATM			
LAN Emulation (LANE)	Next Hop Resolution Protocol (NHRP)	Multiprotocol Encapsulation over ATM (RC 1483)		Native ATM APIs	ATM Name Server (ANS)	Proprietary IP over ATM Designs
AAL5						
ATM Layer						
Physical Layers						

Figure 7.11 User Plane Higher-Layer Protocols for LANs and Internetworking

Figure 7.10 illustrates the SSCS and higher-layer user plane protocols covered in Chapter 9 in support of TDM circuit transport, voice, SMDS, frame relay, video and a frame-based ATM access method.   Once AAL2 is fully standardized, we expect that subsequent voice and video standards will make use of its unique capabilities. Circuit emulation along with voice and telephony over ATM specifications from the ATM Forum make exclusive use of AAL1, while only ATM access to SMDS employs AAL3/4. As indicated earlier, a large majority of packet data over ATM standards employs AAL5. The video-on-demand specification used AAL5 in conjunction with the real-time VBR ATM service category since AAL2 was not standardized at the time of development. The FR-SSCS sublayer is employed only by FR/ATM network interworking, a protocol designed to support trunking of frame relay over ATM networks.

Figure 7.11 illustrates the higher-layer user plane protocols covered in Chapters 10 and 11 that support LANs and internetworks. Since data traffic is growing at a much faster rate than voice traffic, we expect that many readers will be interested in more detail on these subjects. Therefore, as background, Chapter 10 presents a short tutorial on LAN protocols, while Chapter 11 provides an introduction to routing. Chapter 10 describes LAN emulation. Chapter 11 covers the important topic of higher-layer protocol support for multiple internetworking protocols (e.g., IP, IPX, Appletalk, DECnet, etc.) over ATM. Support for the Internet Protocol (IP) over ATM in addition to other protocols is defined in RFC 1483, which is used for well-defined classical IP subnetworks over ATM as well as in the protocol that implements a multicast capability over ATM. The treatment also covers native ATM APIs and an ATM name resolution service based upon the Internet's domain name service. The chapter also surveys several proprietary, leading-edge, high-performance, QoS-aware protocols that support IP networking over an ATM infrastructure, such as IP switching and tag switching.

7.5 MANAGEMENT PLANE

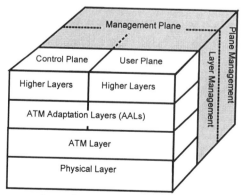

The management plane covers the layer management and plane management functions, as shown in the B-ISDN cube on the left. Layer management interfaces with the Physical and ATM layers, AAL, and higher layers. Plane management is responsible for coordination across layers and planes in support of the user and control planes through layer management facilities. This ensures that everything works properly. Layer management will be discussed first, followed by plane management.

7.5.1 Layer Management

Chapter 12 summarizes the functions of layer management which support the Physical and ATM layers, AAL Common Part, SSCS, and higher-layer protocol entities in both the control and user planes as depicted in Figure 7.12. This two-dimensional view results from cutting the B-ISDN cube open from the back and then folding it out flat. Standards for these management interfaces are being defined by the ITU-T and the ATM Forum for telecommunications equipment using the Common Management Information Protocol (CMIP). Some higher-layer user plane and control plane functions are defined by the IETF and the ATM Forum using the Simple Network Management Protocol (SNMP). Note that standards for the Physical, ATM, and Common Part AALs are identical for both the control and user plane.

Layer management has the responsibility for monitoring the user and control planes for faults, generating alarms, and taking corrective actions, as well as monitoring for compliance with the performance stated in the traffic contract. The operation and maintenance information functions found within specific layers are handled by layer management. These functions include fault management, performance management, and configuration management. The standards for physical-layer management utilize overhead fields within the physical bit stream and are well defend in wide area networks. The standards for ATM-layer fault and performance management are now well defined. Standardization for management for the AAL and higher layers exists mainly in the definition of object-oriented Management Information Bases (MIBs). Standards-based Network Management Systems (NMSs) can then utilize the objects within these MIBs to determine status, detect failures, and automatically configure the managed network element.

7.5.2 Plane Management

Plane management has no defined structure, but instead performs management functions and coordination across all layers and planes in the entire system. The Telecommunication Management Network (TMN) architecture developed by the ITU-T for managing all types of telecommunications networks is being extended to perform the B-ISDN plane management role.

7.6 REVIEW

This chapter took up where the last one left off by introducing higher-layer ATM protocol functions. The text covered an overview of the intended purpose of AALs. The AAL protocol model is comprised of the CS and the SAR sublayer. The CS is further divided into Service-Specific (SS) and Common Part (CP). The CPCS and SAR were explained in more detail for AAL1, AAL2, AAL3/4, and AAL5.

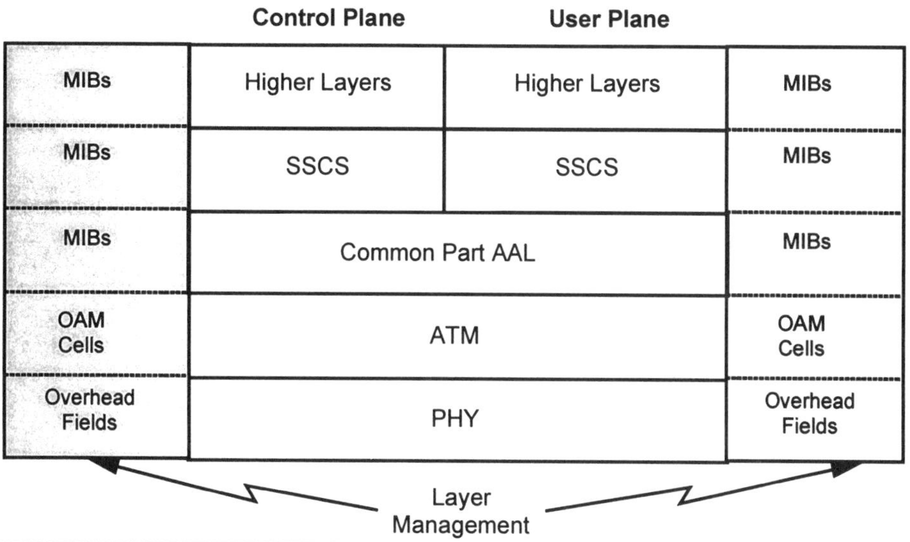

	Control Plane	**User Plane**	
MIBs	Higher Layers	Higher Layers	MIBs
MIBs	SSCS	SSCS	MIBs
MIBs	Common Part AAL		MIBs
OAM Cells	ATM		OAM Cells
Overhead Fields	PHY		Overhead Fields

Layer Management

Figure 7.12 Layer Management in Relation to the User and Control Planes

The treatment then moved on to a brief overview of the subjects covered in the remaining five chapters in this part. First, Chapter 8 covers the all-important aspects of signaling, addressing, and routing which form the foundation for many higher layer user plane protocols. Next, Chapter 9 moves on to higher-layer user protocols in support of voice, video, and WAN data. Chapters 10 and 11 then detail the domain of higher-layer ATM protocol support in the local area network and internetwork environments. Finally, the important but often overlooked topic of network management is covered in Chapter 12.

7.7 REFERENCES

[1]   T. Lyon, *Simple and Efficient Adaptation Layer (SEAL)*, ANSI T1S1.5/91-292, August 1991.

[2]   ATM Forum, *Circuit Emulation Interoperability Specification*, af-saa-0032.000, September 1995.

[3]   ITU-T, *B-ISDN ATM Adaptation Layer (AAL) Specification — Types 1 and 2*, I.363.1, Geneva, May 1996.

[4]   ITU-T, *B-ISDN ATM Adaptation Layer (AAL) Specification*, Recommendation I.363, March 1993.

8

Signaling and Routing in the Control Plane

This chapter covers the B-ISDN control plane, which performs a pivotal role in the switched virtual connection service. First, we summarize the signaling protocol stacks, showing their relationship to basic telephony and ISDN. SVC signaling protocols operate in an analogous manner using a telephone as we described in Chapter 4. However, in ATM there are many more parameters, such as different logical channel and physical network level addresses, quality of service categories, and traffic parameters. Specifically formatted fields, called Information Elements (IEs), within B-ISDN signaling messages convey these user requests. We summarize the definition and usage of signaling messages to help the reader understand the basic functions available to the signaling user. It is important to remember that in many applications employing ATM, a computer program issues the B-ISDN signaling messages, and not a human being, as is frequently the case in the telephone network.

We then summarize the signaling AAL, specifically the Service Specific Coordination Function and Service Specific Connection-Oriented Protocol which provide reliable data transport for the signaling messages. Next, the text covers the UNI signaling protocols by introducing the key signaling messages and their information elements. Simple examples of point-to-point and point-to-multipoint signaling procedures illustrate how users and networks employ the messages to establish and release connections. The chapter then moves on to signaling protocols used between nodes in a network, as well as protocols used between networks. The treatment addresses the simplest network-network protocol first — the ATM Forum's Interswitch Signaling Protocol — before moving on to a more complex protocol, the ATM Forum's Private Network-Network Interface (PNNI). The sophisticated PNNI protocol combines concepts from B-ISDN signaling, local area networks, and Internet routing to automatically provide guaranteed quality and routing in networks that can scale to global proportions. Finally, the chapter concludes with considerations involving signaling between carrier networks at the Broadband Intercarrier Interface using the B-ISDN User Services Part.

8.1 CONTROL PLANE PROTOCOLS

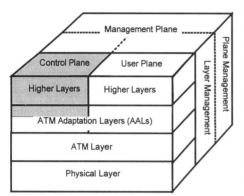

The B-ISDN control plane handles all virtual connection–related functions, most importantly Switched Virtual Circuits (SVCs). The control plane also performs the critical functions of addressing and routing. Analogies with addressing and routing as performed in telephone networks and the Internet are considered where appropriate to leverage the reader's background in these related areas.

The higher-layer and service-specific AAL portions of the signaling protocol are now well standardized. This section covers the functions indicated by the shaded portions of the B-ISDN cube in the figure on the left.

8.1.1 Use of Signaling Protocols

ATM switches are connected together in networks, which in turn may interconnect with other networks as shown in Figure 8.1. These networks employ various types of signaling as indicated in the figure.

Usually, a private switched network is connected to one or more public switched networks. ATM switches are connection-oriented devices which utilize signaling protocols to establish connections. Users interface to switches and communicate the connection request information via a User-Network Interface (UNI) signaling protocol. Between switches an interswitch protocol may be used. Networks are interconnected via a more complex Network-Network Interface (NNI) signaling protocol. Signaling functions may also be emulated by network management protocols which make individual ATM cross-connects, often at a very slow rate. As we shall see later, some higher-layer protocols require ATM devices set up large numbers of connections. For example, in LAN emulation an SVC is set up to each link-layer LAN address. Although each user would typically set up only a few connections to various servers, the aggregate call rate will scale roughly with the number of LAN users. The basic ATM signaling architecture responds to this challenge by distributing intelligence to each device, thus maximizing scalabilty of B-ISDN networks by eliminating any centralized control.

8.1.2 Control Plane Overview

The shaded area of Figure 8.2 illustrates the ATM control plane protocols. The Service-Specific Connection-Oriented Protocol (SSCOP) is first described, which is the foundation for most signaling protocols between AAL 5 and the suite of control plane protocols, as indicated in the figure. The coverage then moves to the ATM Forum's three versions of UNI signaling protocols, numbered 3.0, 3.1, and 4.0. We then move to ITU-T Recommendation Q.2931 [i.e., Digital Subscriber Signaling System 2 (DSS2)], which specifies B-ISDN signaling over the ATM UNI, identifying the alignment and differences with the ATM Forum's UNI 4.0 signaling specification.

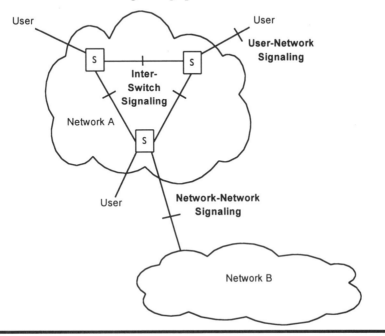

Figure 8.1 Context for Types of Signaling Protocols

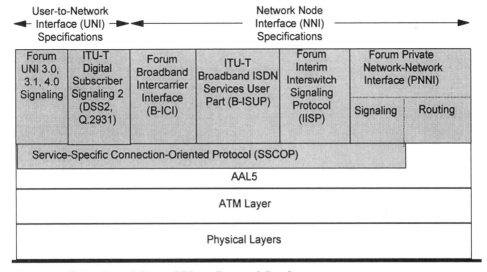

Figure 8.2 Overview of Control Plane Protocol Stack

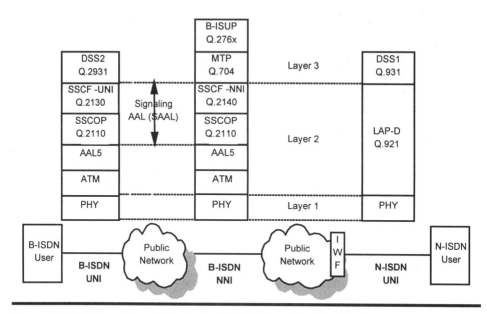

Figure 8.3 Relationship and Context of ITU-T Signaling Standards

The ITU-T's Broadband ISDN User Part (B-ISUP) defines the means to carry UNI signaling between switches and networks. The ATM Forum's adaptation of B-ISUP at the NNI for a Broadband Intercarrier Interface (B-ICI) has two versions, 2.0 and 2.1, aligned with its UNI 3.1 specification. The ATM Forum initially defined an Interim Interswitch Signaling Protocol (IISP) as a simple, multivendor interoperable NNI protocol for private networks. The ATM Forum followed with the Private Network-Network Interface (PNNI) protocol, which defines not only signaling at the NNI, but a scalable, hierarchical topology distribution and routing protocol as well.

8.1.3 Control Plane Architecture and Signaling

Figure 8.3 illustrates the relationships between the major ITU-T signaling standards at the B-ISDN user-network interface. The B-ISDN NNI intercon-nects public networks, and may also be employed between switches within a single network. The right-hand side of the figure also shows the N-ISDN Interworking Function (IWF) and the N-ISDN UNI signaling protocol stack.

The specifications for the Signaling AAL (SAAL) were developed by the ITU-T and subsequently adopted by the ATM Forum, ETSI, and ANSI. ITU-T Recommendation Q.2931 (previously called Q.93B) specifies the B-ISDN signaling on the ATM UNI. The two don't interoperate, so beware of equipment touting support for the older, preliminary Q.93B standard. Q.2931 was derived from both the Q.931 UNI signaling protocol specified for N-ISDN and the Q.933 UNI signaling protocol for frame relay. The formal name for the ATM UNI signaling protocol is the Digital Subscriber Signaling

System 2 (DSS2), the next step after the DSS1 signaling used for ISDN. ITU-T Recommendation Q.2130 (previously called Q.SAAL.2) specifies the Service-Specific Coordination Function (SSCF) for the UNI. ITU-T Recommendation Q.2110 (previously called Q.SAAL.1) specifies SSCOP. The ISDN User Part (ISUP) is being adapted to broadband in a manner similar to the way the UNI protocol was used in defining the parameters of broadband NNI signaling; the result is called B-ISUP. The B-ISUP protocol operates over the Message Transfer Protocol 3 (MTP3), identical to that used in Signaling System 7 (SS7) for out-of-band N-ISDN and voice signaling. This will allow B-ISDN network signaling the flexibility to operate over existing signaling networks or directly over new ATM networks. The series of ITU-T Recommendations Q.2761 through Q.2764 specify the B-ISUP protocol. ITU-T Recommendation Q.2140 specifies the SSCF at the NNI. The NNI signaling uses the same SSCOP protocol as the UNI.

8.1.4 Control Plane Addressing and Routing Defined

Two capabilities are critical to a switched network: addressing and routing. *Addressing* occurs at the ATM Virtual Path Identifier/Virtual Channel Interface (VPI/VCI) level and at the logical network level. Since the VPI/VCI is unique only to a physical interface, there is a need to have a higher-level address that is unique within each network. Ideally, the address should be unique across all networks in order to provide universal connectivity. Once each entity involved in switching virtual connections has a unique address, there is another even more onerous problem: finding a route from the calling party to the called party. *Routing* solves this problem by one of two means: either static, manual configuration, or dynamic, automatic discovery.

8.1.5 ATM-Layer Addressing

The signaling protocol automatically assigns the VPI/VCI values to ATM addresses and physical ATM UNI or NNI ports according to a set of rules. SVCs may be either point-to-point or point-to-multipoint. Each physical ATM UNI port must have at least one unique ATM address in order to support SVCs. An ATM UNI port may have more than one ATM address. Also, in some cases, the same ATM address may be assigned to more than one UNI port within a network. This case is called an anycast address, where the network routes SVCs to the anycast port that is closest to the source.

Recall that a Virtual Channel Connection (VCC) or Virtual Path Connection (VPC) is defined in only one direction; that is, it is simplex. A point-to-point duplex SVC [or a Permanent Virtual Connection (PVC)] is actually implemented as a pair of simplex VCCs or VPCs: a forward connection from the calling party to the called party, and a backward or return connection from the called party, as illustrated in Figure 8.4. Applications may request different forward and backward traffic parameters, for example, as would be used in a video broadcast or in the transfer of a large file or database backup.

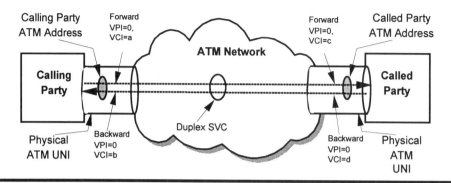

Figure 8.4 Point-to-Point SVC

A point-to-point SVC is defined by the forward and backward VPI (and VCI for a VCC) as well as the ATM address associated with the physical ATM UNI ports at each end of the connection. The VPI and VCI assignment can be different for the forward and backward directions of a VPC or VCC at the same end of the connection as well as being different from the other end of the connection, as illustrated in the figure. In the case of VCCs, the VPI value is often zero, as shown in the figure. A convention in which the VPI (and VCI for a VCC) is identical at the same end of a connection may be used, and is a common implementation method for PVCs because it simplifies operation of ATM networks.

A point-to-multipoint SVC (or PVC) is defined by the VPI and the ATM address associated with the physical ATM UNI port of the root node and the ATM address and VPI and VCI for each leaf node of the connection, as shown in Figure 8.5. There is essentially only a forward direction in a point-to-multipoint connection, because the backward direction is allocated zero bandwidth as stated in the ATM Forum's UNI 3.1 specification. However, there is a backward flow for OAM cells that can also be used by other future protocols. Note that more than one VPI/VCI value and ATM address can be assigned to a physical interface as part of the point-to-multipoint connection. This means that the number of physical ATM UNI ports is always less than or equal to the number of logical leaf endpoints of the point-to-multipoint connection. The implementation of a point-to-multipoint connection should efficiently replicate cells at intermediate switching points within the network as illustrated in the figure. Replication may occur within a public network, or within local switching machines. A minimum spanning tree is an efficient method of constructing a point-to-multipoint connection. Both the LAN Emulation and IP Multicast over ATM protocols make extensive use of point-to-multipoint ATM connections when emulating broadcast LAN protocols. Other applications, such as video teleconferencing, video broadcasts, and dissemination of information to multiple users also utilize the point-to-multipoint ATM connection capability.

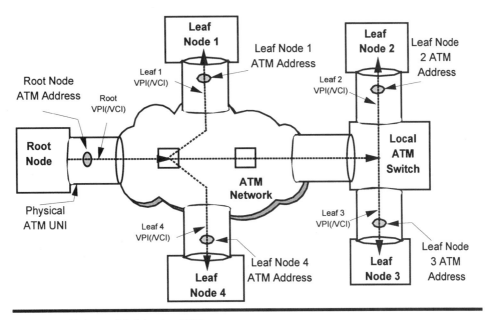

Figure 8.5 Point-to-Multipoint SVC

8.1.6 ATM Control Plane (SVC) Addressing

Currently two types of ATM Control Plane (SVC) addressing plans identify an ATM UNI address: a data-oriented Network Service Access Point (NSAP) format defined by the International Standards Organization and the telephony-oriented ITU-T E.164 standard. We provide an overview of key attributes of these addressing plans in this text. Further details on both can be found in [1].

An important contribution of the ATM Forum UNI 3.0 and 3.1 specifications was the adoption of an address structure based upon the ISO NSAP syntax. UNI 4.0 continued to use this addressing structure and clarified several points. On the other hand, the ITU-T initially adopted the use of telephone number-like E.164 addresses as the addressing structure for public ATM (B-ISDN) networks to interwork with legacy telephone and narrowband ISDN networks. Since E.164 addresses are available only to carriers, preventing the assignment of addresses to the private business sector, the ATM Forum chose NSAP-based addresses, which provide unique ATM addresses for *both* private and public networks. The ITU-T is now also standardizing use of NSAP-based formats.

Figure 8.6*a* illustrates the NSAP-based address format. International (e.g., British Standards Institute) and national (e.g., ANSI) standards bodies assign the Initial Domain Part (IDP) to various organizations, such as carriers, companies and governments, usually for only a nominal fee. The remainder of the 20-octet address is called the Domain-Specific Part (DSP). The network provider supplies the IDP part obtained from an administrative body as well as part of the DSP. The remaining octets are assigned by the end user. The end-user part contains at least 7 octets. The NSAP standards define a structure that is much more rigid than the one adopted by the ATM Forum; this is why we note that the Forum's address structure is NSAP-based. The reason the forum chose a more flexible format was to achieve better scalability through hierarchical assignment of the IDP part of the address. This topic is covered further in the section on PNNI later in this chapter.

Figure 8.6*b* illustrates the ITU-T-specified E.164 address format. This is the same format used for international telephone numbers; it begins with a country code (e.g., 01 for North America, 44 for the UK, etc.), followed by a number defined within that country. This plan has served voice telecommunications well, but it was developed during the era where there was only one major monopoly phone company per country. With the proliferation of fax machines, cellular phones, and multiple phones per residence, the E.164 numbering plan has too few digits, necessitating renumbering of area codes and even individual numbers . Unfortunately, this need to change addresses to continue growth in the telephony sector occurs on an increasingly more frequent basis in response to growing demand. Recent standards work to evolve the E.164 plan to assign a country code to specific carriers is an attempt to address the emerging global competitive nature of networking. The ATM Forum is specifying further details regarding the use of NSAP-based addresses by ATM service providers.

a. ISO Network Service Access Point (NSAP) based Address Format

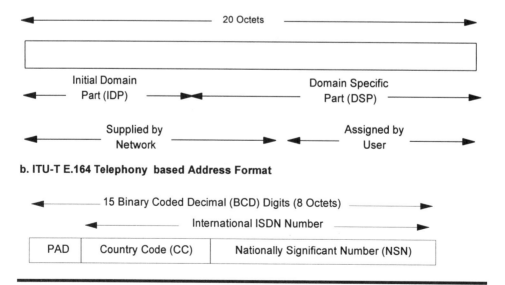

b. ITU-T E.164 Telephony based Address Format

Figure 8.6 ATM Forum UNI Address Formats

NSAP-based numbers can be hard to remember (even if your parents spoke binary code while you were growing up), so the ATM Forum's ATM Names Service [2] provides a means to look up an ATM address based upon a "name," which may be a human-readable name, an IP address, or another ATM address.

The ANS specification represents an ATM End System Address (AESA) as a string of hexadecimal digits with the "." character separating any pair of digits for readability. An example of an NSAP address would be:

39.246f.00.0e7c9c.0312.0001.0001.000012345678.00

The specification represents an E.164 formatted ATM address by a "+" character followed by a string of decimal digits that forms an international E.164 number. Also the "." character separates any set of digits for readability. An example of an E.164 number is:

+01.212.555.1234

8.1.7 Basic Routing Requirements and Attributes

Cells from the same VPC or VCC must follow the same route, defined as the ordered sequence of physical switch ports which the cells traverse from source to destination. The network establishes a connection in response to the following events:

* A SPVC is newly provisioned.
* An SVC connection request is made.
* A failed SPVC is being automatically reestablished.

A connection is cleared in response to the following events:

* An SPVC disconnect order is processed.
* A failure is detected on a restorable SPVC.
* An SVC disconnection request is made by an end user.
* The network performs call clearing in response to a failure.

The route traversed should minimize a cost function including, but not limited to, the following factors:

+ Delay
+ Economic expense
+ Balance utilization on multiple links between node pairs

There are desirable attributes to follow when designing an ATM-layer routing scheme. Attributes of the routing scheme include at least the following:

* Simplicity
* Automatic determination of least-cost route(s)
* Ease of managing changes in the network (e.g., addition or deletion of links and nodes)
* Scaling of the routing scheme to a large network

8.1.8 The Signaling AAL

Figure 8.7 illustrates the protocol model for the SAAL, which provides a layer 2 reliable data transfer service to the layer 3 B-ISDN signaling protocol. The SAAL contain a common part and a service-specific part. The Common Part AAL (CP-AAL) is AAL5 as previously defined in Chapter 7.

The SSCS portion of the SAAL is composed of the following two protocols:

&⟋ SSCF
&⟋ SSCOP

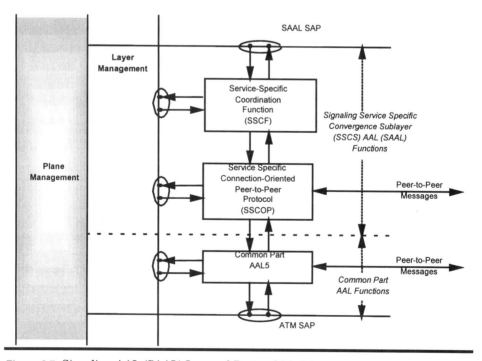

Figure 8.7 Signaling AAL (SAAL) Layered Protocol Model

The SSCF provides the following services to the SAAL user:

- ❖ Independence from the underlying layers
- ❖ Unacknowledged data transfer mode
- ❖ Assured data transfer mode
- ❖ Transparent relay of information
- ❖ Establishment of connections for assured data transfer mode

The SSCF provides these capabilities primarily by mapping between a simple-state machine for the user and the more complex-state machine employed by the SSCOP protocol. The SSCOP is a peer-to-peer protocol that performs the following functions:

- ⬩ Guaranteed sequence integrity, or ordered delivery
- ⬩ Error correction via error detection and retransmission
- ⬩ Receiver-based flow control of the transmitter
- ⬩ Error reporting to layer management
- ⬩ Keep-alive messaging when other data is not being transferred
- ⬩ Local retrieval of unacknowledged or enqueued messages
- ⬩ Capability to establish, disconnect, and synchronize an SSCOP connection
- ⬩ Transfer of user data in either unassured or assured mode
- ⬩ Protocol-level error detection
- ⬩ Status reporting between peer entities

SSCOP is a fairly complicated protocol, but it is specified in the same level of detail as a more successful protocol like HDLC. The unassured mode is a simple unacknowledged datagram protocol, similar to the User Datagram Protocol (UDP). SSCOP Protocol Data Units (PDUs) also employ a 24-bit sequence number that allows for very high sustained rates to be achieved in a window-flow-controlled protocol.

The signaling SSCF and SSCOP protocols and the CP-AAL are all managed as separate layers by corresponding layer management functions as indicated on the left-hand side of Figure 8.7. Layer management sets parameters in the individual layer protocols, such as timers, and monitors their state and performance. For example, the state of SSCOP can be used to determine the state of the underlying physical link or virtual path connecting two ATM devices. Plane management coordinates across the layer management functions to provide the overall end-to-end signaling capability.

8.2 USER-NETWORK INTERFACE SIGNALING

As described in Part 1, ATM signaling shares many characteristics with basic telephony — with extensions that add capabilities to specify bandwidth, quality, end system attributes, different connection topologies, and address formats. Keep in mind that a B-ISDN signaling user will most likely be a computer program and not a human being. First, we introduce some of the basic messages and concepts involved in point-to-point and point-to-multipoint SVC connections. Next, the coverage moves on to some of the key procedures embodied in signaling. Finally, the text presents a comparison of ATM Forum and ITU-T standards with references provided for the reader interested in following up in more detail.

8.2.1 Signaling Messages and Information Elements

The ITU-T's Q.2931 UNI signaling protocol standard and the ATM Forum UNI specification version 4.0 use the following message types for point-to-point and point-to-multipoint connections:

Point-to-Point Connection Control:
☎ Call Establishment Messages
      CALL PROCEEDING
      CONNECT ACKNOWLEDGE
      SETUP
☎ Call Clearing Messages
      RELEASE
      RELEASE COMPLETE
☎ Status Messages
      STATUS ENQUIRY
      STATUS (Response)

Point-to-Multipoint Connection Control:
      ADD PARTY
      ADD PARTY ACKNOWLEDGE
      ADD PARTY REJECT
      DROP PARTY
      DROP PARTY ACKNOWLEDGE
      LEAF SETUP REQUEST
      LEAF SETUP FAILURE

Each signaling message has a number of Information Elements (IEs), some of which are Mandatory (M) and others of which are Optional (O). All messages related to a particular call attempt contain a common mandatory information element, the *call reference,* that is unique at the signaling interface.

The key mandatory information elements used in the UNI signaling protocol are:

- ATM user cell rate requested
- Called party number
- Connection identifier (assigned VPI/VCI value)
- Bearer capability
- Quality of Service (QoS) class requested

8.2.2 Signaling Procedures

Signaling procedures specify the sequence of messages that must be exchanged, the rules for verifying consistency of the parameters, and actions to be taken in order to establish and release ATM-layer connections. A significant portion of the specification is involved with handling error cases, invalid messages, inconsistent parameters, and a number of other unlikely situations. These are all important functions, since the signaling protocol must be highly reliable in order to support user applications. Since the standards bodies based the Q.2931 protocol upon the ISDN Q.931 and frame relay Q.933 protocols, the prospects for interoperability are good. This section gives an example of signaling procedures for the following types of calls:

- Point-to-point connection establishment
- Point-to-point connection release
- Root-initiated point-to-multipoint connection establishment
- Leaf-initiated join point-to-multipoint connection establishment

Figure 8.8 illustrates an example of the point-to-point connection establishment. This example employs a calling party with ATM address A on the left, a network shown as a cloud in the middle, and the called party with ATM address B on the right. Time runs from top to bottom in all of the following examples. Starting from the upper left-hand side of the figure, the calling party initiates the call attempt using a SETUP message indicating B as the called party number IE. The network routes the call to the physical interface on which B is connected and outputs a SETUP message indicating the VPI/VCI to use if the call is accepted. Optionally, the SETUP message may also communicate the identity of the calling party A in the calling party number IE, similar to the calling line ID service in telephony. If the called party chooses to accept the call attempt, it returns the CONNECT message, which the network propagates back to the originator as rapidly as possible in order to keep the call setup time as low as possible. The CONNECT ACKNOWLEDGE message is used from the network to the called party and from the calling party to the network as the final stage of the three-way handshake to ensure that the connection is indeed active.

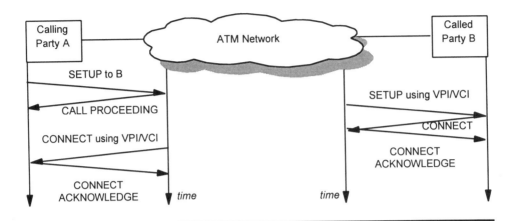

Figure 8.8 Point-to-Point Connection Establishment Example

Figure 8.9 illustrates the point-to-point connection release example, or in other words the process used to hang up the call. The reference configuration and conventions are the same as in the point-to-point connection establishment example above. Either party may initiate the release process, just as either party may hang up first in a telephone call. In this example, the calling party is the one who initiates the disconnect process by sending the RELEASE message. The network then propagates the RELEASE message across the network to the other party, B. The other party acknowledges the RELEASE request by returning a RELEASE COMPLETE message, which is then propagated back across the network to the calling-party RELEASE originator. This two-way handshake completes the call release process.

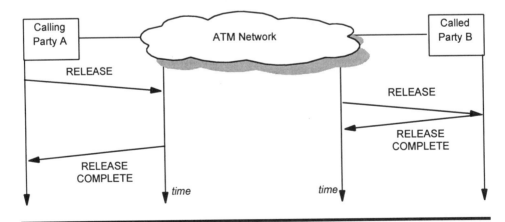

Figure 8.9 Point-to-Point Connection Release Example

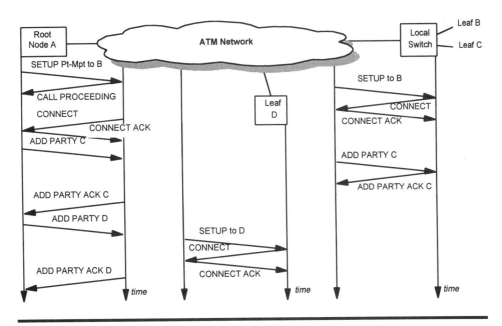

Figure 8.10 Root Initiated Point-to-Multipoint Connection Establishment Example

Figure 8.10 now illustrates an example of a root node setting up a point-to-multipoint call from an originator (root) node A to two leaves, specifically two leaf nodes B and C connected to a local ATM switch on a single ATM UNI, and a third leaf node D connected to a separate ATM UNI. This process is similar to that of three-way telephone calling in which a conference leader (the root) may add one other party to an existing point-to-point call. The root-initiated point-to-multipoint connection procedure meets the needs of audio, video, and multimedia conferencing applications. Root node A begins the point-to-multipoint call by sending a SETUP message to the network requesting setup of a point-to-multipoint call and identifying leaf node B's ATM address. In the example, node A requests a call SETUP to node B, and the network responds with a CALL PROCEEDING message in much the same way as a point-to-point call. The network switches the call attempt to the intended destination and issues a SETUP message to node B identifying the assigned VPI/VCI. The leaf node B then indicates its intention to join the call by returning a CONNECT message that the network in turn acknowledges with a CONNECT ACKNOWLEDGE message. The network informs the calling root node A of the successful addition of party B through a CONNECT and CONNECT ACKNOWLEDGE handshake, as shown in the figure.

Continuing on with the same example, the root node requests that party C be added through the ADD PARTY message, which the network relays to the same ATM UNI as party B through the ADD PARTY message to inform the local switch of the requested addition. Party C responds with an ADD

PARTY ACKNOWLEDGE message that is propagated by the network back to the root node A. The root node A requests that the final leaf party D be added through an ADD PARTY message. The network routes this to the UNI connected to party D, and issues a SETUP message, since this is the first party on this particular ATM UNI. Node D responds with a CONNECT message, to which the network responds with a CONNECT ACKNOW-LEDGE message. The fact that leaf party D has joined the point-to-multipoint call is communicated to the root node A through the ADD PARTY ACKNOWLEDGE message.

The leaves of the point-to-multipoint call may be removed from the call by the DROP PARTY message if one or more parties on the same UNI would remain on the call, or by the RELEASE message if the party is the last leaf present on the same UNI. If the root node initiates disconnection, then it should drop each leaf in turn and finally release the entire connection. Note that the root node is aware of all the parties in the connection, since it added each one to the point-to-multipoint connection.

The ATM Forum's UNI 4.0 specification added a Leaf-Initiated Join (LIJ) protocol that was better suited to data applications. For example, IP multicast internetworking allows users to dynamically join (and leave) multicast groups. This procedure is similar to the popular "meet-me" telephony conference bridges used by many businesses today. Two new message types perform this function in conjunction with the other message types. Figure 8.11 illustrates an example of an LIJ call.

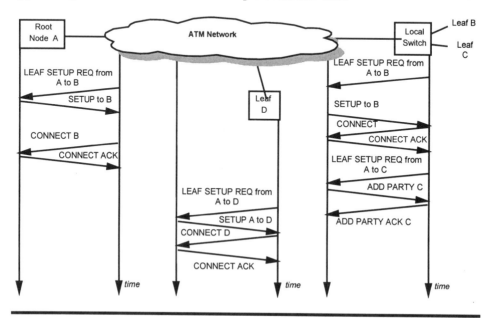

Figure 8.11 Leaf-Initiated Join Point-to-Multipoint Protocol Example

Starting from the right-hand side, leaf B sends a LEAF SETUP REQUEST identifying A as the root, B (itself) as the calling party, and the group address of the point-to-multipoint (pt-mpt) call B wishes to join. The network determines that the point-to-multipoint connection is active and sends the LEAF SETUP REQUEST to the root A. If A accepts the request, then it initiates a SETUP of a point-to-multipoint call to B, identifying it as a call that other leaves may join without notifying the root. The network connects B to the point-to-multipoint call as in the root-initiated case, but includes leaf sequence number information from the LEAF SETUP REQUEST message so that B can associate the SETUP message, with its original request. Leaf B indicates establishment via the CONNECT message, and the network acknowledges in a manner similar to the above examples. Now, when a leaf sends a LEAF SETUP REQUEST for the same point-to-multipoint connection group address, the network adds an additional party to the UNI already supporting the point-to-multipoint connection. In the case of D, the network initiates the SETUP/CONNECT handshake when the first party on the point-to-multipoint connection on the UNI is added. Disconnection from the LIJ point-to-multipoint connection is similar to that for the root-initiated case.

Note that the LIJ point-to-multipoint SVC procedure requires that each leaf use the same group address. This can be either a well-known address or an address determined from a higher-layer protocol, such as IP multicast as described in Chapter 11.

8.2.3 UNI Signaling Standards

The current version of the ATM Forum UNI Signaling Specification version 4.0 [3] and the ITU-T Q.2931 standard are closely aligned in the specification of control plane functions. Table 8.1 compares the capabilities defined in the ATM Forum UNI 4.0 signaling specification and those defined in the applicable ITU-T Q series recommendation. Note that many ATM Forum capabilities are not yet standardized by the ITU-T, while conversely a few ITU-T capabilities are not addressed by the ATM Forum 4.0 specification.

Supplementary services supported include Direct Dialing In (DDI), Multiple Subscriber Number (MSN), Calling Line Identification Presentation/Restriction (CLIP/CLIR), Connected Line Identification Presentation/Restriction (COLP/COLR), subaddressing, and User to User Signaling (UUS) from the N-ISDN world. The End-to-end Transit Delay Information Element allows the calling party to request bounded delay for the connection, a must for delay-sensitive applications such as videoconferencing.

Next, we summarize the features and application of the following extensions to the ITU-T standards by the ATM Forum UNI 4.0 specification:

- Support for group and anycast addresses
- Connection parameter negotiation at setup time
- LIJ point-to-multipoint SVCs
- User-specified QoS parameters

- Switched virtual paths
- Support for multiple signaling channels over one physical UNI

An anycast address identifies a particular service [4], not a specific node. The network efficiently routes a call to an anycast address to the "closest" end system registered within a containing scope to provide the associated service. Anycast supports automatic configuration, name translation and other generic capabilities. Several higher-layer user plane capabilities in LAN emulation and multiprotocol over ATM utilize anycast addressing.

Table 8.1 Comparison of UNI 4.0 and ITU-T UNI Signaling Capabilities

Capability Description	ATM Forum UNI 4.0	ITU-T Recommendation
On-demand (switched) connections	Yes	Q.2931
Point-to-point calls	Yes	Q.2931
N-ISDN signaling interworking	No	Q.2931
E.164 address support	Yes	Q.2931
NSAP-based address support	Yes	Q.2931
Root-initiated point-to-multipoint calls	Yes	Q.2971
Leaf-initiated point-to-multipoint calls	Yes	No
Signaling of individual QoS parameters	Yes	No
ATM anycast	Yes	No
ABR signaling for point-to-point calls	Yes	No
Generic identifier transport	Yes	No
Virtual UNIs	Yes	No
Switched VP service	Yes	No
Proxy signaling	Yes	No
Frame discard	Yes	No
Traffic parameter modification during active calls	No	Q.2963.1
Traffic parameter negotiation during call setup	Yes	Q.2962
Supplementary Services		
Direct Dialing In (DDI)	Yes	Q.2951
Multiple Subscriber Number (MSN)	Yes	Q.2951
Calling Line Identification Presentation (CLIP)	Yes	Q.2951
Calling Line Identification Restriction (CLIR)	Yes	Q.2951
Connected Line Identification Presentation (COLP)	Yes	Q.2951
Connected Line Identification Restriction (COLR)	Yes	Q.2951
Subaddressing (SUB)	Yes	Q.2951
User-User Signaling (UUS)	Yes	Q.2957

The specifications allow a limited form of connection parameter negotiation at call setup time. The user may include, in addition to the desired traffic descriptor, either the minimum acceptable or an alternative traffic descriptor in the SETUP message. The network responds as to whether the original traffic descriptor was supported, or the user-specified minimum/alternative was granted. This is important to applications, such as videoconferencing, that operate best with a preferred bandwidth, but can "step down" to a lower bandwidth in a manner similar to automatic modem speed negotiation adaptation based upon line quality.

Additional signaling information elements allow the end user to specify QoS parameters, such as peak-to-peak Cell Delay Variation (CDV) and Cell Loss Ratio (CLR) in both the forward and backward directions. This feature is useful for connections that require bounded performance, such as multimedia and variable bit rate video.

Signaling 4.0 also supports switched VPCs. The PNNI specification utilizes switched VPCs to "tunnel" across other networks. The specification also defines "virtual UNIs" that allow multiple signaling channels over a single physical UNI. These features are important to private networks implemented with other protocols tunneling over VPC connections, or in public networks where multiple logical customers may be supported on a single physical interface. Further information on the signaling messages and their key parameters, and the basics of the signaling protocol, can be found in [1].

8.3 NETWORK-NODE INTERFACE SIGNALING

The remainder of this chapter covers the Network-Node Interface, also known as the Network-Network Interface. These two meanings of the same acronym identify its dual purpose: use between nodes in a single network, and interconnection between different networks. The treatment in this section begins in the private network domain and then moves to the public network domain and covers the following major NNI signaling protocols:

  * ATM Forum IISP
  * ATM Forum PNNI
  * ATM Forum B-ICI
  * ITU-T B-ISUP

8.4 INTERIM INTERSWITCH SIGNALING PROTOCOL

To build a multivendor ATM SVC network, IISP is the simplest way to get started. However, as your networking needs mature and the ATM network grows, the design should move to PNNI. The ATM Forum recognized the need to produce a standard for a minimum level of interoperability for multi-vendor private ATM networks. Therefore, the Forum rapidly developed and published the IISP in late 1994 [7]. The Forum announced that the IISP standard would fill the void until the complete PNNI specification could be finished. IISP basically extended the UNI 3.0/3.1 protocol to a simple network context.

Figure 8.12 illustrates the conventions that IISP added to the UNI 3.0/3.1 UNI signaling specifications. The IISP physical layer, ATM layer, and traffic management specifications are identical to the UNI 3.0/3.1 specification. IISP employs the UNI cell format, there is no Integrated Local Management Interface (ILMI), and IISP makes policing optional. IISP specifies a limited set of VCIs ranging from 32 to 255 on VPI 0 to ensure interoperability. A key addition of IISP to UNI signaling is identification of each side of a trunk as either the user or the network side, as depicted in the figure. The fact that the UNI signaling protocol implicitly assigns the user and network sides necessitated adoption of this convention in IISP, since the signaling procedures for the user and network sides differ. Simply stated, one may view the network side as the master and the user side as the slave in the signaling protocol. The functions of the user and network sides are symmetrical in the aspects regarding placement or reception of calls, however, and the assignment of user and network side is arbitrary.

IISP utilizes the NSAP-based address format defined previously. IISP defines a simple hop-by-hop routing based upon matching the longest address prefix in a statically configured routing table. Such manual configuration limits the scalability of IISP networks. Also, the switches must clear an SVC call in response to link failures. Support for other features is optional, such as routing over parallel links between nodes, connection admission control for guaranteeing quality of service, and alternative routing. Furthermore, manual configuration of hop-by-hop routing tables may introduce routing loops, a potential problem the IISP specification identifies, but provides no guidance on how to avoid.

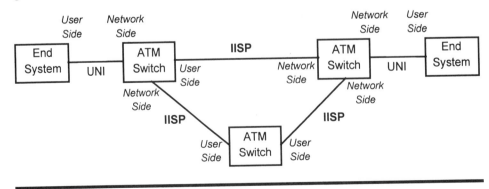

Figure 8.12 IISP Context

8.5 THE ATM FORUM'S ROUTING PROTOCOL — PNNI

A key business driver for the PNNI protocol is to maximize automatic configuration, also called "plug-and-play" operation, and multivendor interoperability of ATM hardware and software. Customers today expect these capabilities based upon their IP networking experience. Early ATM networks required extensive amounts of manual configuration, which led to errors and connectivity failures. The ATM Forum responded to these challenges by designing the mother of all routing protocols, PNNI.

8.5.1 Architecture and Requirements

The abbreviation PNNI stands for either Private Network-Node Interface or Private Network-to-Network Interface, reflecting its two possible uses. The PNNI protocol specifies two separate, but interrelated, protocols and functions to achieve the goal of controlling the user cell stream between nodes and networks as illustrated in Figure 8.13. The PNNI protocol operates on dedicated links or may be tunneled over virtual path connections, as denoted by the VPI=* notation in the figure.

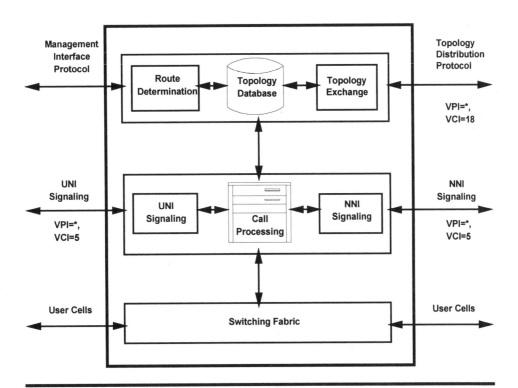

Figure 8.13 PNNI Switching System Architectural Reference Model

A topology distribution protocol defines the methods and messages for distributing topology information between switches and clusters of switches. Information exchanged by this protocol is used to compute optimized paths throughout the network. A hierarchy mechanism enables this protocol to scale well for large ATM networks. A key feature of the PNNI hierarchy mechanism is its ability to automatically configure itself in networks in which the address structure reflects the topology. PNNI topology and routing is based on the well-known link-state routing technique as used in the Open Shortest Path First (OSPF) IP routing protocol, for example.

The PNNI signaling protocol uses message flows to establish point-to-point and point-to-multipoint SVCs and PVCs across an ATM network. The PNNI signaling protocol is based on the ATM Forum UNI signaling standard, augmented with mechanisms to support source routing and the ability to crank back to earlier nodes in order to route around an intermediate node that blocks a call request. The PNNI specification also defines SVC-based Semipermanent Virtual Paths and Channel Connections (SPVPC and SPVCC). Phase 1 of the ATM Forum's PNNI specification has the following characteristics [9]:

- Supports all UNI 3.1 and some UNI 4.0 capabilities.
- Supports hierarchical routing enabling scaling to very large networks.
- Supports QoS-based routing.
- Supports multiple routing metrics and attributes.
- Uses source-routed connection setup.
- Operates in the presence of partitioned areas.
- Provides dynamic routing, responsive to changes in resource availability.
- Uses separate routing protocols within and between peer groups.
- Interoperates with external routing domains, not necessarily using PNNI.
- Supports both physical links and tunneling over VPCs as NNIs.
- Supports SPVPC/SPVCCs.
- Supports anycast.

8.5.2 Network Addressing Philosophy

Network addressing philosophies fall between two ends of a spectrum: flat and hierarchical [8]. Devices with flat addressing, such as bridged LANs, are aware of every other device in the network. Since the routing table of every node must contain every other address, the memory requirements of a flat addressed network design scale linearly with the number of nodes. Typically, scalability refers to how the nodal memory and processor requirements grow with network growth.

On the opposite end of the spectrum, hierarchical addressing assigns significance to portions of the address. A familiar example is the telephone network, which employs E.164 addresses, commonly known as phone numbers. The leftmost digits of an international phone number identify the country in which the addressed device resides. The identified country defines the remaining digits. Most countries employ a geographically oriented addressing scheme. The reason for this convention was scalability in the telephone switch memory requirements. Each node needs to keep track only of how to reach other countries, area codes, and exchanges. If the telephone network used flat addressing, then every switch would require hundreds of millions of address entries. Instead, switches typically get by with hundreds or thousands of entries. Indeed, without this rigid address hierarchy, a global telephone network could not have been built with the technology available in the 1960s. However, the price of memory has dropped precipitously since the 1960s, and so the need to minimize memory has changed markedly, while the telephony addressing plan has not changed accordingly.

Data protocols such as IP also utilize the concept of hierarchical address spaces so that network nodes use scalable routing table sizes and processing requirements. Whereas the telephone network addressing is administered by treaty organizations (i.e., the ITU) and national government–appointed regulators, the Internet runs an address routing registry. The telephone network requires manual administration of the numbering plan, while the Internet offers automatic plug-and-play operation through the use of sophisticated routing protocols. Although there are tens of millions of hosts on the Internet today, the use of hierarchical addressing limits routing table sizes to the order of hundreds of thousands of entries. The Internet primarily utilizes an organizational hierarchy, since address prefixes are assigned to organizations and not countries or geographic areas. However, many organizations have geographic locality, or manage their IP address spaces so that a geographic dimension exists in parallel with the organizational hierarchy. But the standards do not dictate this.

The ATM Forum chose the Internet routing protocol as its addressing and routing model over the older, manually maintained telephone network hierarchy — mainly since private network customers insist upon a high degree of automatic configuration.

An undesirable side effect of hierarchical addressing, however, is the generally low utilization of the total available address space. This sparse filling of the address space occurs because an organization must leave room for growth, or perhaps the fact that the network design dictates peer relationships between groups of devices with widely different population sizes. The ATM Forum's choice of the 20-octet NSAP address format for PNNI meets these requirements well, since there is never likely to be a network that approaches a size anywhere near PNNI's theoretical limit of 2^{160} (approximately 10^{48}) nodes. In practice, however, the real number of useable addresses is much less.

The PNNI addressing plan provides an unprecedented level of hierarchy, supporting up to 105 levels. PNNI exploits the flexibility of such a huge address space with the objective of providing an extremely scalable network in the specification of routing its protocols. In contrast to other network routing protocols developed before it, the PNNI specification begins with global scalability as an underlying requirement instead of an afterthought as now confronts IP in its transition from version 4 to version 6. In the late 1970s, 32 bits of address seemed more than adequate in IPv4. Hindsight similar to PNNI has resulted in selection of a 16-octet IPv6 address, which is actually a subset of the ATM Forum's NSAP-based addressing plan.

8.5.3 A Tale of Two Protocols

Two separate PNNI protocols operate between ATM switching systems connected by either physical or virtual PNNI links: signaling and routing. The signaling protocol sets up the ATM connection along the path determined by the routing protocol. The routing protocol utilizes two types of addresses — topology and end user — in a hierarchical manner. Through exchange of information over PNNI links, every node learns about a hierarchically summarized version of the entire network. The distribution of reachability information along with associated metrics, such as administrative cost to reach a particular address prefix over a PNNI link, is similar to that of the OSPF protocol in IP networks.

Given that the source node has a summarized, hierarchical view of the entire network and the associated administrative and quality metrics of the candidate paths to the destination, PNNI places the burden of determining the route on the source. The information about the source-to-destination path is computed at the source node and placed in a Designated Transit List (DTL) in the signaling message originated by the source. Intermediate nodes in the path expand the DTL in their domain, and crank back to find alternative paths if the call is blocked within their domain. Hence, PNNI DTLs are similar to token ring networks which employ source routing. Also note that source routing prevents loops, therefore, a standard route determination protocol isn't necessary, simplifying interoperability.

Although PNNI builds upon experience gained from older protocols, its complexity exceeds that of any routing protocol conceived to date. As subsequent sections illustrate, the complexity of PNNI stems from requirements for scalability, support for QoS-based routing, and the additional complexities of connection-oriented service, which are not considered in the legacy connectionless protocols of the past.

8.5.4 The PNNI Routing Hierarchy and Topology Aggregation

PNNI employs the concept of embedding topological information in hierarchical addressing to summarize routing information. This summarization of address prefixes constrains processing and memory space requirements to grow at lower rates than the number of nodes in the network. At each level of the hierarchy, the PNNI routing protocol defines a uniform network model composed of logical nodes and logical links. PNNI proceeds upwards in the hierarchy recursively; that is, the same functions are used again at each successive level. The PNNI model defines:

- Neighbor discovery via a Hello protocol
- Link status determination via a Hello protocol
- Topology database synchronization procedures
- Peer-group determination and peer group-leader election
- Reliable PNNI Topology State Element (PTSE) flooding
- Bootstrapping of the PNNI hierarchy from the lowest level upwards

Figure 8.14 depicts the example network used in the remainder of this section to illustrate these concepts. Addresses are expressed in a notation of a.b.c to denote common address prefixes. In this example, we use the labels a.b.c where "a" represents the world region (where P represents the Pacific Rim, A the Americas, and E Eurasia), "b" represents the next lower level of hierarchy, and "c" represents an even lower level of hierarchy. At the lowest level, for example, in a single site, the numbers may be arbitrarily assigned.

Figure 8.15 illustrates the complete PNNI hierarchy for our example. Nodes with the same address prefix are part of a Peer Group (PG), and these groups elect Peer Group Leaders (PGLs), indicated by filled circles within each peer group. The PGLs represent the members of their groups in higher-level groups in a manner similar to elected officials in parliamentary governments. The PGLs communicate summarized information regarding attached peer groups back down the hierarchy so that every node has a hierarchical view of the network.

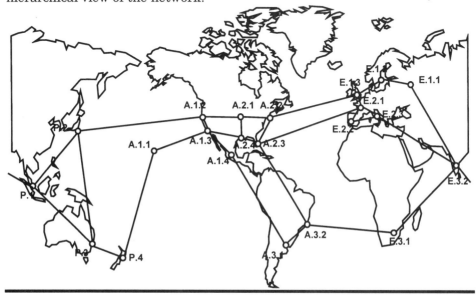

Figure 8.14 Example International Network of Logical Nodes

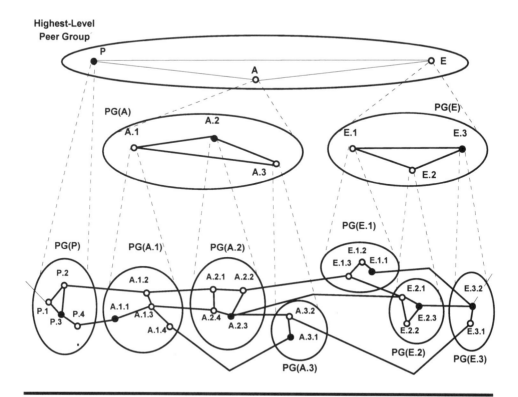

Figure 8.15 Complete PNNI Hierarchy for International Network Example

A complex protocol, such as PNNI 1.0, must have a definition of a minimum interoperable subset; otherwise manufacturers could choose which portions of PNNI they wish to implement, and the resulting networks would fail to meet the goal of multivendor operation. Towards this end, the ATM Forum PNNI 1.0 specification defines base node subsets and options.

8.6 BROADBAND INTERCARRIER INTERFACE (B-ICI)

The B-ICI specification version 2.0 [5] specifies support for UNI 3.1 SVCs across interfaces that connect carrier networks, including support for the following capabilities:

- Bidirectional and unidirectional point-to-point connections
- Unidirectional point-to-multipoint network connections
- Symmetric and asymmetric connections
- Support for UNI 3.1 QoS classes and bearer capabilities
- ATM end system addresses
- Call rejection due to unavailable ATM resources

- Minimum set of signaling network Operations, Administration, and Maintenance (OAM) functions (e.g., blocking, testing, and reset)
- Identification of control plane associations between nodes by means of signaling identifiers.
- Usage measurement procedures for SVCs

Figure 8.16 illustrates the context for use of the B-ICI specification between carriers. The specification not only details message formats and general procedures, but also specifies exact actions required by originating, intermediate, and terminating switches. Note that the B-ICI specification does not specify the protocol used between switches within a carrier's network, only the protocol used between carrier networks.

An addendum, called B-ICI 2.1 [6], added three key features. A call correlation tag provides a means to identify a call across multiple carriers for billing purposes. Support for Variable Bit Rate (VBR) connections was also clarified. Support was also added for NSAP-based addresses between carriers. These capabilities allowed more end-to-end features of UNI 3.1 to be supported in connections across multiple carriers.

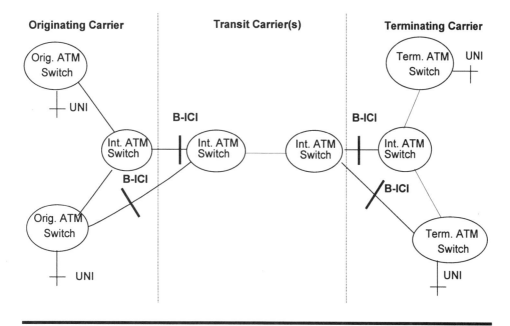

Figure 8.16 B-ICI Reference Model

8.7 B-ISDN USER SERVICES PART (B-ISUP)

The ITU-T specifies the B-ISUP protocol for use at the NNI, and the ATM Forum uses this protocol in the B-ICI specification. The ITU-T B-ISUP specifications for signaling at the NNI match well with the corresponding ITU-T UNI signaling standards, as summarized in Table 8.2. This table provides a road map that provides some structure to the long list of standards in the Q-series recommendations.

The ATM Forum based a large part of the B-ICI specification on the ITU-T's B-ISUP protocol, in a manner analogous to the way the Forum's Signaling 4.0 specification is based largely upon Q.2931. However, B-ICI 2.0 was intended to support UNI 3.1 signaling only, while B-ISUP has already been extended to support Q.2931 capabilities, which are aligned with UNI 4.0. Therefore, in the area of the specification on signaling interfaces between carriers, the ATM Forum B-ICI 3.0 specification, targeted for a 1998 release, will be required for UNI 4.0 support.

Table 8.2 Mapping of ITU-T UNI and NNI Signaling Capabilities

Capability Description	ITU-T UNI Standard	ITU-T NNI Standard
On-demand (switched) connections	Q.2931	Q.2761-4
Point-to-point calls	Q.2931	Q.2761-4
N-ISDN signaling interworking	Q.2931	Q.2660
E.164 address support	Q.2931	Q.2761-4
NSAP-based address support	Q.2931	Q.2726
Root-initiated point-to-multipoint calls	Q.2971	Q.2722.1
Traffic parameter modification during active calls	Q.2963.1	Q.2725.1
Traffic parameter negotiation during call setup	Q.2962	Q.2725.2
Supplementary Services		
Direct Dialing In (DDI)	Q.2951	Q.2730
Multiple Subscriber Number (MSN)	Q.2951	Q.2730
Calling Line Identification Presentation (CLIP)	Q.2951	Q.2730
Calling Line Identification Restriction (CLIR)	Q.2951	Q.2730
Connected Line Identification Presentation (COLP)	Q.2951	Q.2730
Connected Line Identification Restriction (COLR)	Q.2951	Q.2730
Subaddressing (SUB)	Q.2951	Q.2730
User-User Signaling (UUS)	Q.2957	Q.2730

8.8 REVIEW

This chapter introduced the control plane protocols involved in SVCs. We covered the signaling AAL protocol stacks and their relationships to ISDN. Although VPI/VCI usage occurs at the link level in SVCs, the discourse focused on the major issues in network-level addressing. Next, the text introduced UNI SVCs by listing the key signaling messages and their information elements. Drawings and text then showed examples of signaling procedures for both establishing and releasing point-to-point and point-to-multipoint connections using these messages. The chapter then moved on to the simplest NNI protocol first, the ATM Forum's Interswitch Signaling Protocol. The text then introduced the mother of all routing protocols: the ATM Forum's Private Network-Network Interface. Finally, the chapter concluded with considerations of signaling protocols employed between carrier networks at the Broadband Intercarrier Interface using the B-ISDN User Services Part.

8.9 REFERENCES

[1]   D. McDysan and D. Spohn, *ATM: Theory and Application*, McGraw-Hill, 1995.

[2]   ATM Forum, *ATM Name System Specification*, Version 1.0, af-saa-0069.000, November 1996.

[3]   ATM Forum, *User-Network Interface Signaling Specification*, Version 4.0, af-sig-0061.000, July 1996.

[4]   C. Partridge, *Gigabit Networking*, Addison-Wesley, 1994.

[5]   ATM Forum, *BISDN Inter-Carrier Interface (B-ICI) Specification*, Version 2.0, af-bici-0013.003, December 1995.

[6]   ATM Forum, *Addendum to BISDN Inter-Carrier Interface (B-ICI) Specification*, v2.0 (B-ICI Specification, v2.1), af-bici-0068.000, November 1996.

[7]   ATM Forum, *Interim Inter-Switch Signaling Protocol*, Version 1.0, af-pnni-0026.000, December 1994.

[8]   A. Alles, *ATM Interworking*, http://cio.cisco.com/warp/public/614/12.html.

[9]   ATM Forum, *Private Network-Network Interface Specification,* Version 1.0 Addendum (Soft PVC MIB), af-pnni-0066.00, September 1996.

9

ATM Support for Voice, Video, and WAN Data

This chapter covers the carriage of voice, circuit data, video, and WAN data protocols, specifically frame relay (FR) and SMDS, over ATM, as illustrated in Figure 9.1. The story begins with B-ISDN's predecessor, narrowband ISDN, addressing emulation of traditional time-division multiplexed (TDM) circuits and the ATM Forum's Voice and Telephony over ATM initiative. Then, we explore the status of ATM support for video service, including video on demand and residential broadband. The last major section of the chapter covers the general topics of interworking, logical access, trunking, and physical access. We provide specific examples of interworking frame relay with ATM, trunking frame relay over ATM, and providing logical access to SMDS via ATM. The chapter concludes with an overview of low-speed, frame-based ATM protocols, namely the ATM Data Exchange Interface and frame-based UNI.

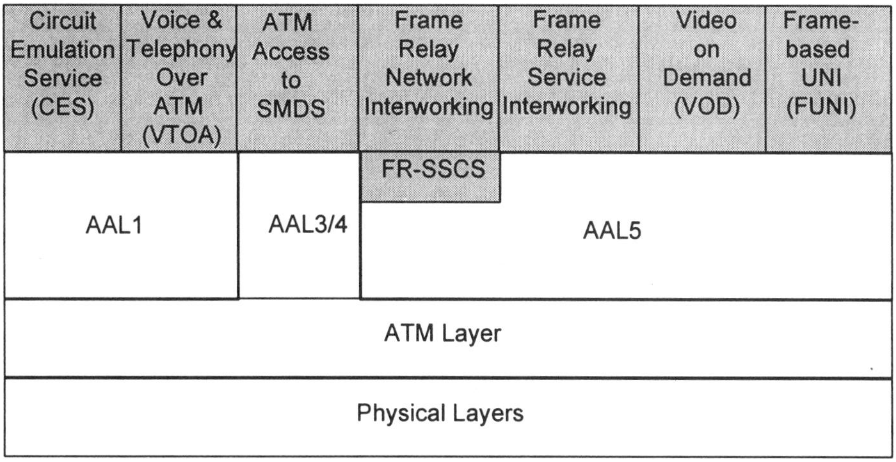

Circuit Emulation Service (CES)	Voice & Telephony Over ATM (VTOA)	ATM Access to SMDS	Frame Relay Network Interworking	Frame Relay Service Interworking	Video on Demand (VOD)	Frame-based UNI (FUNI)
AAL1		AAL3/4	FR-SSCS			
			AAL5			
ATM Layer						
Physical Layers						

Figure 9.1 ATM Protocol Support for Voice, Circuit Data, Video, and WAN Data

193

9.1 INTERWORKING WITH NARROWBAND ISDN

ATM's ancestor in the ITU-T is the Narrowband Integrated Services Digital Network (N-ISDN). Hence, a key focus of this international standards group is to provide seamless interworking between the future Broadband ISDN (B-ISDN) and the legacy N-ISDN. Good business reasons drive this; for example, many networks want new B-ISDN users to be able to interface to many existing users of the older N-ISDN service. Indeed, many manufacturers of the existing switches owned by carriers provide an upgrade path to the new ATM-based B-ISDN technology for this very reason. While, Recommendation Q.2931 specifies the signaling protocol required for interworking between B-ISDN and N-ISDN networks, Recommendation I.580 gives the overall view of interworking between these different generations of integrated networking technologies. Figure 9.2 depicts the scope of I.580 in terms of three interworking scenarios:

1. Covers interworking of 64 kbps–based N-ISDN user circuit-, frame-, and packet mode services with a B-ISDN user
2. Covers the case where 64 kbps–based N-ISDN user circuit-, frame-, and packet-mode services transparently trunk over a B-ISDN to another N-ISDN user
3. Covers the case where only 64 kbps–based N-ISDN circuit-, frame-, and packet-mode services are provided between B-ISDN users

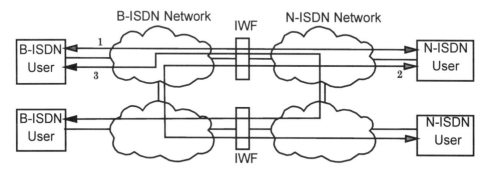

Figure 9.2 Scope of Recommendation I.580 B-ISDN/N-ISDN Interworking Standard

Recommendation I.580 covers an number of potential interworking scenarios and requirements that define mappings between N-ISDN and B-ISDN services as either one-to-one or many-to-one mappings suitable for the trunking of scenario II above. It defines the use of AAL1 for the circuit-mode bearer service in the Interworking Function (IWF), an unspecified AAL for frame mode and FR-SSCS, plus AAL5 as one option for packet mode in the IWF as illustrated in Figure 9.3. Q.922 is the ITU-T recommendation that specifies the frame relay protocol. Link Access Procedure B-channel or D-channel (LAP B/D) is the link-layer protocol of the X.25 packet standard. An IWF may implement one or more of these protocol mapping functions between B-ISDN and N-ISDN. The standard presents several options for performing some of these functions. Therefore, the standards are incomplete at this point, and additional specifications must first be defined in order to achieve full interoperability.

9.2 VOICE AND TELEPHONY OVER ATM

One of ATM's goals is standards support for voice over ATM. Major business drivers and requirements for transporting voice over ATM include [1]:

- Access and/or wide area network consolidation
- Preservation of investments in existing telephone and PBX equipment
- Maintenance of traditional levels of quality and availability in voice services

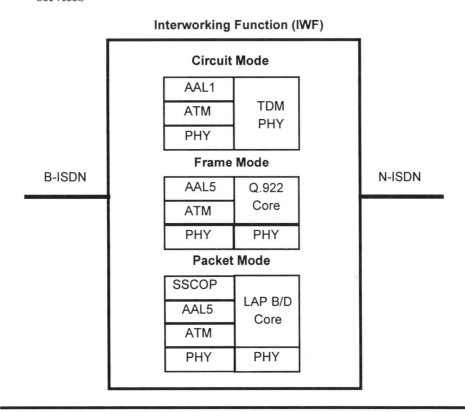

Figure 9.3 Example of I.580 Interworking Function (IWF) Protocol Mappings

- Maintenance of existing line features, such as Calling Line Identification
- Coexistence of desktop voice over ATM with LAN applications

Activities in progress in the ATM Forum's Voice and Telephony over ATM (VTOA) group include the following:

- Trunking for narrowband services over ATM, also called *land-line trunking* [2]
- Voice services at a native ATM terminal, also called *ATM to the desktop* [3]

Figure 9.4 illustrates the reference configuration for ATM trunking for narrowband services. Note that all ATM connections are between IWFs, never directly to an end user. This means that legacy TDM systems can utilize these capabilities without change or additional investment, an important migration consideration. The IWF provides a DS1/E1 physical circuit with N-ISDN signaling. The Roman numerals in the figure illustrate the following narrowband network trunking via ATM network(s):

    I.   Private-to-private narrowband trunked via private ATM
   II. Private-to-private narrowband trunked via public ATM
  III. Public-to-public narrowband trunked via public ATM
  IV. Private-to-public narrowband trunked via private and public ATM
   V. Private-to-private narrowband trunked via private and public ATM
  VI. Public-to-private narrowband trunked via public ATM

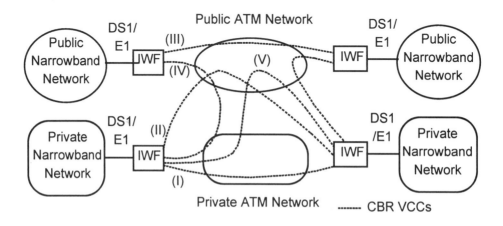

Figure 9.4 ATM Trunking for Narrowband Services Reference Configuration

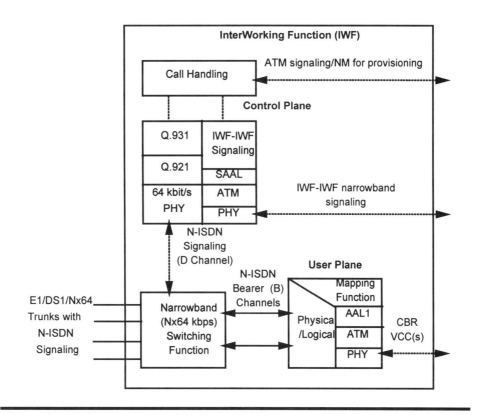

Figure 9.5 ATM Trunking for Narrowband Services IWF

Figure 9.5 illustrates the functions within the ATM trunking for narrow-band services IWF. Note the similarity of interworking for Nx64-kbps circuit emulation to the functional block in the lower right-hand corner. The lower left-hand functional block switches Nx64-kbps connections between DS1 or E1 interfaces — a function commonly performed by telephone switches and ISDN PBXs. Most of the new function and complexity in this specification is covered in the shaded areas, which define interworking between N-ISDN and B-ISDN signaling and the conversion between Time-Division Multiplexed (TDM) circuits and ATM's AAL1. The specification also defines a Management Information Based (MIB) for managing the IWF.

Figure 9.6 illustrates the voice over ATM to the B-ISDN desktop IWF reference configuration utilized by the ATM Forum [3]. The interworking configurations are derived from scenario B, case 1 of Annex A of ITU-T Recommendation I.580. Basically, the specification defines how a voice-enabled ATM desktop device can access either a public or a private ISDN network. Connections between B-ISDN and N-ISDN private networks may be via either P-NNI or ATM UNI, as illustrated in cases *a* (public) and *b* (private) in the figure. The third scenario represented in Figure 9.6*c* utilizes different signaling protocols optimized for private networking using the ATM UNI as detailed below.

Figure 9.7 illustrates the details of the VTOA ATM to the desktop protocol specification. On the right-hand side, the N-ISDN physical interface connects to the IWF, a Primary Rate Interface (PRI) at either the DS1 or E1 rate in this example. A simple TDM multiplexer separates the Bearer (B) channels from the signaling Data (D) channel and provides these streams to user and control plane protocol stacks and mapping functions as illustrated in the lower left-hand part of the figure. The user plane protocol and mapping function is similar to that used for structured-mode circuit emulation described later in this chapter. The protocols in the control plane depend upon the reference configuration, which applies as illustrated in the table in the upper right-hand corner of Figure 9.7. Digital Subscriber Signaling System 2 (DSS2) is specified by the ITU-T Q.2931 standard. The acronym PSS1 stands for Private Integrated Services Signaling System 1. A separate signaling VCC and a CBR VCC for the voice connect the IWF with the private ATM network via either the UNI or PNNI protocol stack, as shown on the left-hand side of the figure.

9.3 CIRCUIT EMULATION SERVICES

The ATM Forum specification for Circuit Emulation Service (CES) [4, 5] defines the means for ATM-based networks to employ AAL1 to emulate, or simulate, synchronous TDM circuits over the asynchronous infrastructure of ATM networks. CES defines support for two types of emulated circuits:

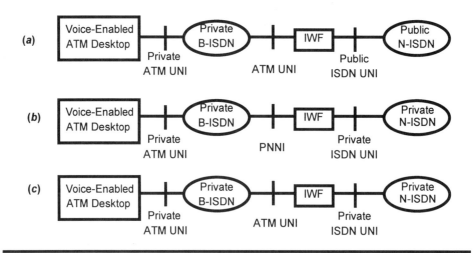

Figure 9.6 Voice over ATM to the Desktop Interworking Reference Configurations

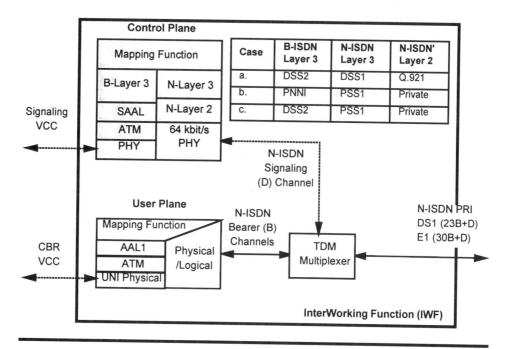

Figure 9.7 Voice over ATM to the Desktop IWF Detail

- Structured DS1/E1 supporting $N{\times}64$ kbps (i.e., fractional DS1/E1)
- Unstructured DS1/E1 (1.544/2.048 Mbps)

Figure 9.8 illustrates the generic CES reference model. On each end, TDM equipment such as a PBX, T1 multiplexer, or a CSU/DSU connects to the CES IWF via either a standard DS1 four-wire or E1 coaxial connector and protocols. The IWF implements the AAL1 Segmentation and Reassembly (SAR) Sublayer and Convergence Sublayer (CS) functions defined in Chapter 7. Logical circuit emulation may also be provided in a reference configuration where the physical DS1/E1 interfaces are not required. CES mandates use of the Constant Bit Rate (CBR) ATM service category and associated quality of service for the Virtual Channel Connection (VCC) that interconnects CES IWFs, so that the play out buffers in the IWF underflow or overflow infrequently. Handling of error cases, such as lost cells, buffer underflow and overflow, and alarm processing, is also detailed. The specification also defines the necessary parameters to set up ATM VCC SVCs to support circuit emulation. The ATM Forum's specification also defines a MIB in support of circuit emulation.

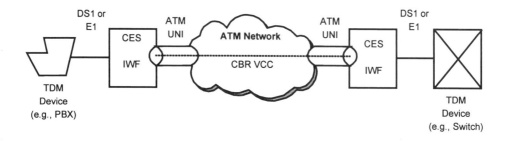

Figure 9.8 Circuit Emulation Service Reference Model

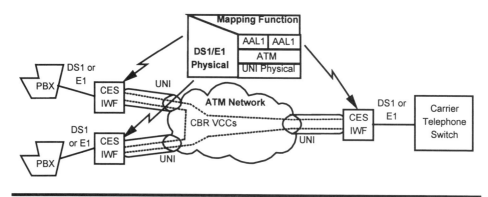

Figure 9.9 Structured-Mode CES Interworking Example and Functions

Figure 9.9 illustrates an example application and key functions of the structured CES IWF, which always provides timing to the connected TDM equipment. The structured capability supports combinations of $N\times64$-kbps bearer channels, where N ranges from 1 to 24 for DS1s and from 1 to 31 for an E1. Optionally, several emulated groups of $N\times64$-kbps circuits may occupy the same DS1, E1, or logical interface, as illustrated in the figure by the two instances of AAL1, one for each CBR VCC in the example. In this example, the CES function performs a mapping of the 64 kbps time slots from the DS1/E1 TDM transmission pipe into separate AAL1 SAR functions. Structured CES also specifies support for Channel-Associated Signaling (CAS), commonly used by PBXs to indicate off-hook and on-hook conditions. Since the structured mapping of the individual time slots does not convey TDM framing information end-to-end, the CAS information is encoded and transported separately.

Figure 9.10 illustrates an example application and key functions of the unstructured mode CES IWF. In the unstructured mode, the CES IWF may either provide timing to the TDM equipment in a synchronous mode or accept timing in an asynchronous mode. The asynchronous mode may use either the Synchronous Residual Time Stamp (SRTS) method, or adaptive clock recovery to transfer timing across the ATM network. Transfer of timing is critical for many legacy TDM networks, specifically T1 multiplexer networks. The unstructured service provides a clear channel pipe at a bit rate of 1.544 Mbps for DS1 or 2.048 Mbps for an E1. This means that the CES IWF supports bit streams with nonstandard framing, such as that commonly used by some video codecs and encryptors, in addition to the standard, framed DS1 and E1 signals used by multiplexers and PBXs. One disadvantage of devices that don't use standard framing is that the CES IWF cannot support DS1/E1 performance monitoring or alarm handling.

One note on optimizing ATM WAN resources: The ATM Forum also specified a dynamic allocation of circuit emulation service [6] which uses a bit mask to indicate when certain 64-kbps time slots in a structured CES connection are active. Although the allocated bandwidth must still support the largest number of active 64-kbps time slots, the bit mask makes the unused bandwidth available to other ATM connections on an ATM network. This bit mask can also be employed to suppress silence in a multiplexed group of emulated 64-kbps timeslots. Studies indicate that this achieves up to a 50 percent gain when multiplexing 10 or more voice sources.

9.4 AUDIO/VISUAL MULTIMEDIA SERVICES

This section covers Audio/Visual Multimedia Service (AMS) market demand, an overview of video coding standards, and the ATM Forum Video on Demand (VOD) specification.

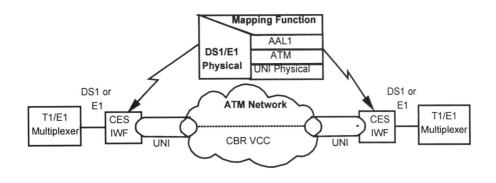

Figure 9.10 Unstructured-Mode CES Interworking Function

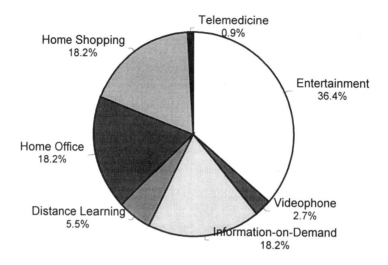

Figure 9.11 RBB Adoption Rate by Early Adopters for Surveyed Applications

9.4.1 Video over ATM Market Demand

A study conducted by IDC Consulting on behalf of the ATM Forum analyzed residential broadband market demand in 1996 [7]. Figure 9.11 shows the breakdown of market opportunity for Residential Broadband (RBB) by application from the survey.

This report predicted that over the next 5 to 15 years, nearly 60 million households are likely to adopt ATM-enabled applications. Furthermore, the strongest demand for ATM-enabled applications will emerge from families with children 10 to 18 years old, home office workers, telecommuters, and World Wide Web users — a population of over 19 million households!

The most promising opportunity to entice leading edge users to invest in ATM hardware, software, and services involves offering entertainment on demand and home office applications. Applications such as home shopping and distance learning are also attractive, but appeal to a smaller subset of the residential population.

The survey identified several barriers to adoption, including price, fear of technology, fear of loss of control, security, and privacy. These barriers will have to be overcome, and the various issues that vendors have regarding infrastructure, standards, and economic viability resolved, before ATM to the home becomes a reality. To create demand for ATM-enabled applications RBB must deliver the following features:

- Graphical User Interface (GUI)/ interactive controller
- Clear, consistent audio/video quality

- Voice activated control of services
- Integrity during file transfer mode
- Full-motion video
- High-speed connectivity to various data sources
- Intelligent agents

The industry is working on standards and implementation agreements to realize these capabilities in response to market demand. For example, one major focus of the current work is achieving efficient coding of full-motion video.

9.4.2 Video over ATM Coding Standards

One of ATM's tenets is support of simultaneous data, voice, and video transmission. While the predominant standard for videoconferencing today is TDM-based, ATM's higher bandwidth and controlled latency and jitter enables many video applications, including the Motion Photographic Experts Group (MPEG1) and MPEG2 video standards.

High-end video applications require accurate bandwidth and delay control, which includes both end-to-end latency and jitter control, for high-quality transmission. Therefore, precise quantification of the tolerable amount of latency and jitter is a key ATM switch and network design consideration. Achievable per-switch requirements for video over ATM are as follows:

- Cell loss ratio across the network on the order of one in a billion
- Cross-network cell transfer delay on the order of the speed of light propagation delay
- Cell delay variation on the order of one millisecond

These are key attributes to look for when selecting an ATM switch. Most modern switches meet these requirements; however, some older switches do not. Network designers must pay close attention to the aggregation of these impairments in larger networks to achieve these objectives.

MPEG and MPEG2 coding removes jitter introduced by ATM networks through the use of internal buffers in the coder/decoders (commonly called codecs). Additionally, the clock signal embedded in MPEG/MPEG2 streams through the use of a phase-locked loop at the decoder enables recovery of timing, even in the presence of network jitter. MPEG protection and recovery techniques include structured packing of encoded video into macroblocks, which enables synchronization by discarding all data until the next macroblock is recognized.

A principal reason that the ATM Forum created the real-time Variable Bit Rate (rt-VBR) service category was to enable variable bit rate video such as MPEG and MPEG2. Table 9.1 summarizes the bandwidth requirements and compression ratio for a representative set of compressed video encodings.

Table 9.1. Bandwidth Requirements for Compressed Video Images

Standard/Format	Bandwidth	Compression Ratio *
Motion JPEG	10–20 Mbps	7–27:1
MPEG-1	1.2–2.0 Mbps†	100:1
H.261	64 kbps–2 Mbps	24:1
DVI	1.2–1.5 Mbps	160:1
CDI	1.2–1.5 Mbps	100:1
MPEG-2	4–60 Mbps‡	30-100:1
CCIR 723	32–45 Mbps	3–5:1
CCIR 601 / D-1	140–270 Mbps	Reference (1:1)
U.S. commercial systems	45 Mbps	3–5:1
Vendor methods	0.1–1.5 Mbps	100:1
Software compression	1–2 Mbps	6:1

* Compared with broadcast quality video.

† Baseline standard; other compression ratios feasible.

‡ Image quality improves only slightly above 8 to 10 Mbps.

9.4.3 ATM Forum Video on Demand Specification

The ATM Forum's Audiovisual Multimedia Services VOD version 1.0 [8] specification defines the carriage of audio, video, and data over ATM. Figure 9.12 illustrates the reference configuration of a client (e.g., a set-top box), a server, an ATM network, and the logical services in control of its connections and the VOD session. The ATM network may be Hybrid Fiber/Coax (HFC), ADSL, xDSL, or a digital fiber network. Users would make an ATM connection to view a particular video in a session. Users then have VOD session-level controls such as "pause," "fast-forward," and "rewind," similar to those available on Video Cassette Recorders (VCRs) today.

9.5 RESIDENTIAL BROADBAND

The ATM Forum established the RBB working group in April 1995 to define a complete end-to-end ATM system both to the home and within the home [9]. The scope of RBB extends beyond the video on demand capability already defined by the forum to other interactive services. This group envisions a Home ATM Network (HAN), called a "toaster net" by some, that interconnects a wide range of household devices, such as PCs, televisions, appliances, security systems, and more.

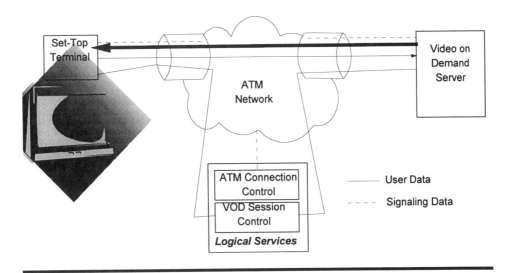

Figure 9.12 Video on Demand Reference Configuration

The large number of choices for physical User-Network Interfaces (UNIs) impedes interoperability in the cost-conscious residential marketplace. Although carriers may deploy different access UNI technologies based upon regulatory, demographic, or business considerations, the group targets a technology-independent interface usable in any home ATM network, possibly through use of an appropriate adapter.

Figure 9.13 illustrates the RBB home ATM network architecture. Starting from the right-hand side of the figure, a backbone, or core, ATM network connects a number of distribution and access subnetworks together, as well as provides ATM-based services, such as video on demand. The access ATM network uses a particular UNI protocol, labeled UNI-a in the figure, to extend ATM to the residence. ATM over an Asynchronous Digital Subscriber Line (ADSL) would be an example of this protocol. Often a carrier will deploy a Network Termination (NT) device in the residence, which provides potentially another UNI to the home ATM network, labeled UNI-b in the figure. The NT may provide a 155-Mbps multimode fiber-optic ATM interface, for example. The home ATM network operates on another UNI protocol, shown as UNI-c in the figure. The HAN may use 25 Mbps over twisted pair as UNI-c to minimize cost, for example. The RBB group is defining the Technology Independent Interface (TII) so that manufacturers can develop a single ATM interface for products, a microwave oven in this example. An adapter that converts between UNI-c and the TTI is, of course, required.

The RBB group maintains a close liaison with other standards bodies working on various aspects of residential broadband networks.

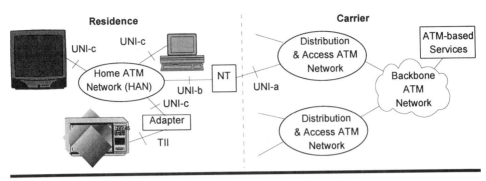

Figure 9.13 Residential Broadband Home ATM Network Architecture

9.6 INTERWORKING, ACCESS, AND TRUNKING

In 1799, Napoleon's army discovered the trilingual Rosetta stone in Egypt, which provided the key to translation of the undeciphered and unknown Egyptian hieroglyphic and demotic writing. The key was that the Rosetta stone also contained the same message in the known Greek. Does ATM perform a similar role in translating the myriad of existing, sometimes arcane data communication languages into the modern language of data communications? Let's look at how ATM-based networks perform translations for common wide area data network protocols.

Figure 9.14 illustrates the relationships defined in standards between the major WAN protocols: X.25, frame relay, ATM, SMDS, and IP. Figure 9.14*a* illustrates true protocol interworking with a thick, solid line. Note that true interworking is defined only between X.25 and frame relay and between ATM and frame relay. The analogy with the Rosetta stone here is that the languages have exactly the same semantics or meaning. True interworking occurs only when protocols have similar semantics. X.25/FR and FR/ATM can interwork because they are all connection-oriented protocols possessing similar status indication methods and connection establishment and release procedures. On the other hand, IP and SMDS are connectionless, and hence cannot directly interwork with a connection-oriented protocol since the basic semantics differ. A similar situation occurs in human languages where different cultural concepts don't translate. Figure 9.14*a* also illustrates a lesser form of interworking, which we call logical access, via directed arrows. Many standards define how one protocol can be accessed via another. For example, a user connected to an ATM network can access an IP network. The terminology used in the figure is the user access IP via ATM. Note that standards exist to access IP via all of these WAN protocols.

Figure 9.14*b* illustrates another key concept of protocols — namely, that almost every one can be used as a trunking method for another. The directed dashed arrows in the figure indicate the cases where one protocol can be trunked over another. Although ATM can trunk any of these other WAN protocols, ATM cannot be trunked over them since they do not currently support quality of service in a standard manner. The business consequence of this fact of protocol trunking is that many carriers and enterprises have announced plans to trunk multiple services over a *common* ATM infrastructure. The figure also illustrates that each WAN protocol has separate physical access requirements. Physical access may be either dedicated or switched, with different requirements for each WAN protocol.

The limited interworking, access, and trunking rules summarized in Figure 9.14 mean that a network designer cannot arbitrarily interconnect protocols over ATM. In fact, the only true interworking design would be to provide access via various protocols to IP and trunk over ATM. Beware of claims that ATM can provide the ultimate translation capability between all protocols — this is simply an incorrect statement at this point in time. The Internetworking Protocol (IP) is the only standard protocol that meets this need today, since it can be accessed via X.25, FR, SMDS, and ATM, as well as served by dedicated or dial access. The next sections cover the interworking, trunking and access protocols for frame relay and SMDS. Chapter 11 covers the subjects of access via ATM to IP and IP trunking over ATM.

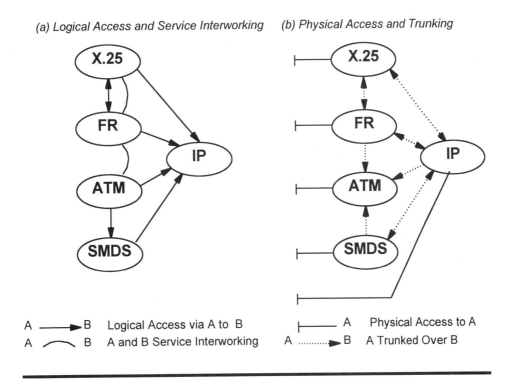

Figure 9.14 Logical Access, Interworking, Physical Access, and Trunking

9.7 FRAME RELAY/ATM INTERWORKING

As we saw in Chapter 2, the frame relay service market in the United States will be over $5 billion in 1999. However, many frame relay users are moving to higher-speed connections and applications that require multiple service categories. Typically, many customer networks need to migrate their largest locations to ATM first, which requires interworking between a few large ATM sites and many smaller frame-relay-connected sites. Furthermore, many carrier networks and large enterprises plan to trunk multiple services over ATM, including frame relay and IP. In response to these business needs, ITU-T Recommendation I.555, the ATM Forum B-ICI specification, and two Frame Relay Forum (FRF) Implementation Agreements (IAs) specify interworking between frame relay and ATM interworking.

ITU-T Recommendation I.555 labels these types of FR/ATM interworking as scenarios one and two, as shown in Figure 9.15. In scenario 1, FR is interworked (or trunked) *over* ATM, while in scenario 2, a FR end system interworks *with* an ATM end system.

Network Interworking Scenario 1: Frame Relay *Over* ATM

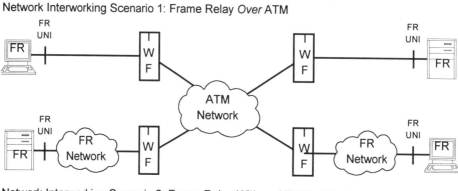

Network Interworking Scenario 2: Frame Relay *With* an ATM End System

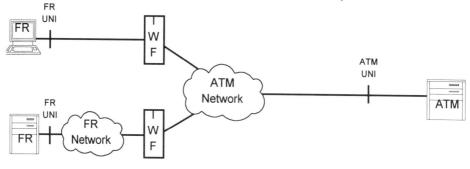

Figure 9.15 FR/ATM Interworking Scenarios and Access Configurations

In scenario 1, FR CPE either directly interfaces to an IWF via a FR UNI or connects via a frame relay network. The access configuration in which an ATM end system connects directly via an ATM UNI, which connects to an IWF, applies to service interworking in scenario 2 only. The Frame Relay Forum details these scenarios in two implementation agreements: FR/ATM Network Interworking [10] and FR/ATM Service Interworking [11]. Let's now explore network and service interworking scenarios in more detail.

9.7.1 Frame Relay/ATM Network Interworking

Figure 9.16 illustrates further details of the FR/ATM network interworking protocol. The FR-to-ATM network IWF converts between the basic frame relay (Q.922 core) functions and the FR Service-Specific Convergence Sublayer (FR-SSCS) defined in ITU-T Recommendation I.365.1, and the AAL5 Common Part (see Chapter 7). The network IWF also converts between the Q.933 Annex A Permanent Virtual Connection (PVC) status signaling for a single, physical FR UNI port and the VCCs that correspond to the frame relay Data Link Connection Identifiers (DLCIs). The FR-SSCS supports multiplexing through the use of the DLCI field, with the ATM layer supporting connection multiplexing using the VPI/VCI. There are two methods of multiplexing FR connections over ATM: many-to-one and one-to-one. Many-to-one multiplexing maps many FR logical connections identified by the FR DLCIs over a single ATM VCC. One-to-one multiplexing maps each FR logical connection identified by DLCI to a single ATM VCC via VPI/VCIs at the ATM layer. Many-to-one multiplexing is best suited for efficiently trunking FR over ATM, since this method efficiently carries the status signaling between FR networks.

The FR traffic parameters include a Committed Information Rate (CIR) and an Excess Information Rate (EIR). Appendix A of the ATM Forum B-ICI specification maps these FR traffic parameters to the ATM traffic parameter in terms of Peak Cell Rate (PCR), Sustainable Cell Rate (SCR), and Maximum Burst Size (MBS). The ATM Quality of Service (QoS) class and service category for the ATM VCC must also be selected. Usually, frame relay utilizes the ATM nrt-VBR service category, however, other categories may also be used in conjunction with prioritized FR service.

9.7.2 Frame Relay/ATM Service Interworking

The ATM Forum worked closely with the Frame Relay Forum to develop a FR/ATM service interworking specification [10]. Figure 9.17 illustrates the user plane protocol stacks for FR/ATM service interworking. Note that a frame relay end system is directly connected to an ATM end system in this scenario. Mapping between different multiprotocol encapsulation standards for FR and ATM, as specified in IETF RFCs 1490 and 1483, respectively, is an optional protocol translation function at the higher layers, as shown in the figure.

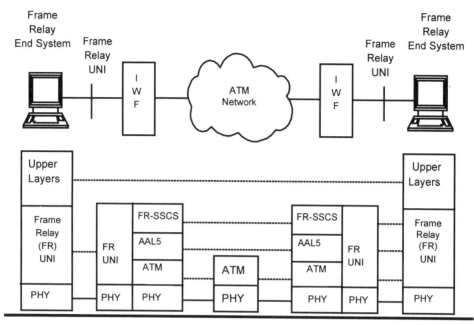

Figure 9.16 FR/ATM Network Interworking

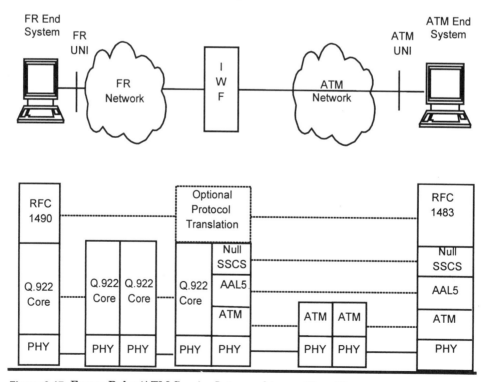

Figure 9.17 Frame Relay/ATM Service Interworking — User Plane

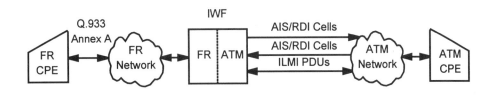

Figure 9.18 Frame Relay/ATM Status Signaling Interworking

Figure 9.18 illustrates the mapping between FR status signaling and ATM AIS and Integrated Local Management Interface (ILMI) PVC status change traps. This mapping communicates the semantics of end-to-end DLCI and VCC status to the FR and ATM end systems, respectively. FR/ATM service interworking is intended to interconnect end users; it was not designed as a trunking protocol, as FR/ATM network interworking was designed for carrier interconnection of FR services over ATM. The mapping of status signaling to ATM Operations, Administration, and Maintenance (OAM) and ILMI traps is less efficient than the many-to-one multiplexing mode of FR/ATM network interworking for use in trunking applications. Status signaling is an important feature for FR users, which this standard preserves when interconnecting FR and ATM users.

9.7.3 FR/ATM Interworking Applied

Large enterprise networks typically have a few large locations that serve as headquarters locations and major traffic sources and sinks. Typical of such applications are large computer centers, large office complexes with many information workers, campuses requiring high-tech communication, server farms, data or image repositories, and large-volume data or image sources. These large locations have a significant community of interest; however, the enterprise usually also has a relatively large number of smaller locations that need at least partial, lower-performance access to the same information. The smaller locations have fewer users, and generally cannot justify a higher cost for equipment or networking facilities. Generally, cost increases as performance, number of features, and flexibility needs increase.

Many users have turned to hybrid networking, using high-speed ATM at the larger sites interworking with lower-speed frame relay at the many smaller locations. These lower-speed access sites require more efficient access rather than high performance, and thus frame relay access through low-end routing and bridging products is often more cost-effective than ATM. This is because the cost per bit per second generally decreases as the public network access speed increases. For example, the approximate ratio of the DS1/DS0 and DS3/DS1 tariffs is approximately 10:1, while the speed difference is approximately 25:1. This means that a higher-speed interface can be operated at 40 percent efficiency at the same cost per bit per second.

Conversely, the lower-speed interface costs 3.5 times as much per bit per second, and therefore efficiency can be important.

What will the virtual enterprise network look like at the beginning of the next century? Figure 9.19 illustrates an ATM-based interworking network cloud connecting a few large ATM sites to many smaller frame relay sites. Such a network is composed of many smaller sites and few larger sites, which is typical of large enterprises, such as corporations, government entities, and other organizations. Principal needs that drive the need for ATM are multiple levels of service, characterized by parameters such as throughput, quality, and billing.

9.8 SMDS ACCESS TO ATM

Switched Multimegabit Data Service (SMDS) was created to bridge the time interval until ATM matured. A number of users employ SMDS, particularly in Europe, where the service is called Connectionless Broadband Data Service (CBDS). Many of these users want to move to ATM, but don't want to write off their investment in SMDS. Also, carriers want to trunk multiple services over ATM. The ATM Forum B-ICI 1.1 specification first defined how SMDS can be transported between carriers. The ATM Forum, SMDS Interest Group (SIG), and European SIG (E-SIG) jointly specified how a user would access SMDS across an ATM UNI to support customers who want to share ATM access lines between SMDS and access to other ATM and ATM-based interworking services.

Figure 9.20 depicts the access configuration and logical placement of function for accessing SMDS features over an ATM (UNI) [12]. An ATM end system accessing SMDS over ATM must format either an AAL3/4 or AAL5 CPCS PDU containing the SMDS Connectionless Service (SIP_CLS) PDU — as shown on the left-hand side of the figure. The ATM network performs a Usage Parameter Control (UPC) function to emulate the SMDS access class. The ATM network relays the cells to an SMDS IWF, which may be implemented in a centralized, regionalized, or distributed manner. The SMDS/ATM IWF converts the AAL stream into the SMDS Layer 2 and 3 protocol stack and passes this to an SMDS network, which implements the SMDS service features, including access class enforcement via the Credit Manager (CM). The SMDS network can interface to a subscriber using the SMDS Subscriber Network Interface (SNI) or an SMDS Data Exchange Interface (DXI) (requiring an SMDS CSU/DSU), as shown in the figure.

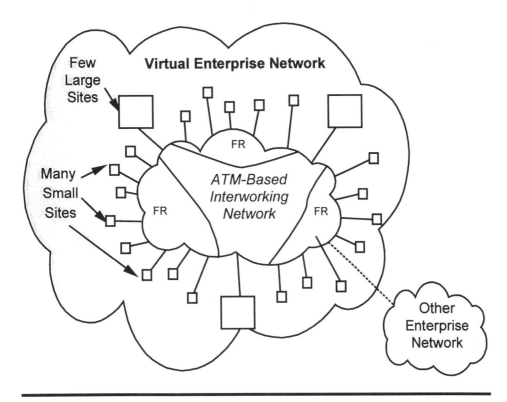

Figure 9.19 Typical FR/ATM-Based Enterprise Network

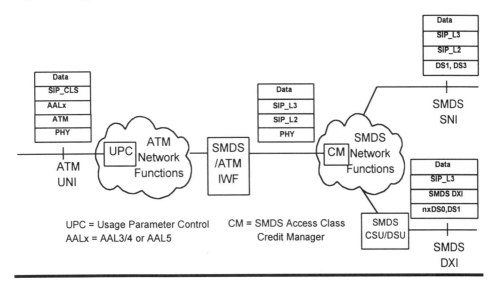

Figure 9.20 Logical Configuration for SMDS Access over ATM

Several of the functions which the SMDS/ATM IWF performs include:

☞ Conversion between SIP_L3 and the SIP_CLS PDU carried via either AAL3/4 or AAL5
☞ Conversion between 802.6 layer 2 PDUs (slots) and either the ATM AAL3/4 or AAL5 SAR
☞ Multiplexing of 802.6 Multiplex IDs (MIDs) into a single ATM VCC

9.9 FRAME-BASED INTERFACES SUPPORTING ATM

Although the ITU-T and the ATM Forum initially focused on the specification of high-speed interfaces for ATM, the expense of high-speed lines in carrier networks along with the costs of early ATM devices drove the need for lower speed interfaces. It also drove a means to utilize existing hardware via software changes only. In response, the ATM Forum defined two types of low-speed, frame-based ATM interfaces to support such connections to ATM networks. The ATM DXI protocol allowed early adopters to utilize ATM with existing routers and data equipment with serial interfaces using a separate piece of equipment to convert between the ATM DXI protocol and an ATM UNI. The ATM Forum then adapted the ATM DXI protocol to a WAN interface and called this specification the ATM Frame-based UNI (FUNI) specification. A main advantage of FUNI is that it eliminates the external CSU/DSU required in the ATM DXI specification. This section provides the context and application of these two important protocols.

9.9.1 ATM Data Exchange Interface

Many users have asked the following question: What if I want the capabilities of ATM over the WAN, but I can't afford the cost of a DS3 or OC-3 access line? The answer could be the ATM Forum–specified ATM DXI [13], which supports either the V.35, RS449, or HSSI DTE-DCE interface at speeds from several kbps up to and including 50 Mbps. ATM DXI specifies the interface between a DTE, such as a router, and a DCE, usually called an ATM CSU/DSU, which provides the conversion to an ATM UNI, as illustrated in Figure 9.21. Like the SMDS DXI on which the ATM DXI specification was patterned, the context is a limited-distance DTE-DCE interface.

The ATM DXI interface is managed by the DTE through a Local Management Interface (LMI), while the ATM UNI Interim Local Management Interface (ILMI) Simple Network Management Protocol (SNMP) messages are passed through to the DTE as shown in Figure 9.21.

Table 9.2 summarizes the key attributes of the various modes of the ATM DXI specification. All modes support AAL5, and some modes also support AAL3/4. The maximum number of VCCs differs in the various modes, as does the maximum frame size as a result of the address bits in the DXI header and the length of the Frame Check Sequence (FCS).

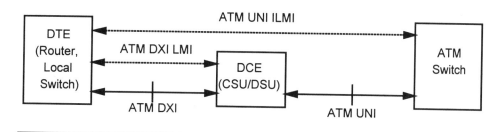

Figure 9.21 ATM DXI Configuration

Table 9.2 Summary of ATM DXI Mode Characteristics

Characteristic	Mode 1a	Mode 1b	Mode 2
Maximum number of VCCs	1023	1023	16,777,215
AAL5 support	Yes	Yes	Yes
AAL3/4 support	No	Yes	Yes
Maximum DTE SDU length			
AAL5	9232	9232	65,535
AAL3/4	N/A	9224	65,535
Bits in FCS	16	16	32

9.9.2 Frame Relay User-to-Network Interface

The ATM Forum specified the FUNI specification [14] so that CPE without ATM hardware capabilities, such as many currently deployed routers, could interface to ATM networks with only minor software changes. Most importantly, the ATM FUNI specification required no hardware changes or the costly external ATM DXI converter. FUNI provides low-speed, WAN ATM access protocol rates of nxDS0, DS1, and E1. Figure 9.22 illustrates how frame-based CPE sends frames using the FUNI data link protocol to a network-based ATM switch, which then segments the frames into standard ATM cells using the AAL5 protocol. The destination ATM switch reassembles cells and delivers frames to the FUNI user. Thus, FUNI users communicate transparently across an ATM network with either other FUNI users (FUNI-to-FUNI) or ATM UNI users (FUNI-to-ATM UNI).

The FUNI data link layer specification utilizes a framing structure based upon the ATM DXI modes in providing the following functions [15]:

- VPI/VCI multiplexing
- SVC signaling
- Network management
- Traffic policing
- ATM Operations, Administration, and Maintenance (OAM) functions
- VBR and Unspecified Bit Rate (UBR) traffic

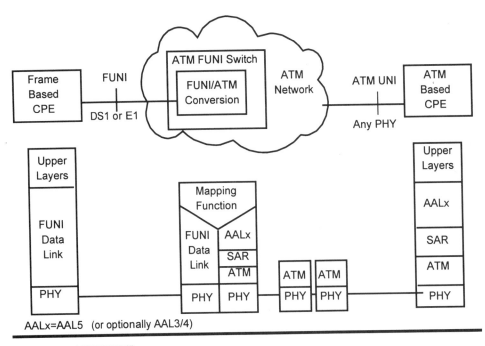

Figure 9.22 ATM FUNI

There are two key functional differences between FUNI and DXI. FUNI provides improved access line utilization compared with the cell-based access of an ATM DXI CSU/DSU. For example, at a typical packet size of 300 bytes, FUNI is 15 to 20 percent more efficient than ATM. The second difference is that FUNI supports nx64 kbps rates, while the lowest speed supported by ATM DXI is DS1/E1.

A paper published by the Frame Relay Forum [16] analyzes the relative advantages and disadvantages of FUNI versus frame relay, since frame relay and ATM technologies overlap. The paper asserts that the following business considerations drive a choice between FR and FUNI:

- Existing installed base of user and network equipment
- Availability of equipment and service from multiple suppliers
- Cost of network and user equipment
- Recurring cost of service
- Cost of managing the network
- Bandwidth utilization efficiency
- Service classes provided by the network
- Performance (interface speed, delay, throughput)
- Interoperability between vendors

In discussions on the frame relay mail exploder, experts believe that wide availability of the FUNI interface in user equipment won't occur until public service providers offer FUNI access service at a cost comparable to that of frame relay. Without that, there is little market demand to drive the end system (CPE) vendors to implement it. Even if this situation occurs, users must incur a migration cost to switch their FR sites to FUNI to connect to presumably higher-bandwidth ATM sites for reasons such as increased peak rates, QoS support, or seamless networking. Some users believe that FUNI offers a number of capabilities that FR does not at lower speeds, using frames that do not incur the ATM cell and AAL5 overhead. Capabilities that FUNI provides, but FR does not, are:

- Access to richer, better-defined QoS support in ATM
- Elimination of the need for complex FR/ATM signaling interworking
- Eliminates LLC/NLPID conversion required at FR/ATM boundary
- AAL5 for longer frames (64K) than FR (4K), eliminating fragmentation at the FR/ATM boundary (note that this requires the optional 32-bit CRC in FUNI)
- Direct support for ATM's scalable NSAP addressing
- Direct participation of FUNI interfaces in PNNI networks
- Elimination of traffic descriptor conversion in FR/ATM interworking

9.10 REVIEW

This chapter covered higher-layer ATM protocol support for voice, video, and wide area data. First, we summarized how the ITU-T focuses on interworking between the next-generation broadband ISDN and the legacy narrowband ISDN by summarizing the user and control plane functions. Next, we covered the circuit emulation service in support of nx64-kbps TDM circuits using structured mode and support of standard DS1 and E1 signals in the unstructured mode. We then covered the specific protocols being developed in the ATM Forum's Voice and Telephony over ATM (VTOA) working group. The coverage then surveyed the business drivers for video over ATM, focusing on the ATM Forum's video on demand and residential broadband efforts. Next, the text described the concepts of interworking, logical access, trunking, and physical access. Specific examples of frame relay trunking over ATM using the network interworking protocol, true service interworking between frame relay and ATM, and access to SMDS via ATM illustrated these concepts. Finally, we covered the ATM Forum's specifications on the frame-based interfaces defined by the ATM DXI and FUNI protocols. ATM DXI and FUNI make ATM available to existing non-ATM CPE cost-effectively via external converters and a software-defined protocol, respectively.

9.11 REFERENCES

[1]   G. Onyszchuk, "Will Voice Take Over ATM?" *ATM Forum 53 Bytes*, October 1995.

[2]   ATM Forum, *ATM Trunking Using AAL1 for Narrow Band Services* v1.0, af-vtoa-0089.000, July 1997.

[3]   ATM Forum, *Voice and Telephony Over ATM to the Desktop*, af-vtoa-0083.000, May 1997.

[4]   ATM Forum, *Circuit Emulation Interoperability Specification*, af-saa-0032.000, September 1995.

[5]   ATM Forum, *Circuit Emulation Service,* V2.0, af-vtoa-0078.000, January 1997.

[6]   ATM Forum, *(DBCES) Dynamic Bandwidth Utilization in 64 KBPS Time Slot Trunking Over ATM - Using CES*, af-vtoa-0085.000, July 1997.

[7]   ATM Forum, "Families Lead the Way in Demand for ATM Applications," ATM Forum Press Release, September 3, 1996.

[8]   ATM Forum, *Audiovisual Multimedia Services: Video on Demand,* Specification 1.0, af-saa-0049.000, December 1995.

[9]   S. Ooi, "The Rhyme and Reason of Residential Broadband," *ATM Forum 53 Bytes*, Volume 4, Issue 1, 1996.

[10] Frame Relay Forum, *Frame Relay/ATM PVC Network Interworking Implementation Agreement*, FRF.5, December 20, 1994.

[11] Frame Relay Forum, *Frame Relay/ATM PVC Service Interworking Implementation Agreement*, FRF.8, April 14, 1995.

[12] SMDS Interest Group, *Protocol Interface Specification for Implementation of SMDS over an ATM-based Public UNI*, Revision 2.0, October 31, 1996.

[13] ATM Forum, *Data Exchange Interface,* Version 1.0, af-dxi-0014.000, August 1993.

[14] ATM Forum, *Frame-Based User-to-Network Interface (FUNI) Specifications*, af-saa-0031.000, September 1995.

[15] ATM Forum, *Frame-Based User-to-Network Interface (FUNI),* Specification v2.0, af-saa-0088.000, July 1997.

[16] Frame Relay Forum, *Frame Relay and Frame-Based ATM: A Comparision of Technologies*, http://www.frforum.com/4000/fratm/fratm.toc.html.

10

ATM in Local Area Networks

This chapter covers ATM's support for Local Area Networks (LANs). Most major enterprises embraced LANs in the 1980s, and now even some residences have LANs. The ATM industry developed LAN Emulation (LANE) to provide a means to seamlessly interconnect legacy LANs with new, high-performance ATM LANs. The LANE protocol allows ATM host and server applications to interwork with devices already resident on existing, legacy LANs. LANs involve some unique concepts; therefore, we begin by summarizing some terminology related to bridging, routing, and internetworking employed in this chapter and the next. Next, we review LAN protocol standards and bridging functions in some depth as an introduction to LAN Emulation (LANE). Finally, we show how the LANE protocol supports seamless ATM host and server interconnection with both legacy Ethernet and Token Ring LANs.

10.1 BRIDGING, ROUTING, AND INTERNETWORKING

Let's first review some basic LAN and internetworking terminology for bridging and routing with reference to Figure 10.1, based upon RFC 1932 [1] defines the framework for the IETF's work on IP over ATM.

A h*ost* (also called an end system) delivers and receives IP packets to/from other hosts. A host does not relay packets. Examples of hosts are workstations, personal computers and servers.

A *router* (also called an Intermediate System) delivers and receives IP packets and relays IP packets among end and intermediate systems. Internet Service Providers (ISPs) and large enterprises often utilize routers made by companies like Cisco and Bay Networks.

All members of an *IP subnet* are capable of directly transmitting packets to each other. There may be repeaters, hubs, bridges, or switches between the physical interfaces of IP subnet members. An Ethernet or Token Ring LAN is an example of an IP subnet. However, multiple Ethernets may also form a subnet. The assignment of IP addresses and subnet masks determines the specific subnet boundaries as described in more detail in Chapter 11.

Bridging makes two or more physically disjoint media appear as a single bridged IP subnet. Bridging implementations occur at the medium access control level or via a proxy address resolution protocol (ARP). We covered a taxonomy of bridging devices in Chapter 4.

A *broadcast subnet* allows any system to transmit a packet to all other systems in the subnet. An Ethernet LAN is an example of an broadcast subnet.

A *multicast-capable subnet* provides a facility that enables a system to send packets to a subset of the subnet members. For example, a mesh of ATM point-to-multipoint connections provides this capability.

A *Nonbroadcast Multiple Access (NBMA) subnet* doesn't support a convenient multidestination connectionless delivery capability, like broadcast and multicast capable subnetworks do. A set of point-to-point ATM VCCs is an example of an NBMA subnet.

An *end-to-end path* is an arbitrary number of routers and subnets over which two hosts communicate, as illustrated in Figure 10.1.

An *internetwork* is a concatenation of networks, often employing different media and lower-level encapsulations, that form an integrated larger network supporting communication between hosts. Figure 10.1 illustrates a relatively small internet when judged in comparison with the Internet, which comprises over 40,000 networks.

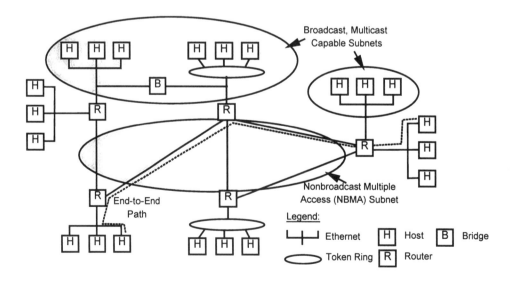

Figure 10.1 Basic LAN and Internetworking Terminology

Vendors of intermediate and end systems strive to implement an efficient process for deciding what should be done with a received packet. Possible decisions are local delivery, or forwarding the packet to another external interface. The process of deciding what to do with a received IP packet is called *IP forwarding*, which may also require replacement or modification of the media-layer encapsulation when transiting between different LAN media.

IP routing involves the exchange of topology information that enables systems to make IP forwarding decisions that cause packets to advance along an end-to-end path towards a destination. This is sometimes called a topology distribution protocol.

An *IP address resolution protocol (ARP)* provides a quasi-static mapping between an IP address and the media address on the local subnet.

Scalability refers to the ability of routing and resolution protocols to support a large number of subnets as well as handle the dynamics of a large internetwork. When large numbers of subnets are interconnected, routers must exchange large amounts of topology data and store the resultant forwarding information in high-speed memory. Furthermore, as network size increases, so does the likelihood that some network elements are changing state, creating the need to update routing topology information across the network. Hence, scalability affects the required processing power and storage for the routing protocols.

IP over ATM either extends IP address resolution beyond IP subnet boundaries or interconnects IP subnets. The first approach directly connects classic IP subnets via NBMA media, such as ATM, in the *classical IP over ATM* approach, while the second involves IP routing and IP forwarding in the *next-hop resolution protocol* approach. Now, that we've given an overview of LAN and internetworking terminology, let's start with some more details on the specifics of LAN operation.

10.2 LOCAL AREA NETWORKING STANDARDS

LAN protocols implement the protocol stack shown in Figure 10.2. The Logical Link Control (LLC) and Media Access Control (MAC) sublayers map to the OSIRM data link layer, while the actual physical medium that interconnects stations on a LAN maps to the OSIRM physical layer. The MAC layer manages communications across the physical medium, defines frame assembly and disassembly, and performs error detection and addressing functions. The LLC layer within a particular system interfaces with the network-layer protocols through one or more Service Access Points (SAPs), as shown in Figure 10.2. These SAPs provide a means for multiplexing within a single host over a single MAC-layer address as illustrated in the figure. A range of addresses in the data link frame determines which SAP is being addressed.

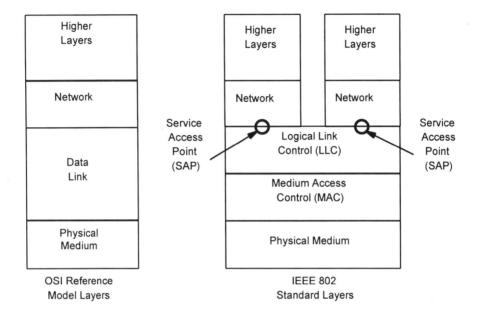

Figure 10.2 LAN Protocol Standards Layered Model

10.2.1 Logical Link Control Sublayer

IEEE Standard 802.2 defines the LLC protocol that hides the differences between various MAC sublayer implementations from the network-layer protocol. This allows systems on very different types of LANs, for example, Token Ring and Ethernet, to communicate. LLC provides services to the network layer that are either connection-oriented or connectionless. Connection-oriented service uses peer-to-peer communications and provides acknowledgments, flow control, and error recovery. There are two classes of connectionless, or datagram, services provided in the LLC: class 1, or *unacknowledged datagram*, which requires both the sending and receiving station addresses to be contained in each packet, and class 2, or *acknowledged datagram*.

When the LLC layer receives user data, it places it in the information field and adds a header to form an LLC Protocol Data Unit (PDU) as shown in Figure 10.3. A Destination and Source Service Access Points (DSAP and SSAP) address field and a control field precede a variable-length information field in the PDU. The size of these address fields determines the number of possible addresses in a device. The address field is either 2 bytes long as shown in the figure, or optionally configured as a 6-byte field.

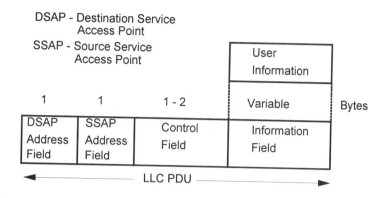

Figure 10.3 IEEE 802.2 LLC Protocol Data Unit (PDU)

10.2.2 Medium Access Control Sublayer

The MAC sublayer manages and controls communications across the physical medium, assembles and disassembles frames, and performs error detection and addressing functions. Table 10.1 summarizes some key attributes of the IEEE 802 series of standards for MAC sublayer protocols.

Table 10.1 Important Attributes of MAC Sublayer Standards

IEEE Number	Standard Title	Media Speed (Mbps)	Physical Media Supported	Maximum Payload Size (Bytes)
802.3	Ethernet	10, 100	Coax, 2W UTP, STP, Fiber	1500
802.4	Token Bus	1, 5, 10	Coax	8191
802.5	Token Ring	1, 4, 16	STP	5000*
802.6	Distributed Queue Dual Bus (DQDB)	34, 44, 155	Coax, Fiber	8192
802.9a	IsoEthernet	16	2W UTP, STP	
802.12	100VG-AnyLAN	100	4W UTP, STP, Fiber	

Notes:
2W UTP   2-Wire Unshielded Twisted Pair
4W UTP   4-Wire Unshielded Twisted Pair
STP   Shielded Twisted Pair
* Computed for 4 Mbps media speed and a token-holding time of 10 ms.

The MAC layer adds a header and trailer to the LLC PDU prior to transmission across the physical medium. Figure 10.4 shows how the 802.3 Ethernet MAC layer encapsulates the LLC PDU to yield a MAC PDU. The 6-octet (48-bit) MAC addresses are uniquely assigned by the IEEE and are used by the MAC layer to identify physical stations on the network. Each station on an Ethernet compares the destination MAC address in a received frame to determine if the frame should be passed up to the LLC entity addressed by the DSAP field in the LLC PDU.

10.3 BRIDGING PROTOCOLS

Bridging performs several critical functions in local area networks. Bridging between LANs with different MAC sublayers requires conversion of frame formats, recompilation of checksums, in some cases speed conversion, and sometimes even a reordering of the bits for transmission. Unfortunately, the IEEE committees developing the standards did not agree on the same conventions, thus creating the need for bridging and MAC conversion.

Early bridge implementations focused on a transparent bridge [2] which targeted completely plug-and-play operation. These devices worked fine as long as the LAN physical network topology had only a single path between any bridges. Unfortunately, if a single link or bridge failed, then the transparent bridge network was down. The IEEE's 802.1 Spanning Tree Learning Bridge Protocol (STP) solved this problem and delivered reliable, automatically configuring network bridging. The spanning tree protocol dynamically discovers network topology changes and changes the frame forwarding tables to automatically recover from failures or revert to an optimized configuration once links are repaired.

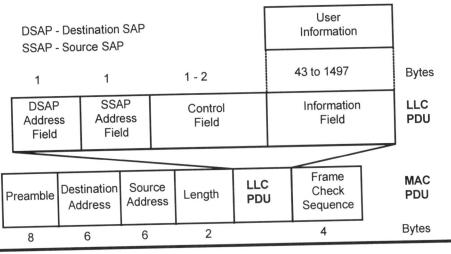

Figure 10.4 802.3 Ethernet MAC PDU Containing LLC PDU

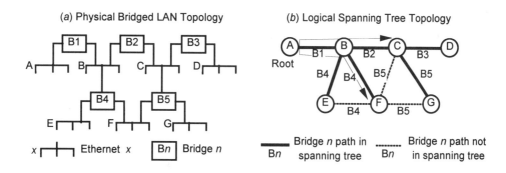

Figure 10.5 Example of IEEE 802.1 Spanning Tree Protocol Operation

IEEE 802.1 provides reliable networking by utilizing an algorithm that determines a loop-free topology. The resulting path through the bridged network looks like a tree rooted at the bridge with the lowest numerical MAC address. All other bridges forward packets up the tree to this root bridge, which then forwards packets back down the tree to the destination leaf, or to the destination where the bridge simply transmits the frame onto the destination LAN.

Figure 10.5 illustrates a simple example that illustrates this property of the spanning tree algorithm. Figure 10.5a illustrates the physical topology of seven LANs, labeled A through G, connected by five bridges, labeled B1 through B5. The physical topology has multiple paths between LANs B through G, which the spanning tree algorithm resolves to a single logical topology of a tree rooted in the port on LAN A in Bridge 1 (B1), as shown in Figure 10.5b. Note that traffic in such a bridged network often does not take the most direct path. For example, LAN frames between LANs C and F will not flow through B5, but instead flow through B2 up to the root B1 and back down to B4. Therefore, care must be taken in the application of STP bridged networks to WANs to minimize traffic flowing across the WAN to the root of the spanning tree, otherwise, the STP protocol will send all traffic to the lowest numerical address on the bridged network. The STP algorithm runs continuously to react to link failures as well as automatically add and delete stations and LANs.

Although STP bridges offer the convenience of plug-and-play operation, they utilize link and bridge port capacity inefficiently, as illustrated in the previous example. The token group of IEEE 802.5, with support from IBM, responded to this challenge by designing the Source Routing Protocol (SRP) where each LAN station specifies the end-to-end routing for each frame for bridging between token LANs. Stations utilize SRP for frames destined to stations on other LANs by setting the multicast bit in the source address. This convention works because no station should ever transmit from a multicast address. Each frame contains a complete set of routing information that describes the sequence of bridges and LANs the frame must traverse from the source to the destination station. LAN stations obtain the information to compute this optimal path from explorer packets broadcast periodically throughout the bridged network.

SRP utilizes an addressing scheme in the routing information field illustrated in Figure 10.6, which shows the IEEE 802.5 (Token Ring) MAC PDU fields. The Routing Information (RI) field starts with a 2-byte control header, made up of a type field to distinguish explorer packets from source-routed packets, a length field that limits the source route to 14 hops, a direction bit indicating left-to-right or right-to-left route scanning, and a largest frame size indicator. The remainder of the RI field contains a sequence of 12-bit token ring and 4-bit bridge numbers, defining the hops from source to destination. In real implementations each bridge uses a pair of ring–bridge number pairs, so in practice the maximum number of bridges traversed on a source route is seven. Note that the ATM Forum's Private Network-to-Network Interface (PNNI) routing protocol also utilizes a source routing paradigm in the interest of efficiently utilizing link and port capacity.

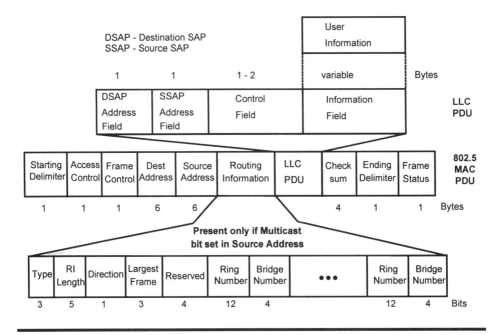

Figure 10.6 IEEE 802.5 Token Ring MAC Frame and Routing Information Field

10.4 LAN EMULATION

LAN emulation could well be the killer application that brings ATM networking into the mainstream. A key reason for this prediction is that LANE provides an interoperable transition from legacy Ethernet and Token Ring networks to ATM. Prior to LANE, legacy LAN and WAN protocols (Ethernet, Token Ring, FDDI, etc.) required proprietary conversion devices to benefit from ATM.

A key challenge for LANE is resolving the fundamental difference between ATM's connection-oriented, point-to-point protocol and connectionless, shared-media LANs (e.g., Ethernet and Token Ring). The ATM Forum's LANE 1.0 specification [4, 5] defines operation over the ATM best effort, or UBR service class, similar to existing LANs. The LANE 2.0 [6] specification adds QoS guarantees, giving ATM-based LAN emulation a characteristic that distinguishes it from most other LAN protocols.

LANE literally bridges ATM and LANs by interworking at the MAC layer, which provides device-driver interfaces such as Open Data-Link Interface (ODI) and Network Driver Interface Specification (NDIS) to higher-level applications.

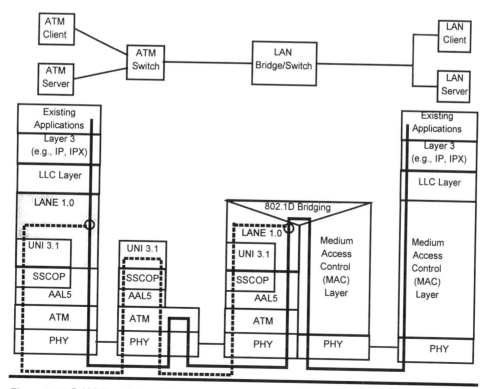

Figure 10.7 LAN Emulation Protocol Model

Figure 10.7 illustrates how LANE enables legacy applications to run essentially unchanged using existing device-driver interfaces, simultaneously enabling computers running the same applications to directly connect to ATM-enabled systems on high-performance ATM networks. Starting on the left-hand side, an ATM host or server runs an existing application and networking protocol, such as IP or IPX. Note how the LANE software provides the same interfaces to the network layer that Ethernet-attached hosts and servers on the right-hand side of the figure do. Moving to the right, an ATM switch interconnects ATM clients and servers. A LAN bridge and/or switch with an ATM interface converts from the ATM-based LANE protocol to the MAC sublayer — for example, Ethernet. These two functions may be implemented in the same device. The LANE 1.0 protocol has two types of data flows, as illustrated in Figure 10.7: a signaling connection, shown by the dashed line, and a data path connection, shown by the solid line. The signaling connection sets up an SVC for the data direct path between the ATM client or server and the LAN bridge or switch.

Each emulated LAN is one of two types: Ethernet/IEEE 802.3 or IEEE 802.5 (Token Ring). LANE specifications define communication among all users, independently of other emulated LANs and other ATM logical networks, similar to a physical LAN. Routers or bridges typically interconnect emulated LANs.

10.4.1 LANE Components and Connection Types

Figure 10.8 illustrates how logical components in the LANE specification are interconnected by virtual channel connections. The four logical components in the LANE specification are :

- LAN Emulation Client (LEC)
- LAN Emulation Server (LES)
- Broadcast and Unknown Server (BUS)
- LAN Emulation Configuration Server (LECS)

The LEC is an end system that provides a standard LAN service interface to higher-layer interfaces. An LEC performs data forwarding, address resolution, and other control functions in this role. ATM Network Interface Card (NICs) and LAN switches are examples of LEC implementations. A unique ATM address, which the LANE protocol associates with one or more MAC addresses reachable through its ATM UNI, identifies each LEC. A LAN switch dynamically associates all the MAC addresses reachable through its LAN ports to a single ATM address.

A single LES implements the control function for a particular emulated LAN. A unique ATM address identifies the LES.

The BUS is a multicast server that floods unknown-destination address traffic and forwards multicast and broadcast traffic to clients within a emulated LAN. An emulated LAN may have multiple BUSs for throughput reasons, but each LEC is associated with only one BUS. A unique ATM address identifies the BUS to each LEC. Typically, the association of the broadcast MAC address (e.g., "all ones") is configured into the LES.

The LECS assigns individual LANE clients to particular emulated LANs by directing them to the controlling LES. Logically, one LECS serves all clients within an administrative domain. The LECS is often utilized to implement virtual LANs, a capability where an administrator controls the allowed interconnection of sets of ATM users.

Figure 10.8 also illustrates the control and data virtual channel ATM connections between LANE components via directed arrows. The control connections are:

- A bidirectional, point-to-point *configuration direct VCC*, set up by the LEC to the LECS.
- A bidirectional, point-to-point *control direct VCC*, set up by the LEC to the LES.
- A unidirectional *control distribute VCC*, set up from the LES back to the LEC. Typically, this is a point-to-multipoint connection, but it may be implemented as a set of unidirectional point-to-point VCCs.

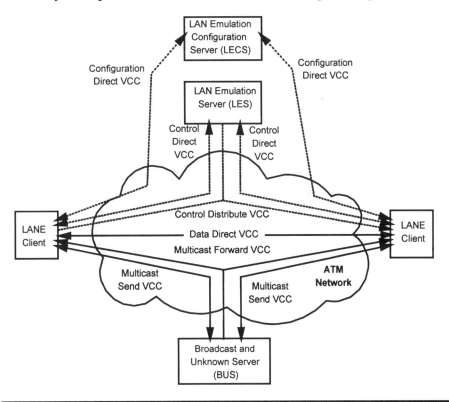

Figure 10.8 LAN Emulation Components and Interconnections

The data connections are:

- A bidirectional, point-to-point *data direct VCC*, set up between two LECs to exchange data. Usually, LECs use the same data direct VCC to carry all packets between them, instead of setting up a new VCC for each MAC address pair between them. This is done to conserve connection resources and avoid connection setup latency.
- A bidirectional, point-to-point *multicast send VCC*, set up by the LEC to the BUS.
- A unidirectional *multicast forward VCC*, set up from the BUS to the LEC. Typically, this is a point-to-multipoint connection with each LEC as a leaf, but it may also be a set of unidirectional point-to-point connections.

10.4.2 LANE Implementation Considerations

An LEC resides on every ATM-attached station in an emulated LAN. Although Figure 10.8 depicts all server functions implemented separately, the LANE protocol does not specify where any of the server components should be located. Indeed, any device or devices with ATM connectivity may implement the LANE server functions. For the purposes of reliability and performance; however, most vendors implement these server components on networking equipment, such as ATM switches or routers, rather than on a workstation or host.

Each LEC is part of an ATM end station. It represents a set of users identified by their MAC address(es). Communication among LECs and between LECs and the LES is performed over ATM VCCs. Each LEC must communicate with the LES over control and data VCCs. Emulated LANs operate in any of the following environments: Switched Virtual Circuit (SVC), Permanent Virtual Circuit (PVC), or mixed SVC/PVC. There are no call setup and release procedures in a PVC-only LAN; instead, layer management sets up and clears connections. However, the large number of connections required in PVC networks make all but the smallest emulated LAN networks too complex to manage.

Since MAC addressing is flat (i.e., no logical hierarchy exists), bridges must flood connectivity data throughout the emulated LAN. LANE makes the same tradeoff that bridges do, achieving plug-and-play operation at the cost of decreased scalability. A further differentiating advantage of ATM LAN emulation over LAN switching is that it implements LANs at aggregate speeds on the order of gigabits per second. Also, emulated LANs make efficient use of WAN bandwidth, avoiding the problems in spanning tree bridging.

ATM NIC cards enable ATM-connected workstations to communicate with LAN-attached workstations and servers. Since LANE protocols use standard ATM signaling procedures, ATM switches are convenient platforms for implementing LANE server components. LANE provides a standard way to connect LAN switches, which effectively act as fast multiport bridges. Basically, the LANE protocol resolves MAC addresses into ATM addresses, and hence implements bridging, which makes it a natural extension to current LAN switches. Routers also use LANE to implement bridged virtual LANs.

A LAN bridge learns about MAC addresses on adjacent LAN segments and doesn't propagate this information. Hence, a bridge shields LAN segments from each other by *not* propagating broadcast information. Several LANE functions specifically support the operation of LAN bridges.

10.4.3 Optional LANE Capabilities

An intelligent BUS shares knowledge of MAC address reachability with the LES. The intelligent BUS can then forward packets received from other LECs directly to the appropriate LEC across the bidirectional multicast send VCC, instead of over the point-to-multipoint multicast forward VCC. The intelligent BUS allows a minimal LEC implementation. The performance, of course, is limited by the forwarding capacity of the intelligent BUS. The LANE protocol, while allowing for intelligent BUSs, does require all LECs to set up data direct VCCs whenever possible, and also restricts the number of flooded (unicast) packets sent to the BUS over a specified interval.

Vendors utilize LANE as the basis for Virtual LAN (VLAN) service over ATM backbones. A VLAN capability can be implemented through extensions to the LECS. Employing network management interfaces, a network administrator can establish multiple emulated LANs over a common ATM network by controlling the LES and BUS assignments to end systems, bridges, and LAN switches. VLANs overcome the limitation of many early bridges that associated physical ports on a particular device with a specific LAN segment. VLANs place the control of LAN connectivity within software so that enterprises can dynamically move, add, and change users across LAN segments without having to physically move workstations and servers. This benefit often justifies LANE deployment, especially in a multivendor environment.

Since LANE is a bridging protocol, it is subject to the limitations and problems of other bridged protocols. One limitation is scalability, hence LANE is applicable to smaller private networks. Also, bridged networks are subject to broadcast storms. Users should plan to utilize routers to interconnect emulated LANs in a manner similar to that commonly in use today to connect smaller bridged networks. LANE allows high-performance ATM routers to be utilized. In an IP-based network, LECs would have the same IP subnet address, and use LANE procedures to establish data direct VCCs between themselves. If the destination IP address is not on the same subnet, then the LEC would use the MAC address of the default router; which then can route the packet towards its destination using its next-hop table. Of course, eventually the capacity of the router becomes the limiting factor in such networks.

10.4.4 LANE Work in Progress: LUNI 2.0 and LNNI

The LANE 1.0 protocol specifies only the operation of the LAN Emulation User to Network Interface (LUNI, pronounced "Loony") between a LEC and the network providing the LANE service in a nonredundant mode. The phase 1 LANE protocols specify only the LUNI operation; furthermore, the phase 1 LANE protocol does not allow for the standard support of multiple LESs or BUSs within an ELAN. Hence these components represent both single points of failure and potential bottlenecks.

The ATM Forum plans to extend the specification in a version 2.0 specification that also adds a LAN emulation NNI (LNNI, pronounced "Lenny") interface, which operates between the server components within a single emulated LAN. The LANE 2.0 LUNI specification also added support for ATM's quality of service.

10.5 REVIEW

This chapter introduced the important topics of ATM in LANs and internetworks. We then summarized important terminology and concepts at the data link layer critical to LANs, namely LLC, Medium Access Control, and bridging. Next, we covered some layer 2 protocol concepts used in the popular Ethernet and Token Ring LAN protocols to convert to ATM compatibility. The text then described how the ATM Forum's LAN emulation supports seamless interconnection of ATM hosts and servers with their legacy LAN counterparts.

10.6 REFERENCES

[1]   R. Cole, D. Shur, and C. Villamizar, *RFC 1932: IP over ATM: A Framework Document*, IETF, April 1996.
[2]   R. Perlman, *Interconnections*, Addison-Wesley, 1992.
[3]   A. Tannenbaum, *Computer Communications*, 3d ed., Prentice-Hall, 1996.
[4]   ATM Forum, *LAN Emulation over ATM: Version 1.0 Specification*, af-lane-0021.00, January 1995.
[5]   N. Finn and T. Mason, "ATM LAN Emulation," *IEEE Communications*, June 1996.
[6]   ATM Forum, *LAN Emulation over ATM — LUNI Specification*, Version 2, af-lane-0084.000, July 1997.
[7]   D. Spohn, *Data Network Design*, 2d ed., McGraw-Hill, 1997.

11

Internetworking Using ATM

This chapter covers ATM's support for internetworking protocols, such as the popular Internet Protocol (IP). The emergence of the World Wide Web (WWW) as the killer application for data communications has established IP as the de facto standard for internetworking to the corporate desktop as well as the home office and residential user. The promulgated standards and some proprietary implementations have also made significant progress in addressing the more difficult problem of seamless interoperation with existing internets. This task is daunting because of the fundamental difference between ATM's nonbroadcast, connection-oriented protocol and the Internet's broadcast, connectionless orientation. Nonetheless, where there is a will, there is a way. We now delve into this important subject and show how industry experts have crafted various designs involving servers and clever paradigm shifts to emulate broadcast, connectionless LANs and internets using ATM's nonbroadcast, connection-oriented infrastructure.

Figure 11.1 illustrates the higher-layer user plane protocols covered in this chapter that support internetworking protocols, primarily IP, over an ATM infrastructure. But first a tutorial on the Internet Protocol suite. We then move on to some of the earliest designs supporting IP over ATM via multiprotocol encapsulation to enable efficient ATM virtual circuit connection resource sharing. On top of this infrastructure, we will then describe support for classical IP subnetworks and emulation of the IP multicast group service. Next, we will introduce several proprietary, leading-edge, high-performance, Quality of Service (QoS)-aware designs which support IP networking over an ATM infrastructure. These IP and tag switching techniques offer promise — which meets the rapid growth created by the information content of the Web. The chapter briefly covers an ATM name resolution service based upon the Internet's Domain Name Service (DNS) designed to ease usage of the lengthy 20-byte NSAP addresses. A survey of native ATM Application Programming Interfaces (APIs), which will likely play a key role in next-generation operating systems for true multimedia support, will be given in conclusion.

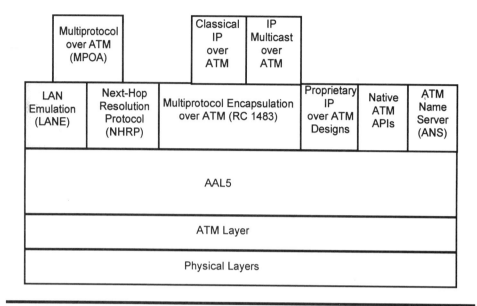

Figure 11.1 User Plane Higher-Layer Protocols for LANs and Internetworking

11.1 THE INTERNET PROTOCOL

The Internet has become a household word in the 1990s with the introduction of user-friendly, multimedia browser applications accessing the World Wide Web. Banks, auto dealerships, retail stores, book publishers, and even children's television programs beckon users to look at their "Web pages." Information is the new currency, and the Web is the marketplace. Gone are the good old days when the Internet was the haven of university researchers and government organizations. If you want information, to purchase goods, or just to play computer games against other players — do it on the Web. The Web offers the ultimate in interoperability — all you need is Internet access and a Web browser, and let the Web do the rest. Let's take a look under the hood at the internetworking protocol engine that powers the Web before delving into how various protocols and procedures support IP over ATM.

11.1.1 The TCP/IP Suite

Figure 11.2 illustrates the layered Internet protocol suite built atop IP. The User Datagram Protocol (UDP), Internet Control Message Protocol (ICMP), routing control protocols, and the Transmission Control Protocol (TCP) interface directly with IP, making up the transport layer in the Internet architecture.

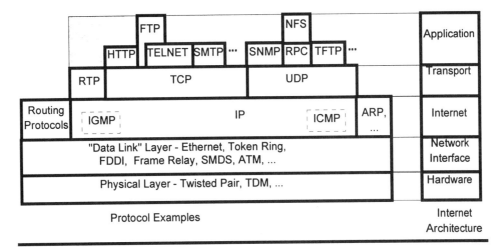

Figure 11.2 Internet Protocol (IP) Suite

Both TCP and UDP provide the capability for the host to distinguish among multiple applications through port numbers. TCP provides a reliable, sequenced delivery of data to applications. TCP also provides adaptive flow control, segmentation and reassembly, and prioritized data flows. UDP provides only an unacknowledged datagram capability. The recently defined Real Time Protocol (RTP) provides real-time capabilities that multimedia applications can access.

IP is a datagram protocol that is highly resilient to network failures, but does not guarantee "in-sequence" delivery. IP works with TCP for end-to-end reliable transmission of data across the network. TCP controls the amount of unacknowledged data in transit by automatically reducing either the window size or the segment size. The reverse is also true; window or segment size values can be increased to pass more data if error conditions are minimal. This increases throughput.

A number of applications interface to TCP and UDP, as shown in Figure 11.2. The File Transfer Protocol (FTP) application provides for secure server log-in, directory manipulation, and file transfers. TELNET provides a remote terminal log-in capability. The Hypertext Transfer Protocol (HTTP) supports the popular World Wide Web. The Simple Network Management Protocol (SNMP) supports configuration setting, data retrieval, and alarm reporting. The Trivial FTP (TFTP) provides, as its name indicates, a simplified version of FTP which is intended to reduce implementation complexity. The Remote Procedure Call (RPC) and Network File Server (NFS) capabilities allow applications to dynamically interact over IP networks. DNS provides a centralized name service, and can run over UDP or TCP.

Routers send error and control messages to other routers using ICMP. ICMP also provides a function in which a user can send a *ping* (echo packet) to verify reachability and round trip delay of an IP-addressed host. The IP layer also supports the Internet Group Multicast Protocol (IGMP), which we cover later in this chapter.

The Address Resolution Protocol (ARP) directly interfaces to the data link layer, for example, Ethernet. The purpose of ARP is to map a physical address (e.g., an Ethernet MAC address) to an IP address. We cover the routing protocols after introducing the IP packet format and addressing in the following sections.

11.1.2 IPv4 Packet Formats

Figure 11.3 illustrates the format of the IP version 4 (IPv4) packet. The version field specifies the IP protocol version. The IP Header Length (IP HL) field specifies the datagram header length in units of 32-bit words, the most common length being 4 words, or 20 octets. Use of the Type of Service (TOS) field varies across the industry. Either each particular bit is treated as an individual flag (a 3-bit precedence of 1 to 7 – 1 bit to indicate delay sensitivity, 1 bit to indicate high throughput, and 1 bit to indicate a request for high reliability), or a 3-bit field is used with values of 0 through 7 (or 1 through eight, even) and eight levels of precedence or service qualities. The total length field specifies the total IP datagram length for the header and the user data.

The identification, flags, and fragment offset fields control fragmentation (or segmentation) and reassembly of IP datagrams. The Time to Live (TTL) field specifies how many routers the packet can pass through before a router declares the packet "dead." Intermediate nodes or routers decrement TTL, and when it reaches zero, they discard the packet. The protocol field identifies the higher-level protocol type (e.g., TCP or UDP), which identifies the format of the data field. The header checksum ensures integrity of the header fields through a simple bitwise calculation that is easy to implement in software. Source and destination IP addresses are required, and the user data is placed in the data field. The field for options can specify routing and time-stamp information.

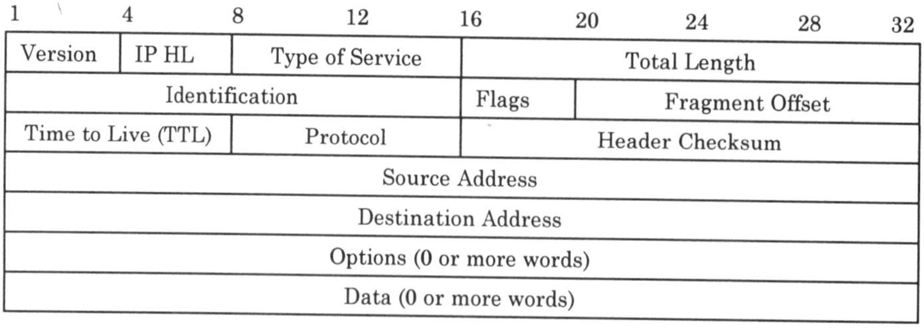

1	4	8	12	16	20	24	28	32
Version	IP HL	Type of Service		Total Length				
Identification				Flags	Fragment Offset			
Time to Live (TTL)		Protocol		Header Checksum				
Source Address								
Destination Address								
Options (0 or more words)								
Data (0 or more words)								

Figure 11.3 IP version 4 (IPv4) Datagram Format

11.1.3 Internet Protocol Addressing

The Internet uses a 32-bit global network addressing scheme. Each user — or "host," in Internet parlance — has a unique IP address which is 4 octets in length, represented in the following dotted decimal notation:

XXX.XXX.XXX.XXX

where XXX ranges from 0 to 255 decimal, corresponding to the range of 00000000 to 11111111 binary. There are 2^{32}, or over 4 billion, possible IP addresses. You would think that this would be enough addresses, but the Internet recently had to drop a previously used strict hierarchical structure that grouped addresses into classes A, B, and C, where the class determined the maximum network size, measured in number of hosts. The Internet reserved another block of Class D addresses for multicasting. The high-order bits represented the network address, and the remaining bits represented the hosts in the network. Although network classes no longer formally exist in the Internet today, they are briefly described here as an introduction to classless addressing. Table 11.1 illustrates the key properties of the legacy Internet address classes.

Table 11.1 Characteristics of Legacy Internet Address Classes

IP Address Class	Bits for Network Address	First Byte Network Address Range	Total Number of Networks	Bits for Host Address	Hosts per Network
A	7	0–127*	126	24	16,777,214
B	14	128–191	16,384	16	65,534
C	21	192–223	2,097,152	8	254
D†	NA	224–254	NA	NA	NA

* Values 0 and 127 are reserved for the "all zeroes" and "all ones" addresses.
† Values reserved for multicast.

A central authority, the Internet Assigned Numbers Authority (IANA), assigns IP addresses to ensure that they are unique. A network administrator could assign the host addresses within its class A, B, or C address space however it wished, as long as the assignment was unique. Reusing IP addresses is a bad idea, since address conflicts arise when networks are interconnected. This assignment scheme worked fine until the public's addiction to the information content of the Web made the Internet enormously popular. Then problems arose because anyone asking for a IP address asked for the largest size they could justify. In the early days of the Internet, the address space seemed limitless. This inefficient allocation meant that a lot of IP addresses remained unused. The Internet community resolved the crisis by reallocating Class C and A addresses to the many new service providers, who then dynamically allocated addresses to individual users clamoring to get on the Internet. Now, modern routing protocols treat IP addresses as 32-bit numbers without a class structure .

The Internet called this new scheme Classless Interdomain Routing (CIDR) and began deployment in 1993 [1, 2, 3] to improve scaling of the Internet routing system. CIDR generalizes the concept of Variable-Length Subnet Masks (VLSMs) and eliminates the historical network classes (A, B, and C). Interior (intradomain) routing protocols supporting CIDR are OSPF, RIP II, Integrated IS-IS, and E-IGRP. Only one exterior (interdomain) routing protocol, BGP-4, currently supports CIDR.

11.1.4 Next Generation IP — IPv6

It is true: The Internet is running out of addresses! The more efficient allocation of IPv4 addresses through CIDR, along with the availability of routing protocols that support the variable-length subnet masks, have bought at best a few years time for growth in the Internet. For example, CIDR is now moving into the Class A address space reserved for expansion (64.0.0.0 through 126.0.0.0) [1]. Anticipating the exhaustion of the IP address space, the IETF issued RFC 1752, the recommendation for the IP next-generation protocol (IPng) in July 1994. IPng supersedes IPv4, and is now formally referred to as IPv6. IPv6 contains the following additions and enhancements to IPv4:

* Address field size expanded from 32 to 128 bits
* Simple dynamic autoconfiguration capability
* Easier multicast routing with addition of "scope" field
* Anycast feature, where a host sends a packet to an anycast address which the network delivers to the closest node supporting that function
* Capability to define quality of service for individual traffic flows
* Reduction of overhead by making some header fields optional
* More flexible protocol design for future enhancements
* Authentication, data integrity, and confidentiality options
* Easy transition from, and interoperability with, IPv4
* Support for all IPv4 routing algorithms (e.g., OSPF, RIP, etc.)

IPv6 supports all the traditional protocols that IPv4 did, such as datagram service, FTP file transfers, E-mail, X-windows, Gopher, and of course, the web. Furthermore, IPv6 also supports approximately 340×10^{36} individual addresses. To ease migration, IPv4 addressing is a proper subset of the Ipv6 address space.

Figure 11.4 illustrates the IPv6 packet format. The version field allows routers to examine the first 4 bits of the packet header to determine the IP version. Note that the IPv4 packet header has the same field in the first 4 bits. The priority field defines eight values (0 through 7) for sources that can be flow-controlled during congestion, and eight values (8 through 15) for sources that cannot respond to congestion (e.g., "real-time" constant bit rate traffic, such as video and voice). Within each priority group, lower-numbered packets are less important than higher-numbered ones. The flow label field is intended for use by protocols such as the Resource Reservation Protocol (RSVP) to guarantee bandwidth and QoS for related streams of packets. The next header field identifies the subsequent header extension field. There are six (optional) header extensions. The last extension header identifies the protocol type, using the same values as IPv4. The hop limit field is a count that decrements by 1 each time the packet is forwarded, analogous to the TTL field in IPv4. The source and destination addresses are extended to 128 bits. Therefore, the IPv6 header is a constant 40 bytes; however, the optional extensions can make the header considerably larger.

11.2 ROUTING PROTOCOLS

Larger networks usually implement some form of routing. As described in Chapter 3, routing protocols build tables for use in determining the next hop that a packet should be forwarded to and through. Routing protocols automatically discover neighbors, distribute topology, and compute optimized routes. We survey in this section only the modern link-state routing protocols, and not older historical protocols. We then cover how larger networks scale through subnetting.

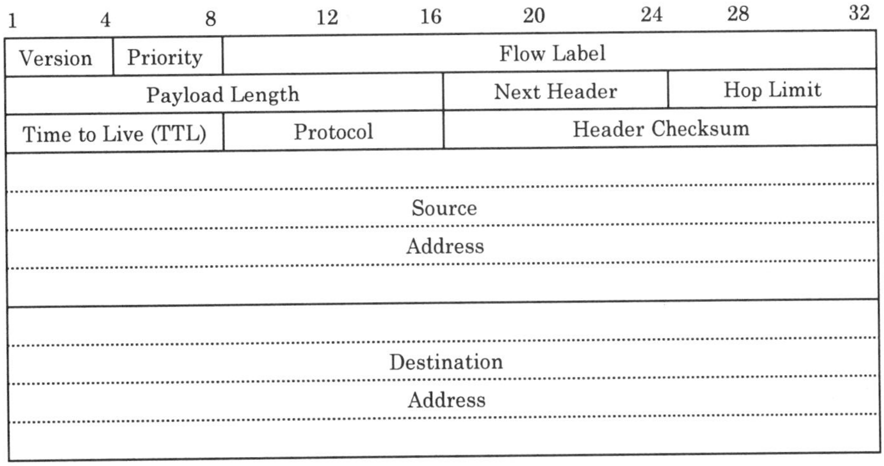

1	4	8	12	16	20	24	28	32
Version	Priority		Flow Label					
Payload Length				Next Header			Hop Limit	
Time to Live (TTL)		Protocol		Header Checksum				
Source Address								
Destination Address								

Figure 11.4 IPv6 Packet Format

11.2.1 Link-State Routing Protocols Defined

The class of routing protocols that use the link-state paradigm replaced an earlier protocol that used a distance vector algorithm in the Internet beginning in 1979. The link-state method overcame the slow convergence times of the prior method. Routers implementing link-state protocols perform the following four basic functions [4]:

1. They say hello to their neighbors, learn addresses, and collect routing "cost" information.
2. They collect the state information from all their links and place these in advertisements transmitted to their neighbors.
3. They reliably and efficiently "flood" the link-state packets throughout the network so that every router quickly converges to an accurate view of the entire network's topology.
4. They compute the least-cost path to every other router in the network.

Let's look into each of these steps a little further with reference to the simple example in Figure 11.5. Neighboring routers run a "hello" protocol once they boot up or once a link activates, as shown in Figure 11.5a. The hello protocol messages contain routing "cost" information, which may be economic information about the link or may reflect some other information such as the distance, latency, or bandwidth of a particular link. Routers also detect link failures when they stop receiving the periodic heartbeat of the hello protocol messages from a neighbor.

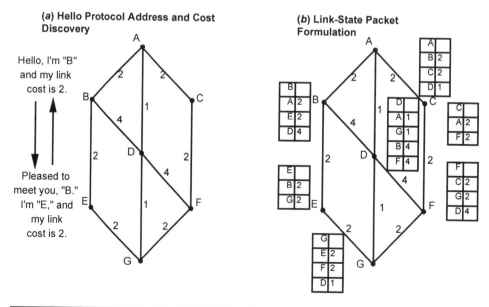

Figure 11.5 Examples of Hello Protocol and Link-State Packets

Each node in the network assembles its view of the current link state into a packet and forwards it to each of its neighbors as shown in Figure 11.5b. The link-state packet identifies the source router in the first line, and the destination routers and link costs in each of the subsequent lines in the figure. Routers send these link-state packets upon start-up, or whenever a significant change occurs in the network, such as a link failing or coming on line.

Intermediate nodes forward link-state packets on to other nodes as illustrated in Figure 11.6a for router A, in a procedure called *flooding*. Flooding involves replicating the link-state packets in an efficient and reliable manner so that every node quickly obtains an identical copy of the entire network link-state topology. Note that some nodes receive multiple copies of the link-state packets. Additional fields in the link-state packets that record a sequence number and an aging count eliminate duplicate packets and handle other error scenarios. Routers acknowledge flooded link-state packets to ensure reliable topology distribution.

Finally, each router computes the least-cost path to every other router in the network. Figure 11.6b illustrates the result of this calculation for router A in the solid, bold lines. The net effect of the routing calculation, using the Djikstra algorithm, for example, is a minimum spanning tree rooted at each node as shown by the upside down tree rooted in node A in the figure. When a link or node fails, a new node or link is added, or a link or node is deleted; then the above procedure repeats. The time for this entire process to complete its routine is called the *convergence time*. Current link-state routing algorithms converge within a matter of seconds in moderate-sized networks.

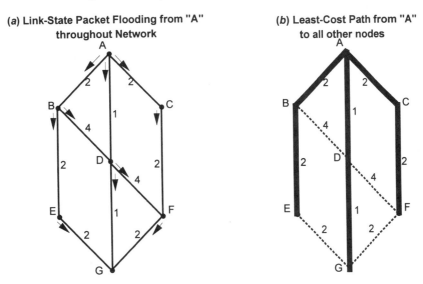

(a) Link-State Packet Flooding from "A" throughout Network

(b) Least-Cost Path from "A" to all other nodes

Figure 11.6 Examples of Flooding and Least-Cost Route Determination

Three major implementations of link-state routing protocols dominate the market: the OSI's Intermediate System to Intermediate System (IS-IS) Routing Protocol, the Internet's Open Shortest Path First (OSPF) protocol, and Novell's NLSP. A popular implementation of link-state routing is OSPF, which uses the Dijkstra, or Shortest Path First (SPF), algorithm, for determining routing. All costs for links are designated on the outbound router port, so that costs may be different in each direction (unlike the simple example above). OSPF also supports a limited form of hierarchical routing by sectioning the network into independent lower-level areas interconnected by a backbone area.

OSPF routing supports three types of networks: point-to-point, broadcast, and Nonbroadcast Multiaccess (NBMA). Point-to-point links join a single pair of routers. Broadcast networks attach more than two routers, with each router having the ability to broadcast a single message to multiple routers. Nonbroadcast multiple-access networks, such as ATM, interconnect more than two routers but do not have broadcast capability. OSPF also supports subnetting, which we will discuss next. OSPF supports only IP networks, unlike IS-IS, which supports multiple protocols simultaneously. OSPF also supports bifurcated routing, the ability to split packets between two equal paths.

11.2.2 Routing and Logical IP Subnetworks

A critical concept of routing in large networks is summarization of host addresses, called *subnetting*. If every router in a network needed to have a routing table entry for every host, then the routing tables would become unmanageably large. Furthermore, routing table size is not the most critical constraint – in practice, the message processing to update the routing tables limits routing table size before physical storage does.

How does an IP network determine when routing is necessary? For example, how do two hosts on the same LAN know that they can transmit packets to one another directly without using routing? The answer in general is that when the two hosts are *not* on the same (bridged) LAN, then routing is needed. Historically, IP preceded LANs. Therefore, IP adopted the convention of a subnetwork bit mask that constrains address assignments. This allowed hosts to determine whether routing was required based solely upon the source and destination address. The subnet mask convention dictates that IP hosts are in the same Logical IP Subnet (LIS) if a certain number of high-order bits of their IP addresses match. A station determines if two IP addresses are in the same subnet by bitwise ANDing the subnet mask with each address and comparing the results. If both addresses ANDed with the subnet mask result in the same value, then they are on the same subnet. CIDR generalized the concept of subnet masks even further by allowing them to be of variable length for different subnetworks within the same administrative domain.

Subnet masks are expressed as in the same IP address format where a certain number of the high-order bits all have the value of binary 1. In dotted decimal notation this means that the four decimal values of a subnet mask have one of the values listed in Table 11.2. The table also lists the number of consecutive 1s in the subnet mask along with the number of networks and hosts allowed in the 1-byte subnet mask. See Appendix C of [5] for more details on subnet mask values.

Table 11.2 Valid Subnet Mask Decimal Values and CIDR Length fields

Subnet Mask Number	Consecutive 1s	Number of Networks	Number of Hosts								
255	8	254	0	1	1	1	1	1	1	1	1
254	7	126	0	1	1	1	1	1	1	1	0
252	6	62	2	1	1	1	1	1	1	0	0
248	5	30	6	1	1	1	1	1	0	0	0
240	4	14	14	1	1	1	1	0	0	0	0
224	3	6	30	1	1	1	0	0	0	0	0
192	2	2	62	1	1	0	0	0	0	0	0
128	1	1	126	1	0	0	0	0	0	0	0
0	0	1	254	0	0	0	0	0	0	0	0

For example, the old IP class A, B, and C addresses had implicit subnet masks as follows:

Class A	255.0.0.0
Class B	255.255.0.0
Class C	255.255.255.0

The old IP class address structure suffered from a degenerate variant of Goldilocks' syndrome from the Three Bears fairy tale: Class A with over 16 million hosts, was much too big for all but the largest networks; class B with 65,000 addresses, was also too big for most networks, yet Class C, with only 254 hosts, was too small for most networks. Although the 32-bit address enabled 2 billion networks, the inefficiency of assigning addresses in only these three sizes threatened to exhaust the Class B address space in 1993. CIDR usage of a variable-length subnet mask allowed Internet administrators to split up the IP address space more efficiently and to keep the Internet growing until the next IP version (IPv6) could be deployed. CIDR also defines the concept of supernetting, where multiple Class C–style addresses are combined into a single route advertisement.

Let's look at simple example like the Alamo Trader's Market in Texas. This network has an old-style class C address range of 198.62.193.1 to 198.62.193.254. Our example network has four routers, one at the headquarters in Austin and three remote sites at Dallas, Houston, and San Antonio as illustrated in Figure 11.7. Each site requires up to 10 hosts per router; therefore, we can use the subnet mask of 255.255.255.240, since this allows up to 14 hosts per network (i.e., site), as shown in Table 11.2. This choice allows the network administrator to add more sites in the future. The 14 network addresses available under the subnet mask 255.255.255.240 are (see [5], Appendix C):

198.62.193.16

198.62.193.32

198.62.193.48

198.62.193.64

198.62.193.80

198.62.193.96

198.62.193.112

198.62.193.128

198.62.193.144

198.62.193.160

198.62.193.176

198.62.193.192

198.62.193.208

198.62.193.224

The network administrator assigns the address 198.62.193.16 to the headquarters subnetwork in Austin, 198.62.193.32 to the Dallas subnetwork, 198.62.193.48 to the Houston subnetwork, and 198.62.193.64 to the San Antonio subnetwork, as shown in Figure 11.7. The administrator assigns addresses to hosts and servers at each of the locations. Starting in the Dallas 198.62.193.32 subnetwork, the administrator assigns addresses, .34, .35, and .36, to the three hosts (Ken, Sue, and Julie) attached to Ethernet segment .33 (we leave out the common Class C address prefix 198.62.193 for clarity). Note that the administrator can add up to 10 more addresses within this subnet. Moving on to the next subnet, Houston, the network administrator assigns .49 to the Ethernet segment and .50, .51, and .52 to the hosts named Bill, Kelly, and Joe, respectively. Finally, she assigns addresses within the San Antonio subnet to the Ethernet segment (.65), Rodney (.66), Kim (.67), and Steve (.68). The same address assignment process also applies at the Austin location.

The network administrator in this example must now assign IP addresses and subnet masks to the WAN links in the example of Figure 11.7. Planning for growth of her network, the administrator chooses a different subnet mask for the point-to-point links, since the 255.255.255.240 subnet mask reserves 14 addresses per WAN link, when in fact only two are needed. This is possible because the routers run a version of OSPF that supports CIDR's variable length subnet masks. Therefore, the administrator assigns WAN links the subnet mask 255.255.255.252, which allows exactly two hosts. The network administrator chooses to use this longer subnet mask to split up the

198.62.193.224 network, leaving room to add other networks. Hence, the valid network numbers are .224 through .252 in increments of 4 (see [5], Appendix D). The administrator assigns the network address 198.62.193.224 with a subnet mask of 255.255.255.252 to the link between Austin and Dallas as shown in Figure 11.7. The router port in Austin gets the IP address 198.62.193.225 and the Dallas router gets 198.62.193.226. Note that these address choices avoid the "all 0s" and "all 1s" host addresses on the WAN link subnet. The other WAN links are then assigned sequential addresses under the longer 255.255.255.252 subnet mask.

This assignment allows the administrator to add another 9 subnets under the 255.255.255.240 mask and another 11 WAN links out of the 198.62.193.224 network under the 255.255.255.252 mask. If the routers had not used CIDR, then the administrator would have needed to assign a separate network to each WAN link, and the expansion would have been limited to 6 additional subnets and/or WAN links. Patting herself on the back for such a forward-looking address assignment and clever use of variable-length subnet masks, the LAN administrator in this example heads out of the office for a well-deserved, ice-cold Lone Star beer at her favorite watering hole on Sixth Street in Austin.

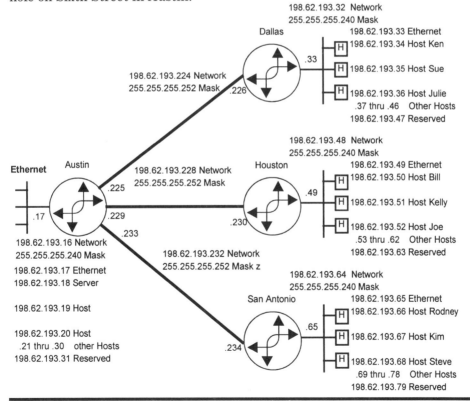

Figure 11.7 Network Example for IP Address Assignment and Subnet Masks

11.3 MULTIPROTOCOL ENCAPSULATION OVER AAL5

IETF standard RFC 1483 [6] defines how a number of commonly used protocols can be routed or bridged over ATM Adaptation Layer 5 (AAL5) using either protocol encapsulation or VC multiplexing. *Protocol encapsulation* allows for multiple protocols to be multiplexed over a single ATM Virtual Circuit (VC) [which is a commonly used shorthand name for Virtual Channel Connection (VCC)]). The *VC multiplexing* method assumes that each protocol is carried over a separate ATM VC. Both of these encapsulation methods utilize the AAL5 payload format. We will cover the protocol encapsulation method and then the VC multiplexing method.

11.3.1 Protocol Encapsulation

Protocol encapsulation operates by prefixing the Protocol Data Unit (PDU) with an IEEE 802.2 Logical Link Control (LLC) header, and hence the RFC 1483 document calls this *LLC encapsulation*. The LLC header identifies the PDU type. This method is designed for public network or wide area network environments where a premises device would send all protocols over a single VCC, such as in a Permanent Virtual Circuit (PVC) environment where the ATM carrier pricing structures often favor a small number of PVCs, similar to frame relay. In other words, this design saves money by sending multiple protocols over on VCC, avoiding the expense of ordering a separate VCC for each protocol. Note that all packets get the same QoS since they share a single VCC.

Figure 11.8a illustrates protocol encapsulation by routers, showing a network of three routers, each multiplexing separate Ethernet and Token Ring LANs over a single VCC interconnecting the locations. The Ethernet and Token Ring PDUs are multiplexed onto the same VCC between routers using the encapsulation described below. The drawing in Figure 11.8b illustrates how bridges multiplex PDUs from Ethernet and Token Ring interfaces to yield a bridged LAN. The Ethernet bridges only use a spanning tree of the ATM VCCs at any one point in time, which the example illustrates by a dashed line to indicate the unused VC link in the spanning tree where the center bridge assumes the role of the spanning tree root. The Token Ring bridges will make more efficient use of the ATM VCCs through source routing as described in Chapter 10.

11.3.2 VC-Based Multiplexing

The second method of carrying multiple protocols over ATM is through VC-based multiplexing, which supports a single protocol per virtual connection. In other words, the VCs are multiplexed rather than the protocols themselves as done by protocol encapsulation. With this method, different protocols can have different bandwidth allocations and QoS, unlike the multiprotocol encapsulation method.

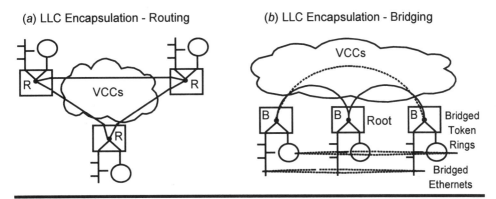

Figure 11.8 Routing and Bridging Use of LLC Encapsulation

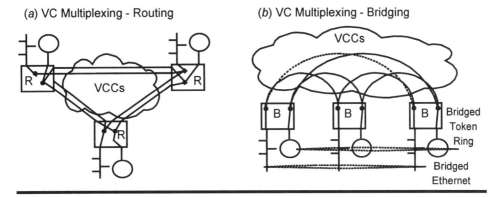

Figure 11.9 Routing and Bridging Usage of VC Multiplexing

Figure 11.9*a* illustrates the VC multiplexing concept for routed protocols, showing a separate VCC connecting the routing point for Ethernet and Token Ring. Figure 11.9*b* illustrates the same point for bridged protocols, again requiring twice as many VCCs as for protocol encapsulation. In the example, the source-routed bridged token ring load balances across all VCCs, while the spanning tree Ethernet does not use the VCC indicated by a dashed line. Comparing this to Figure 11.8, observe that the only difference is the use of one VCC for each protocol being routed or bridged versus one VCC between each pair of routers or bridges — Ethernet and Token Ring. The bridged PDU payload is devoid of the LLC and SNAP protocol identifiers used in protocol encapsulation, resulting in less overhead, less processing, and higher overall throughput at the expense of the lost routing function. This method is designed for environments where the user can dynamically create and delete large numbers of ATM VCCs in an economical fashion, as occurs in private ATM networks or service provider ATM Switched Virtual Circuit (SVC) networks.

11.3.3 Selection of Multiplexing Method

Either of the two types of multiplexing method, encapsulated or VC multiplexing, can be used with PVCs and SVCs. The method is selected by a configuration option for PVCs. SVCs require information elements in the signaling protocol for the two routers to communicate whether protocol encapsulation or VC multiplexing is being used. Signaling also indicates when using VC multiplexing, depending on whether the original LAN FCS is being carried in the PDU.

11.4 IP MAXIMUM TRANSFER UNIT OVER AAL5

RFC 1626 defines the Maximum Transfer Unit (MTU) negotiation over the Internet using AAL5 [7]. This standard specifies the default MTU size over ATM AAL5 at 9180 bytes, aligning it with the default MTU size for IP over SMDS specified in RFC 1209.

The standard also specifies procedures to use with SVCs that allow negotiation of larger MTU sizes, up to the AAL 5 limit of 64 kbytes. Larger MTU sizes are more efficient because they minimize AAL5 overhead and processing overhead. This standard also specifies that all routers utilize the IP path MTU discovery mechanism in RFCs 1191 and 1435 so that IP packet fragmentation is avoided, resulting in the greatest efficiency. Use of the path MTU discovery mechanism is important because ATM uses a default MTU size significantly different from that used by older subnet technologies such as Ethernet and FDDI. The consequence of choosing too large an MTU size is reduced performance, due to the high overhead process of IP packet fragmentation and reassembly at intermediate routers.

11.5 CLASSICAL IP OVER ATM

A basic concept involved in all methods supporting IP over ATM is resolution of an IP address to a corresponding ATM address. End stations must have both IP and ATM addresses in classical IP over ATM subnetworks. IETF RFC 1577 specifies classical IP over ATM for the use of ATM as a direct replacement for the "wires" interconnecting IP end stations, LAN segments, and routers in an LIS [9]. An LIS consists of a group of hosts or routers connected to an ATM network belonging to the same IP subnet; that is, they all have the same IP subnet number and mask. These procedures apply to both PVCs and SVCs. We cover the PVC case first. See the referenced RFCs or our previous book *ATM: Theory and Application* for more detail.

A standard method for routers to automatically learn the IP address of the router on the far end of each ATM PVC, called the *Inverse Address Resolution*

Protocol (Inverse ARP), is defined by RFC 1293 [10]. Basically it involves a station sending an InARP message containing the sender's IP address over the ATM VCC PVC. This situation occurs in PVC networks when a PVC first initializes or when a router reloads its software because the VCC is known, but the IP address that can be reached on this VCC is not known. The station on the other end of the ATM VCC PVC then responds with its IP address, establishing an association between the IP addresses of the pair and the ATM VCC's Virtual Path Identifier/Virtual Channel Identifier (VPI/VCI) on each ATM interface.

Having to manually configure large numbers of PVCs is not a desirable situation. Therefore, RFC 1577 specifies an automatic method using SVCs as well. The standard requires an ATMARP server for each LIS. The ATMARP server resolves the ARP requests for all IP stations within the LIS. IP stations first register with the route server, then act as clients to the server when making address resolution requests. Hosts must also "age" their ARP table entries to remove old data.

IP stations register with the ATMARP server by placing an SVC "call" to the ATMARP server. Each station has a hardware address (which is specified in the signaling message) and the address of the server located within the LIS. The ATMARP server may either transmit an Inverse ARP request to the newly attached client to determine the node's IP and ATM addresses, or else determine this information from ARP requests. In either case, the ATMARP server stores the association of a node's IP and ATM addresses in its ATMARP table. The route server time-stamps entries and may periodically test that the IP station is still there by using a ping command. Old entries are "aged" using this time stamp so that unresponsive IP stations are removed. The key server function is then to enable IP stations to resolve the association of an IP address with an ATM address. Armed with the destination's ATM address, the originating station dynamically sets up an ATM SVC. After a period of inactivity, the station takes down the SVC to efficiently utilize bandwidth.

Figure 11.10 illustrates the operation of multiple interconnected LISs. Each of the three LISs operates and communicates independently of all other LISs, even if they are all on the same ATM network. The classical model of RFC 1577 requires that any packet destined outside the source host or router's LIS must be sent to an IP router. For example, a host on LIS-1 must send packets for delivery to hosts or routers on LIS-2 or LIS-3 to router 1 (i.e., the default router for packets not on its LIS). Routers 1 and 2 are configured as endpoints of the LISs to which they are connected. RFC 1577 notes that this configuration may result in a number of disjoint LISs operating over the same ATM network, but the standard states that hosts on different LISs must communicate via an intermediate IP router, even though said hosts could open a direct VC between themselves. If the stations did not follow this rule, then routing loops could result.

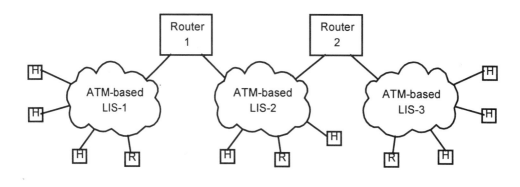

Figure 11.10 Router Interconnection of Logically Independent Subnets

11.6 NEXT-HOP RESOLUTION PROTOCOL

The classical model for IP over ATM specified in RFC 1577 requires that all communication between different LISs occur through a router. Such networks fail to take advantage of more efficient, ATM-only "cut-through" routes enabling direct communication between nodes that are connected to the same ATM network, but members of two different LISs, hence bypassing expensive intermediate router hops.

The IETF spent several years evaluating protocols designed to overcome this limitation. After considering various approaches, the IETF has advanced a protocol known as the Next-Hop Resolution Protocol (NHRP) [11]. NHRP supports a multiprotocol internetworking layer environment over an NBMA subnetwork (e.g., ATM, FR, and SMDS subnetworks). NHRP enables different LIS to be present on the same NBMA network to decouple the local versus remote forwarding decision from the addressing convention that defined the LISs. Thus, NHRP enables systems to directly interconnect over an NBMA network, independent of addressing based upon considerations such as traffic parameters or QoS characteristics.

NHRP utilizes the concept of administrative domains, where a separate instance of the NHRP applies separately to each domain. These domains may be separate NBMA networks or a partitioning of a single larger NBMA network into multiple, *logical NBMA subnetworks*. The NHRP standard assumes that no closed user groups or address screening will partition the underlying NBMA network.

NHRP stations (i.e., hosts or routers) utilize the NHRP protocol to determine the internetworking layer address (e.g., IP, IPX, and AppleTalk) and NBMA subnetwork addresses of the *NBMA next hop* on the path towards a destination station. Stations act as either servers or clients.

Within each administrative domain, *Next-Hop Servers (NHSs)* implement the NHRP protocol. An NHS is always closely associated with a router;

however, the RFC assumes that all routers connected to an NBMA may not participate in NHRP. The standard defines the last NHS along the routed path to a client as the *serving NHS*. NHSs maintain *next-hop resolution* cache tables that map internetworking addresses to NBMA addresses. NHSs construct this cache from *NHRP Register packets, NHRP Resolution Request/Reply,* or manually configured table entries. NHSs automatically populate their interworking address tables through internetworking routing protocols.

Next-Hop Clients (NHCs) also maintain a cache mapping internetworking addresses to NBMA addresses, populated through NHRP Resolution Reply packets or manual configuration. Administrators may configure the NHS NBMA address into stations connected to an NBMA network, the NHS may be the station's default router, or the station may utilize the ATM Anycast address to connect to the closest NHS. Stations register their NBMA address and reachable internetworking addresses with the NHS determined by the above rule using NHRP Register packets.

If the destination is connected to the same NBMA subnetwork, then the NBMA next hop is simply the destination station itself. Otherwise, the RFC defines the NBMA next hop as the egress router on the NBMA subnetwork that is closest to the destination station. The example of Figure 11.11 illustrates this concept for a case of two separate NBMA ATM networks interconnected by an IP router labeled R3. In this example, the source station with IP address S utilizes the same procedure, and ends up setting up a "cut-through" SVC to the egress router, R3. Meanwhile, R3 has determined through use of the NHRP protocol with R4 and R5 that a cut-through SVC can be set up through the second NBMA network to access destination D through egress router R5. Once the cut-through SVCs are established, packets flow from station S to station D over the efficient ATM SVC cut-through routes and the LAN connection between R5 and R6.

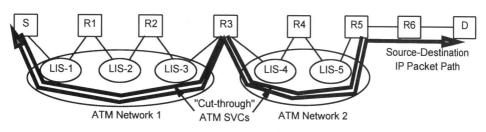

Figure 11.11 Illustration of NHRP Operation for Multiple Domains

As the NHRP Resolution Reply traverses the return path, intermediate NHSs learn and cache the IP-to-ATM mapping so that the NHS can respond directly to subsequent packet flows between these same domains without creating a Resolution request. The RFC defines an option where an originating node may request an authoritative mapping option, in which case

NHSs must not utilized cached information. The RFC identifies how to employ this method to ferret out closed user groups that may be implemented in NBMA networks by requesting a trace of the NHSs along the routed path and using the ATM address information to determine which NHSs are reachable over the NBMA network.

So far, so good, you say — such is the case with many of the best-laid plans. Figure 11.12 adds some traditional LANs and routers to the previous example, a realistic assumption in the hybrid environment expected in many networks adding ATM as part of the infrastructure. To start with, the "cut-through" SVCs are set up as in the previous example. The example adds another router, R7, which is interconnected via subnets which preserve the exchange of IP routing information as indicated in the figure. Now for the important part — *NHRP cut-through SVCs do not pass IP routing information.* Let us examine what happens in a failure scenario. While the cut-through SVCs are in operation, the link between R6 and destination D fails as step 1. Router R6 determines that the next best path is through R3. R3 still has the cached association indicating that the cut-through SVC through the second ATM network is the best route to D, and forwards the packet back to R5, which then sends it on to R6 and a routing loop forms step 2. Such a stable routing loop is a very bad thing, because once a packet begins looping, it doesn't stop! It's the Massachusetts Transit Authority (MTA) under the streets of Boston, forever (so the song goes).

The "back door" path from R6 to R3 is utilized because R5 is unable to inform R3 through the cut-through SVC that the routing distance to the destination D has changed; if it could, the IP routers would converge on the less desirable low-speed path via R1 through R7 to D. The RFC gives several guidelines for avoiding routing loops, but leaves the automatic avoidance of routing loops as an area for further work. For example, directly connected stations cannot have this problem, since if they become physically disconnected, the ATM cut-through SVC disconnects as well. Another guideline points out the danger of "back door" routes, as illustrated earlier.

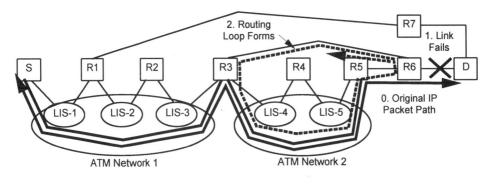

Figure 11.12 Illustration of a Routing Loop in NHRP via a Back Door Path

The draft RFC details other procedures regarding cache time-outs, cache purging, and the handling of error conditions. NHRP also supports optional features, such as route recording to detect loops and address aggregation which allows the protocol to return a subnet mask and consequently identify a range of reachable addresses instead of a single address.

11.7 MULTIPROTOCOL OVER ATM

The ATM Forum initiated the Multiprotocol over ATM (MPOA) work in response to a widespread industry consensus that it was necessary to extend ATM to protocols other than IP (e.g., IPX, Apple Talk, and DECnet) and to enhance native mode protocols. This section gives an overview of the current standards direction and the challenges that still lie ahead in handling MPOA.

11.7.1 MPOA Version 1.0

The ATM Forum worked closely with the IETF in developing the MPOA version 1.0 specification. Drafts of the MPOA specification and ATM Forum member contributions, normally accessible to members only, were made available to the public. This summary is based upon the final version of the MPOA specification [12] and other descriptions [13]. This area of work is an important one for the future.

Figure 11.13 illustrates the components in an MPOA network. LAN Emulation Clients (LECs) interconnect MPOA edge devices (also called hosts) and MPOA-capable routers. An MPOA edge device also contains an MPOA Client (MPC) and a layer 3 forwarding function. Edge devices reside on the periphery of ATM networks, usually supporting traditional LAN interfaces such as Ethernet and Token Ring. Edge devices are capable of bridging with other edge devices and hence can be part of virtual LANs. They also have a limited amount of layer 3 processing capability based upon information fed from MPOA servers. MPOA edge devices do not participate in routing protocols.

On the right-hand side of Figure 11.13, an MPOA-capable router contains a MPOA Server (MPS), which includes the NHRP NHS function and a routing function. MPOA synthesizes bridging and routing with ATM. LAN Emulation (LANE) performs the bridging function, while extensions of the IETF's NHRP perform the layer 3 forwarding function. MPOA separates switching (or forwarding) from routing in a technique called virtual routing. The routing function in MPOA servers exchange topology information and calculate routes, while the edge devices perform the majority of the layer 3 forwarding. Since the edge devices perform layer 3 forwarding, latency is reduced and higher throughput is achieved more cost-effectively than with router-based forwarding capabilities. The NHRP NHS distributes layer 3 forwarding information to MPOA clients via NHRP with the addition of a cache management protocol.

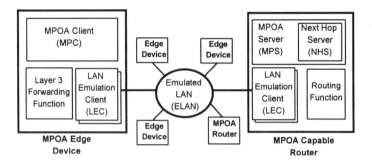

Figure 11.13 MPOA Network Components

MPOA specifies that a single route server may serve multiple edge devices, and that multiple route servers may support a single edge device. This many-to-many mapping provides redundancy for the route server function and eases administration, since route servers are simply configured to join the virtual LAN for the edge devices they serve. MPCs use LANE bridging for communication within their own emulated virtual LAN.

11.7.2 Challenges Ahead

Users with large emulated LANs supporting thousands of clients, such as McDonald's and Amoco [14], require MPOA as soon as possible. Many manufacturers have announced MPOA products, most with proprietary extensions. MPOA offers the promise of true multivendor interoperability of new, high-performance ATM networks with the legacy multiprotocol networks present in today's enterprises.

11.8 IP MULTICAST OVER ATM

IETF RFC 2022 specifies the means to implement multicast over ATM [15], enabling interworking with IP multicast specified in RFC 1112 [16]. The IETF's choice of AAL5 for carriage of IP over ATM has important consequences [17]. An inherent property of AAL5 is that all cells from a packet are transmitted sequentially on a single VCC. This is in sharp contrast to AAL3/4, which has a Multiplex ID (MID) inside each cell, enabling cells from multiple packets to be interleaved on a single VCC. In practice this means that each system must have a separate Segmentation and Reassembly (SAR) engine for each VCC, in either point-to-point or point-to-multipoint configurations. The sequential receipt requirement of AAL5 also means that in a point-to-multipoint connection, transmission is strictly from the root to each of the leaves. If the leaves were to transmit to the root, then cells from multiple packets could be interleaved when arriving at the root, resulting in AAL5 SAR failures and loss of packet data.

The IETF recognized that ATM requires a true multicast capability, since most existing protocols rely upon a broadcast, inherently multicast-capable facility, such as that occurring naturally on an Ethernet. RFC 2022 defines two methods for implementing ATM multicast:

- Multicast server
- Full mesh point-to-multipoint

In the multicast server approach illustrated in Figure 11.14, all nodes join a particular multicast group by setting up a point-to-point connection with a Multicast Server (MCS). The MCS may have a point-to-multipoint connection as shown in the figure, or alternatively it may emulate the broadcast connection via a set of point-to-point connections. The MCS receives packets from each of the nodes on the point-to-point connections and then retransmits them either on the return direction of the point-to-point connection, or across the point-to-multipoint connection. This design ensures that the serialization requirement of AAL5 is met, that is, all cells of an entire packet are transmitted prior to any other cells being sent.

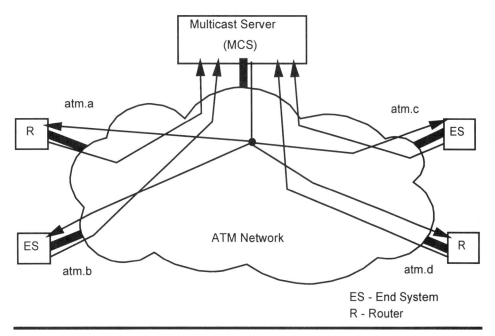

Figure 11.14 Multicast Server ATM Multicast Option

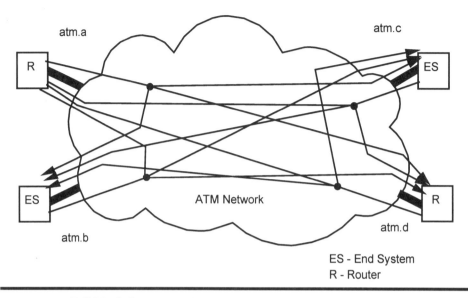

atm.a

atm.c

R

ES

ES

ATM Network

R

atm.b

atm.d

ES - End System
R - Router

Figure 11.15 Full-Mesh Point-to-Multipoint ATM Multicast Option

The full-mesh point-to-multipoint connection approach, illustrated in Figure 11.15, involves establishment of a point-to-multipoint connection between every node in the multicast group. Hence, as seen from inspection of the figure, every node is able to transmit to and receive from every other node.

Each of these approaches has advantages and disadvantages for a multicast group of N nodes. The point-to-multipoint mechanism requires each node to maintain N connections for each group, while the multicast server mechanism requires at the most two connections per node. The point-to-multipoint method places a connection burden on each of the nodes and the ATM network, while the multicast server approach requires that only the server support a large number of connections. Hence, the multicast server mechanism is more scalable in terms of being able to dynamically change multicast group membership, but presents a potential bottleneck and a single point of failure in ATM networks supporting IP multicast.

IP multicast over ATM utilizes the Unspecified Bit Rate (UBR), or best effort ATM service class as specified in RFC 1755. The current RFC does not define how to request a guaranteed ATM quality of service.

RFC 2022 supports IP multicast requirements [16] using a Multicast Address Resolution Server (MARS) connected to a cluster of end system nodes via another point-to-point VCC as shown in Figure 11.16. The separate VCC is required to separate address resolution and connection setup messages from the multicast application packets, since they cannot be interleaved on AAL5. End systems employing SVCs are configured with the ATM address of the MARS. The MARS keeps mappings of IP multicast addresses to a list of ATM addresses that are currently members of the particular multicast group. The IP multicast over ATM protocol allows end systems that operate on Ethernets to seamlessly interoperate with ATM end systems.

11.9 REINVENTING IP OVER ATM

Recently, network-layer switching has emerged on the scene, biting at the heels of LAN switching in the continual quest to improve networking price-performance. Network switches operate at the edges of backbone networks with the goal of performing routing and switching decisions only once, and not for every packet that is sent through the network to the same destination. While the IP and ATM standards bodies were developing the protocols described earlier in this section, manufacturers were building better mousetraps in response to the tremendous growth in IP internetworking. Interestingly, these manufacturers published at least an overview of their approach in IETF informational RFCs, in addition to issuing public proclamations that their approach would be an open, nonproprietary solution. The first company to break with the momentum and direction of the standards bodies was a start-up company in Silicon Valley, Ipsilon Networks, whose IP switching approach proposed placing IP over ATM on a strict protocol efficiency diet. A similar approach from Toshiba proposed cell switch routers for efficiently interconnecting classical IP over ATM and MPOA networks.

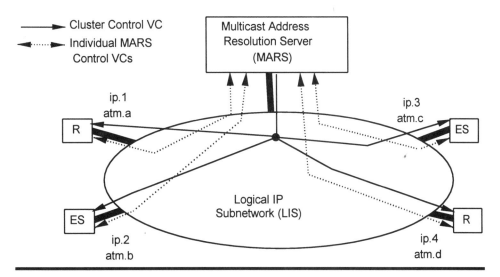

Figure 11.16 Multicast Address Resolution Server

The latest entrant onto the scene is Cisco Systems' Tag Switching architecture, which works with not only ATM but a number of legacy technologies as well. The IETF has now formed a Multiprotocol Label Switching (MPLS) working group to sort this all out and come up with a common standard. The following sections present a brief overview of each approach, concluding with a comparison of the various approaches. We cover the other competing alternatives composed of switched 100-Mbps Ethernets and gigabit Ethernets in Part 6.

11.9.1 Ipsilon's IP Switching

Beginning in 1995, Ipsilon Networks introduced a fresh idea into the industry. The company accurately asserted that ATM had already lost the battle for the desktop to Fast Ethernet, that LANE did little more than LAN switching, and that the software burden of the complex ATM protocols made proposing IP implementations over ATM prohibitive [18]. Furthermore, Ipsilon's publications questioned the direction of the ATM Forum and the IETF — LANE, NHRP, MPOA, and the entire approach for implementing IP over ATM. They pointed out duplication of function, scaling problems, and difficulties in multicast implementations. The answer to all of these problems was a simplified form of IP over ATM that Ipsilon called IP switching.

Ipsilon also rediscovered the original intent of the Internet and published the key aspects of its protocol in Internet RFCs 1953, 1954, and 1987. This bold move made the aspects of the protocol open not only to all manufacturers, not only were the algorithms available to hosts and routers that would use Ipsilon's devices, but to competitors as well. The company even made source code available to the research community free of charge. This was definitely a different approach.

The basic philosophy of Ipsilon's approach was to classify traffic into short- and long-lived flows. The IP switching approach applied only to the longer-duration flows, such as FTP, long TELNET sessions, HTTP, and extended Web multimedia sessions. IP switching now handled short-lived, interactive traffic, such as DNS, E-mail, and SNMP, in exactly the way IP routers handle it today.

In order for IP switching to improve performance, a majority of the total traffic must be in long-lived flows. If the majority of the traffic were in short-lived flows, then the performance of IP switching is no better than that of routers. A number of studies published by Ipsilon of corporate networks indicate that although a high percentage of flows are of short duration, these short-lived flows carry a small percentage of the overall packet traffic. Indeed, these studies report that the small number of long-lived flows carry the majority of packet traffic.

Figure 11.17 illustrates the components, interfaces, and protocols of Ipsilon's IP switching functional architecture [19]. An IP switch is composed of two logical components: an ATM switch and an IP switch controller. Any ATM switch with a switch controller capable of making and breaking hundreds of virtual channel connections per second can be part of an IP switch. Ipsilon manufactures IP switch controllers, which connect via an ATM User-Network Interface (UNI) to the ATM switch, and multiplexes ATM cells at the VCC level to an IP router and Ipsilon protocol controllers. ATM UNIs connect the IP switch to a number of upstream and downstream nodes as indicated in the figure. Nodes (i.e., hosts or routers) connect to interfaces carrying IP data packets. These nodes must be capable of adding labels to IP packets, as well as multiplexing various flows of IP packets associated with the labels onto different VCCs. These nodes interface to the IP switch controller via Ipsilon's Flow Management Protocol (IFMP) as specified in IETF RFCs 1953 [20] and 1954 [21], as the text below describes in an example. The IP switch controller also implements a Generic Switch Management Protocol (GSMP) as specified in RFC 1987 [22], to make and break ATM VCC connections through interaction with the ATM switch's controller.

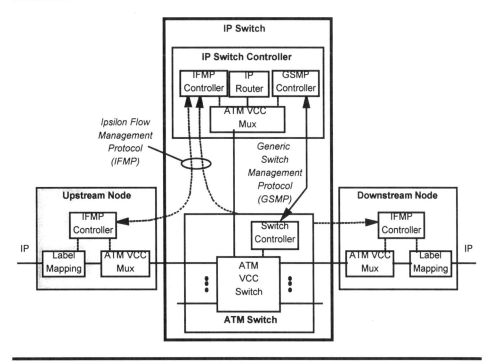

Figure 11.17 Ipsilon Networks IP Switching Architecture

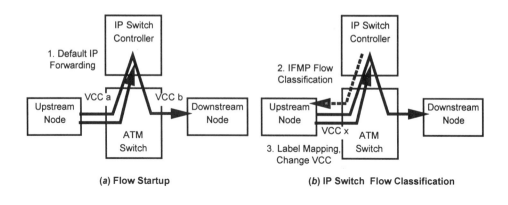

Figure 11.18 Ipsilon IP Switching Example (1 of 2)

Figures 11.18 and 11.19 illustrate the operation of Ipsilon's IP switching and protocols through a simple example [18, 19]. Initially, each IP node sets up a default forwarding VCC a to the IP switch controller's IP router in step 1, which forwards the packet to the next hop on VCC b as determined by standard IP routing protocols. Simultaneously, the IP switch controller performs flow classification by detecting long-lived sequences of IP packets sent between a particular source and destination address pair employing the same protocol type (e.g., UDP or TCP) and type of service, as determined from the IP packet header. Once the IP switch controller identifies a long-lived flow as a candidate for optimization, its IFMP controller requests that the upstream node label the traffic for that flow and use a VCC x different from the default forwarding VCC a (steps 2 and 3). If the upstream node's IFMP controller concurs, then the flow begins on the new VCC x, which is still handled by the IP router in the IP switch controller.

Independently, the downstream node may request via IFMP that the IP switch controller set up an outgoing VCC for the same flow (steps 4 and 5). The IP switch controller responds to the downstream node and directs the flow to VCC y, which differs from the default forwarding VCC b. Finally, in step 6 the IP switch controller's GSMP process instructs the ATM switch's controller to connect the ATM VCCs between the upstream and downstream nodes, thereby removing the IP router from the IP packet data path.

Ipsilon claims that first-generation IP switches using their approach support throughputs of over 5 million packets per second using the above protocols. Flow classification and switching are local, soft-state decisions that time out within seconds unless refreshed. Hence, the system is resilient to failures. Additionally, flow characterization allows IP Switches to allocate quality of service to different flows in conjunction with ATM switch QoS capabilities. Also, IP switches support IP multicast transparently.

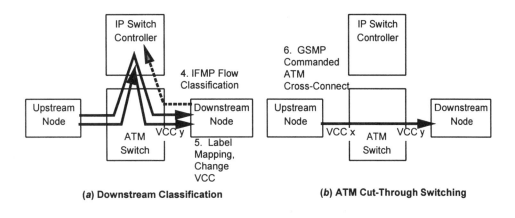

(a) Downstream Classification   (b) ATM Cut-Through Switching

Figure 11.19 Ipsilon IP Switching Example (2 of 2)

11.9.2 Toshiba's Cell Switch Router

RFC 2098 [23] describes another vendor proprietary proposal for handing IP over ATM networks. Further insights are also given in a white paper by Toshiba [24]. A Cell Switch Router (CSR) has ATM cell switching capabilities in addition to conventional IP datagram routing and forwarding, as illustrated in Figure 11.20. Note that this architecture is very similar to Ipsilon's IP switch at this functional block diagram level.

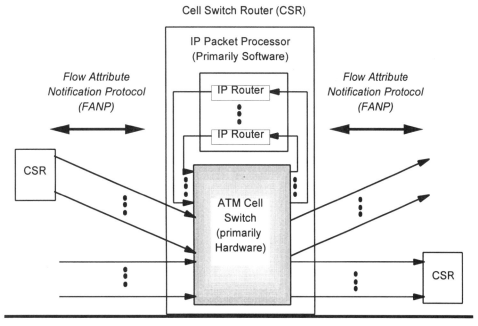

Figure 11.20 Toshiba Cell Switch Router (CSR) Architecture

The routing function in the CSR normally forwards IP datagrams along hop-by-hop paths via a routing function, exactly as in the IP switching approach. The routing function automatically recognizes long-lived flows and either assigns or establishes efficient cut-through ATM paths, similar to IP switching again. But CSR adds several new concepts. First, it proposes to handle more than the IP protocol. Second, it allows cut-through connections to be pre-configured, or established via interaction with RSVP. CSR also proposes setting up cut-through routes that may bypass several routers. CSRs interact using a Flow Attribute Notification Protocol (FANP) as indicated in the figure. CSRs also implement standard IP routing protocols, the ATM Forum PNNI protocol, and ATM signaling.

The CSR proposal also focuses strongly on meeting application-specific QoS and bandwidth requirements, even over non-ATM networks. Furthermore, CSR purports to interconnect classical IP over ATM, MPOA, and switched IP networks [24], as illustrated in Figure 11.21. One of CSR's goals is to internetwork these various flavors of IP over ATM at much higher throughput than the current interconnection methods, as indicated by the thicker lines in the figure. The current RFC gives only an overview of the CSR approach, and further details must be specified before interoperable implementations can be specified.

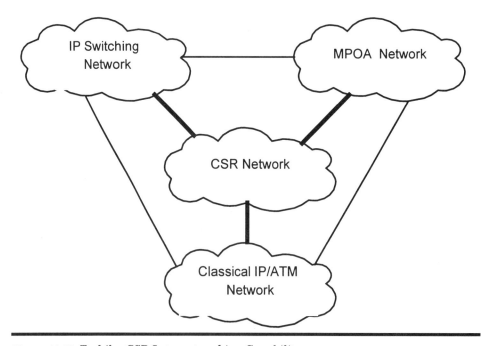

Figure 11.21 Toshiba CSR Internetworking Capability

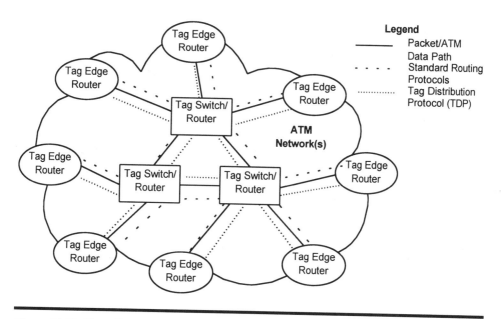

Figure 11.22 Cisco Systems' Tag Switching Architecture

11.9.3 Cisco's Tag Switching

Now, just when it appears that all major problems are solved about IP over ATM, someone comes up with a different idea, albeit better in some respects. Cisco announced its tag switching architecture in September 1996. A white paper on Cisco's Web page [25] and informational RFC 2105 [26] give an overview of the architecture and protocols involved in tag switching. Figure 11.22 illustrates the basic components and interfaces of Cisco's tag switching architecture in an ATM network environment. Tag edge routers at the boundaries of an ATM network provide network-layer services and apply tags to packets. Tag switches/routers at the core of the network switch tagged packets or cells based upon tags determined via information piggybacked on to standard routing protocols, or via Cisco's Tag Distribution Protocol (TDP). Tag switch/routers and tag edge routers implement standard network-layer routing protocols, such as OSPF and Border Gateway Protocol (BGP), as shown in the figure. Additionally, they implement TDP in conjunction with standard network-layer routing protocols to distribute tag information.

Tag switching is a high-performance packet forwarding technique based on the concept of label swapping. A label is a generic name for a header. By swapping labels at intermediate nodes, an end-to-end connection results. Since ATM VCC switching directly implements a special case of the general label swapping using the VPI/VCI fields in the cell header, the switch/routers know whether to switch cells or assemble the cells and route the resultant packets based upon information derived from TDP.

Tag switching operates as follows. First, tag edge routers run standard routing protocols and populate their next-hop tables with the most desirable routes based upon the routing criteria, such as the destination prefix. Tag routers and switches utilize these next-hop tables and distribute VCC tag information via TDP. Tag edge routers examine network-layer headers of received packets, perform network services (e.g., filtering), select a next-hop route, and then apply a tag. For example, a tag edge router may apply a VCC tag such that several tag switch/routers may switch the cells directly through to the destination tag edge router *without performing any routing*! At the destination edge router the tag is removed; that is, the packet is reassembled and forwarded to the destination.

Since this destination-based forwarding approach is topology-driven, rather than traffic-driven, tag switching does not require high call setup rates or depend on the longevity of flows to achieve increased throughput. Tag switching makes ATM switches peers of other routers since they participate in standard network-layer routing protocols with edge routers.

11.9.4 Comparison of Alternative IP over ATM Approaches

Table 11.3 compares some key attributes of these alternative vendor proposals in support of IP (and other network-layer internetworking protocols) over ATM. Some of the assessments are subjective, since details for some of these protocols are still being defined and published.

Table 11.3 Comparison of Alternative IP/ATM Protocols

Attribute	Ipsilon's IP Switching	Toshiba's Cell Switch Router (CSR)	Cisco Systems' Tag Switching
Throughput	High	Potentially very high	Medium to high
Throughput sensitivity to traffic	Degrades for short-lived flows	Degrades for short-lived flows	None
Scope	Link-by-link	Link or subnetwork	Edge-to-edge
Hierarchy	None	None	Standard routing
Mapping basis	Long-lived flows	Long-lived flows or preconfigured	Derived from routing topology
State persistence	Soft, refresh required	Soft, refresh required	Hard, tied to network routing protocol
Required VCC setup connection rate	High	High	Low
Complexity	Low	High	Medium

11.10 ATM NAME SYSTEM

The ATM Forum adopted the DNS concept from the Internet to resolve names into ATM addresses in ATM Name Service (ANS) [27]. Both NSAP-based and E.164 ATM addresses are supported. In the Internet, a DNS resolves a host name and organization in an E-mail address (i.e., user@host_name.org) to an IP address. Most human beings find it easier to remember a name rather than a number. There are exceptions among us, such as those capable of rattling off IP addresses and other numeric data more readily than their own children's names; however, you won't likely encounter them at too many cocktail parties.

ANS is a native ATM application defined by the Native ATM Services (NAS) API that employs ATM SVCs for clients to communicate with ANS servers. The protocol also specifies the means for servers to communicate in the processing of providing service to ANS clients. The basic directory services defined in ANS are:

- Domain name–to–ATM address translation using existing top-level domain names
- ATM address–to–domain name translation using a new domain name, ATMA.INT

Figure 11.23 illustrates the operation of the ANS protocol. In the first step, ANS clients either get the ATM address of an ANS server via the Integrated Local Management Interface (ILMI) or use a well-known ANS address. In step 2, an ANS client sets up a connection to an ANS server using the SVC procedure, using the address determined in step 1. Once the client establishes a connection with the server, it can send ANS requests in step 3, to which the ANS server responds. The ATM Forum specification advises that the client and server should release the connection if no activity occurs for a long period of time (e.g., minutes) so that other clients may access the ANS server.

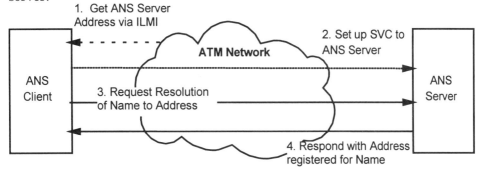

Figure 11.23 Illustration of DNS Lookup of ATM Address from ATM Name

11.11 NATIVE ATM SERVICE SEMANTICS

The ATM Forum defines a set of services available to higher-layer applications in its NAS Semantic Description [28]. This document articulates the services available to higher-level application programs independently of any programming language or operating system environment. Hence, the ATM Forum's document is *not* an Application Programming Interface (API), which is a set of software libraries/interfaces that enable applications to use their native language to access lower-level functional modules, such as operating systems, graphical user interfaces, and communication protocols. Instead, the ATM Forum's stated objective is to influence the development of API interfaces, such as Microsoft's Winsock version 2.0 and the X/Open Transport Interface (XTI) protocol for UNIX and Apple machines. Apple and Fore Systems announced that they plan to ship ATM API software in 1997 supporting both the Winsock and XTI protocols.

Note that legacy applications don't require ATM, and new applications requiring ATM have been slow to emerge. Legacy equipment not built for ATM may require upgrades or even replacement to utilize native ATM capabilities. This presents a dilemma, since unless the underlying operating system provides access to native ATM capabilities, application developers cannot develop applications to take advantage of ATM.

Figure 11.24 illustrates the ATM Forum NAS reference model. The model applies between the API interfaces and the ATM UNI services lines indicated in the figure. These could be implemented in an operating systems kernel, a PBX, or an ATM switch. Native ATM services include the following:

- Data transfer, supporting both reliable and unreliable delivery modes employing both ATM and ATM adaptation layers
- Means for specifying the parameters and setting up SVCs
- Means for specifying the parameters and setting up PVCs
- Means for supporting traffic management capabilities, such as different service categories and quality of service guarantees
- Distribution of connections and associated data to the associated application – a multiplexing/demultiplexing function, for example — using the higher- and lower-layer information elements in signaling messages
- Means for participation in ATM network management, such as the ILMI and Operations, Administration, and Management (OAM) cell functions

Good news for native ATM APIs is just over the horizon, however [29]. Winsock version 2 provides support for much of what is required to utilize ATM features, and the XTI protocol standard used by UNIX and Apple will provide QoS support. In 1997 Winsock 2 began shipping with Windows NT version 4, and XTI extended support for ATM was available as well. The next enabler for ATM is for independent software vendors to use these APIs as the basis for mainstream applications. Something of the old chicken-and-egg situation also exists for ATM-aware applications. Many report that since no applications require or support ATM, many users don't see compelling reasons for networking ATM to the desktop. Many early ATM adopters are putting in ATM networks in anticipation of its supporting real-time inter-active applications better than any other alternative on the horizon. The linchpin will likely be popular applications that run better over an all-ATM network than over networks of routers and LAN switches supporting other protocols.

The introduction of ATM may move the bottleneck from the network to the PC/workstation adapters. The speeds easily supported by ATM may tax software and drivers on adapters and workstations. Furthermore, there may be timing problems in supporting synchronous traffic. A next generation of workstations with hardware assists may be necessary to fulfill the vision of true end-to-end multimedia networked applications. Many factors will decide the issue: costs, dependability, manageability, ease of support, marketing skill of vendors, etc.

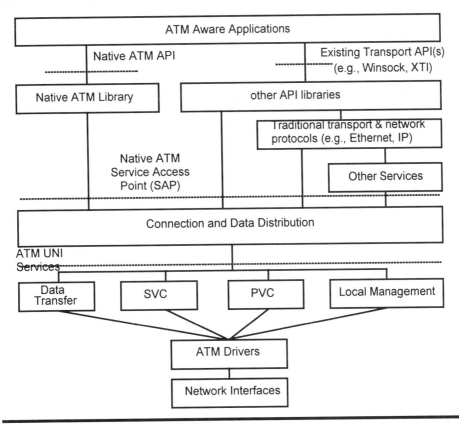

Figure 11.24 Native ATM Services (NAS) Reference Model

11.12 REVIEW

This chapter moved up the protocol stack to the network layer by providing a short primer on IP addressing and subnetworks followed by a brief introduction to routing protocols. Building up the protocol stack, we then covered how systems can encapsulate multiple protocols over ATM as well as ensure efficient operation through proper negotiation of the maximum transfer unit size in hybrid networks. We then covered the simplest design supporting a single Logical IP subnetwork (LIS) over ATM employing the classical IP over ATM protocol. As background we then introduced the next-hop resolution protocol designed by the IETF to support larger internetworks involving multiple IP subnets. We then reviewed the latest output from the IETF and the ATM Forum, the MPOA standard, which promises to provide multivendor, interoperable, high-performance internets using an ATM-based infrastructure. The text also presented an overview of how the inherently nonbroadcast ATM infrastructure supports IP multicast over ATM.

Then recent industry innovations supporting IP over ATM were reviewed and compared, in particular, Ipsilon's IP switching, Toshiba's cell switching router and Cisco's tag switching. Unlike the standards-based implementations, these proprietary schemes require the same equipment throughout the network. Whatever the future brings, the cross-fertilization afforded by the exchange of ideas between the ATM Forum, the IETF, and the Internet manufacturers will benefit everyone. Finally, we concluded with some recent work that extends native ATM capabilities to applications through the ATM name system and the native ATM service API.

11.13 REFERENCES

[1]   Y. Rekhter, *CIDR and Classful Routing*, IETF, August 1995.
[2]   Y. Rechter and T. Li, *An Architecture for IP Address Allocation with CIDR*, IETF, September 1993.
[3]   V. Fuller, T. Li, J. Yu, and K. Varadhan, *Classless Inter-Domain Routing (CIDR): An Address Assignment and Aggregation Strategy*, IETF, September 1993.
[4]   A. Tannenbaum, *Computer Communications*, 3d ed., Prentice-Hall, 1996.
[5]   D. Spohn, *Data Network Design*, 2d ed., McGraw-Hill, 1997.
[6]   J. Heinanen, *RFC 1483: Multiprotocol Encapsulation over ATM Adaptation Layer 5*, IETF, July 1993.
[7]   R. Atkinson, *RFC 1626: Default IP MTU for Use over ATM AAL 5*, IETF, May 1994.
[8]   J. Mogul and S. Deering, *RFC 1191: Path MTU Discovery*, IETF, November 1990.
[9]   M. Laubach, *RFC 1577: Classical IP and ARP over ATM*, IETF, January 1994.
[10] T. Bradley and C. Brown, *RFC1293: Inverse Address Resolution Protocol*, IETF, January 1992.

[11] J. Luciani, D. Katz, and D. Piscitello, *NBMA Next Hop Resolution Protocol (NHRP)*, 10/1/1996, IETF draft-ietf-rolc-nhrp-10.txt.

[12] ATM Forum, *Multi-Protocol Over ATM*, Version 1.0, ATM Forum/BTD-MPOA-MPOA-01.13 Draft, February 1997.

[13] G. Swallow, "MPOA, VLANS and Distributed Routers," *ATM Forum 53 Bytes*, Volume 4, Issue 3, 1996.

[14] E. Nolley, "MPOA Goes Under the Microscope at User Panel Discussion", *ATM Forum 53 Bytes*, Volume 4, Issue 3, 1996.

[15] G. Armitage, *RFC 2022: Support for Multicast over UNI 3.0/3.1 based ATM Networks*, IETF, November 1996.

[16] S. Deering, *RFC 1112: Host Extensions for IP Multicasting*, IETF, August 1992.

[17] A. Alles, "ATM Interworking," http://cio.cisco.com/warp/public/614/12.html.

[18] Newman, T. Lyon, and G. Minshall, "Flow Labelled IP: Connectionless ATM Under IP," Networld + Interop Presentation, April 1996, ttp://www.ipsilon.com/staff/pn/presentations/interop96.

[19] Ipsilon Networks, "IP Switching: The Intelligence of Routing, the Performance of Switching," February 1996.

[20] *RFC 1953, Ipsilon Flow Management Protocol*, IETF, May 1996.

[21] *RFC 1954, The Transmission of Flow Labelled IPv4 on ATM Data Links*, IETF, May 1996.

[22] RFC 1987, *Ipsilon General Switch Management Protocol*, IETF, August 1996.

[23] Y. Katsube, K. Nagami, and H. Esaki, *RFC 2098: Toshiba's Router Architecture Extensions for ATM: Overview*, IETF, February 1997.

[24] H. Esaki, Y. Katsube, S. Matsuzawa, A. Mogi, K. Nagami, and T. Jinmei, *Cell Switch Router*, Version 1.0, Toshiba, November 1996.

[25] Cisco Systems, "Scaling the Internet with Tag Switching," http://www.cisco.com/warp/public/732/tag/pjtag_wp.html, 2/4/97.

[26] Y. Rekhter, B. Davie, D. Katz, E. Rosen, and G. Swallow, *RFC 2105: Cisco Systems' Tag Switching Architecture Overview*, IETF, February 1997.

[27] ATM Forum, *ATM Name System Specification*, Version 1.0, af-saa-0069.000, November 1996.

[28] ATM Forum, *Native ATM Services: Semantic Description*, Version 1.0, af-saa-0048-000, February 1996.

[29] R. Jeffries, "Three Roads to Quality of Service: ATM, RSVP, and CIF," *Telecommunications*, April 1996.

12

Managing and Testing It All

With any new network technology, management of the network typically follows network in implementation, and ATM is no exception. Standardization of management protocols and interfaces, as well as implementation, lags behind network capabilities. Many standards exist at the ATM layer; however, they largely treat the ATM network in a manner similar to private lines by using Operations, Administration, and Maintenance (OAM) cells. Another set of network management standards focuses on the multivendor management model incubated in the Internet using management information bases and the Simple Network Management Protocol. Carrier-oriented standards and implementations look to the ITU-T and the ATM Forum for guidance and normally use the competing Common Management Interface Protocol. Despite all of the standardization activity, proprietary network management system implementations exhibit the most advanced features available today. However, a number of companies plan to offer full-featured, standards-based, multivendor management systems. Or there are the options of outsourcing or outtasking. Thus an experienced company can manage your network. Finally, we cover the important matter of testing to ensure that the ATM equipment meets specifications, and will interoperate in a multivendor environment. This chapter explores the state of managing and testing ATM networks today, and provides a road map for the future.

12.1 NETWORK MANAGEMENT PRINCIPLES

This section introduces the overarching principles of ATM network management. We will then describe the concept of functional layers defined by the ITU-T standards, which involves managing the hybrid of transmission and ATM layers using operational flows. In the physical transmission media layers, overhead fields carry these flows, while in the ATM virtual path and virtual channel levels, OAM cells carry these flows.

12.1.1 OSI Fault Management Functional Areas

OSI defines five generic functional areas for network management, commonly abbreviated as "FCAPS" [1]:

◆ Fault management
◆ Configuration management
◆ Accounting management
◆ Performance management
◆ Security management

Currently, ATM OAM-based management primarily covers fault management and performance management. Some aspects of configuration management, fault management, and performance management are covered by ATM Forum specifications, the ATM Forum Integrated Local Management Interface (ILMI), and the IETF-defined Management Information Bases (MIBs). Unfortunately, a great deal of work still remains in configuration and accounting management. Work in fault management is the most mature, and meets the minimum requirements for initial ATM deployment.

12.1.2 Operations, Administration, and Maintenance Flows

The ITU-T defines OAM flows for SONET/SDH and the ATM layer [2]. Figure 12.1 shows a real-world example of end-to-end OAM flows for an end-to-end ATM Virtual Channel Connection (VCC) connecting two end systems.

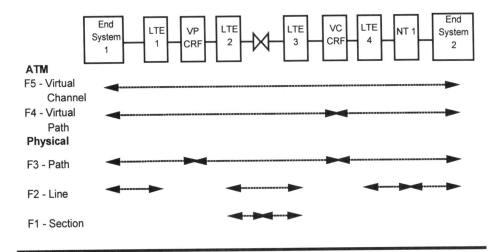

Figure 12.1 Illustrative Example of OAM Flow Layering

Starting from the left-hand side, end system 1 is connected to Lightwave Terminal Equipment (LTE) 1, which terminates the digital section OAM flow (F2). The transmission path flow (F3) terminates on the Virtual Path (VP) Cell Relaying Function (CRF). The VP flow (F4) passes through the VP CRF, since it is only a connection point; that is, only the Virtual Path Identifier (VPI) value changes in cells that pass through that specific VP. The Virtual Channel Identifier (VCI) value is not changed.

Next, the example traverses a typical transmission path across the wide area network from LTE 2 to LTE 3 through a repeater (indicated by the "bow tie" symbol in Figure 12.1). The regenerator section flow (F1) operates between LTEs 2 and 3 and the repeater, as well as between repeaters. The OAM flow between LTE 2 and LTE 3 is an example of a digital section flow (F2). The transmission path (F3) flow terminates on the VC CRF. The VP flow (F4) also terminates on the VC CRF because in its relaying function it can change the VCI as well as the VPI. A separate digital section OAM flow (F2) then extends from LTE4 to a Customer Premises Equipment (CPE) device (NT 1) as another line flow (F2). The OAM flow to end system 2 from NT 1 is also a digital section level flow (F2). The transmission path flow (F3) extends from VC CRF to end system 2, as does the VP flow (F4) since the VPI cannot change in this portion of the connection. Finally, note that the Virtual Channel (VC) flow (F5) is preserved from end system 1 to end system 2.

12.2 ATM-LAYER MANAGEMENT

The ATM-layer management standards define cells with a special format, called OAM cells, for VP flows (F4) and VC flows (F5) on either an end-to-end or a switch-to-switch (i.e., segment) basis.

Figure 12.2 depicts the format of these special F4 and F5 OAM cells, illustrating the specific coding used to distinguish end-to-end and segment flows within a virtual path or a virtual connection. Note that this use of VCIs within a virtual path and use of Payload Type (PT) within a virtual channel forces OAM cells to implicitly follow the same sequence of switches as user cells. This fact enables many of the ATM OAM functions covered below.

Standards define generic types of OAM functions and specific functions within them as follows:

- Fault management
  - Alarm indication signal/remote defect indication
  - Loopback
  - Continuity check
- Performance management
  - Forward reporting
  - Backward reporting
  - Monitoring and reporting

F4 (VPC) OAM Cell Format

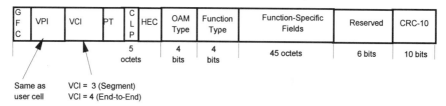

F5 (VCC) OAM Cell Format

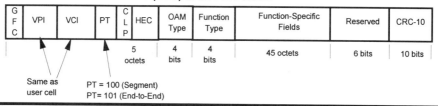

Figure 12.2 ATM OAM Cell Types and Format

  ✍ Activation/deactivation
     ☞ Performance monitoring
     ☞ Continuity check

Each of these generic types is covered briefly as well as how they are used to manage real ATM networks.

12.2.1 Fault Management

Fault management determines when there is a failure, notifying other elements of the connection regarding the failure and providing the means to diagnose and isolate the failure. Let's consider an analogy for fault management with vehicular traffic where the road itself actually fails! For example, imagine a divided highway with separate bridges crossing a river. A flash flood may wash out one or both of the bridges. The vehicles crossing one bridge cannot see the other bridge because this is very rugged country. The motorists who just passed over the bridge and saw it collapse will travel to the next police station and report the bridge failure. If both bridges wash out, then the police know they must divert traffic away from the bridge in both directions. If the bridge washes out in one direction, then the failure must be reported in one direction, and another vehicle must travel across the remaining bridge in the other direction in order to divert traffic away from the failed bridge. This example illustrates the basic principle of Alarm Indication Signal (AIS) and Remote Defect Indication (RDI) [also called Far End Reporting Failure (FERF)] shown in Figure 12.3. We cover two failure cases: (a) the failure occurs in both directions simultaneously, and (b) the failure occurs in only one direction. In both examples there is a VP (or VC) connection between node 1 and node 4.

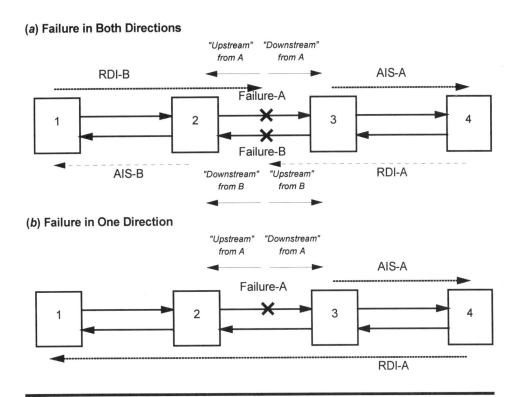

(a) Failure in Both Directions

(b) Failure in One Direction

Figure 12.3 Illustration of AIS and RDI/FERF Theory and Operation

Figure 12.3*a* illustrates a typical failure in both directions of the physical layer between nodes 2 and 3 that causes the underlying VPs and VCs to simultaneously fail. The failures in each direction are indicated as "Failure-A" and "Failure-B" in the figure so that the resulting AIS and RDI/FERF cells can be traced to the failure location. A node adjacent to the failure generates an AIS signal in the downstream direction to indicate that an upstream failure has occurred, as indicated in the figure. As can be seen from example *a*, both ends of the connection (nodes 1 and 4) are aware of the failure because of the AIS alarm that they receive. However, by convention, each generates an RDI/FERF signal.

Example *b* in the same figure illustrates the purpose of the FERF (or RDI) signal. In most communications applications the connection should be considered failed even if it fails in only one direction. This is especially true in data communications where each packet often requires acknowledgment in the reverse direction. Example *b* illustrates the case of a failure that affects only one direction of a full-duplex connection between nodes 2 and 3. Node 3, which is downstream from the failure, generates an AIS alarm, which propagates to the connection end (node 4), which in turn generates the RDI/FERF signal. The RDI/FERF signal propagates to the other connection end (node 1), which is now aware that the connection has failed. Without the

RDI/FERF signal, node 1 would not be aware that there was a failure in the connection between nodes 2 and 3. This method will also detect any combination of single-direction failures. Note that the node(s) that generate the AIS signals know exactly where the failure is, and could report this to a centralized network management system or take a distributed rerouting response.

Figure 12.4 illustrates how the segment and end-to-end loopback cells can be used to diagnose a failure that AIS and RDI/FERF cannot. An example of such a failure would be a misconfigured VP or VC Permanent Virtual Connection (PVC). The example shows two endpoints and two intervening networks, each with three nodes. Part *a* shows the verification of end-to-end continuity via an end-to-end loopback to endpoint 1. If this were to fail, then network 2 could diagnose the problem as follows. Part *b* shows verification of connectivity between a node in network 2 and endpoint 2 via an end-to-end loopback. If this fails, then the problem is between network 2 and endpoint 2. Part *c* shows verification of connectivity to endpoint 1 via an end-to-end loopback. If this fails, there is a problem in the link between endpoint 1 and network 1, a problem in network 1, or a problem in the link between networks 1 and 2. Part *d* shows verification of connectivity across networks 1 and 2 via a segment loopback. If this succeeds, then the problem is the access line from endpoint 1 to network 1. Part *e* shows verification of connectivity from entry to exit in network 1. If this succeeds, then the problem is in network 1. Verification within any of the networks could also be done using the segment loopback.

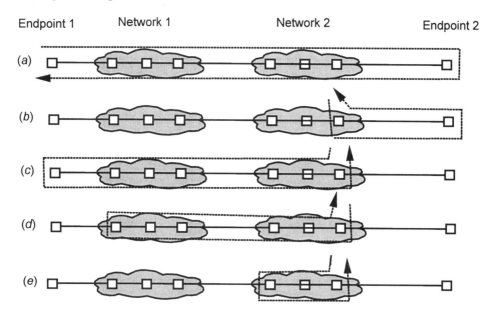

Figure 12.4 Usage of Loopback in Verification/Problem Diagnosis

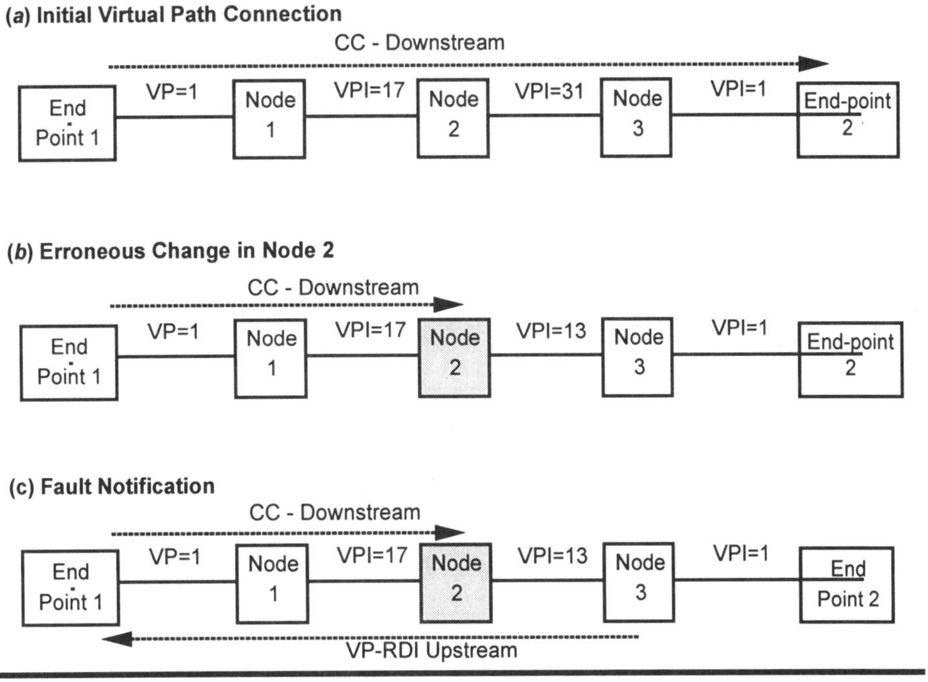

(a) Initial Virtual Path Connection

CC - Downstream

```
                    VP=1            VPI=17           VPI=31           VPI=1
┌─────────┐      ┌──────┐      ┌──────┐      ┌──────┐      ┌──────────┐
│  End    │      │ Node │      │ Node │      │ Node │      │ End-point│
│ Point 1 │      │  1   │      │  2   │      │  3   │      │    2     │
└─────────┘      └──────┘      └──────┘      └──────┘      └──────────┘
```

(b) Erroneous Change in Node 2

CC - Downstream

```
                    VP=1            VPI=17           VPI=13           VPI=1
┌─────────┐      ┌──────┐      ┌──────┐      ┌──────┐      ┌──────────┐
│  End    │      │ Node │      │ Node │      │ Node │      │ End-point│
│ Point 1 │      │  1   │      │  2   │      │  3   │      │    2     │
└─────────┘      └──────┘      └──────┘      └──────┘      └──────────┘
```

(c) Fault Notification

CC - Downstream

```
                    VP=1            VPI=17           VPI=13           VPI=1
┌─────────┐      ┌──────┐      ┌──────┐      ┌──────┐      ┌─────────┐
│  End    │      │ Node │      │ Node │      │ Node │      │   End   │
│ Point 1 │      │  1   │      │  2   │      │  3   │      │ Point 2 │
└─────────┘      └──────┘      └──────┘      └──────┘      └─────────┘
```

VP-RDI Upstream

Figure 12.5 Illustration of Continuity Check OAM Cell Usage

The idea behind the continuity check cell is that the endpoint sends a cell periodically at some predetermined interval if no other traffic is sent on the connection so that the connecting points and the other endpoint can distinguish between a connection that is idle and one that has failed. Continuity checking is activated and deactivated by the procedures that we described earlier. The continuity check detects failures that AIS cannot, such as an erroneous VP cross-connect change as illustrated in Figure 12.5. Part *a* shows a VP connection traversing three VP cross-connect nodes with VPI mappings shown in the figure carrying only Continuity Check (CC) cell traffic downstream, interleaved with the user's VP cells. In part *b* an erroneous cross-connect is made at node 2, shown shaded in the figure, interrupting the flow of CC cells. In part *c* node 3 detects this continuity failure and generates a VP-RDI/FERF OAM cell in the opposite (upstream) direction.

12.2.2 Performance Management

Figure 12.6 illustrates the operation of the performance measurement (PM) OAM in cell insertion and processing. The connection or segment endpoints A and B that are involved are determined by the activation/deactivation procedure. In this example the PM cell flow in each direction has different block sizes, every 4 cells from left to right, and every 2 cells from right to left. The functions involved are insertion of OAM cells, counting user cells, and computing the BIP-16 parity on the transmit side. On the receive side, OAM cells are extracted. The same counts are made, and the BIP-16 parity is recomputed for comparison with the value received in the monitoring cell as determined by the transmitter. Note that the monitoring cell contains the results for the cells in the preceding block.

Performance monitoring OAM cells detect the following types of impairments on ATM virtual path and channel connections:

☞ Missing or lost cells
☞ Many bit error patterns
☞ Extra or misinserted cells
☞ Delay and delay variation

Higher-level network management systems can then utilize this data to determine if the desired ATM-level Quality of Service (QoS) is being delivered. Calculations based upon the above measurements readily estimate ATM quality of service parameters, such as Cell Loss Ratio (CLR), Cell Error Ratio (CER), and Cell Transfer Delay (CTD). Another means to estimate QoS is to connect ATM test equipment to test connections in the same service category that traverse the same switches and trunks that user cells traverses.

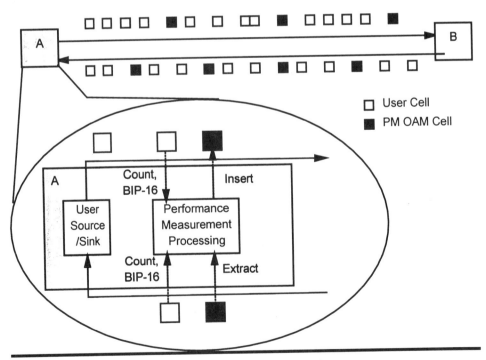

Figure 12.6 ATM OAM Performance Measurement Procedure

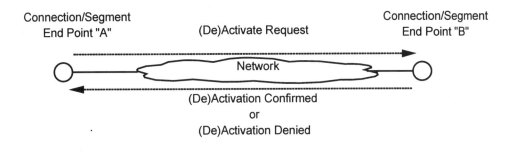

Figure 12.7 Illustration of Activation/Deactivation Flow

12.2.3 Activation/Deactivation

Figure 12.7 illustrates the activation/deactivation procedure for performance monitoring or continuity checking. In the example, connection/segment endpoint A generates a De(Activate) request toward B requesting action on either the A-to-B, B-to-A, or both directions. If B can comply with all of the requests, then a (De)Activation Confirmed message is returned. If B cannot comply with the request(s), a (De)Activation Request Denied message is returned. A denial can result if the endpoint is unable to support the performance management function. If the deactivation refers to a single function that is currently not operating, then the request is also denied. If the deactivation request refers to both directions, yet only one direction is operating, then the request is confirmed, with the reference to the nonoperational function ignored. These activation and deactivation procedures allow performance measurement and continuity checking to be performed on selected VPCs and VCCs. This keeps the total processing load required for performance measurements manageable.

12.3 SIMPLE NETWORK MANAGEMENT PROTOCOL (SNMP)

The IETF's network management (NM) philosophy, protocol, and database structure, called SNMP for short, is widely used in the data communications industry. We begin by defining the overall object-oriented network management model, summarize the SNMP messaging protocol itself, and conclude with a review of the major SNMP-based ATM-specific network management standards.

12.3.1 Object Model of Network Management

SNMP is the simplest part of the IETF's network management philosophy: It alone will not manage your network [6]. Figure 12.8 illustrates the key components of an SNMP-based NM system. Typically, a single computer system interfaces to a number of network elements. The NM connections may not be physical, and indeed may be carried by the underlying network itself. SNMP is only a basic set of messages for monitoring and controlling the state of the network elements. The intelligence of an NM system is in understanding what the state variables [called Management Information Based (MIB) objects in SNMP parlance] in the network elements actually mean. The condition of a physical interface — active or inactive — is an example of a state variable modeled by a MIB object. Continuing this example, knowing that two physical interfaces are supposed to be connected together requires intelligence. Many network management engineers model more complex network conditions as finite-state machines. The MIB objects that are retrievable and configurable via the basic SNMP messaging protocol reflect and control certain aspects of the network element's state, Hence, look for value in the insight conveyed in the vendor's MIB documentation — if the comments aren't detailed and don't reflect specifics of the implementation, beware. Also, when looking for a network management system, we suggest looking at the one provided by the vendor, or else one provided by a third party who is extremely knowledgeable about the type of equipment being managed.

12.3.2 SNMP Message Types

Amazingly, SNMP allows a complex management system to monitor and control a large network of complex devices using only the following five simple messages:

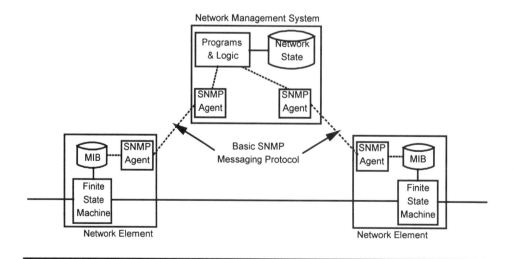

Figure 12.8 SNMP-based Network Management System

- GET
- GET NEXT
- SET
- RESPONSE
- TRAP

The GET message retrieves a particular object, while the GET NEXT message retrieves the next object in the management database structure. The SET message modifies a management object. The RESPONSE message is always paired with a stimulus SET, GET, or GET NEXT message. The TRAP message is very important, since it is the unsolicited notification of an unexpected event, such as a failure or a system restart. SNMP normally operates over the User Datagram Protocol (UDP), which then usually operates over IP in the Internet Protocol (IP) stack, but may operate over some other protocol. Note that the UDP/IP protocol does not guarantee delivery of packets, because there is no retransmission or sequence numbering. This means that if a TRAP is lost, then a management system relying on TRAPs alone would miss a failure notification. Real systems resolve this problem by periodically sending out traps for major failure conditions, or else the management system periodically polls the ATM network devices for status.

SNMP utilizes a subset of Abstract Syntax Notation 1 (ASN.1) to define a MIB as a data structure that can be referenced in SNMP messages. The MIB defines objects in terms of primitives such as strings, integers, and bit maps, using a simple form of indexing. Each object has a name, a syntax, and an encoding. The MIB variables have a textual Object Identifier (OID) which is commonly used to refer to the objects. The MIB objects are defined as a tree structure that allows organizational ownership of subtrees to be defined. The branches of the tree are identified by a dotted decimal notation. For example, the prefix of the subtree registered to the ATM Forum is 1.3.6.1.4.1.353.

12.3.3 Management Information Bases

MIBs were first widely used in local area network and Internet environments. MIBs have achieved the greatest degree of interoperability using the SNMP protocol, because of simplicity. SNMP has only five message types with very clearly defined encoding and processing rules. This section covers the major standardized MIBs available today in many vendor implementations. The usage of MIBs also extends beyond standards. Many vendors utilize SNMP-based MIBs for proprietary extensions. A good degree of interoperability results when users compile these proprietary MIBs into third-party management systems.

12.3.3.1 ATM Forum Integrated Local Management Interface

When the ATM Forum created the Interim Local Management Interface in 1992, it anticipated that ITU-T and ANSI standards would create a final interface management solution. Four years later, the Forum changed the initial "I" in the acronym to Integrated, since the ILMI [3] now performs the following critical functions:

- Basic configuration information
- PVC status indication in FR/ATM service interworking
- ILMI connectivity detection and auto neighbor discovery
- Address registration for SVCs and PNNI
- ABR attribute setting
- Autoconfiguration of a LAN Emulation Client (LEC)

Figure 12.9 illustrates the reference configuration for the ILMI. ATM Interface Management Entities (IMEs) communicate using the ILMI protocol through the SNMP over AA5, each in turn over physical or virtual links. IMEs may operate in either a user, network, or symmetric mode.

Address registration using ILMI is a key component of automatic configuration of Private Network-Network Interface (PNNI) reachability information in the ATM Switched Virtual Circuit (SVC) capability. Basically, address registration allows the network to communicate to the user which address prefixes are valid on the User-Network Interface (UNI). The user can then register the valid remaining portions of the address(es) present locally. It also provides source authentication for virtual private networks, since the originating switch may screen the calling party information element in the SETUP message against the set of registered addressed prefixes.

The Service Registry MIB information portion of the ILMI provides a general-purpose service registry for locating ATM network services, such as the LAN Emulation Configuration Server (LECS) and the ATM Name Server (ANS).

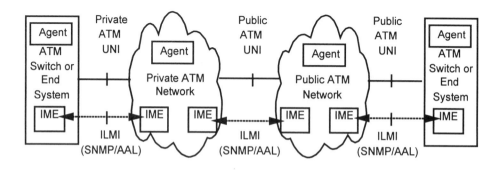

Figure 12.9 Integrated Local Management Interface Connections

12.3.3.2 IETF AToMMIB

IETF RFC 1695 defines an ATM Management Information Base, called the "AToMMIB" [4], which covers the management of ATM PVC-based interfaces, devices, and services. This standard defines managed objects for ATM interfaces, ATM VP/VC virtual links (VPL/VCL), ATM VP/VC cross-connects, AAL5 entities, and AAL5 connections supported by ATM end systems, ATM switches, and ATM networks.

The AToMMIB's structure collects objects pertaining to related information in groups. The AToMMIB defines the following groups:

- ⊙ ATM interface configuration
- ⊙ ATM interface DS3 PLCP
- ⊙ ATM interface TC Sublayer
- ⊙ ATM interface virtual link (VPL/VCL) configuration
- ⊙ ATM VP/VC cross-connect
- ⊙ AAL5 connection performance statistics

The ATM interface configuration group contains ATM cell layer information and configuration of local ATM interfaces. This includes information such as the port identifier, interface speed, number of transmitted cells, number of received cells, number of cells with uncorrectable HEC errors, physical transmission type, operational status, administrative status, active VPI/VCI fields, and the maximum number of VPCs/VCCs.

The ATM interface DS3 PLCP and the TC sublayer groups provide the physical-layer performance statistics for DS3 or SONET transmission paths. This includes statistics on the bit error rate and errored seconds.

The ATM virtual link and cross-connect groups allow management of ATM VP/VC virtual links and VP/VC cross-connects. The virtual link group is implemented on end systems, switches, and networks, while the cross-connect group is implemented on switches and networks only. This includes the operational status, VPI/VCI value, and physical port identifier of the other end of the cross-connect.

The AAL5 connection performance statistics group is based upon the standard interface MIB for IP packets. It is defined for an end system, switch, or network that terminates the AAL5 protocol. It defines objects such as the number of received octets, number of transmitted octets, number of octets passed to the AAL5 user, number of octets received from the AAL5 user, and number of errored AAL5 CPCS PDUs.

12.3.3.3 Other ATM MIBs

The ATM Forum has defined a number of additional MIBs in support of specific functions as summarized in Table 12.1. NMSs using SNMP can utilize these MIBs to manage devices performing these functions.

Table 12.1 Other ATM-Related MIBs

Function(s) Supported MIB	Reference(s)
ATM Data Exchange Interface (DXI)	af-dxi-0014.000
ILMI extensions for LAN emulation	af-lane-0021.000
Private Network-Network Interface	af-pnni-0055.000
Inverse Multiplexing over ATM (IMA)	af-phy-0086.000
Circuit Emulation Service (CES) MIB	af-saa-0032.000
Physical interfaces	RFC 1595, 1407, 1406

12.4 ATM FORUM NETWORK MANAGEMENT ARCHITECTURE

Figure 12.10 depicts the ATM Forum's network management reference architecture [5], which identifies five distinct management interfaces. Interfaces M1 and M2 define the interfaces between a private network management system for one or more customer sites and private networks and ATM end stations. The M3 interface allows public network carriers to provide standardized Customer Network Management (CNM) services. The M4 interface targets standardization of the interface to switches and element managers. M5 provides the management interface between different carriers' network management systems. The only interface in this structure specified in detail by the ATM Forum to date is the M4 interface. The currently approved ATM Forum documents cover the M4 interface requirements and logical view. These specifications provide a protocol-independent MIB for M4 that supports SNMP objects defined in accordance with the SNMP Structure of Management Information (SMI), as well as Common Management Information Protocol (CMIP) objects that conform to GDMO (Guidelines for Development of Managed Objects).

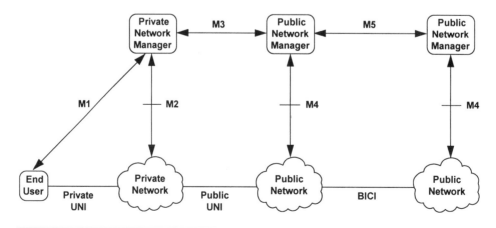

Figure 12.10 The ATM Forum Management Interface Reference Architecture

Although the ATM Forum has not standardized the other interfaces yet, many current standards fit into this framework [7, 8]. Because SNMP is widely deployed by end users, the M1 and M2 interfaces embrace SNMP-based specifications defined by the IETF. These include relevant standard MIBs for DS-1, DS-3, and SONET physical interfaces and the AToM MIB described in the previous section. The M3 CNM interface gives a customer a view into its carrier's network. Several carriers have announced plans to extend CNM offerings to the point where customers dynamically control their services. But in reality these capabilities, as provided by ATM service providers, are probably still some way off. The M4 interface provides network-wide and single-element-level views of the carrier's network management system for public ATM networks. Many promises have been made in this area, but few results have been achieved so far. Thus, the M4 interface is where the different approaches to management converge, both the private network manager and the carrier who provides the service must be able to cooperatively control and monitor ATM service. This situation presents a dilemma. On the one hand, the private network manager requires cost-effective public services, but insists on retaining a degree or modicum of monitoring and control to assure bandwidth and quality of service guarantees. The carrier, on the other hand, wants to monitor and control customer networks to offer end-to-end, value-added network management services. The M5 interface targets the complex area of automatic management connections between carrier network management systems. M5 is perceived as the most complicated of the management interfaces.

12.5 ITU-T TELECOMMUNICATIONS MANAGEMENT NETWORK

Figure 12.11 depicts the ITU-T M.3010 specification's layered model for the Telecommunications Management Network (TMN) operations functions [9]. We will define later the interfaces between the layers, labeled Q3, and the interfaces between the layers and their peers, labeled X. This model abstracts lower-level details further up the hierarchy, enabling effective service and resource management.

Starting at the bottom of the figure, physical network elements are devices, such as ATM switches, LAN bridges, routers, or workstations. The element management layer manages network elements, either individually or in groups, to develop an abstraction of the network element functions to higher-layer operations functions. Many vendors provide proprietary element managers that control an entire network of their devices. The network management layer addresses functions required across an entire geographic or administrative domain. This layer also addresses network performance by controlling network capabilities and capacity to deliver the required quality of service. The service management layer is responsible for the contractual aspects of services provided by carriers to customers. This includes statistical data reporting, interfaces with other carriers, and interactions with other services. The scope of the business management layer is the entire enterprise, encompassing proprietary functions. Since this layer performs proprietary functions, it does not usually provide the standard X interface to a peer NMS layer. Please note that the layers in this model represent functional components, not physical systems. The ITU-T standard indicates that other models are valid, so that systems without all of these layers, or systems with different layers, are also acceptable.

Figure 12.12 illustrates several possible implementations of the above referenced architecture, showing how the lowest three logical layers may be mapped to physical systems. Figure 12.12a shows separate systems implementing each layer, where element management is performed on a one-for-one basis for each network element. This design could use computers at the element level to convert from a proprietary network element interface to a standard interface, which is then managed by a standard NMS. Figure 12.12b illustrates a system which integrates the network- and element-level management into a single overall management system. Proprietary vendor management systems often implement this type of architecture. Figure 12.12c illustrates a system in which network management intelligence and standard interfaces are distributed to each network element. Switch vendors who implement all MIB standards and provide open access to their proprietary MIBs follow this model. Finally, Figure 12.12d illustrates a hierarchical system in which element management systems manage groups of Network Elements (NEs) and then feed these up into a centralized NMS that manages an entire network. Sometimes the processing requirements of larger networks dictate this hierarchical structure.

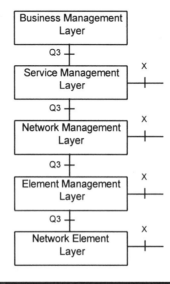

Figure 12.11 The Multilayered Reference Architecture for Operations

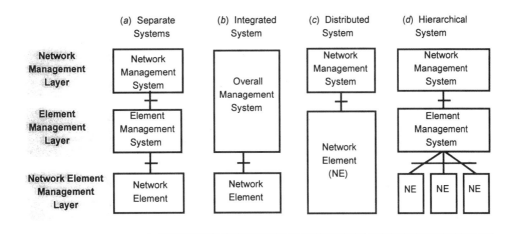

Figure 12.12 Physical Realization Examples of the Multilayered Model

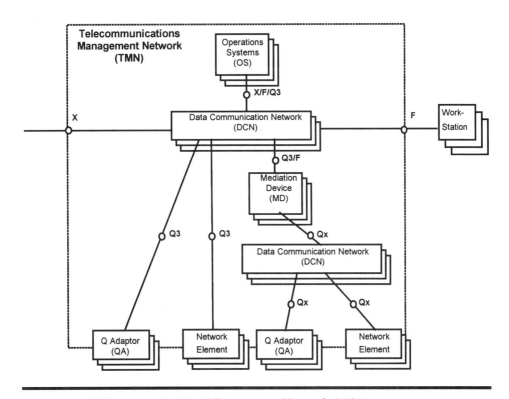

Figure 12.13 Telecommunications Management Network Architecture

Figure 12.13 depicts the ITU-T's vision for the standardized TMN architecture [9]. Starting at the top of the figure, a carrier's Operations Systems (OS) connect to a packet- or circuit-switched Data Communications Network (DCN) using one of the TMN standard interfaces, denoted by the letter X, F, or Q. The X interface supports connections to TMNs in other carriers. For example, the X interface supports coordination of restoration requests between carriers. The F interface allows humans to retrieve and modify management information, for example via a workstation as shown in the figure. The Q3 interface comprises layers 4 through 7 of the OSI protocol reference model. The ITU-T utilizes the OSI standardized Common Management Information Service Elements (CMISE) and the associated CMIP for the Q3 interface. The Qx interface supports protocols other than the standard Q3 interface, such as SNMP. Mediation Devices (MDs) convert from these Qx interfaces to the standard Q3 interface.

12.6 NETWORK MANAGEMENT SYSTEM IMPLEMENTATIONS

Several vendors implement generic NMSs that utilize the standard SNMP and CMIP MIBs described earlier in this chapter. The most commonly used NMS implementations are HP's Open View, Sun's Enterprise Network Manager, and IBM's NetView/AIX. Many users employ these NMSs to manage networks composed of devices from many vendors. These NMSs can also be loaded with vendor proprietary MIBs, supplementing the standard MIB functions and variables.

Web/Java-based network management is a new possibility, first pioneered by Sahara networks in 1996. With Web-based Java, new NM software is downloaded automatically to a Web agent in the network element, and so the NMS is never out of date! Newbridge markets a sophisticated network management system, called the 46020, which manages not only ATM but frame relay as well. See Chapter 17 for more details on these approaches and those of other vendors.

Third-party vendors also supply NMSs for ATM. For example, Stanford Telecom provides the NetCoach ATM management system — including support for fault and performance management, simulation and modeling, and distributed management capabilities.

12.7 MAKING CERTAIN THAT IT ALL WORKS — TESTING

This section briefly summarizes standard testing methodologies and specifications. It also compares the key capabilities of a number of test equipment manufacturers.

12.7.1 Testing Standards

The ATM Forum's testing group defines specifications targeted to ensure that different products conform to specifications, meet measurable performance metrics, and interoperate [11]. These documents fall into three basic categories:

* Protocol Implementation Conformance Statement (PICS)
* Conformance test suites
* Performance testing

A PICS is employed prior to any testing. A PICS is basically a checklist, or questionnaire, in which the tester or vendor indicates whether the implementation under test meets major functional, interface, or performance requirements. PICSs form the basis for conformance and interoperability test suites.

A tester develops a suite of conformance tests from the PICS checklist and relevant specifications. These conformance tests verify that an ATM product complies with every feature and function defined in an ATM Forum (or other standards body) specification. A conformance test suite targets a specific layer or protocol — for example, singling out the physical layer or only the ATM layer. Thus, a specific implementation may conform at one layer but not at another. Further, conformance testing helps identify the offending implementation when an interoperability problem arises.

Performance testing measures QoS and Network Performance (NP) parameters under normal and overload conditions. For example, the accuracy of an implementation's policing function (i.e., usage parameter control) would be the subject of performance testing.

Interoperability testing first determines whether two vendor devices implement complementary mandatory and optional features. If the two systems under test implement different subsets of the mandatory features (for example, because of different specification versions) or implement different optional features, then they may not be interoperable. The ATM Forum documentation notes that systems that do not meet the standard specification may still interoperate. Also, this phase of testing attempts to resolve ambiguities in the underlying specifications through specifically designed test cases.

12.7.2 Test Equipment

Table 12.2 lists interfaces and ATM-layer functions tested by leading ATM test equipment vendors. The table lists the vendor name, model number, physical-layer interface(s) tested (DS3, OC-3, STM1), and ATM-layer interface(s) tested (PVC traffic generation and monitoring, UNI 3.0 and 3.1 SVC generation and monitoring). Physical-layer standard support includes the Universal Test and Operations PHY Interface (UTOPIA) and the Level 2/MultiPHY (Multiple Physical Interfaces) standards.

Other devices are available from Able Communications (AC-500 and 1000 protocol analyzers and AC-2000 Load Generator) and Nitech's NiteOwl analyzer, but they are not summarized in this table since information is awaiting and forthcoming.

Desirable functional capabilities in an ATM test tool include:

- Analyze LAN and WAN
- Plug into/run on any PC
- User-friendly GUI
- Multiple ports/test slots
- Export to other tools (i.e., trend, management, reporting)
- Low cost
- Field upgradablility
- Cost-effective and scalable platform

Table 12.2 Industry Leading Test Equipment by Vendor

Vendor & Model	Interfaces Tested			ATM-Layer Functions Tested	
	DS3	OC3	STM1	PVC traffic	UNI 3.0/3.1 SVC
Adtech AX-400	Y	Y	Y	Y	Y
Cerjac 156 MTS	—	Y	—	Y	—
Desknet OC3port+	—	Y	—	Y	—
Desknet DS3port	Y	—	—	Y	—
DTI LANE DS3port	Y	—	—	Y	—
Duke MultiModd	Y	Y	Y	Y	Y
Fluke	Y	Y			
HP 75000, E4200/E4210 E4829B	Y	Y	Y	Y	Y
Net2Net CellBlaster and LT	—	Y	—	Y	Y*
Network General Sniffer	—	Y	—	—	Y*
Radcom RC-200	—	Y	—	—	Y
Tekelec Chameleon Open	Y	Y	Y	Y	Y
TTC T-bird 310	—	Y	—	Y	—

* Monitoring only.

Key technical capabilities of an ATM test tool include [12]:

- >100,000 cell bursts/generation for cells from 16 to 128 bytes in length
- Capability to generate high rates of SVC calls
- Capability to capture more than 1 million cells
- Ability to emulate multiple interfaces

- Test capability for switch latency
- Point-to-point and multipoint call generation
- Test ATM signaling protocol addressing polling and signaling
- OAM channel monitoring and transmission
- Interfaces covered
- ATM service categories supported (CBR, rt-VBR, nrt-VBR, UBR, ABR)
- Ability to verify ATM-layer functions (bandwidth and traffic shaping, cell insertion and discarding, policing)
- Higher-layer protocol support (AALs, SSCS, etc.)
- QoS testing (e.g., CDV, CTD, CLR)
- IP ping capability
- Bit Error Rate Test (BERT) and Header Error Check (HEC) capability
- PVC and SVC test capability

12.8 REVIEW

This chapter began with a summary of ATM operations, administration and maintenance cell functions. These provide the critical functions of fault identification and localization, as well as performance measurement. We then covered the SNMP and its use in conjunction with MIBs to support status queries and configuration via external NMSs. Next, the text covered the ATM Forum's network management architecture, which defines a structure for future MIB definitions. We then moved on to the ITU-T's Telecommunications Management Network architecture, which lays out a common structure for managing transmission, voice, and data networks. Several examples of real NMS implementations concluded the coverage of network management. Finally, we summarized the standards for conformance and interoperability testing, along with a survey of ATM test equipment capabilities.

12.9 REFERENCES

[1]   U. Black, *Network Management Standards*, McGraw-Hill, 1992.
[2]   CCITT, I.610, *OAM Principles for the B-ISDN Access*, Geneva, November 1995.
[3]   ATM Forum, *Integrated Local Management Interface (ILMI) Specification*, Version 4.0, af-ilmi-0065.000, September 1996.
[4]   M. Ahmed and K. Tesink, *RFC 1695 — Definitions of Managed Objects for ATM Management Version 8.0 using SMIv2*, August 25, 1994.
[5]   ATM Forum, *M4 Network-View Interface Requirements, and Logical MIB*, AF-NM-0058.000, March 1996.
[6]   T. Cikoski, "The Complexities and Future Evolution of SNMP as a Management Protocol," *Telecommunications*, August 1996.

[7]   P. Alexander and K. Carpenter, "ATM Net Management: A Status Report," *Data Communications*, September 1995.

[8]   IBM, "ATM Network Management Strategy," http://www.networking.ibm.com/atm/atmnman.html#mgt, 1996.

[9]   ITU-T, *Recommendation M.3010 — Principles for Telecommunications Management Network*, Geneva, May 1996.

[10] I. Rubin and T. Cheng, "The Effect of Management Structure on the Performance of Interconnected High-Speed Packet-Switched Networks," GLOBECOM, December 1991.

[11] ATM Forum, *Introduction to ATM Forum Test Specifications*, af-test-0022.000, December 1994.

[12] iNews articles.

3

ATM DEVICES

This section provides the reader with an overview of commercially available ATM hardware and software devices. The first chapter begins by defining ATM switch types, ranging from the carrier backbone all the way down to the end user's desktop. This can be used in the comparisons given in subsequent chapters. We divide switch types into three categories: central office–based or backbone and edge switches; enterprise switches that interface to the WAN as well as interconnecting LAN/campus backbone switches; and workgroup switches and the desk area networks they serve. We then define the characteristics used in a tabular comparison of switch vendors. The second chapter in this part focuses strictly on WAN Edge and Backbone switches, which make up the core of most carrier ATM networks. We then move on in the next chapter to detail the switches, routers, hubs, and servers in the LAN or campus environment. This chapter also covers enterprise switches, also called customer premises equipment access switches, because they often interface the customer premises environment to the WAN. Moving closer to the end user, the fourth chapter in this part focuses on the Desktop Area Network (DAN) or workgroup environment. The DAN environment includes workgroup switches, ATM application programming interfaces, and network interface cards. As ATM moves to the desktop, powerful workstations require ATM interface cards. The last chapter in this part contains details provided by vendors as a result of our survey.

13

Categorization of ATM Devices

This chapter begins by reviewing basic switch models, including the major architectures and buffering models. We next define ATM switches of the following types: workgroup, LAN or campus backbone, enterprise customer premises equipment (CPE), carrier edge, and core or carrier backbone. We then group these into three categories of ATM switches: backbone or core and edge, LAN backbone or enterprise, and workgroup switches. This chapter then defines the parameters of an in-depth analysis of vendors in the ATM equipment marketplace at the time of publication. Subsequent chapters provide the results of this analysis for each switch category.

13.1 SWITCH MODELS

ATM switches have several distinguishing characteristics. First, a switch architecture is either blocking, virtually nonblocking, or nonblocking, which determines the load a device can carry. Next, the architecture of the switch fabric at the heart of the machine determines the scalability and maximum switch size. Finally, the buffering method used and its implications on performance are discussed.

13.1.1 ATM Switch Blocking Performance

A figure of merit, called blocking, attributed to ATM switches has been adapted from circuit switches. In circuit switches, if an inlet channel can be connected to any unoccupied output channel, up to the point where all inlets are occupied, then the switch is said to be strictly nonblocking. Circuit switches are often then specified as virtually nonblocking, meaning that a small blocking probability occurs as long as no more than a certain fraction of inlet channels are in use.

This blocking concept has been extended to ATM switches, although ATM switches utilize a completely different paradigm from circuit switches. When an inlet is connected to an outlet in a circuit switch, bandwidth is reserved and completely isolated from other connections. This is generally not true in an ATM switch — there are Virtual Path and Virtual Channel Connections (VPCs or VCCs) which arrive on input ports destined for potentially *different* output ports. Cell loss can occur, depending upon the statistical nature of this virtual connection traffic as it is handled by the cell switching fabric and the switch's buffering strategy. *Cell loss* in an ATM switch is the analog to *call blocking* in a circuit switch. Most analyses make the assumption that arriving virtual connection traffic is uniformly and randomly distributed across the outputs. The switch performance is then normally cited as virtually nonblocking (sometimes called nonblocking), meaning that up to a certain input load a very low cell loss ratio occurs. Most vendors surveyed cite nonblocking performance at full load per the traffic patterns specified in Bellcore's GR-1110 specification.

The ATM switch blocking performance is sensitive to the switch architecture and the source traffic assumptions. This is an important practical consideration, since, depending upon traffic characteristics, one switch type may be better than another.

13.1.2 Switch Architectures

Figure 13.1 illustrates several of the more common published switching architectures implemented in the current ATM switches. These are also called switch fabrics, or switch matrices. Of course, some switch designs are hybrids, employing one larger switch fabric to connect another, smaller switch fabric to yield one larger overall switch fabric. We now describe each architecture in terms of its complexity, maximum overall speed, scalability, ease of support for multicast, blocking level, and other unique attributes.

The single bus shown in Figure 13.1a is the simplest switch type. Basically, ports connect to a single bus, usually implemented via a large number of parallel circuit board traces. The total speed of such a bus usually ranges between 1 and 10 Gbps. Some complexity is introduced by the need for bus arbitration, which in combination with the buffering strategy controls the blocking level. Multicast is easily implemented, since all output ports "listen" to the common bus.

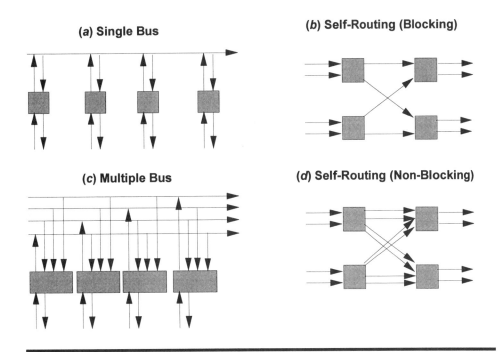

(a) Single Bus

(b) Self-Routing (Blocking)

(c) Multiple Bus

(d) Self-Routing (Non-Blocking)

Figure 13.1 Example Switch Architectures

The multiple-bus switch fabric shown in Figure 13.1*b* extends the single-bus concept by providing a broadcast bus for each input port. This design eliminates the need for bus arbitration, but shifts additional requirements for controlling blocking to the outputs. In general, each bus runs at slightly greater than the port card speed (usually between 100 Mbps and 1 Gbps) and uses multiple circuit traces on a shared backplane that all the other cards plug into. Therefore the switch bandwidth is comparable to that of the single-bus switch. An early version of this switch architecture was called the "knockout" switch because the outputs could receive cells from only a limited number of inputs at the same time in an attempt to make the architecture more scalable. For smaller switches, every output can receive from every input simultaneously. Another method employs arbitration to ensure that the output port does not receive too many cells simultaneously; however, this creates a need for input buffering and adds complexity. Multicast is a natural in this switch type, as it was for the single bus, since each input is broadcasting to every output.

The self-routing switch fabrics shown in Figure 13.1*c* and 13.1*d*, such as Batcher Banyan networks, employ more complex internal switching elements; however, these can be scaled to larger sizes due to the regular nature of the individual switching elements in Very Large Scale Integration (VLSI) implementations. These types of networks have been the subject of a great deal of research and investigation. See [1] for an in-depth review of these switch architectures. These switches generally do not support multicast well, often requiring either a separate copy network or special processing in the internal switching elements. If the self-routing network runs at the same speed as the input ports, blocking can be quite high. Hence, many of these switch designs run at a higher internal speed. Self-routing networks generally have some buffering within the switching elements. An augmented self-routing fabric basically runs the internal matrix at a faster speed or has multiple connections between switching elements, as shown in Figure 13.1*d*.

Table 13.1 summarizes a comparison of the characteristics for these switch fabric architectures.

Table 13.1 ATM Switch Characteristics

Characteristic	Single Bus	Multiple Bus	Self-Routing	Augmented Self-Routing
Complexity	Low	Medium	Higher	Higher
Maximum speed	1–10 Gbps	1–20 Gbps	1–200 Gbps	1–800 Gbps
Scalability	Poor	Better	Good	Best
Point-to-multipoint support	Good	Good	Poor	Poor
Blocking level	Low	Low to medium	Medium	Low
Unique attributes	Inexpensive	Inexpensive	Amenable to VLSI	Amenable to VLSI

Space-division crosspoint switches can also be used as an ATM switch fabric. The crosspoints are rearranged every cell time in a crosspoint switch.

13.1.3 Switch Buffering Methods

The buffering strategy employed in the switch also plays a key role in the switch blocking (i.e., cell loss) performance. Figure 13.2 illustrates various ATM switch buffering strategies employed in real-world switches.

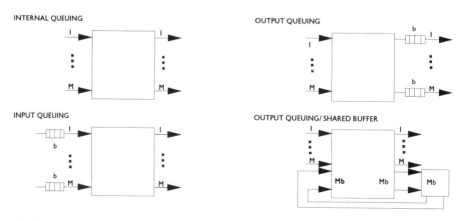

Figure 13.2 Switch Buffering Methods

The following parameters define the notation used in the figure:

$$M = \text{ number of ATM switch ports}$$
$$b = \text{ number of effective buffer positions per port}$$

Switch fabrics built with internal queuing have the potential to scale to large sizes. On the other hand, it is difficult to provide other functions — such as priority queuing, large buffers, and multicast — with internally queued switching fabrics.

Input queuing was simple to implement; however, it can suffer from a fatal flaw. With input queuing, when the cell at the Head of Line (HOL) cannot be switched through the fabric, all the cells behind it are delayed. Note that input queuing limits switch throughput to only 50 to 60 percent of the port speed. Therefore, input queuing alone is not adequate for many applications, and it is usually employed in conjunction with other queuing methods. One way around the HOL blocking problem is to provide an input queue for each virtual connection. In this way, a congested port does not delay cells destined for other uncongested ports.

Output queuing is theoretically optimal, and shared output queuing is the best in terms of achieving the maximum throughput with the fewest cell buffer positions. Most ATM switches employ at least some output queuing for this reason. Real ATM switches may have a combination of input, output, and internal queuing.

13.1.4 Other Aspects of ATM Switches

Other factors which are important in comparing switch architectures are listed below.

- Modularity, which is defined as the minimum increment of ports that can be added to a switch
- Maintainability, which measures the isolation of a disruption or failure from the remainder of the switch
- Availability, which means that the operation continues in the presence of single or multiple faults
- Complexity, often measured by logic gate counts, chip pinout, and card pinout in comparing switch implementations
- Flexibility, which covers the capability to implement further packet processing functions easily
- Expandability, which considers the maximum number of switch ports and increased speeds supportable by the architecture

13.2 ATM SWITCH TYPES AND CATEGORIES

ATM technology has appeared in many of the major internetworking devices used and services offered today, from the switching backbone of large carriers to being used in Internet Service Provider (ISP) networks. Users are deploying ATM all the way down to the local network environment with switches, routers, bridges, hubs, multiplexers, ATM interface cards for high-end workstations, and even application programming interfaces (APIs). Thus, ATM is disintegrating the fine line between wide area, campus, and local area networking using a broadband, cell-based architecture that scales well in terms of distance, speed, and network size.

Most ATM vendors target their hardware for five different environments, corresponding to the following ATM switch device types:

☞ Core or carrier backbone (also called a central office switch)
☞ Carrier edge
☞ Enterprise backbone (also labeled as CPE access switches)
☞ LAN or campus backbone
☞ Workgroup

We briefly introduce these five switch types, working down from the carrier backbone switch, through the edge and into the enterprise switch, across the campus backbone, and arriving at the workgroup and ultimately the end user. Figure 13.3 illustrates the commonly used hierarchical view of these ATM switch types. The carrier backbone switch resides in a Central Office (CO) and forms the core of a public ATM service network. Edge switches located in carrier Points of Presence (PoPs) feed into the core, backbone switch network. The carrier backbone and edge switches may also interwork with voice and other data networks as shown in the figure. Moving out of the carrier domain onto the customer's premises, the enterprise ATM switch connects the other local switches to the WAN via an ATM User-to-Network Interface (UNI) (e.g., DS3, OC-3). Enterprise switches interconnect LAN backbone switches, high-performance legacy LANs (such as FDDI), ATM-capable PBXs, and large Routers (R), Servers (S), and Bridges (B). Enterprise ATM switches often provide access to public data and voice services. The LAN, or campus, backbone has a key role in large customer local area networks, often replacing FDDI backbone networks to interconnect LANs, bridges, routers, and servers. The LAN backbone switch also interconnects the ATM workgroup switches directly supporting native ATM Clients (C), Routers (R) and Servers (S) in virtual networks. ATM workgroup switches may also support legacy LANs, such as Token Ring (TR) or Ethernet.

We group these five switch types in the next three chapters in this part for a comparative analysis of key switch attributes as follows:

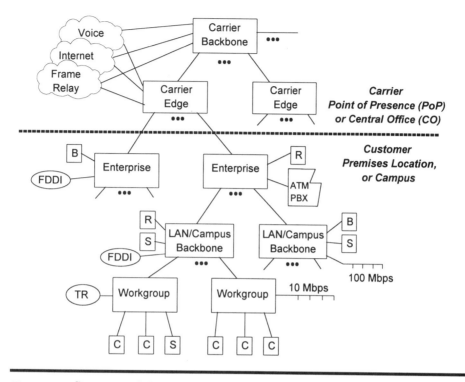

Figure 13.3 Campus and Central Office Switching Roles

Chapter 14 - Carrier Backbone and Edge Switches
Chapter 15 - Enterprise and LAN/Campus Backbone Switches
Chapter 16 - Workgroup Switches and Network Interface Cards

13.3 ATM SWITCH COMPARISON OVERVIEW

The next few sections summarize the features and functions of ATM switches used in the analyses in subsequent chapters that shows how industry leaders compare based on a survey conducted by the authors. All equipment providers were asked to provide full contact information, including their company name, address, contact name and phone number, Web page, annual sales, number of customers actually using the switch, number of switches sold, maximum and minimum switch price and configuration, and a paragraph on the company strengths. We have attempted to include as much of this information as possible in the charts in the next few chapters. We also requested product graphics, some of which are also included to illustrate the various switch types.

Many vendors responded to this survey and provided information on products commercially available as of mid-1997. A few vendors either chose not to respond or did not have products available by this timeframe. Current publications were used for details on vendor announcements for those vendors who did not respond. The next few sections summarize the switch characteristics compared in the remainder of this part:

- General features and functions of ATM switches
- Questions asked of the vendors on each subject
- Traffic management
- Protocols and standards
- Network management support

13.3.1 Manufacturer, Product Name, and Category of Switch

The equipment vendors who responded to our survey are shown in Table 13.2, along with their product name and category of switch. Switch types are indicated by a WG for workgroup, LB for LAN backbone, E for Enterprise, CA for Carrier Access, CE for Carrier Edge, and CB for Carrier Backbone. Some switches can be categorized as more than one type. A Y was used to indicate the vendor's preference on switch type.

We also requested company information, some of which is provided in each vendor analysis, including:
- Name and address, Web page address, and strengths
- Primary point of contact for public inquiries, including the person's title and phone number
- Sales information, including annual sales, number of ATM customers, switches sold, ATM ports sold, and maximum and minimum switch price and configuration

13.3.2 Power

Does the switch support AC power, DC power, or both? If the switch is to be placed in a CO environment, DC power is almost always required, whereas in a wiring closet AC power is typically preferred.

13.3.3 Minimum/Maximum Switch Price/Configuration

The minimum and maximum configuration of the switch, along with the price for each of these configurations, tells the minimum cost of entry for a single port and the maximum number of ports that can be used before an additional switch is required. Maximum configurations bound scalability.

13.3.4 Switch Architecture and Bus Capacity

Switch architectures vary as defined above (matrix, crossbar, etc.). The bus capacity is defined in Mbps or Gbps, and is scalable on both the backplane and the switching modules/cards.

Table 13.2 ATM Switch Vendors

Company Name	Product Name	WG	LB	E	CE	CB	Switch Fabric/Bus Capacity
3Com	CoreBuilder 7000		Y			Y	5 Gbps matrix
ADC Kentrox	ATM Access Concentrator - 3		Y	Y			524 Mbps
Bay Networks	Centillion 100	Y	Y	Y			3.2 Gbps
Bay Networks	System 5000	Y	Y	Y			3.2 Gbps
Cabletron Systems Sales & Service	Smartcell ZX-250			Y	Y	Y	2.5 Gbps
Cascade Communications Corp.	CBX 500	Y		Y	Y		5 Gbps
Cisco	Lightstream 1010	Y	Y	Y			5 Gbps
Digital Equipment Corporation	GIGAswitch/ATM (14 Slot)		Y	Y	Y		Crossbar fabric of 10.4 Gbps
Digital Equipment Corporation	GIGAswitch/ATM (5 Slot)		Y	Y	Y		Crossbar fabric of 3.2 Gbps
Digital Equipment Corporation	ATMswitch 900		Y	Y	Y		Memory switch with 1.6 Gbps bandwidth
Digital Equipment Corporation	VNswitch 900EA		Y	Y	Y		400 Mbps for in-hub configuration
FORE Systems, Inc.	ES-3810	Y		Y			640 Mbps
FORE Systems, Inc.	ASX-200BX	Y		Y			2.5 Gbps
FORE Systems, Inc.	ASX-1000			Y	Y		10 Gbps
FORE Systems, Inc.	PH7000			Y			3.2 Gbps shared memory
FORE Systems, Inc.	PH6000	Y					1.6 Gbps shared memory
FORE Systems, Inc.	CellPath 90						2 Mbps
FORE Systems, Inc.	ASX-200WG			Y			2.5 Gbps (nonblocking)
Fujitsu	AstralSwitch EA 1550		Y	Y			10 Gbps
General DataComm	APEX Strobos, NPX, DV2, MAC, MAC1 Switches			Y	Y	Y	Up to 25.6 Gbps
IBM Corporation	IBM 2220 Nways BroadBand Switch, Models 300/500			Y		Y	4.2 Gbps
IBM Corporation	IBM 2225 Nways Multiservice Switch, Model 400/450			Y	Y	Y	1.2 Gbps FDX
IBM Corporation	IBM 2230 Nways ATM Switch Model 600/650			Y	Y		2.5 to 5 Gbps (Model 600, 650)
IBM Corporation	8260 Nways Switching Hub			Y			4.2 Gbps
IBM Corporation	8285 Nways Workgroup Switch			Y		Y	4.2 Gbps
NEC America, Inc.	Atomnet/M20				Y		10 - 160 Gbps
NewBridge Networks	Vivid Workgroup Switch	Y		Y			1.6 Gbps
NewBridge Networks	MainStreetXpress 36190					Y	>1 Tbps
NewBridge Networks	MainStreetXpress 36170				Y	Y	Scalable 800 Mbps to 51.2 Gbps
NewBridge Networks	MainStreetXpress 36150			Y	Y		>2.5
Sahara Networks, Inc.	SA-100 Broadband Service Unit			Y			1 Gbps of cell and packet simultaneously
Sahara Networks, Inc.	SA-600 Broadband Service Concentrator			Y			*
Sahara Networks, Inc.	SA-1200 Service Access Multiplexer			Y	Y		*
Siemens Stromberg-Carlson	MainStreetXpress 36190					Y	>1 Tbps
Siemens Stromberg-Carlson	MainStreetXpress 36170				Y		Max.12.8 Gbps
Siemens Stromberg-Carlson	MainStreetXpress 36150						>2.5
Telematics International	Telematics switch				Y		3.5 Gbps
Xylan	OmniSwitch w/Omnicell			Y			13.2 Gbps

13.3.5 Maximum Sum of Port Speeds

It is important to understand the maximum sum of ports, by speed, supported by the switch. This includes a maximum port speed expressed in Gbps. Some switches offer only WAN ports, leaving LAN support to workgroup and edge switch vendors. Most enterprise switches provide both WAN and LAN ports.

13.3.6 Percent Blocking at Load per GR-1110

The key attribute for a switch architecture is the degree to which it is virtually nonblocking. Switches are typically nonblocking, although some are virtually nonblocking with the probability of blocking defined as 1*10-X. Each vendor was asked to provide the percent blocking that occurs at specified load per Bellcore's GR-1110. The blocking or nonblocking performance is compared to the bus capacity in Gbps. Some switches define half- or full-duplex operation differently.

13.3.7 Point-to-Multipoint Capability

Does the switch support point-to-multipoint connections? (This is sometimes referred to as multicast.) Is the point-to-multipoint supported spatial or logical? Spatial means that the leaves of point-to-multipoint trees are physical ports, while logical means that the leaves are VCCs, where many may exist on one physical port.

13.3.8 Minimum Switch Transit Delay

Delay is measured (in microseconds) as the total one-way delay through the switch. The delay varies widely based on switch fabric architecture, ranging from a few to hundreds of microseconds.

13.3.9 VPI/VCI Bits on UNI/NNI

ATM switches vary in the number of Virtual Path Identifier (VPI) and Virtual Channel Identifier (VCI) address bits they support on a UNI and Network-Network Interface (NNI). Some switch vendors support all VPI and VCI addressing bits. Others use part of them in a proprietary manner.

13.3.10 VPC and VCC Support (Maximum per Card/Switch)

What is the maximum number of Permanent Virtual Connection (PVC) VPCs and VCCs that can be supported per card and per switch? How many Switched Virtual Connections (SVCs) can be supported per card and per switch? Are the PVCs and SVCs compliant with the ATM Forum and ITU-T Q.2931 specifications?

13.3.11 Redundancy

ATM hardware may offer some level of redundancy at the node, card, module, and port level. M for N (abbreviated M:N) redundancy is defined as M spares for a set of N active components, such as CPUs, port cards, ports, power supplies, or switching matrix. We also asked what level of common equipment redundancy was available in the power cards, controller cards, switching fabric, and bus. Note that true redundancy is achieved when a module, card, or processor can fail and the redundant spare automatically assumes the role with no appreciable traffic or user service interruption. Reliability can be further increased with separate processors on each card/module.

13.3.12 Distinguishing Features

Vendors were requested to provide a narrative of any distinguishing features of their product. We collected these inputs from the vendor and present them in Chapter 17.

13.3.13 ATM Interfaces

Chapter 6 defines interfaces typically found in these switches as listed in Table 13.3.

Table 13.3 Typical Interfaces on ATM Devices

ATM UNI Interfaces	Non-ATM Interfaces
nxDS1 IMA	Ethernet
DS3	100-Mbps Ethernet
OC3	FDDI
OC12	4-Mbps Token Ring
OC48	16-Mbps Token Ring
Cell-based clear channel TC	FR nxDS0
E1	FR DS1
E3	FR >DS1
E4	SMDS DS1
STM-1	SMDS DS3
STM-4	SMDS DXI nxDS0
J1	SMDS DXI DS1
J2 (6.312 Mbps)	HDLC V.35
25-Mbps UTP	HDLC HSSI
51.84-Mbps UTP	
155-Mbps UTP	
155-Mbps MMF	

13.3.14 Switch Type

Switch types can fit into three categories: fabric, bus, or other.

13.3.15 Buffering

Buffer capacity defines the total number of input, internal (fabric), and output storage positions for cells per port. The buffering method can be input, fabric, or output. More buffer capacity can mean better throughput for protocols such as Transmission Control Protocol (TCP); however, large buffers can create more latency and delay during peak traffic conditions. As a basic rule, the larger the buffers, the less traffic will be dropped, but the greater the average and variation in delay. Buffer capacity can be measured in cells per port, in cells per switch, or in the delay for a certain line rate. Vendors were also asked to describe the fabric/bus operation with the buffering scheme.

13.3.16 Congestion Control and Available Bit Rate

Does the switch support congestion control as defined by the ATM Forum? There are three major modes of standard ABR congestion control: Explicit Forward Congestion Identification (EFCI), Explicit Rate (ER), and Virtual Source /Virtual Destination (VS/VD) as previously defined in Chapter 6.

13.3.17 Cell Loss Probability (CLP)

Is Cell Loss Probability (CLP) supported? We also asked the vendors how they use the CLP — for example, is it used for tagging or selective discard as defined in Chapter 6.

13.3.18 Policing and Shaping

Is policing performed at Peak Cell Rate (PCR), or for both PCR and Sustainable Cell Rate (SCR)? Again, refer to Chapter 6 for definitions of these terms.

13.3.19 Connection Admission Control (CAC)

Is Connection Admission Control (CAC) supported, and if so, is Generic CAC (GCAC) also supported?

13.3.20 Early/Partial Packet Discard

There are two major forms of packet discard: Early Packet Discard (EPD) and Partial Packet Discard (PPD). Frame policing is also an option.

13.3.21 OAM Performance Measurement

Is performance measured per the ITU-T's I.610 Operations, Administration, and Maintenance (OAM) standard?

13.4 PROTOCOL AND STANDARDS SUPPORT

This section defines typical product support for protocols and standards for ATM devices.

13.4.1 ATM Forum Signaling

Vendors were asked to detail what forms of signaling they support. The ATM Forum has specified Versions 3.0, 3.1, and 4.0 for UNI, point-to-point SVC, and point-to-multipoint SVC signaling.

13.4.2 ITU-T Signaling

The ITU-T has specified UNI signaling in both an older standard (Q.93*B*) and the latest standard (Q.9231). NNI signaling is defined in the ITU-T B-ISUP standards.

13.4.3 LAN Emulation

LAN Emulation (LANE) server and client signaling are specified in LANE 1.0 and RFC 1483, as described in Chapter 10.

13.4.4 Virtual LAN Capability

Some campus and LAN ATM switches support a Virtual LAN (VLAN) capability. "Virtual LANs" use software to define "virtual workgroups" which logically band together multiple users on different LANs in the same VLAN segment. Thus, each workstation can belong to multiple VLANs. VLANs will be defined in greater detail in Chapter 22.

13.4.5 Classical IP over ATM

Classical IP over ATM client and server signaling are specified in RFCs 1577 and 1755, as described in Chapter 11.

13.4.6 Multiprotocol over ATM

Multiprotocol over ATM (MPOA) signaling is specified by the ATM Forum, as described in Chapter 11.

13.4.7 Next-Hop Resolution Protocol

Enterprise or LAN backbone routers implement the IETF-defined Next-Hop Resolution Protocol (NHRP) for IP networks that encompass multiple subnets, as described in Chapter 11.

13.4.8 Tested Interoperability with Other Switches

Each vendor was asked to provide a matrix of its interoperability certification with other switches. Chapter 17 presents the interoperability matrix we collected in our survey.

13.4.9 Distinguishing Features

Each vendor was asked to detail distinguishing features of its products. We report on the narratives provided by vendors in response to our survey in Chapter 17.

13.5 NETWORK MANAGEMENT SUPPORT

This section defines typical network management support for ATM devices. The ATM Forum has defined the Integrated Local Management Interface (ILMI) and several other network management interfaces. Other management protocol support includes: Management Interface Bases (MIBs), OAM cells, automatic configuration and restoration, and support for de facto standard Network Management Systems (NMSs).

13.5.1 Full ATM Forum ILMI

Is the full ATM Forum ILMI supported for versions 3.0, 3.1, and 4.0?

13.5.2 ILMI Address Registration

Is ILMI address registration supported?

13.5.3 RFC 1695 (AToMMIB)

Is RFC 1695 (the AToMMIB) supported?

13.5.4 Per Port/VC Statistics

Can the switch support statistics per virtual path, per virtual channel, or per port?

13.5.5 OAM Cell VPC/VCC AIS/RDI and Loopback

Does the switch support OAM cell functions as defined in ITU-T I.610? Does it support VPC/VCC Alarm Indication Signal/Remote Defect Indication (AIS/RDI) and loopback as defined in Chapter 12?

13.5.6 ATM Forum NM I/F Support

The ATM Forum has specified five network management interfaces: M1, M2, M3, M4, and M5, as described in Chapter 12. Ask which of these interfaces the switch vendor currently supports, or plans to support?

13.5.7 Automatic PVC Configuration and Restoration

Does the switch support automatic PVC configuration and restoration using the PNNI standard SPVPC/SPVCCs method defined in Chapter 8? Does the switch use a proprietary method?

13.5.8 NMS Support

Vendors were asked to provide a narrative on how they used industry standard NMSs, such as HP's OpenView, Cabletron Spectrum Enterprise Manager, Sun's Enterprise Network Manager, and IBM's NetView 6000, or whether they offered their own proprietary system. Some vendors detailed specific MIB support in their survey responses.

13.5.9 Distinguishing Features of Network Management Support

Vendors were asked to detail any distinguishing features of their network management support.

13.6 REVIEW

ATM hardware and switching systems take many forms. The chapter began with a discussion of switch network models — the building blocks of ATM hardware. The set of all ATM devices was then broken down into workgroup, LAN, enterprise, edge, and backbone or core switch types. These were further categorized as workgroup, LAN/enterprise, and edge/core, corresponding to the organization of an exhaustive vendor analysis in the next three chapters. This survey covered ATM switch products on the market as of mid-1997. We concluded this chapter by defining the switch characteristics compared in the remainder of this part: general features and functions, traffic management, protocols and standards, and network management support.

13.7 REFERENCE

[1]   P. Newman, ATM Technology for Corporate Networks," *IEEE Communications Magazine*, April 1992

14

ATM in the WAN Edge and Backbone

This chapter compares a sampling of backbone and edge switches that make up the public carrier and Internet Service Provider ATM networks. Figure 14.1 illustrates the role of WAN backbone and edge switches in relation to an enterprise's ATM implementations in the shaded boxes. We first define WAN backbone and edge switches, then follow with a detailed analysis and comparison of 18 leading ATM switch vendors' products.

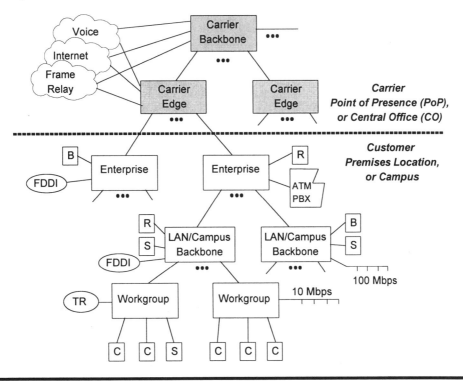

Figure 14.1 Campus and Central Office (CO) Switching Roles

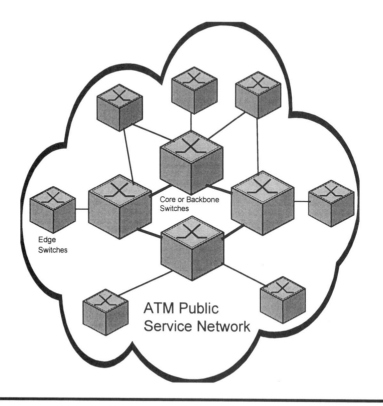

Figure 14.2 ATM Backbone Switch Configuration

14.1 CORE OR BACKBONE SWITCHES

Core or backbone switches are generally larger and more industrial-strength than their edge counterparts. Figure 14.2 illustrates a typical ATM edge switch configuration. Carriers deploy ATM WAN backbone switches to form the core of their backbone switching and transport fabric, as they offer the highest-speed trunks available. The Central Office (CO) environment where core backbone and edge switches reside dictates DC power and the capability to scale to a large number of very high speed ports and trunks. Core or backbone switches often tout throughput in excess of 10 Gbps up to 1 terabit per second, and usually support only native ATM User-Network Interfaces (UNIs).

Figures 14.3 and 14.4 illustrate two leading vendors' backbone switches, the Cascade 9000 and General DataComm's APEX DV2. Details on both vendors' products can be found in Chapter 15. Backbone switches have multiple interconnected shelves arranged in multiple shelves. Literally, these are large switches. They often support SONET/SDH automatic protection switching to work hand in hand with automated restoration in the modern, synchronous digital transmission network. Backbone switches also often have multiple processors in support of management functions and Switched Virtual Connections (SVCs). These switches often support the ITU-T-defined CMIP management interface.

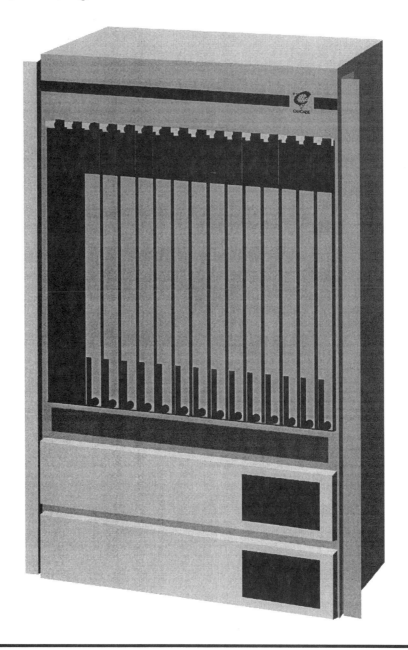

Figure 14.3 Cascade 9000 ATM Backbone Switch

Figure 14.4 General DataComm's APEX DV2 Backbone Switch

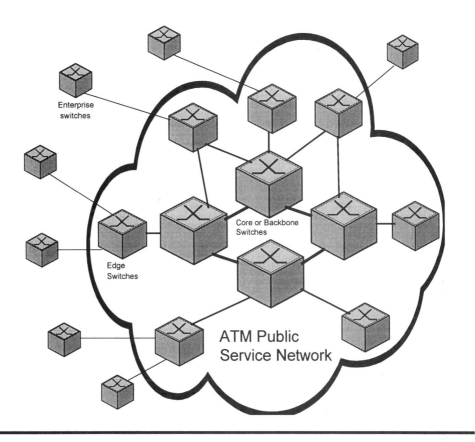

Figure 14.5 ATM Edge Switch Configuration

14.2 EDGE SWITCHES

When CPE ATM switches interface to an ATM WAN, they typically do so through an edge switch. Figure 14.5 illustrates a typical ATM edge switch configuration. Carrier networks often deploy many edge switches at smaller Point-of-Presence (PoP) access points to minimize backhaul. Edge switches are characterized by high port densities and capacities of between 5 and 20 Gbps. Edge switch designs target high reliability by making common components redundant with automatic switchover.

Figures 14.6 and 14.7 show two leading vendor's ATM edge switches: Cascade's CBX500 and FORE Systems' ForeRunner ASX-1000. Edge switches often fit within a single shelf, although more modern designs now support multiple interconnected shelves to increase port fan-out. Interfaces are often on the rear for rack mounting and easy access in central offices. These switches support redundant DC power feeds and have hot standby switch fabrics and controllers.

Figure 14.6 Cascade's CBX500 ATM Edge Switch

Figure 14.7 FORE Systems' ForeRunner ASX-1000 Switch

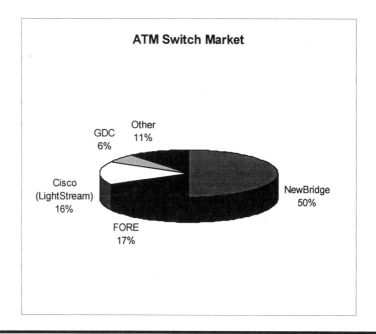

Figure 14.8 WAN ATM Switch Market Share Statistics

According to a report from InStat titled *1995 ATM Market analysis*, NewBridge holds a dominant position with 50 percent of the ATM market for WAN switch ports. FORE and Cisco (LightStream) follow, with 17 percent and 16 percent, respectively. It is interesting to note here that General DataComm only captured 6 percent of the WAN switch ports market. Figure 14.8 summarizes these market statistics.

14.3 WAN BACKBONE AND EDGE SWITCH SURVEY

Table 14.1 lists the WAN backbone and edge switches surveyed in this chapter. Table 14.1 shows the responses from these WAN backbone and edge switch vendors to the survey questions contained in Chapter 13.

14.4 REVIEW

This chapter defined WAN backbone and edge switches, and then presented the results of our survey in a table-based comparison. If you plan to select a vendor for a WAN ATM network, this style of comparison table analysis can be quite useful. We used a representative set of questions; however, your priorities, requirements, and network philosophy may differ.

Table 14.1 Comparison of WAN Edge and Backbone Switches

Company Name	Product Name	WG	LB	E	CE	CB	Switch Fabric/Bus Capacity
ADC Kentrox	ATM Access Concentrator - 3			Y	Y		524 Mbps
Cascade Communications Corp.	CBX 500			Y	Y	Y	5 Gbps
Cisco	Lightstream 1010	Y	Y	Y			5 Gbps
Digital Equipment Corporation	GIGAswitch/ATM (14 Slot)	Y	Y	Y	Y		Crossbar fabric of 10.4 Gbps
Digital Equipment Corporation	GIGAswitch/ATM (5 Slot)	Y	Y	Y	Y		Crossbar fabric of 3.2 Gbps
Digital Equipment Corporation	ATMswitch 900	Y	Y	Y	Y		Memory switch with 1.6 Gbps bandwidth
Digital Equipment Corporation	VNswitch 900EA	Y	Y	Y	Y		400 Mbps for in-hub configuration
FORE Systems, Inc.	ForeRunner ASX-1000			Y	Y		10 Gbps
General DataComm	APEX Strobos, NPX, DV2, MAC, MAC1 switches			Y	Y	Y	Up to 25.6 Gbps
IBM Corporation	IBM 2225 Nways Multiservice Switch, Model 400/450			Y	Y		1.2 Gbps FDX
IBM Corporation	IBM 2230 Nways ATM Switch Model 600 and 650			Y	Y	Y	2.5 to 5 Gbps (Model 600, 650)
NEC America, Inc.	Atomnet/M20				Y	Y	10 - 160 Gbps
NewBridge Networks	MainStreet*Xpress* 36190				Y	Y	>1 Tbps
NewBridge Networks	MainStreet*Xpress* 36170			Y		Y	Scalable 800 Mbps to 51.2 Gbps
NewBridge Networks	MainStreet*Xpress* 36150			Y	Y		>2.5
Sahara Networks, Inc.	SA-1200 Service Access Multiplexer			Y	Y		*
Siemens Stromberg-Carlson	MainStreet*Xpress* 36190				Y	Y	>1 Tbps
Siemens Stromberg-Carlson	MainStreet*Xpress* 36170			Y			Max.12.8 Gbps
Telematics International	Telematics switch			Y			3.5 Gbps

Table 14.1 Comparison of WAN Edge and Backbone Switches (continued)

Name	ADC Kentrox	Cascade Communications	Digital Equipment Corporation	Digital Equipment Corporation	Digital Equipment Corporation	Digital Equipment Corporation
Address	14375 NW Science Park Drive, Portland, OR 97229	5 Carlisle Road, Westford, MA 01886	LKG1-2/W06, 550 King Street, Littleton, MA 01581	LKG1-2/W06, 550 King Street, Littleton, MA 01581	LKG1-2/W06, 550 King Street, Littleton, MA 01581	LKG1-2/W06, 550 King Street, Littleton, MA 01581
Web Page	kentrox.com	cascade.com	networks.digital.com	networks.digital.com	networks.digital.com	networks.digital.com
Annual Sales 1994	n/a	$58.1M				
Annual Sales 1995	n/a	$134.8M				
Annual Sales 1996	$135M	$230.6M				
Number of Customers	100	n/a	n/a	n/a	n/a	n/a
Number of Switches Sold	650 ATM Access Concentrators	n/a	n/a	n/a	n/a	n/a
Number of ATM Ports Sold	25,000	n/a	n/a	n/a	n/a	n/a
Product Information						
Product Name	ATM Access Concentrator-3	CBX 500	GIGAswitch/ATM (14 Slot)	GIGAswitch/ATM (5 Slot)	ATM switch 900	ATM switch 900
Product Categories						
Workgroup			Y	Y	Y	Y
Campus Backbone			Y	Y	Y	Y
Enterprise	Y	Y	Y	Y	Y	Y
CPE Access	Y	Y	Y	Y	Y	Y
Carrier Edge	Y	Y	Y	Y	Y	Y
Carrier Backbone	Y	Y	Y	Y	Y	Y
AC Power	Y	Y	Y	Y	Y	Y
DC Power	Y	Y	Y	Y	Y (hub only)	Y (hub only)
Minimum Switch Price	$15,000	$25k	$13,695	$12,600		$13,695
Configuration	Four slot, power supply, T1 ATM unit, 2 PKT ports, 2 CBR ports		GIGAswitch Chassis, Clock Module, Dual AC Power Supply, 622 SMF	GIGAswitch Chassis, Clock Module, AC Power Supply, 4 ports 155Mbps UTP	ATM switch 900 8 port ATM switch with 6 UTP and 2 ModPHY (UTP) ports	ATM switch 900 Module with 6UTP and 2 ModPHY (UTP) ports
Maximum Switch Price	$60,000	$500k	$275,500	$86,250		$20,995
Configuration	Fully loaded, eight slot, with 24 ports, T1/FT1, redundant power, T3 ATM unit		GIGAswitch Chassis, Clock Module, Dual AC Power Supply, 13 ports 622 SMF	GIGAswitch Chassis, Clock Module, Dual AC Power Supply, 4 ports 622 Mbps SMF	ATM switch 900 Module, 6ports MMF and 2 ports SMF	Memory switch with 1.6 Gbps bandwidth
Switch Fabric/Bus Capacity	524 Mb/s	5 Gbps	Cross Bar fabric of 10.4Gb/s	Cross Bar fabric of 3.2Gb/s	Cross Bar fabric of 3.2Gb/s	Memory switch with 1.6 Gbps bandwidth
Max Sum of Port Speeds	524 Mb/s	5 Gbps	155Mbps x 52 ports = 8.060Gb/s, 622Mbps x 13 ports = 8.086Gbps	155Mbps x 16 ports = 2.48Gb/s, 622Mbps x 4 ports = 2.488Gbps	155Mbps x 8 ports = 1.24Gb/s	
% Blocking at Load per GR-1110			Non blocking cross-bar fabric	Non blocking cross-bar fabric	Non blocking cross-bar fabric	Non blocking cross-bar fabric
CBR	non-blocking	0	Now for CBR & VBR	Now for CBR & VBR	Now for CBR & VBR	Now for CBR & VBR
VBR	non-blocking	0	Now for UBR	Now for UBR	Now for UBR	Now for UBR
Point-to-Multipoint Capability						
Spatial	Y		n/a	n/a	n/a	n/a
Logical	Y	Y	Y	Y	Y	Y
Min Switch Transit Delay	N/A (not a switch)	15 msec	<15us port to port	<15us port to port	<15us port to port	<15us port to port
VPI/VCI Bits on UNI	8 / 16	8/14	8bits/12bits	8bits/12bits	8bits/12bits	8bits/12bits
VPI/VCI Bits on NNI	N/A / No NNI available	12/16	12bits/16bits	12bits/16bits	12bits/16bits	12bits/16bits
Max PVC VPCs per card/switch	512	16k/14	4 VPs / 52 VPs	4 VPs / 52 VPs	98/98	98/98
Max PVC VCCs per card/switch	4096	16k/14	4096/16K	4096/16K	4096/16K	4096/16K
Max SVCs per card/switch	2098	16k/14	28K/28K	28K/28K	28K/28K	28K/28K
Port Redundancy (1:1, 1:N, other)	n/a	1:1	Line Card Redundancy	Line Card Redundancy	Line Card Redundancy	Multiple modules
Common Eqpmt Redundancy						
Power	Y	Y	Y	Y	Y	Y (in hub)
Fabric/Bus	Y	Y	Y	Y		
Controller	future	Y	Y	Y		
Other			Line card redundancy	Line card redundancy	n/a	n/a
Distinguishing Features	*	*	*	*	*	

Table 14.1 Comparison of WAN Edge and Backbone Switches (continued)

Interface Information	ADC Kentrox	Cascade Communications	Digital Equipment Corporation	Digital Equipment Corporation	Digital Equipment Corporation	Digital Equipment Corporation
ATM UNI Interfaces						
DS1	Y	Y	Y	Y	Y	Y
nxDS1 IMA	Y	-	-	-	-	-
DS3	Y	Y	Y	Y	Y	Y
OC3	Y	Y	Y	Y	Y	Y
OC12	-	Y	Y	Y	Y	-
OC48	-	-	-	-	-	Y
155Mbps SMF	-	-	Y	Y	Y	-
622Mbps SMF	-	-	Y	Y	-	-
Cell-Based Clear Chan TC/HSSI	Y	Y	Y	Y	Y	Y
E1	Y	Y	Y	Y	Y	Y
E3	Y	Y	Y	Y	Y	Y
E4	-	-	-	-	-	-
STM-1	Y	Y	Y	Y	Y	Y
STM-4	-	Y	Y	Y	-	-
J1	-	-	-	-	-	-
J2 (6.312 Mb/s)	Y	98	-	-	-	-
25 Mb/s UTP	-	-	-	-	-	-
51.84 Mb/s UTP	-	-	-	-	-	-
155 Mb/s UTP	-	-	Y	Y	Y	Y
155 Mb/s MMF	Y	Y	Y	Y	Y	Y
TAXI 100Mbps	-	-	-	-	-	-
Other						
Non-ATM Interfaces						
10 Mbps Ethernet	Y	-	Y	Y	Y	Y
100 Mb/s Ethernet	*	-	-	-	97	Y
FDDI	*	-	-	-	97	Y
4 Mb/s Token Ring	*	-	-	-	-	Y
16 Mb/s Token Ring	*	-	-	-	-	Y
Frame Relay nxDS0, DS1, >DS1	Y	-	-	-	-	Y
Frame Relay E1						
SMDS DS1 & DS3	Y	-				
SMDS DXI nxDS0 & DS1	X	-				
HDLC V.35 & HSSI	Y	-				
Circuit Emulation DS1						
Circuit Emulation						
Serial IO Circuit Emulation (EIA 530, EIA 449, X.21, V.35)						
M-JPEG,H.320 Video						
JPEG-PAL, JPEG-NTS						
H.320 Video						
FUNI						

Table 14.1 Comparison of WAN Edge and Backbone Switches (continued)

Traffic Management	ADC Kentrox	Cascade Communications	Digital Equipment Corporation	Digital Equipment Corporation	Digital Equipment Corporation	Digital Equipment Corporation
ATM Service Classes Supported						
CBR		Y	Y	Y	Y	Y
rt-VBR		Y	Y	Y	Y	Y
nrt-VBR	Y	Y	Y	Y	Y	Y
UBR	Y	Y	Y	Y	Y	Y
ABR	Y	Y	Y	Y	Y	Y
Switch Type (Fabric, Bus, Other)	Fabric	Fabric	13 x 13 Non-blocking cross bar fabric	4 x 4 Non-blocking cross bar fabric	Memory based switch	
Switch Buffering						
Input		Y	Y	Y	Y	Y
Fabric		Y				
Output		•				
Switch Buffer Quantity/Port	4700 cells / HSCPM	Fabric 128,000; Output 24,000/port				
Switch Architecture (Narrative)	2000 cells / LSCPM	•	•	•	•	
ATM Forum Congestion Control						
EFCI	Y	Y	Y	Y	Y	Y
ER	Y	-	98	98	98	98
VS/VD		-	98	98	98	98
Other	Y	-	QFC in 1998/GFC in 97 FLOWmaster: Hop by hop credit based flow control	QFC in 1998/GFC in 97 FLOWmaster: Hop by hop credit based flow control	FLOWmaster: Hop by hop credit based flow control	FLOWmaster: Hop by hop credit based flow control
Congestion Control	•	•	0	0	0	0
Cell Loss Probability						
CBR	10^-x at GR-1110 Specified Load	0	0 with Flow Control	0 with Flow Control	0 with Flow Control	0 with Flow Control
VBR	10^-x at GR-1110 Specified Load	VBR adjustable 10^-1 to 10^-12, CDV objectives defineable	0 with Flow Control	0 with Flow Control	0 with Flow Control	0 with Flow Control
CLP Bit Usage						
Tag	Y	Y	Y	Y	Y	Y
Selective Discard	Y	Y				
Other						
Policing						
PCR		Y	Y	Y	Y	Y
PCR+SCR	Y					
Other			Late 97	Late 97	Late 97	Late 97
Shaping						
PCR		No	Y	Y	Y	Y
PCR+SCR	Y	No	Y	Y	Y	Y
Other						
Connection Admission Control						
GCAC		Y	97	97	97	97
Other	Y	CAC with Crankback	CAC with Crankback	CAC with Crankback	CAC with Crankback	CAC with Crankback
Packet Discard						
EPD	Y	Y	Y	Y	Y	Y (traffic shaping for CBR ckts)
PPD	Y	Y				
Frame Policing						
Other	Y	Now (Traffic Shaping for CBR)	Now (Traffic Shaping for CBR)	Now (Traffic Shaping for CBR)	Now (Traffic shaping for CBR)	
I.610 OAM Performance Measurement		97 - F4 and F5 Flows	97 - F4 and F5 Flows	97 - F4 and F5 Flows	97 - F4 and F5 Flows	
Measurement	Y	Y				

Table 14.1 Comparison of WAN Edge and Backbone Switches (continued)

Protocol/Standards Support	ADC Kentrox	Cascade Communications	Digital Equipment Corporation	Digital Equipment Corporation	Digital Equipment Corporation	Digital Equipment Corporation
ATM Forum						
UNI Signaling						
3.0	Y	Y	Y	Y	Y	Y
3.1	Y	Y	Y	Y	Y	Y
4.0	Y	Y	Y	Y	Y	Y
Other		97	97	97	97	97
Pt-Pt SVC Signaling						
3.0		Y	Y	Y	Y	Y
3.1		Y	Y	Y	Y	Y
4.0		Y	Y	Y	Y	Y
Other		97	97	97	97	97
Pt-Mpt SVC Signaling						
3.0		Y	Y	Y	Y	Y
3.1		Y	Y	Y	Y	Y
4.0		Y	Y	Y	Y	Y
Other	Y	97	97	97	97	97
NNI Signaling						
IISP		Y	Y	Y	Y	Y
PNNI 1.0		97	97	97	Y	Y
BICI 2.0		97	97	97	97	97
ITU-T		97	98	98	98	98
UNI Signaling						
Q.93B						
Q.2931	Y	Y	Y	Y	Y	Y
NNI Signaling						
BISUP		Y	Y	Y	Y	Y
Other	97	97				
LAN Emulation Client		No	No	No	No	No
LANE 1.0		IISP and DECNNI	IISP and DECNNI	IISP and DECNNI	IISP and DECNNI	IISP and DECNNI
RFC 1483	Y	Y	Y	Y	Y	Y
LAN Emulation Server		Y	Y	Y	Y	Y
LANE 1.0						
RFC 1483	Y	Y	Y	Y	Y	Y
Virtual LAN Capability	Treat it transparently	Y	Y	Y	Y	Y
		*	*	*	*	*
IP/ATM Client: RFC 1577	n/a	n/a	n/a	n/a	n/a	n/a
IP/ATM Server: RFC 1577	n/a	*	*	*	*	*
MPOA: ATM Forum	future	98	98	Y	Y	Y
NHRP	future	98	98	98	*	*
Tested Interoperation with others	*	98	98	98	98	98
Distinguishing Features		*	*	*	*	*

Table 14.1 Comparison of WAN Edge and Backbone Switches (continued)

Network Management Support	ADC Kentrox	Cascade Communications	Digital Equipment Corporation	Digital Equipment Corporation	Digital Equipment Corporation
Full ATM Forum ILMI					
3.0		Y	Y	Y	Y
3.1		Y	Y	Y	Y
4.0		97	97	97	97
Other					
ILMI Address Registration					
3.0		Y	Y	Y	Y
3.1		Y	Y	Y	Y
4.0		97	97	97	97
Other					
RFC 1695 (ATOM MIB)		Y	Y	Y	Y
Per Port Statistics		Y	Y	Y	Y
Per VC Statistics		Y	Y	Y	Y
OAM Cell VPC AIS/RDI		98	98	98	97
OAM Cell VCC AIS/RDI		Y	Y	Y	Y
OAM Cell Loopback		Y	Y	Y	Y
ATM Forum NM I/F Support					
M1					
M2					
M3		97			
M4		Y	Y		
M5		Y	Y		
Automatic PVC Configuration					
SPVPC/SPVCC		98 / 97	98 / 97	98 / 97	98 / 97
Other					
Automatic PVC Restoration					
SPVPC/SPVCC		98 / 97	98 / 97	98 / 97	98 / 97
Other			Automatic PVC restoration supported now	Automatic PVC restoration supported now	Automatic PVC restoration supported now
NMS Support					
HPOV	Y				
Cabletron Spectrum Enterprise					
SunNet Manager					
NetView 6000/AIX					
Others					
MIB Support			MIB-II, SONET MIB (RFC 1595), ILMI, ATM, DEC ATM MIB	MIB-II, SONET MIB (RFC 1595), ILMI, ATM, DEC ATM MIB	MIB-II, SONET MIB (RFC 1595), ILMI, ATM, DEC ATM MIB
Distinguishing Features		•	•		•

Table 14.1 Comparison of WAN Edge and Backbone Switches (continued)

Name	Digital Equipment Corporation	FORE Systems, Inc	General DataComm	IBM Corporation	IBM Corporation
Address	LKG1-2/W06, 550 King Street, Littleton, MA 01581	1000 FORE Drive, Warrendale, PA 15086	6520 Powers Ferry Road, Suite 370, Atlanta, GA	Old Orchard Road, Armonk, NY 10504	Old Orchard Road, Armonk, NY 10504
Web Page	networks.digital.com	fore.com	gdc.com	raleigh.ibm.com	raleigh.ibm.com
Annual Sales 1994		$39.3M	$211M	n/a	n/a
Annual Sales 1995		$106.2M	$221M	n/a	n/a
Annual Sales 1996		$235.2M	$235M	n/a	n/a
Number of Customers	n/a	2000	>200	n/a	n/a
Number of Switches Sold	n/a	5519 (3/4 CY96)	1,500+	n/a	n/a
Number of ATM Ports Sold	n/a	55,000 (3/4 CY96)	16,000+	n/a	n/a
Product Information					
Product Name	VNswitch 900EA	ASX-1000	APEX Strobos, NPX, DV2, MAC, MAC1 Switches	IBM 2225 Nways 400/500 Multiservice	IBM 2230 Nways 600/650 ATM Switch
Product Categories					
Workgroup	Y				
Campus Backbone	Y				
Enterprise			Y		Y
CPE Access	Y		Y		Y
Carrier Edge	Y		Y		Y
Carrier Backbone			Y		Y
AC Power	Y (in hub)		Y	Y	Y
DC Power	Y (in hub)		Y	Y	Y
Minimum Switch Price	?		$13,000	n/a	n/a
Configuration	VNswitch 900EA Module with 12 Ethernet 10BaseT ports and 1 ModPHY (155 Mbps MMF) port	1 fabric, no ports	List Price: APEX MAC1 w/1 MM Oc3c and 1 ATM serial link	n/a	Model 600 Base + 4 OC3
Maximum Switch Price/Configuration	?	?	$554,500	n/a	n/a
Configuration	Module w/12 Ethernet 10BaseT ports & 1 ModPHY 155 Mbps SMF port	4 fabrics, 64 OC-3c ports	NPX w/redundant switch fabrics, common logic, power and 30 OC-3c ports	n/a	Model 650 Base + 56 OC3
Switch Fabric/Bus Capacity	Bus bandwidth of 400Mbps for in hub configuration	10 Gbps	Fabric: from 1.6 to 25.6Gbps (w/Strobos)	1.2 Gb/s FDX	2.5 to 5 Gbps (Model 600, 650)
Max Sum of Port Speeds	155Mbps x 1 port + 10Mbps x 12 ports = 275Mb/s	10 Gbps	19.9 Gbps (Strobos) through 630 Mbps FDX 1.24 Gbps (MAC1)		3.8 to 9 Gbps (Model 600, 650)
% Blocking at Load per GR-1110	n/a		n/a	n/a	n/a
CBR			n/a		n/a
VBR			n/a		n/a
Point-to-Multipoint Capability					
Spatial	0		Y		
Logical	0		Y		Y
Min Switch Transit Delay	<19us Eth-Eth port	14 us	< 10 microsecs	n/a	n/a
VPI/VC Bits on UNI	8bits/12bits		8/16		full ATMF bit range
VPI/VC Bits on NNI	12bits/16bits		12/16		full ATMF bit range
Max PVC VPCs per card/switch	4 VPs	32k/128k	4 VPs/4VPs		2K/23K
Max PVC VCCs per card/switch	4K/4K	32k/128k	750/1000	4 K VC Trunk/Card	16K/224K
Max SVCs per card/switch	4K/4K	32k/128k	750/1000	n/a	16K/224K
Port Redundancy (1:1, 1:N, other)	Multiple modules		750/1000	1:1	1:1
Common Eqpmt Redundancy			1:1		
Power	Y (in hub)			Y	
Fabric/Bus	n/a		Y		Y
Controller	n/a		Y		Y
Other	n/a		Y		Y
Distinguishing Features	•	•	•		•

Table 14.1 Comparison of WAN Edge and Backbone Switches (continued)

Interface Information	Digital Equipment Corporation	FORE Systems, Inc	General DataComm.	IBM Corporation	IBM Corporation
ATM UNI Interfaces					
DS1	Y	Y	Y	-	Y
nxDS1 IMA	-	-	Y	-	-
DS3	Y	Y	Y	Y	Y
OC3	Y	Y	Y	Y	Y
OC12	-	97	97	-	Y
OC48	-	-	98	-	-
155Mbps SMF	Y	-	Y	-	-
622Mbps SMF	-	-	-	-	-
Cell-Based Clear Chan TC/HSSI	Y	-	-	-	-
E1	Y	Y	Y	Y	Y
E3	Y	Y	Y	-	Y
E4	-	-	-	-	-
STM-1	Y	Y	Y	Y	Y
STM-4	-	97	97	-	Y
J1	-	-	-	-	-
J2 (6.312 Mb/s)	-	Y	Y	-	-
25 Mb/s UTP	-	Y	-	-	-
51.84 Mb/s UTP	-	-	-	-	-
155 Mb/s UTP	Y	Y	-	-	-
155 Mb/s MMF	Y	Y	Y	Y	Y
TAXI 100Mbps	-	-	-	-	-
Other			E2, DX21, DX27		
Non-ATM Interfaces					
10 Mbps Ethernet	Y		Y		
100 Mb/s Ethernet	Y		97		
FDDI	Y				
4 Mb/s Token Ring	Y				
16 Mb/s Token Ring	Y				
Frame Relay nxDS0, DS1, >DS1	Y		Y		
Frame Relay E1			Y		
SMDS DS1 & DS3			Y		
SMDS DXI nxDS0 & DS1			Y		
HDLC V.35 & HSSI			Y		
Circuit Emulation DS1			Y		
Circuit Emulation			Y		
Serial IO Circuit Emulation (EIA 530, EIA 449, X.21, V.35)			Y		
M-JPEG H.320 Video			Y		
JPEG-PAL, JPEG-NTS					
H.320 Video			Y		
FUNI			Y		

Table 14.1 Comparison of WAN Edge and Backbone Switches (continued)

Traffic Management	Digital Equipment Corporation	FORE Systems, Inc	General DataComm.	IBM Corporation	IBM Corporation
ATM Service Classes Supported					
CBR	Y	Y	Y	Y	Y
rt-VBR	Y	Y	Y	Y	Y
nrt-VBR	Y	Y	Y	Y	Y
UBR	Y	Y	Y	Y	Y
ABR	Y	Y	Y		Y
Switch Type (Fabric, Bus, Other)	Edge switch	Distributed shared memory	Fabric	Fabric	Fabric
Switch Buffering					
Input	n/a				
Fabric			Y		
Output		Y	Y		
Other					
Switch Buffer Quantity/Port	*		Input 64,000; Fabric 1,024; Output 64,000	•	16K Cells
Switch Architecture (Narrative)	*	*	*		•
ATM Forum Congestion Control					
EFCI	Y	Y	Y	Y	Y
ER		97	97		
VS/VD			98		
Other	FLOWmaster				Y
Congestion Control	FLOWmaster: Hop by hop credit based flow control		Open-loop and shaping		
Cell Loss Probability					
CBR	0	0			
VBR	0 with Flow Control	0	3.286×10^{-11}		
CLP Bit Usage					
Tag	Y	Y	Y	Y	Y
Selective Discard	n/a	Y	Y	Y	Y
Other					
Policing					
PCR	Y	Y	Y		Y
PCR+SCR	n/a	Y	Y		Y
Other					
Shaping					
PCR	n/a	97	Y		
PCR+SCR	n/a		Y		
Other					
Connection Admission Control					
GCAC	n/a	Y	Y		
Other	n/a		Effective Bandwidth	PCR,SCR	Proprietary
Packet Discard					
EPD	n/a	Y	Y	Y	Y
PPD	n/a	Y	Y		
Frame Policing	Y (traffic shaping for CBR ckts)	Y	Y		
I.610 OAM Performance Measurement	n/a	Y	Y	F4, F5 Alarm, Loopback	F4, F5 Alarm, Loopback

Table 14.1 Comparison of WAN Edge and Backbone Switches (continued)

Protocol/Standards Support	Digital Equipment Corporation	FORE Systems, Inc	General DataComm.	IBM Corporation	IBM Corporation
ATM Forum					
UNI Signaling					
3.0	Y	Y	Y	Y	Y
3.1	Y	Y	Y	Y	Y
4.0	97	97	97		4Q97
Other					
Pt-Pt SVC Signaling					
3.0	Y	Y	Y	Y	Y
3.1	Y	Y	Y	Y	Y
4.0	97	97	97		4Q97
Other					
Pt-Mpt SVC Signaling					
3.0	Y	Y	Y		Y
3.1	Y	Y	Y		Y
4.0	97	97	97		4Q97
Other					
NNI Signaling					
IISP	Y	Y	Y		Y
PNNI 1.0	n/a	97	97		4Q97
BICI 2.0	n/a		98		
ITU-T					
UNI Signaling					
Q.93B	Y		Y		
Q.2931	Y	Y	Y		Y
NNI Signaling					
BISUP	No		98		
Other					
LAN Emulation Client					
LANE 1.0	Y	Y	RFC 1483_Now		
RFC 1483	Y	Y			
LAN Emulation Server					
LANE 1.0	n/a	Y			
RFC 1483	Y	Y			
Virtual LAN Capability	*	LEC/BUS can run on switch controller			
IP/ATM Client: RFC 1577	Y	Y			
IP/ATM Server: RFC 1577	*	Y			
MPOA: ATM Forum	98				
NHRP	n/a				
Tested Interoperation with others	*	*			*
Distinguishing Features	*				*

Table 14.1 Comparison of WAN Edge and Backbone Switches (continued)

Network Management Support	Digital Equipment Corporation	FORE Systems, Inc	General DataComm.	IBM Corporation	IBM Corporation
Full ATM Forum ILMI					
3.0	Y	Y	97		
3.1	Y	Y	97		Y
4.0	97	97	97		
Other					
ILMI Address Registration					
3.0	Y	Y	Y		
3.1	Y	Y	Y		Y
4.0	97	97	97		
Other					
RFC 1695 (ATOM MIB)	Y	Y	Y		Y
Per Port Statistics	Y	Y	Y		Y
Per VC Statistics	n/a	Y	Y		Y
OAM Cell VPC AIS/RDI	98		Y	Y	Y
OAM Cell VCC AIS/RDI	Y		Y	Y	Y
OAM Cell Loopback	Y		Y	Y	Y
ATM Forum NM I/F Support					
M1	n/a				
M2	n/a				
M3	n/a		97		
M4	n/a		97		
M5	n/a				
Automatic PVC Configuration					
SPVPC/SPVCC	n/a	Y	Y		
Other					
Automatic PVC Restoration					
SPVPC/SPVCC	n/a	Y	Y		
Other	Automatic PVC restoration supported now				
NMS Support			*see chapter		
HPOV	Y	Y			Y
Cabletron Spectrum Enterprise					
SunNet Manager	Y	Y			
NetView 6000/AIX	Y	Y			
Others					
MIB Support	MIB-II, SONET MIB (RFC 1595), ILMI, ATM, DEC ATM MIB				
Distinguishing Features	*		*		*

Table 14.1 Comparison of WAN Edge and Backbone Switches (continued)

Name	NEC America, Inc.	NewBridge Networks	NewBridge Networks	NewBridge Networks	Sahara Networks, Inc.
Address	1525 W Walnut Hill Lane, Irving, TX 75038	593 Herndon Parkway, Herndon, VA 22070	593 Herndon Parkway, Herndon, VA 22070	593 Herndon Parkway, Herndon, VA 22070	860 North Main Street, Wallingford, CT 06492
Web Page	nec.com	newbridge.com	newbridge.com	newbridge.com	info@saharanet.com
Annual Sales 1994	n/a	n/a	n/a	n/a	n/a
Annual Sales 1995	n/a	n/a	n/a	n/a	n/a
Annual Sales 1996	$41 B	n/a	n/a	n/a	n/a
Number of Customers	n/a	n/a	n/a	n/a	n/a
Number of Switches Sold	M20 = 30, M7 = 500	>200 carriers in 80+ countries	>200 carriers in 80+ countries	n/a	n/a
Number of ATM Ports Sold	n/a	n/a	n/a	n/a	n/a
Product Information					
Product Name	Atomnet/M20	MainStreet*Xpress* 36190	MainStreet*Xpress* 36170	MainStreet*Xpress* 36150	SA-1200 Service Access Multiplexer
Product Categories					
Workgroup					
Campus Backbone					
Enterprise					
CPE Access		Y	Y	Y	Y
Carrier Edge		Y	Y	Y	Y
Carrier Backbone	Y	Y	Y	Y	Y
AC Power	Y	Y	Y	Y	Y
DC Power	N	Y	Y	Y	
Minimum Switch Price	n/a	$25,000	$25,000	n/a	$19,000
Configuration	n/a	n/a	n/a	n/a	
Maximum Switch Price/Configuration	n/a	$1M	n/a	n/a	$125,000
Configuration	n/a	n/a	n/a	n/a	
Switch Fabric/Bus Capacity	10 - 160 Gbps	>1Tbps	scaleable 800 Mbps to 51.2 Gbps	>2.5 Gbps	*
Max Sum of Port Speeds	10 - 160 Gbps	1Tbps	2.5		max 72 ports
% Blocking at Load per GR-1110					
CBR	n/a	non-blocking	non-blocking	non-blocking	
VBR	n/a	non-blocking	non-blocking	non-blocking	
Point-to-Multipoint Capability	Y	Y	Y	Y	Y
Spatial	Y	Y	Y	Y	
Logical	Y	Y			
Min Switch Transit Delay	125 ms	16us	<25 microsec.	<18 μs *	
VPI/VCI Bits on UNI	8 bits/14 bits	16 / 16	8 / 16	6 / 9	
VPI/VCI Bits on NNI	12bits/14bits	16 / 16	12 / 15	6 / 9	
Max PVC VPCs per card/switch	4K/32K	8192/2,000,000	6000/16000	2000/node	4,096/24,576
Max PVC VCCs per card/switch	4K/32K	8192/2,000,000	6000/16000	2000/node	4,096/24,576
Max SVCs per card/switch	TBD/TBD	8192/2,000,000	6000/16000	0	4,096/120,000
Port Redundancy (1:1, 1:N, other)	1:1	1:1, 1:N	1:1 & 1:N planned		1:1 3Q97
Common Eqpmt Redundancy					
Power					
Fabric/Bus	Y	Y	Y	Y	Y
Controller	Y	Y	Y	Y	2Q97
Other	Y	Y	Y	Y	Y
Distinguishing Features		•	•	•	•

Table 14.1 Comparison of WAN Edge and Backbone Switches (continued)

Interface Information	NEC America, Inc.	NewBridge Networks	NewBridge Networks	NewBridge Networks	Sahara Networks, Inc.
ATM UNI Interfaces					
DS1	-	Y	Y	Y	Y
nxDS1 IMA	-	-	-	-	Y
DS3	Y	Y	Y	Y	Y
OC3	Y	Y	Y	Y	Y
OC12	Y	Y	Y	-	Y
OC48	-	-	-	-	-
155Mbps SMF	-	-	Y	-	-
622Mbps SMF	-	-	-	-	-
Cell-Based Clear Chan TC/HSSI	-	-	-	-	-
E1	Y	Y	Y	Y	Y
E3	Y	Y	Y	Y	Y
E4	-	-	-	-	-
STM-1	Y	Y	Y	Y	Y
STM-4	Y	Y	Y	-	Y
J1	-	-	-	-	-
J2 (6.312 Mb/s)	-	-	-	-	Y
25 Mb/s UTP	-	-	-	-	Y
51.84 Mb/s UTP	-	-	-	-	-
155 Mb/s UTP	-	-	Y	-	Y
155 Mb/s MMF	-	-	Y	-	Y
TAXI 100Mbps	-	-	-	-	-
Other				140 Mbps	
Non-ATM Interfaces					
10 Mbps Ethernet				Y	Y
100 Mbps Ethernet					Y
FDDI				Y	Y
4 Mb/s Token Ring				Y	Y
16 Mb/s Token Ring				Y	Y
Frame Relay nxDS0, DS1, >DS1			Y		Y
Frame Relay E1					Y
SMDS DS1 & DS3				DS1 only	Y
SMDS DXI nxDS0 & DS1				Y	
HDLC V.35 & HSSI				Y	Y
Circuit Emulation DS1	nxDS0 only		all except nxDS0	Y	Y
Circuit Emulation					
Serial IO Circuit Emulation (EIA 530, EIA 449, X.21, V.35)					Y
M-JPEG,H.320 Video					Y
JPEG-PAL, JPEG-NTS				Y	
H.320 Video					Y
FUNI					

Table 14.1 Comparison of WAN Edge and Backbone Switches (continued)

Traffic Management	NEC America, Inc.	NewBridge Networks	NewBridge Networks	NewBridge Networks	Sahara Networks, Inc.
ATM Service Classes Supported					
CBR	Y	Y	Y	Y	Y
rt-VBR	Y	Y	Y	Y	Y
nrt-VBR	Y	Y	now	Y	Y
UBR	Y	Y	Y	Y	Y
ABR	Y	Y	Y	Y	•
Switch Type (Fabric, Bus, Other)	Fabric	Fabric	Broadcast matrix	Fabric	•
Switch Buffering					
Input	Y (32K)	Y		Y	Y
Fabric			Y		Y
Output	Y (32K)	Y		Y	Y
Switch Buffer Quantity/Port	n/a	224 k cells per SMU shared among all ports. Up to 31 SMUs per switch	Fabric 25,000 cells, Output 4000–32,000 cells	Output 1188/4 ports	•
Switch Architecture (Narrative)	•	•	•	•	•
ATM Forum Congestion Control					
EFCI	Y		Y	Y	Y
ER	1Q98	Y	planned		Y
VS/VD			planned		3Q97
Other					
Congestion Control	•	Y		EPD, PPD, CLP Packet discard for AAL5	•
Cell Loss Probability					
CBR	10^{-11}	10^{-10}	1.70E-10	1.00E-07	n/a
VBR	Yes (depends on loading of switch)	10^{-10}	1.00E-07		n/a
CLP Bit Usage					
Tag	Y	Y	Y	Y	Y
Selective Discard	Y	Y	Y	Y	Y
Other					
Policing					
PCR	Y	Y	Y	Y	Y
PCR+SCR	Y	Y	Y	Y	Y
Other	Y - MBS for VBR			CDVT	
Shaping					
PCR	Y	Y	planned	Y	Y
PCR+SCR	Y	Y	planed	Y	Y
Other				VPI/VCI, ABR	
Connection Admission Control					
GCAC	Y	Y			
Other	n/a	Sigma Rule		CAC	Y
Packet Discard					
EPD	Y	Y - Logical Queue Discard	Y	Y	Y
PPD	Y	Y	planned	Y	Y
Frame Policing			planned	Y	Y
Other				Logical Queue Discard	
I.610 OAM Performance Measurement	2H97	Y - also supports GR 1248	Y	Y	Y

Table 14.1 Comparison of WAN Edge and Backbone Switches (continued)

Protocol/Standards Support	NEC America, Inc.	NewBridge Networks	NewBridge Networks	NewBridge Networks	Sahara Networks, Inc.
ATM Forum					
UNI Signaling					
3.0					
3.1	Y	Y	Y	Y	Y
4.0	4Q97	Y	4Q97	98	Y
Other					
Pt-Pt SVC Signaling					
3.0	Y	Y	Y		Y
3.1	Y		Y	98	Y
4.0	4Q97	Y			Y
Other					
Pt-Mpt SVC Signaling					
3.0	Y	Y	planned		Y
3.1	Y				Y
4.0	4Q97	Y			
Other					
NNI Signaling					
IISP	Y	Y	Y		Y
PNNI 1.0	Y	Y	now		
BICI 2.0	Y	Y	now		
ITU-T					
UNI Signaling					
Q.93B	Y				Y
Q.2931	Y	Y	Y		
NNI Signaling					
BISUP	4Q97	Y	planned		97
Other	Y - NISUP				
LAN Emulation Client					
LANE 1.0	planned	planned	FR/ATM SIW		3Q97
RFC 1483	planned	planned			Y
LAN Emulation Server					
LANE 1.0	planned				Y
RFC 1483	planned				Y
Virtual LAN Capability	planned		Layer 3 LAN/WAN integration planned		3Q97
IP/ATM Client: RFC 1577	planned				3Q97
IP/ATM Server: RFC 1577	planned				3Q97
MPOA: ATM Forum					No
NHRP	planned				
Tested Interoperation with others	*				
Distinguishing Features	*		*		*

Table 14.1 Comparison of WAN Edge and Backbone Switches (continued)

Network Management Support	NEC America, Inc.	NewBridge Networks	NewBridge Networks	NewBridge Networks	Sahara Networks, Inc.
Full ATM Forum ILMI					
3.0		planned			
3.1	Y	planned	Y	Y	Y
4.0	4Q97	planned		98	Y
Other					
ILMI Address Registration					
3.0		planned			
3.1	Y	planned	Y		Y
4.0	4Q97	planned			Y
Other					
RFC 1695 (ATOM MIB)	Future	planned	Y		Y
Per Port Statistics	Y		Y		Y
Per VC Statistics	Y	Y	Y	Y	Y
OAM Cell VPC AIS/RDI	Y	Y	Y	Y	Y
OAM Cell VCC AIS/RDI	Y	Y	Y	Y	Y
OAM Cell Loopback	Y	Y	Y	Y	Y
ATM Forum NM I/F Support					
M1					
M2	Y	Y			
M3					4Q97
M4	Future	Y	Y		4Q97
M5					
Automatic PVC Configuration					
SPVPC/SPVCC	planned	planned		98	Y
Other	in conjunction w/BNMS		SPVCC now		
Automatic PVC Restoration					
SPVPC/SPVCC		planned		98	
Other	in conjunction w/BNMS		Y		Y
NMS Support	*see chapter		*see chapter		*see chapter
HPOV					
Cabletron Spectrum Enterprise					
SunNet Manager					
NetView 6000/AIX					
Others					
MIB Support					
Distinguishing Features	*		*		*

Table 14.1 Comparison of WAN Edge and Backbone Switches (continued)

Name	SIEMENS Stromberg-Carlson	Siemens Stromberg-Carlson	Telematics International
Address	900 Broken Sound Parkway, Boca Raton, FL 33487	900 Broken Sound Parkway, Boca Raton, FL 33487	1201 W. Cypress Creek Road, Fort Lauderdale, FL 33309
Web Page	SSC.Siemens.com	SSC.Siemens.com	
Annual Sales 1994	n/a	n/a	n/a
Annual Sales 1995	n/a	n/a	$2.6M
Annual Sales 1996	n/a	n/a	n/a
Number of Customers	n/a	n/a	10
Number of Switches Sold	n/a	n/a	26
Number of ATM Ports Sold	n/a	n/a	156
Product Information			
Product Name	MainStreetXpress 36190	MainStreetXpress 36170	Telematics switch
Product Categories			
Workgroup			
Campus Backbone			
Enterprise			
CPE Access			
Carrier Edge			Y
Carrier Backbone	Y		Y
AC Power	Y		Y
DC Power	n/a	n/a	
Minimum Switch Price	n/a	n/a	$60K
Configuration	n/a	n/a	n/a
Maximum Switch Price/Configuration	n/a	n/a	$300K
Configuration	n/a	n/a	n/a
Switch Fabric/Bus Capacity	>1Tbps	max 12.8 GB/s	3.5 Gbps
Max Sum of Port Speeds	1Tbps	14.6 Gb/s	2.5 Gbps
% Blocking at Load per GR-1110	non-blocking	non-blocking	0
CBR	non-blocking	non-blocking	0
VBR			
Point-to-Multipoint Capability	Y	Y	switch
Spatial	Y	Y	IOCs
Logical	Y	Y	
Min Switch Transit Delay	16us	<25 microsec	23 us
VPI/VCI Bits on UNI	16_/16_	8/16	12/16
VPI/VCI Bits on NNI	16_/16_	12/16	256/4k
Max PVC VPCs per card/switch	8192/2,000,000	6000/16000	1k/16k
Max PVC VCCs per card/switch	8192/2,000,000	6000/16000	1k/16k
Max SVCs per card/switch	8192/2,000,000	6000/16000	
Port Redundancy (1:1, 1:N, other)	1:1, 1:N	N+1 card redundancy	1:1, 1:N
Common Eqpmt Redundancy			
Power	Y		Y
Fabric/Bus	Y		Y
Controller	Y		Y
Other			
Distinguishing Features			

Table 14.1 Comparison of WAN Edge and Backbone Switches (continued)

Interface Information	SIEMENS Stromberg-Carlson	Siemens Stromberg-Carlson	Telematics International
ATM UNI Interfaces			
DS1	Y	Y	Y
nxDS1 IMA	-	Y	98
DS3	Y	Y	Y
OC3	Y	Y	Y
OC12	Y	Y	98
OC48	-	-	98
155Mbps SMF	-	-	Y
622Mbps SMF	-	-	-
Cell-Based Clear Chan TC/HSSI	-	-	-
E1	Y	Y	-
E3	Y	Y	Y
E4	-	-	-
STM-1	Y	Y	Y
STM-4	Y	Y	98
J1	-	-	-
J2 (6.312 Mb/s)	-	-	-
25 Mb/s UTP	-	-	-
51.84 Mb/s UTP	-	-	-
155 Mb/s UTP	-	Y	-
155 Mb/s MMF	-	Y	97
TAXI 100Mbps	-	-	-
Other			
Non-ATM Interfaces			
10 Mbps Ethernet			
100 Mb/s Ethernet			
FDDI			
4 Mb/s Token Ring			
16 Mb/s Token Ring			
Frame Relay nxDS0, DS1, >DS1		Y	1Q97
Frame Relay E1			
SMDS DS1 & DS3			
SMDS DXI nxDS0 & DS1			
HDLC V.35 & HSSI			
Circuit Emulation DS1	Y		
Circuit Emulation	all except E1,E3		
Serial IO Circuit Emulation (EIA 530, EIA 449, X.21, V.35)			
M-JPEG,H.320 Video			
JPEG-PAL, JPEG-NTS			
H.320 Video			
FUNI			

Table 14.1 Comparison of WAN Edge and Backbone Switches (continued)

Traffic Management	SIEMENS Stromberg-Carlson	Siemens Stromberg-Carlson	Telematics International
ATM Service Classes Supported			
CBR	Y	Y	Y
rt-VBR	Y	Y	Y
nrt-VBR	Y	planned 2Q98	Y
UBR	Y	Y	Y
ABR	Y	Y	97
Switch Type (Fabric, Bus, Other)	Fabric	Fabric	Time-shared bus
Switch Buffering			
Input	Y	Y	
Fabric		Y	
Output	Y	Y	Y
Other			
Switch Buffer Quantity/Port	224k cells per SMU shared among all ports. Up to 31 SMUs per switch today	Input 256, Fabric 2000, Output 4000	8K per IOC, 140K/switch
Switch Architecture (Narrative)		output buffered broadcast matrix	*
ATM Forum Congestion Control			
EFCI	Y	Y	Y
ER			97
VS/VD			97
Other			
Congestion Control	Y		
Cell Loss Probability			
CBR	10^-10	1.70E-10	Zero
VBR	10^-10	1.00E-07	Zero with Flow Control
CLP Bit Usage			
Tag	Y	NOW	Y
Selective Discard	Y	planned 4Q97	Y
Other			
Policing			
PCR	Y	Y	planned 4Q97
PCR+SCR	Y - MBS for VBR	Y	planned 4Q97
Other			
Shaping			
PCR	Y	*see chapter	Y
PCR+SCR			Y
Other			
Connection Admission Control			
GCAC	Sigma Rule		Y
Other			
Packet Discard			
EPD	Y - Logical Queue Discard	Y	97
PPD	Y	planned 4Q97	Y
Frame Policing			Y
Other			
I.610 OAM Performance Measurement	Y - also supports GR 1248		Y

Table 14.1 Comparison of WAN Edge and Backbone Switches (continued)

Protocol/Standards Support	SIEMENS Stromberg-Carlson	Siemens Stromberg-Carlson	Telematics International
ATM Forum			
UNI Signaling			
3.0			Y
3.1	Y	Y	Y
4.0	Y	4Q97	98
Other			
Pt-Pt SVC Signaling			
3.0			
3.1	Y	4Q97	97
4.0	Y		98
Other			
Pt-Mpt SVC Signaling			
3.0			
3.1	Y		98
4.0	Y		98
Other			
NNI Signaling			
IISP	Y	Y	Y
PNNI 1.0	Y	4Q97	97
BICI 2.0	Y		
ITU-T			
UNI Signaling			
Q.93B			
Q.2931	Y	4Q97	Y
NNI Signaling			
BISUP	Y	Y	
Other	Y - NISUP		
LAN Emulation Client			
LANE 1.0	planned		98
RFC 1483	planned		98
LAN Emulation Server			
LANE 1.0	planned		98
RFC 1483	planned		98
Virtual LAN Capability	planned		
IP/ATM Client: RFC 1577	planned		98
IP/ATM Server: RFC 1577	planned		98
MPOA: ATM Forum		Y	Y
NHRP	planned		
Tested Interoperation with others			
Distinguishing Features			

Table 14.1 Comparison of WAN Edge and Backbone Switches (continued)

Network Management Support	SIEMENS Stromberg-Carlson	Siemens Stromberg-Carlson	Telematics International
Full ATM Forum ILMI			
3.0	planned		
3.1	planned	4Q97	Y
4.0	planned		
Other			
ILMI Address Registration			
3.0	planned		
3.1	planned		Y
4.0	planned		
Other			
RFC 1695 (ATOM MIB)	planned		Y
Per Port Statistics		4Q97	Y
Per VC Statistics	Y	4Q97	98
OAM Cell VPC AIS/RDI	Y	4Q97	Y
OAM Cell VCC AIS/RDI	Y	4Q97	Y
OAM Cell Loopback	Y	Y	Y
ATM Forum NM I/F Support			
M1			
M2			
M3	Y		
M4	Y	Y	Y
M5			
Automatic PVC Configuration			
SPVPC/SPVCC	planned		Y
Other			
Automatic PVC Restoration			
SPVPC/SPVCC	Y		Y
Other			
NMS Support			
HPOV			*See Chapter
Cabletron Spectrum Enterprise			Y
SunNet Manager			
NetView 6000/AIX			
Others			
MIB Support			
Distinguishing Features			

ATM in the Enterprise
and LAN Backbone

This chapter provides a comparison of ATM switches and devices in the enterprise and LAN/campus backbone. We start by defining enterprise and LAN backbone classes of switch. We next take a tour through the many device types found in the enterprise and LAN that contain ATM switching and interfaces, including routers, switches, hubs, and end systems. The detailed vendor analysis concludes the chapter. The shaded areas of Figure 15.1 show the context for ATM enterprise and LAN backbone switches in relation to other ATM switch categories.

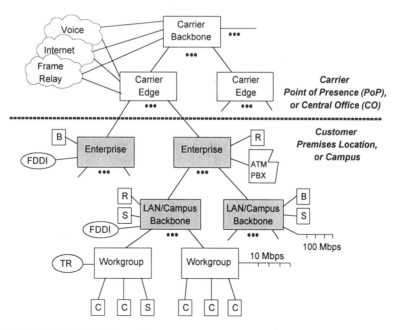

Figure 15.1 Enterprise and LAN Backbone Switching Roles

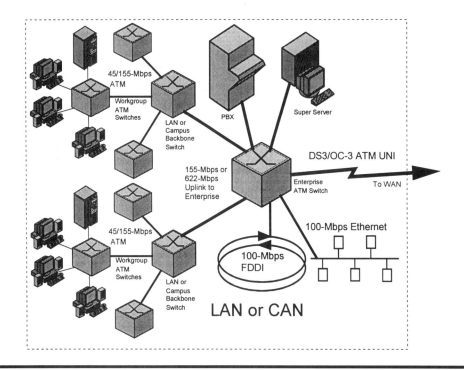

Figure 15.2 ATM Enterprise Switch

15.1 ENTERPRISE ATM SWITCHES

Enterprise ATM switched typically support [1]:
- Local networking
- Basic user-to-network interface connections
- LAN Emulation
- Multiple Quality of Service (QoS) classes and traffic management
- Switched Virtual Circuit (SVC) signaling
- Available bit rate support
- WAN connectivity

Enterprise ATM switches interface the customer premises to the wide area network. Figure 15.2 illustrates a typical ATM enterprise switch configuration.

ATM enterprise switches provide connectivity for both LAN backbone and workgroup ATM switches, as well as for high-speed LANs, such as FDDI and 100-Mbps Ethernet. An enterprise switch would be deployed when the requirements warrant a large switch that can provide many interfaces not found in larger ATM switches, such as native LAN (i.e., Ethernet and Token Ring), MAN (i.e., FDDI and DQDB), SNA, X.25, serial devices, and voice equipment (i.e., PBX). They are differentiated from LAN/campus backbone switches by their high-speed WAN access ports. Some also provide protocol conversion, LAN emulation, and virtual networking. Enterprise switches typically run on AC (i.e., wall outlet) power. They may have smaller port capacity than LAN backbone switches, but they sport higher-speed ports for interconnecting multiple LAN backbone switches and WAN interfaces at DS3 and OC-N speeds. Typically, these devices range in switching capacity from 5 to 10 Gbps and are designed for the customer premises [as opposed to the Central Office (CO)] environment. All ATM premises equipment — such as switches, routers, hubs, and bridges — plays an important role in ATM end-to-end networking.

Figures 15.3, 15.4, and 15.5 show FORE's Powerhub 7000, ForeRunner ASX-200WG, and CellPath 90 and 300 enterprise switches, respectively. These products span the enterprise from hub through workgroup and into WAN access, and provide a complementary set of switches for all enterprise needs.

Enterprise switches may be either AC- or DC-powered. Many enterprise switches also serve a dual role as carrier edge switches, personalized by the purchaser's choice of interface cards and redundant common equipment. Enterprise switches often have a management system that controls a network of switches. These devices are the Swiss army knife of ATM switches, supporting a multitude of various interface types.

15.2 LAN BACKBONE SWITCHES

LAN backbone switches typically support [2]:

- Workgroup switch connectivity
- Local networking
- Basic LAN interface connections
- LAN emulation
- Data-oriented traffic management
- SVC signaling
- Available bit rate support

ATM LAN or campus backbone switches provide hierarchical connectivity for workgroup ATM switches, with higher-speed uplinks of 155 Mbps at a minimum, and typically 622 Mbps. Figure 15.6 illustrates a typical LAN or campus backbone switch configuration, providing connections for local devices at ATM backbone speeds within a confined geographic area, such as a campus environment. The LAN/campus backbone often aggregates traffic into one or more uplinks to an enterprise switch and thus has only local interfaces, since the enterprise switch has WAN interfaces. LAN switches typically run on AC (i.e., wall outlet) power and make up for smaller port capacity and less processing power by being modular or stackable. These devices are usually located in wiring closets, in the main distribution frame (MDF), or in the data center area. Some level of redundancy is required, especially in processor cards and power supplies. For the purposes of our study, these devices range in switching capacity from approximately 1.0 to 5 Gbps.

Figure 15.3 FORE Systems' PowerHub 7000

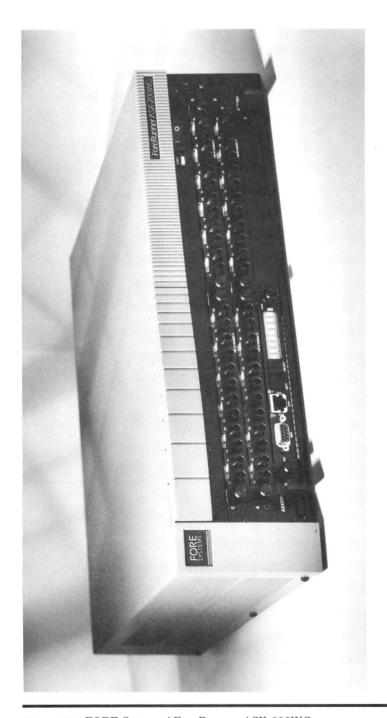

Figure 15.4 FORE Systems' ForeRunner ASX-200WG

Figure 15.5 FORE Systems' CellPath 90 and 300

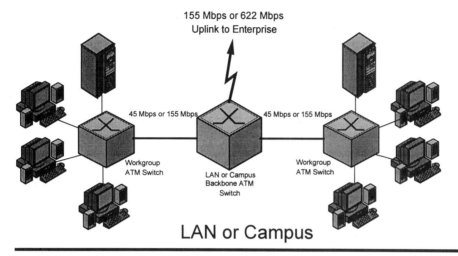

155 Mbps or 622 Mbps
Uplink to Enterprise

45 Mbps or 155 Mbps   45 Mbps or 155 Mbps

Workgroup
ATM Switch

LAN or Campus
Backbone ATM
Switch

Workgroup
ATM Switch

LAN or Campus

Figure 15.6 ATM LAN or Campus Backbone Switch

Figure 15.7 shows General Datacomm's APEX MAC LAN or campus backbone switch. The main characteristics of this switch can be found in Chapter 17. LAN/campus backbone switches usually support short-reach and long-reach interfaces. Interfaces are often on the front of the switch to allow wall mounting or installation in a telephone wiring closet.

15.3 ATM ENTERPRISE AND LAN BACKBONE DEVICES

This section reviews the various other types of ATM-based equipment used primarily in the local area customer premises, as opposed to within the service provider's network. These include routers, hubs, bridges, service access multiplexers, and CSU/DSUs. In some cases these devices serve as the backbone of the LAN/MAN/enterprise, and other times they interface to the WAN.

The rush of router, bridge, and hub manufacturers to embrace ATM in the industry trade press is dizzying. Simultaneously, it appears that everyone is moving into everyone else's area of functionality. Indeed, many products have a split personality: hubs and switches with router cards, hubs doing switching, and routers doing switching. Some ATM hardware contains some or all of these features and functions. This chapter focuses on ATM switching devices that serve many of these functions. Representative manufacturers and products are mentioned as examples in the following narrative, but this is by no means an exhaustive list.

Figure 15.7 General DataComm's APEX MAC ATM LAN Backbone Switch

15.3.1 Evolution of Routers, Bridges, and Hubs

Perhaps the greatest driving factor for routers, bridges, and hubs has been the LAN. Due to diverse markets, technologies, and protocol suites, a need evolved to make diverse LANs speak one language (or at least to provide a translation between similar languages on similar types of LANs — e.g., Ethernet to Ethernet, Token Ring to Token Ring). When bridges and routers first came along, they were designed to deal with local area networking. Now the functions of both are beginning to merge through the use of increased processor speeds and technologies [i.e., Reduced Instruction Set (RISC) processors and Application-Specific Integrated Circuits (ASIC)]. These advances yield reduced costs and enable devices to support both local and wide area networking at speeds ranging from analog modem speeds up to gigabits per second speeds over ATM and SONET interfaces.

The functions provided by routers, bridges, and hubs can be provided either separately or together in one piece of equipment. Each type of device provides protocol support for certain levels of the OSI reference model. Bridges provide level 1 and 2 support, while routers and hubs support layers 1, 2, and 3. Figure 15.8 illustrates this relationship to the OSI Reference Model (OSIRM) layers for bridges and routers.

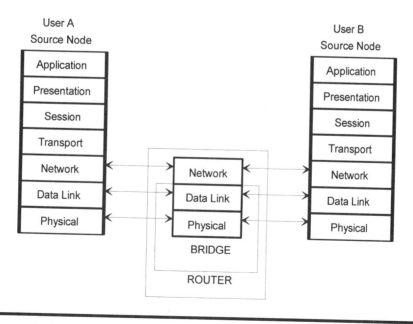

Figure 15.8 Bridge and Router Support for the OSI Protocol Layers

15.3.2 ATM Routers

Current high-end routers can forward on the order of 1 million IP packets per second and route at gigabits per second. Most LAN backbone–class routers have support for LAN emulation, as well as ATM user-network and network-network interfaces. The current generation of ATM routers reassemble packets and then process them. The ATM conversion is done on interface cards. Therefore, ATM capable routers accept multiple protocols and either route them to non-ATM ports or send them to ATM ports for conversion from packets to ATM cells for transport over an ATM switch. Examples of routers with ATM capabilities include the Cisco 7000 series, 3Com's OnCore product line, and Bay Networks' BCN routers.

15.3.3 ATM Hubs

Figure 15.9 illustrates the wiring collection, segmentation, and network management function a hub typically performs. Usually many Ethernet or Token Ring twisted pair lines, in some cases FDDI or ATM over twisted pair to individual workstations, are run to a hub, usually located in the wiring closet. Hubs allow administrators to assign individual users to a resource (e.g., an Ethernet segment), shown as an ellipse in the figure, via network management commands. Lower-level hubs are often connected in a hierarchy to higher-level hubs, sometimes via higher-speed protocols such as FDDI and ATM over optical fiber and high-grade twisted pairs. Hubs are often employed in a hierarchical manner to concentrate access for many individual users to a shared resource, such as a server or router as shown in Figure 15.9. The highest level hubs are candidates for a collapsed backbone architecture based on ATM, also supporting high-speed access to shared resources such as routers and switches.

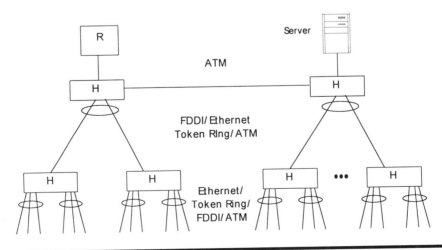

Figure 15.9 Hub Interfaces, Functions, and Architecture

Router and hub ATM interface cards support a wide range of industry standard interfaces, such as UTP, DS1, DS3, 100 Mbps (4B/5B), 140 Mbps (4B/5B0), 155 Mbps Fiberchannel, OC-3, and even OC-12. They typically come equipped with their own microprocessors. Hub cards have a broad range of functionality, including Permanent Virtual Circuits (PVCs) and SVCs, multicast (point-to-multipoint) and broadcast, AAL and guaranteed QoS support; support TCP/IP and ATM Application Programming Interfaces (APIs); and are SNMP MIB, CMIP, and RMON (1 and 2) compliant.

15.3.4 Other Local ATM Devices

This section covers the following other categories of local ATM devices: ATM multiplexers/concentrators, ATM bridging devices, and ATM Channel Service Units/Digital Service Units (CSU/DSUs). Figure 15.10 presents a pictorial representation of the interfaces and function of these devices. An ATM multiplexer takes multiple, often lower-speed ATM interfaces and concentrates them into smaller, often higher-speed ATM trunk interfaces. A bridging device takes a bridgeable protocol, such as Ethernet or Token Ring, and connects it over an ATM network. This makes it appear to the user devices as if they were on the same shared medium, or segment, as shown by the ellipse in the figure. A CSU/DSU takes the frame-based ATM Data Exchange Interface (DXI) over a High-Speed Serial Interface (HSSI) and converts it into a stream of ATM cells.

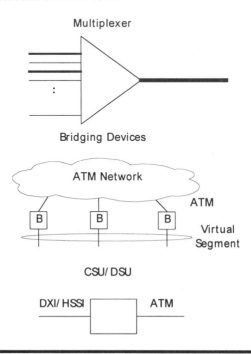

Figure 15.10 ATM Multiplexers, Bridges, and CSU/DSUs

15.3.4.1 ATM Multiplexers / Concentrators

A multiplexer, or concentrator, takes multiple ATM interfaces as input and concentrates them into a single ATM interface. A switch can also perform multiplexing; however, multiplexers are usually less expensive than switches because they have fewer functions. ATM multiplexers are available from ADC Kentrox, Fujitsu, Hitachi, and Sahara Networks. ATM access concentrators (like those from Yurie Systems, ADC Kentrox, and NetEdge Systems) have seen a booming business as users demand alternative lower-speed methods to access ATM public services.

15.3.4.2 ATM Bridging Devices

A bridging device encapsulates a bridged protocol, such as Ethernet, and emulates the encapsulated protocol's bridging functions. These include self-learning and self-healing capabilities. Examples of ATM bridging devices are the Ethernet bridging port cards in the NewBridge 36150 and the Cisco LightStream 1010.

15.3.4.3 ATM CSU/DSUs

A CSU/DSU performs the conversion from a HSSI DTE/DCE interface operating at up to 50 Mbps utilizing the frame-based ATM DXI protocol to an ATM user-network interface. ATM CSU/DSU vendors include ADC Kentrox and Digital Link.

15.4 LAN Enterprise and Backbone Switch Study

Table 15.1 shows a summary of all enterprise and LAN/campus backbone switch survey respondents. Table 15.2 shows the results of the survey for enterprise and LAN/campus backbone switches.

15.5 REVIEW

This chapter covered the basics of enterprise and LAN backbone switches, complete with an in-depth vendor analysis. We also reviewed the characteristics of other LAN devices that have ATM interfaces, such as routers, hubs, bridges, multiplexers, and CSU/DSUs.

Table 15.1 Enterprise and LAN/Campus Backbone Switch Survey Respondents

Company Name	Product Name	WG	LB	E	CE	CB	Switch Fabric/Bus Capacity
Bay Networks	System 5000			Y		Y	3.2 Gbps
Cabletron Systems Sales & Service	Smartcell ZX-250			Y			2.5 Gbps
Cisco	Lightstream 1010	Y	Y				5 Gbps
FORE Systems, Inc.	ASX-200BX	Y	Y				2.5 Gbps
FORE Systems, Inc.	PowerHub 7000			Y			3.2 Gbps shared memory
FORE Systems, Inc.	CellPath 90						2 Mbps
FORE Systems, Inc.	ASX-200WG		Y				2.5 Gbps (nonblocking)
Fujitsu	AstralSwitch EA 1550		Y	Y			10 Gbps
General DataComm.	APEX Strobos, NPX, DV2, MAC, MAC1 Switches			Y	Y	Y	Up to 25.6 Gbps
IBM Corporation	IBM 2220 Nways BroadBand Switch, Models 300/500			Y			4.2 Gbps
IBM Corporation	8260 Nways Switching Hub			Y			4.2 Gbps
IBM Corporation	8285 Nways Workgroup Switch			Y			4.2 Gbps
Sahara Networks, Inc.	SA-100 Broadband Service Unit			Y			1 Gbps of cell and packet simultaneously
Sahara Networks, Inc.	SA-600 Broadband Service Concentrator			Y			*
Siemens Stromberg-Carlson	MainStreet*Xpress* 36150						> 2.5 Gbps
Xylan	OmniSwitch w/Omnicell		Y				13.2 Gbps

Table 15.2 Comparison of Enterprise and LAN/Campus Backbone Switches

Company Name	Bay Networks	Cabletron Systems	Cisco	FORE Systems, Inc	FORE Systems, Inc
Address	4401 Great America Parkway, Santa Clara, CA	35 Industrial Way, Rochester, NH 03867	170 West Tasman Dr. San Jose, CA 95134	1000 FORE Drive, Warrendale, PA 15086	1000 FORE Drive, Warrendale, PA 15086
Web Page	baynetworks.com	ctron.com	www.cisco.com	fore.com	fore.com
Annual Sales 1994	n/a	$598M	n/a	$39.3M	$39.3M
Annual Sales 1995	n/a	$810 M	n/a	$106.2M	$106.2M
Annual Sales 1996	n/a	$1.07 B	n/a	$235.2M	$235.2M
Number of Customers	n/a	n/a	n/a	2000	2000
Number of Switches Sold	n/a	n/a	n/a	5519 (3/4 CY96)	5519 (3/4 CY96)
Number of ATM Ports Sold	n/a	n/a	n/a	55,000 (3/4 CY96)	55,000 (3/4 CY96)
Product Information					
Product Name	System 5000	Smartcell ZX-250	Lightstream 1010	ASX-200BX	PH7000
Product Categories					
Workgroup			Y	Y	
Campus Backbone	Y		Y	Y	
Enterprise	Y	Y	Y	Y	Y
CPE Access				Y	
AC Power	Y	Y		Y	Y
DC Power				Y	Y
Minimum Switch Price	$18,000	$7995 List		$15,995	$14,320
Configuration	2 ports ATM	n/a		no ports	5-slot w/ 6 10BaseT ports
Maximum Switch Price	$110,000	$22,000 List		$33,885	$62,800
Configuration	48 ports ATM	n/a	8 - 622 Mbps ports	Loaded w/16 OC-3c ports	10 slot w/ 216 10BaseT ports
Switch Fabric/Bus Capacity	3.2 Gbps	2.5 Gbps	5 Gbps	2.5 Gbs	3.2 Gbps shared memory
Max Sum of Port Speeds	3.2 Gbps	2.5 Gbps	5 Gbps	2.5 Gbps	
% Blocking at Load per GR-1110					
CBR	non-blocking	0		0	n/a
VBR	non-blocking	0		0	n/a
Point-to-Multipoint Capability					
Spatial	Y	Y		Y - on TDM	n/a
Logical				Y - on shared mem	n/a
Min Switch Transit Delay	n/a	9us min, 11uS max	19 us	7 us	n/a
VPI/VCI Bits on UNI	n/a	n/a			n/a
VPI/VCI Bits on NNI	n/a	n/a			n/a
Max PVC VPCs per card/switch	255	n/a	7/256	16k/16k	n/a
Max PVC VCCs per card/switch	3072	n/a	7/32k	16k/16k	n/a
Max SVCs per card/switch	n/a	n/a		16k/16k	n/a
Port Redundancy (1:1, 1:N, other)	n/a	n/a		No	1:1
Common Eqpmt Redundancy					
Power	Y	Y		Y	Y
Fabric/Bus					Y
Controller					
Other				Y	Y
Distinguishing Features	.	.		.	

Table 15.2 Comparison of Enterprise and LAN/Campus Backbone Switches (continued)

Interface Information	Bay Networks	Cabletron Systems	Cisco	FORE Systems, Inc	FORE Systems, Inc
ATM UNI Interfaces					
DS1	-	-	Y	Y	-
nxDS1 IMA	-	-		-	-
DS3	Y	97	Y	Y	Y
OC3	Y	Y	Y	Y	Y
OC12	-	97	Y	Y	-
OC48	-	-		-	-
155Mbps SMF	-	-	Y	-	-
622Mbps SMF	-	-	Y	-	-
Cell-Based Clear Chan TC/HSSI	-	-		-	-
E1	Y	-	Y	Y	-
E3	-	97	Y	Y	Y
E4	-	-		-	-
STM-1	-	-		Y	-
STM-4	-	-		-	-
J1	-	-		-	-
J2 (6.312 Mb/s)	-	-		Y	-
25 Mb/s UTP	-	-	Y	Y	-
51.84 Mb/s UTP	-	-		-	-
155 Mb/s UTP	-	Y		Y	Y
155 Mb/s MMF	Y	Y		Y	Y
TAXI 100Mbps	-	-		-	-
Other					
Non-ATM Interfaces					
10 Mbps Ethernet				Y	Y
100 Mb/s Ethernet					Y
FDDI					Y
4 Mb/s Token Ring					
16 Mb/s Token Ring					
Frame Relay nxDS0, DS1, >DS1					
Frame Relay E1					
SMDS DS1 & DS3					
SMDS DXI nxDS0 & DS1					
HDLC V.35 & HSSI					
Circuit Emulation DS1					
Circuit Emulation					
Serial IO Circuit Emulation (EIA 530, EIA 449, X.21, V.35)					
M-JPEG,H.320 Video					
JPEG-PAL, JPEG-NTS					
H.320 Video					
FUNI					

Table 15.2 Comparison of Enterprise and LAN/Campus Backbone Switches (continued)

Traffic Management	Bay Networks	Cabletron Systems	Cisco	FORE Systems, Inc	FORE Systems, Inc
ATM Service Classes Supported					
CBR	Y	Y	Y	Y	
rt-VBR	Y	Y	Y	Y	
nrt-VBR	Y	Y	Y	Y	
UBR	Y	Y	Y	Y	
ABR	Y	Y	Y	Y	
Switch Type (Fabric, Bus, Other)	Fabric			Distributed shared memory	
Switch Buffering					
Input		Y			
Fabric					
Output				Y	
Other					
Switch Buffer Quantity/Port	*		65k cells shared	64k cells map	
Switch Architecture (Narrative)	*		n/a	*	
ATM Forum Congestion Control					
EFCI		Y	Y	Y	
ER				97	
VS/VD					
Other		Backward RM cell marching			
Congestion Control	input and output buffering	n/a		Open-loop and shaping in 97	
Cell Loss Probability					
CBR		0%	0	0	
VBR		10 -9 or less	0	0	
CLP Bit Usage					
Tag				Y	
Selective Discard		Y	Y	Y	
Other					
Policing					
PCR		n/a	Y	Y	
PCR+SCR		n/a		Y	
Other					
Shaping					
PCR		n/a	Y	97	
PCR+SCR		n/a			
Other					
Connection Admission Control					
GCAC			Y	Y	
Other		Y			
Packet Discard					
EPD		Y	Y	Y	
PPD		Y	Y	Y	
Frame Policing					
Other				97	
I.610 OAM Performance Measurement		97			

Table 15.2 Comparison of Enterprise and LAN/Campus Backbone Switches (continued)

Protocol/Standards Support	Bay Networks	Cabletron Systems	Cisco	FORE Systems, Inc	FORE Systems, Inc
ATM Forum					
UNI Signaling					
3.0		Y	Y	Y	Y
3.1		Y	Y	Y	Y
4.0		97		97	97
Other					
Pt-Pt SVC Signaling					
3.0		Y		Y	Y
3.1		Y		Y	Y
4.0		97		97	97
Other					
Pt-Mpt SVC Signaling					
3.0		Y		Y	Y
3.1		Y		Y	Y
4.0		97		97	97
Other					
NNI Signaling					
IISP	Y	Y	Y	Y	Y
PNNI 1.0	Y	97	Y	97	97
BICI 2.0					
ITU-T					
UNI Signaling					
Q.93B	Y	Y		Y	Y
Q.2931	Y	Y		Y	Y
NNI Signaling					
BISUP		No			
Other		No		PNNI & ATM FUNNI	
LAN Emulation Client					
LANE 1.0	Y	Y	Y	Y	Y
RFC 1483	Y	Y	Y	Y	Y
LAN Emulation Server					
LANE 1.0	Y	Y	Y	Y	Y
RFC 1483	Y	Y	Y	Y	
Virtual LAN Capability				LEC/BUS can run on switch controller	Port,MAC,subnet-based VLANs, 802.1g tagging in 97
IP/ATM Client: RFC 1577				Y	Y
IP/ATM Server: RFC 1577				Y	Y
MPOA: ATM Forum		97		97	97
NHRP				97	97
Tested Interoperation with others				*	
Distinguishing Features		*			

Table 15.2 Comparison of Enterprise and LAN/Campus Backbone Switches (continued)

Network Management Support	Bay Networks	Cabletron Systems	Cisco	FORE Systems, Inc	FORE Systems, Inc
Full ATM Forum ILMI					
3.0		Y		Y	Y
3.1		Y		Y	Y
4.0		97		97	97
Other					
ILMI Address Registration					
3.0		Y		Y	Y
3.1		Y		Y	Y
4.0		97		97	97
Other					
RFC 1695 (ATOM MIB)		Y		Y	Y
Per Port Statistics		Y		Y	Y
Per VC Statistics		Y			Y
OAM Cell VPC AIS/RDI		n/a			Y
OAM Cell VCC AIS/RDI		97			Y
OAM Cell Loopback		97		Y	Y
ATM Forum NM I/F Support					
M1		now			
M2		now			
M3		now			
M4		now			
M5		now			
Automatic PVC Configuration					
SPVPC/SPVCC		VC in 97		Y	SPVCC
Other					
Automatic PVC Restoration					
SPVPC/SPVCC				Y	SPVCC
Other					
NMS Support					
HPOV			Y	Y	Y
Cabletron Spectrum Enterprise Mgr		Y		Y	Y
SunNet Manager			Y	Y	Y
NetView 6000/AIX				Y	Y
Others	Optivity				
MIB Support					
Distinguishing Features		*			
Legend	Y = Supported/Available Now * = See chapter				

Table 15.2 Comparison of Enterprise and LAN/Campus Backbone Switches (continued)

Company Name	FORE Systems, Inc	FORE Systems, Inc	Fujitsu	IBM Corporation	IBM Corporation
Address	1000 FORE Drive, Warrendale, PA 15086	1000 FORE Drive, Warrendale, PA 15086	3190 Miralama Ave., Anaheim, CA 92806	Old Orchard Road, Armonk, NY 10504	Old Orchard Road, Armonk, NY 10504
Web Page	fore.com	fore.com	n/a	raleigh.ibm.com	raleigh.ibm.com
Annual Sales 1994	$39.3M	$39.3M	n/a	n/a	n/a
Annual Sales 1995	$106.2M	$106.2M	n/a	n/a	n/a
Annual Sales 1996	$235.2M	$235.2M	n/a	n/a	n/a
Number of Customers	2000	2000	n/a	n/a	n/a
Number of Switches Sold	5519 (3/4 CY96)	5519 (3/4 CY96)	n/a	n/a	n/a
Number of ATM Ports Sold	55,000 (3/4 CY96)	55,000 (3/4 CY96)	n/a	n/a	n/a
Product Information					
Product Name	CellPath 90	ASX-200WG	AstralSwitch EA 1550	IBM 2220 Nways 300/500 BroadBand	8260 Nways Switching hub
Product Categories					
Workgroup			Y		
Campus Backbone			Y	Y	Y
Enterprise		Y	Y	Y	Y
CPE Access	Y		Y	Y	Y
AC Power	Y	Y		Y	Y
DC Power				Configuration Dependent	Configuration Dependent
Minimum Switch Price	$4,495	$9,995			Configuration Dependent
Configuration		18 ports, 25 Mbps			Configuration Dependent
Maximum Switch Price	$5,495	$20,950			
Configuration		16 ports, 155M bps			Configuration Dependent
Switch Fabric/Bus Capacity	2 Mbps	2.5 Gbps (non-blocking)	10 Gbps	4.2 Gbps	4.2 Gbps
Max Sum of Port Speeds	2 Mbps	622 Mbps OC-12c	n/a	2.17 Gbps	4.3 Gbps
% Blocking at Load per GR-1110					
CBR	0	0		Non-blocking switch	0
VBR	20	0		Non-blocking switch	0
Point-to-Multipoint Capability					
Spatial		Y - on TDM		No	
Logical		Y - on shared mem		No	Y
Min Switch Transit Delay	250 us	7us	25 us	3.4 us, Node=35 us	33 us for OC3 rate
VPI/VCI Bits on UNI	8 _ 8	16k/16k		8/16	6_/14
VPI/VCI Bits on NNI		16k/16k		12/16	6_/14
Max PVC VPCs per card/switch	n/a	16k/16k	?/32K	1500/7000	8128_/12k
Max PVC VCCs per card/switch	256	16k/16k	?/32K	1500/7000	8128_/12k
Max SVCs per card/switch	n/a	16k/16k		0_/_0	4064_/6k
Port Redundancy (1:1, 1:N, other)	None	No		other	
Common Eqpmt Redundancy					
Power				Y	Y
Fabric/Bus				Y	Y
Controller					
Other				Y	Y
Distinguishing Features					ATM control point

Table 15.2 Comparison of Enterprise and LAN/Campus Backbone Switches (continued)

Interface Information	FORE Systems, Inc	FORE Systems, Inc	Fujitsu	IBM Corporation	IBM Corporation
ATM UNI Interfaces					
DS1	Y	Y	Y	-	Y
nxDS1 IMA	-	-	-	-	-
DS3	-	Y	Y	Y	Y
OC3	-	Y	Y	Y	Y
OC12	-	Y	-	-	Y
OC48	-	-	-	-	-
155Mbps SMF	-	-	Y	Y	-
622Mbps SMF	-	-	Y	-	-
Cell-Based Clear Chan TC/HSSI	-	-	-	-	Y
E1	Y	Y	Y	-	Y
E3	-	Y	-	Y	Y
E4	-	-	-	-	-
STM-1	-	Y	Y	Y	Y
STM-4	-	Y	-	-	-
J1	-	-	-	-	Y
J2 (6.312 Mb/s)	-	Y	-	98	-
25 Mb/s UTP	-	Y	-	-	Y
51.84 Mb/s UTP	-	-	-	-	-
155 Mb/s UTP	-	Y	-	-	Y
155 Mb/s MMF	-	Y	-	Y	Y
TAXI 100Mbps	-	Y	-	-	Y
Other	-	-	-	-	-
Non-ATM Interfaces					
10 Mbps Ethernet	Y	mgmt only	-	-	Y
100 Mb/s Ethernet	-	-	Y	-	Y
FDDI	-	-	-	-	Y
4 Mb/s Token Ring	-	-	-	-	Y
16 Mb/s Token Ring	-	-	-	-	Y
Frame Relay nxDS0, DS1, >DS1		TBD		Y	
SMDS DS1 & DS3	-	-	-	-	-
SMDS DXI nxDS0 & DS1	-	-	-	Y	-
HDLC V.35 & HSSI	V.35 only	-	-	Y	Y
Circuit Emulation DS1	Y	-	-	Y	Y
Circuit Emulation	-	-	-	-	-
Serial IO Circuit Emulation (EIA 530, EIA 449, X.21, V.35)	Y	-	-	-	-
M-JPEG,H.320 Video	-	-	-	-	-
JPEG-PAL, JPEG-NTS	-	-	-	-	-
H.320 Video	-	-	-	-	-
FUNI	-	-	-	-	-

Table 15.2 Comparison of Enterprise and LAN/Campus Backbone Switches (continued)

Traffic Management	FORE Systems, Inc	FORE Systems, Inc	Fujitsu	IBM Corporation	IBM Corporation
ATM Service Classes Supported					
CBR	Y		Y	Y	Y
rt-VBR	Y		Y	Y	Y
nrt-VBR	Y		Y	Y	Y
UBR	Y		Y	Y	Y
ABR	Y		Y		Y
Switch Type (Fabric, Bus, Other)	n/a	Distributed shared		Fabric	Fabric
Switch Buffering					
Input					
Fabric				Y	
Output	Y			Y	Y
Other			Y		
Switch Buffer Quantity/Port	n/a	Max 13k cells/port: 52k per 64k switch		Shared buffer, 128 cells	8k
Switch Architecture (Narrative)	n/a	2.5 Gbps non-blocking			
ATM Forum Congestion Control					
EFCI	Y			Y	Y
ER		Y			Y
VS/VD		Y			
Other					
Congestion Control	*			NBBS Congestion Prevention	RR in 4Q97 *
Cell Loss Probability					
CBR	0			Y	
VBR	0			Y	
CLP Bit Usage					
Tag					
Selective Discard	Y			Y	Y
Other	Y			Y	
Policing					
PCR	Y				
PCR+SCR	Y			Y	4Q97
Other	Y				4Q97
Shaping					
PCR	Y				
PCR+SCR	Y			Y	4Q97
Other					
Connection Admission Control					
GCAC	n/a				
Other	Y		Y	NBBS Route Selection and Reservation	*
Packet Discard					
EPD	Y			Y	Y
PPD	Y			Y	Y
Frame Policing					
Other	Y			Y	
I.610 OAM Performance Measurement	Cell loss, erred cells	Y		Y	Not supported

Table 15.2 Comparison of Enterprise and LAN/Campus Backbone Switches (continued)

Protocol/Standards Support	FORE Systems, Inc	Fujitsu	IBM Corporation	IBM Corporation
ATM Forum				
UNI Signaling				
3.0		Y	Y	Y
3.1		Y	Y	Y
4.0	TBD			Y
Other				
Pt-Pt SVC Signaling				
3.0	Y	Y		Y
3.1	Y	Y		Y
4.0	TBD			Y
Other				
Pt-Mpt SVC Signaling				
3.0	Y	Y		Y
3.1	Y	Y		Y
4.0	TBD			Y
Other				
NNI Signaling				
IISP	Y	Y		Y
PNNI 1.0	TBD	Y		Y
BICI 2.0				
ITU-T				
UNI Signaling				
Q.93B	Y			Y
Q.2931	Y			Y
NNI Signaling				
BISUP				Y
Other				
LAN Emulation Client				
LANE 1.0	Y	Y		Y
RFC 1483	Y	Y		
LAN Emulation Server				
LANE 1.0	Y	Y		Y
RFC 1483	Y	Y		
Virtual LAN Capability	Y *See ForeView V-LAN			*
IP/ATM Client: RFC 1577	Y			Y
IP/ATM Server: RFC 1577	Y			Y
MPOA: ATM Forum	Y			97/98
NHRP	TBD			Y
Tested Interoperation with others	*			*
Distinguishing Features	FTBW management			*

Table 15.2 Comparison of Enterprise and LAN/Campus Backbone Switches (continued)

Network Management Support	FORE Systems, Inc	FORE Systems, Inc	Fujitsu	IBM Corporation	IBM Corporation
Full ATM Forum ILMI					
3.0					Y
3.1	Y				Y
4.0	TBD				Y
Other					
ILMI Address Registration					
3.0					Y
3.1	Y				Y
4.0	TBD				Y
Other					
RFC 1695 (ATOM MIB)	*			Y	Y
Per Port Statistics				Y	Y
Per VC Statistics	per port only			Y	4Q97
OAM Cell VPC AIS/RDI	No			Y	Y
OAM Cell VCC AIS/RDI	No			Y	
OAM Cell Loopback	No			Y	Y
ATM Forum NM I/F Support					
M1				Y	
M2				Y	
M3				Y	
M4				Y	
M5				Y	
Automatic PVC Configuration					
SPVPC/SPVCC					
Other				Y	Y
Automatic PVC Restoration					
SPVPC/SPVCC				Y	
Other				Y (NPDS)	
NMS Support					
HPOV	Y			Y	
Cabletron Spectrum Enterprise Mgr					
SunNet Manager	Y				
NetView 6000/AIX	Y			Y	Y
Others					
MIB Support				TMN 2000	Y
Distinguishing Features	*				*

Legend

Table 15.2 Comparison of Enterprise and LAN/Campus Backbone Switches (continued)

Company Name	IBM Corporation	Sahara Networks, Inc.	Sahara Networks, Inc.	SIEMENS Stromberg-Carlson	Xylan
Address	Old Orchard Road, Armonk, NY 10504	860 North Main Street, Wallingford, CT 06492	860 North Main Street, Wallingford, CT 06492	900 Broken Sound Parkway, Boca Raton, FL 33487	26679 West Agoura Rd, Calabasas, CA 91302
Web Page	raleigh.ibm.com	info@saharanet.com	info@saharanet.com	SSC.SIEMENS.COM	xylan.com
Annual Sales 1994	n/a	n/a	n/a	n/a	$0
Annual Sales 1995	n/a	n/a	n/a	n/a	$29.6M
Annual Sales 1996	n/a	n/a	n/a	n/a	$82.5M
Number of Customers	n/a	n/a	n/a	n/a	600
Number of Switches Sold	n/a	n/a	n/a	n/a	10,500
Number of ATM Ports Sold	n/a	n/a	n/a	n/a	11,000
Product Information					
Product Name	8285 Nways Workgroup Switch	SA-100 Broadband Service Unit	SA-600 Broadband Service Concentrator	MainStreet*Xpress* 36150	OmniSwitch w/Omnicell
Product Categories					
Workgroup					
Campus Backbone					
Enterprise	Y	Y	Y		Y
CPE Access	Y	Y	Y	Y	Y
AC Power	Y	Y	Y	Y	Y
DC Power	Y	Y	Y	Y	Y
Minimum Switch Price	Configuration Dependent	$6,000	$15,000	n/a	$24,100
Configuration					8 port OC-3c multimode
Maximum Switch Price	Configuration Dependent	$25,000	$55,000	n/a	$96,450
Configuration					64 port OC-3c multimode
Switch Fabric/Bus Capacity	4.2 Gbps	1 Gb/s of cell & packet simultaneously		n/a	13.2 Gbps
Max Sum of Port Speeds	1.85 Gbps	max# of ports of 12, up to 5 full duplex OC-3c's	max 36 ports	>2.5	9.95 Gbps
% Blocking at Load per GR-1110					
CBR	0	n/a		non-blocking	0
VBR	0	n/a		non-blocking	0
Point-to-Multipoint Capability					
Spatial	Y	Y	Y	Y	n/a
Logical	Y	Y	Y		n/a
Min Switch Transit Delay	33 us for OC3 rate	<18 µs *	<18 µs *		15 us
VPI/VCI Bits on UNI	6 / 14	6 / 9	6 / 9		n/a
VPI/VCI Bits on NNI	6 / 14	6 / 9	6 / 9		n/a
Max PVC VPCs per card/switch	8128 / 12k	4,096/4,096	4,096/12,288		n/a
Max PVC VCCs per card/switch	8128 / 12k	4,096/4,096	4,096/12,288		n/a
Max SVCs per card/switch	4064 / 6k	4,000/20,000	4,096/60,000		n/a
Port Redundancy (1:1, 1:N, other)		*see chapter	1:1 3Q97		1:1
Common Eqpmt Redundancy					
Power				Y	Y
Fabric/Bus			2Q97	Y	Y
Controller				Y	Y
Other	*				
Distinguishing Features	*	*		*	*

Table 15.2 Comparison of Enterprise and LAN/Campus Backbone Switches (continued)

Interface Information	IBM Corporation	Sahara Networks, Inc.	Sahara Networks, Inc.	SIEMENS Stromberg-Carlson	Xylan
ATM UNI Interfaces					
DS1	Y	Y	Y	Y	97
nxDS1 IMA	-	Y	Y	-	97
DS3	Y	Y	Y	Y	97
OC3	Y	Y	Y	Y	Y
OC12	-	Y	Y	-	Y
OC48	-	-	-	-	
155Mbps SMF	-	-	-	-	Y
622Mbps SMF	-	-	-	-	Y
Cell-Based Clear Chan TC/HSSI	Y	Y	Y	Y	
E1	Y	Y	Y	Y	97
E3	Y	Y	Y	Y	97
E4	-	Y	Y	-	Y
STM-1	Y	Y	Y	Y	Y
STM-4	-	Y	Y	-	Y
J1	Y	-	-	-	
J2 (6.312 Mb/s)	-	Y	Y	-	97
25 Mb/s UTP	Y	Y	Y	-	
51.84 Mb/s UTP	-	-	-	-	97
155 Mb/s UTP	Y	Y	Y	-	Y
155 Mb/s MMF	Y	Y	-	-	Y
TAXI 100Mbps	Y	-	-	-	
Other				140 Mbps	
Non-ATM Interfaces					
10 Mbps Ethernet	Y	Y	Y	Y	Y
100 Mb/s Ethernet	-	Y	Y	Y	Y
FDDI	-	Y	Y	Y	Y
4 Mb/s Token Ring	Y	Y	Y	Y	Y
16 Mb/s Token Ring	Y	Y	Y	Y	Y
Frame Relay nxDS0, DS1, >DS1	-	Y	Y	Y	-
Frame Relay E1	-	-	-	-	-
SMDS DS1 & DS3	-	-	-	-	-
SMDS DXI nxDS0 & DS1	-	Y	Y	Y	Y
HDLC V.35 & HSSI	-	Y	Y	Y	-
Circuit Emulation DS1	Y	Y	Y	Y	-
Circuit Emulation	-	Y	Y	Y	-
Serial IO Circuit Emulation (EIA 530, EIA 449, X.21, V.35)	-	Y	-	Y	-
M-JPEG H.320 Video					
JPEG-PAL, JPEG-NTS	-	Y	-	Y	-
H.320 Video					
FUNI					

Table 15.2 Comparison of Enterprise and LAN/Campus Backbone Switches (continued)

Traffic Management	IBM Corporation	Sahara Networks, Inc.	Sahara Networks, Inc.	SIEMENS Stromberg-Carlson	Xylan
ATM Service Classes Supported					
CBR	Y	Y	Y	Y	Y
rt-VBR	Y	Y	Y	Y	Y
nrt-VBR	Y	Y	Y	Y	Y
UBR	Y	Y	Y	Y	Y
ABR	Y	Y	Y	Y	Y
Switch Type (Fabric, Bus, Other)	Fabric	*	*	Fabric	Other
Switch Buffering					
Input	Y	Y	Y		
Fabric	Y	Y	Y		
Output	Y	Y	Y	Y	
Other					Y
Switch Buffer Quantity/Port	8k	*	*	Output 1188/4 ports	*
Switch Architecture (Narrative)	*	*	*	*	*
ATM Forum Congestion Control					
EFCI	Y	Y	Y		Y
ER		Y	Y		Y
VS/VD		Y	Y		
Other	RR in 4Q97	3Q97			
Congestion Control	*	*	*		*
Cell Loss Probability					
CBR	n/a	n/a	n/a		virtually 0%
VBR	n/a	n/a	n/a		virtually 0%
CLP Bit Usage					
Tag	Y	Y	Y	Y	Y
Selective Discard	Y	Y	Y		Y
Other					
Policing					
PCR	4Q97	Y	Y	Y	Y
PCR+SCR	4Q97	Y	Y		Y
Other					
Shaping					
PCR	Y	Y	Y	Y	Y
PCR+SCR	4Q97	Y	Y		Y
Other					
Connection Admission Control					
GCAC	Y	Y	Y		Y
Other	*	Y	Y		
Packet Discard					
EPD	Y	Y	Y		Y
PPD	Y	Y	Y		Y
Frame Policing		Y	Y		Y
Other					Y
I.610 OAM Performance Measurement	Y	Y	Y	planned	Y 97

Table 15.2 Comparison of Enterprise and LAN/Campus Backbone Switches (continued)

Protocol/Standards Support	IBM Corporation	Sahara Networks, Inc.	Sahara Networks, Inc.	SIEMENS Stromberg-Carlson	Xylan
ATM Forum					
UNI Signaling					
3.0	Y			Y	Y
3.1	Y	Y		Y	Y
4.0	Y	Y		planned	97
Other					
Pt-Pt SVC Signaling					
3.0	Y				Y
3.1	Y	Y			Y
4.0	Y	Y			97
Other					
Pt-Mpt SVC Signaling					
3.0	Y				Y
3.1	Y	Y			Y
4.0	Y	Y			97
Other					
NNI Signaling					
IISP	Y				Y
PNNI 1.0	Y	Y			Y
BICI 2.0					
ITU-T					
UNI Signaling					
Q.93B	Y				
Q.2931	Y	Y			Y
NNI Signaling					
BISUP	Y	97			Y
Other					
LAN Emulation Client					
LANE 1.0	Y	3Q97			Y
RFC 1483		Y			Y
LAN Emulation Server					
LANE 1.0	Y	3Q97			Y
RFC 1483		Y			Y
Virtual LAN Capability	*				*
IP/ATM Client: RFC 1577	Y	3Q97			Y
IP/ATM Server: RFC 1577	Y				Y
MPOA: ATM Forum	97/98	3Q97			Y
NHRP	Y	No			Y
Tested Interoperation with others	*				
Distinguishing Features	*	*			*

15.6 REFERENCES

[1] R. Bellman, "An Enterprise View of ATM," *Business Communications Review,* April 1995.

[2] M. Cooney, "IBM Lays Out ATM and LAN Switching Road Map," *Network World,* January 30, 1995.

16

ATM in the Workgroup and Desktop Area Network

This chapter explores ATM in the local area, focusing on the devices and services that allow end users their first access to ATM. We define this environment as the Desktop Area Network (DAN); it includes the workstations and servers, their operating systems, Application Program Interfaces (APIs), and the ATM Network Interface Cards (NICs) inside them. After summarizing the market outlook in the battle for the desktop, we review the key features of ATM network interface cards operating at speeds of 25, 51, and 155 Mbps. Although ATM interface cards may never replace the inexpensive Ethernet card widely deployed in current PCs, end-to-end ATM networks are a reality today for many companies. We then present a comparison of workgroup ATM switches.

The shaded area of Figure 16.1 shows the workgroup and DAN ATM switching environment in relation to an enterprise-wide ATM implementation. Workgroup ATM switches provide direct connection to ATM workstations equipped with 25- or 155-Mbps NICs. Figure 16.2 illustrates a typical workgroup switch configuration. Workgroup switches usually support high-speed devices, such as super servers or multimedia workstations, by providing direct ATM connectivity with guaranteed bandwidth and multiple Quality of Service (QoS) classes. Workgroup ATM switches are typically low-cost devices that also support legacy LAN interfaces (i.e., Ethernet and Token Ring). A common configuration multiplexes many lower-speed legacy LAN or lower-speed ATM interfaces onto a single, higher-speed ATM uplink connected to a LAN backbone switch. These devices typically run on AC (i.e., wall outlet) power and have much smaller port capacity and less processing power than most ATM LAN and WAN switches.

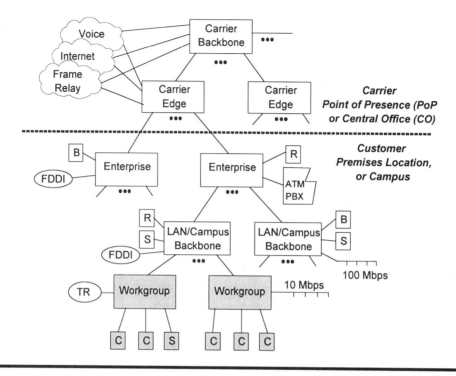

Figure 16.1 Workgroup Switching Context

Workgroup or LAN

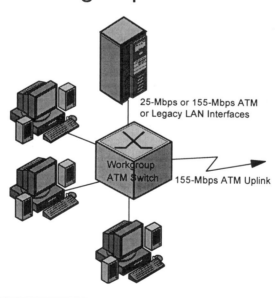

Figure 16.2 ATM Workgroup Switch Configuration

Figure 16.3 DEC GigaSwitch ATM Workgroup Switch

Figures 16.3 and 16.4 show the DEC GigaSwitch and FORE Powerhub 4000 ATM workgroup switches, respectively. Details on these switches can be found in Chapter 17. Other attributes of a workgroup switch are small physical size, interfaces on the front to allow wall mounting, and Simple Network Management Protocol (SNMP) network management interfaces allowing the switch to be managed by an umbrella management system.

16.1 INTEGRATING ATM TO THE DESKTOP

Users realize the greatest benefits from ATM when it is used from end system to end system. Thus, the natural starting place for our analysis is within the desktop. This section reviews ATM's battle with Ethernet for control of the desktop, complete with a market study and recent moves by the standards groups to assist ATM in the DAN. The most critical application for ATM DANs is high-performance ATM workgroups where the high bandwidth, multiple classes of service, and flexibility require ATM to the desktop.

Figure 16.4 FORE PowerHub 4000 ATM Workgroup Switch

16.1.1 The Battle for the Desktop

ATM did not make its way into the mid-1990s generation of workstation motherboards. There were many reasons for this. First of all, the workstations of the mid-1990s had internal bandwidth constraints of 33- to 50-MHz buses, where an ATM LAN offered speeds of 100 Mbps and 140 Mbps. And even when the bus speeds were matched, peripheral speeds were not. New Pentium PC buses operate at speeds in excess of 100 MHz and are now capable of providing true multimedia to the desktop.

What makes a user require an ATM interface on the end system? One reason is the requirement for higher bandwidth and performance in the LAN. Users typically first try to segment their existing Ethernet LAN into smaller and smaller segments until they reach the threshold of Ethernet switching, which provides 10 or 100 Mbps to each user. This is the point where ATM takes over by providing full-duplex 51 and 155 Mbps to the desktop. From an application standpoint, desktop videoconferencing — the integration of the phone, computer, and video — is becoming a reality for many corporations, along with integrated multimedia applications; all of these require the capabilities of ATM.

For some users, ATM to the desktop is too costly at this point, especially when installation and support costs are added to hardware costs. However, the price for ATM interface cards is dropping rapidly, so that very soon the cost of Ethernet and ATM adapter cards may be close. But support costs for ATM remain high. Although ATM speeds are greater than those required by many current applications, the rapid growth in computer performance and increased need for communications is rapidly changing this situation. When the workstation becomes faster than the current LAN, then an upgrade is in order. An upgrade to ATM will be the choice of many.

But is ATM too late? The battle for the desktop is really between IP over legacy LAN protocols like 100-Mbps Ethernet, and ATM. ATM has an uphill battle to fight to become a major contender, let alone attain the role of dominant desktop LAN interface. Beating 100-Mbps switched Ethernet and eventually gigabit Ethernet is a formidable challenge for ATM. ATM is faced with the chicken-and-egg situation — legacy applications that don't require the features of ATM are the chicken; in fact, much legacy equipment isn't compatible as a direct interface to ATM systems. Furthermore, native ATM applications have been slow to hatch (egg) as ATM struggles for ubiquitous access. Many independent marketing studies show deployment of ATM to the desktop (NICs) far behind Ethernet. A comparison of revenue for ATM and Ethernet NIC shipments is shown in Figure 16.5 [1]. From this study it is clear that while the percentage of ATM NICs to Ethernet will increase over time, desktop deployment of ATM will need to become much more ubiquitous if ATM is to become the dominant desktop technology.

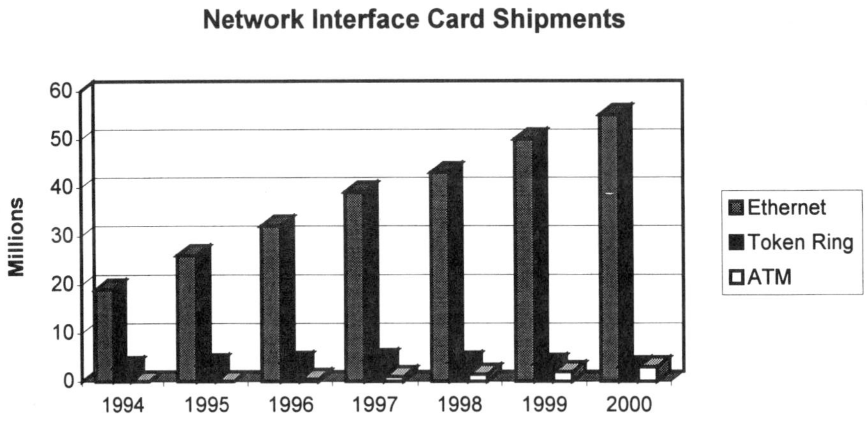

Network Interface Card Shipments

Figure 16.5 ATM NIC Shipments Compared to Ethernet and Token Ring

Averaging several different studies, we estimate that vendors will sell over 20 million 100-Mbps Ethernet NICs in 1997, as opposed to only a few hundred thousand ATM NICs.

In the campus environment, bandwidth is close to free, once the labor and construction charges for laying fiber have been incurred. Therefore, the cost of the local networking equipment and workstation interface cards is important as an incremental investment. Adapter cards are also available that can encapsulate IPX and DECnet. At present, 25-Mbps ATM NICs can be purchased for as little as $400, and prices are decreasing. Table 16.1 shows ATM, Ethernet, and Token Ring NIC card pricing as of early 1997, along with the cost per node for workgroup switches as determined by a study [2] and our estimates.

Figure 16.6 shows that the total revenue market for 25-Mbps ATM grew rapidly between 1995 and 1996, and continues to grow.

Table 16.1 Network Interface Card (NIC) Pricing

Media Type	Speed (Mbps)	Price per NIC	Price per Switched Port
ATM	25	$200	$200
ATM	51	$400	$600
ATM	155	$500	$1000
Ethernet	10	$60	$200
Ethernet	10/100	$100	$500
Token Ring	16	$500	$1100

Revenue ($M)

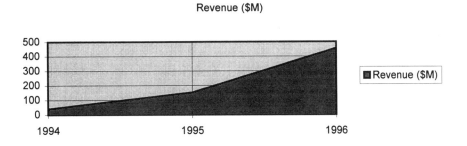

Figure 16.6 25-Mbps ATM Market

16.1.2 Standards Watch

ATM at the desktop has a champion — the ATM Forum — which continues to promote ATM to the vendor and user community as the technology of choice for desktops, especially for multimedia applications. Some challenges for the ATM Forum to help enable ATM at the desktop include:

- Voice telephony over ATM
- Switch-to-switch connections (trunking)
- Low bit rate voice compression

A new 155-Mbps physical-layer spec for short-wavelength lasers also was released for approval, as well as some new testing documents.

Most major chip manufacturers have developed ATM chip sets used by many of the ATM devices described in this chapter. What are the latest developments in ATM chip sets and processors? Check out the ATM Chip Web page at www.infotech.tu-chemnitz.de/~paetz/atm, which has a listing of over 50 ATM chip vendors.

One interesting development effort currently under way by AT&T Bell Labs and LSI Logic is called Euphony. Euphony integrates a RISC processor with an ATM interface, thus combining the ATM Forum UTOPIA Level-1 interface with a DPI interface. The targets for this technology are the smart packet telephone, personal communicators, and residential network markets. Integrated Device Technology (IDT) is building chips for 155 Mbps ATM using RISC technology [3].

16.1.3 Operating System and Application Programming Interfaces — Where Are They?

APIs form the bridge between the network operating system (such as Windows NT) and the ATM interface or NIC. It appears that the soon to be dominant operating system will be Windows 97 and NT. ATM Windows Socket (WinSock) 2.0 Service Provider Interface (SPI) for NT 4.0 and

Windows 95 is the gateway that allows applications to open connections and specify QoS requirements to the ATM network. WinSock 2.0 bundled with Windows NT 4.0 has the capability, as defined by the WinSock Forum, to map a generic quality-of-service capability to the ATM Forum's quality of service definitions. The WinSock 2.0 API also added support for ATM addressing and User-to-Network Interface (UNI) signaling. This new API will have a dramatic effect on the increased adoption of desktop ATM. Native ATM with WinSock 2.0 SPI provides a common set of developers' tools for x86/Windows environments, over which developers can now build native ATM applications that take full advantage of ATM's QoS features through programming directly to the ATM protocol stack. One example is the MPEG video over native ATM product by Optivision, over which multimedia applications like distance learning, telemedicine, and videoconferencing are sent. Another example is FORE Systems' ForeThought ATM APIs within ForeThought NIC software, incorporating WinSock 2.0 and X/Open Transport Interface (XTI) applications. These APIs enable programmers to take advantage of ATM QoS and point-to-multipoint communications for applications like videoconferencing, video on demand, security monitoring, and medical imaging. The X-Open XTI specification creates the bridge from ATM to the Macintosh, IRIX, and Solaris operating systems [4].

The contrasting view to this optimism is that while Microsoft's WinSock 2.0 does indeed enable ATM, it is really specified as a transport independent interface. These same generic QoS commands do not specify, or require, a specific transport infrastructure. Thus, delay-sensitive applications such as videoconferencing can run over ATM or non-ATM transport infrastructures, such as IP running Reservation Protocol (RSVP). And WinSock 2.0 does not support an isochronous bit stream, relying on the packetized stream to achieve best effort.

But the QoS experienced with the use of ATM as the transport infrastructure offers far better performance and flexibility, as we will see later in Chapter 22 in our analysis of IP RSVP versus ATM QoS. Furthermore, desktop-to-desktop ATM networking eliminates the chance of quality-sensitive traffic traversing a legacy system somewhere in the network infrastructure that doesn't support the end-system-specified QoS parameters.

16.1.4 ATM Servers

Modern high-performance servers employ ATM technology. One example of an ATM-enabled server is the Virata Store Server produced by Advanced Telecommunications Modules Ltd. This server has an 8-gigabyte storage capacity and is optimized for ATM video transmission, guaranteeing picture quality even when handling multiple simultaneous video streams. Thus, the device can handle up to 4 feature-length films and stream up to 25 simultaneous audio clips and video images on its 155-Mbps ATM interface. This server can be directly attached via an ATM adapter card to a Virata ATM workgroup switch — making it one of the first such systems that can offer a smooth migration path from Ethernet while delivering on ATM's promise of 25 Mbps to the desktop and 155 Mbps to the workgroup switch. The 8-Gbyte Video Store Server is the key component of the Virata family.

16.2 EVALUATING ATM NETWORK INTERFACE CARDS

What are the key criteria for selection of an ATM NIC? The key features include:

- Type of bus and media supported
- Operating System (OS) support
- Throughput
- Features and functionality
- ATM switch interoperability
- Performance
- Ease of use and installation
- Documentation quality and technical support
- Pricing

Let's look at each area in more detail.

16.2.1 Bus Structure and Media Supported

What type of bus do your workstations and servers use? Here is a listing (roughly) in order of introduction:

- VME
- Industry Standard Architecture (ISA)
- Extended ISA (EISA)
- Micro Channel Architecture (MCA)
- S-bus
- Peripheral Computer Interface (PCI bus)
- TURBOChannel
- NeXTbus
- NuBus (Apple)
- GIO32 and GIO64
- FutureBus

Most PC ATM workstations are moving toward the PCI bus. What speed adapter (i.e., NIC) card can your wiring/cabling support or require?

- 25 Mbps over STP, UTP-3, 4, or 5
- 51 Mbps
- 155 Mbps over UTP-5, MMF, or SMF

What media types are you currently using or planning to install?

- Unshielded Twisted Pair (UTP) 3 or 5
- Shielded Twisted Pair (STP)
- Single or Multimode Fiber (SMF or MMF)

Note that all 25-Mbps adapters work on copper cable.

16.2.2 Operating Systems Support

Is the NIC certified to operate under one or more of the following operating systems?

- Sun Solaris 2.3, 2.4, X86
- SunOS V4.x or higher (V4.1.3)
- DOS
- Windows 3.x, Windows 95, Windows-for-Workgroups 3.11, Windows NT
- HPUX/DEC UNIX/LINUX/IRIX 5.x
- IBM's OS-2
- IBM's AIX 3.2x
- NetWare 3.12 or 4.x
- MacOS 7.5

16.2.3 Throughput

Throughput is defined as the ability to transmit at near the ATM specified rate of 25, 51, or 155 Mbps. ATM cards, like any high-speed NIC, share the central processor chip of the workstation, and their cell processing may have an impact on overall workstation performance. NIC on-board processors help minimize the load on the workstation processor. Ask for benchmark testing results from the manufacturer for your hardware, operating system, higher-layer protocols, and application before you buy.

16.2.4 Features and Functionality Supported

Performance and functionality studies show that adapters all provide the same standard higher-layer protocol capabilities, such as ATM Forum UNI V3.0/3.1 signaling, LAN emulation, and the IETF's classical IP over ATM. Some cards also support new standards, such as Multiprotocol over ATM (MPOA), Next-Hop Resolution Protocol (NHRP), and IP multicast over ATM. See Chapter 11 for definitions of these protocols. Some questions to ask are:

- Is there an on-board processor?
- What LANE schemes are supported?
- How many emulated LANs can be handled?
- Is classical IP supported?

16.2.5 ATM Switch Interoperability

Ask the NIC card vendor for interoperability test results from leading ATM switch vendors.

16.2.6 ATM NIC Performance

The two key areas of performance to review include the absence of hardware and software conflicts and stated interoperability.

16.2.7 Ease of Use and Installation

Here are some questions you should ask. How easy is it to configure and install the NIC? What network and ATM knowledge is required on your part to install the NIC? How quickly can devices be installed and configured? What drivers are standard? How are they updated? Is the current version of your operating system supported? Are drivers updated via flash memory, or is a hardware change required?

16.2.8 Documentation and Technical Support

Review documentation for clarity, completeness, and ease of reading. Call technical support before purchasing the product to see if they have the requisite knowledge, and respond within a timely fashion.

16.2.9 Management

Almost all ATM NIC cards can be managed via SNMP. Eventually you will also want support for RMON. Ask what MIBs the NIC adapter supports. Does it support the Integrated Local Management Interface (ILMI)? The IETF's AToMMIB?

16.2.10 NIC Cost Comparison

100BaseT adapters now cost an average of less than $100 each, and most Ethernet adapters sold today have the capability and option to run either 10BaseT or 100BaseT Ethernet. ATM NIC cost depends on speed; 25-Mbps ATM cards can be purchased for as low as $295 each (IBM) but typically average around $500, and 155 Mbps cards can be purchased for as low as $650 (Interphase) but typically average around $900.

However, there is still a huge installed base of 10- and 100-Mbps NIC cards that can be used and reallocated for some time. This installed base is an impediment to ATM in the LAN given the current, economically motivated usage of LANs. Therefore, a fundamental paradigm shift must occur in computing applications and user requirements if ATM is to make a significant splash in the LAN.

The other event facing ATM is the eventual implementation of the LAN interface card directly on the motherboard. For example, Intel plans to put 10/100 Mbps Ethernet ports on all new computers. ATM chip set and NIC vendors would be wise to be ahead of this curve and work to have the ATM chip set built into these motherboards rather than an Ethernet chip set.

As far as comparing ATM versus Fast Ethernet NICs, Intel provides 10/100 auto-sensing PCI Fast Ethernet NICs for less than $100, while the cheapest ATM NIC sells for less than $300. For more information, see www.intel.com.

16.3 NIC VENDORS

Presented below are a few of the leading NIC vendors and their products as of publication date [5, 6]:

- 3Com ATMLink ISA, PCI, and Sbus
- Adaptec ANA-5200, 5600, 5900 series of MCA, PCI, and Sbus
- ATM Limited Virata
- ATM Inc. VL1000, VL2000 ISA, and PCI
- Cabletron SmartCell Sbus 155
- Cabletron SmartCell PCI 155
- CrossComm (Olicom) RapidFire ATM 155
- Data General PCI
- DEC ATMworks line of PCI, Sbus, and Turbo
- Digiboard
- DTI Sbus
- Efficient Networks ENI-25p, ENI-155, and 155 Sbus, Aruba, PCI, EISA
- FORE ForeRunner
  - 25-Mbps and 155-Mbps PCI (PC, Apple Power Macintosh)
  - PCA-200EPC PCI Bus 155 Mbps
  - SBA-200E Sbus 155 Mbps
  - PCA-200EUX PCI Bus 155 Mbps
- Hewlett-Packard S700, S800 EISA
- IBM Turboways ISA, PCI, Sbus
- Integrated Micro Solutions 25 and 155 Mbps
- Interphase 4615/4815/5215/5515 Sbus, EISA, VME, and PCI
- Madge 740 PCI and EISA
- NCR
- NewBridge VIVID EISA, Sbus, VME, PCI
- Olicom RapidFire ATM PCI
- Sumitomo 3700 MER
- Sun Microsystems SunATM-155 Sbus
- Transcell
- Trillium
- ZeitNet 1211/1215 ATM Sbus
- ZeitNet ZN 1221/1225 ATM PCI-bus

Almost all of these cards are OC-3/155-Mbps ATM-compliant. Some ATM switch vendors also make their own adapters [7], as shown in the list above. This is a great way to avoid interoperability problems between the workstation's adapter card and the switch. HP and FORE are also collaborating on producing ATM 155- and 622-Mbps NICs. Note that Zeitnet was recently acquired by Cabletron, and that FORE has led the market in ATM NIC shipments as of publishing time.

16.3.1 Efficient Networks Adapters

Although there are over 25 ATM adapter card manufacturers, we chose Efficient Networks of Dallas as an example. This section reviews the ATM adapter cards manufactured and sold by Efficient Networks [8].

Efficient Networks, Inc. develops custom ATM hardware that meets the demanding requirements of high-performance computer attachment, as well as the software needed for seamless operation with popular ATM switches. These hardware/software solutions fully integrate with the buses and operating systems of high-end personal computers and workstations. Because Efficient controls the underlying technology, ATM adapters provide consistently high performance and value.

The ENI-25p ATM PCI bus adapter connects PCI-based desktop computers to ATM networks via full-duplex, 25 Mbps over UTP Category 3, 4, or 5 wiring. This card is ideal for high-throughput data functions, such as image distribution, multimedia, and other delay-sensitive applications. The ENI-25p offers a tightly integrated design based on Efficient's custom Lanai Application-Specific Integrated Circuit (ASIC), which supports a PCI bus version 2.1–compliant interface, utilizing a high-performance Segmentation and Reassembly (SAR) engine supporting up to 1024 open VCs, and 25-Mbps physical-layer functions.

The ENI-155 ATM PCI and EISA bus adapters attach PCI- or EISA-based servers and desktop computers to high-speed ATM networks via 155 Mbps over MMF or UTP Category 5 (UTP-5) wire. This adapter enables high-throughput data applications such as server attachment on a switched LAN backbone. Furthermore, image distribution, multimedia, and other delay-sensitive applications on desktop computers especially benefit from Efficient's 155-Mbps ATM adapters.

The ENI-155 incorporates the high-performance Midway ASIC, which provides AAL5 SAR and Direct Memory Access (DMA) for efficient bus and CPU utilization. This fully integrated chip executes complex ATM protocol hardware functions for optimized performance. Additional features include onboard buffer memory that limits consumption of host computer memory and traffic shaping across multiple rate queues to assure adherence to traffic contracts.

Efficient's ATM 155-Mbps SBus adapters' hardware design also utilizes the Midway ASIC to optimize communication within Sun's high-performance workgroup environments. The Midway provides the SAR and high-speed DMA required for ATM to operate most efficiently.

As a complete solution, Efficient Networks' ATM SBus adapters are ideally suited for UNIX workgroup and server applications. They are specially designed for all high-performance Sun workstation/workgroup networks, including SPARCcenters, SPARCstations, SPARCservers, and ultraSPARCs, with software support for Solaris and SunOS.

Efficient Networks' adapters interoperate with ATM switches, routers, and edge devices from major manufacturers, including 3Com, ATM Ltd., Avidia, Bay Networks, Cisco Systems, Cabletron, Digital Equipment Corporation, Fore Systems, General DataComm, IBM, NEC, SMC, Sumitomo, Whitetree, and Xylan. PC and motherboard compatibility is verified by Efficient for popular brands, including Compaq, Dell, Digital, Hewlett-Packard, and Intel.

The following is an example of a NIC specification sheet, reproduced with permission from Efficient Networks. This illustrates the format you'll see when reviewing information on ATM NIC adapter product literature.

16.3.1.1 Software Features

OS versions supported:
- Windows NT 3.51, 4.0, and Windows 95
- NetWare 4.1X, NetWare Client32
- SunOS 4.1.3_U1, 4.1.4 (155 SBus only)
- Solaris 2.4, 2.5.1 (155 SBus only)

UNI version:
- UNI 3.0, 3.1 signaling, and ILMI

LAN Emulation:
- Ethernet LANE, multiple clients, LECS autodiscovery

RFC 1577 Classical IP over ATM:
- SVC and PVC support, multiple clients
- ATMARP Server (155 SBus only)

RFC1483:
- 802.3 Bridged PDU PVCs

Traffic Management:
- Configurable Peak Cell Rate per PVC/ELAN/LIS

Other features:
- Configurable MTU size

Other features (155 SBus only):
- ECM remote management tool
- LANE services, software development kit available

16.3.1.2 Hardware Features

Form Factor:
- Single-slot adapter, half-size card (not Sbus)

Memory Configurations (for ENI-155 only):
- 512-kbyte client adapter
- 2-Mbyte server adapter

Bus Interface (for ENI-25p only):
- 32-bit, 33-MHz PCI bus version 2.1
- Bus Master capability with DMA bursting

Bus Interface (for ENI-155 only):
- 32-bit EISA bus
- 33-MHz PCI bus version 2.1
- Bus Master capability with DMA bursting up to 64 bytes

Bus Interface (for Sbus only):
- 32-bit, 16–25-MHz SBus Interface Support
- Bus Master capability with DMA bursting up to 64 bytes

AAL and ATM Support:
- Custom ASIC implements full AAL5 adaptation in hardware
- 1024 VCI address range

Physical Layer:
- ATM Forum 25 Mbps (ENI-25p)
- 155.52 Mbps, configurable for SONET or SDH (ENI-155 & SBus)

Visual Indicators:
- LED indicates network status

Cabling:
- Unshielded twisted pair Category 3, 4, or 5 (UTP-3, UTP-4, or UTP-5) (ENI-25p)
- Multimode Fiber (MMF) or unshielded twisted pair Category 5 (UTP-5) (ENI-155 & SBus)

Connectors (ENI-25p):
- Eight-contact, shielded RJ-45

Connectors (ENI-155 & SBus):
- MMF - SC Style optical Interface
- UTP-5 - Eight-contact, shielded RJ-45

Board Specifications (ENI-25p):
- Dimensions: 3.9" x 5.375"
- Weight: 3 oz

Board Specifications (ENI-155):
- Dimensions: PCI: 4.2 x 6.875 EISA: 5.0 x 6.875
- Weight: 4 oz

Board Specifications (Sbus):
- Dimensions: 3.3" x 5.776"
- Weight: 4 oz

Power Requirements (ENI-25p):
- 1 A max @ +5 V ± 5%

Power Requirements (ENI-155):
- PCI: 1.5 A max @ +5 V ± 5%; 0.2 A max @ +12 V
- EISA: 2 A max @ -5 V ± 5%; 0.2 A max @ +12 V

Power Requirements (155 Sbus):
- 1.5 A max @ +5 V ± 5%
- 0.2 A max @ +12 V ± 5%

Operating Temperatures:
- 0°C to 70°C

Nonoperating Storage Temperatures:
- -10°C to 85°C

Relative Humidity:
- Operating: 10% to 90% (noncondensing)

Compliance and Certification:
- FCC Class B, EN55022, EN50082, EN55022 (ENI-155 only)
- EN50082-1 (ENI-155 only), VCCI-2, CE, UL1950, CSA, EN60950
- FCC Class B (ENI 155s-MF)
- FCC Class A (ENI 155s-U5)
- EN55022, EN50082-1 VCCI-2, CE UL1950, CSA, EN60950 (Sbus)

Warranty
- 1 year parts and labor for hardware; software updates via Web site

16.4 WORKGROUP SWITCH SURVEY RESULTS

Table 16.2 shows the summary of all workgroup switch survey respondents. Table 16.3 shows the results of the vendors surveyed and research on workgroup switches.

Table 16.2 Workgroup Switch Vendor Survey Respondents

Company Name	Product Name	WG	LB	E	CE	CB	Switch Fabric/Bus Capacity
3Com	CoreBuilder 7000		Y				5 Gbps matrix
Bay Networks	Centillion 100	Y	Y				3.2 Gbps
FORE Systems, Inc.	ES-3810	Y					640 Mbps
FORE Systems, Inc.	PH6000	Y					1.6 Gbps shared memory
NewBridge Networks	Vivid Workgroup Switch	Y				Y	1.6 Gbps

Table 16.3 Workgroup Switch Vendor Survey

	3Com	Bay Networks	FORE Systems, Inc	FORE Systems, Inc	NewBridge Networks
Address	5400 Bayfront Plaza, PO Box 58145, Santa Clara, CA 95052	4401 Great America Parkway, Santa Clara, CA 95052	1000 FORE Drive, Warrendale, PA 15086	1000 FORE Drive, Warrendale, PA 15086	593 Herndon Parkway, Herndon, VA 22070
Web Page	3Com.com	baynetworks.com	fore.com	fore.com	newbridge.com
Annual Sales 1994	n/a	n/a	$39.3M	$39.3M	n/a
Annual Sales 1995	n/a	n/a	$106.2M	$106.2M	n/a
Annual Sales 1996	n/a	n/a	$235.2M	$235.2M	n/a
Number of Customers	n/a	n/a	2000	2000	n/a
Number of Switches Sold	n/a	n/a	5519 (3/4 CY96)	5519 (3/4 CY96)	n/a
Number of ATM Ports Sold	n/a	n/a	55,000 (3/4 CY96)	55,000 (3/4 CY96)	n/a
Product Information					
Product Name	CoreBuilder 7000	Centillion 100	ES-3810	PH6000	Vivid Workgroup Switch
Product Categories					
Workgroup		Y	Y	Y	Y
Campus Backbone	Y	Y	Y	Y	Y
Enterprise					Y
AC Power		Y	Y	Y	Y
DC Power					
Minimum Switch Price	$22,000	$7,000	$10,750	$8,950	$25,995
Configuration	4 ports OC-3	2 ports ATM	w/ATM uplink	3 slot chassis with 12 ports switched Ethernet	n/a
Maximum Switch Price	$73,000	$50,000	$69,950	$24,850	$75,000
Configuration	32 ports OC-3	24 ports ATM		fully loaded 3 slots SW Eth with ATM uplink	n/a
Switch Fabric/Bus Capacity	5 Gbps matrix	3.2 Gbps	640 Mbps	1.6 Gbps shared memory	1.6 Gbps
Max Sum of Port Speeds	5 Gbps matrix	3.2 Gbps	up to 72 - 10Mbps Ethernet ports		1.8 Gbps
% Blocking at Load per GR-					
CBR	non-blocking	non-blocking			
VBR	non-blocking	non-blocking			
Point-to-Multipoint Capability					
Spatial	n/a	n/a	n/a		Y
Logical	n/a	n/a	n/a		
Min Switch Transit Delay	n/a		n/a		26 us
VPI/VCI Bits on UNI	n/a		n/a		VPI 0-15, VCI 32-1023
VPI/VCI Bits on NNI	n/a		n/a		VPI 0-15, VCI 32-1023
Max PVC VPCs per card/switch 8/port	255		n/a		16
Max PVC VCCs per	512/port		n/a		1200
Max SVCs per card/switch	3072		n/a		2000
Port Redundancy (1:1, 1:N)	n/a		1:1		1:1
Common Eqpmt Redundancy	n/a				
Power	Y		Y	Y	
Fabric/Bus	Y				Y
Controller	Y				
Other				*	
Distinguishing Features					

Table 16.3 Workgroup Switch Vendor Survey (Continued)

Interface Information	3Com	Bay Networks	FORE Systems, Inc	FORE Systems, Inc	NewBridge Networks
ATM UNI Interfaces					
DS1	-	-	-	-	-
nxDS1 IMA	-	-	-	-	-
DS3	Y	Y	-	Y	-
OC3	-	Y	Y	Y	Y
OC12	-	-	-	-	-
OC48	-	-	-	-	-
155Mbps SMF	Y	-	Y	-	Y
622Mbps SMF	Y	-	-	-	-
Cell-Based Clear Chan					
TC/HSSI					
E1	Y	Y	-	-	-
E3	-	-	-	-	-
E4	-	-	-	-	Y
STM-1	-	-	-	-	Y
STM-4	-	-	-	-	-
J1	-	-	-	-	-
J2 (6.312 Mb/s)	-	-	-	-	-
25 Mb/s UTP	-	-	-	-	-
51.84 Mb/s UTP	-	-	-	Y	Y
155 Mb/s UTP	-	-	Y	Y	Y
155 Mb/s MMF	Y	Y	Y	Y	Y
TAXI 100Mbps	-	-	-	-	-
Non-ATM Interfaces					
10 Mbps Ethernet	-	-	Y	Y	Y
100 Mb/s Ethernet	-	-	Y	Y	-
FDDI	-	-	-	-	-
4 Mb/s Token Ring	-	-	-	-	-
16 Mb/s Token Ring	-	-	-	-	-
Frame Relay nxDS0, DS1,	-	-	-	-	-
Frame Relay E1	-	-	-	-	-
SMDS DS1 & DS3	-	-	-	-	-
SMDS DXI nxDS0 & DS1	-	-	-	-	-
HDLC V.35 & HSSI	-	-	-	-	-
Circuit Emulation DS1	-	-	-	-	-
Circuit Emulation DS3,nxDS0,E1,E3	-	-	-	-	-
Serial IO Circuit Emulation (EIA 530, EIA 449, X.21, V.35)	-	-	-	-	Y
M-JPEG,H.320 Video	-	-	-	-	-
JPEG-PAL, JPEG-NTS	-	-	-	-	-
H.320 Video	-	-	-	-	-
FUNI	-	-	-	-	-

Table 16.3 Workgroup Switch Vendor Survey (Continued)

Traffic Management	3Com	Bay Networks	FORE Systems, Inc	NewBridge Networks
ATM Service Classes Supported				
CBR	Y	Y	n/a	Y
rt-VBR	Y	Y	n/a	Y
nrt-VBR	Y	Y	n/a	Y
UBR	Y	Y	n/a	Y
ABR	Y	Y	n/a	Y
Switch Type (Fabric, Bus,				Broadcast Matrix
Switch Buffering				
Input				
Fabric				
Output				Y
Other				
Switch Buffer Quantity/Port	600 cells/port			4000 cells
Switch Architecture (Narrative)		input and output buffering		Broadcast Matrix Output Buffered
ATM Forum Congestion Control				
EFCI	Y			Y
ER				
VS/VD				
Other	CLP-bit			
Congestion Control				
Cell Loss Probability				
CBR				
VBR				
CLP Bit Usage				
Tag				
Selective Discard				Y
Other	Y			
Policing				
PCR				Y
PCR+SCR				Y
Other				
Shaping				
PCR				
PCR+SCR				
Other				
Connection Admission Control				
GCAC	Y			Y
Other				
Packet Discard				
EPD				
PPD				
Frame Policing				
Other				
I.610 OAM Performance Measurement				Y

Table 16.3 Workgroup Switch Vendor Survey (Continued)

Protocol/Standards Support	3Com	Bay Networks	FORE Systems, Inc	FORE Systems, Inc	NewBridge Networks
ATM Forum					
UNI Signaling					
3.0	Y	Y		Y	Y
3.1	Y	Y		Y	Y
4.0				97	97
Other					
Pt-Pt SVC Signaling					
3.0	Y			Y	
3.1	Y			Y	Y
4.0				97	97
Other					
Pt-Mpt SVC Signaling					
3.0	Y			Y	
3.1	Y			Y	Y
4.0				97	97
Other					
NNI Signaling					
IISP	Y	Y			
PNNI 1.0		Y			97
BICI 2.0					
ITU-T					
UNI Signaling					
Q.93B		Y		Y	
Q.2931				Y	Y
NNI Signaling					
BISUP					Y
Other					
LAN Emulation Client					
LANE 1.0	Y	Y		Y	
RFC 1483	Y	Y		Y	
LAN Emulation Server					
LANE 1.0	Y	Y			
RFC 1483	Y	Y			
Virtual LAN Capability			Port and MAC address based	Port,MAC,subnet-based VLANs, 802.1g tagging in 97	Y
IP/ATM Client: RFC 1577	Y			Y	
IP/ATM Server: RFC 1577	Y			Y	
MPOA: ATM Forum			Ready for MPOA	97	Y
NHRP				97	
Tested Interoperation with others			*		
Distinguishing Features			*		

Table 16.3 Workgroup Switch Vendor Survey (Continued)

Network Management Support	3Com	Bay Networks	FORE Systems, Inc	FORE Systems, Inc	NewBridge Networks
Full ATM Forum ILMI					
3.0			Y	Y	Y
3.1			Y	Y	Y
4.0			97	97	97
Other					
ILMI Address Registration					
3.0			Y	Y	Y
3.1				Y	Y
4.0				97	97
Other					
RFC 1695 (ATOM MIB)				98	Y
Per Port Statistics			Y	Y	Y
Per VC Statistics			Y	Y	Y
OAM Cell VPC AIS/RDI				Y	Y
OAM Cell VCC AIS/RDI				Y	Y
OAM Cell Loopback				Y	Y
ATM Forum NM I/F Support					
M1					
M2					
M3					
M4					
M5					
Automatic PVC Configuration					
SPVPC/SPVCC			SPVCC	SPVCC	
Other					Y
Automatic PVC Restoration					
SPVPC/SPVCC			SPVCC	SPVCC	
Other					Y
NMS Support					
HPOV			Y	Y	Y
Cabletron Spectrum Enterprise Mgr					
SunNet Manager			Y	Y	
NetView 6000/AIX			Y	Y	
Others		Optivity			Systems Manager
MIB Support					
Distinguishing Features			*		
Legend	Y' = Supported/Available Now * = See chapter				

16.5 REVIEW

This chapter reviewed ATM devices in the workgroup and desktop area network. We covered ATM NIC adapters in detail. The chapter then concluded with a survey of leading workgroup switch vendors. Note that some of the enterprise and campus/LAN backbone switches in the previous chapter could also serve as workgroup switches.

16.6 REFERENCES

[1] IDC Report, May 96.
[2] Inews assorted sources and news stories.
[3] *EE Times*, January 20, 1997.
[4] E. Roberts, "The ATM-ready Desktop Is Just an API Away," *Communications Week*, May 1995.
[5] D. Hibner, F. Groom, and G. Early, "The real status of ATM cards," *Communications News; Nokomis,* January 1996.
[6] *Communications News* study by The Center for Information and Communication Sciences at Ball State University Applied Research Institute.
[7] K. Cholewka, "Affordable ATM," *Data Communications*, December 96.
[8] Provided by G. Landon at Efficient Networks. Contact www.efficient.com for more details.
[9] Courtesy of Cascade.
[10] M. Cooney, *Network World*, July 15, 1996.

17

ATM Switch Vendor Survey Details

This chapter provides vendor responses from the survey that either were too detailed or required further explanation. The vendor submitting the response is identified in boldface type at the beginning of the paragraphs and figures of their response. Italics indicate where we make clarifying comments within vendor responses. Some sections contain no vendor responses, and we insert a brief summary of the survey results presented in the earlier chapters.

17.1 GENERAL PRODUCT INFORMATION

This section provides specific product details not included in the spreadsheet, along with the author's comments. The same format will be used consistently throughout this section.

17.1.1 Manufacturer, Product Name, and Category of Switch

Some of the vendors surveyed chose to provide a few paragraphs on their company's strengths.

ADC Kentrox — Third-generation ATM access products. Large carrier market and CPE base of customers. First to market with innovative solutions like IMA, high-speed frame relay. Large deployment of products.

Cabletron — The company continues to grow as we build the next generation of network infrastructures. Our research and development is guided by listening to customers and delivering what we promise. This simple, powerful philosophy is one we've used since the founding of Cabletron, and is what helped us become the billion-dollar company we are today.

Cascade is at the forefront of broadband data communications with its family of scalable, carrier-class frame relay, ATM, and remote access switching products. Used by public carriers and Internet service providers worldwide, Cascade's products are forming the foundation of the public network infrastructure for global communications.

Note: Cascade and IBM have an alliance through which IBM resells Cascade switches.

Digital Equipment Corporation is the world's leader in open client/server solutions, from personal computing to integrated worldwide information systems. Digital's approach to virtual networking integrates hub, switching, and routing functionality using standard protocols to deliver flexible, secure, low-latency access to the full complement of network services regardless of technology or physical location. Digital offers a modular, "building block" architecture and enables the customer to take full advantage of new technologies as they are needed, while making the most of existing technologies. Digital now provides the complete core switching infrastructure for all levels of the organization, the desktop, the department, and the enterprise. Digital is the only vendor shipping Ethernet, FDDI, ATM, and IP switching today.

FORE Systems is a worldwide leader in the design, development, manufacture, and sale of high-performance networking products based on ATM technology. According to industry analysts, FORE Systems offers more ATM-based networks than any other vendor in the world. FORE ATM switches also carry approximately two-thirds of the world's Internet traffic.

FORE offers a complete line of ATM switches, adapters, WAN and LAN access devices, and ATM video products as well as comprehensive ATM-based solutions for emerging service providers. These solutions provide seamless managed infrastructures in both LAN and WAN service providers' networks, including competitive access providers, Internet service providers, and cable companies.

Note that FORE and NorTel have a joint development and marketing alliance through which NorTel resells FORE switches [1].

General DataComm, founded in 1969, has over 25 years of experience in designing and manufacturing transmission products and in installing and supporting networks. The company currently enjoys leadership in the ATM WAN market, with numerous recent industry surveys showing its product as being #1 or #2 in market share in the edge ATM switching market. GDC's APEX family of ATM switches is currently used in numerous carrier and enterprise ATM networks around the world, including MCI, Deutsche Telecom, France Telecom, and MFS. GDC's APEX switches are also sold through partnerships with Lucent, Ericsson, and Digital Switch Corporation. The company's ATM strategy is based on proven technology innovations and industry leadership in customer network deployment. GDC currently has four R&D centers focused on ATM/broadband research in ATM switching technology, LAN protocols, signaling, multimedia, and network management.

IBM creates, develops, and manufactures the world's most advanced information technologies, including computer systems, software, networking systems, storage devices, and microelectronics. The IBM Networking Hardware Division develops and manufactures leading-edge networking technologies and products, providing global end-to-end solutions for ATM, Token Ring, Ethernet, and SNA networks. With headquarters in Research Triangle Park, N.C., the Networking Hardware Division also offers consultation, education, services, and support worldwide to help customers achieve their business objectives. For further information about IBM, its products and services, you can contact http://www.ibm.com, http://www.raleigh.ibm. com or call 1-800-IBM-3333.

NEC is a world leader in all aspects of the electronics industry. NEC has expertise in computers, semi conductors, and telecommunications equipment. NEC also employs leading-edge design and manufacturing techniques.

NewBridge Networks — NewBridge Networks offers a comprehensive suite of networking solutions to meet business, government, and service provider requirements for high-speed digital communications systems.

NewBridge is a recognized global leader in end-to-end communications solutions incorporating traditional technologies such as Time Division Multiplexing (TDM) as well as frame relay, wide area ATM systems, and switched routing solutions for local area environments, all manageable by a single platform. The comprehensive family of ATM products includes the MainStreetXpress 36150 Access Switch for the wide area, the MainStreetX-press 36170 Multiservices Switch, which can support both ATM and frame relay from the same platform, and the new MainStreetXpress 36190 Core Services Switch. NewBridge also offers the VIVID Switched Routing solution for enterprise networks. The company's recent acquisition of UB Networks further strengthens NewBridge Networks' position in the local area network marketplace.

The company maintains a unique position in the industry with a standards-based, fully managed, multimedia networking product line which has technical approvals in more than 100 countries. NewBridge Networks' U.S. corporate headquarters is in Herndon, Va., with facilities throughout Canada, the United States, Latin America, Europe, the Middle East, Asia, and Australia.

NewBridge offers a complete ATM service infrastructure product line — core, edge, and access — unified under advanced service and network management systems suite. It supports core network consolidation and multiple full-service solutions, including FR, carrier-scale internetworking, video/LAN services, and digital "private line" overlay services.

Note that NewBridge and Siemens have entered into a joint development and marketing agreement through which Siemens is to resell NewBridge ATM switches [2]. Thus you will note that these switch types are very similar in many features and functions.

Sahara — Founded on June 2, 1995, with a mission: "To deliver leading edge integrated broadband access products for the internet era." Sahara Networks develops high-speed access systems for broadband-based networks. These products provide telecommunications service providers and corporate end users with the flexibility to serve many applications over a single cell- or frame-based wide area network infrastructure. The Sahara products enable a variety of applications to be supported over a common broadband network. These units may be located at customer site, central office, or point-of-presence (PoP), providing access for multiple service types with speeds ranging from T1/E1 up to 155 Mbps. Sahara products provide superior fault tolerance and redundancy, enabling nonstop operation of critical network facilities. Sahara places great emphasis on ease of use and network management, offering a unique Java-based World Wide Web management capability, sophisticated security enhancements, and industry-standard SNMP-based management.

Sahara Networks has focused on five key areas with its broadband access systems. They are: a scalable family of products; Web- and Java-based management; high performance and redundancy features; cross-flow switching; and handling multiple traffic types including data, voice, and video over broadband frame or ATM wide area networks at price points not seen in the marketplace.

Telematics offers a complete line of ATM carrier edge switching, frame relay switching, and multiservice access products. Telematics' switching products are differentiated by their industry-leading traffic management attributes which enable true multiservice adaptation switching within single platforms while simultaneously enabling high trunk utilization and low cost of operation via sophisticated network management.

17.1.2 Power

Nothing noteworthy was said on power requirements. Most premises switches supported AC power, and most WAN switches supported AC and DC power.

17.1.3 Minimum/Maximum Switch Price/Configuration

Minimum price per switch ran from $4500 to $60,000, while the maximum price quoted was $1M. Note that some of the vendors chose not to provide the configuration for minimum and maximum pricing. Configuration should always be a consideration when purchasing from a vendor, as most vendors charge by the chassis with an additional cost per card/interface.

Of note are switches manufactured by FORE Systems, which can achieve a workgroup price per 155-Mbps port of less than $700! With adapters at less than $300 each, the total price for an ATM 155-Mbps switch port and NIC is less than $1000 — compared to $600 for 100-Mbps Ethernet.

17.1.4 Switch Architecture, Bus Capacity, and Blocking

Bus capacity and switch fabric/matrix size ran from 500 Mbps to greater than 1 terabit per second. All three types of switching fabrics described in Chapter 13 were represented in the survey responses.

Sahara — SA-600 has 1 Gbps of cell and 1 Gbps of packet simultaneously per ICM. The SA-600 can hold up to 3 ICMs. The SA-1200 can hold up to 6 ICMs.

17.1.5 Maximum Sum of Port Speeds

This value ranged from equaling the switch architecture bus capacity to values substantially less than the fabric or bus capacity. This number is more important than raw switch capacity, since it determines how much usable capacity the switch actually supports.

17.1.6 % Blocking at Load per GR-1110

Most switches offered nonblocking performance at full offered load. The key is to offer full bandwidth to every port on the switch.

17.1.7 Point-to-Multipoint Capability

Most vendors supported spatial multicast (that is, one destination per physical port), while some also provided logical multicast, with multiple destinations per physical port.

DEC's GIGAswitch supports both CBR and VBR point-to-multipoint capability. Cell replication is done in hardware, hence keeping very low latency for point-to-multipoint circuits.

17.1.8 Minimum Switch Transit Delay

Minimum switch transit delay varied from 3.4 to 250 μs.

DEC GIGAswitch and 900: The variation of this latency across the crossbar switch fabric is +/- 1 μs per Virtual Channel (VC) contending for the same output port (with 95 percent confidence interval). For the VN900EA, latency varies if translation of packet to and from FDDI is required

Sahara's family of products is targeted at the WAN access market. As such, these products usually help bridge non-ATM traffic into broadband traffic. Under these conditions, most of the delay experienced occurs at the adaptation layers. Switching delay is relatively minimal when compared to the delay introduced by the adaptation and applications layers (one order of magnitude). The delay introduced by the adaptation layer depends on the type of interface and its configuration (nx64 kbps, Ethernet, MPEG, etc.).

The switching delay (includes cell routing, and processing/accounting) on the SA-100 is no more than 6 cell interval times (<18 μs).

17.1.9 VPI/VCI Bits on UNI/NNI

Responses ranged from 8 to 16 bits for both the User-Network Interface (UNI) and the Network-Network Interface (NNI).

17.1.10 VPC and VCC Support (Max per Card/Switch)

Vendor responses varied, and we assumed that when a single number was provided, it meant "per switch." Maximum Virtual Path Connections (VPCs) responses ranged from 4 to 32,000 per card and from 4 to 2,000,000 per switch. Responses on maximum Virtual Channel Connections (VCCs) per card ranged from 14 to 32K and from 256 to over 2,000,000 per switch.

17.1.11 SVC Support (Max per Card/Switch)

Some vendors did not yet support Switched Virtual Connections (SVCs). Those that did support SVCs reported support for a maximum per card of 14 to 32,000, and a maximum per switch ranging from 1000 to 2,000,000 Most vendors reported plans to support SVCs by the end of the 1997 calendar year.

17.1.12 Redundancy

About half the respondents said they supported 1:1 redundancy, and most of the rest either did not support redundancy or did not specify any. Some vendors, like Telematics, specified which cards had what redundancy, such as broadband cards being 1:1, and T1/E1 multiport cards being 1:N. This type of redundancy is typical, where the common processor cards are 1:1 and the port cards are 1:N.

Sahara — The SA-100 is designed to be a low-cost customer premises piece of equipment. Generally, this is used in nonredundant applications (due to cost constraints). If the customer requires redundancy at the customer premises, the SA-600/SA-1200 is available and supports full redundancy. The SA-1200 is designed to be a customer premises / remote PoP or edge of carrier network piece of equipment. Customer redundancy requirements vary greatly in this market. As redundancy is an option, each customer can choose the configuration which best suites its needs.

17.1.13 Distinguishing Features

Many of the vendors provided narratives, which we repeat below.

ADC Kentrox — Support multiple services with a variety of interfaces within a single platform. Can be used as an ATM product, frame relay switch or a mini DSLAM (HDSL).

Cabletron — Advanced shared-memory architecture provides high performance, yet low cost. Excellent connection management features include advanced CAC (policy) for call admission. Permanent Virtual Circuit (PVC) and SVC connection support: Private Network-Network Interface (PNNI) ph 0 routing, full Quality of Service (QoS) and traffic class support including ABR. Congestion management features include early packet discard, configurable floor/ceiling limits for central buffer store, Explicit Forward Congestion Identification (EFCI), and backward RM congestion notification.

Cascade — Quad Plane Architecture: The CBX 500 implements a Quad Plane switch architecture by subdividing the buffer pool into four parallel arrays, each of which is tailored in size to support different traffic requirements. This architecture builds an independent buffer plane for each of the four classes of services defined by the ATM Forum.

Virtual Network Navigator (VNN): VNN is QoS-enhanced network-routing technology based on Open Shortest Path First (OSPF) routing that creates a single-domain multiservice network routing topology across Cascade's family of broadband switches. VNN allows the CBX 500 to share a common routing domain with Cascade's B-STDX multiservice switches, which allows seamless end-to-end VC establishment across frame relay, ATM, or SMDS networks.

Call Admission Control (CAC): The basic CAC principle is real-time generation that maps an effective bandwidth for the parameters of an SVC call or PVC provision command, plus a metric of link state at each buffer site in the network. The effective bandwidth is checked against the remaining bandwidth, and, if the route is suitable, the call is connected.

Distributed Routing: The routing tables used to look up the topology of the network are stored on every line card. There is no centralized routing server to cause delay or bottlenecks.

Distributed SVC processing: The CBX offers a dedicated SVC signaling processor on every line card; this distributed approach allows the signaling performance to scale with port density. SVC processing is the highest in the industry, supporting up to 3,000 SVC per second per switch.

VC Capacity: 224,000 per switch.

FORE — ASX-200BX has nonblocking multicast, per-VC queuing with weighted RR queue draining. ASX-200WG has Forethought Bandwidth Management [3].

The ASX-1000 has Head of Frame (HOF) upgradable bandwidth from 2.5 Gbps to 10 Gbps in 2.5-Gbps increments, nonblocking multicast, per-VC queuing with weighted RR queue draining.

The PH 7000 is a multilayered switch with ATM uplink (Powercell 700).

The PH 6000 is a workgroup multilayered switch with ATM uplink (Powercell 700) that provides ATM connectivity to legacy LANs, Ethernet, and Fast Ethernet networks at a very competitive price.

GDC's APEX family provides comprehensive solutions for enterprise and carrier customers needing access and switching solutions for voice, video, and data. GDC customers enjoy a wide array of interfaces including ATM, frame relay, FUNI, M-JPEG video, H.320 video, MPEG-2 video (1997), circuit emulation, and Ethernet, which allows them to concurrently support legacy applications and ATM switching in a scalable product family. Interface speeds in the family range from 56 kbps to 622 Mbps. GDC's focus on the carrier marketplace has caused the company to adhere to industry standards such as NEBS and has been a key factor in the architectural decisions made to allow for redundancy and clocking/synchronization/timing.

GDC has also taken the lead in video over ATM research, offering its customers robust, flexible solutions for narrowband, wideband, and broadband multimedia services. Its APEX VIP interfaces offer integrated video CODECs on its APEX family of switches, while the APEX Multimedia Multipoint Server (MMS) is the industry's first "Anyband" MCU allowing integrated narrowband, wideband, and broadband multimedia conferences.

IBM — 2220 and 2225 Nways BroadBand Services (NBBS), Non-Disruptive Path Switching (NPDS). Multiprotocol support in same adapter. Multiservice support — voice, video, and data. An IBM 2230 distinguishing feature is a very high SBC setup rate — 2000 VCs per second.

The 8260 provides N+1 power load sharing with up to four power supplies. Hot standby and automatic configuration mirroring is provided by the redundant switch/control points. Cell buffer pools use a separate memory bank from VCC/VPC memory blocks. Only ATM switch on the market to support shared LANs, switched LANs, and ATM on one chassis/power supply. Integrated ATM routing/LANE bridging/ARP server/LANE server/RFC1483 and super VLAN support with the ATM switch with Multiprotocol Switched Services (MSS). Same PNNI 1.0 code available in backbone 8260 and workgroup 8285 switch providing scalable reusable design point.

IBM 8285 — Cell buffer pools use a separate memory bank from VCC/VPC memory blocks, ATM WAN modules, 25 Mbps, 155 Mbps, 100 Mbps, LAN-Bridge module. MSS used in Backbone 8260 and Workgroup 8285.

NewBridge 36170 — Unparalleled scalability from 800 Mbps to 51.2 Gbps switching capacity. Capacity is modular in 800-Mbps or 1.6-Gbps increments. SVC/PNNI is scalable with redundancy. Multiservice platform that supports cell relay, FR, circuit emulation, and internetworking. NEBS compliant. The NewBridge 36150 has the most interface options in the industry. The industry's best-of-breed product for high-quality Interactive Distance Learning (IDL) and medical imaging applications, the 36150 has the only integrated MPEG II card in the industry with the option of a windows-based GUI video scheduler and a turnkey solution.

Sahara — All access products use common hardware and software; as such, the SA-100 is easily upgraded to an SA-600 or SA-1200, and the SA-600 is easily upgraded to an SA-1200 or downgraded to an SA-100. Sahara access products employ a unique cross-flow switching architecture for unprecedented performance and flexibility. Cross-flow switching enables service providers and end users to interwork circuit-, packet-, and cell-based applications across a variety of media and transmission types. Parallel subsystems on every Interface Control Module (ICM) switch packets and cells simultaneously at 1 gigabit per second each. Multiple ICMs can be combined in a single chassis for multigigabit switching rates. Third-generation traffic management — including advanced traffic shaping capabilities and available bit rate class of service — conserves network bandwidth while guaranteeing the proper quality of service to each application.

An object-oriented, component-based software architecture enhances Sahara Access system reliability and lets customers integrate new capabilities with minimal disruption to network operation. Open PODCONNECT hardware and software interfaces help strategic partners tailor Sahara Access systems for specialized applications.

With its SaharaView network management system, Sahara has pioneered the use of Java-based Web technology to deliver low-cost, platform-independent management and control. The use of Java, plus support for standard protocols such as FTP, SNMP, and Telnet, provides easy integration with existing network management platforms like HP OpenView, NetView 6000, SunNet Manager, and others. Sophisticated client/server techniques maintain rigid end-to-end security and automatically track software revisions by dynamically uploading applets from the device to be managed.

Sahara Access products meet all of the criteria for successful broadband access:

- A scalable product portfolio
- Exceptional reliability and availability
- Integrated packet, circuit, and cell processing
- Blazing performance
- An open software architecture
- Revolutionary network management

17.1.14 ATM Interfaces

DS1, DS3, OC-3, E1, E3, and 155-Mbps Unshielded Twisted Pair (UTP) and Multimode Fiber (MMF) were the most commonly supported interfaces. Of the non-ATM interfaces, 10- and 100-Mbps Ethernet and FDDI were the most popular, with some support for Token Ring and frame relay. Many vendors used the terms 155- and 622-Mbps Single Mode Fiber (SMF) synonymously with OC3/OC12. Beware that although SDH and SONET interfaces have the same speed, they are not plug-compatible.

17.2 TRAFFIC MANAGEMENT FEATURES

This section summarizes vendor responses to switch traffic management features.

17.2.1 ATM Service Classes Supported

Most vendors surveyed supported all five of the ATM Forum defined service categories: CBR, rt-VBR, nrt-VBR, UBR, and ABR.

17.2.2 Switch Type

Fabric/matrix was by far the most popular switch type.

17.2.3 Buffering

Since cell discard has a negative impact on applications using ATM, the switch's buffering scheme is a critical component. Most vendors offered output and/or input switch buffering, with some in the fabric as well, as indicated in the tabulation of the vendor responses. The following survey responses provide additional insights into some vendors' strategies.

DEC — GIGAswitch ATM 14 and 5 slot: Primarily input-buffered with limited output buffers. Per VC buffer allocation and accounting. SWITCH-master algorithm does parallel iterative matching to avoid head of line blocking and results in fabric throughput of greater than 97 percent. The DEC ATMSwitch 900 is primarily input-buffered with limited output buffers. Per VC buffer allocation and accounting.

17.2.4 Switch Buffer Quantity/Port

The specific number of cells at each point (input, fabric, output) per port.

Cabletron — The ZX-250 is based on an advanced shared-memory architecture implemented in high-performance Application-Specific Integrated Circuits (ASICs). A single fast SRAM buffer store is used in conjunction with a multiple-priority queue controller to provide excellent separation of traffic flows between VCs of different classes of service and QoS guarantees. The base ZX-250 provides 16K cells of buffer, while the ZX-250i and the ZX-250r provide 32K.

DEC — GIGAswitch ATM 14 and 5 slot: Minimum 2400 cell buffers/port; can be increased to 30,000 cell buffers per congested port, or approximately 250K cell buffers per output port. The ATMswitch 900 has 8000 buffers per port, 64,000 cell buffers per congested port. The VNswitch 900EA has 4 MB of shared buffer allocated dynamically.

IBM 2230 — Cross-point switch fabric 8/8, 640 Mbps per thread for Model 650; 4 4x640 for Model 600. 8 Mb of buffer (128K cells) distributed into 4 buffer planes: CBR, VBR-Nrt, VBR-Rt, UBR/ABR. ATM adapters have large buffers: OC3/STD-1: 24K cells per port. 10 QoS classes: CBR, UBR/ABR, 4 for VBR-Nrt, 4 for VBR-Rt.

NEC America — Based on NEC-developed chip set. TDM input/output-buffered nonblocking single-stage switch fabric. The switch and buffer capacities for the M20 are:

- ATM switch capacity — 10 Gbps (622 Mbps x 16) (expandable to 160 Gbps)
- Input Expandable Buffer (IXB) capacity per switch port — 32,768 cells
- Output buffer capacity per switch port — 128 cells
- Output Expandable Buffer (OXB) capacity per switch port — 32,768 cells

Sahara — Buffer resources are modular in nature (can be upgraded by replacing SIMMs). Sahara Access products provide user and network connections via modules called PODs (Protocol Option Devices). There are two version of PODs, basic and enhanced. Sahara products may or may not require buffering (depending on the application), basic PODs do not provide buffering while enhanced PODs do. The current buffer sizes for enhanced PODs are:

- Input: Cell subsystem: 6000 packet subsystem: 16,000 or 64,000 packets (modular)
- Fabric: 32 cell buffer pools
- Output: 4000

The input and output buffers can be increased via SIMM upgrade. All buffer resources are controlled via a "back-pressure" technique which allows all buffer resources to be flow-controlled based on output buffer load levels.

17.2.5 Architecture Narrative

Vendors were asked to provide any additional narrative on their switch architecture, and some are provided below.

ADC Kentrox - Nonblocking, dynamically allocated bandwidth architecture, 524 Mbps.

Cascade — The CBX 500 is an overspeeded, output-buffered, cross-point matrix switch and has no input buffers. Per QoS class and per VC queue buffer allocation are supported, which allocate different buffers for the different class of service QoS definitions on the I/O ports. Cell buffers are located on the individual line cards and on the switch fabric itself.

The switch provides a total of 16,000 cell buffers per I/O channel, for a total of 128,000 cell buffers integrated in the switch fabric. The 128,000 Cell buffers in the fabric are divided into 4,000 cells per queue (CBR, rt-VBR, nrt-VBR, and UBR), per thread.

The line card buffering implements a weighted round-robin scheduling to deliver QoS guarantees. A weighted round-robin transmission scheduler selects one of the buffer planes per cell interval. The CAC algorithm provides the weights applied to the scheduler. The scheduler has programmable time slots with a buffer plane selected per time period. The bit setting for that time period determines which plane should be sent. If that selected plane is empty, then it uses pure priority against the other planes to select the plane to be sent. Within that search, the planes that are empty are skipped until one with a cell is found. If no cells are found, the server is left with no cell to send. The weighted round-robin priority is in the following order: CBR, rt-VBR, nrt-VBR, ABR/UBR. It should be noted that CBR traffic receives strict priority over the other planes.

DEC — The DEC GIGAswitch architecture is a 13 x 13 crossbar with a total of 10.4 Gbps. Each port is mapped to the crossbar port on a TDM schedule. Since the sum of the port speeds is lesser than slot bandwidth, no cells are delayed. In case of contention, cells are buffered. The 900 offers a shared memory architecture with logical partitioning of memory with 8000 cell buffers per port and total bandwidth of 1.6 Gbps. The VNswitch 900EA offers multiple processors for routing and switching to provide line rate throughput. Multiple modules can configured in hub to interconnect via 400-Mbps VNbus to provide Ethernet, Fast Ethernet and FDDI ports.

FORE — ASX200-BX and ASX-1000 have distribution of cells to shared memory output queues by TDM bus. Note that the PH 6000 is not truly an ATM switch, but rather supports ATM uplink.

GDC — The APEX family of ATM switches is designed for up to 1.6 Gbps of ATM switching capacity in the APEX MAC1, and up to 6.4 Gbps in the APEX NPX. A high degree of flexibility allows each switch to act as a pure cell switch and also as an adaptation switch for interconnecting non-ATM networks (such as LANs, frame relay, T1/E1 multiplexers) or front-end processors via the ATM backbone.

The APEX switches use a mid-plane architecture with slot controller modules plugging into the front of the unit, providing easy access for maintenance and repair. The rear of the shelf accommodates Link Interface Modules (LIMs), which house the physical interface circuitry and line drivers. All modules may be hot-swapped with power applied, without affecting the operation of the switch.

At the core of the APEX switch architecture is a cross-point fabric that provides a switching bandwidth of up to 6.4 Gbps. The switch fabric is a busless, enhanced broadcast matrix design. It provides connections for up to 16 independent slot controller modules. Connections from the switch fabric to each slot controller are made via dedicated cell buses. There is no common bussing or contention. Besides providing the speed necessary to handle the high data rates required, the dedicated buses eliminate the common failure points found in many other designs, where a failure on one card can affect all other cards sharing the same bus.

Furthermore, each cell carries its own switching information into the switch fabric. Residual switching information is not retained within the switch fabric, which makes it highly reliable. A 3-byte tag is attached to the 53-byte ATM cell and sent to the switch fabric by a slot controller that wishes to exchange cells with another slot controller. The Switch Fabric uses the 3-byte tag to switch the ATM cell from one cell bus to another, which takes it to the destination slot controller. The switch fabric also uses information within the 3-byte tag to perform multicast, whereby the incoming cell stream from one slot controller is replicated and forwarded to the outgoing slot controllers as determined in the system configuration. The outgoing slot controllers will independently multiply the received cell stream to all defined VPI/VCIs.

Each slot controller operates as a completely separate subsystem. All communications with other cards in the switch take place through the switch fabric. There is no shared bus or other communications link to form a point of contention or common failure point.

Redundancy and fault tolerance, critical to a network's availability, are also key elements of the APEX switch architecture. There is provision for a standby switch fabric module for automatic switchover. In redundant configurations, power-supply modules within the APEX can be configured to provide 1-for-N redundancy load sharing. Environmental monitoring facilities enable the network manager to monitor temperature, voltage, and fan rotation for early detection of possible failures.

For APEX switches, the slot controller located in slot 0 is responsible for systemwide facilities, such as overall control of fault tolerance and redundancy and control of PVC and SVC routing information. A dedicated standby slot position (slot 0) is provided for a redundant slot controller. Presently, the MS/QEDOC, Ethernet Adaptation Control Card, is capable of acting as the slot 0 redundant controller to provide nondisruptive redundancy.

APEX employs a distributed buffering scheme with three distinct buffering mechanisms. Input and output buffers reside on each APEX ATM slot controller, while Head-of-Line (HOL) blocking relief buffers are used within the XH switch fabric. Distributed buffering enables the APEX family to scale quite well. As each slot controller is added to the system, the amount of buffering available increases without dramatic cost increases.

Input Buffering — As cells enter the APEX, the "ATM Engine" performs traffic policing and real-time cell processing functions, including statistics gathering and QoS management. CBR or high-priority VBR traffic is placed into a high-priority, 31-cell-deep input buffer that is switched as high-priority traffic through the switch fabric. Low-priority traffic is placed into a separate input buffer as large as 64K cells deep, and is switched at a lower-priority by the switch fabric. (For actual sizes of the lower priority buffer, see below for purchasing options.)

Switch Fabric Buffering — The XH switch fabric has a four-cell-deep buffer for each possible cross-connect point (i.e., 16 x 16 x 4 cells). This is used for HOL blocking relief. Potential HOL blocking can occur when multiple cell inputs are destined for the same output port. This small four-cell-deep buffer ensures that blocking does not occur in this instance. The use of a distributed buffering system, including input buffering, output buffering, and HOL blocking relief buffers, provides a highly flexible architecture.

Output Buffering — As cells leave the switch fabric, APEX again uses a unique output buffering mechanism for different types of traffic. Again, two independent output buffers are used. CBR and high-priority VBR traffic (VBR-rt) is placed into the high-priority 63-cell-deep output buffer, while medium-priority VBR (VBR-nrt) and best efforts traffic is placed into an even larger buffer that can be as large as 64K cells deep. Cells residing within the high-priority buffer are given transmission priority over those residing in the lower-priority buffer.

The combination of distributed input, switch fabric, and output buffering, together with traffic prioritization through the switch, yields the most flexible set of capabilities available in this class of ATM product, while maintaining a low entry cost.

Congestion Control and Management — A series of programmable thresholds are included in the ingress and egress buffers to allow customization of operation in congestion scenarios. Three thresholds have been defined, one for maximum buffer size (to software restrict the egress buffer for certain applications), a second for the point at which the controller signals the onset of congestion (i.e., sets all cells as EFCI bit = 1), and the last for the point at which the buffer should start discarding CLP=1 cells at the egress point.

Expanding Ingress and Egress Buffer Sizes for Low-Priority Buffer. Purchasable Options — Ingress and egress low-priority buffer size can be expanded by plug-in memory cards. Depending on the memory requirements needed, the ingress and egress buffer size can range from 4K, 8K, or 16K to 64K cells per port. This will allow up to 256K cells of buffering per two-port controller card, or up to 4 million cells of buffering per APEX node. The buffer size requirement will depend on the traffic characteristics, e.g., voice/video vs. data, the amount of delay the application can handle, plus the amount of link oversubscription needed.

IBM — The 2220 has an integrated cell switch with shared output buffer and built in expansion modes. Expansion modes are speed expansion, port expansion, and link paralleling. The IBM 2230 has a cross point switch fabric, 8×8, 640-Mb per thread for Model 650, 4×4×640 for Model 600. 8 MB of buffer distributed into four buffer levels: CBR, VBR-nrt, VBR-rt, UBR/ABR. ATM adapters have large buffer, i.e., OC3/STM-1: 24K cells per port. 10 QoS classes: CBR, UBR/ABR, 4 for VBR-nrt, 4 for VBR-rt.

NewBridge — The Xpress 36170's output-buffered broadcast matrix delivers a scalable fabric with low blocking probability. Head-of-line blocking is prevented. Fabric inherently supports multipoint. Types of connections include symmetric, asymmetric, bi-directional, point-to-point, and point-to-multipoint. The Xpress 36150 offers switching for voice, data, image, and video interfaces manageable from a single network management system. It is important to note that with the optional Starvision Video Scheduler Package, the 36150 is the industry's best-of-breed switch for video services featuring a fully GUI scheduler.

Sahara — The switching architecture of Sahara is classified as distributed and fully meshed. It is distributed because switching is performed on each interface card (ICM). It is fully meshed because each interface card is interconnected to every single other card in a system. Generically, Sahara's architecture is based on two levels of switching. The first level, local switching, is performed on the input device or ICM. The second level, off-board switching, is performed on other input devices (interface cards). This is depicted in Figure 17.1.

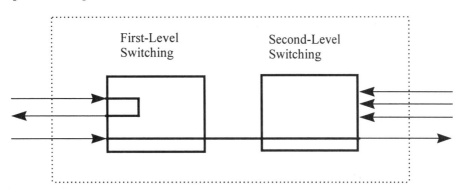

Figure 17.1 Sahara Switching Architecture

Thus Sahara's family of interface cards provides the physical interface to the transmission media in addition to performing the local switching. In addition, all ICMs are equipped with a control RISC processor to configure and manage the lines, and to route connections. This architecture was chosen because it provides maximum performance and flexibility. In addition, it can easily be upgraded to handle OC-12 speeds. The architecture of the SA-100 is based on a crossbar space-division switch element. The SA-600 and the SA-1200 are classified as fully meshed architecture based on a crossbar space-division switching element capable of switching 400-Mbps-per-slot streams in a nonblocking manner. The SA-600 and the SA-1200 are two-stage switches. The first level of switching determines if the input stream needs to be switched locally or off-board. The first level adds the appropriate routing header and sends the traffic to the right interface card to perform the second level of switching.

Sahara's products have two types of buffers: frame and cell buffers. Frame buffers are used by frames originating from Customer Premises Equipment (CPE) devices connected to IPODs. These buffers are needed for frame processing, traffic shaping, or implementing ABR rate adaptation. Frame buffers are implemented on SIMMs located on the main ICM board. The maximum number of frames that can be buffered is 16,000 (on a 1-Mbyte SIMM). These buffers are shared among all frame-based line interfaces (e.g., Ethernet, FUNI, frame relay). They can be upgraded to handle more connections for bandwidth-hungry users. Cell buffers are available for all ATM traffic sources. Cell buffers are dedicated to each IPOD (circuit switching and ATM), XPOD, and the Protocol Engine. These buffers service all ATM-capable CPE devices connected to IPODs, ATM WAN network links (connected to XPODs or IPODs), and the Protocol Accelerator Engine. Two types of cell buffers are present: input and output buffers. The total number of buffers depends on the type and number of interface ports present (e.g., DS1/E1 vs. OC3c). In fact, Sahara's architecture is flexible so as to allow different amounts of buffers to be allocated according to the interface ports present. This translates into high performance at the lowest prices to customers. The maximum number of cell buffers is 10,000 cells (input and output) per IPOD and XPOD for all traffic types. The maximum number of cell buffers for the Protocol Accelerator is 19,000 cells. These buffers incorporate such advanced features as per VC accounting, packet-level discard, backpressure, and multiple service priorities. Sahara has developed a superior and advanced cell buffering scheme. First buffers can be divided into fixed-length queues to service different classes of service (CBR, VBR-rt, VBR-nrt, ABR, UBR). It is also possible to allocate cell memories pooled among queues. This allocation technique can maximize traffic throughput. All queues can be enabled for AAL5 early packet discard and partial packet discards. This technique is useful to increase the "goodput" of TCP/IP traffic. Furthermore, a specialized queue can be dedicated to Operations, Administration, and Maintenance (OAM) cell processing only. Finally, worth noting is that all buffers are linked using a backpressure mechanism. This allows the discard of excessive cells at the input buffers rather than crowding the output buffers and congesting the switching elements.

Telematics — The NCX 1E6 has a space-time-space nonblocking switch architecture. Each IOC has discrete input/output paths, with output path bandwidth being 4 times input path bandwidth, enabling cells to exit output buffers on the egress side of the switch fabric at such rates that blocking is virtually eliminated. With the exception of statistically sized output buffers on the output side of the time switch, all buffering is resident on the transmit side of each IOC. Buffering is designed to provide logically discrete buffer spaces for VBR, CBR, and UBR traffic, enabling loss- or delay-sensitive traffic to be queued and shaped consistent with individual VC/VP service-level agreements.

17.2.6 Congestion Control

The ATM Forum defines three types of ABR congestion control standards: EFCI, Explicit Rate (ER), and Virtual Source/Virtual Destination (VS/VD). Most vendors supported the EFCI standard, and many intend to support the ER and VS/VD standard in late 1997 or 1998 as adoption of the standard by CPE devices increases. Details on the specific congestion control schemes used by vendors are listed below.

ADC Kentrox — Early packet discard and partial packet discard. A levels of priorities.

Cascade — The flow control–enabled I/O modules will support flow control functionality that will benefit all non-real-time service: nrt-VBR, ABR, and UBR. The hardware brings an additional 128K cells of buffering, per VC queuing, and a dedicated microprocessor to support buffer management and RM cell handling. Flow control for up to 12,000 VCs can be simultaneously supported. Cascade implements closed-loop flow control that enables congestion control inside your ATM network without requiring TM 4.0 upgrade to CPE equipment. The flow control system makes ATM service fair and deterministic even in the face of congestion.

Cascade's flow control scheme differs slightly from the generic approach in a few interesting ways. Cascade implements flow control using RM cells on a hop-by-hop basis, which is initiated by the destination rather than the source. The system can take proactive action as soon as downstream congestion is apparent. A feedback mechanism, based on monitoring six buffer thresholds on a per VC and global basis, is used to either increase, decrease, or make no change in the rate of transmission for the subject VC at the source switch. The hardware allocates buffer resources in proportion to the MCR of each circuit, for a fair and efficient resource utilization. Both per VC and global thresholds are maintained for EFCI indication, and discard based on CLP bit marking or Early Packet Discard (EPD).

DEC — ATM Forum–compliant rate-based flow control with "Fair" EPD/Partial Packet Discard (PPD). GIGAswitch/ATM supports FLOWmaster flow control, a credit-based congestion management scheme that provides zero cell loss for ABR VCs. Digital's FLOWmaster flow control is supported in the hardware. Flow control is provided for each virtual circuit, on each link (that has FLOWmaster support at each end of the link), through a credit-based scheme. Each virtual circuit has an input buffer, and the credit scheme ensures that when the buffer is filled to a certain point, backpressure to the sender prevents continued sending of cells and eliminates buffer overflow or cell loss. The latest generation of line cards add EFCI, to support the ATM

Forum's rate-based flow control mechanism. Fair EPD is also available on the new-generation cards. EPD improves ABR (and UBR) throughput in cases of cell losses not prevented by rate-controlled ABR.

ATM Switch 900 FLOWmaster: Hop-by-hop credit-based flow control ABR: ATM Forum–compliant rate-based flow control with "Fair" EPD/PPD. ATMswitch 900/ATM supports FLOWmaster flow control, a credit-based congestion management scheme that provides zero cell loss for ABR VCs. Digital's FLOWmaster flow control is supported in the hardware. Flow control is provided for each virtual circuit, on each link (that has FLOWmaster support at each end of the link), through a credit-based scheme. Each virtual circuit has an input buffer, and the credit scheme ensures that when the buffer is filled to a certain point, backpressure to the sender prevents continued sending of cells and eliminates buffer overflow or cell loss. The latest generation of linecards add EFCI, to support the ATM Forum's rate-based flow control mechanism. Fair EPD is also available on the new-generation cards. EPD improves ABR (and UBR) throughput in cases of cell losses not prevented by rate-controlled ABR.

VNswitch 900EA supports FLOWmaster flow control, a credit-based congestion management scheme that provides zero cell loss for ABR VCs. Digital's FLOWmaster flow control is supported in the hardware. Flow control is provided for each virtual circuit, on each link (that has FLOWmaster support at each end of the link), through a credit-based scheme. Each virtual circuit has an input buffer, and the credit scheme ensures that when the buffer is filled to a certain point, backpressure to the sender prevents continued sending of cells and eliminates buffer overflow or cell loss.

FORE — ASX-200WG supports EPD/PPD, smart buffers, dual leaky bucket, per VC queuing [3].

IBM — The 2230 CBR buffers have priority over cells in the buffers. The other three buffers (UB/ABR, VBR-nrt, VBR-rt) are serviced in a round-robin queuing algorithm.

The weights are determined by the effective bandwidth, which is computed based on (SCR, FCR, MBS) by CAC, for each connection. Weighting based on effective bandwidth, calculated by the CAC algorithm, ensures that the bandwidth assigned to each service is adequate to guarantee the QoS contract. The combination of priority queuing and weighted round-robin queuing provides the mechanism to ensure minimal CDU for CBR traffic and provide QoS guarantee for VBR and UBR traffic.

Trip points are used in the buffers to allow for priority queuing as well as CLP = s discard capability. One trip point is configured for the CBR and UBR/ABR buffer such that cells with CLP=1 are discarded after the queue exceeds the threshold specified by the trip point.

VBR buffers (VBR-rt, VBR-nrt) have four separate trip points. At each trip point, cells are discarded according to priority and CLP setting. Trip points can be customized.

In addition, an optional closed-loop congestion control based on RN cells is supported (pie-ABR). This mechanism ensures that the congestion in the network is limited and that the network resource usage is optimized and cell loss ratio reduced.

This control mechanism will evolve to a standard ABR buffer (UNI 4.0) by 4Q97.

IBM 8260 Nways Switch — Input and output buffer pools are provided with various thresholds; every ATM module is equipped with a traffic management ASIC that is capable of processing the cells and extracting the RM cells. The relative rate ABR flow control implements the backward notification method for quicker end-system reaction

NEC America — The M20 uses selective cell discard and EFCI. Selective cell discard applies to all ATM service categories, whereas EFCI applies to ABR service only. It is enforced at the IXB. When congestion occurs, ATM cells start to accumulate within the IXB queues. When the cells contained in the queue exceed the cell discard threshold, low-priority cells with CLP=1 or cells belonging to low-priority connections with the P bit marked are discarded until the number of cells contained in the queue falls below the threshold. Calls with CLP=0 or belonging to high-priority connections are not affected.

EFCI is a congestion notification mechanism to end-user equipment that the ATM-layer service user can use to improve ATM-layer utility. When congestion occurs in the IXB, the M20 sets an EFCI in the cell header for explanation by the destination end user. The M20 detects congestion status when the number of cells in the IXB queue exceeds the software selectable congestion (EFCI) set threshold. When the number of cells in the IXB queue is less than the software-selectable congestion reset threshold, M20 stops setting an EFCI in the cell header.

Sahara — Congestion is usually declared whenever buffers exceed a predetermined level. Sahara Networks uses two congestion control variables: EPD and EFCI. The EPD threshold is tied to the buffer fill level (e.g., 70 percent) and is used to determine when EPD is activated or deactivated. The EFCI threshold is also tied to the buffer fill level (e.g., 80 percent) and is used to determine when to tag all incoming cells.

17.2.7 Cell Loss Probability

Vendor responses varied, but most vendors stated either virtually zero or zero Cell Loss Probability (CLP). The most popular use of the CLP bit was for selective discard.

17.2.8 Policing and Shaping

In addition to the responses to the policing and shaping standards defined in Chapter 6, several vendors offered additional clarifications repeated below. Most vendors supported either PCR, PCR+SCR, or both for policing.

IBM — If leaky bucket defined by ATM Forum, using PCR, SCR, MBS, and CLP. Dual leaky bucket.

NewBridge — The 36170 (also used by Siemens) traffic shaping on the ATM side is performed in conjunction with the FR policing function.

Sahara — Currently provides shaping for all packet-based traffic. Cell-based shaping will be available in 3Q/97.

17.2.9 Connection Admission Control

Many vendors supported Generic CAC (GCAC), while some vendors supported other, more sophisticated mechanisms, as indicated in the following responses.

DEC — The GIGAswitch and ATMswitch 9000 CAC is implemented as a function of DECNNI, and a crankback feature is supported in case a CAC fails. GIGAswitch ATM performs a CAC function based on the traffic parameters and requested QoS of the connection. GIGAswitch will support GCAC as per Forum standards with the implementation of PNNI 1.0.

The default cascade CAC algorithm tries to improve the available resources' utilization (and statistical gains) through adopting the notion of defining an equivalent bandwidth associated with a number of connections and not only the equivalent bandwidth of a single connection. The equivalent bandwidth calculation is based on both fluid flow and gaussian approximate traffic models.

On a given physical port, the connection acceptance decision is taken by computing the effective bandwidth of the total number of connections passing through that port (including the connection initiating the connection request). The connection is accepted if the resultant effective bandwidth is less than the statistically configured BW for the connection's QoS class and is less than the physical port capacity. This may be seen to correspond to a two-level admission decision, ensuring at a first level that there is enough bandwidth on the logical port (complying with the configured bandwidth values for the port) and on a second level (more important) ensuring that the physical port capacity is not exceeded and that the QoS can be guaranteed.

Oversubscription. The oversubscription factor percentages enable you to optimize the number of PVCs and SVCs you can configure on the network by allowing you to oversubscribe the logical ports. You can configure oversubscription for the VBR and UBR classes of service. However, QoS is no longer guaranteed. Configuring the oversubscription factor at the minimum value of 100 percent ensures that the port will deliver all user data for that service class without unanticipated delays or excessive cell loss. A value of 200 percent effectively doubles the available virtual bandwidth that is available for that service class.

FORE — CAC now supports regular CAC algorithm, VBR overbooking, and CBR overbooking.

IBM — The 2230's ICAC computes an effective bandwidth that is indicative of the bandwidth required to satisfy the QoS of the connection as well as the QoS of existing ones. If enough bandwidth is available, accept the connection. CAC is in each node. CAC can be customized. CAC support objectives defined for CLR, CTD, CDV, (PCR, BCR, MBS).

The 8260 and 8285 now provides now control of the bandwidth at connection set up. Later in 1997, the 8260 will be able to even police the incoming traffic to verify that the contracted PCR/SCR are respected by the ATM devices.

Sahara — Access products provide routing and connection establishment via SNNI (Sahara NNI). The initial release of products will implement SNNI. Full PNNI support will be provided soon.

17.2.10 Early/Partial Packet Discard

Most vendors supported either PPD, EPD, or both.

DEC — In implementation of frame policing, they support traffic shaping for CBR circuits.

17.2.11 OAM Performance Measurement I.610

Many vendors reported that they will support this important standard by 1998.

DEC — Fault management support, including loopback, AIS/FERF, and continuity check. Performance Management: Includes forward and backward monitoring. Activation/Deactivation: Essentially the control component for performance management and periodic loopback. For the GIGAswitch, user control of OAM, particularly those functions after fault management. CLI control, SNMP, and/or Web-based UI.

17.3 PROTOCOL AND STANDARDS SUPPORT

This section defines typical product support for protocols and standards for ATM devices.

17.3.1 ATM Forum Signaling

Most vendors support both 3.0 and 3.1 standards for UNI, point-to-point SVC signaling, and point-to-multipoint SVC signaling, and plan to support the 4.0 version of these standards by 1998. Some products, such as the IBM 8260, support autoconversion between UNI 3.0 and UNI 3.1. The IBM 2220 and 2225 offer a nonstandard NNI signaling protocol. IISP was by far the most popular NNI signaling protocol. Other vendors reported plans to support PNNI V1.0 and B-ICI V2 in late 1997 and 1998, respectively.

17.3.2 ITU-T Signaling

Q.2931 is by far the most popular standard for UNI signaling, followed by support for its predecessor, Q.93B. Some vendors support both standards. The most popular planned protocol to support NNI signaling is B-ISUP (in early 1998), with some supporting NISUP and IISP. See Chapter 8 for definitions of the signaling terminology

17.3.3 LAN Emulation

Most vendors support or plan to support both the LAN Emulation (LANE) 1.0 and RFC 1483 client and server standards. Note that the IBM 8285 supports both Token Ring and Ethernet LANE.

17.3.4 Virtual LAN Capability

Vendor support for Virtual LANs (VLANs) varied widely. Here are some highlights.

Cabletron — The LANE servers available on the ZX-250 can provide LANE services for up to 127 emulated LANs. The switch may also provide RFC 1577 classical IP over ATM ARP services with support up to 64 IP-ATM Logical IP Subnets (LISs).

DEC — The GIGAswitch ATM supports multiple ELANS per port. GIGAswitch ATM supports all the LANE servers (LECS, LES, and BUS), and using the edge switches, VLANS can be mapped to ELANS for trunking of VLAN information across the ATM network. GIGAswitch ATM currently supports up to 16 ELANS, increasing to 64 ELANS in mid-1997.

The DEC ATMswitch 900 supports multiple ELANS per port. ATMswitch 900 supports all the LANE servers (LECS, LES, and BUS), and using the edge switches, VLANS can be mapped to ELANS for trunking of VLAN information across the ATM network. ATMswitch 900 currently supports up to 16 ELANS.

The DEC VNswitch 900EA supports multiple ELANS. VLANS can be mapped to ELANS for trunking of VLAN information across the ATM network. VNswitch 900EA currently supports up to 16 ELANS or 16 bridge tunnels or 16 LISs or a mix of them.

IBM 8260 — Virtual LAN's capability is based on ATM Forum LANE with the ability to create up to 64 independent virtual LANs per MSS module (Multiprotocol Switched Services).

Reference [6] describes IBM's MSS as an enhancement to the ATM Forum's LANE with routing and broadcast control, improving performance and reducing latency in multiprotocol networks. With MSS, IBM enhances the LANE Broadcast Unknown Server with a tool that controls broadcasts across emulated LANs. IBM's Broadcast Manager monitors network traffic and makes sure broadcasts are forwarded only to those end stations that need them. IBM's server can manage both virtual LAN and emulated LAN characteristics for end stations on ATMF-compliant networks. The server includes IP and IPX routing capabilities for directing traffic between VLANs.

17.3.5 IP over ATM

Vendor support for IP over ATM varied widely. Here's what DEC had to say.

DEC — IP over ATM ARP server is implemented on an attached station. Only one ATM ARP server is required per physical network.

17.3.6 MPOA

Most vendors said they planned to support the ATM Forum Multiprotocol over ATM (MPOA) standard in the future.

17.3.7 Next-Hop Resolution Protocol

Most vendors said they planned to support the Next-Hop Resolution Protocol (NHRP) standard in the future.

17.3.8 Tested Interoperability with other switches

To what degree has the vendor performed interoperability testing with other ATM products, and where can the user obtain the results? Table 17.1 shows the vendor responses stating some form of interoperability with other vendors.

The chart is interpreted by reading how a vendor listed in the left-hand column has been tested with a vendor across the top row.

17.3.9 The Interoperability Forum

No one would disagree that the ATM industry needs more interoperability standardization. Many trade shows and industry events have multivendor interoperability exhibits, and most vendors talk a lot about how they are "interoperable" with other vendors who conform strictly to the standards. But few vendors actually have the goal of creating an interoperability forum that has the common goal of true plug-and-play. One of the most recent efforts in the ATM community is the Network Interoperability Alliance (NIA) started by 3Com Corp., Bay Networks, and IBM in May of 1996 [4, 5, 6].

Table 17.1 Vendor Tested Interoperability Matrix

	3Com	ADC Kentrox	Bay Networks	Cabletron Systems	Cascade Communications	Cisco	CrossCom	Digital Equipment Corporation	FORE Systems, Inc	Fujitsu	General DataComm.	IBM Corporation	NEC America, Inc.	NewBridge Networks	Sahara Networks, Inc.	Siemens Stromberg-Carlson	Telematics International	Xylan
3Com	-																	
ADC Kentrox	Y	-	Y	Y	Y				Y	Y	Y			Y				
Bay Networks			-															
Cabletron Systems	Y		Y	-		Y	Y		Y		Y							
Cascade	Y	Y	Y	Y	-	Y	Y	Y	Y	Y	Y	Y	Y	Y	Y			Y
Cisco						-												
Crosscom							-											
DEC	Y		Y			Y		-	Y		Y	Y	Y					Y
FORE Systems, Inc	Y		Y			Y			-									Y
Fujitsu										-								
General DataComm.		Y		Y	Y	Y	Y	Y	Y		-	Y		Y				Y
IBM Corporation	Y		Y	Y		Y	Y	Y	Y	Y	Y	-				Y		Y
NEC America, Inc.									Y				-					
NewBridge Networks					Y	Y			Y					-				
Sahara Networks, Inc.															-			
Siemens Stromberg-Carlson																-		
Telematics International	Y				Y				Y		Y			Y			-	
Xylan	Y		Y	Y		Y			Y	Y				Y				-

Vendor in row states interoperability with vendors in columns.

The NIA bridges the gap left in the evolving ATM standards, drawing unlikely vendors together with the common purpose of testing and assuring that their products interoperate. This combination of companies that have spanned from the Network Interface Card (NIC) card to the mainframe has a good chance at setting an end-to-end interoperability to enable true QoS and related services from the NIC in the desktop machine (DAN), through the hub/switch/router enterprise network, and into the WAN backbone frame/packet/cell network. We quote [4] for more detail on this effort.

There are four key aspects of the framework. The first involves the addition of network intelligence to the computer systems that plug into the net. The NIA's members have a built-in advantage here: Bay, IBM, and 3Com together control some 38 percent of the nearly 200 million network connections, which include network adapters and hub and switch ports. Cisco Systems Inc. (San Jose, Calif.), on the other hand, has less than a 1 percent share of such products (but is nearly neck and neck with 3Com on switch ports, which is the fastest growing segment of this market).

By building more network intelligence into desktops and servers, it's possible to create autoconfigurable virtual LANs (VLANs), inter-VLAN links that don't require routers, and quality-of-service offerings. The NIA is doing all it can to see these possibilities come to fruition: It has embraced a host of protocols, including IEEE 802.q, zero-hop routing, Lane (LAN emulation), NHRP (next hop routing protocol), IEEE 802.1p, reservation protocols within ATM, and RSVP (resource reservation protocol) and related specs. If those offerings are to be delivered, a client-server relationship needs to be established between desktops and servers. That in turn means that adapters and switches must be guaranteed to work together.

The second aspect of the NIA framework is the edge network — which furnishes switching, switching with core routing, edge routing, short-cut routing via zero-hop protocol, and quality-of-service routing. ATM UNI (user-network interface) and I-PNNI (integrated private network-to-network interface), IEEE 802.1p, IGMP (Internet Group Management Protocol), and RSVP are some of the protocols involved here.

The third key is the core network, which is linked to the edge of the network. The core supports the backbone routers; it makes use of routing protocols like OSPF (open shortest path first) and ATM standards like I-PNNI and Lane. I-PNNI is clearly a big part of the logical networking that goes on at the core, since it makes use of a single protocol for routing traffic among routers, directory servers, and ATM switches.

The fourth component of the framework is network management. The group's aims here are to align the enterprise MIBs (management information bases) already in place, promote the development and standardization of new MIBs, and promote the development of Java tools. The group also plans to develop a network topology protocol.

The net management aspect is the most vital part of the framework. If the NIA is successful here, it will have more than justified its existence — since it would permit the effective management of the entire enterprise with a common set of tools.

THE PROSPECTS

Still, none of this really answers the basic question: Why have these particular vendors gotten together to form the NIA?

What's at stake here is the site, campus, and backbone network markets — a multibillion dollar trifecta if there ever were one. And each vendor has its own motivation: 3Com needs systems sales, IBM needs to be a player again, and Bay needs to make sure that Cisco isn't completely dominant. (Right now, the NIA's main rival is Cisco's IOS/Fusion architecture.)

Can the NIA succeed? I'd say the group's viability depends most on whether it can grow well beyond its three original members. Microsoft and Netscape have to join, particularly since Microsoft's Winsock 2.0 is a key piece of quality of service. I would even go so far as to say that without Microsoft or Netscape the NIA is doomed.

I'd also recommend that an outside firm manage the alliance's day-to-day activities. This will ensure that no one company dominates and that the organization is managed as a truly independent entity open to the industry. Next, there has to be a way for users to be represented. Otherwise, the group faces an all-too-familiar fate: falling out of touch with what network managers need and becoming irrelevant.

Also, timing is key — and if the NIA wants to be a player it has to establish its identity quickly. That means getting the independent interoperability lab up and running by this fall, if not sooner. The lab should devise an NIA logo that can be slapped on products that conform to the NIA interoperability standards. On top of that, interoperability demonstrations can be run at all of the major trade shows.

If the NIA can pull all this off, net managers are in for some big benefits — namely, heterogeneous networks that will work together and cost a lot less to manage. If not, then the consortium will at least be in some good company.

17.3.10 Distinguishing Features

A number of vendors provided feedback on their most distinguishing features, which we provide below.

Cabletron — Fully ATMF-compliant signaling, routing, and LANE implementations. High-performance signaling engine guarantees high connection processing throughput in a predominantly switched connection environment.

DEC — The GIGAswitch and ATM900 offer:
o Traffic shaping for CBR virtual circuits provides zero cell loss.
o VP shaping provides zero cell loss for bursty traffic across the WAN.
o Per VC buffer allocation and buffer allocation enforcement prevent a misbehaving VC from grabbing all of the buffer space and forcing other VCs to lose cells.
o Our distributed processing architecture allows us to have unmatched scalability.
o FLOWmaster credit-based flow control mechanism ensures that the cell loss is subject to only the bit error rate of the link. In other words zero cell loss.
   The GIGAswitch only supports:
o GIGAswitch ATM supports port speeds from T1/E1 (1.544 Mbps) to OC-12 (622 Mbps).
o Cell buffers can be expanded from 2400 cells to more than 15,000 cells.
   The VNswitch 900EA is part of the VNswitch family of products for DEChub 900 Multiswitch. First wave of these products are:
o VNswitch 900EA, Ethernet to Ethernet and ATM edge switch with 12 Ethernet and 1 ATM (OC3) port
o VNswitch 900EX, 12 ports 10baseT and 2 ports 100baseT
o VNswitch 900EF, 12 ports 10baseT and 1 port (DAS) FDDI
o VNswitch 900EE, 24 ports 10baseT
All these modules can communicate with each other via three 400-Mbps VNbuses in the DEChub 900 Multiswitch backplane.
o Nonzero VP support.
o Can be an edge switch and an IP switch gateway.

o Distributed processing architecture allows switching and routing without performance degradation.

o FLOWmaster credit-based flow control mechanism ensures that the cell loss is subject to only the bit error rate of the link. In other words, zero cell loss.

All DEC switches can support IP switching and ATM Forum software simultaneously.

FORE — ES-3810 has redundant load-balancing ATM uplinks, low-cost, ASCI-based, segment support and desktop support for Ethernet, 10/100 autosensing, high-performance ATM uplink.

GDC — Presently, GDC is working with several LAN vendors to provide an industry-standard solution to LANE, MPOA, and NHRP signaling requirements. Although we do not presently implement LANE client/server software on our product, we do support the point-to-multipoint signaling necessary for such devices to successfully interoperate. Given GDC's market share in the edge market, we feel this is a strength of GDC, and allows us to offer solutions for other vendors' products.

GDC was also the first major switch vendor to announce support for Ipsilon's IP switching protocol family (RFCs 1953, 1954, and 1987). GDC's Boston Research Center is currently developing WAN solutions based on these protocols that will allow our customers to efficiently utilize the benefits of IP and ATM.

IBM — The 2230 has a high port density, very high VC capacity, very high VC setup and reroute performance, bulletproof quality of service, seamless integration with IBM Nways 2225 ATM/Frame Relay Switch supporting FR, SMDS, ATM. Same network architecture, network management.

IBM 8260 and 8285 integrate a Multiprotocol Switched Server with ATM routing and LANE bridging; they include also cut-through LANE bridging for greater performance; a broadcast manager over ATM is also available for reduction of broadcast frames of IP, IPX, Netbios, and T/R SR. Routing between LANE and classical IP (RFC 1577) is also available. ATM access control for security Multiservice platform — Integrated Video Distribution Module (MPEG-2 decoder function) for video broadcast, Hybrid Fiber Coax Module for Cable-On-Line solution. PNNI extensions for fast route setup and call crankback. Network management support.

NEC America — High-performance switch fabric incorporating redundancy and scalability.

NewBridge — The Xpress 36170 future plans include support of layer 3 (and above) awareness through the application of ATM Forum MPOA. This will enable carriers to support routed data applications with carrier-class features such as scalability, high reliability, billing, and security.

Sahara — The Protocol-Accelerator is a micro-coded super-RISC-based processor. This device allows Sahara to provide the performance required by today's demanding applications. Due to its micro-coded design, developers can rapidly integrate new features and protocols as needed. The Protocol-Accelerator can support up to 200,000 packets per second.

Telematics — Offers Subscriber-Oriented Networking; Myrtle Queueing; industry-leading cell latency under multiservice CBR/VBR traffic load; STM-1/OC-3, T3/E3, T1/E1, NxMx64 provisioning of ATM, frame relay, circuit emulation, and bitsynchronous services in a single switch platform; full NEBS/ETSI compliance; and full redundancy.

17.4 NETWORK MANAGEMENT SUPPORT

This section summarizes typical network management support for ATM devices.

17.4.1 Full ATM Forum ILMI

Most vendors support both 3.0 and 3.1 ATM Forum standards for ILMI, and plan to support the 4.0 version of these standards by the time this book is in print.

17.4.2 ILMI Address Registration

Most vendors support both 3.0 and 3.1 ATM Forum standard address registration for ILMI, and plan to support the 4.0 version of these standards by the time this book is in print.

17.4.3 RFC 1695 (AToMMIB)

About half the vendors now support or plan soon to support the RFC 1695 AToMMIB.

17.4.4 Per Port/VC Statistics

Most vendors support the capability to collect statistics on a per port and per VC basis.

17.4.5 OAM Cell VPC/VCC AIS/RDI and Loopback

Many vendors supported the capability to perform both F4 (VP) and F5 (VC) AIS/RDI and loopback test.

17.4.6 ATM Forum NM I/F Support

Very few vendors supported or planned to support the ATM Forum NM M1 through M5 interfaces. The ones that did primarily claimed support for the only completed standard, M4.

17.4.7 Automatic PVC Configuration and Restoration

Very few vendors support using SPVPC and/or SPVCCs for automatic PVC configuration and reconfiguration. Some planned to support it in 1998. More vendors claimed support for VCs than for VPs.

17.4.8 NMS Support

It is important to understand how easy it is to manage the switch, and what industry-standard management platforms are supported, such as Cabletron Spectrum Enterprise Manager, HP OpenView, NetView 6000/AIX, and SunNet Manager. Vendors were asked to provide a narrative on how they used these industry-standard NMSs or the attributes of their proprietary system. HP OpenView was by far the most popular platform supported, with half as many vendors supporting NetView 6000/AIX and SunNet Manager.

FORE — Web server–based, browser access, packaged with ForeView 4.1.1.

IBM — The 2220 Network Management Support is provided by the IBM Nways Enterprise Manager for AIX, which runs on an RS/6000 system under TME 10 NetView for AIX. The Nways Enterprise Manager uses the OSI Common Management Interface Protocol and Services (CMIP/CMIS) and provides fault management, accounting management, performance management, operational control, and automation capabilities. It also includes alarm filtering, thresholding, discrimination, and logging. NetView DM/6000, a feature of SystemView for AIX, remotely manages 2220 code changes.

The IBM 2225 and 2230 provide support for provisioning, configuration, fault management, statistics collection, accounting, and network topology.

NewBridge — MainStreet Xpress 46020 provides an advanced and easy-to-use GUI for NMS. Application is Sun-based and can be integrated with HP OpenView.

Sahara Networks believes that network management requires a whole new approach that emphasizes ease of use, cost-effective platform independence, ubiquitous access capabilities, and effective security. To that end, Sahara has developed SaharaView, the industry's first Web-based network management architecture to combine the power of Java-based network computing with existing and emerging network management standards. Figure 17.2 shows SaharaView network management.

Functionality: SaharaView provides secure, real-time monitoring and control for the entire Sahara Access portfolio with an architecture based on the standard World Wide Web client/server model.

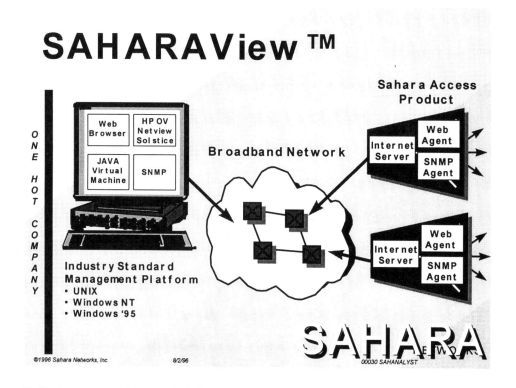

Figure 17.2 SaharaView ATM Management

The client is an off-the-shelf Java-enabled Web browser such as Netscape Navigator, Microsoft Internet Explorer, or equivalent. A Web server, or agent, is embedded in every Sahara Access system.

Network operators manage Sahara Access systems using friendly point-and-click Web pages. Java applets are downloaded from the Web server to support more complex functions and provide displays of real-time data, such as traffic statistics. Applets are small software modules that run on a Java virtual machine inside the Web browser.

The architecture organizes management tasks into discrete functional areas:

- System administration and accounting
- Interface management
- Provisioning and connection management
- System status
- Diagnostics
- Event & fault management

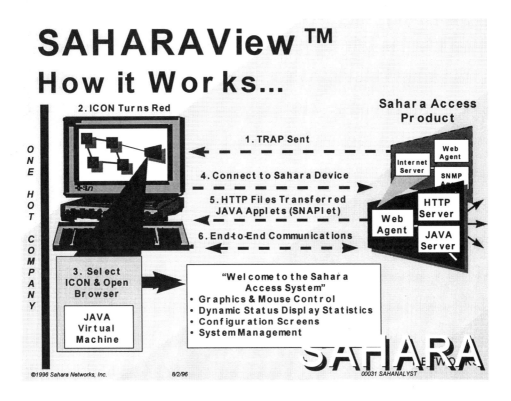

Figure 17.3 SaharaView

Additionally, a full complement of utilities supports file management, real-time software upgrades, and other functions necessary for proper system maintenance.

How It Works — Figure 17.3 shows how the SaharaView system works when hosted by a standard platform like HP OpenView:

• *Step 1*. An event occurs in a Sahara Access system — a line failure, for example — that triggers the delivery of an SNMP trap to OpenView. An icon representing the access system turns red on the network map.

• *Step 2*. The network operator selects the red icon, and OpenView automatically launches the Web browser. (Traditionally, a proprietary application specific to the network device would be launched instead.)

• *Step 3*. The Web browser connects to the Sahara Access system using its IP address. The Web agent in the access system returns a "welcome" page and a Java applet, which displays the activities that the operator can invoke.

• *Step 4*. The operator decides, in this example, to display real-time traffic statistics and selects the appropriate menu item. The Web browser signals the access system, which sends back the next Java applet.

• *Step 5.* The applet interacts with software in the Sahara Access system to gather and display real-time statistics.

Telematics — SNMP-based, open management architecture which provides full configuration/change, fault, and performance management subsystems via HP OpenView environment.

17.4.9 Distinguishing Features of Network Management Support

Vendors were asked to elaborate on the distinguishing features of their network management support. Here's what some of them said.

Cabletron — SPECTRUM is the fastest-growing enterprise manager contending with HP OpenView. It can manage a wide variety of other vendors' equipment in addition to Cabletron's. Some of the main features are:

• Integrated VLAN management
• Available expert system modules
• Alarm and event management
• Full standards-based SNMP MIB support, including IETF and ATM Forum based

Cascade NMS Support — ATM network management support is provided through a product called CascadeView. CascadeView's competitive advantage is that it provides multiservice support on one platform, ranging from ATM to frame relay and including SMDS, ISDN, X.25 encapsulation, and IP switching support. Although CascadeView is a proprietary application managing the Cascade switches, it sits under HP OpenView to provide a standard open management interface to the network. Communication to the CBX 500 ATM switches is via SNMP. The HP OpenView application displays the Cascade ATM switches on the top-level map through the graphical user interface. When the user clicks on the switch, he or she launches into the CascadeView application seamlessly. It is transparent to the operator that he or she is now working under CascadeView, since the Common Desk Top, Solaris and Motif are used across both applications. Once in CascadeView, the user can graphically access the ATM CBX 500 back panel, front panel, slot, port, trunk, and circuit, allowing him or her to intuitively configure and manage an ATM network. The application runs with Sybase and is supported on Sun stations.

HP OpenView has been used as a springboard from which Cascade has enhanced its application to provide some key differentiating features. Using the Network Management functional areas, the following are some strong features supporting ATM.

Configuration — CascadeView allows the user easy provisioning through point and click to establish end-to-end connectivity. The operator simply provisions the two endpoints of the ATM network, and through the VNN (Virtual Network Navigator) routing algorithm the path is built end to end without having an operator set up the routes. CascadeView also provides a template function to allow rapid provisioning of SVCs and PVCs. Using a copy and paste function, programmers can now provision hundreds of PVCs with less operator error. The user can also set up QoS priorities and CAC parameters. In addition, VPN and customer ID can be set up through configuration management. A customer can be assigned to a circuit and that circuit can be assigned to a VPN with a preference on routing that trunk over the public network if it goes down or not rerouting. This feature is used for customer network management to identify partitions of customers.

Performance — CascadeView provides three ways of obtaining critical ATM performance information. The user can click on the summary statistics screen to view real-time SVC and PVC physical port, logical port, trunk, and circuit information. The user can also invoke the bulk statistics application that gathers ATM statistics every 5 minutes and uploads to CascadeView once an hour with the 5-minute peak and delta measurement. Information like User and OAM cells with a CLP of 0 and 1 transmitted, received, and discarded is provided as well as utilization information. The user can also click on the monitor statistics screen to view ILMI information.

Security — CascadeView provides the HP Administrator password and has added an Operator password to log into CascadeView and a provisioning password to perform only certain functions. There is also customer view access, which allows a customer access to only his or her circuits. There is also an audit trail log to identify users and their actions.

Accounting — CascadeView provides an accounting function to collect key ATM statistics for ATM billing. The information is collected from the switches using GR 1110 and uploaded to the NMS station. The NMS station formats the data into an AMA format so that it can be retrieved via FTP to a customer's Revenue and Accounting System in order to generate an invoice to bill customers.

Fault Management — CascadeView uses HP OpenView's Network Node Manager application to log traps to the event categories window. In addition, Cascade has added a Fault Management Server product with a Web interface to address the large number of traps and events that an ATM network generates. The Fault Management Server is inference engine–based and receives a trap and puts it through a sequences of steps, including parsing, filtering, aging, and correlating, so that if a trap doesn't fit any of these categories, it gets reported as a major service-affecting trap. The user can then concentrate on only service-affecting traps and retrieve noncritical traps through the log history.

All of these features that were added above the HP OpenView functionality provide a much more robust solution as well as provide key differentiators. All applications can be distributed and run on separate servers or under the one CascadeView platform, and all have open interfaces to forward information to other OSSs.

DEC — All DEC switches support complete management using clearVISN, a graphical user interface to SNMP. ClearVISN can be layered on HP OpenView, NetView, or SunNet Manager for alarms, statistics, and configuration management support. The clearVISN Multichassis manager will support both historical and real-time network performance monitoring statistics, including peak and average traffic, error rate, and configuration details. Traffic summary information in the Multichassis Manager displays information based on the following parameters: most congested, most errors, most traffic, and total traffic.

In addition, the VNswitch 900EA supports multiple VLANs with port-based VLANs in the first release. MAC and protocol VLANs will be in subsequent release of firmware.

Additionally, DEC supports the following standards: ANSI T1.630, ANSI T1.635, ITU-TI.363, section 6, ITU/CCITT G.703, G707, G708, G709, G804, G823, G832, ITU/CCITT I.363, T1E1.2/92-020R2, Q.2110, Q.2130, Q.2931, Q.93B, ANSI T1.408, AT+T TR-62411, ANSI T1.105, ANSI T1.102, ITU/CCITT I.432, B-ISDN UNI-Physical Interface Spec, ANSI T1.107 and T1.107a, ITU-T G.804 Draft ATM Cell Mapping into PDH, and Bellcore recommendation for Jitter Transfer for TR-NWT-000499.

The ATMswitch 900 supports the same software and standards functionality as GIGAswitch products. The VNswitch 900 family provides:

- High-density switched Ethernet to Fast Ethernet, FDDI, and ATM
- 1,000,000 pps switching capacity per VNswitch 900 module
- Line-rate switching of all LANs on all ports
- Optional full-duplex operation on all front-panel LAN interface ports
- Mbytes of packet buffer per module, dynamically shared across all ports
- 1.2-Gbps switching fabric distributed across three 400-Mbps interconnects
- Support for 8000 MAC addresses per module
- Full-featured industry-standard, 802.1d-compliant bridging and bridge filtering
- Software-configurable switch communication fabric for packets, cells, and multitechnology switch interconnects
- Robust, IEEE-based VLAN capability supporting Digital's enVISN architecture, including interoperability with ATM Emulated LANs
- Distributed routing capability via software upgrade option
- Cable media flexibility via modular Fast Ethernet, FDDI, and ATM uplinks
- Chassis-based distributed switching capability available through firmware upgrade
- Fully manageable operation in both stand-alone and chassis-based configurations

FORE — ES-3810 provides port-level RMON (9 groups).
Cellpath 90 provides:

- Support for Ethernet, T1 voice, H.320 video, HDLC data on low-cost T1 access unit
- Integral T1 ESF CSU
- User-friendly Web-based GUI
- Standards-based VBR shaping and VBR, CBR, UBR, QoS support

GDC's APEX family of ATM switches is managed via APEX ProSphere, a family of network management applications. ProSphere is composed of the NMS-3000, the Service Provisioning Manager, the Routing Manager, and the Accounting Manager.

The APEX-NMS3000 is a program tool for monitoring and managing the family of GDC switches. It provides extensive fault management capabilities, a topology manager/discovery process, and an object-oriented GUI manager that automates the graphical depiction of GDC APEX nodes found in the discovery process. APEX-NMS3000 uses SNMP Version 1, as defined in RFC 1155 and RFC 1157. Both MIB I and MIB II (RFC 1156 and RFC 1213) variables and enterprise-specific MIBs for the APEX ATM switch family are supported. This level of SNMP implementation, plus the system's ability to automatically parse any enterprise MIB that conforms with RFC 1212 and RFC 1215, enables management of not only APEX switches but other IP-addressable network elements, including bridges, routers, and access products. The NMS3000 also supports parent/child management relationships, allowing hierarchical network management systems to be built in public or private networks.

The APEX-Service Provisioning Manager enables the ease of point-and-click operation for the configuration of permanent and switched virtual circuits. This application provides the customer the ability to quickly create circuits and all defined QoS parameters via customer-defined templates, and also allows in-depth tracing of customer routes through the network.

The APEX-Routing Manager provides static routing table generation for a network of GDC APEX switches utilizing SVC signaling for SVCs, SPVCs, etc. Routing tables are generated from this point-and-click application and are automatically downloaded to each APEX switch in the network. Feature advantages include primary route allocations based on least-cost routing, optional fallback routes in least-cost order, and traffic loading across routes based on random or predefined choices.

The APEX Accounting Manager allows for the generation, collection, consolidation, formatting, and delivery of usage-based accounting data for each virtual circuit in the APEX network. The Accounting Manager system is based on distributed processes at various points in the network, and has been tested with several large carriers.

These applications currently run on a UNIX-based Sun SPARC workstation under Solaris. GDC will soon provide a gateway to HP OpenView, and later HP OpenView will be able to connect to APEX directly with all network management functionality.

IBM — NMS supports simplified network management, cost reduction, and common management interface protocols. The IBM 2225 and 2230 offer a distributed architecture for high scalability. Provisioning Server for significant workload reduction (programmed interface).

IBM 8260 — Auto-topology is provided and connection tracking over the entire network of ATM switches for point-to-multipoint connections. Management also of the attached ATM devices. Integrated management with LAN network applications: seamless navigation between LAN view and ATM views. One database for all network objects and search for a resource using any parameter: IP, ATM, or MAC address logical name, etc.

NEC America — ATOMNET/BNMS Broadband Network Management System. The BNMS is a CMIP-based network management system developed by NEC. The BNMS is based on a distributed, scalable architecture and provides high reliability via primary/backup server configurations. It utilizes an intuitive GUI and comprises an extensive suite of features. Functions include network configuration, switch configuration, connection management, fault/alarm management, performance/traffic management, and security/account/log management. Migration to SNMP is offered using ATOM-View as a module under the BNMS umbrella management system.

ATOMView is an SNMP-based network management system developed by NEC. ATOMView can run under HP OpenView as a stand-alone management system for a homogeneous network of SNMP switches, or it can be operated as a module within the BNMS for managing a heterogeneous mix of SNMP and CMIP ATM switches.

NewBridge Xpress 36170 — Offers the following:

- Integrated management which spans TDM, voice and data, FR, X.25, LDM, and DTM under one system
- Simplified path management
- Network performance analysis with real time alarm and statistics collection
- Management of rerouting and restoration
- Unsurpassed network scalability and flexibility
- Networks can be partitioned into hundreds of virtual networks
- NMS architecture based on TDM model with applications for business management, service management, network management, and element management
- Open architecture to SNMP and CMIP
- Scalable to multiple GUIs
- 5000-node support

17.5 VENDORS WHO DECLINED TO ANSWER

Some vendors declined to answer for specific reasons, as cited below.

Hughes was not able to respond.

Ipsilon — Ipsilon's business is IP switching, rather than ATM switches. Therefore, Ipsilon responded that its products should not be included in this book.

Loral decided not to place information in the book.

Network Security Corporation (NSC) — NSC does not provide an ATM switch that fits into our categories as defined. NSC does, however, resell the NorTel Passport ATM switch. NSC has an ATM security product called ATLAS (ATM Line Access & Security system).

Whitetree stated that Ascend's support of its switches was in question, and declined to provide information on products that may not exist at time of publishing.

Verilink decided not to submit any information for the book.

Also of note:
Siemens is an alliance partner with **NewBridge**, and thus resells its MainStreetXpress product line: 36190 core switch, 36170 edge switch, 36150 access switch, and 46020 network management platform. Note that there are some differences in the two vendors' product features, although they carry the same name.

17.6 ADDITIONAL RFP QUESTIONS

Additional items for consideration on the RFI checklist included [7]:

- How much of the end-to-end solution does the vendor provide — from desktop to desktop?
- Service and support history and reputation of the vendor
- Customer references

17.7 REVIEW

This chapter provides vendor information from the survey that was either too detailed or required further explanation. This chapter summarized the vendor responses and gave insight into the more and less popular standards supported across a wide sample base.

17.8 REFERENCES

[1]   FORE, "Northern Telecom and FORE Systems Partner to Deliver End-to-End ATM Solutions," http://www.fore.com/press/archive/ntpartner.html, January 24, 1995.
[2]   NewBridge, "Siemens, NewBridge Form Alliance to Speed Availability of High-Speed, ATM-Based Broadband Communication Networks," http://www.New-Bridge.com/Investors/NewsReleases/PRQ496/MAR04_96.html, March 4, 1996.
[3]   FORE, "Forethought Bandwidth Management, Version 1.0," http://www.fore.com/atm-edu/pdf_files/bandwidt.pdf.
[4]   N. Lippis, "A New Vendor Alliance: Doomed or Destined?" *Data Communications,* August 1996.
[5]   S. Lawson, *InfoWorld,* Sep 30, 1996.
[6]   M. Petrosky, "The Gang of Three May Well Push Networking to a Higher Level," *Network World,* June 17, 1996.
[7]   J. Cohen, M. Csenger, and J. Duffy, *Network World,* February 27, 1995.

Part

4

ATM SERVICES

This part provides the reader with an overview of ATM service access methods and a comprehensive study of ATM services and their providers both in North America and worldwide. Chapter 18 begins by looking at the various ATM service access methods, spanning a range of speeds from nx64 kbps up to hundreds of megabits per second. We highlight industry leading efforts to place ATM over Digital Subscriber Loop (xDSL) technologies using existing copper pairs, delivering integrated voice and data to small businesses and a significant number of residences. These technologies may move ATM into upscale residences and become the information superhighway on-ramp for the Home Area Network. The chapter concludes with a discussion of the prognosis for voice over ATM in the PBX and wide area networks traditionally served by time-division multiplexing. We then move on to a review of major North American carriers in Chapter 19, providing details obtained in our survey, including pricing. Chapter 20 then covers other trials and carrier services available around the globe. Hopefully, the facts presented in this part will convince you that ATM has already crossed the chasm to success in commercial wide area carrier networks.

18

ATM Service Access Methods

While dial-up and ISDN access remains the predominant technology for smaller business locations and residences, the trend begun by frame relay to increase speeds to nx64 kbps levels will likely continue. We believe that ATM will effectively compete and coexist with frame relay at nxDS0, DS1, and nxDS1 speeds. Of course, ATM has little competition at DS3 and higher speeds. ATM will likely excel when higher-speed voice, data, and video traffic are combined — nxDS1 ATM may be the service of choice. ATM must interoperate and interwork with frame relay, ISDN, legacy LANs, and the Internet to provide a common WAN infrastructure.

This chapter looks at the predominant access methods to ATM. We characterize the types of ATM services available today. There are many options in addition to the basic ATM Forum–defined User-to-Network Interface (UNI), including DS1 circuit emulation for N-ISDN access, nxDS0 and DS1 ATM Frame-based UNI (FUNI), frame relay/ATM service inter-working, and LAN extension services — sometimes referred to as a native mode "bit pipe" service because it operates in LAN native mode and effec-tively provides a data pipeline between sites [5]. While previous chapters covered the specifics of access protocols, this chapter looks at key issues involved with access to ATM services.

The chapter next explores alternative access methods for ATM services, including ATM over SONET restored transmission facilities, ATM over Asymmetrical Digital Subscriber Line (ADSL), cable modem access to ATM, and wireless access to ATM. We also take a look at set-top ATM boxes and the home area network. Next, we look at where ATM services and the PBX are heading or merging, followed by a discussion of carrying voice over ATM.

18.1 ATM PUBLIC SERVICE ACCESS METHODS

ATM offers the ability to consolidate access from the smallest remote branch offices to the largest headquarters and data centers. ATM services allow users to consolidate access that would typically require the provisioning and cost of three separate services:

- Public Switched Telephone Network (PSTN) for voice traffic
- Frame relay, private line, and Internet networks for data traffic
- ISDN network for nx64-kbps video traffic

18.1.1 Basic UNI Connectivity

Chapter 7 covered basic UNI connectivity. This is the most prevalent form of access to ATM services today, typically at DS1, DS3, or OC3 speeds. The DS1 service is very popular, because it is relatively inexpensive, giving customers a chance to try out ATM without making the large investment typically involved in installing a DS3 line. Most ATM service providers offer DS3 (45 Mbps) ATM access, but most businesses either don't need or can't afford this much bandwidth yet.

18.1.2 nxDS0 and DS1 ATM and Frame-Based UNI

The ability to provide ATM access speeds using the FUNI method in DS0 increments (called nxDS0) up to DS1/E1 speeds, along with the ability to provide DS1 ATM access speeds, gives greater flexibility and some potential cost savings for many enterprises. ATM at DS1 offers more than just bandwidth — it also offers a guaranteed Quality of Service (QoS) and a clear upgrade path for even the smallest branch office user. DS1 ATM service is suitable for many applications, such as multimedia applications employing packetized voice and video [9].

NxDS0 and DS1 FUNI offers the best method of entry for corporations into higher-speed ATM services. Flat-rate DS1 ATM pricing makes the cost of WAN access predictable, and SVC usage-based services make it cost-effective for low connect and usage times connected with occasional users. In fact, the price of DS1 ATM services is now at the point where they are more attractive than dedicated private lines.

18.1.2.1 DS1 Service Provider Benefits

DS1 ATM also offers the service provider many benefits. An all-ATM network offers reduced operating costs, since the carrier needs only a single, integrated infrastructure for voice, video, and data services. CO-based equipment that aggregates many low-speed DS1 ATM ports into a single high-speed trunk allows carriers to gain economies of scale, which in a competitive environment usually translates to lower prices to the end user. Thus, DS1 ATM could lower costs and help spur ATM services at all rates. DS1 ATM has been a strong seller within ATM public services, and some studies predict that over 70 percent of all ATM ports used in the United States will be DS1 by 1999 [6]. In fact, PacBell cited planned growth for DS1 ATM coming from medical clinics, retail store chains, and small businesses, and has been offering a low speed nxDS0 service since March 1997. DS1 ATM may be the true competitor to take away private line business, similar to a parallel trend where frame relay displaced fractional T1 private lines in the early 1990s [7].

18.1.2.2 Public nxDS0 and DS1 ATM Accessible Services

Carriers currently offer the following types of nxDS0 and DS1 ATM-accessible services [8]:

- Native ATM DS1 user network interface as defined by the ITU-T and the ATM Forum.
- Frame relay/ATM Permanent Virtual Connection (PVC) network interworking encapsulates and multiplexes frames and status signaling over an ATM network for trunking applications.
- Frame relay/ATM PVC service interworking specifies how frame relay traffic and status signaling is converted to and from ATM cells.
- FUNI provides simple, frame-oriented access to ATM without expensive CSU/DSUs on the customer premises.

18.1.2.3 Some DS1 ATM Service Offerings

MCI Communications Corp. has a T1 (1.544-Mbit/s) ATM service that boasts usage-based billing for Constant Bit Rate (CBR), Variable Bit Rate (VBR), and Unspecified Bit Rate (UBR) transmissions.

AT&T sells T1 ATM for VBR and CBR service categories.

Both carriers allow oversubscription, a scheme that lets net managers save money by allocating more PVCs to a port (or connection) than the bandwidth can support. Oversubscription relies on the statistical probability that not all the PVCs will be used at once.

Sprint (Kansas City, Mo.) offers T1 ATM for CBR and VBR traffic, with oversubscription on a case-by-case basis.

18.1.3 nxDS1 ATM

The ATM Forum's Inverse Multiplexing over ATM (IMA) specification standardizes nxDS1 and nxE1 access. IMA allows multiple DS1/E1 paths to be treated as a single aggregate path, similar to traditional nxDS1 TDM multiplexers of private lines. Figure 18.1 illustrates the operation of an IMA system. Cells arriving from the sending ATM layer originate at the upper left-hand side of the figure. The IMA transmitter multiplexes these cells in a round-robin manner onto the three physical links in the IMA group, interleaving IMA Control Protocol (ICP) cells for control and synchronization purposes. The link selected by the IMA transmitter is indicated by the shading of the cells in the figure. At the receiver, the cells on each of the physical links arrive after different delays. The IMA receiver employs the ICP cells to realign the cells before multiplexing them back into an accurately reproduced version of the original high-speed ATM cell stream, which is then delivered to the destination ATM layer in the upper right-hand corner of the figure. The net effect of the IMA is that the end equipment sees an ATM cell stream operating at an nxDS1 or nxE1 aggregate rate.

Many ATM switch, access multiplexer, and concentrator vendors now offer support for IMA. NxDS1 IMA offers a cost-effective way to garner greater than DS1 bandwidth across the WAN, without having to lease a full DS3 access line. Bandwidth can be added in DS1 increments, typically up to 8 DS1s, at which point a user must purchase a more expensive DS3 or SONET access line. Carriers began offering NxDS1 IMA services in 1997.

18.2 ATM OVER SONET

While some view ATM and SONET as competing technologies, they actually complement one another to improve the user's end-to-end service availability and QoS. ATM and SONET work together to provide high availability by one of several methods:

- ATM VP-based rings to restore VCs
- SONET/SDH self-restoring rings or digital cross-connects
- Hybrid ATM and SONET/SDH restoration schemes

The method of SONET/SDH and ATM working together is the most reliable, but also the most complex. Here the self-healing nature of SONET rings protects ATM links and ports. For high reliability, SONET/SDH becomes the physical layer of choice for ATM. Both methods could then be managed in an integrated manner using the ITU-T's Telecommunications Management Network (TMN) architecture [11].

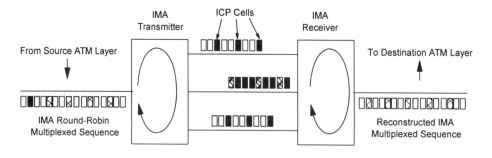

Figure 18.1 Illustration of Inverse Multiplexing over ATM

Some studies indicate that ATM-based restoration is 30 to 40 percent more efficient than Time-Division Multiplexing (TDM)-based digital cross-connect restoration systems [12]. ATM even enables the potential of hitless protection switching by broadcasting the cell stream using diversity coding at the transmitter in conjunction with a very intelligent receiver [13].

18.3 DIGITAL SUBSCRIBER LINE TECHNOLOGIES

Digital Subscriber Line (or DSL for short) technology is a hot topic in communications networking today. First, we explain what this technology is by defining the technical parameters and reference configuration. Next, we summarize the standards activity in xDSL. The section then moves onto a summary of xDSL trials and the forecasted market for xDSL. We then discuss the advantages of xDSL technology for carriers, and conclude with some speculation about the future role of xDSL technologies.

18.3.1 xDSL Explained

The term *xDSL* refers to a family of communication technologies based around the DSL technology, where "x" corresponds to standard upstream and downstream data rates, defined from the perspective of the end user. *Upstream* is from the user to the service provider, while *downstream* is from the service provider to the end user. Several groups of manufacturers, carriers, and entrepreneurs are actively standardizing and promoting this technology in several forums [1, 2]. One group, the ADSL Forum, has even coined a new acronym for ATM: Another Telecommunications Medium. They've also coined a new set of acronyms, explained in Table 18.1.

DSL technology harnesses the power of state-of-the-art modem design to "supercharge" existing twisted-pair telephone lines into information super-highway on-ramps. ADSL technology enables downlink transmission speeds of over 1 Mbps to a subscriber, while simultaneously supporting transmissions of at least 64 kbps in both directions. xDSL achieves bandwidths orders of magnitude over legacy access technologies, such as ISDN and analog modems, using existing cabling, albeit over shorter distances.

Many experts expect xDSL to play a crucial role over the coming decade as consumers' demand for video and multimedia information increases, since it uses existing unshielded twisted pair cabling, while the installation of new, higher-performance cabling (e.g., optical fiber) will take decades.

We now describe a typical xDSL configuration with reference to Figure 18.2. The equipment on the left-hand side is located on the customer premises. Devices which the end user accesses, such as a personal computer, television, and ISDN video phone, connect to a premises distribution network via service modules. These service modules employ either STM (i.e., TDM), ATM, or packet transport modes as depicted at the bottom of the figure. An existing twisted pair telephone line connects the user's xDSL modem to a corresponding modem in the public network. The xDSL modem creates three information channels — a high-speed downstream channel ranging from 1.5 to 52 Mbps, a medium-speed duplex channel ranging from 16 kbps to 2.3 Mbps, and a POTS (Plain Old Telephone Service) channel. Analog splitters separate the POTS channel from the digital modem using filters that pass only the lower 4 kHz of spectrum to the local telephone devices. This design guarantees uninterrupted telephone service, even if the xDSL system fails.

Moving to the center of Figure 18.2, multiple xDSL modems connect to an access node within the public network. Splitters carve off analog voice signals to the PSTN. The access node interfaces to packet, broadband, video, or service networks as shown on the right-hand side of the figure. Depending upon the transport mode employed by the customer, the conversion to/from ATM may be performed as indicated by the lines at the bottom of the figure. If the customer employs ATM end-to-end, then cost and administration of such conversions is eliminated. Experts envision these access networks connecting to a variety of service providers' private networks supporting a wide range of applications, such as Internet access, on-line services, remote LAN access, videoconferencing, and video on demand.

Table 18.1 The Family of Digital Subscriber Line (xDSL) Acronyms Explained

Acronym	Full Name	Twisted Pairs	Upstream Rate	Down-stream Rate	Example Applications
DSL	Digital Subscriber Line	1	160 kbps	160 kbps	ISDN service for voice and ISDN modem data
HDSL (DS1)	High Data Rate Digital Subscriber Line	2	1.544 Mbps	1.544 Mbps	North American T1 service
HDSL (E1)	High Data Rate Digital Subscriber Line	3	2.048 Mbps	2.048 Mbps	European and international E1
SDSL (DS1)	Single-Line Digital Subscriber Line	1	1.544 Mbps	1.544 Mbps	North American T1 service
SDSL (E1)	Single-Line Digital Subscriber Line	1	2.048 Mbps	2.048 Mbps	European and international E1
ADSL	Asymmetric Digital Subscriber Line	1	16 to 640 kbps	1.5 to 9 Mbps	Video on demand, LAN and Internet access
VDSL	Very High Data Rate Digital Subscriber Line	1	1.5 to 2.3 Mbps	13 to 52 Mbps	High-quality video, high-performance Internet/LAN

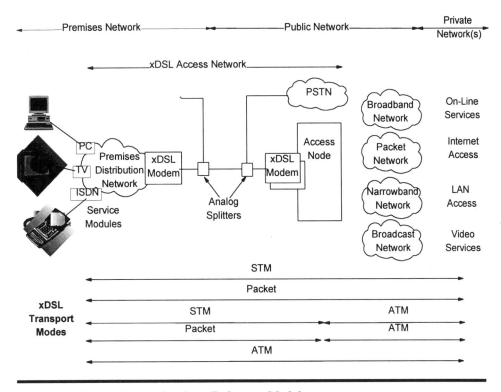

Figure 18.2 Digital Subscriber Line Reference Model

Current xDSL modems provide data rates aligned with North American and European digital STM hierarchies at a constant bit rate. Future plans include LAN interfaces and direct incorporation of xDSL modems and service modules directly into TV set-top boxes and PC interface cards. The ADSL Forum plans to support ATM at variable rates when the ATM market matures. Since real-time signals, such as digital video, can't employ link- or network-level error control procedures because of the delay they cause, xDSL modems incorporate forward error correction that dramatically reduces errors caused by noise.

The achievable high-speed downstream data rate depends upon a number of factors, such as the length of the twisted pair line, the wire gauge, presence of bridged taps from the old party line days, and cross-coupled interference from other lines. Without bridged taps, ADSL can support a 1-Mbps downstream rate over distances in excess of 3 miles. While the measure varies according to geographic area, studies indicate that ADSL capabilities cover up to 95 percent of a loop plant. Premises outside the 3-mile limit must be served by fiber-based digital loop carrier systems.

From a system viewpoint, xDSL looks simple — high-speed data rates over ordinary telephone lines. Of course, several miracles of modern technology work together to achieve this quantum leap in performance over existing

POTS analog modems and even ISDN technologies. ADSL modems divide up the 1-MHz telephone line bandwidth using either Frequency Division Multiplexing (FDM) or TDM echo cancellation. The FDM method assigns a frequency band for downstream data and a smaller band for upstream data. Echo cancellation assigns the upstream band to overlap the downstream, and separates the two by means of local echo cancellation, as V.32 and V.34 modems do. Echo cancellation uses bandwidth more efficiently, but at the expense of complexity and cost. ADSL multiplexing, interleaving, and error correction coding create up to 20 ms of delay. This process achieves high resistance to impulse noise that can be generated by electrical appliances. Both techniques split off the 4-kHz passband for POTS using low-pass filters.

Figure 18.3 summarizes speed and distance limitations for 24-gauge twisted pair. The double-headed arrows are placed vertically at the maximum speed for the DSL technology, with their horizontal dimension indicating the range of feasible operation.

18.3.2 Standards Activity

A coalition of vendors formed the ADSL Forum in December of 1994 to promote the ADSL concept and facilitate development of ADSL system architectures, protocols, and interfaces. The American National Standards Institute (ANSI) approved an ADSL standard at rates up to 6.1 Mbps (ANSI Standard T1.413). The European Technical Standards Institute (ETSI) provided an Annex to T1.413 reflecting European requirements. The ATM Forum and the Data and Video Council (DAVIC) have both recognized ADSL as a physical-layer transmission protocol for unshielded twisted pair media.

The ADSL Forum, working in conjunction with the ATM Forum and ANSI, wrote Technical Report TR-002. This pre-standard specifies how to interwork ATM traffic over ADSL modem links. The ATM Forum Residential Broadband Working Group is working on its version of an ADSL/ATM standard that will work with either xDSL or cable modem technologies.

18.3.3 Trials and Market Forecast

Alcatel and Pacific Bell demonstrated 6-Mbps ATM rates over ADSL technology in May 1997. Alcatel used Discrete Multitone (DMT) technology that allows the ATM transfer rate to adjust its speed automatically in response to varying line conditions and interface parameters. Some methods provide IP packets over ATM cells, which in turn run over an ADSL transmission scheme, all with the security inherent within ATM. ADC Communications is also producing ATM/DSL access devices [15].

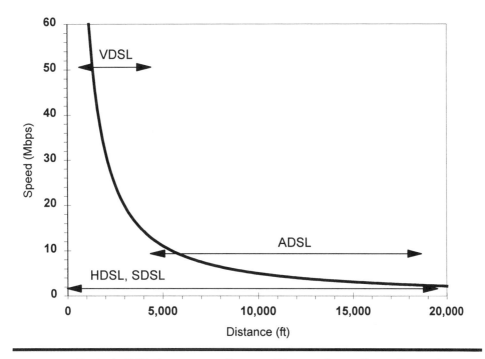

Figure 18.3 Typical xDSL Downstream Rate vs. Distance for 24-Guage Twisted Pair

Central office vendors, such as DSC Communications Corp., are also beginning to modify their equipment to support ATM over xDSL, along with the traditional Regional Bell Operating Companies (RBOCs) like Bell Atlantic. The most popular protocol for session establishment and release is the Point-to-Point Protocol (PPP). This brings all the features of PPP (authentication, encryption, compression, etc.) to bear for all ATM communications.

Market forecasts project significant growth in xDSL penetration in the United States [4] at markedly different rates for residences and small businesses, as shown in Figure 18.4.

The relative fraction of residences and small businesses with Internet access is projected to be almost the same, growing at a rate of approximately 30 percent per year. However, the penetration of xDSL into small businesses is likely to occur much more rapidly than penetration into residences. Indeed, xDSL may only be present in such homes as those visited by Robin Leach in *Lifestyles of the Rich and Famous* for quite some time to come.

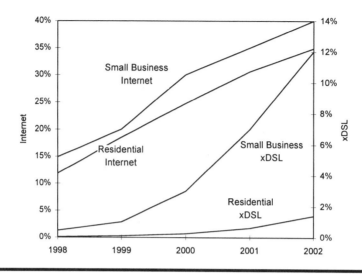

Figure 18.4 U.S. Projected Growth in Residential Internet and xDSL Access

18.3.4 Equipment Vendors

ATM over DSL networking technology is accomplished through a variety of devices:

- Digital Subscriber Loop Access Multiplexers/modems (DSLAMs)
- DSLAM Network Interface Cards (NICs)
- Fiber to the Curb (FTTC)
- XDSL stand-alone Set-top Boxes (STBs)

The access node (DSLAM) provides ADSL subscriber line termination, as well as concentration and multiplexing of subscriber lines into the ATM network. This device acts similar to legacy modem pools. Key vendors providing ATM over ADSL products include Alcatel, Ariel, Dagaz, Efficient, and Motorola Semiconductor [16].

18.3.5 ATM and xDSL — Advantages for Carriers

ADSL, or for that matter any of the xDSL technologies, is basically an access technology to public network services. ATM is a networking and transport technology that can be offered as a service over xDSL access, where the xDSL line provides the user access at a lower cost per Mbps. This combination is very attractive to service providers, as it leverages the existing copper plant and offers ATM services over it without the requirement to replace existing copper with fiber-optic cabling. In fact, ATM offers virtual connections at specified bandwidths with guaranteed QoS [14].

A real advantage of the use of ATM over ADSL exists for the Local Exchange Carriers (LECs). Since LECs already own the (unshielded) twisted pair into almost all residences, as well as many businesses, a combination of ATM service for video (TV channels), data (for Internet or telecommuting access), and voice (for residential dial-tone services) could allow them to keep a lock-in on existing customers for some time to come. LECs could offer lower-speed ADSL services, video on demand, home shopping and banking, local and long distance phone services, and Internet access over ADSL more cost-effectively than they could be offered through separate providers. The benefits to be gained are enormous: fewer access lines, less termination equipment, consistent QoS, and more. Of course, the downside for the consumer could be the lack of competition from multiple providers.

18.3.6 ATM over xDSL — Future Internet Access Method of Choice?

Will ATM over ADSL become the preferred method for high-performance Internet access? While dial access via analog modems is the preferred method of Internet access for consumers today, many telecommuters and remote offices requiring remote LAN access have moved to faster (128 kbps) ISDN access. Most Internet access traffic is small requests upstream from the user to the network, interleaved with much larger data streams coming from the remote Web site downstream to the requesting user. It's the old inquiry/response routine well known in data applications. Thus, xDSL technologies promise a tenfold increase in speed over today's top-of-the-line ISDN modems.

Currently, Internet providers are faced with the problem of how to provide different quality of service to different applications over the Internet. ATM offers the best method today of guaranteeing end-to-end QoS across the WAN. Potentially, these facts position ATM over xDSL services as the Internet access method of choice, especially for large corporations with many telecommuters, or remote offices that want to send voice, video, and data traffic over the Internet.

18.4 ATM CABLE MODEMS

xDSL services compete with cable modems that can operate at much higher speeds (up to 30 Mbps). Both technologies are optimized for high speed transmission rates from the network service provider toward the user — in other words, designed for distribution from server to user, rather than for peer-to-peer, user-to-user traffic patterns.

Cable modems operate typically from 10 to 30 Mbps, full duplex. Yet the one-way-only nature of today's cable networks remains a major barrier to complete realization of cable modems. Also, most office buildings still lack coaxial cable, the necessary transport medium. These cable modem standards can be found in IEEE 802.14. Despite the short time cable modems have been available, Motorola has already shipped 1 million units. Cable modems are manufactured by many traditional modem companies like COM21, Motorola, and DEC, as well as Bay Networks, LANcity, and Media General.

This higher-speed option for running ATM over existing cable plant skips the lower-bandwidth ATM over ADSL alternative and goes directly to 30-Mbps ATM over cable modems. This technology could give cable companies a jump on the LECs. But if history is an indicator, cable companies may have a struggle providing these services as competently as the LECs.

18.5 PCS DIGITAL AND CELLULAR ANALOG ACCESS TO ATM

There is also a move to provide cellular and PCS access to ATM services. PCS digital networks are quickly replacing cellular analog networks. While cellular transport has severe bandwidth and throughput limitations, packetized voice can be aggregated at the Central Office (CO), and from there transported via either ATM or TDM uplinks to the switching centers. PCS service providers are now rolling out CDPD data services that offer even higher bandwidth and better service for data and voice traffic. We cover the topic of wireless ATM in greater depth in Chapter 25.

18.6 SET-TOP ATM

CATV providers have had the ability to offer interactive services over their existing infrastructure, such as telephony services and video on demand, for some time. Yet they have been unable to offer these types of services successfully. ATM can play a key enabler along with other technologies to deliver these services to devices like set-top boxes within a Home Area Network (HAN) from video servers resident within the ATM service network. Some manufacturers, such as Acorn, have produced an ATM STB that combines ATM25 and Ethernet interfaces along with MPEG2 decoding capability and support for Java applications. The focus of the product is toward corporate and consumer applications. Standards groups like the ATM Forum have working groups — Residential Broadband (RBB) — that focus on ATM in the HAN.

18.7 TELECOMMUTING OPTIONS COMPARISON

Table 18.2 compares the likely choices for telecommuters requiring high amounts of bandwidth, defined as greater than 56 kbps modem speeds. The most promising telecommuting solution is ATM over xDSL .

Table 18.2 ISDN, ATM over ADSL, Cable Modem Comparison

	ISDN	ATM over ADSL	Cable Modems
Downstream speeds	Up to 128 kbps	Up to 6 Mbps	Up to 30 Mbps
Upstream speeds	Up to 128 kbps	Up to 640 kbps	Up to 30 Mbps
Cabling requirements	Copper	Copper	Coaxial
Cost per access device	Low	Medium	Medium
Service monthly cost	Low	Low	Low
Length of local loop		Max 18K ft	
Issues		No load coils or bridged taps	

Both DSL and cable modems promise low-cost access, perhaps as little as $50 a month per connection. By comparison, users now pay at least $300 for 1.5 Mbps of bandwidth. ISDN costs vary but can be found as low as $50 a month, yet ISDN delivers just 64 or 128 kbps. One major drawback of ADSL is that it cannot process signals through load coils or bridged taps This may require an overhaul of the local loop copper plant to support ADSL.

18.8 ATM AND THE PBX

Some vendors are adopting the ATM switching approach to Private Branch Exchanges (PBXs), where the PBX becomes a server on an ATM LAN. However, the rich set of PBX features and embedded handset functions inhibit rapid migration to other technologies. Some ATM vendors are building traditional PBX call control features into their ATM switching architectures. At the same time, PBX vendors see ATM-ready PBX products replacing ATM LAN switches. The most likely scenario will be a coexistence of ATM-ready PBXs and ATM switches with call processing and control capability in both the campus and wide area. ATM interfaces are beginning to appear in PBXs. One example is the Siemens and ROLM product.
There are advantages to replacing a PBX with an ATM switch:

- An ATM switch is less expensive than a PBX.
- PBXs still resemble mainframes in architecture and administration.
- Eliminating the PBX leaves a single wiring infrastructure for voice and data.

- This cuts out duplicate maintenance, installation, management, and staff support costs.
- Wouldn't it be easier to just add a headset to your workstation?

The disadvantages to using an ATM switch as a PBX include:

- The call handling features on the PBX may not all be available.
- PBXs are historically more reliable than LAN devices
- There is a lack of standard interoperability between ATM switch manufacturers supporting telephony functions.
- Additional investment in end-station software and hardware is required.
- Gateway to the PSTN is required.

Other issues must be analyzed. If a LAN is very busy, the voice quality may not be acceptable without quality of service support. Another issue is how to handle all the call processing, signaling, and enhanced PBX features within the ATM network. One answer involves running a voice processing application on a low-cost, ATM network-based server which stores voice messages and executes calling features. For example, using this single network approach, a user retrieves voice mail through the ATM LAN using a Switched Virtual Connection (SVC) call request for a VBR VCC. Using a Pentium computer as a server on the LAN to perform these functions could end up being more cost-effective than a expensive, legacy PBX.

18.9 VOICE OVER ATM

One of the primary benefits of end-to-end ATM is the capability to integrate voice and data traffic. In this section we review integration design alternatives, first looking at the endpoint aggregation methods, and then at ATM service category selection.

The options today for placing voice over ATM include:

- Circuit emulation over CBR
- Voice with silence suppression over rt-VBR

Three APIs are available for applications to access call processing feature and control voice calls:

- Telephony API
- Telephony Services API
- WinSock 2.0

18.9.1 Service Class Selection

Voice traffic can be categorized as:

- Human speech
- Fax data
- Modem data
- Recorded audio (e.g., music, nature sounds, etc.)

There are two methods of transmitting voice traffic over ATM: CBR and real-time VBR service categories. Circuit emulation (AAL1) via CBR service category or vendor proprietary solutions have been the standard way to date to place voice over ATM. While CBR guarantees a specific amount of bandwidth, it does not free up bandwidth during periods of voiceband inactivity. Yet CBR service remains the most popular method for voice transport among ATM concentrators and switches, since the ATM Forum's standard has promoted interoperability between vendors. Use of the rt-VBR service category offers a more cost-effective alternative for human voice, since the ATM network doesn't use any bandwidth during periods of silence. The unused bandwidth during these inactive intervals is then available to other ATM service categories.

18.9.1.1 Constant Bit Rate Service Category

Table 18.3 shows five standard methods for transmitting voice as CBR service category traffic. Each of these is offered over SVCs.

Table 18.3 Voice as CBR Service Category Traffic

Voice Format	Standard
64-kbps Pulse Code Modulation (PCM)	ITU-T G.711
64-kbps Adaptive Differential Pulse Code Modulation (ADPCM)	ITU-T G.722/G.725
16/24/32/40-kbps ADPCM	ITU-T G.726
9.6/12.8/16-kbps linear prediction	ITU-T G.728
1–8-kbps voice for 20-ms packets	IS-54/95 wireless voice

Note that 64-kbps ADPCM supports signals with bandwidths up to 7 kHz, whereas 64-kbps PCM only supports 3.1 kHz of bandwidth. Support for standard PCM was the first effort of the ATM Forum's Voice and Telephony over ATM (VTOA) group. The difference will be heard in the upper harmonics of a person's voice — 3.1 kHz will sound much flatter and less recognizable than 7 kHz, especially for female voices, which are usually higher in pitch. Fax and modem modulation are best supported by the CBR service category, or by transcoding to the native bit rate using methods employed by Digital Circuit Multiplication Equipment (DCME).

18.9.1.2 Real-time Variable Bit Rate Service Category

The rt-VBR ATM service category improves efficiency by not transmitting cells during periods of silence [18, 20, 21]. This method is sometimes referred to as gap-mode CBR, because the conversion protocol listens for gaps in the speech where no one is talking and doesn't generate traffic during these gaps. An integrated system can send lower-priority data traffic during these gaps. However, the gaps may be several seconds in duration. Telephone engineers have a great deal of experience in how to make silence suppression yield high-fidelity speech transmission on undersea cable communication systems. These gaps in human speech constitute over 60 percent of the average conversation, allowing for approximately a 50 percent bandwidth savings when using rt-VBR compared with CBR. A future standard to watch for from the ITU-2 for voice compression is AAL2 in I.363.2. An additional method for gaining bandwidth efficiency is to prevent the insertion of idle bits normally transmitted when phones are off hook.

One example of a product that offers rt-VBR voice over ATM service is General DataComm's APEX ATM switch. Please refer to the switch vendor survey in Chapter 17 for additional details.

Table 18.4 compares the benefits and cost of placing voice traffic over a CBR VC versus a rt-VBR VC.

Table 18.4 Comparison of CBR to rt-VBR Voice Traffic

Attribute	CBR	rt-VBR
Cost of VC	Highest	Lower
Bandwidth usage	Less efficient	More efficient
Voice quality	Effectively lossless	Possibility of loss

With the statistical multiplexing inherent in rt-VBR, there is a possibility of loss. As a rule of thumb, between 10 and 20 voice connections can multiplexed onto a single ATM port with approximately a 50 percent reduction in required VCC bandwidth (i.e., SCR) and suffer acceptable loss. Loss of voice signal may sound like a click, or occasionally may render a single word unrecognizable.

18.9.1.3 ATM Forum Voice and Telephony over ATM Specification

The ATM Forum VTOA specification defines the use of predefined PVCs over which to connect voice calls. The two efforts within VTOA include Circuit Emulation Services (CES) that emulate a point-to-point private line similar to CBR service, and a voice trunking specification where the ATM network acts as the voice switch for PBXs. The real gain for VTOA will be enhancing the direct connection between a PBX and ATM switch — providing call-by-call switching — establishing an SVC for each voice call. This group is also working on a silence suppression specification.

18.9.1.4 Use SVCs, not PVCs!

Future voice over ATM applications will ride SVCs instead of PVCs [19]. SVCs free up unused bandwidth when not in use, whereas PVCs reserve it 100 percent of the time. Once service providers offer SVCs for CBR and rt-VBR service categories, we expect to see more demand for voice and circuit emulation over ATM. SVCs have been a challenge for service providers, as they are hard to administer and manage, and require large amounts of switch processing time and signaling overhead, along with complex pricing and billing schemes. But clearly SVCs are the way to go for voice over ATM.

18.9.2 Handling ATM Network Delay and Echo

The ITU looked at the basic tradeoff between efficiency and packetization delay versus cell size before it finally decided on the 53-byte cell in 1990. Packetization delay is the amount of time required to fill the cell at a rate of 64 kbps, that is, the rate to fill the cell with digitized voice samples. Ideally, high efficiency and low delay are both desirable, but they cannot be achieved simultaneously. Better efficiency occurs at large cell sizes at the expense of increased packetization delay. In order to carry voice over ATM and interwork with two-wire analog telephone sets, the total delay should be less than about 15 ms; otherwise echo cancellation must be used. Two TDM-to-ATM conversions are required in the round-trip echo path. Allowing 3 ms for propagation delay and two ATM conversions, a cell size of 32 octets avoids the need for echo cancellation. Thus, the ITU-T adopted the fixed-length 48-octet cell payload as a compromise between data's drive for large cell sizes to achieve high efficiency and voice's need for constrained delay. There are two key areas where a designer can reduce the effects of delay on the ATM network: cell transfer delay between nodes and cell delay variation (CDV). If the round-trip delay is greater than 15 ms, then objectionable "echo" occurs. For delays that exceed 15 ms, ensure that the design includes an echo canceler.

18.9.3 Applications of Voice over ATM

Multimedia workstations offer the perfect platform on which to combine voice communications and visual data, such as desktop videoconferencing. Integration of the phone into the desktop workstation and thus LAN interface is one of the benefits of using ATM to the desktop. The next most common method is to provide a direct connection of a telephone, fax machine, or modem to an ATM network switch. Another method of placing voice over ATM is through a direct connection of a PBX voice switch to an ATM network switch, as discussed earlier in this chapter.

The main drivers for placing voice over ATM in a corporate environment typically include:

- Strong requirement for desktop multimedia
- Volume of voice traffic is lower than that of the data traffic
- Majority of voice traffic is intranet, versus extranet to public switched voice network

18.10 REVIEW

While earlier chapters introduced many of the methods of accessing an ATM network, this chapter discussed issues involved with the actual implementation along with vendor specifics. The chapter began with a review of low-speed ATM access alternatives, ranging from nxDS0 through DS3. The chapter then showed that ATM can provide the network technology over a variety of legacy and new access methods (SONET, xDSL, cable modems, and cellular) at a variety of speeds (nxDS0 through OC-N). We concluded this chapter with a look at the comparisons using an ATM network versus a PBX, along with an in-depth study of the methods for placing voice traffic over ATM services.

18.11 REFERENCES

[1] ADSL Forum, "ADSL Forum Home Page," http://www.adsl.com/adsl/.
[2] Telechoice, "The Telechoice Report on xDSL On-line, " http://www.telechoice.com/xdslnewz/.
[3] K. Maxwell, "Asymmetric Digital Subscriber Line: Interim Technology for the Next Forty Years," *IEEE Communications*, October 1996.
[4] "Digital Subscriber Line Technologies Highlight Supercomm '97," *Broadband Networking News*, June 10, 1997.
[5] "ATM — The Next Generation," *Business Communications Review*, February, 1996.
[6] Vertical Systems Study, 1997.
[7] D. P. Haas, "The Case for Slowing Down ATM," *America's Network*, June 15, 1997.
[8] K. Taylor, "From Frames to Cells: Low-Speed Access to ATM," *Data Communications*, May 1995.
[9] S. Taylor, "T1 ATM: Less than Meets the Eye," *Data Communications*, February 1994.
[10] D. Rohde, "'Transparent' LAN Services Look Good," *Network World*, March 20, 1995.
[11] T. Landegem, "Self-Healing Networks for SDH and ATM," *IEEE Communications,* September 1995.
[12] J. Anderson, B. Doshi, S. Dravida, and P. Harshavardhana, "Fast Restoration of ATM Networks," IEEE JSAC, January 1994.
[13] E. Ayanoglu and R. Gitlin, "Broadband Network Restoration," *IEEE Communications*, July 1996.

[14]   J. Caruso, "DSL Goes Hybrid by Adding ATM," *Communications Week*, June 1997.
[15]   *Broadband Networking News*, May 13, 1997.
[16]   WWW references at Ariel.com, Dagaztech.com, Efficient.com, Motorola.com.
[17]   ATM Forum/95-1428, Issues for ATM over Wireless.
[18]   D. Wright, "Voice over ATM: An Evaluation of Network Architecture Alternatives," *IEEE Network*, September/October 1996.
[19]   ATM Forum, "Voice Networking in the WAN," http://www.atmforum.com/atmforum/library/vtoa.html.
[20]   *Broadband Networking News*, May 13, 1997.
[21]   *ATM Report*, April 15, 1996.
[22]   T. L. Nolle, "AIN and ATM, Collision or Coexistence," *America's Network*, September 1996.

19

ATM Services in North America

This chapter provides a detailed analysis of North American public ATM WAN services. We start by defining the services market and key players, then move on to defining the key evaluation criteria for ATM service vendors. The chapter closes with an analysis of pricing structures. The next chapter covers international ATM services.

19.1 ATM PUBLIC SERVICES OVERVIEW

There are many factors to consider when choosing a public network ATM-based service: the access facility, ATM service categories offered, interworking support, network management, Customer Premises Equipment (CPE) support, and pricing and billing options, just to name a few. We start by examining public ATM network architectures and services. We also examine the challenges and benefits to public network ATM services.

19.1.1 Public ATM Network Architectures

As ATM technology proliferates, it provides an evolutionary path from the traditional networks based on a Time-Division Multiplex (TDM) architecture to an ATM-based architecture. An architecture based upon ATM technology utilizes ATM switches both in the Central Office (CO) and at the CPE. Carriers can also deploy ATM in cross-connects, routers, gateways, workstations, and Interworking Functions (IWFs), as shown in Figure 19.1. Furthermore, most public ATM-based networks employ a SONET backbone in North America and SDH internationally. Figure 19.1 also shows a network example where users either interface to the ATM network directly via an ATM User-Network Interface (UNI), an ATM DXI interface, ATM DS1, ATM nxDS1 Inverse Multiplexing over ATM (IMA), or a frame relay interface; access an SMDS connectionless server; or even access the Internet via an IP interworking function. Part 2 of this book detailed these access types and interworking functions.

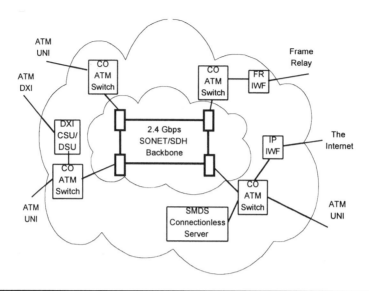

Figure 19.1 ATM-Based Network Services Using a SONET Backbone

19.1.2 ATM Service Suite

The suite of possible ATM services includes the following:

- ATM Cell Relay Service (CRS)
- Virtual Path or Virtual Channel Connections (VPC or VCC)
- Point-to-point or point-to-multipoint connections
- Permanent Virtual Connection (PVC)
- Switched Virtual Connection (SVC)
- Bandwidth reservation
- Frame relay network and service interworking with ATM
- SMDS access over ATM
- Access to IP via ATM
- Voice over ATM

19.1.3 Public ATM Services and Providers

Commercial and private ATM service offerings abound, offered by the traditional Local Exchange Carriers (LECs), Competitive Access Providers (CAPs), Internet Service Providers (ISPs), Interexchange Carriers (IXCs), value-added service providers, and international Postal Telephone and Telegraph (PTT) operators. The leading service providers in the United States include Ameritech, AT&T, Bell Atlantic, BellSouth, COMSAT, GTE, MCI, NYNEX, Southwestern Bell Communications, WorldCom, and US West. The next chapter covers leading international service providers.

Many carriers are banking their data networking futures on ATM. In fact, many of the nation's largest data transport networks have a switching infrastructure built upon ATM technology. One of the largest examples, next to large carriers like AT&T, is the Internet itself. The Internet is one of the biggest drivers of ATM deployment —ATM switching accounts for more than 75 percent of the Internet's backbone.

Most ATM service backbones are composed of OC3 trunks running at 155 Mbps, with plans to later upgrade to OC12 running at 622 Mbps.

19.2 PUBLIC ATM SERVICES COMPARISON OVERVIEW

The next few sections summarize the features and functions of ATM public services available as of late 1997. First, the text defines each feature and function for use in a survey of ATM service providers presented in this chapter and the next one. We asked all service providers to provide full contact information, including their company name, address, contact name and phone number, Web page, annual sales, number of customers actually using the service, date the service was launched, number of customers, number of ATM ports sold, and a paragraph on the company's strengths. We have attempted to include as much of this information as possible in the charts in this chapter. We also requested graphics depicting the service layout, some of which are also included.

Many vendors responded to a survey for this book providing information on services commercially available as of late 1997. A few vendors either chose not to respond or did not have products available by this timeframe. Current publications were used for details on vendor announcements for those vendors that did not respond [2, 3, 4, 5]. If your company offers an ATM service, and you want it included in the next revision of this book, please contact the authors at their E-mail address listed in the back of this book.

The key features for ATM services are the capability to support Available Bit Rate (ABR) traffic, nxDS1 and DS1 speeds, frame relay to ATM inter-working, and cost-effective pricing. Billing features and flexibility, geographic coverage, management features, and SVCs follow as a close second.

19.3 ATM SERVICES GENERAL INFORMATION

This section summarizes the general features and functions of ATM services. Each feature and function will be defined and service provider specifics provided based on a survey conducted by the authors.

This section presents the service provider responses to the survey questions. Sections on service support details and interfaces supported will follow. Note that the responses provided by the ATM service providers surveyed are presented as provided to the authors.

19.3.1 Service Provider, Service Name, and Service Availability

The service providers who responded to our survey are listed, along with their service name and both nationwide United States and international coverage.

19.3.1.1 Company Information

Company information requested includes:
- Name and address, Web page address, and strengths
- Primary point of contact for public inquiries, including the person's title and phone number
- Sales information

19.3.1.2 Corporate Strengths

We asked service providers to list their strengths. The boldfaced type indicates the respondent.

AT&T — AT&T is a leader in the high-speed services market and integrated frame relay and ATM service offerings. AT&T was an innovator of services like FR and ATM interworking, is the first interexchange service provider to offer ATM SVCs, and offers comprehensive service features such as ATM network management and AT&T lab testing and trials.

AT&T InterSpan ATM Service is designed to meet high-speed data, voice, and video connectivity needs. Developed in concert with the AT&T ATM Customer Advisory Council and built on AT&T's ATM experience, InterSpan ATM Service carries forward proven concepts from InterSpan Frame Relay Service. These concepts include: a truly committed Committed Information Rate (CIR), reliable sustained bursting, multiprotocol internetworking, a global seamless infrastructure with globally deployed Network Operations Centers (NOCs), and standards-based Customer Network Management Services (CNMS).

Bell Atlantic's comprehensive approach to LAN Office Backbone solutions utilizes the FORE Systems ASX-200 Forerunner ATM switch. The ASX-200 brings ATM connectivity to LAN workgroup, LAN backbone, and LAN/WAN internetworking applications. Together with the Forerunner series of ATM network adapter cards, the ASX-200 delivers the advanced networking capabilities needed by today's distributed, time-critical applications. It provides high-performance server switching, thereby removing bottlenecks and enhancing server-based applications.

Recognizing the need to work within diverse ATM LAN office backbone environments, Bell Atlantic's approach is engineered to fit the exact customer need. The ATM LAN Office Backbone solution is scalable to support applications ranging from small office environments to mainframe computer operations. Solution sets include multiple platforms to provide an offering robust enough to meet the most demanding needs for data and video support.

COMSAT World Services — COMSAT Corporation (NYSE: CQ) is a global provider of international communications services and products. COMSAT World Systems is the U.S. Signatory to INTELSAT and a 19 percent owner of the INTELSAT system.

Teleport offers the most complete line of data services available from any local exchange carrier in the United States. The same services are available in every TCG market, coast to coast. Services include transparent LAN: Ethernet (10 Mbps), Token Ring (16 Mbps), FDDI (100 Mbps), Fast Ethernet (100 Mbps). User-network interfaces include: 45 Mbps ATM, 155 Mbps ATM, and frame relay via network interworking.

WorldCom prides itself on being known in the industry as "the carrier's carrier," signifying the trust put in us by our competition. A build will be completed during 1997 which will position WorldCom with a 100 percent fiber, self-healing SONET infrastructure. The ATM commercialization unit is staffed with advanced-degreed engineers with more than four years experience with ATM and its implementation. The result is a professional design and implementation which fulfills the customer's needs.

Note that MFS and WorldCom merged in 1996. A few vendors did not submit information, such as Sprint and some of the traditional Regional Bell Operating Companies (RBOCs), and thus publicly available information was used in the tables below.

19.3.2 Product Name and Switch Used

Table 19.1 shows the switch types used by each of the service providers surveyed. This survey indicates that NewBridge and Cascade hold the predominant share of service provider backbone switching equipment.

19.3.3 Service Availability

We requested the date that the service became commercially available. International service coverage and specifics were also requested. Note that Sprint announced the first commercially available ATM service in the United States. Also note that MCI announced deployment of the first national OC3 backbone ATM network in September 1994. MCI turned up the NSF's very high-speed Backbone Network Service (vBNS) in April 1995. In October 1997 MCI announced its new family of SONET networkMCI broadband connections, offering DS3, STS-1, OC-3, and OC-3c. AT&T is one of the largest carriers, with more than 500 T1.5 and more than 300 T3 Points of Presence (PoPs) nationwide.

Table 19.1 Matrix Depicting Service Provider Usage of Switch Platforms

Switch Used in Service	Ameritech	AT&T	Bell Atlantic	Bell South	GTE	MCI	PacTel	SBC	Sprint	TCG	US West	WorldCom
AT&T GlobeView 2000	BB				BB							
Cascade CBX 500		AF	BB	BB	BB							
Cisco 7000, 1010	ED									ED		BB
FORE ASX-1000, ASX-200BX										BB		
Fujitsu Fetex 150				BB	BB							
GDC APEX NPX						ED						
Lucent Technologies GlobeView(TM)		BB										
NEC Model 20									BB			
NewBridge 36150, 36170	ED			BB	BB	BB	BB	BB			BB	
NorTel Vector									ED			
StrataCom BPX	ED											BB

19.3.4 ATM Forum UNI Support

The service should support the UNI as defined by the ATM Forum Version 3.0 and 3.1, or another standard.

COMSAT World Services — Note that satellite ATM service operates at the transport level, and thus does not implement traffic management features. All ATM traffic can be supported.

19.3.5 ATM Service Categories Supported

What ATM service categories does the service provider support? These include Constant Bit Rate (CBR), real-time Variable Bit Rate (rt-VBR), non-real-time Variable Bit Rate (nrt-VBR), Unspecified Bit Rate (UBR), and ABR. See Chapter 6 for definitions of these service categories.

CBR service operates on only the peak rate, whereas VBR service adds a Sustainable Cell Rate (SCR) traffic parameter. ABR service requires the CPE to adjust its transmission rate based on the congestion feedback received from the network provider. UBR offers the lowest class of service — similar to flying standby at the airport.

19.3.6 Congestion Control

Providers were requested to explain their method of congestion control. These are the responses we received.

AT&T — ReliaBURST is available on the frame relay and ATM services. The ReliaBURST feature gives your applications the capability to reliably burst traffic into the network at sustained rates higher than your PVC's or SVC's committed information rates, up to the peak cell rate. This capability can give you:

- Higher throughputs and more efficient bandwidth utilization
- Truly committed minimum throughput levels (CIRs)
- A fair share of excess network capacity
- Lower costs, using lower committed bandwidths

The ReliaBURST feature consists of two parts: (1) a feedback mechanism that determines the state of congestion of the network, and (2) a method of changing the amount and rate of traffic that is admitted to the network in response to the changing state of the network. The feedback mechanism is internal to the AT&T ATM service network and works on a port-to-port basis.

ReliaBURST works by tracking network status indicators and reporting this information back to the sending port. The status information is used at the source port to determine whether to increase or decrease the rate of transmission of extra cells for that particular virtual circuit. ReliaBURST allocates additional bandwidth to virtual circuits (either virtual paths or virtual channels) above and beyond the CIR for that circuit, for Connection-Oriented Data (COD) virtual circuits. The amount of excess bandwidth is determined by a feedback mechanism that probes the network periodically. This allows for extended bursts to be transmitted equitably and reliably when excess bandwidth is available, while maintaining customers' CIR during times of heavy overall network usage.

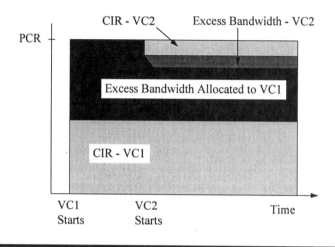

Figure 19.2 AT&T's ReliaBURST Congestion Control

An example of how ReliaBURST adjusts bandwidth is shown in Figure 19.2. Let's assume that two users are getting ready to send traffic onto the network. User 1 has a CIR of 20 Mbps, which we'll call VC1, and User 2 has a CIR of 4 Mbps on VC2. Further, as VC1 starts, we will assume there is no traffic on the network. Therefore, it not only receives its CIR, but can also burst up to the full Peak Cell Rate (PCR) available on that port. As VC2 starts, the value of the CIR of VC2 is taken from the excess bandwidth above VC1's CIR. Then, a proportional share of the excess bandwidth is allocated to VC2. This is shown by the ramping after VC2 starts. VC1 and VC2 then each receive a proportional share of the excess bandwidth, in this case 20:4 or 5:1.

Additionally, ReliaBURST does not affect a customer's conforming user traffic and is designed to prevent the increased traffic loss rates that are possible when using open-loop bursting systems.

COMSAT World Services — Several mechanisms are implemented. For example, the service allows for guaranteed bandwidth for CBR services. The satellite interface also acts as a virtual source, virtual destination in that it has the ability to generate RM cells for congestion notification.

WorldCom — Congestion control is maintained through a policing action referred to by the ATM Forum as Usage Parameter Control (UPC). The UPC algorithm used by WorldCom adheres to the GCRA (Generic Cell Rate Algorithm), otherwise known as the double-leaky-bucket algorithm, defined by the ATM Forum. Six important traffic control functions are used to maintain network performance. They are: UPC, Connection Administration Control (CAC), Network Resource Management, Traffic Shaping, Explicit Forward Congestion Indication (EFCI), and Selective Cell Discarding. WorldCom allows CBR cells to be served first, VBR cells next, and ABR cells last.

19.3.7 PVC VPC and VCC Service

ATM services should support VPCs and VCCs for PVCs.

19.3.8 SVC Service

ATM service should support SVCs. SVCs can help reduce costs and provide additional provisioning and administration flexibility for large networks. But SVCs cause a huge burden on the provider from a provisioning, accounting, and billing perspective.

SVCs allow users to connect end ATM stations "on the fly," rather than having to preprovision PVCs. This enables users to establish temporary high-speed links to other sites. SVCs use signaling in each cell to establish calls "on demand." Benefits of SVCs include:

- Flexibility — They give the ability to add devices to the network more quickly than with the PVC provisioning process.
- Scalability — PVCs need $n(n-1)/2$ PVCs to have every end talk to every other end. SVCs can be set up and taken down on demand. Good for large numbers of users or high volumes of traffic.
- Ease of use
- Quality of Service (QoS) granularity — Use of SVCs for different application requirements offers greater granularity to QoS.
- Ease of network management — SVCs simplify network administration by eliminating the manual update requirement inherent in maintaining PVCs.
- Lower Cost — SVCs have a lower cost than PVCs if billing is usage-based and the call volumes and duration are low (there is a breakeven point where PVCs would be less expensive).
- Redundancy — SVCs can be used to reroute traffic dynamically around a failed PVC link.

There are a few drawbacks to SVCs. Vendors may support the SVC standards, but SVCs that span multivendor environments may not work as planned. Many vendors have yet to prove cross-platform interoperability. Ask your vendor for details. SVCs will also provide a better method of enabling FR to ATM service interworking.

19.3.9 FR/ATM Service Interworking

ATM services should provide for frame relay–to–ATM service interworking. Thus, corporations can use frame relay as the feeder technology at their many remote sites and ATM at the headquarters site.

19.3.10 Access to SMDS

Does the service provide user access to SMDS services?

19.3.11 Access to Internet

Does the service provide user access to Internet services? As many carriers turn into Internet service providers, Internet access from the ATM service is more likely to be available.

19.3.12 LAN Connectivity

Does the service support native LAN connectivity?

19.3.13 Voice over ATM

Does the service support voice over ATM?

19.3.14 Pricing Method and Strategy

We asked respondents whether they supported a flat rate or usage pricing method. We also asked them to elaborate on their pricing strategy. We purposefully left pricing out of the study, as most is either tariff-based or individual pricing per customer. More detail on pricing structures and a few examples can be found later in this chapter. Some vendors had additional information as provided below. Note that with greater proliferation of ATM services, the increase in price competition should lower user rates.

AT&T — AT&T offers pricing in either a customized quote or flat rate based on port speed and PVC CIR. All pricing is publicly available.

COMSAT — The service is offered as an enhancement to COMSAT's existing carrier lease-based space segment offerings. To make our typical services ATM-ready, the ATM enhancement service places ATM satellite interfaces on both ends of the satellite link. These interfaces can be leased to the customer on a monthly basis, or alternatively, the interfaces can be purchased outright by a user. The monthly lease cost for an ATM satellite interface is approximately $300 to $400 per month. Unit costs for interfaces purchased outright are between $7K and $10K, depending on quality.

MCI — Monthly recurring port charge is based on port speed and type selected (DS1, DS3, OC3). PVCs are priced per service class and SCR selected.

Teleport — Pricing varies by region of country. Pricing components include port charges, logical channels, CIR, and mileage.

WorldCom — VPC service and VCC service for CBR, VBR, and ABR are billed at a flat rate. Usage-sensitive billing with the offering of SVC services should be available by time of publishing.

19.3.15 Customer Premises Equipment (CPE)

Here we asked for the type of CPE provided with the service, and CPE certified for use with the provider's network. Some service providers offer specific CPE with their service. Bundling of CPE with the service was also available.

AT&T provides a CPE compatibility testing program for vendor's ATM CPE. If your CPE has not yet been tested with the ATM Service, we will work with you and your equipment vendor to have it tested for compatibility with ATM Service.

19.3.16 Customer Network Management

Some providers offer a customer network management options. We asked what network management features and services are available to the end user.

AT&T's ATM Service also offers Customer Network Management Options. Customer Network Management Options allow you to monitor and manage your ATM network. Reports track network loading, performance (including discards), and configuration. These reports are a necessary adjunct for a network manager to manage capacity, design, engineer, track, and plan networks.

Through an industry standard interface (SNMP), you have the ability to directly monitor your network status and obtain network performance on a continuous basis, or receive long-term reports. Real-time status and alarm information, as well as access to near-real-time performance and configuration data, is provided through SNMP Access. Longer-term reports that offer a trended analysis over a period of time are provided through Customer Network Management Advanced Reports.

With a Network Management SNMP interface, you have the ability to monitor the network status directly and obtain network performance information on a continuous basis. This includes real-time status and alarm notification as well as access to real-time performance and configuration data. This system allows for seamless management of both ATM and frame relay services from an SNMP platform.

Information is available on a demand basis. You can establish a session through your SNMP workstation to the Network Management Server, and request information on the Management Information Base (MIB) modules of interest. The server will then interrogate the particular ATM switch registers for your PVCs and return those register readings to you.

Advanced Reports let you evaluate your usage and modify your network configurations to take maximum advantage of your ATM network. These reports show utilization patterns on ports and circuits over time. You can then modify your network parameters to optimize the network. AT&T will assist in interpreting reports when necessary. Advanced Reports are updated on a weekly basis. Access to Advanced Reports is the same as it is for SNMP (access requires a minimum 32-kbps PVC).

Worldcom — Customer network management for WorldCom's ATM services will be available by publish time. It will be similar in concept to the Frame/Private Line Web-based tool announced at Fall Interop 1996. Customers will be allowed to view near-real-time statistics from a server. Statistics will be historical, less than 15 minutes old.

19.3.17 Referenced and Announced Customers

We asked respondents to cite some network examples from their referenced or announced customers. Some of these were included in our case studies in Chapter 23.

19.3.18 Differentiating Features

We also asked for some of their differentiating features. Some of the more notable ones are included below. Vendors were requested to provide a narrative.

COMSAT — Cost-effective, global reach, meets stringent ITU Recommendation I.356 performance objectives for Class 1 ATM service, data compression feature for greater efficiency.

MCI
- OC3, fully redundant backbone, currently being upgraded to OC12.
- Stable, mature switching platform
- Highly experienced operations staff
- Aggressive pricing
- Free interoperability testing for customer applications and CPE in lab
- ATM service to UK and Canada

Teleport — The most complete line of data services available from any local exchange carrier in the United States. The same services are available in every TCG market, coast to coast.

WorldCom — In order to remain a preferred vendor of ATM services, WorldCom follows a strict set of policies which ensure that the customer's applications are served properly, and that the customer's CPE has been tested, certified, and properly configured for optimum performance. WorldCom maintains the ATM network backbone in a superior manner in order to ensure the automatic availability of reroute bandwidth in the event of route failure. With WorldCom, reliability and customer service are essential.

19.3.19 ATM Interfaces Supported By Service

ATM UNI physical interfaces supported by these services include:

ATM UNI Interfaces	Non-ATM Interfaces
nxDS1 IMA	Ethernet
DS3	100-Mbps Ethernet
OC3	FDDI
OC12	4-Mbps Token Ring
OC48	16-Mbps Token Ring
Cell-based clear-channel TC	FR nxDS0
E1	FR DS1
E3	FR >DS1
E4	SMDS DS1
STM-1	SMDS DS3
STM-4	SMDS DXI nxDS0
J1	SMDS DXI DS1
J2 (6.312 Mbps)	HDLC V.35
25-Mbps UTP	HDLC HSSI
51.84-Mbps UTP	
155-Mbps UTP	
155-Mbps MMF	

Table 19.2 presents the results of the service provider survey of ATM services.

Table 19.2 Comparison of ATM Service Providers

Name of Service Provider	Ameritech	AT&T	Bell Atlantic	Bell South	COMSAT World Systems
Address	n/a	295 North Maple Ave. Basking Ridge, NJ 07920	n/a	n/a	6560 Rock Springs Drive, Bethesda, MD 20817
Web Page	n/a		bell-atl.com	n/a	comsat.com
Annual Sales					
1994	n/a	not disclosed	n/a	n/a	$827M
1995	n/a	not disclosed	n/a	n/a	$852M
1996	n/a	not disclosed	n/a	n/a	TBD
Date ATM Service Launched	1994	May-94	1996	Jun-95	Feb-97
Number of Customers	n/a	not disclosed	45+	n/a	10
Number of ATM Ports Sold	n/a	not disclosed	n/a	n/a	n/a
One paragraph on Company Strengths	n/a	*	n/a	n/a	*

Table 19.2 Comparison of ATM Service Providers (Continued)

Name of Service Provider	Ameritech	AT&T	Bell Atlantic	Bell South	COMSAT World Systems
Service Name	Advanced Data Services	ATM Service	Cell Relay Service	Broadband ATM Service	Satellite ATM Enhancement Service
Switch(es) Used	AT&T GlobeView 2000 backbone; Stratacom BPX, NewBridge 36150, Cisco 7000 Edge	Lucent Technologies GlobeView (TM), Cascade (ATM-FR interworking)	Cascade 500 Model 20	Fujitsu Fetex 150, Cascade 500, NewBridge 36170	Satellite
Service Availability	7+ cities in region	All DS1 & DS3 PoPs	3+ cities in PA	Tennessee	Feb-97
International Service	No	Trials - see chapter	No	No	Everywhere
ATM Forum UNI Support					
3.0	Yes	Y	Y	Y	Y*
3.1	Yes	Y	Y	Y	Y
ATM Service Categories Supported					
CBR	Y	Y	◄	Y	Y
rt-VBR	Y			Y	Y
nrt-VBR	Y	Y	Y	Y	Y
UBR		Y		Y	Y
ABR		Y		Y	Y
Congestion Control	overengineered	*	CAC		*
PVC VPC Service	Y	Y	Y	Y	n/a
PVC VCC Service	Y	Y	Y	Y	n/a
SVC Service	1997	Y		2H97	98
FR/ATM Service Interworking	Yes	Y		Y	4Q97
Access to SMDS		n/a			4Q98
Access to Internet	Yes	y		Y	4Q97
LAN Connectivity		n/a			Y

Table 19.2 Comparison of ATM Service Providers (Continued)

Service Support	Ameritech	AT&T	Bell Atlantic	Bell South	COMSAT World Systems
Pricing Method (Flat or Usage)					
Flat Rate	Now	for PVC	Y	Y	Y
Usage		for SVC			
Pricing Strategy	n/a	*	tariff and individual contracts	tariff and individual contracts	tariff and individual contracts *
CPE Provided with Service	Yes	*	Y	Y	Y
CPE Certified for Use with Network	FORE, NewBridge, Cisco	*	FORE		GlobeView, FORE, Cascade, GDC, others
Customer Network Management	No	*	n/a		console or IP-based, SNMP-based soon
Reference/Announced Customers	Amoco, Argonner National Lab	ComDisco, Dept of Defense, Prudential, Unisys	Commonwealth of Pennsylvania, Virginia Tech, US Government Agencies	Sate of North Carolina, MCNC, US Department of Energy	n/a
Differentiating Features	n/a	*	n/a	n/a	*

Table 19.2 Comparison of ATM Service Providers (Continued)

ATM UNI Interfaces	Ameritech	AT&T	Bell Atlantic	Bell South	COMSAT World Systems
DS1	Y	Y	Y	Y	Y
nxDS1 IMA					
DS3	Y	Y	Y	Y	Y
OC3	Y	Y	Y	Y	
OC12	Y				
OC48					
Cell Based Clear Chan TC					
E1					Y
E3					Y
E4					
STM-1					
STM-4					
J1					
J2 (6.312 Mb/s)					
25 Mb/s UTP					
51.84 Mb/s UTP					
155 Mb/s UTP				Y	
155 Mb/s MMF				Y	
Non-ATM Interfaces					
Ethernet	Y			Y	
100 Mb/s Ethernet				Y	
FDDI	Y			Y	
4 Mb/s Token Ring	Y			Y	
16 Mb/s Token Ring	Y			Y	
Frame Relay nxDS0		Y			
Frame Relay DS1		Y			
Frame Relay >DS1					
SMDS DS1					
SMDS DS3					
SMDS DXI nxDS0					
SMDS DXI DS1					
HDLC V.35					Y
HDLC HSSI		Y			
Circuit Emulation					

* = See Chapter for Details

Table 19.2 Comparison of ATM Service Providers (Continued)

Name of Service Provider	GTE	MCI Telecommunications Inc.	Pacific Bell	SBC
Address	n/a	901 International Parkway, Richardson, TX 75081	n/a	n/a
Web Page	gte.com	mci.com	pacbell.com	n/a
Annual Sales				
1994	n/a	n/a	n/a	n/a
1995	n/a	n/a	n/a	n/a
1996	n/a	n/a	n/a	n/a
Date ATM Service Launched		Nov-95	Oct-96	Jul-97
Number of Customers		30	60+	2+
Number of ATM Ports Sold		120		n/a
One paragraph on Company Strengths		See corporate report.		n/a

Table 19.2 Comparison of ATM Service Providers (Continued)

Service Information	GTE	MCI Telecommunications Inc.	Pacific Bell	SBC
Service Name	ATM Service	HyperStream ATM Service (HSATM)	FasTrak ATM Cell Relay Services	ATM Cell Relay Service
Switch(es) Used	ATM GlobeView 2000, Fujitsu Fetex 150, Cascade 500, NewBridge 361X0	GDC Apex NPX , Newbridge 36170	NewBridge 36170	NewBridge 361X0
Service Availability	Nationwide	490 PoPs nationwide	5 LATAs in CA	Jul-96
International Service	No	UK, Canada	No	No
ATM Forum UNI Support				
3.0	Y	Y	Y	
3.1	Y	No	Y	Y
ATM Service Classes Supported				
CBR	Y	Y	Y	Y
rt-VBR			Y	Y
nrt-VBR	Y	Y	Y	
UBR	Y	Y	Y	Y
ABR			98	
Congestion Control		UPC based on dual leaky bucket algorithms, selective cell discard (CLP=1), EFCI closed loop	based on SCR/PCR contract	None
PVC VPC Service	Y	Y	Y	Y
PVC VCC Service	Y	Y	Y	Y
SVC Service	No	1998	98	1Q98
FR/ATM Service Interworking	Y	Now	97	97
Access to SMDS		1997		
Access to Internet	97	1997	97	No
LAN Connectivity		n/a		trial
Voice over ATM	No	1998	No	

Table 19.2 Comparison of ATM Service Providers (Continued)

Service Support	GTE	MCI Telecommunications Inc.	Pacific Bell	SBC
Pricing Method (Flat or Usage)				
Flat Rate	Y	Y	Y	Y
Usage		End 1997		
Pricing Strategy		*	tariff and individual contracts	All ICBs
CPE Provided with Service	Y	available for lease	Y	Y
CPE Certified for Use with Network	n/a	no equipment certified, but various vendors tested for interoperability		n/a
Customer Network Management	Y	provided under HyperScope offering 6/97	97	No
Reference/Announced Customers	UCLA, Texas Instruments, University of Hawaii, State of NC, State of VA	National Science Foundation (NSF), US Navy, NetCom	ARIES, Northrop-Grumman, Tandem Computers, USC	Texas Instruments
Differentiating Features	n/a	*	n/a	

Table 19.2 Comparison of ATM Service Providers (Continued)

ATM UNI Interfaces	GTE	MCI Telecommunications Inc.	Pacific Bell	SBC
DS1		Y	Y	97
nxDS1 IMA		2Q97		
DS3	Y	Y	Y	Y
OC3	Y	Y	Y	Y
OC12	97	3Q97	97	
OC48				
Cell Based Clear Chan TC				
E1		Y (UK too)		
E3		Y (UK too)		
E4				
STM-1		Y (UK too)		
STM-4				
J1				
J2 (6.312 Mb/s)				
25 Mb/s UTP				
51.84 Mb/s UTP				
155 Mb/s UTP				
155 Mb/s MMF				
Non-ATM Interfaces				
Ethernet		ICB		
100 Mb/s Ethernet				
FDDI		ICB		
4 Mb/s Token Ring				
16 Mb/s Token Ring				
Frame Relay nxDS0		Y		
Frame Relay DS1		Y		
Frame Relay >DS1		2Q97		
SMDS DS1		3Q97		
SMDS DS3		3Q97		
SMDS DXI nxDS0		3Q97		
SMDS DXI DS1		3Q97		
HDLC V.35				
HDLC HSSI		ICB		
Circuit Emulation				

Table 19.2 Comparison of ATM Service Providers (Continued)

Name of Service Provider	Teleport Communications Group	US West	WorldCom, Inc.
Address	1 Teleport Drive, Staten Island, NY 10311	n/a	One Williams Center, Tulsa, OK 74172
Web Page	tcg.com	n/a	wcom.com
Annual Sales			
1994	n/a	n/a	$230K
1995	n/a	n/a	$1.2M
1996	n/a	n/a	$9M
Date ATM Service Launched	Dec-95	Jan-95	Aug-93
Number of Customers	120	15+	31
Number of ATM Ports Sold	500	n/a	200+
One paragraph on Company Strengths	*	n/a	*

Table 19.2 Comparison of ATM Service Providers (Continued)

Service Information	Teleport Communications Group	US West	WorldCom, Inc.
Service Name	OmniLAN Transparent LAN Service, OmniStream User-Network Interface Service	ATM Cell Relay Service	ATM Services, Data Broadband Concourse
Switch(es) Used	Core: Fore ASX 1000, Fore 200 BX, Cisco 1010; CPE: NetEdge ATM Connect, Cisco 4700, Cisco 7000	NewBridge 36170	cisco/StrataCom BPX
Service Availability	57 Major Markets. 28 of the 30 largest	entire US West region	Lower 48 States
International Service	None	No	U.K., France, Germany
ATM Forum UNI Support			
3.0	Y		
3.1	Y	Y	Y
ATM Service Classes Supported			
CBR	Y	Y	Y
rt-VBR	TBD		Y
nrt-VBR	TBD	Y	Y
UBR	No	1997	4Q97
ABR	Y	No	Y
Congestion Control	available in 1997	police on ingress	*
PVC VPC Service	Y	Y	Y
PVC VCC Service	Y	Y	Y
SVC Service	available in 1997	No	available in 1997
FR/ATM Service Interworking	No plans, possible 1998.	1997	Y
Access to SMDS	No plans. Strategic decision not to support SMDS		
Access to Internet	Yes. Acquired CERFnet in 1997		1997
LAN Connectivity	Yes. Via TDM in 1994. Via ATM in 1995.		Now
Voice over ATM	Plans depend on ATM Forum. Expected in 1997.		1997

Table 19.2 Comparison of ATM Service Providers (Continued)

Service Support	Teleport Communications Group	US West	WorldCom, Inc.
Pricing Method (Flat or Usage)			
Flat Rate	Now	Y	Now
Usage	Not planned		3Q97
Pricing Strategy	*	tariff	*
CPE Provided with Service	NetEdge ATM Connect, Cisco 4700, Cisco 7000	Y	None
CPE Certified for Use with Network	All ATM Forum compliant	Bay, 3Com, Cisco, Kentrox	Cisco 7000 & 7500, Newbridge 36150, LightStream 2020, Stratcom BPX & IGX, Nortel Passport, Fore ASX 200.
Customer Network Management	Limited. To be expanded first half of 1997	No	
Reference/Announced Customers	ARIES Project, American Petroleum Institute, Staten Island University Hospital, Dallas Community College District	n/a	Tandem Computers, Sun Microsystems, NetCom, AGIS, Motorola, and GoodNet.
Differentiating Features	*	n/a	*

Table 19.2 Comparison of ATM Service Providers (Continued)

ATM UNI Interfaces	Teleport Communications Group	US West	WorldCom, Inc.
DS1	2Q 97	Y	2Q97
nxDS1 IMA			2Q97
DS3	Yes	Y	Now
OC3	Yes	Y	3Q97
OC12			1Q98
OC48			3Q99
Cell Based Clear Chan TC			4Q97
E1			2Q97
E3			Now
E4			3Q93
STM-1			3Q97
STM-4			1Q98
J1			3Q97
J2 (6.312 Mb/s)			3Q97
25 Mb/s UTP			
51.84 Mb/s UTP			
155 Mb/s UTP			
155 Mb/s MMF			
Non-ATM Interfaces			
Ethernet	Yes		2Q97
100 Mb/s Ethernet	Yes		4Q97
FDDI	Yes		2Q97
4 Mb/s Token Ring	ICB (no demand)		2Q97
16 Mb/s Token Ring	Yes		2Q97
Frame Relay nxDS0			Now
Frame Relay DS1	Yes		Now
Frame Relay >DS1			Now
SMDS DS1			
SMDS DS3			
SMDS DXI nxDS0			
SMDS DXI DS1			
HDLC V.35			2Q97
HDLC HSSI	ICB only		2Q97

19.4 ATM SERVICE PRICING STRUCTURES

ATM services may have any or all of the following charge elements.

- Installation charge (nonrecurring/one-time) —typically for access port, Virtual Channels and Virtual Paths (VCs and VPs), and equipment (if purchasing or leasing new equipment).
- Monthly service charge (recurring/monthly) — again, per UNI port, VC/VP, and equipment if new and depreciated. Based on physical access port speed, bandwidth used, class of service. Frequently, this charge is distance-sensitive.
- Variable usage charge (recurring/monthly) — typically in units of megacells per VC/VP. Can be based on time of day, connection duration, total frames sent, or total cells received
- Implementation fee (nonrecurring/one-time) — sometimes a provider will charge an additional implementation fee regardless of whether new ports or equipment is purchased.
- SCR, PCR (variable pricing schemes) — some providers charge by sustainable cell rate and peak cell rate increments for VBR and CBR service. This pricing takes the form of cost per 1-Mbps increment per month. This pricing scheme is similar to what is found in frame relay with CIR, where users pay for a specific CIR rate, yet can burst above it but not expect guaranteed delivery.
- SVC pricing is based on a unit of usage charge — such as cents per minute.

ATM tariffs are based primarily on the standard service categories: CBR, rt-VBR, nrt-VBR, UBR, and ABR.

Future tariffs may become more granular, focusing on traffic contract parameters such as PCR, SCR, MBS, and CDVT. This would provide the savvy user much greater capability to match traffic types with pricing schemes that would offer a greater granularity to cost savings.

19.4.1 LEC/RBOC/CAP Pricing

Most LEC pricing is filed under a tariff. One example is Pacific Bell's ATM service. The service is available at two speeds — 45 Mbps and 155 Mbps. Rates for 45-Mbps access are $5,000 for installation and $4,850 per month. Rates for 155-Mbps access are $8,500 for installation and $7,899 per month. There are no usage or mileage charges. Bell Atlantic offers DS1 ATM service for as little as $400 per month.

19.4.2 Carrier/ISP Pricing

Carrier and ISP pricing also varies greatly based on the parameters defined above. As an example, Table 19.3 shows AT&T's InterSpan ATM rates.

Table 19.3 AT&T ATM Pricing

(CLASS C) ATM PVC CIR	Two-Way PVC Monthly Charge	(CLASS A) ATM PVC CIR	ATM PVC MonthlyCharge	VBR ATM SVC CIR	ATM SVC Charge Per Miniute	CBR ATM SVC CIR	ATM SVC Charge Per Min
4	$17	56 Kbps	$173	4	$0.006	4	$0.012
8	$21	64 Kbps	$173	8	$0.008	8	$0.016
16	$30	128 Kbps	$386	16	$0.012	16	$0.023
32	$58	192 Kbps	$583	32	$0.021	32	$0.035
48	$85	256 Kbps	$780	48	$0.031	48	$0.05
56/64	$99	320 Kbps	$969	56/64	$0.035	56/64	$0.06
128	$225	384 Kbps	$1,166	128	$0.081	128	$0.14
192	$338	448 Kbps	$1,473	192	$0.13	192	$0.22
256	$450	512 Kbps	$1,748	256	$0.16	256	$0.29
320	$563	576 Kbps	$1,993	320	$0.21	320	$0.36
384	$675	640 Kbps	$2,229	384	$0.24	384	$0.43
448	$854	704 Kbps	$2,473	448	$0.31	448	$0.54
512	$1,012	768 Kbps	$2,717	512	$0.37	512	$0.64
576	$1,153	832kbps	$3,023	576	$0.43	576	$0.72
640	$1,290	896kbps	$3,327	640	$0.47	640	$0.82
704	$1,430	960kbps	$3,633	704	$0.52	704	$0.91
768	$1,575	1024kbps	$3,785	768	$0.58	768	$0.99
832	$1,723	1.5 Mbps	$4,313	832	$0.63	832	$1.10
896	$1,872	2 Mbps	$4,888	896	$0.68	896	$1.22
960	$2,025	3.1 Mbps	$5,865	960	$0.74	960	$1.32
1024	$2,175	4.1 Mbps	$7,038	1024	$0.79	1024	$1.38
1536	$2,415	4.6 Mbps	$7,935	1536	N/A	1536	$1.44
2048	$2,625	5.1 Mbps	$8,798	2048	$1.09	2048	$1.85
3.1 Mbps	$3,450	6.1 Mbps	$10,557	3.1 Mbps	$1.69	3.1 Mbps	$2.88
4.1 Mbps	$4,140	6.2 Mbps	$10,695	4.1 Mbps	$2.76	4.1 Mbps	$4.69
5.1 Mbps	$5,175	7.2 Mbps	$12,317				
6.1 Mbps	$6,210	7.7 Mbps	$13,283	4.6 Mbps	N/A	4.6 Mbps	$5.51
7.2 Mbps	$7,245	8.2 Mbps	$14,076	5.1 Mbps	$3.92	5.1 Mbps	$6.67
8.2 Mbps	$8,280	9.2 Mbps	$15,836	6.1 Mbps	$5.18	6.1 Mbps	$8.80
9.2 Mbps	$9,315	10.2 Mbps	$17,595	6.2 Mbps	N/A	6.2 Mbps	$8.91
10.2 Mbps	$10,350	10.8 Mbps	$18,630	7.2 Mbps	$7.11	7.2 Mbps	$12.08
11.3 Mbps	$11,385			7.7 Mbps	N/A	7.7 Mbps	$13.83
12.3 Mbps	$12,420			8.2 Mbps	$8.63	8.2 Mbps	$14.66
13.3 Mbps	$13,455			9.2 Mbps	$9.71	9.2 Mbps	$16.49
14.3 Mbps	$14,490			10.2 Mbps	$11.50	10.2 Mbps	$19.55
15.4 Mbps	$15,525			10.8 Mbps	N/A	10.8 Mbps	$20.70
16.4 Mbps	$16,560						

(CLASS C) ATM PVC CIR	Two-Way PVC Monthly Charge		
17.4 Mbps	$17,595		
18.4 Mbps	$18,630	DS3 Port	$12,650
19.5 Mbps	$19,665	DS1 Port	$2,415
20.5 Mbps	$20,700		
21.5 Mbps	$21,735	SVC UBR (2way)	
22.5 Mbps	$22,770	Per Minute	$0.035
23.6 Mbps	$23,805	Per MegaCell	$3.57
24.6 Mbps	$24,840		
25.6 Mbps	$25,875		
26.6 Mbps	$26,910		
27.6 Mbps	$27,945		
28.7 Mbps	$28,980		
29.7 Mbps	$30,015		
30.7 Mbps	$31,050		
31.7 Mbps	$32,085		
32.8 Mbps	$33,120		
33.8 Mbps	$34,155		
34.8 Mbps	$35,190		
35.8 Mbps	$36,225		

19.4.3 SVC Pricing

SVCs have recently appeared on the scene, and pricing schemes vary greatly. One example is AT&T's InterSpan service, which offers pricing from 1 cent to $18 per minute depending on interface speed [6].

19.5 INTEROPERABILITY BETWEEN SERVICES

As of publication date there existed little or no interoperability between service providers' ATM networks. This service capability also does not exist for more simplistic services like frame relay, a sign that ATM service interworking may not occur until SVC services become ubiquitous.

19.6 REVIEW

This chapter introduced the basic environment of service provider ATM networks and some of the challenges facing them. This chapter reviewed the leading North American ATM service offerings along with specific details on a number of the carriers. Pricing structures were included as a means of education, but the user should check with each vendor for current pricing. Design recommendations based on the features and capabilities found in this chapter will be used later in Chapter 22.

19.7 REFERENCES

[1]   ATM Report newsletters, Broadband Publishing Corporation, Rockville, MD 20852. Circa 1996.

[2]   The ATM Report, *Inside: The ATM Report Guide to ATM Public Services — Part One*, Broadband Publishing Corporation, November 29, 1996.

[3]   The ATM Report, *Inside: The ATM Report Guide to ATM Public Services — Part Two*, Broadband Publishing Corporation, December 31, 1996.

[4]   "ATM Service Providers," *Broadband Networking News*, May 13, 1997.

[5]   K. Hodges and J. Hamer, "Carrier Implementation of ATM Services," *Telecommunications,* April 1995.

[6]   J. Wexler, "ATM Makes Strides," *InfoWorld*, February 10, 1997.

20

Global Service Providers

This chapter reviews the status of ATM service providers around the globe. While many U.S. ATM providers offer international ATM services, there are also regional and nationally owned entities that offer ATM services. This chapter provides a thorough review of most international ATM service providers, and concludes with a study of ATM over satellite.

20.1 INTERNATIONAL ATM SERVICE PROVIDERS

There are many examples of international ATM services. This section covers the global alliances and international trial activities. Subsequent sections will cover European, Pacific Rim service providers.

20.1.1 Global Alliances

The three main competing global alliances include:

- Global One
- Concert
- WorldSource

In 1995 Sprint, Deutsche Bundespost, and France Telecom formed an international partnership named "Global One." Their objective was to compete against the BT and MCI "Concert" Alliance announced in 1992. Soon thereafter AT&T partnered with the PTTs of the Netherlands, Spain, Switzerland, Sweden, the UK, and Japan (KDD) to form the Unisource consortium, which is soon to be called WorldSource.

20.1.2 International Trails

Many international trials have been underway. The Pan European Trials encompassed over 15 countries and employed switching equipment from manufacturers such as Alcatel, Ericsson, and Siemens-Stromberg-Carlson. A follow-on effort, called Project JAMES (Joint ATM Market Evaluation Study), intends to test new ATM-based technology and move it into commercial services.

In May of 1996 Sprint announced an ATM test bed between the United States, France, Germany, and Canada. Efforts were coordinated between Sprint and its partners, Deutsche Telekom and France Telecom. Their objective was to implement a high-speed research network to be used both by government and commercial customers. Applications included collaborative research and testing across continents, as well as sharing of information between government and commercial entities on a global basis. The remaining G-7 countries -- Japan, Italy, and England -- are in discussions to join the test bed to make it the first comprehensive G-7 high-speed test-bed project.

Table 20.1 lists the leading European countries that are currently in ATM trials or in the process of introducing ATM services:

These efforts are detailed below by country as reported in the ATM Forum's Marketing and Awareness report.

Table 20.1 ATM Public Network Operator ATM Trials

Country	Public Network Operator	Efforts
Belgium	Belgacom	European ATM Pilot network participation
Denmark	Tele Danmark	ARAMIS (RACE II), Batman Project
Finland	Telecom Finland	World's first commercial ATM pilot
France	France Telecom	BREHAT Project, TRANSREL, IRLE network, RENATER research centers backbone, SOCRATE network, BETEL (RACE)
Germany	Deutsche Bundespost (DBP)	International B-ISDN services
Ireland	Telecom Eireann	European ATM Pilot network
Italy	Telecom Italia	Italian ATM Pilot project
Norway	Telenordia	Supernet, RACE, Eurescom, Pan-European network
Portugal	TLP and Telecom Portugal	RACE CATALYST, EXPLOIT, ISABEL, IBER, TEN-IBC project STEN, BINET, READA, BARCA
Span	Telefonica	RECIBA II, ISABEL
Sweden	Telia AB	Service trial, EXPANA, ARAMIS
Switzerland	Swiss Telecom PTT	European ATM Pilot
Netherlands	PTT Telecoms	Service trials
United Kingdom	BT	Service trials, SuperJANET

20.1.2.1 Belgium

The Belgian public network operator, Belgacom, is participating in the European ATM Pilot with 34 Mbps links to Paris, London, Cologne, and Amsterdam.

Customers can be connected in three ways:

* Access link transporting ATM at 34 Mbps PDH
* Access link transporting ATM at 155 Mbps SDH (available soon)
* 2 Mbps access link

Belgacom will support the following services over the ATM network: frame relay, structured and unstructured Constant Bit Rate (CBR) service, interconnection of Ethernet LANs, and interconnection of the MAN (Metropolitan Area Network) in Brussels.

20.1.2.2 Denmark

The international Tele Danmark cross-connect situated in Copenhagen serves as a national service node for the Copenhagen area (KTAS). The ATM cross-connect is connected to the western part of the country (Jydsk Telefon) via SDH transmission links. Tele Danmark is participating in two major projects:

* ARAMIS (RACE II): Airline Realtime Application for Maintenance Information Systems from Copenhagen airport to Arlanda airport in Stockholm, Sweden, via a 34 Mbps PDH link.
* Batman Project (collaboration between Tele Danmark and DTH): 155-Mbps STM-1 broadband services for LAN interconnect, switched access TV, and 2-Mbps isochronous and multimedia traffic.

20.1.2.3 Finland

Telecom Finland launched the world's first commercial ATM pilot in May of 1993, and now is one of the leading European service providers, competing with Helsinki Telecom.

20.1.2.4 France

France Telecom is participating in several projects:

* BREHAT Project (FT), an ATM Virtual Path (VP) cross-connect network between Lannion, Rennes, and Paris over 34-Mbps PDH links to transport R&D labs, industry, and medical applications.
* TRANSREL provides LAN interconnect; connectionless (CL) data service over ATM using CBDS; access speeds from 64 kbps to 34 Mbps; and gateways to lower-speed Transpac Service.

 * IRLE network offering CLNS and CONS; Internet Protocol (IP) service, SMDS/CBDS (over ATM and HDLC); and ATM VP service.
 * RENATER research centres backbone.
 * SOCRATE network (Ministry of Defense) offering PBX services, leased line emulation, N-ISDN (30B+D, 2B+D), X.25/X.75, VP service, and LAN interconnection.
 * BETEL: Broadband Exchange over Trans European Links (RACE project) for trans-border ATM to Lyon, Sophia, Antipolis, Geneva, and Lausanne.
 * EDID: Environment for Distributed and Integrated Design (RACE project) for distributed and collaborative CAD/CAM for the Aerospace industry.

20.1.2.5 Germany

Deutsche Bundespost (DBP) offering includes Broadband ISDN (B-ISDN) services: CONS, CLNS, voice, data, video, international B-ISDN dedicated circuits.

20.1.2.6 Ireland

Telecom Eireann participated in the European ATM Pilot network, and now offers ATM VP bearer service, SMDS/CBDS, and CBR for circuit emulation support.

20.1.2.7 Italy

The Italian ATM pilot project by Telecom Italia was the forerunner to ATM services. Italy also participated as an international gateway for the European Pilot in Rome. Services offered include ATM VP-based LAN and Local ATM (LATM) interconnection, CBDS/SMDS, frame relay, and CBR services.

20.1.2.8 Norway

Norway is working within several initiatives: Supernet, RACE, Eurescom, and Pan-European network, along with local ATM test beds.

20.1.2.9 Portugal

Portugal sports a national ATM network with international connectivity to the European ATM Pilot. Services include a virtual path service (ETSI specifications), CBDS/SMDS, and CBR circuit emulation at 2 Mbps. The participation of TLP and Telecom Portugal in ATM-related technical trials and projects includes:

 * RACE CATALYST and EXPLOIT (participation of CET, the R&D center of Telecom Portugal)
 * ISABEL and IBER projects ATM interconnection between Aveiro and Madrid [participation of CET and Telefonica (Spain)]
 * TEN-IBC project STEN, Scientific Trans-European Network, (CET and TLP) and BINET, Broadband Interconnection Network (CET)

* National projects READA (CET with national R&D and industry partners) and BARCA (Telecom Portugal and TLP with national R&D and university partners)

20.1.2.10 Spain

Telefonica has a test bed called RECIBA.II with ATM cross-points over 155-Mbps SDH and 2-Mbps PDH, using single mode optical fiber and coax, based on ETSI/ITU standards and leads the ISABEL project.

20.1.2.11 Sweden

Telia AB international offers national and international services supporting circuit emulation and frame relay. Related research initiatives include EXPANA, which is an experimental test bed mainly intended for resource management and signaling experiments. The ARAMIS test bed located in the Arlanda airport in Stockholm will be connected via the node in Gothenburg to the ARAMIS test site in the Copenhagen airport (Danmark).

20.1.2.12 Switzerland

Swiss Telecom PTT has an ATM virtual path network connected to the European ATM Pilot, cross-connecting Zurich, Berne, Geneva, and Lugano via 34-Mbps PDH and 155-Mbps SDH. Services include VP bearer service, CBR, SMDS/CBDS, and LAN bridging. The first phase involved R&D labs, universities, and selected industry participants.

20.1.2.13 The Netherlands

PTT Telecom national/international networks lead their European counter-parts. Bearer services include T1/E1 private circuits, LAN bridging, frame relay, and bandwidth on demand.

20.1.2.14 United Kingdom

Collaboration between BT and the UK academic community has led to an advanced broadband switching platform based on ATM and optical fiber network, with migration from data services to multiservice (i.e., JANET to SuperJANET).

20.2 European Networks

ATM awareness in Europe has increased drastically in the last few years, with a forecast for 20,000+ ATM connections in Europe by the year 2000. Many ATM services have rolled out since the publishing of an article [1] on a low awareness by the ATM Forum and later *53 Bytes* newsletter. The Netherlands and the UK have clearly led the ATM public services market, with Germany, Belgium, and Portugal lagging, possible due to their contin-ued usage of CBDS/SMDS for LAN interconnection.

The lead sectors for ATM adoption in Europe include education and entertainment — primarily for multimedia information retrieval and desktop videoconferencing — and printing and publishing. Health care, aerospace, automotive, travel, and transport are lesser targets, which is surprising given the level of automation and communications required in these industries to remain competitive.

20.2.1 European ATM Services Market

There are three key ATM markets in Europe, as shown in Table 20.2 [2].

The major differences in the ATM infrastructure market in the United States and in Europe are in the WAN infrastructure (not the LAN) and are caused by the differences in regulation and standards compliance.

20.2.2 European LAN Infrastructures

Will ATM have a major presence in European LANs? Probably not for some time. The legacy LAN product market in Europe is very similar to that in the United States, if not a few years behind. In fact, most LAN technologies developed in the United States make their way to Europe years later. The regulatory and standards environments are also similar in the LAN for both the United States and Europe.

20.2.3 European WAN Infrastructures

Table 20.3 provides a comparison of the U.S. and European ATM WAN markets. We compare key WAN players, tariffs, common speeds, status of voice and data integration, predominant low speed access protocol, and the cost of ATM WAN services between the United States and Europe [3, 4].

Table 20.2 ATM Service Markets in Europe

Market	Services	Providers	Degree of Regulation
Public network infrastructure	Residential broadband, leased line, WAN services (i.e., FR), public telephony, broadcast TV, CATV	U.S. Local Exchange Carriers (LECs), US Interexchange Carriers (IXCs), European Public Telephone Operators (PTOs), CATV providers	Heavy
LAN	Workstation, workgroup, adapters, campus, backbone products	Many diverse players	Low to none
WAN	Enterprise networks, leased lines, VPNs, FR and packet switching interworking	Small but growing number of service providers	Varies widely

Table 20.3 ATM Wide Area Network Market Comparison

	United States	Europe
Key players	IXCs, LECs	Value-Added Service providers (VAS), Public Network Operators (PNOs)
Tariffs	Leased lines cheaper	Leased lines expensive (4x U.S.)
Common speeds	DS1, DS3	64k, E1
Voice/data integration	Many networks integrated	Networks often separate, some VPNs
Predominant low-speed access protocol	Frame relay	X.25
Cost of ATM services	Very high	High

20.2.4 Standards Environment

U.S. ATM service providers comply with standards as set by the ITU-T and ATM Forum in the United States, whereas European service providers rely more on ITU-T and the European Telecommunications Standards Institute (ETSI).

20.2.5 Regulatory Environment

U.S. telecommunications services and network regulatory powers are centralized and standardized, being subject to regulation by the Federal Communications Commission (FCC) and the U.S. government. European services are regulated by the European Union (EU) and by individual governments. All states within the United States are under the centralized jurisdiction of the FCC, whereas in Europe jurisdiction is splintered between countries. Even within many European countries, different types of services can be provided. For example, EU telecommunications policy separates services provisions from infrastructure provisions in an attempt to encourage the establishment of competition.

In the late 1990s, data services in the United States were labeled as "enhanced services" to escape the requirement to standardize and publish tariff pricing. A similar phenomenon has happened in Europe, where full deregulation and thus limited restrictions have been placed on services labeled "Value-Added Data Services." Even cellular services have created their own loophole to be called "mobile telephony" and also become deregulated. Each nation is still required to issue a license to their suppliers in addition to the original monopoly PTTs. This has caused many national voice services to become deregulated and thus open to foreign competition from global alliances, such as BT/MCI Concert, Unisource, or Global One. Some countries, like the United Kingdom, Netherlands, France, and Germany, have swung fully toward deregulation. Others, like Spain, will soon be deregulated, and still others, like Ireland, Luxembourg, Spain, Portugal, and Greece, probably will not follow until the next decade. This massive deregulation movement has already had a major impact on the proliferation of ATM services throughout Europe. For more information, see references [5] and [6].

20.2.6 European ATM Service Providers

Table 20.4 lists the major European ATM network providers. The table provides their service name, corporate headquarters location, phone number, Internet address, city coverage, estimated number of customers, access speeds offered in Mbps, traffic service classes supported, and whether they support distance-sensitive pricing. More information can be found at www.data.com [7].

20.2.7 European Leaders

A few European service providers that have led ATM efforts in Europe are worthy of mention.

20.2.7.1 Telecom Finland

Telecom Finland Ltd. was the first public network operator to offer long-distance commercial ATM services outside the United States launched as Datanet ATM and other ATM-based LAN interconnect services in 1994. In fact, ATM service in Finland is cheaper than in the United States. The Finnish ATM service is one example of free and open competition where PTT monopolies that relied heavily on cross-subsidation once stood firm [8].

Table 20.4 Survey of European ATM Service Providers

	British Telecom	Deutsch Telekom	Energis	Finnet Group	France Telecom
Service name	Cellstream	T/NET ATM	Callconnect	LAN Link ATM	ATM Multiservice
Location	London, UK	Bonn, Germany	London, UK	Helsinki, Finland	Paris, France
Phone	+44-1473-293-622	+49-228-181-0	+44-171-206-55-55	+358-9-400-2320	+33-1-44-44-53-14
URL	bt.com	dtag.de	energis.co.uk	hpy.fi	francetelecom.fr
Coverage	UK nationwide, connections to U.S.	Germany: 19 cities	UK nationwide	Finland nationwide	France: 12 cities
Estimated # customers YE96	7	10	1	3+	20
Access speeds (Mbps)	34, 155	2, 34, 155	2, 4, 6, 8, 34, 155	34, 155, 622	2, 34, 155
Traffic Type					
ABR	N	N	Y	N	N
CBR	Y	Y	Y	Y	Y
VBR	Y	Y	Y	Y	N
UBR	N	N	Y	N	N
Dist-dependent pricing	Y	Y	N	Y	Y

Table 20.4 Survey of European ATM Service Providers (continued)

	Mercury	MFS/HCI	Swiss Telecom	Telecom Finland	Telecom Italia
Service name	Datalink ATM	MFS/HCI	Swiss WAN	Datanet ATM	ATMosfera
Location	London, UK	Vienna, VA	Bern, Switzerland	Helsinki, Finland	Rome, Italy
Phone	+44-1789-265-217	+1-703-287-2400	+41-31-338-1111	+358-2040-2964	+1670-080082
URL	mercury.co.uk	mfst.com	telecom.ch	tfi.net	telecomitalia.it
Coverage	UK nationwide	Frankfurt, London, Paris, Stockholm	Switzerland: 15 cities	Finland: 22 cities, Stockholm, Sweden	Italy: 16 cities
Estimated # customers YE96	0	10	?	28	30
Access speeds (Mbps)	2, 8, 34, 45, 155	2 to 155	2, 34	155	2 to 34
Traffic Type					
ABR	N	N	N	N	Y
CBR	N	N	Y	Y	Y
VBR	Y	Y	N	Y	Y
UBR	N	N	N	Y	N
Dist-dependent pricing	N	N	N	Y	Y

	Tele Danmark	Telefonica de Espana	Telenor	Telia	Telenordia
Service name	Nordicom ATM	Gigacom	Nordicom ATM	Telia City Services	Nordicom ATM Service
Location	Aarhus, Denmark	Madrid, Spain	Oslo, Norway	Stockhold, Sweden	Stockhold, Sweden
Phone	+45-89-47-3100	+34-1-589-764	+47-23-16-66-39	+46-8-707-6801	+46-85-87-87-0
URL	teledanmark.dk	telefonica.es	telenor.no	telia.se	telenordia.se
Coverage	Denmark: 12 cities, Finland, Norway, Sweden connections	Spain: 11 cities	Norway: 6 cities, Denmark, Sweden connections	Sweden: 25 cities, Norway: 5 cities	Sweden: 3 cities, Denmark, Norway connections
Estimated # customers YE96	2	12	5	100	10
Access speeds (Mbps)	2, 34	64k, 2, 34	34	2, 34, 155	34
Traffic Type					
ABR	N	N	N	N	N
CBR	Y	Y	Y	Y	Y
VBR	Y	N	Y	Y	Y
UBR	N	N	N	N	N
Dist-dependent pricing	Y	Y	Y	Y	Y

20.2.7.2 Nordicom

Nordicom, a consortium of Nordic countries' service operators Tele Danmark, Telenordia, and Telenor, and partners with BT/Concert, offered the first commercial, international ATM-based broadband network between operators in the world. This service competes with Telia/Unisource and GlobalOne.

20.2.8 Other European Network Initiatives

The TEN-34 Trans-Euro network is a trans-European network linking 16 national research networks in Europe via an IP-over-ATM network covering France, Germany, Switzerland, Netherlands, Spain, UK, and the Nordic countries. For more information, contact www.dante.net/ten-34.

20.2.9 Pricing

Pricing is the biggest decision factor in choosing ATM services in Europe. This is not surprising when one understands the inflated price of bandwidth in Europe compared with the United States. Pricing structures are similar to those in North America, with the exception of a reliance on geographic zones. Tariff rates are less public than in the United States. In general, the average price per month per Mbps worth of bandwidth is around $500, with Telecom Finland and Telia AB (Sweden) charging the lowest at about $300.

There are also several European development initiatives for commercial billing systems and pricing models for public ATM services that can be shared across multiple service providers. Two examples are the ACTS CA$HMAN project (www.isoft.intranet.gr/cashman) and the CAN-CAN project (www.teltec.dcu.ie/cancan).

20.2.10 Future European ATM Efforts

While ATM service providers plan to offer everything from voice, data, and video transport services to telephony services over the existing CATV infrastructure, one thing is clear — ATM has a very good chance of becoming the common transport infrastructure for Europe. ATM will coexist for some time with 34-Mbps PDH and 155-Mbps SDH transport services down to the lowly dial access and X.25 services. ATM will also play a key role in delivering broadband residential services.

20.3 PACIFIC RIM NETWORKS

A number of service providers have been performing trials with ATM. Recently, a number of carriers have announced commercial services, or international trials. Overall, the Pacific rim region has seen a heightened interest in ATM since 1996 [9]. We summarize some of the activities that have gone commercial in the following sections.

20.3.1 Australia

A large number of private ATM networks have been deployed. In 1996, NASA conducted an ATM-over-satellite trial between Pasadena, California, and Canberra, Australia. The trial supported voice, video, and two priorities of data traffic. Experts expect commercial services to be introduced in 1997.

20.3.2 Hong Kong Telecom

Hong Kong Telecom announced a broadband multimedia network based on ATM in March 1996 [11] with connections running at speeds up to 155 Mbps. The service offers both VBR and CBR options. The carrier stated a vision that this network would eventually carry all the data and multimedia traffic in Hong Kong. The service can achieve up to 75 percent savings over comparable private line services. The carrier plans to integrate this ATM network with its frame relay network, called FrameLink, in 1997. The carrier also plans to establish international links in late 1997. The carrier announced satellite link testing with Sprint in August 1997.

20.3.3 Japan

Japan has long been a test bed for ATM equipment and various multimedia and video trials. The Japanese interest group is a focal point within the ATM Forum's Asia Pacific Market Awareness Committee (APMAC).

20.3.3.1 Nippon Telephone & Telegraph (NTT)

Nippon Telegraph and Telephone launched a new, cheaper ATM service in Japan, called Megalink, in March 1997 [10], running at rates ranging from 1 Mbps to 135 Mbps in 1-Mbps increments. Megalink has three different service options: Double Class, Extra Class, and Single Class. Under the Double Class service option, the customer has a primary connection, plus a backup connection in the event of a failure. The Extra Class service offers the primary connection along with a backup connection that can also carry traffic during nonfailure periods. In the event of a failure on the primary connection, then the customer has use of only the backup connection. The Single Class service offers only the primary connection. The pricing of these services is between 25 and 50 percent of a comparable private line service.

20.3.3.2 Kokusai Denshin Denwa (KDD)

In May 1996 AT&T announced that it would partner with KDD of Japan to test interoperability of high-speed, broadband networks between the United States and Japan in support of the Group of Seven Nations' (G7) Global Interoperability of Broadband Networks project (GIBN) [12] to provide trans-Pacific connectivity at 155 Mbps. The announcement stated that AT&T would connect its InterSpan ATM network in San Francisco to KDD's network in Tokyo using ATM technology. Customers from each country participated in trial applications that included brainwave monitoring, remote interactive education, high-definition motion picture transmission, and high-performance protocol (e.g., TCP/IP) testing. Expected benefits were real-time sharing of education and research information, medical and health-care collaboration to augment patient care, and experimentation with high-speed network protocols, multimedia, and imaging.

20.4 ATM OVER SATELLITE TRIALS AND SERVICES

A number of trials and demonstration networks have used ATM over satellite [17] since 1994. The American Petroleum Institute's ATM Research and Industrial Enterprise Study (ARIES) project was an early adopter that used a NASA high-speed satellite and terrestrial ATM networks to demonstrate interactive seismic exploration in 1994. In subsequent years, ARIES demonstrations included shipboard exploration and simulated medical emergencies. In the remote parts of Canada, satellites are the only cost-effective way to transmit communications signals, which motivated North-wesTel to conduct trials of ATM over satellite for telemedicine and distance learning applications.

The prize for highest-speed performance by ATM over a satellite goes to the Jet Propulsion Laboratory and NASA Lewis Research Center, which achieved TCP/IP data transfers at over 600 Mbps over NASA's Advanced Communica-tion Technology Satellite (ACTS) [18]. In fact, the field of ATM over satellites is an area of active research [19]. Areas of projected advances include higher capacity, support for multimedia, and sophisticated on-board processing specifically designed to support ATM.

The ATM over satellite market is now just beginning to take off. COMSAT appears to be the leader in satellite ATM services in the United States. In Europe, the RACE program has spawned the Catalyst Project to provide interconnection of regional ATM services. This section provides an analysis of ATM performance over satellite, and the reader will find that it is surprisingly close to terrestrial performance, except, of course, for the delay.

20.4.1 Benefits of ATM over Satellite

ATM over geostationary satellites (satellites that remain 36,000 kilometers above the earth and have a view of approximately one-half of the earth's surface) allows ATM service to be provided to geographically diverse areas, many of which are difficult to reach with the terrestrial fiber required to carry these large bandwidths. This allows near-ubiquitous worldwide service. Since remote areas may wait years for fiber-optic cable installation, ATM satellite provides a fast deployment alternative. Initially, ATM satellite speeds run at fractional DS1 through DS3 speeds. ATM service can even be offered over existing Very Small Aperture Satellite (VSAT) stations. Special termination equipment is required, of course.

20.4.2 TCP Transmission Issues When Using Satellites

TCP transmissions historically have not worked well over networks that caused long end-to-end delays (latency), and they are also affected by excessive noise. Satellite transmissions experience a ½-s delay end-to-end — ¼ s in each direction. To many TCP implementations, this is a large delay. Thus, protocol changes within the frame windowing method were required to transport TCP traffic over satellite transmissions. Efforts are under way by

BBN Inc. (funded by the National Aeronautics and Space Administration) to improve TCP's performance over networks with so-called high-latency links, such as satellite transmissions. In fact, NASA's Research and Educational Network (NREN) has tested TCP/IP data transfers at speeds of OC-12 over satellite.

20.4.3 Performance Measurements

The ITU-T I.356 standard was developed to define ATM performance requirements for transmission over any media. The goals of ATM service are presented in Table 20.5. The high latency of a satellite circuit (minimum of 43-ms delay one-way for data) has been proven not to degrade ATM's performance compared to terrestrial fiber-optic transmission media. Protocol improvements such as forward error correction and priority queuing have been implemented to account for the increase in delay and error rates inherent in satellite transmissions. Low- and mid-earth-orbit satellites can even reduce the amount of delay due to operating in a vacuum vs. fiber optics [13].

Now compare these goals to those of standard ITU-proposed end-to-end performance objectives for satellite Bit Error Rates (BERs) as shown in Table 20.6. Note that these calculations are based on ITU-specified 35 percent allocation for satellite portion of the connection. We see that they are not too far out of line, in fact in some cases better.

Table 20.5 ATM Quality of Service (QoS) Parameters

	CTD	CDV	CLR_{0+1}	CLR_0	CER	CMR
Default objectives	No default	No default	No default	No default	4.0×10^{-6}	1/day
Class 1 (stringent)	400 ms	3 ms	3.0×10^{-7}	None	Default	Default
Class 2 (tolerant)	U	U	1.0×10^{-5}	None	Default	Default
Class 3 (bi-level)	U	U	U	1.0×10^{-5}	Default	Default

Table 20.6 ITU End-to-End Satellite BER

	CLR_{0+1}	Sat. BER	CLR_0	Sat. BER	CER	Satellite BER
Default objectives	No default		No default		4.0×10^{-8}	4.4×10^{-8}
Class 1 (stringent)	3.0×10^{-7}	1.1×10^{-8}	None		Default	
Class 2 (tolerant)	1.0×10^{-5}	1.4×10^{-8}	None		Default	
Class 3 (bi-level)	U		1.0×10^{-5}	1.4×10^{-8}	Default	

Comsat's Network Technology Division has developed equipment that supports high performance data applications over satellite operating at 45-Mbps speeds developed for a series of experiments and demonstrations of ATM via satellite for the Defense Information Systems Agency under the Commercial Satellite Communications Initiatives (CSCI) contract. The ATM Link Enhancer (ALE) operates at 45 Mbps in support of TCP/IP over the SSCOP protocol running over AAL5 using the DS3 PLCP. A separate ATM Link Accelerator (ALA) utilizes an adaptive, dynamically adapted speed cell-based, Reed-Solomon-based Forward Error Correction (FEC) to transform noisy satellite or wireless point-to-point links into fiberlike quality, achieving BERs better than 1×10^{-9}. Interleaving eliminates bursty errors. The ALA's Time Sequence Protocol (TSP) improves efficiency from the 75 percent using FEC to nearly 100 percent in sunny day (i.e., low noise) intervals. Standard ATM traffic management and control standards are implemented per the ATM Forum. Recently, Comsat deployed this equipment in a worldwide ATM over satellite service operating at speeds ranging from fractional DS1 to DS3 speeds [16]. Major customers include Amoco and Sprint.

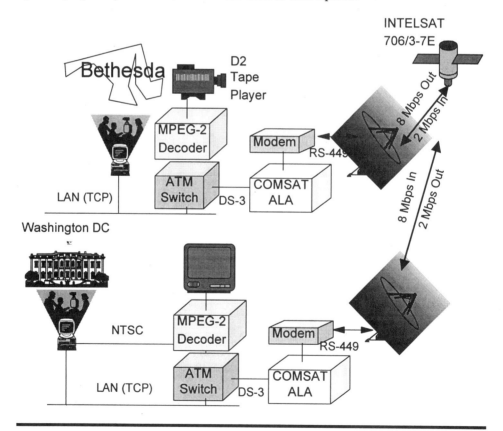

Figure 20.1 ATM via Satellite

Figure 20.1 shows a sample application of ATM via satellite provided by COMSAT's service. Here, two workgroups in Washington, D.C., and Bethesda, Md., communicate via multimedia over ATM via satellite. An ALA enables ATM traffic to be placed over a point-to-point satellite link operating at fractional T1 to 8 Mbps information rates.

20.4.4 Applications

COMSAT's service offers a DS3/E3 channel that allows duplex asynchronous 8.448 Mbps/2 Mbps in/out operation. Applications that have been tested over ATM satellite include circuit emulation, VBR traffic, MPEG-2 video, desktop videoconferencing, and Internet access.

20.4.5 When Is ATM Satellite Cheaper Than Terrestrial Fiber?

ATM satellite services can be very cost-effective when compared to the fiber land-line alternative. This is especially true outside of head-end cable pair cities like London, Frankfurt, Paris, etc. For example, if a user wanted DS3 ATM service from Dublin, Ireland, to Zweibrucken, Germany, the fiber endpoints would be far from London and Frankfurt. Thus, large amounts of very expensive fiber backhaul or high-speed leased lines would be required that are not required with ATM satellite [14].

Specific pricing information was not available from COMSAT, but it was stated that international satellite service was either slightly lower (thick routes such as United States to Western Europe) or appreciably lower (thinner routes from United States to African continent) than undersea fiber optic cable. For more information on COMSAT's services, contact [15].

20.5 REVIEW

This chapter presented the leading providers of ATM services in Europe and the Pacific Rim. The past 3 to 5 years have yielded a slew of international ATM trials that have enabled many of the national PTTs and Public Network Operators to offer commercial ATM services. Each of these services was presented and compared, along with the LAN and WAN infrastructure, standards, and regulatory environment issues. Finally, we presented an overview of ATM over satellite, along with the COMSAT method of providing ATM services over satellite.

20.6 REFERENCES

[1]   T. Bosser, K. Distler, and M. Grant, ATM Forum study, *53 Bytes*, Spring 1996.
[2]   ATM Forum European Market Awareness Committee (EMAC).
[3]   info@atmforum.com.

[4]   ATM Forum European Market Awareness Committee White Paper.

[5]   The European Commission Green Paper.

[6]   The Commission of the European Community (CEC).

[7]   D. Greenfield, *Data Communications on the Web*, February 1997.

[8]   P. Heywood, "Can ATM Really Be This Cheap?" *Data Communications*, January 1995.

[9]   T. Kubo, "Asia-Pacific Region Shows Heightened Interest in ATM," ATM Forum *53 Bytes*, June, 1997, www.atmforum.com/atmforum/library/53bytes/current/article-52_02.html

[10] M. Williams, "NTT Announces New ATM, Frame Relay Services," *Newsbytes Pacifica Headlines*, www.nb-pacifica.com/headline/, March 26, 1997.

[11] E. Lai, "Hong Kong Telecom Launches Broadband Network," *Newsbytes Pacifica Headlines*, www.nb-pacifica.com/headline/, September 3, 1996.

[12] AT&T, "AT&T, KDD Partner to Support Global Broadband Networks Initiative," AT&T Press Release, http://www.att.com/press/0596/960513.bsb.html, May 13, 1996.

[13] D. M. Chitre and S. P. Miller, COMSAT's ATM Satellite Services white paper.

[14] S. Masud, "TCP Overhaul Needed for Satellites," *Computer Reseller News*, September 23, 1996.

[15] S. Miller, information provided by COMSAT, 1997.

[16] J. Rendleman, "ATM Goes Into Orbit," *Communications Week*, March 17, 1997.

[17] V. Oakland, "Broadband from Above," *Telephony*, February 17, 1997.

[18] A. Rogers, ". . . While IP Gets Speedy in Space," *Communications Week*, March 17, 1997.

[19] IEEE, "Broadband via Satellite," *IEEE Communications*, July 1997.

5

SURVEY OF NETWORK DESIGNS

This part surveys several key aspects of network designs from a practical, hands-on point of view. We summarize earlier material and apply it to requirements analysis, network design, economic reality, and the ultimate proving ground: actual case studies. Chapter 21 begins by providing the reader with an overview of the network design process, starting with business and application requirements analysis through switch selection. This chapter also covers the emerging high-performance video teleconferencing for use by businesses as an example of a multimedia application for ATM. We also address performance and migration considerations in this chapter. Next, Chapter 22 assists the reader in designing a private, public, or hybrid ATM network, complete with more detailed information on testing and security. Key topics covered here are the economics of dedicated WAN bandwidth, virtual path tunneling, the high port speed and large switch sizes achievable with ATM, hybrid network designs, and management considerations. Chapter 23 then presents sample case studies of actual ATM network designs.

21

Understanding Your Business and Application Needs

This chapter walks through the business and application requirements that warrant using ATM. First, we define the user requirements followed by the all-important traffic forecast. We then review the application requirements, and the options for taking advantage of ATM. The text highlights videoconferencing over ATM as a prime application design example. We next move to application performance considerations, complete with design recommendations. Finally, we explore FR to ATM migration design issues and alternatives.

21.1 DEFINE THE USER REQUIREMENTS FIRST

As a network designer or architect, your first step in designing an ATM network is to clearly define and understand the business requirements of your users. Often these requirements come directly from the end users, but in other situations corporate executives define them. The network designer, or planner, has to ensure that the network design achieves the requirements of both the end user and the business. First, find out what business requirements are required and which are not being met with the existing network. Some typical business requirements include:

- Ubiquitous access for all users to all network resources
- Near zero downtime and near 100 percent service availability
- Predictable and consistent Quality of Service (QoS) delivered to end users
- Required performance in terms of throughput and/or response time
- Effective price-performance
- Feature- and option-rich service

- LAN/DAN/desktop extension across the WAN
- Efficient use of expensive WAN capacity (often the bottleneck)
- Intranet, Internet, and extranet resource sharing

There are also network requirements that may not be as obvious to the users but make managing the network easier, including:

- Proactive network management and problem resolution
- Standards-based solutions
- Future-proofed solutions
- Dynamic capability to modify network with minimal user interruption
- Flexible means of adding, moving, and deleting users

Make sure you poll the user community for present and future requirements. The user community consists of both end users and executives — providing requirements ranging in time frames from near-term tactical to long-term strategic. Look at these requirements from both a technology and a business perspective. Technology requirements include bandwidth needs, protocol support, and network size, while business needs determine corporate work-flows, geographic deployment, features, and management. More information on business planning can be found in [1]. Remember, there is no substitute for good project planning.

21.2 TRAFFIC FORECAST

Forecasting your present and future traffic load requirements is the next crucial step in ATM network design. The traffic forecast should look at the following characteristics:

- Traffic Type (e.g., voice, video, data)
- Aggregate traffic volume (bps) and user connections (ports) per site
- Quality of service requirements (e.g., loss, delay, jitter)
- Traffic patterns, or matrix of traffic volume between sites

Collect as much specific information as you can: It's a lot easier to remove extra details than to make assumptions without supporting data. Look to the current voice, video and data networks to understand the current traffic volumes and community of interest.

21.2.1 Traffic Type

There are three major categories of traffic:

- Voice (e.g., 64-kbps PCM, 32-kbps ADPCM, G.729 packet voice)
- Video (e.g., H.261 or H.320 N-ISDN, MPEG1, MPEG2)
- Data (e.g., Ethernet, Token Ring, FDDI, native ATM)

Add as much ATM specific details as you can using the terminology defined in Part 2 when collecting the traffic forecast data. Try to estimate the Peak and Sustainable Cell Rates (PCR and SCR), and understand your needs for Maximum Burst Size (MBS). This will also help you better understand application requirements and migration strategies and fill out the traffic matrix.

21.2.2 Traffic Volume

Traffic volume is typically measured in minimum, average, and peak rates. These may be measured in bits per second (bps), packets per second, or cells per second over a specific measurement interval (e.g., 5 minutes). For example, the average traffic volume across a 10-Mbps Ethernet LAN may be 2.5 Mbps, whereas the LAN connectivity across a DS1 WAN link may have an average traffic volume of 500 Mbps. Don't confuse traffic volume with utilization, which is expressed by in-use bandwidth as a percentage of total bandwidth. For example, a 50 percent utilized 10-Mbps Ethernet LAN segment has an average traffic volume of 5 Mbps.

Understand the volume of traffic generated and thus bandwidth requirements for each device on the network — such as a server or a workstation. Just because you provide 155 Mbps to every desktop doesn't mean that an older PC bus can pump enough data onto its output port to ever fill that pipe. This limit can vary depending on the ATM adapter model and type and software drivers, the configuration of the processor, the disk access throughput, and the applications being run.

Also, keep an eye toward the future — faster machines and buses with software optimized for high-performance networking will produce even greater amounts of traffic. The design rule here is to provide enough LAN bandwidth to support the maximum transport rate and not cause the LAN to be a bottleneck, while enabling some future room for growth. For example, a high-powered NT server that uses a 25-Mbps ATM interface may be constrained in a year, and thus it may be better to start with a 155-Mbps dedicated LAN switch port.

Remember that the four key bottlenecks in a network are:

- Processing power (CPU speed) and hardware assists
- Input/output speeds
- LAN performance
- WAN performance

Look at each of these points for potential bottlenecks when designing a network. Of course, processing speed and hardware assists, such as those for full motion video, are the first point on the shopping list. Next, let's look at the I/O speeds on a typical workstation. For high-performance applications, avoid the ISA or EISA architectures, which are capable of only 128 or 256 Mbps I/O bus throughput. The I/O bus is used for all peripherals, including the disk drive. A Pentium processor operating on a PCI bus has a bandwidth of almost 1 Gbps, which should give a good deal of future potential. Currently, many LANs use a shared 10-Mbps Ethernet because of its extremely low cost. As users connect higher-performance machines to these shared LAN segments, productivity declines because the shared Ethernet media operates at approximately 40 percent utilization. Typically, network administrators eliminate the LAN bottleneck by installing more expensive Ethernet switches with more ports than the shared Ethernet hubs they replaced. Visionary network planners may replace the 10-Mbps hub ports with autosensing 10/100-Mbps Ethernet ports on the switch. The next bottleneck is the WAN. The LAN switch aggregates the LAN traffic and then, in many cases, provides this to a router. Most WAN connections are still DS1 or less, effectively imposing a WAN performance bottleneck of 1.5 Mbps on your application. Here, ATM access comes into play, by allowing users to prioritize the traffic types and flows over this bottleneck and more efficiently use the limited available bandwidth and dynamically allocate limited bandwidth resources as required. Furthermore, ATM allows the flexibility to upgrade to nxDS1 Inverse Multiplexing over ATM (IAM), DS3, or SONET 155-Mbps WAN links as traffic growth increases [2]. Additionally, ATM allows the network designer to efficiently share expensive WAN bandwidth on a time of day basis.

21.2.3 Defining Quality of Service Requirements

The next step is to select the right ATM service category to deliver the required QoS. ATM offers many different quality of service categories, including Constant Bit Rate (CBR), real-time Variable Bit Rate (rt-VBR), non-real-time Variable Bit Rate (nrt-VBR), Available Bit Rate (ABR), and Unspecified Bit Rate (UBR). The type of traffic requiring transport should be mapped to the appropriate service category. We repeat Table 21.1 from Chapter 5 to illustrate a mapping between the recommended ATM service category for major traffic types. For example, you should place voice over a rt-VBR or CBR connection, while best effort LAN interconnection would be best served by ABR across the WAN.

Table 21.1 Suitability of ATM Forum Service Categories for Various Applications

Applications	CBR	rt-VBR	nrt-VBR	ABR	UBR
Critical data	Good	Fair	Best	Fair	No
LAN interconnect	Fair	Fair	Good	Best	Good
WAN transport	Fair	Fair	Good	Best	Good
Circuit emulation	Best	Good	No	No	No
Telephony, videoconferencing	Best	TBD	TBD	No	No
Compressed audio	Fair	Best	Good	Good	Fair
Video distribution	Best	Good	Fair	No	No
Interactive multimedia	Best	Best	Good	Good	Fair

Note: TBD = to be determined.

21.2.4 Estimating Traffic Patterns — Gone are the Days of 80/20

The ATM bandwidth parameters (i.e., PCR, SCR, and MBS) along with the service category precisely define the traffic volume of a particular type between sites. The ideal scenario would be to precisely understand the current and future connectivity requirements down to the individual end user. Practically, this level of detail either isn't available in many larger enterprises, or is too expensive and too time consuming to collect. One way to measure current traffic is to either rent or purchase analyzers, or outsource to someone the measurement of traffic patterns of the existing networks. Many design and analysis tools are available to help obtain valuable information on the current network, ranging from less than $1000 probes to $20,000+ protocol analyzers and design tool software. If you do not already own these tools, choose them wisely. It is easy to underestimate the postpurchase support requirements in training and staffing to make these tools actually produce results. And rarely can a tool produce results "right out of the box." Beware of vendors who claim this to be true.

Don't stop if you can't get this data; however, be creative — use existing trunk sizes between PBXs, private line interface speeds between routers, or T1 multiplexer trunk sizes to estimate the traffic matrix. Use estimated growth rates to scale current traffic estimates into the future, and consider multiple scenarios so that you can analyze the sensitivity of your design to different traffic assumptions. Finally, remember that predicting the future is an imprecise science at best.

Also, beware of time-honored network design rules: The networking times, to use a Bob Dylan song, are "a changing." For example, the traditional rule of thumb in LAN and WAN design was that a majority of the traffic would remain local (typically 80 percent) while a smaller portion required transport across the WAN (typically 20 percent). Designers referred to this as the 80/20 rule, reflecting the percentage split of LAN/WAN traffic. However, as times and means of doing business change, the mix of LAN to WAN traffic deviates further and further from this rule. Trends like the Internet, extranets, and virtual LANs spanning the WAN have caused traffic patterns to diverge and become almost unpredictable. Indeed, as discussed in Chapter 1, the accelerating bandwidth principle increasingly sends users out over the WAN to obtain the most up to date information, as evidenced by the World Wide Web phenomenon. Thus, the best planning approach is to start with a low amount of WAN bandwidth, implement performance measurement from the outset, and increase the WAN bandwidth as required to achieve the required performance level.

21.3 GETTING APPLICATIONS TO ATM

Your ATM network design must accommodate both new, state-of-the-art applications and existing applications which you plan on migrating to ATM. In fact, most mission-critical applications in use today are written for legacy systems: SNA, IP, and Ethernet, to name a few. This section looks at both the new and migration scenarios.

21.3.1 New Applications on ATM

New application development is the easiest way to place applications over ATM and realize its benefits. Specifically, applications programmed directly through an ATM Application Programming Interface (API) are ideal for ATM networks. Using these APIs, programmers can write applications that concurrently run voice, video, and data. APIs can also tie non-ATM-aware protocols, such as IP, IPX, and NetBEUI, to ATM virtual channel and path connections and provide them with the guaranteed bandwidth, quality of service, and prioritization benefits of ATM. The key challenge here is for the API developer to take advantage of ATM's 53-byte cell-oriented, connection-oriented architecture. The fact that many data networking protocols (e.g., IP) operate on a completely different variable packet length, connectionless architecture makes this especially challenging. Always make sure the workstation and server hardware you choose supports the ATM API drivers your applications require.

21.3.2 Converting Legacy LAN Applications to ATM

How can legacy applications be ported to run on ATM? This is a key question, since a majority of business-critical applications targeted for ATM networks are already written to interface to legacy LAN and WAN systems. Legacy applications can run over ATM via one of two migration methods:

- Map the application to ATM at the LAN device driver protocol level through use of ATM Forum's LAN Emulation (LANE) client driver software in the ATM Network Interface Card (NIC) in the workstation or server. LANE Level 3 traffic can then be routed across the ATM network via either Multiprotocol over ATM (MPOA) or Integrated Private Network-to-Network Interface (I-PNNI) as defined in Chapter 11. No changes in the applications are required when using LANE, but QoS features are limited in LANE 1.0.
- Map the application directly to ATM via an ATM middleware API like WinSock 2.0, resident within a common operating system like Microsoft's Windows. ATM APIs are the best choice for ATM-to-the-desktop users — Microsoft's WinSock Version 2 for Windows users, and X/Open X/Sockets, or X/TLI APIs for UNIX users.

See Chapters 10 and 11 along with references [3] and [4] for more information on these topics.

21.3.3 Application Dependencies

Sometimes the transition from legacy application or networking to ATM is not clean, and dependencies remain. To better manage this, try to identify up front any application dependencies that are related to subjects like physical wiring, networking protocols, routing protocols, other switching protocols, operating systems, computing platforms, and people requirements. Develop a plan that accommodates or eliminates the requirement for these dependencies. Remember that hybrid operating environments may exist for some time, since migrations rarely occur overnight.

21.4 VIDEOCONFERENCING OVER ATM

Since videoconferencing, and in particular desktop videoconferencing in a multimedia environment, has been a driver for ATM in the LAN, this section is dedicated to bandwidth requirements, market, APIs, operating systems, and standards. Video coder-decoders, or CODECs for short, play an important role in converting the video digital stream into a format that transportable by ATM. We also take a quick look at residential video, and complete with a discussion on design tips.

21.4.1 Market and Application Defined

Desktop videoconferencing offers the ability for users to join in a workgroup to collaborate through real-time data sharing while visually demonstrating things using a virtual whiteboard application. Desktop video-conferencing is a huge market: estimated to be in excess of $1B by the year 2000 according to International Data Corporation (IDC) forecasts. Video-conferencing applications create variable, high-rate bit streams of data — a perfect application for ATM transport. These applications require a lot of bandwidth ranging from 4 to 60 Mbps for a real-time, full-motion, color MPEG2 video stream. And in playback mode one minute's worth of video can easily consume 100 Mbytes of storage!

How does ATM enable business savings with videoconferencing support? Using an ATM access device that accepts a video stream directly from an ATM NIC has the important benefit of reducing the requirement for physical attendance at a meeting, thus avoiding additional productivity-draining travel. ATM networking achieves high-quality video networking by operating at speeds far in excess of today's ISDN alternatives as discussed later in this chapter. ATM thus offers the performance required for business quality videoconferencing while offering scalability that far exceeds that of legacy technologies like ISDN [5].

21.4.2 ATM Videoconferencing APIs and Operating Systems

One example of an ATM videoconferencing API is Insoft's Communique application, based on Insoft's Open Digital Video Everywhere API development environment. This product is specifically designed and optimized to run over an ATM network. Insoft's clients for this product include financial trading, mission-critical telemedicine, and concurrent engineering.

One example of an operating system designed and optimized to ATM is First Virtual Corporation's Media Operating System (MOS). MOS lets PC-based multimedia applications run over an ATM network without having to write code that tells the switch to set up the requisite real-time circuits. Like other kinds of ATM API middleware, MOS buffers the application from the ATM network, thus eliminating the need for programmers to understand the protocol details of ATM. Some vendors sell switches and adapters that require the user to develop software that tells the switch when to establish real-time VCs. Alternatively, they transport multimedia using LAN emulation — over circuits that cannot deliver the service level needed for delay-sensitive traffic. LAN emulation for multimedia works, but quality suffers markedly as usage grows and congestion becomes an issue. MOS redirects application calls, thus fooling applications into thinking they are executing locally [6, 7].

21.4.3 Videoconferencing Standards

Table 21.2 lists the leading video compression standards, their bandwidth requirements, compression ratios, and typical video applications. Note that most desktop and in-room videoconferencing applications today use the N-ISDN H.261 and H.320 standards. There are also many proprietary standards that can provide lower compression ratios, operating at speeds less than 2 Mbps.

Table 21.2 Standard Video Compression Ratio, Bandwidth, and Applications

Compression Standard	Compression Ratio Achieved	Bandwidth Required (Mbps)	Video Applications
ITU H.261 and H.320	24:1	0.064 – 2.0	Desktop and in-room videoconferencing
ISO MPEG 1	100:1	1.2 – 2.0	VHS quality, desktop videoconferencing
ISO MPEG 2	30–100:1	4 – 60	Theater quality broadcasting and entertainment distribution
ITU Motion JPEG	7–27:1	10 – 20	Full motion video

21.4.4 CODEC Requirement

A video compression/decompression system is required when converting a video bit stream to a standard digital format for transmission over ATM. Sample CODEC vendors include AG Communications Systems, K-Net Limited, Litton-FiberCom, and NUKO Information Systems Inc.

21.4.5 Residential Video

Residential video service is now appearing over newly deployed Local Exchange Carrier (LEC) fiber/coaxial cables using ATM. In the local loop, fiber/coax media and video services are replacing copper and basic telephone service, enabling LECs to deliver voice, data, and video dial tone over the same plant [8].

21.4.6 Video over ATM Design Requirements

When designing ATM networks to carry video traffic, the engineer must carefully measure end-to-end delay and jitter. For interactive videoconferencing, end-to-end delay should not exceed 150 ms, and jitter (variations in playback delay) should not exceed a few milliseconds, or the user will become annoyed by the time lag or jerky video playback.   Pay close attention to the jitter, or cell delay variation, absorption specs of your video CODEC.

Also, ensure that each video stream has the appropriate quality of service and thus enough bandwidth to achieve the video quality of service desired. For example, achieving an effective throughput of 384 kbps will deliver what is considered business-quality videoconferencing [delivering 15 frames per second (fps) of a 352 x 288 pixel frame]. A desirable feature of ATM switches would be support for per video-stream buffering to ensure fairness among multiple streams destined for the same switch port.

21.5 APPLICATION PERFORMANCE CONSIDERATIONS

What are the major application performance considerations when operating over ATM? Applications should perform better than over any other technology — if designed correctly. In fact, no current technology handles multimedia and distributed applications better than ATM.

Many network variables have an effect on application performance, for example:

- Network architecture
- Network topology, routing parameters, and link speeds
- Switch type, size, capacity, etc.
- Traffic type and protocol mix
- Quality of service requirements
- Congestion control and policing mechanisms
- Interoperability and/or gateway requirements

It is the network engineer's job to isolate and quantify the effect of each of these, making sure they do not create a bottleneck.

21.5.1 Effects of Network Congestion on Data Applications

Network congestion affects end-to-end transport layer (e.g., TCP) and ultimately application layer (e.g., HTTP) performance. A key design issue for ATM networks is to select ATM service categories and bandwidth parameters that minimize the chance of loss and congestion. Furthermore, the network should respond rapidly to congestion so that high-priority applications continue performing well, even during periods of congestion.

Most data transport protocols use a scheme where a window of sequence number packets can be sent prior to receipt of any acknowledgments. Historically, this was an issue for data communications over satellite, since the round-trip delays were on the order of half a second. Once the transmitter reaches the end of its transmit window, it stops sending until it receives an acknowledgment. If an acknowledgment is not received, then the transmitter eventually times out and begins transmitting at the packet sequence number immediately after the last acknowledgment. Therefore, when a packet (or its acknowledgment) is either lost or delayed, the transport layer throughput is markedly decreased. Add to this the fact that standard TCP implementations only support a 64-kbyte window size, and you'll find that you can't send at 10-Mbps Ethernet speeds across the WAN. Look for TCP window scaling extensions found in IETF RFC 1323 to enable operation over networks with large bandwidth-delay products. A general rule of thumb is that the total throughput of TCP (in kbps or Mbps) increases with the window size in kbytes linearly up to the point where either the maximum window size is reached or the window equals the product of the round trip delay and the bottleneck bandwidth. See [9] for the performance impacts of window size and delay on the TCP windowing protocol. Also, be aware that errors cause lost packets and result in throughput-robbing retransmissions [10].

21.5.2 TCP over ATM: UBR and ABR

This section looks at a few more issues concerned with placing TCP traffic over the ATM service categories called UBR and ABR as defined in Chapter 6. TCP/IP is the most common data traffic running over ATM networks today. TCP's adaptive windowing protocol dynamically acts to fill the available bandwidth, if user demand is high enough. Thus, ATM is an ideal network infrastructure to support TCP's ability to fill in bandwidth unused by higher-priority multimedia traffic like voice and video. TCP can use either the ABR or UBR service category, with advantages and disadvantages that as summarized below.

Many UBR implementations use a simple cell discard threshold in a buffer based upon the Cell Loss Priority (CLP) bit in the ATM cell header. Once the buffer fills beyond the threshold, the switch discards lower-priority cells (i.e., CLP = 1 – tagged UBR cells). ATM switches should have large buffers, sized to be on the order of the product of the round-trip delay and bandwidth bottleneck, when supporting TCP over UBR.

During congestion conditions and subsequent loss of cells, the ATM network device does not notify the sender that retransmission is required — instead, higher-layer protocols, like TCP, must notice the loss via a timeout and retransmit the missing packets. One cell loss causes not only the missing packet, but all packets after it up to the end of the transmit window to be retransmitted. Excessive packet discards within a TCP window can degrade the recovery process and cause host time-outs — causing interruptions on the order of minutes. Loss also touches off TCP's slow-start adaptive windowing mechanism, further reducing throughput. If you plan to operate TCP/IP over UBR, be sure that your ATM switches support Early/Partial Packet Discard (EPD/PPD) as defined in Chapter 6. The EPD/PPD functions ensure that the switch discards *entire packets* during periods of congestion. This is especially important when a relatively large number of TCP sources contend for a particular bottleneck.

Possibly the best ATM service category for TCP traffic is ABR, which employs a closed-loop rate-based mechanism for congestion control using explicit feedback. For ABR traffic, the TCP source must control its transmission rate. ABR defines a Minimum Cell Rate (MCR) for each virtual connection, which defines the lowest acceptable value of bandwidth. The MCR may be zero. Operating in an ATM network, the ABR protocol utilizes Resource Management (RM) cells to control the input rate of each source (and thus each connection) based upon the current level of congestion in the switches along the route carrying that connection's traffic. In ABR, the switch buffer size requirements are similar to those in the UBR case.

The network may police ABR connections to ensure that they conform to the traffic contract. The standards allow networks to do this so that an unregulated user on a single connection cannot affect the service of all other users sharing bandwidth with that connection [11, 12].

21.6 FR TO ATM MIGRATION ISSUES — INTERWORKING

ATM offers two key features not found in FR — high-speed access and trunking, and QoS support. We believe that FR and ATM will coexist for a long time for several reasons: Users who've already invested in FR want to get the payback, FR service operates best at lower speeds, and many CPE devices seamlessly interoperate over FR today. However, many FR users want to take advantage of ATM technology and services at critical sites requiring greater bandwidth and QoS support. Fortunately, users don't need to make a decision for exclusively FR or ATM networking. Two design options allow users to mix and match FR and ATM ports on their networks: FR/ATM network and service interworking. We now look at the design issues of both [13].

21.6.1 FR/ATM Network Interworking

The Frame Relay Forum's FRF.5 standard defines FR/ATM network interworking. This standard allows users to transport FR transparently across an ATM network — a procedure also called "tunneling" in the trade press. Indeed, the ATM Forum's Broadband Intercarrier Interface (B-ICI) specification specified this protocol for carriers to interconnect their FR networks across a shared ATM interface. Users must have FR switching equipment at both network ingress and egress. Figure 21.1 illustrates an application of FRF.5. Note that FR Permanent Virtual Circuits (PVCs) can be carried over individual ATM PVCs, or all FR PVCs can be multiplexed onto a single ATM PVC.

21.6.2 FR/ATM Service Interworking

The Frame Relay Forum's FRF.8 standard defines FR/ATM service interworking. This standard allows users to enter the network via FR and exit via ATM, or vice versa. Either the FR or the ATM network must convert between the FR and ATM protocols, map DLCI and Virtual Path Identifier/Virtual Channel Identifier (VPI/VCI) values, and convert status signaling. Figure 21.2 shows an example of FR/ATM service interworking between a headquarters' ATM circuit and multiple remote (A, B, and C) FR access devices. Many FR and ATM service providers are now offering service interworking as a way to offer both services to users as well as preserve their existing FR equipment investments. The most critical design issues in service interworking are the mapping of frame sizes to the 53-byte cells maintaining traffic shaping and QoS, address mapping, and signaling.

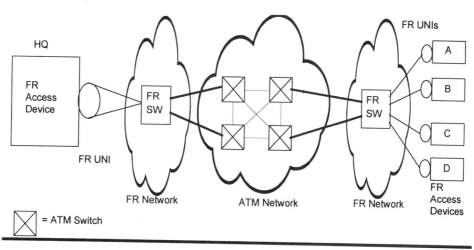

Figure 21.1 FR/ATM Network Interworking

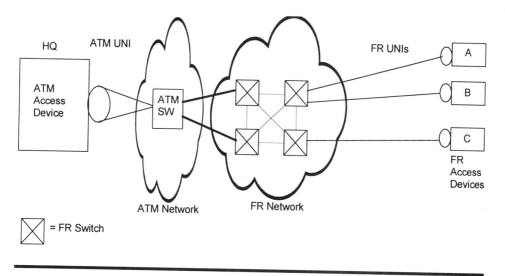

Figure 21.2 FR/ATM Service Interworking

21.7 REVIEW

This chapter first reviewed the key user and business requirements, along with strategies to run existing and new applications on ATM. The text then covered some details of traffic forecasting and network planning. We then covered high-performance business videoconferencing as an example of an application. The chapter then addressed some application performance implications, in particular the performance of TCP/IP over the UBR and ABR ATM service categories. The chapter concluded with examples of how to migrate from FR to ATM and, in the interim, use hybrid frame relay and ATM functions. Now, armed with this knowledge, the next chapter will show how to design a private network or a hybrid private-public ATM network.

21.8 REFERENCES

[1]   D. Spohn, *Data Network Design*, 2d ed., McGraw-Hill, 1997.
[2]   A. Edmonds, *ATM Network Planning and Implementation*, Thompson Computer Press, 1997.
[3]   T. Nolle, "Getting Applications for ATM," *Network World,* March 11, 1996.
[4]   B. Nance, "Teach Your Apps to Speak ATM," *BYTE*, August 1996.
[5]   J. Paone, "ATM Pumps Video-conferences to Desktop," *Internetworking*, January 1995.
[6]   J. Johnson, "Plug-and-Play ATM Multimedia," *Data Communications*, January 1995.
[7]   R. Gross, "ATM: The Key to Harnessing the Power of Networked Multimedia," *Telecommunications*, November 1996.
[8]   R. Karpinski, "New Technology Drives New Network Management," *Telephony*, March 28, 1994.
[9]   D. McDysan and D. Spohn, *ATM: Theory and Application*, McGraw-Hill, 1995.
[10] T. Bowers and T. Lu, "Covering Traffic on the ATM," *EE Times*, January 15, 1996.
[11] C. Pazos, M. Gerla, and V. Signore, *Comparing ATM Controls for TCP Sources*, IEEE, 1995.
[12] H. Li, K-Y Siu, and H-Y Tzeng, *A Simulation Study of TCP Performance in ATM Networks with ABR and UBR Services*, IEEE, 1996.
[13] R. Sullebarger, "ATM and FR Making the Connection," *Data Communications*, June 1997.

22

Designing Private and Public ATM Networks

Public network planners are used to thinking with a long-term perspective. Increasingly, private network managers are now thinking that over a 7- to 10-year interval, an ATM backbone network is a very attractive alternative [1]. This chapter looks at the key issues to understand when building a private network, also using services provided by a public ATM network, or a hybrid of the two. ATM networks may be implemented by using an ATM WAN backbone as a private network (or use a carriers' public shared ATM network), and then moving ATM switching into your enterprise and LAN backbone, or taking it all the way through the workgroup to the desktop. Design tips for selecting and managing Permanent Virtual Connections (PVCs) and Switched Virtual Connections (SVCs) are offered, along with methods of improving ATM network performance and using virtual LANs. This chapter offers advice that will save you money while ensuring a reliable design that will scale for growth or contraction for many years to come.

22.1 PRIVATE VERSUS PUBLIC — BUILD OR BUY?

The choice between private versus public networking is a key one. Basically, as the network designer you must decide either to design and build your own network using facilities from a carrier and ATM CPE, or to lease ATM services from a public provider. Which network design is right for you? The answer depends upon several factors. If your company makes ATM switches, then at least part of your network should be private. You should do this to gain experience with ATM networking in the networking market that your product targets. After all, would you buy a product from someone who didn't use it themselves? Outside of ATM device manufacturers, the decision to build or buy is not so clear-cut. Another key factor is whether networking is a key competency for your enterprise. If it is, then you should consider building at least part of your network. If you work for a carrier, the decision will usually be to build your own; however, in some cases, it may make good business sense to resell another carrier's service.

You should also consider other key differences between private networks and public carrier networks when making your decision. Service provider or public ATM network design varies from private network design in several respects. First, private network designers typically know the locations, speeds, and needs of their users at design time during the discovery cycle of user's needs, whereas public network providers usually have only generic forecasts on the exact speed, location, and composition of access circuits until customers actually order service. Second, the cost basis for private and public network designers differs markedly. Facilities-based public service providers have much lower costs for transmission than do private network designers. Finally, public networks achieve an economy of scale when aggregating multiple customers onto a single infrastructure that can be achieved only in extremely large private networks.

Recall that we covered public and private ATM network architectures in Part 3. This sequel describes and analyzes a range of architectures that employ private and public network capabilities. Our analysis focuses on an important topic to many network designers: saving money. However, don't forget the other cornerstone of modern capitalism — making money — when determining where to deploy ATM. Deploying leading-edge ATM-based applications and networking may give your enterprise a competitive advantage against the competition. For other network designs, integrating the newer ATM technology into existing legacy network environments may be of paramount importance. The next sections summarize various design issues in the LAN, private line–based wide area networks, and the use of public data services.

22.2 PRIVATE LOCAL AREA ATM NETWORKS

Our discussion of network design begins in the local area private network, by covering the following three topics:

- Native ATM to the desktop and workgroup
- Interworking with legacy LANs
- Upgrading to a ATM LAN backbone

The key issues and solutions presented here center around how to combine routing and switching between legacy protocols and ATM. Consolidation of voice, video, and data traffic while mapping real-time protocol flows into ATM service categories is the most critical area of focus in these designs.

22.2.1 Native ATM to the Desktop and Workgroup

ATM designs that take advantage of the end-to-end capabilities of ATM begin at the desktop. Chapter 16 presented the leading technologies and implementations of ATM to the desktop. The only true way to guarantee Quality of Service (QoS) and cost-effective bandwidth is to design a network that uses ATM all the way from the WAN backbone switch, down through the enterprise into the corporate LAN backbone, then through the workgroup, and down to the workstation and server Network Interface Cards (NIC).

One method of designing an ATM network is from the workstation out toward the network. To do this, the designer starts by grouping users into workgroups based upon resource sharing, organizational structure, and/or information exchange patterns. The designer should use these traffic patterns to determine bandwidth allocation, switch topology, and routing metrics. Decide where legacy LAN technologies will remain, and which workgroups require direct ATM access based upon performance needs. Utilize test equipment to measure performance as a design input.

Utilize PVCs when the potential for call blocking is unacceptable, or when interconnected ATM devices have incompatible SVC signaling. Take advantage of SVCs whenever possible to realize the benefits of automatic address resolution built into LAN emulation, classical IP over ATM and Multiprotocol over ATM (MPOA). Make sure to match the service category and traffic parameters with the application requirements, so that each application receives the required QoS and bandwidth.

22.2.2 Interworking with Legacy LANs

Most user environments have an existing legacy protocol used in the workgroup (i.e., Ethernet, Token Ring, FDDI, IP, IPX). ATM provides several options for native ATM users to interwork with this legacy workgroup environment, namely LAN emulation for *bridged* networks, along with MPOA and classical IP over ATM for *routed* networks. These protocols allow an organization to move to ATM only where performance of application needs dictate, consequently preserving the legacy LAN and existing desktop (NIC) investments in the remainder of the network. The move to ATM may be accompanied in parallel by the deployment of LAN switching and 100-Mbps or gigabit Ethernet to resolve legacy LAN bottlenecks.

ATM-based LANs provide a more scaleable, lower cost per Mbps, higher bandwidth solution than legacy LAN protocols, and also connect seamlessly across the wide area. ATM LAN emulation and MPOA also reduce the requirement to purchase additional routers; however, the existing routers may require upgrades to support higher loads in the legacy LAN and interworking points with the native ATM applications and workgroups.

A designer must select some method of converting LAN frames into ATM cells. The most popular method to date is to deploy LAN Emulation (LANE) on routers and/or LAN switches at the intersection or boundary of the legacy LAN and ATM environments. Be careful when using classical IP over ATM and MPOA when routing between different subnets, because the required routers can be a more expensive solution than ATM switching. Network management is also a key consideration when interworking with legacy LANs. Beware of the methods used by these routers and/or switches to filter and route traffic, and make sure they fit with the QoS schemes you plan to use on the ATM side. Carefully size legacy LAN environments to emulate ATM QoS features by monitoring performance and balancing the load using LAN switching.

22.2.3 Upgrading to an ATM LAN Backbone

Often, large private networks already have a LAN backbone — for example, FDDI. If performance measurements indicate that the LAN backbone is a bottleneck, then upgrading to a higher-performance, more scalable ATM backbone could be the answer for you. Select ATM switching devices to meet specific LAN needs, but keep an eye on WAN capabilities as well. Also, consider anticipated growth and increased capacity needs in the initial design phase. Most large LAN backbone and enterprise switches and routers offer ATM WAN interfaces. Therefore, you may be able to upgrade some of your existing investment by replacing cards and loading new software. For those devices that don't have an ATM upgrade path, consider using ATM devices to convert to an ATM cell format.

22.3 PRIVATE ATM WIDE AREA NETWORKS

Now that you've decided to use ATM in the LAN, you need to connect sites across the wide area network. Should you do it with private lines or use a public ATM service? The answer depends upon several factors. First, the volume of traffic going across the WAN limits the economies of scale achievable in a totally private solution when compared with a public network. Second, your enterprise's service availability requirements dictates the required access line redundancy, which can be a significant cost factor.

22.3.1 Economics of Private Line–Based Networking

A private ATM-based network comprises devices located on customer premises interconnected via dedicated transmission facilities, either owned by the customer or leased from a carrier. Most building and campus area networks are private, since the enterprise owns the right of way for transmission facilities, which run the gamut from twisted pairs through coax to fiber and microwave links. In general, if you own the transmission facilities, plan on building that part of the network yourself. But, if you are designing for the WAN where you don't own the transmission facilities, then a principal economic motivation is the relatively high cost of leased wide area transmission facilities. Let's look into this subject further.

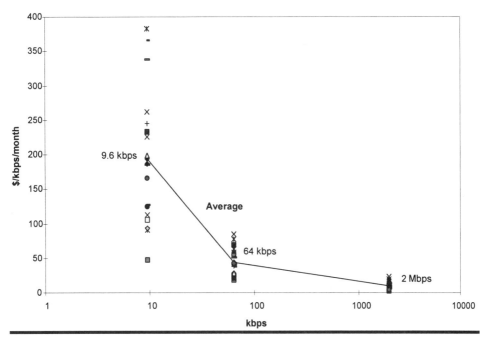

Figure 22.1 Monthly Unit Transmission Cost versus Speed for International Private Lines

Tariffs for DS1 and DS3 private lines in the United States create an economic motivation for customers to upgrade from multiple DS1s to a single DS3 when the recurring monthly tariffs are about equal. This occurs at a crossover point of between 5 and 10 times the monthly DS1 tariff, depending upon geographic region [2]. Internationally, a similar situation exists for 9.6-kbps, 64-kbps and 2-Mbps private lines.

For lower-speed access at smaller sites, efficiency is a more significant concern than the flexibility and higher performance of ATM. This is because the cost per bit per second (bps) decreases as the public network access speed increases. For example, the approximate ratio of DS1/DS0 and DS3/DS1 tariffs is approximately 10:1, while the speed difference is approximately 25:1. This means that a higher-speed interface can be operated at 40 percent efficiency at the same bit per second unit cost. Conversely, the lower-speed interface costs 2.5 times as much per bit per second, and therefore efficiency is much more important. Figure 22.1 graphically illustrates this concept for international private line tariffs.

The average cost per unit of bandwidth for a 9.6-kbps international private line is approximately $200/kbps/month; however, there is considerable variation about this average, as seen from the figure. The average cost of bandwidth decreases to less than $50/kbps/month for a 64-kbps circuit, and falls even further for a 2-Mbps circuit, to $10/kbps/month.

Why is there such a wide disparity in the cost per unit of bandwidth? Several factors contribute to the overall cost. First, the cost of the copper wire–based infrastructure dominates over all other considerations. These private lines all utilize the same twisted pair copper to the end subscriber; the only difference is the equipment that interfaces to the wires. Of course, in some countries and cities the pairs of wires must be carefully selected, and in some cases, new wires may have to be run to the subscriber to handle the digital signals. This ubiquity of copper plant to many subscribers will also enable broadband access to the business and residence well into the twenty first century through Asymmetric Digital Subscriber Loop (ADSL) technology [3].

Now, before you get too excited and run off to tell your boss you've discovered a way to save a mint on international private lines, read on. The above analysis considered the cost per kbps; therefore, the total monthly cost is the product of the cost per unit of bandwidth and the line rate bandwidth. Figure 22.2 plots this total monthly cost. The average monthly cost of a 9.6-kbps leased line is less than $2,000, while the average monthly cost of a 2-Mbps E1 private line exceeds $20,000!

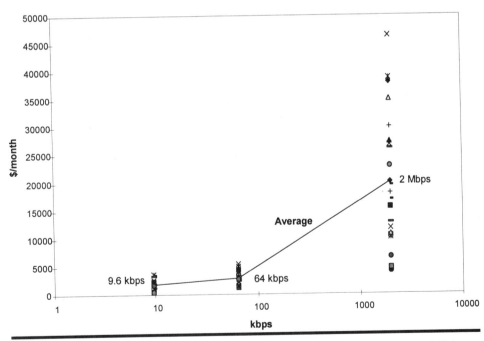

Figure 22.2 Monthly Total Transmission Cost versus Speed for International Private Lines

The lesson here is that the lower unit cost of bandwidth will be a benefit only if you can fill a substantial portion of the bandwidth with traffic. These economics drive several networking strategies. First, a cost-conscious network designer (and cost-consciousness should be one of your goals) should strive to aggregate all traffic onto a common backbone. Second, even if the common backbone technology is not the most efficient, the economics of higher-speed lines usually more than overcome such inefficiencies. The 1980s saw network designers apply these concepts to T1 Time-Division Multiplexed (TDM) networks. The 1990s witnessed the advent of these same economic principles using integrated packet networks and ATM networks.

22.3.2 The Effect of Traffic Volume on Efficiency

As seen from the previous section, the aggregate traffic volume plays a key role in the economic viability of a high-speed network. If you can fill up a higher-speed pipe, then the cost per Mbps drops drastically. If you can't fill up the next larger size pipe, then your unit costs are higher. Since ATM service providers using public ATM service offerings aggregate traffic from many customers, they achieve economies of scale impossible in all but the very largest private networks. Public networks also employ statistical multiplexing for variable bit rate service categories to further improve their economics. Normally, users select traffic parameters for individual PVCs to meet periods of peak demand. Users must do this if they want guarantees on QoS at specified traffic rates. However, most PVCs do not carry this peak period traffic simultaneously. Therefore, if a PVC is active only a certain percentage of time, then a carrier can statistically multiplex the traffic. In fact, the name chosen by the ITU-T for the VBR service category — namely the Statistical Bit Rate (SBR) ATM transport capability — reflects this design philosophy.

Figure 22.3 illustrates this concept by plotting the maximum achievable utilization efficiency for a fully loaded trunk versus the ratio of the source Peak Cell Rate (PCR) and the link rate using Guerin's equivalent capacity formula [4]. The source peak to average rate (i.e., PCR/SCR) was 2 in this example, meaning that with conservative peak rate Connection Admission Control (CAC), the utilization would still be 50 percent. The figure plots utilization for two ATM service categories, real-time and non-real-time Variable Bit Rate (rt-VBR and nrt-VBR), modeling the relative Maximum Burst Size (MBS) to the switch buffer size at 100 percent and 10 percent, respectively. Since real-time VBR must deliver a constrained cell delay variation, the buffer size in a switching device supporting this service category must be relatively small. This means that the achievable efficiency declines for high peak to link ratios. On the other hand, the non-real-time VBR service category allows very large delay variation, which means that switching devices may employ very large buffers to smooth out longer-term fluctuations in traffic. Hence, the achievable utilization for nrt-VBR is higher, provided your ATM devices have enough buffering.

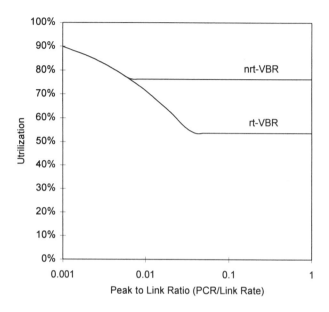

Figure 22.3 Utilization Efficiency versus Peak to Link Ratio

We can extract several important lessons from this result. First, if all you can afford is a DS1 or nxDS1 private ATM network, a carrier with a DS3 ATM backbone will achieve better utilization than you can. Furthermore, the higher the carrier's trunk speed, the more efficient the carrier's network can be. Also, pay attention to the relationship between ATM service category, the MBS, and the switch buffer sizes. Look for switches with buffer sizes at least ten times as large as the MBS value when considering non-real-time VBR. Look for switches with buffers that are on the same order as the delay variation budget allocated to each switch when planning for real-time VBR services. And most of all, look at the relative economics. Although a carrier's network might be more efficient, it still may not be more cost-effective for your particular traffic needs and network topology.

22.3.3 Impact of Service Availability on Access Line Design

The access line is often the Achilles heel of a wide area network design. Failure of a single access line into a public service isolates the affected site from all others in the network. Estimate what the impact will be on business if a site becomes isolated. Try to place an economic impact on such a failure, since this analysis will be necessary to justify the additional cost of access lines. If a large number of sites require redundant access, then a private line–based network may meet your redundancy requirements more cost effectively than a dual homed access line public network. If only a few key sites require dual homing, then the public design will likely be better.

22.4 HYBRID PUBLIC-PRIVATE NETWORKS

A virtual circuit on a public network is more economical than a real circuit interconnecting private sites when the offered traffic is: bursty, of multiple types, or has multiple destinations. This section covers several topics involved when interconnecting private local networks via public networks. We begin by discussing the flexibility of ATM and the popular hybrid public-private architecture employing "tunneling" of private virtual channels over public virtual paths. Next, we cover popular topologies for hybrid networks, such as the hub and spoke design. Also, we discuss how the relative dynamics of your traffic usually determine whether you'll need switched or permanent virtual connections. Finally, the section concludes with the topics of using carrier LAN interconnect services and selecting ATM service categories and traffic parameters to optimize the price-performance tradeoff.

22.4.1 ATM's Forte: Flexibility

Generally, for any single communication need except native ATM, another networking technology is superior. Since ATM supports a diverse range of applications — voice, video, and data — ATM best suits an environment with multiple requirements, or a multimedia-oriented set of applications. Flexibility takes on another facet if the enterprise's needs are either uncertain or time-varying.

Carrier SVC services afford tremendous flexibility to time-varying applications. However, the blocking probability for high-bandwidth connection attempts may be significant in public networks during busy intervals.

22.4.2 Tunneling over Virtual Paths

A common technique employed in hybrid private-public networks is to "tunnel" Virtual Channel Connections (VCCs) over Virtual Path Connection (VPC) PVCs provided by a public ATM network as shown in Figure 22.4. In this example, the network designer has ordered three nrt-VBR service class VPC PVCs to interconnect private ATM switches A, B, and C. A good example using this technique is Fore Systems' early implementation of enterprise ATM switches that placed proprietary VCC SVC connections over VPC PVC trunks leased from public ATM service providers [5].

In essence, VP tunneling enables the enterprise switches to dynamically allocate bandwidth to individual VCCs out of the total VPC bandwidth. Of course, each underlying VCC has the same QoS as the leased VPC. A hybrid VP tunneling network requiring multiple QoS class support must subscribe to multiple VPC trunks with different QoS classes between enterprise nodes, as illustrated in the example of Figure 22.5, which adds a CBR service category VPC between each of the three sites. The private ATM switches would select either the nrt-VBR VPC or the CBR VPC based upon the end user's application. The users could make this decision statically in the case of a PVC network, or dynamically if using SVCs. For example, the users of this network could use LAN emulation over the nrt-VBR VPCs and on-demand videoconferencing over the CBR VPCs. This example also illustrates another advantage of public networking, namely combining multiple logical connections onto a single physical User-Network Interface (UNI) connected to the public network.

22.4.3 Optimizing Network Topologies

A commonly used network topology homes many remote offices to either centralized or regionalized servers. The applications best suited to this topology should be using the client-server paradigm. The literature often refers to this type of design as a hub and spoke network, with an example illustrated in Figure 22.6. Here, sites 1, 2, and 3 have a primary connection to server A, while sites 4, 5, and 6 have a primary connection to server B. Each site has a secondary connection to the other server. The servers are also interconnected. This design requires only 13 PVCs, compared with the 28 required in a full-mesh PVC design.

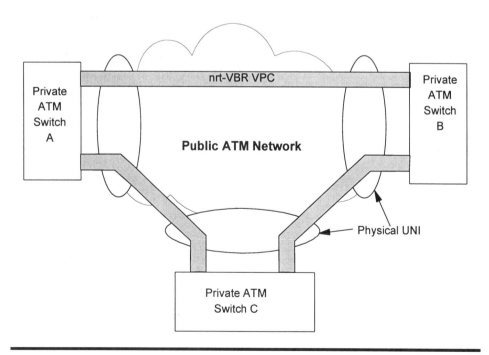

Figure 22.4 Hybrid Public-Private VP Tunneling Network Supporting a Single QoS Class

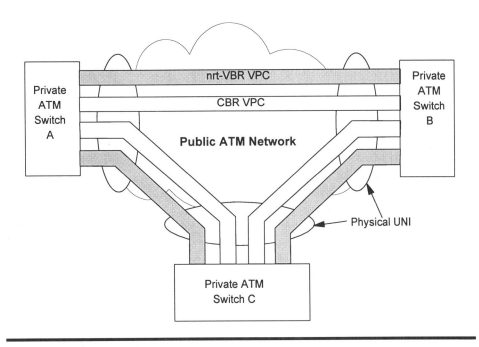

Figure 22.5 Hybrid Public-Private VP Tunneling Network Supporting Multiple QoS Classes

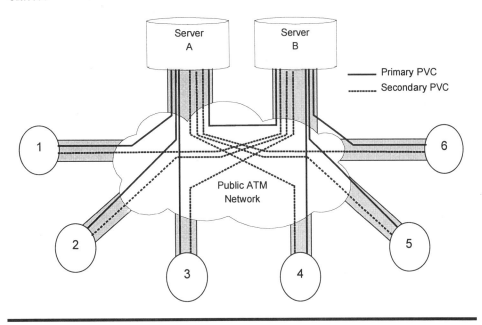

Figure 22.6 Hub and Spoke Design for Private Network Sites Connected via a Public Network

Another popular hybrid private-public network design is a hierarchy of backbone and edge switches. This topology works best when applications utilize a peer-to-peer paradigm. The hierarchy significantly reduces the required number of links compared with a full mesh of point-to-point ATM connections. Figure 22.7 shows an example of a hierarchical hybrid private-public ATM network. Backbone nodes A through D are interconnected via a full PVC mesh, shown by solid lines on each of the UNIs traversing the public network cloud. Each edge node, numbered 1 through 8, is dual homed via separate PVCs to two backbone nodes. An advantage of this design is that it allows the edge node to remain connected to the rest of the network even if a backbone node or its access line fails. This example utilizes 22 PVCs, compared with 66 required in a full-mesh PVC design.

Although this design significantly reduces the required number of connections, note that a great deal of traffic traverses additional, expensive access lines on its way to the destination. This may still save you money if the carrier passes on enough of its economies of scale efficiency to you. Another cost-cutting move could be to collocate backbone nodes on a carrier's premises to avoid additional access line charges.

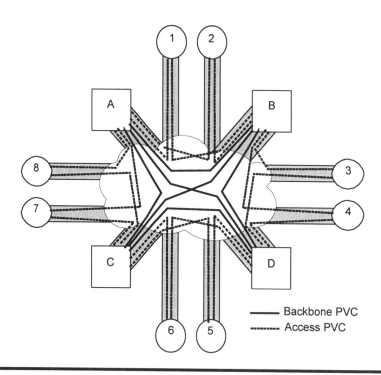

— Backbone PVC
-------- Access PVC

Figure 22.7 Hierarchical Private-Public Network Design

22.4.4 Permanent versus Switched Virtual Connections

The decision to use PVCs versus SVCs applies in the private as well as the public environment; hence we discuss this topic in the next section on general design considerations. However, certain aspects are unique to the public network environment. In public networks, SVCs can help reduce costs and provide additional provisioning and administration flexibility. Look carefully at your traffic patterns and carrier pricing to determine whether SVCs will save money. Note that SVCs are more difficult than PVCs for service providers to implement from a capacity planning, provisioning, and billing perspective.

22.4.5 Building a Bigger, Better (Emulated) LAN

The ATM Forum's LAN Emulation (LANE) standard empowers a significant innovation: construction of a wide area LAN which is scalable to hundreds of megabits per second. The technology required to achieve this impressive goal is necessarily complicated by the fundamental semantic differences between connection-oriented ATM and connectionless LANs. As if this weren't enough, LANE must hurdle another formidable obstacle — emulating a broadcast network over a fundamentally point-to-point media. Chapter 10 provides more details on LANE.

Transparent LAN extension services have grown in popularity, particularly as offered by traditional RBOCs, CLECS, and ISPs. The service providers offer service in city centers where users cannot install their own infrastructure, and where traditional carrier services are either too expensive or short on bandwidth. This enables users to connect traditional shared Ethernet, Token Ring, or FDDI LANs extended across the ATM WAN — and eliminates the need for expensive routers on the LAN. The biggest markets for these services have been the financial services and health-care industries. This also enables user connectivity to the Internet via ATM at native LAN speeds.

MFS provides a large emulated LAN service within the United States with extensions into Europe trunked over an ATM infrastructure. LAN users are unaware that their traffic is chopped into cells, carried across a backbone network, and reconstituted at the far end. To them the emulated LAN service appears as a cost-effective, higher-performing alternative to DS1 trunked private line networks. A number of carriers employ ATM to effectively resell higher-speed transmission facilities to many emulated LAN customers.

22.4.6 Designing the Network to Fit the Service Cost or Tariff

A key objective of this book is to help users design ATM networks. Thus, when designing an ATM network that employs a public ATM service, the user, to achieve the most cost-effective result, must keep the provider's pricing and tariff schemes in mind when selecting traffic parameters and PVC topology. The public and private network designers have different objectives. While the ATM service provider designs its network to achieve a maximum bandwidth utilization (in order to maximize return on investment), the private network designer chooses a topology and traffic parameters to minimize cost.

Correct selection of service categories and bandwidths are key to minimizing cost while assuring that users receive their required QoS. Selection of bandwidth parameters that are too small can cause excessive loss within the network, while selection of parameters that are too large increases cost unnecessarily. This method of selecting the correct traffic parameters *a priori* can be difficult, and often requires some tuning. See Part 2 for guidelines on selecting the ATM service category and bandwidth parameters. Our advice is to start with smaller traffic parameters, measure the resultant load and performance, and increase the traffic parameters as needed.

The Available Bit Rate (ABR) standard offers an attractive alternative to network designers. In this approach, the user's equipment responds to network indications of congestion by *decreasing* the offered traffic [6]. ABR allows a Minimum Cell Rate (MCR), which is the minimum guaranteed bandwidth. In this method, the network service provider communicates network congestion to the end user using the Explicit Forward Congestion Indication (EFCI) bit in the ATM header or ABR resource management cells (see Chapter 6). Service providers that implement ABR services can maximize the cost-effectiveness of ATM services while maintaining consistent QoS to the end users [6]. Indeed, users must respond to congestion indications from service provider networks in order to maximize application throughput and meet end user quality expectations according to the ABR specifications.

22.5 SELECTING VENDORS AND SERVICE PROVIDERS

It is now time to select an ATM switch and/or WAN service providers to meet your networking needs. Don't just use the information in this book: because vendor and carrier information is constantly changing. Ask the same questions of your candidate suppliers, request detailed documentation, and ask for a demonstration and explanations at trade shows or meetings. Remember that you are the customer; they are in business because of you.

To summarize, the primary factors influencing the selection of ATM equipment and a service provider(s) include:

- Feeds and speeds (i.e., interface types and their transmission rates)
- Throughput – peak and average rates
- Performance — delay, delay variation, and loss
- Scalability — planning for growth
- Functionality — feature and functions supported
- Stability and redundancy
- Upgrade path

- Price
- Support

Refer to Chapters 13 through 17 for a detailed switch selection guide and Chapters 18 through 20 for guidance in selecting a WAN vendor. We now review these criteria in more detail [5].

22.5.1 Selecting Equipment Vendors

Decide the basis on which you will make your equipment vendor selection before shopping around for vendors. Survey the marketplace, read several books on ATM networking, surf the Web, and collect vendor brochures to become familiar with what's out there. As a guideline, we suggest that your decision be based primarily upon the vendor's ability to meet your network design requirements. Beyond that, there are a few additional selection criteria that should be considered when evaluating hardware vendors [7, 8]:

- Product integration (especially a company that has grown through acquisition)
- Product architecture (expandability, redundancy, reliability)
- Adherence to standards
- Support structure and options
- Future product vision and market/industry leadership
- Financial stability of company
- Proven interoperability
- Effective functional partitioning between hardware and software
- Upgrade path to comply with future standards (in software rather than hardware.
- Support for legacy protocols — they'll be there for a while!
- Field upgrade hot swap capability
- Additional capacity easy to add — scalability!
- Defined and tested interoperability
- Cross-product common card usage — not different cards for different size chassis!
- Adequate documentation

22.5.2 Selecting an ATM Service Provider

This section presents some of the key criteria for selecting an ATM service provider.

Any ATM service provider should offer:

- Geographic coverage near your locations
- 7-day by 24-hour (7 x 24) proactive support
- Network management support

- Redundant ATM switch hardware, software, and power systems
- Automatic alternative and redundant routing capabilities

Be sure to base service provider selection on specific feature, cost, and support requirements. In addition, some things to consider include:

- Service integration and protocol interworking
- Service architecture (switch type, access methods, backbone trunking design)
- Adherence to standards
- Support structure and options
- Future service vision and market/industry leadership
- Financial stability of company
- Customer network management options
- Service-level guarantees offered

22.6 OTHER DESIGN CONSIDERATIONS

This section contains some other design considerations. One key issue covered is the choice between the use of PVCs and SVCs. Another key consideration is designing for specific objectives of delay, delay variation, and throughput. Virtual LANs are also briefly discussed, along with methods for improving network performance and security considerations.

22.6.1 Selecting and Managing PVCs and SVCs

There are a few key design tips to selecting and managing PVCs and SVCs.

22.6.1.1 Selecting PVC Traffic Parameters

Select the initial PVC rate at a lower value and measure usage over the first few weeks or months. Ramp up the PVC traffic parameters if you experience excessive loss or unacceptable throughput or response times. Periodically review the selection of ATM service categories against traffic types and usage patterns.

22.6.1.2 Advantages of SVCs

LANE, MPOA, and classical IP over ATM work best over SVCs. Actually, for all but the smallest networks, the complexity of PVC administration is too great for these layer 2 and 3 interworking standards. SVCs allow users to connect end ATM stations "on the fly" rather than having to pre-provision PVCs. This enables users to establish temporary high-speed links to other sites. SVCs use signaling protocols to establish calls "on demand." Benefits of SVCs include:

- Flexibility —Devices can be added to the network more quickly than with the PVC provisioning process.
- Scalability — PVCs need $n(n - 1)/2$ connections for full connectivity of n nodes.
- Ease of use – As with routing, once the end station address is configured, the user can dynamically connect to others.
- Ease of network management — Eliminating the manual update requirement inherent in maintaining PVCs simplifies network administration.
- Lower cost — SVCs have lower cost than PVCs for intermittent usage (see the next section for more details).
- Redundancy — SVCs can be used to reroute traffic dynamically around a failed link or switch.

There are a few drawbacks to SVCs. Vendors may support the SVC standards, but SVCs that span multivendor environments may not work as planned. Many vendors have yet to prove cross-platform interoperability. Ask your vendor for proof of this. SVCs will also provide a better method of enabling FR to ATM service interworking.

22.6.1.3 Determining SVC Requirements

Consider using SVCs for infrequent connectivity. SVCs also provide more accurate cost accounting to end-user addresses (i.e., IP). Designing networks with cross-corporation (i.e., extranet) SVCs can also be very powerful — when this option is available from carriers. SVCs also make sense when the destination changes over time — for example, in a corporate videoconferencing network.

Placing voice alongside data has always been one of ATM's key advantages. With the advent of SVCs, any network manager should study the tariffs for ATM SVCs and telephone calls when building a private network, at least for intracompany voice communications. SVCs could eventually replace voice services. It's worth investigating!

Ensure that the maximum number of concurrent SVC connections and SVC call setup rate meet your traffic requirements. For example, an analysis performed for the entire set of Georgia Tech LANs [9] determined that the need was for 2000 concurrent SVC connections and 30 SVC connections/second. Your requirements may be more or less than these values.

22.6.1.4 When to Use PVCs versus SVCs

Providing a PVC from every host in a network to every other host in an n-node network, requires $n(n - 1)/2$ PVCs. For example, a network with 1,000 hosts, each of which wanted to communicate with each of the others, would require 499,500 PVCs! And 1,000 hosts is a relatively small network. Would you realistically consider having someone type in the parameters for almost half a million connections? Hopefully, this shows how PVC management quickly can become unmanageable.

The saving grace is that in fact, rarely do all hosts need to communicate simultaneously with all other hosts. However, even with limited host-to-host traffic, the total number of PVCs can become quite large, making the network much more difficult to manage. This also requires a huge amount of switch resources to manage all these PVCs. SVCs are the solution to this problem, bringing scalability to large networks by being established and terminated as required. But keep an eye on SVC creation rates, as they can get out of hand. Make sure the switch you choose does not limit the number of SVCs that can be created or simultaneously maintained.

22.6.2 Virtual LANs (VLANs)

Some campus and LAN ATM switches support a Virtual LAN (VLAN) capability. "Virtual LANs" use software to define "virtual workgroups" which logically band together multiple users on different LANs in the same virtual LAN segment. Thus, each workstation can belong to multiple virtual LANs.

The primary objectives of VLANs include:

- Provide high-speed connectivity for LAN users.
- Provide virtual workgroups across the enterprise.
- Reduce administrative overhead involved in moves, adds, and changes.

The three primary LAN switch models for VLANs (in migration order) include:

- Parallel cabling
- Proprietary shared media
- ATM VLANs

While ATM provides tremendous scalability and interoperates with existing LAN technologies, it does have a steep learning curve [10]. VLANs offer a powerful alternative to workstation management. VLANs can offer the benefits of:

- No requirement to move workstations to access changing resource requirements — just give them logical access to shared resources

VLANs drastically reduce the cost of moves, adds, and changes.

- No requirement to change IP addresses as users' access requirements begin to move or span the network

22.6.3 Improving ATM Network Performance

Improving application performance over ATM starts at the workstation, but can also be performed within the LAN.

There are many methods that can improve ATM workstation performance [11]:

- Increase packet size (up to 20,000 bytes).
- Try increasing block size of transfers (watch 53-byte cell overhead).
- Try increasing PDU size.
- Try a different operating system — different operating systems have varying levels of performance.
- Try a different transmission protocol — performance can vary drastically by protocol (for example, UDP can achieve 30 percent greater throughput than TCP).
- Use an ATM-layer API — this can boost performance dramatically, sometimes to near wire speed!
- Check disk access speed of workstation — this can have an impact on performance.
- Use a PCI card — PCI can achieve better performance than ISA or EISA NIC cards.
- Check your higher-layer protocol performance — higher-layer protocols can have different impacts on throughput.

Note that most EISA cards rarely achieve throughputs of greater than 50 Mbps, while PCI cards can achieve a full 100 Mbps throughput. There are also a few things to check on LAN performance before throwing more bandwidth or more LAN switching at the problem. Besides the obvious sniffing for abusive users or degraded service due to failing parts or cables, understand exactly what bandwidth is available [12].

22.6.4 Delay, Jitter, and Buffering

Always pay attention to the delay (latency) and jitter imposed by ATM switches. From a technical standpoint, there are three ways in which switches impact your application performance:

- Latency – how long it takes a switch to process each cell
- Jitter – fluctuations in the rate of cells delivered by the destination switch
- Loss – the fraction of cells lost in switches due to congestion

Both delay and jitter are detrimental to time-sensitive traffic like video and voice, where excessive latency and jitter become noticeable to the end user and must be kept to a minimum. Most switches have latency of less than 250 µs, which is acceptable. On the other hand, jitter depends on the switch design, port speeds, and the overall load. In the Constant Bit Rate (CBR) service category, look for jitter that is in the range of hundreds of microseconds, since the end-to-end jitter should be on the order of milliseconds. Both delay and jitter are increased by the number of switches that the application must transit (see Chapter 5 for more details on delay and jitter).

The other key switch attribute that can affect your design is loss, which is largely determined by the amount and type of buffering employed by the ATM switch. When a network becomes congested, bursts of traffic may occasionally overload the network. Buffering allows the congested switch port to ride through the period of overload by delaying the cells and transmitting them later. Thus, if you are planning on sending traffic that has frequent and extremely large bursts, you may want to select a switch with a large buffering capability. Switch designs which share a large pool of buffers across multiple interfaces can provide this capability cost-effectively. Be sure that the allocation of a shared-memory design is equitable across users and applications.

22.6.5 ATM Security

ATM security is a relatively new technology covering closed user groups, encryption, and firewalls. ATM address screening provides the ability for ATM switches to specify a list of ATM addresses (per port) that users are allowed, or not allowed, to receive or initiate SVC calls.

GTE offers its InfoGuard 100 ATM encryptor, an ATM cell encryptor that uses standard Data Encryption Standard (DES) and Diffie-Hellman protocols. Storage Technology Corp. (StorageTek) provides an ATM line access and security system (ATLAS) which operates at OC-3 speeds and creates a firewall at the ATM switch. Finally, NSC has announced a firewall designed specifically for ATM. ATM security standards information can be obtained by going to the ATM Forum's Security Working Group Web page.

22.7 REVIEW

This chapter covered the basic design of a private or hybrid private-public ATM network. The chapter referred back to earlier material as required, focusing on the key issues involved in actual network design. Here the focus was on economic, complexity, and operational considerations. Design considerations were also provided in the key areas of PVC and SVC design and management. We also covered the subjects of virtual LANs, workstation and LAN performance tuning, and the emerging field of ATM security.

22.8 REFERENCES

[1]   S. Salamone, "Life in the Fast Lane," *Byte*, July 1996.
[2]   D. McDysan, "Public Data Multi-Service Interface Interworking using ATM (Balancing Connectivity, Efficiency and Performance)," Globecom '94, Houston.

[3]   K. Maxwell, "Asymmetric Digital Subscriber Line: Interim Technology for the Next Forty Years," *IEEE Network*, October, 1996.

[4]   R. Guerin, "Equivalent Capacity and Bandwidth Allocation," IEEE JSAC, September 1991.

[5]   D. McDysan and D. Spohn, *ATM: Theory and Application*, McGraw-Hill, 1995.

[6]   M. Incollingo, K. Schulz, and H. Uhrig, "Taking Advantage of ATM Services and Tariffs: The Importance of Transport Layer Dynamic Rate Adaptation," *IEEE Networks*, April 1997.

[7]   D. Spohn, *Data Network Design*, 2d ed., McGraw-Hill, 1997.

[8]   J. White, "ATM Networking: How Users Can Protect Their Investments," *Telecommunications,* July 1996.

[9]   R.J. Clark, R. R. Hutchins, and S. Register, "Deploying ATM in a Data Network: An Analysis of SVC Requirements," IEEE Conference on Local Communications, October 16–19, 1995.

[10] S. King, "It's an Adventure," *Network World*, April 10, 1995.

[11] ATM Report, January 1996.

[12] R. Mandeville and J. Till Johnson, "Forget the Forklift," *Data Communications,* September 1996.

23

Case Studies

This chapter presents case studies from various walks of life. Most of the networks covered below are in full production, but some are still in the trial phases. Early ATM trials starting in the early 1990s were mostly on research or educational networks. Most of the more recent trials in the second half of the 1990s involved TCP/IP over ATM and were designed specifically to solve business problems. Also, there are many more private ATM networks being built. We have tried to find at least one case study from each vertical market. You are encouraged to select the case studies that best fits your application and business requirements and research them using the references cited at the end of this chapter.

23.1 SOURCES OF CASE STUDY MATERIAL

Case studies presented in this chapter were primarily provided by the vendors responding to our switch and service survey. Other information was available on the World Wide Web or through vendor or service provider press releases. All material used was publicly available as of publication time.

23.2 INTERNET SERVICE PROVIDER NETWORKS

Public Internet and data transport service providers are probably the biggest users of ATM technology. ATM brings a high-throughput and effective traffic management to Internet Service Provider (ISP) backbones. ATM's higher speed backbone circuits (155 and 622 Mbps) provide better performance than routers — offering switching times in the microseconds as compared to packet forwarding times in the milliseconds for routers. Per port and per Mbit, ATM switches remain much more cost-effective than routers, and offer much greater port densities. Bandwidth management is also more granular, offering many options per Virtual Channel (VC). These economies are so great that some providers are offering ATM access at less than one-third the price of equivalent dedicated access.

The lead switch vendor for carriers and ISPs offering frame relay services (as listed by Vertical Systems Group) has been Cascade Communications (now part of Ascend). This is due in part not only to the quality and functionality of the product, but also due to the fact that Cascade has been able to drive a high level of scalability in ports and processing. One example is Cascade's channelized DS3 access module, which crams 392 DS1 ports into a single chassis. Scalability and port density remains one of the key drivers of service providers, a lesson that any equipment vendor needs to take to heart when selling to this type of customer.

Some report that large Internet service providers are dividing into two camps: those who scale their IP backbones using ATM and those who don't. MCI announced plans to upgrade its domestic DS3 IP network to an OC3 ATM backbone in 1995. Continuing to ramp up its network in responsive to explosive Internet traffic growth, MCI announced plans to upgrade its network to OC12 ATM by year-end 1996 and set its sights on OC48 ATM for futures. Other service providers extol the efficiency virtues of high-performance, frame-based routers using a protocol referred to as IP over SONET. But there are trade offs between IP over ATM and IP over SONET as we will discover.

23.3 FOOD SERVICES

23.3.1 McDonald's Corp.

McDonald's Corporation owns and operates an ATM network designed to support client-server applications, including cash-register transactions, that reach out to all of the company's almost 30,000 restaurants. Chuck Rush, McDonald's global-network architect, says ATM makes the most sense as a carrier for the multimedia data that it was designed for, thus justifying the cost by carrying voice and video on the same network. In 1996, McDonald's network designer viewed LAN Emulation (LANE) over ATM as the only viable technology to migrate away from FDDI [1]. Since LANE is not the optimal solution, the company then planned to move to the ATM Forum's Multiprotocol over ATM (MPOA) standard when it became available.

23.4 MEDICAL

23.4.1 Pennsylvania's Allegheny Health, Education and Research Foundation (AHERF)

At Pennsylvania's Allegheny Health, Education and Research Foundation (AHERF), a statewide academic health system, neurosurgeons perform surgery while medical students in multiple remote locations observe and pose questions to the doctors all simultaneously over the ATM network. The ATM network was designed by FORE Systems for AHERF and connects its major facilities in Pittsburgh and Philadelphia, 300 miles apart. Each node is equipped with a redundant communications path. Here's how the system works: Operating rooms at Allegheny General Hospital in Pittsburgh are wired with video cameras and a monitor. ForeRunner ATM switches take the digitized signals from the cameras, convert them to ATM cells, and transmit them to ForeRunner ATM switches located at the local carrier's point of presence. A 45-Mbps fiber optic link terminates in Philadelphia, where the transmissions are distributed to lecture halls at AHERF hospitals and colleges via ForeRunner ATM switches thus providing the networking components needed for a live, interactive medical class.

Today, in medical education and research, skilled surgeons have obligations to both the operating room and the lecture hall. To help physicians handle these obligations, the AHERF ATM network enables surgeons to conduct training directly from the operating room. Doctors use the ATM network to conduct live, interactive medical classes at multiple locations even during surgical procedures. The same ATM network can transfer medical images for remote diagnostics and handle complex data transmissions files, records, and billing information. With all these capabilities, the network helps AHERF to increase efficiency, save time, and reduce costs by moving information, not people and paper.

ATM was chosen primarily for the ability to link multiple sites in Pittsburgh and Philadelphia to participate in an interactive videoconference — a requirement for 10 megabits of bandwidth. AHERF runs four or five concurrent videoconferences, each requiring 10 Mbps of bandwidth, from multiple locations. AHERF needed a technology that would allow the physicians to do a better job of showing what the students need to know. ATM provided a better solution than traditional desktop video, which was reaching its limitations in size and resolution. This was one of the first medical digital video networks of its kind using ATM.

ATM helped AHERF integrate its bridges and routers into ATM, reduce the number of T1s, and yet maintain the response time and throughput of the network — critical for its data applications, some of which are actually life support.

By using ATM from FORE, AHERF has established a new information systems paradigm for the health-care industry. It is a model that has proven to be technically superior, as well as demonstrably cost-effective [2].

23.5 FINANCIAL SERVICES — BANKING

The first major banking network using Asynchronous Transfer Mode (the other ATM) was Boatmen's Bank. But Boatmen's is not alone anymore. The Bank of New York also now uses an ATM communications network. And if you think about it, banks have more to overcome in adopting ATM than any other industry, given that they have the same acronym that sometimes causes confusion — ATM (Automatic Teller Machines).

23.5.1 Boatmen's Bank

Boatmen's Bank is based in St. Louis and operates 700 remote-banking sites, with a growth rate of 400 percent in 6 to 7 years, with assets in the $40 billion range. It was one of the first banks to deploy ATM technology in a mission-critical use [3].

Boatmen's data center was previously a heterogeneous environment with IBM 3090 mainframes and a variety of UNIX machines that communicated over a DS1 backbone. After analyzing a Time-Division Multiplexing (TDM) vs. ATM solution on the basis of price/performance, present capabilities, and future growth, the bank decided to deploy ATM. The bank replaced its DS1 backbone with a DS3 and OC-3 ATM backbone offering 1 Gbps capacity to their headquarters location. It built a dark fiber network so that bandwidth between key facilities would not become an issue.

The network uses General DataComm's APEX ATM switch along with services from AT&T, MCI, and Sprint, and some other competitive access providers. The Boatmen's management team is using ATM-enabled applications, including 30-Mbps broadcast-quality videoconferencing — motion JPEG running on ATM-NIC-enabled workstations along with internal codecs (coder/decoders) within the ATM switches.

23.6 RESEARCH AND EXPLORATION

23.6.1 Schlumberger Geco-Prakla

Schlumberger Geco-Prakla, a division of Schlumberger Technology Corporation, an $8 billion global technology company, provides high-resolution, three-dimensional seismic profiles to oil company geologists and geophysicists, who analyze this data on high-end workstations in order to determine the most likely places to drill for oil. Schlumberger Geco-Prakla is a Houston-based company that specializes in helping oil companies find oil. ATM helped Schlumberger Geco-Prakla reduce the costs and time involved in determining where oil wells should be drilled [4]. Schlumberger Geco-Prakla uses FORE ATM products to process and transmit seismic data to oil companies, which then use the data to locate subterranean oil. Schlumberger Geco-Prakla installed FORE ATM switches to connect elements of a High-Performance Parallel Interface (HiPPI) LAN at its supercomputer center to high-end desktops. The ATM workgroup switch connects a cell of six nodes to the center's HiPPI LAN through an ATM backbone switch. Workstations are SGIs, Indigos, Crimsons, and high-end SPARCs. Servers on the ATM backbone are IBM and SPARCs. The network uses IP exclusively.

By using ATM, Schlumberger Geco-Prakla has been able to realize significant cost savings while, at the same time, providing better service to customers. "We acquire a 2- or 3-terabyte data set and process it down to 50- or 60-gigabyte images that we provide to oil companies," explained Dennis O'Neill, technical manager for data processing at Schlumberger Geco-Prakla. By interpreting these data sets, the geophysicists attempt to identify salt domes, faults, or other places where subterranean oil might be located and where wells should be drilled. "The problem," O'Neill noted, "is that the data sets are huge, and the analysis techniques are very computationally and graphics-intensive. It's a common problem in the oil industry." As a result, Schlumberger Geco-Prakla teamed with several companies (Amoco, Chevron and Shell), government agencies (NASA and the Department of Energy), and the Minnesota Supercomputer Center in a joint effort to explore using ATM to speed data transmission and processing of these data sets. The collaboration was dubbed the ARIES project, with the acronym standing for the ATM Research and Industrial Enterprise Study. Based on the initial success of the ARIES project, Schlumberger Geco-Prakla incorporated ATM into its own companywide internal production network.

"Conventional delivery medium is magnetic tape. The amount of time it takes just to spin those tapes, write to them, and then read them back can be days, if not weeks. ATM technology can enable us to deliver that same data set overnight. So we've gotten real value out of ATM, using it daily in our production center in Houston, as well as in the ARIES project."

"I certainly know how much cheaper it is for me to run an ATM switch rather than HiPPI," said O'Neill, comparing ATM to Schlumberger Geco-Prakla's previously installed HiPPI network. "The HiPPI switch, by itself, cost about $25,000, and depending on the machine that we brought into that HiPPI network, interfaces ran from $15,000 to over $100,000. By contrast, with FORE ATM, we've been able to add Ultra Sparcs and SP-2s on the order of $2,000 a port. We've been able to bring ATM performance on-line at much less cost than HiPPI. That has been a driving factor."

"The initial application was to tie the supercomputers together via ATM. Our next step was to move ATM out into the hands of high-end SGI users. The next step will be to bring in the more mid-range desktop users, or at least their servers."

23.6.2 Bayer AG

The biotechnology division of German drugmaker Bayer AG, based in Berkeley, California, used ATM to upgrade its LAN backbone [5]. The division began its migration to ATM in 1995, and has had to evaluate the new alternative of a gigabit Ethernet backbone. The Bayer network manager viewed ATM as a solution designed to meet LAN backbone needs for 5 years into the future, but doubted that gigabit Ethernet's jury-rigged backbone solution could meet his needs. The initial applications required support for imaging and document management, both bandwidth hogs. The ATM network also supports unplanned applications for video training and corporationwide use of Lotus Notes. Although Bayer deployed fiber-optic cabling, it still runs a switched 10-Mbps Ethernet backbone. For now, the network manager, Ron Puccinelli, must run video traffic on its own subnetwork to avoid overloading this hybrid ATM and switched Ethernet infrastructure. For Bayer, Berkeley is a model for other potential ATM sites, of which the West Haven, Connecticut, location is the next likely pharmaceutical site to adopt ATM. The company stated that it plans to integrate DS1 connections between Private Branch Exchanges (PBXs) in Berkeley and West Haven along with data and video traffic over a connection running ATM over a DS3 private line. Eventually, the company expects to realize a 75 percent savings (!) on WAN access fees from this design.

Bayer built its ATM backbone around CoreBuilder 5000 switches from 3Com Corporation connecting ATM by uplink modules to FORE Systems' enterprise backbone switches. A Cisco Systems Inc. AGS+ router connects to the FORE switches. Sprint, the WAN ATM vendor, uses an ATM switch from FORE Systems Inc. at the customer premises to link to the carrier's backbone. It made sense to managers at Bayer's headquarters in Pittsburgh to standardize on FORE equipment at all Bayer sites to take advantage of FORE's value-added services throughout the enterprise. Bayer plans to move to ATM Switched Virtual Circuits (SVCs) to overcome the throughput limitations of routers, as well as to avoid the frequent moves, adds, and changes between the current 17 IP subnetworks. The Bayer network is an example of an enterprise that considers ATM networking to changing core competencies. So far, ATM has served Bayer well and promises to continue to meet the networking needs of this company.

23.7 ENTERTAINMENT/TRAVEL

23.7.1 Carnival

Carnival cruise lines uses 3Com Corporation's Cellplex 7000 ATM backbone switches for the company's LAN backbone and support switched Ethernet to the desktop. An older FDDI LAN backbone will remain in place until the company can migrate several core business applications from an old Unisys mainframe to new client-server configuration. Workgroup switches are used to connect to Ethernet at the desktop. Future uses of ATM may be for videoconferencing and interactive TV aboard Carnival's cruise ships.

23.7.2 I Want My MCI HDTV!

MCI used its ATM network to broadcast the nation's first coast-to-coast live broadcast from a High Definition Television (HDTV) station — a 20-Mbps video digital stream.

23.7.3 Equant (Scitor) Circle

Equant (Scitor) Circle uses Cisco BPX ATM switches to provide global voice and data Virtual Private Network (VPN) services to international businesses as well as an airline reservation system.

23.7.4 Videotron and SohoNet

No matter what the source or direction within the London-based MAN, the SohoNet ATM network can quickly transmit film scenes, entire movies, graphic images, text, videoconferencing, or sound. At the core of SohoNet is a ForeRunner ASX-1000 ATM switch located at the headquarters of Videotron, London's largest cable company [6]. Each of the postproduction houses on the network is currently connected to Videotron's facility by a single mode fiber STM-1 155-Mbps link. Bandwidth requirements are so great that many of the links are being upgraded to 622 Mbps. The network uses ForeThought internetworking software and is managed via ForeView network management software in conjunction with HP OpenView.

London's cosmopolitan Soho district has emerged as a world-class center for the production of computer-generated animation and special effects for the movie industry. Because this work is so graphics-intensive, it requires extremely broad bandwidth and high data transfer speeds. To answer the need for more bandwidth and faster transmissions, several of the leading production facilities installed ATM equipment and then connected their internal ATM networks together in a metropolitan area network called SohoNet.

The Computer Film Company, VTR, Cinesite, and the Moving Picture Company had independently arrived at the decision to use FORE ATM adapters and switches for their internal networks. "The main reason we had for choosing ATM is its combination of high speed and price/performance," explained Neil Harris, director of the Computer Film Company. "We think LAN connectivity is a good thing to have. But once you've got a network, you see it has multiple uses. Postproduction companies, although competitive with one another, also end up being one another's customers and suppliers, as work on various projects is subcontracted from one house to another. Since we were already making movies in collaboration with one another, we thought, Why not have an ATM network that we can all use?"

Mike Farrell, chairman of SohoNet, Ltd., explained, "With an ATM network like SohoNet, you can work more efficiently on collaborative projects. At the click of a button, you can see work in progress. This makes you more competitive and opens all sorts of commercial opportunities because you can do more work. Much of the work must be turned around quickly, no matter what the cost. If you can't turn the work around in, say, 24 hours, you won't get the job. The FORE ATM network eliminates the time delays associated with transferring film images to tape, transporting the tape, and reloading it from the tape onto another machine."

The benefits of SohoNet's ATM network have been impressive. Companies on SohoNet are able to "drag and drop" film segments created by other production houses into their own system for editing. Film segments can be transferred from celluloid to digital format in minutes, and transferred between sites on the network as easily as sending E-mail messages. Producers and directors are able to videoconference with artists and editors using an electronic whiteboard, which enables them to view a common image and make revisions to it, in real time. This speeds approvals, so movies can be completed faster than ever, which means that they can be released to the public sooner and provide a quicker return on investment than could be achieved otherwise.

Other benefits accrued from ATM include saving money by optimizing installed hardware: servers, routers, workstations, and the like. You can do that by spreading the workload among different companies on the network, even if they're your competitors. It's a very mature approach to doing business. By doing that, you can level the peaks and troughs of traffic on your installed hardware. It's a way to best utilize the hardware you've invested in already. Scalability is also important. Plans are being laid to extend the network via British Telecom to ad agencies, prepress companies, and film studios in the UK and Europe, even to ATM sites in Hollywood. Harris added, "We see SohoNet as a network for the media industry." Observed Farrel, "It is going to change the way our industry works."

23.8 THE ARTS

23.8.1 City Library in Valenciennes, France

Equipped with ForeRunner ATM switches from FORE Systems, the city library in Valenciennes, France, now digitizes its documents to make them easily accessible across a high-speed ATM network [7]. At the center of the Valenciennes network is an ATM switch which provides 155-Mbps ATM links to the library's two IBM AS/400 servers. The network's two Ethernet switches link 30 personal computers to the ATM switch by converting the LAN protocols into ATM cells.

In France, the city of Valenciennes has long been known as a destination for tourists seeking a Renaissance-era flavor complete with ancient architecture and leisurely strolls along quaint pathways. Now, with help from ATM, Valenciennes is becoming known for a technological renaissance that involves 155-Mbps ATM architecture and multimedia transmissions across optical fiber paths. The city's library, home to ancient parchments and manuscripts, now digitizes library documents to make them easily accessible across a high-speed network called the Culture Ring. The network uses ATM to transmit voice, video, and data at extremely high speeds. Conceived by Valenciennes officials as a means to protect and promote the city's rich cultural history, the Culture Ring links the city's museum, library, and theater via a fiber optic cable network. Plans for the network were supported by the European Community, which identified Valenciennes as one of its new technology pilot zones.

At the library, one of the first projects was to compile documentary archives into an information technology system. Library officials purchased an IBM AS/400 minicomputer to store the data. Later, when they began to set up a multimedia catalogue, their goal was to offer direct access to 72 on-line CD-ROMs located in optical disk libraries, with each digitized document featuring its own one-minute, audiovisual abstract. To achieve that goal, library officials recognized the need for technical expertise. With support from Valenciennes Mayor Jean-Louis Berloo, officials evaluated bids from vendors, and awarded the contract for network services and cabling to Archimed, a multimedia development company based in Lille, France. Offering a network solution based on ATM technology, Archimed designed OPAC (Open Public Access Catalogue), a system that allows users of the network to simultaneously access all digitized elements from the library's catalogue of CD-ROMs.

The ATM network architecture is centered on an ATM switch which connects two servers using the Windows NT operating system with 30 workstations via two 16-port Ethernet switches. All ATM network connections operate at 155 Mbps. The network's servers hold the multimedia features of the documents that are stored on the AS/400. At present, the library has more than 300 video clips and 300 fixed images. On the client side, 30 workstations are equipped with multimedia cards. Mr. Mongi Zidi, project manager at Archimed, explains. "The PC acts as a standard terminal, and access is completely transparent to the users. They have the impression that they are looking at local data when, in fact, it comes from the server."

Now that the ATM-based network has been operating for more than a year, the City of Valenciennes Library operates several networked multimedia applications. In addition to using multimedia to reclassify literature, documentaries, and audiovisual collections, personnel at the library also use the system to administer the city's municipal archives. From the city's point of view, the ATM network has helped stimulate interest in the new library. The number of visitors has increased tenfold, and the library has quadrupled its membership.

Now, the designers of the Culture Ring project want to take it even further. They are considering placement of multimedia terminals throughout the city, including possible access to the network from the homes of city residents. Other plans call for connections to the University of Valenciennes and several sites in the sister city of Mons, Belgium. By basing the network infrastructure on ATM, the designers of the Culture Ring Project have positioned the network for the future, creating a technological renaissance in a venerable Renaissance city.

23.9 RETAIL

23.9.1 Gemological Institute of America (GIA) Gem Trade Laboratory (GTL)

The GIA GTL is the industry leader in diamond grading, gem identification, and research. The GIA built an ATM network based on the NewBridge VIVID switching platform [8]. ATM offered a high-performance MPOA-based solution that allows gemologists to accurately register and track diamonds and support subnetworks for education and training.

The VIVID system, based on the ATM Forum's MPOA standard, supports GIA's new Horizon relational database, designed to capture important characteristics on the world's most significant diamonds, colored stones, and pearls. The VIVID solution also supports a variety of GIA's subnetworks used for gemology education, management consulting in the retail jewelry industry, and industry manufacturing.

"The data we capture requires huge amounts of bandwidth," said Richard Testa, GIA Director of Information Technology and Chief Information Officer. "We needed a solution that could deliver 155 Mbps, with the ability to go as high as 622 Mbps, to our servers and backbone. Only NewBridge Networks, with its VIVID switched routing solution, was able to offer these capabilities, allowing us to create virtual local area networks and improve load balance demand on the network as well as provide the highest level of support and engineering."

To handle the bandwidth demand of transmitting images from its Horizon relational database, GIA has installed a highly scalable VIVID system that incorporates 42 VIVID Yellow Ridge Ethernet switches and 12 VIVID workgroup switches. VIVID systems are located at GIA's New York City headquarters and a new, recently completed, state-of-the-art facility in Carlsbad, California.

Prior to deploying the VIVID solution, GIA used a more traditional approach to manually grade and certify precious stones. When the Horizon client/server system was cut over in August 1996, GIA moved quickly to implement the VIVID switched routing solution to support the institute's extremely high bandwidth requirements.

In addition to supporting the GIA Gem Trade Laboratories in New York, the VIVID switched routing solution will create virtual LANs that provide a subnetwork used in educating thousands of students annually at the new Carlsbad campus, while other subnetworks will support GIA divisions that provide manufacturing and consulting.

"This is an excellent example of how an MPOA-based switched routing architecture can alleviate many of the congestion, management, and performance problems network managers face today," said John Morency at The Registry, an information technology consulting firm. "The VIVID switched routing solution is a proven industry standards–based architecture that enables users to automatically configure networks which dramatically reduce the cost and time requirements of servicing large and complex systems such as the GIA network."

The VIVID switched routing system is a powerful solution for meeting the demands of today's LAN internetworking environments. The VIVID system eliminates the performance bottlenecks and management complexity of conventional router network designs. With its highly scalable, wire-speed routing capacity, the VIVID switched routing solution is ideal for meeting the performance requirements of high-speed LAN, multimedia, and intranet environments. Switched routing also enables extensive virtual networking capabilities, enabling customers to define policies for governing user behavior and enhancing application performance.

23.10 TRANSPORTATION

23.10.1 Canada's Highway 407

ATM has enabled implementation of the world's first electronic toll collection system on Canada's Highway 407 near Toronto for billing, planning, and other management functions, easing congestion and reducing pollution at the road's 28 interchanges. The FORE ATM communications system for the Highway 407 project features both wide and local area components [9]. ForeThought internetworking software provides end-to-end network management across the ATM network, which features ForeRunner ASX-200BX ATM switches located at 28 electronic toll collection interchanges. The ATM switches at these interchanges transmit video images and data to the system's operation center, which features servers, PowerHub LAN switches, and Vector ATM switches. FORE ATM Network Interface Cards (NICs) are in the servers as well as the roadside toll collection units.

Running 69 km through Ontario, Canada's most populous province, Highway 407 serves the congested Toronto metropolitan area as the first public/private partnership highway project in the area's history. To ease congestion caused by an estimated 55,000 daily users, and reduce pollution at the road's 28 interchanges, the highway relies on an ATM-based system that eliminates toll collection booths by utilizing broadcast transponders and video imaging to record highway usage by individual vehicles. The data gathered by the system is relayed to central toll transaction processors, which forward pertinent information to a Revenue Management System (RMS) that calculates and creates bills and distributes them to drivers' homes, posts revenues to accounts, and manages other related transactions.

In planning the tollway's communications system, the project design team looked for a networking technology that could effectively transmit both data and digital images. The system also demanded an architecture that would work effectively for both wide and local area networks. Other requirements for the networking technology included speed, reliability, scalability, and cost-effectiveness. Ethernet, SONET, and FDDI technologies were considered, but they were ultimately rejected in favor of ATM technology, which met all of the project's requirements.

ATM's ability to contain bandwidth costs was a key reason it was selected as the networking technology for the Highway 407 project. ATM consolidates both data and digital images on one network, which reduces bandwidth costs significantly, explained Dave Lester, senior designer of systems engineering, Bell Canada, and a member of the network design team for Highway 407. ATM enables high-speed file transfers, improving the performance efficiency of the ETC servers. In addition, ATM is a connection technology that supports SVCs, providing transparent fault isolation and simplified operation and management.

This ATM network can be easily expanded to accommodate future growth. The network currently operates at a rate of 155 Mbps, but the data rate on the WAN can be increased to 622 Mbps simply by adding an expansion module in each ForeRunner ATM switch. This future-proofing capability is important because, while Highway 407 is designed to handle an initial 55,000 vehicles a day on its six lanes, it has the capacity to expand up to ten lanes, and the electronic toll collection network must be able to handle the additional traffic.

23.11 ELECTRONIC COMMERCE

23.11.1 Intuit Services Corporation (ISC)

Intuit's electronic commerce offering uses the NewBridge Networks VIVID MPOA-based switched routing solution and MainStreetXpress 36170 multiservices switch to support Intuit's Quicken on-line banking services [10]. ATM services based on the NewBridge switch are used to enhance and expand the on-line banking capabilities of Quicken, the leading personal finance software application.

Located in Chicago, ISC is responsible for architecting and managing the company's electronic commerce network that links 6 million Quicken customers with more than 40 financial institutions. ISC is leveraging the VIVID switched routing architecture to facilitate more than 60,000 daily electronic transactions, including on-line banking and bill payment. The Quicken network also incorporates Newbridge MainStreetXpress 36170 Multiservices Switches, which extend the VIVID switched routing solution transparently across a wide area network to two separate data centers. In addition, the switches provide the traffic management features needed for large-scale ATM deployment and service offerings.

"The network is fundamental to our entire business, and the Newbridge technology ensures that our electronic commerce network is resilient, robust, and highly reliable," said Erik Stillman, Voice and Data Manager, Intuit Services Corporation. "Our customers expect fast, error-free on-line banking every day. The VIVID switched routing solution with support for MPOA further solidifies NewBridge Networks' leadership role in ATM. The MainStreetXpress 36170 switch completes the total network infrastructure we need to provide a range of electronic banking services addressing the dynamic needs of Quicken users."

"VIVID is the first solution to deliver switched-based routing, and provides Intuit with a competitive advantage as well as solid underlying technology to support a mission-critical on-line banking system," said Eric Andrews, Director of VIVID Product Marketing for NewBridge Networks. "The VIVID architecture will enable Intuit to easily handle today's electronic commerce applications as well as future multimedia on-line banking services."

When an Intuit customer dials into the ISC network using Quicken software and a modem, the requested financial transactions are routed through the VIVID switched routing solution, which distributes the data to local servers or to the appropriate financial institution.

The majority of ISC's current network traffic is financial data; however, the company is planning to add services that incorporate videoconferencing, imaging, and other multimedia services over the ATM network.

"Companies introducing network-based service offerings are facing the hard facts about network reliability and the demands that high traffic and multimedia applications place on the infrastructure," said John McConnell, McConnell Consulting, Inc. "The NewBridge local area network and wide area network switching and routing architecture addresses the immediate and long-term performance and reliability requirements that enable companies such as Intuit to deploy mission-critical network applications."

23.11.2 Lloyd's Bank

Derivatives trading in financial markets requires access to timely, accurate information. Lloyd's Bank uses a FORE ATM network to transmit risk assessment reports to its derivatives dealers at any time [11]. An ATM network reduces risk exposure for Lloyd's Bank. End-to-end ATM from the switch to the PCI adapter cards produces excellent throughput for the Treasury Division's network at Lloyds Bank in the United Kingdom. This network enables Lloyd's derivatives dealers to obtain crucial reports quickly at any time of the day as opposed to just twice daily, which was the case before Lloyd's installed its ATM network.

In the late 1980s, the Systems Team at Lloyd's Treasury Products Group installed a PC-based derivatives processing application running on a Novell server over a Token Ring network. The network was designed to generate dealer exposure reports, which the group's dealers use to assess and manage the level of risk associated with every deal. However, the 4-Mbps Token Ring network provided the risk assessment reports only twice a day. Because every derivatives transaction represents a potentially significant loss, it is critical to generate timely, accurate reports.

In the early 1990s, the network was upgraded to incorporate a 100-Mbps FDDI connection to the backbone. Lloyd's network managers soon recognized, however, that the number of bottlenecks increased with the level of data transmitted across the FDDI network. Plus, the crucial exposure reports could still be transmitted only twice a day.

In 1994, Lloyd's Systems Group developed and applied a rigorous test procedure to evaluate a broad array of standards-based network technologies, including Ethernet, Fast Ethernet 100Base-T, Token Ring and FDDI networks. After in-depth testing and evaluation, Lloyd's network managers concluded that these conventional shared network technologies could not meet their needs for reliable, near-instantaneous report transmission.

Recognizing that a higher-bandwidth network technology, one that offered better performance and scalability, was needed to reduce bottlenecks and provide the exposure reports at any time of day, Lloyd's Systems Group began to assess ATM switches and adapter cards. High-speed, 155-Mbps connections to the desktops of dealers enable them to obtain up-to-the-minute transaction exposure reports at any time. In addition, the ability to add more processing engines to handle the dealer requests means that the system is scalable — an important consideration for Lloyd's.

Today, FORE's ATM switch and PCI adapter cards at Lloyd's Bank support its Treasury Products Division's network of Pentium PCs that provide parallel processing for dealer transaction exposure requests.

23.12 GOVERNMENT NETWORKS

23.12.1 vBNS

The highest-performance hybrid public-private network in existence in 1997 provides a private IP service over a public ATM network. This network is the United States National Science Foundation's very-high-speed Backbone

Network Service (vBNS). In April 1995 MCI turned up this ATM-based OC3 network between five supercomputer centers distributed across the United States. Figure 23.1 illustrates this network [12]. The OC3 connections are provided by Virtual Path Connections (VPCs) between the five Super Computer Centers (SCCs) over MCI's commercial HyperStream ATM service. The local ATM switches split the VPCs up into two full mesh connections of VCCs: one for meshing the vBNS routers which utilize the OSPF protocol and a second which acts as a Logical IP Subnet (LIS) planned for use with SVCs in early 1997. The NSF plans to use the LIS Virtual Channel Connections (VCCs) for applications like video over ATM. As part of the vBNS effort, engineers collect traffic statistics and report on these regularly [13]. An inexpensive IBM-based PC with an OC3 ATM interface card connected to the network via a passive optical splitter is the basis of much of this data. The OC3MON captures the first cell of an AAL5 packet, enabling engineers to analyze all the TCP/IP information [14].

In early 1997 the NSF and MCI announced plans to upgrade this network to OC12 trunking and add additional universities with meritorious high-bandwidth applications. Basically, the network topology looks identical to that above, except that the trunks are upgraded to OC-12 (622 Mbps) speeds and FORE ASX 1000 ATM switches replace the Lightstream 2020 switches [13].

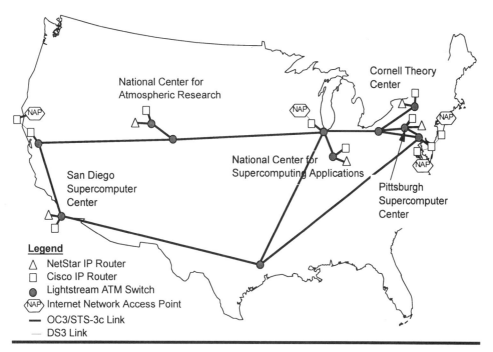

Figure 23.1 1995 National Science Foundation Very-High-Speed Backbone Network Service

23.13 REVIEW

This chapter reviewed case studies from trials, early adopters, and production networks employing ATM-based applications, switching devices and services across a broad range of industry segments.

23.14 REFERENCES

[1] B. Wallace, "Is It Real, or Is It LAN Emulation Software?" *Computerworld*, November 13, 1995, http://www.computerworld.com/search/data/cw_951106-960108/951113SL45atm.html.
[2] AHERF case study provided by FORE Systems.
[3] *Communications Week*, July 29, 1996, p. 45, via Individual Inc. Contact: Lloyd Bollinger at Boatmen's.
[4] Case study provided by FORE Systems.
[5] M. McLean, "Case Study: Standing Firm on ATM — Bayer Pharmaceutical's Network Manager Stays with Backbone Plans Despite Gigabit-Ethernet Hype," *LAN Times*, June 1997, http://www.lantimes.com/97/97jun/706b055a.html.
[6] Videotron case study provided by FORE Systems.
[7] Valenciennes case study provided by FORE Systems.
[8] Gemological Institute of America (GIA) Gem Trade Laboratory (GTL) case study provided by NewBridge Networks.
[9] Canada's Highway 407 case study provided by FORE Systems.
[10] Intuit case study provided by NewBridge Networks.
[11] Lloyd's Bank case study provided by FORE Systems.
[12] J. Jamison and R. Wilder, "vBNS: The Internet Fast Lane for Research and Education," *IEEE Communications*, January, 1997.
[13] MCI, vBNS Home Page, www.vbns.net.
[14] "oc3mon happenings," http://www.nlanr.net/NA/Oc3mon/.

6

Technology
Comparisons
and Futures

This final part provides the reader with an overview of technologies that compete with ATM in the LAN and WAN in Chapter 24. Recently, gigabit Ethernet emerged surrounded by tremendous hype as a contender for the LAN backbone. The text surveys how ATM stacks up against the lower-speed 10- and 100-Mbps Ethernet technologies along with this new speedster and the traditional FDDI LAN backbone. Chapter 24 then investigates alternative means proposed for delivering end-to-end Quality of Service (QoS) to end applications. Next, Chapter 25 gazes into the crystal ball for a glimpse at ATM's potential future, focusing on wireless ATM. We compare the forecast for highest interface speed, switch size, and issues in achieving multimedia applications. This final chapter also touches on some fundamental issues involved in achieving QoS with frame-based networks and the need for high-performance switched virtual connections driven by higher-layer protocols operating over ATM's connection-oriented infrastructure. Finally, we discuss the key issues and work in progress expected to have a major impact on the future of ATM.

24

Technology Comparisons

This chapter provides a detailed comparison of ATM with competing LAN and WAN technologies as well as alternatives to providing Quality of Service (QoS) support. Competing LAN technologies include 100-Mbps Ethernet, gigabit Ethernet, and FDDI. Despite its apparent benefits over legacy LAN technologies, like Ethernet and FDDI, ATM is still not making significant progress in the LAN. In this analysis we show how ATM fares more favorably in the LAN backbone environment than in the cost-driven desktop and workgroup area networks. Next, we look at the WAN competitors and partners to ATM: private lines, frame relay, multimegabit FR, and IP over SONET. Finally, we explore and compare ATM with alternative methods for delivering QoS on an end-to-end basis, namely IP's Resource Reservation Protocol, and a new initiative called cells in frames.

24.1 LAN TECHNOLOGY COMPARISON

This section provides the reader with the criteria required to chose a LAN backbone and access technology. Technology, business, and cost attributes are presented in a risk/benefit analysis. This section analyzes the following technologies competing in the enterprise LAN backbone environment:

- Legacy LAN contention-based protocols (e.g., 10/100/1000-Mbps Ethernet)
- Token-passing protocols (4/16-Mbps Token Ring and FDDI)
- ATM

The general rule when building LAN backbones is switch whenever possible and share media only when necessary. This remains true because switching achieves much greater throughput and alleviates the contention problems inherent in shared Ethernet media. Ethernet technologies have moved into the switching mainstream in recent years with LAN Layer 2 (L2) switching in an attempt to move toward switching with legacy LAN protocols. Token rings play a much smaller role in LAN backbones because of their lower speeds, and have not seen a speed upgrade to compete with ATM. Therefore, we don't include them in these comparisons.

24.1.1 Technology Comparison — Ethernet vs. FDDI vs. ATM

ATM was designed to handle multimedia. A key protocol difference between ATM and Ethernet is in the segmentation and reassembly of the user Protocol Data Units (PDU). ATM breaks data (the PDU) into fixed-length cells. It then establishes a *connection-oriented* virtual circuit that guarantees bandwidth and quality to the recipient. In contrast, Ethernet encapsulates user PDUs into frames on a shared media in a *connectionless* broadcast fashion, relying on its collision-detection mechanism to manage user contention for the shared bandwidth. If the user PDUs are too large for the shared media, then a higher-layer protocol must segment and reassemble them.

Despite all the hype surrounding gigabit Ethernet, ATM remains very much a viable option in the LAN. While ATM remains the future WAN technology of choice, one must look deeper into the economics of placing ATM in the LAN. This is especially true when analyzing the existing legacy LAN environment, whose cost-effective, embedded base of 10/100 Mbps shared and switched Ethernet technology creates a tremendous barrier to entry for ATM. To date, the key for ATM's foray into the LAN environment has been its extension and integration with a new breed of LAN switches and routers. These devices provide a viable and more cost-effective LAN backbone technology than FDDI, as well as a more cost-effective per Mbps technology than 10/100-Mbps Ethernet to the desktop. Now let's look at the advantages and disadvantages of switched 10/100-Mbps Ethernet, gigabit Ethernet, FDDI, and ATM presented in Table 24.1.

Table 24.1 Advantages and Disadvantages of Competing LAN Technologies

Technology	Advantages	Disadvantages
10-Mbps switched	Simple, cheap, incremental upgrade path to 100-Mbps switched as required, easy to manage	Collision-based, not scalable, no QoS, distance limitations
100-Mbps Ethernet switched	Scalable, simple, investment protection (NIC, wiring, equipment), some QoS support	Distance limitations
100-Mbps Ethernet shared	Inexpensive, simple, speed improvement over 10-Mbps, investment protection (NIC, wiring, equipment), easy to manage	Collision-based, distance limitations, no QoS
FDDI	Fault-tolerant	Expensive, no upgrade path, no QoS
Gigabit Ethernet	Speed increase to 1 Gbps, simple, potential for cost decrease	Expensive, no QoS, distance limitations, collision-based
ATM 25, 155, 622 Mbps	End-to-end QoS, no distance limitations, scalable to OC-48	Expensive

Table 24.2 Attributes Comparison of FDDI, Fast Ethernet, and ATM

Attributes	FDDI	Switched 100-Mbps Ethernet	1-Gbps Ethernet	ATM
Throughput	100-Mbps simplex	100-Mbps simplex	1000-Mbps simplex	25-Mbps to 622-Mbps duplex
Evolution potential	Little	Some	Some	Best
Reserved bandwidth	No	Yes	No	Yes
Isochronous support	No	Yes	No	Yes
Multiple traffic classes	No	Planned in 802.1p	Planned in 802.1p	Yes
Projected costs	High	Low	Medium	Medium
Use of existing wiring	No	Yes	No	Yes
Scalable in speed	No	Yes	No	Yes
Scalable to wide area	No	No	No	Yes

From this table we see that while Ethernet technologies offer a simpler and cheaper alternative, they lack the scalability, WAN reach, end-to-end integration, and QoS features required by tomorrow's applications [1]. Note that only switched 100-Mbps Ethernet offers any QoS support.

Table 24.2 compares the key technology and business attributes of FDDI, switched 100-Mbps Ethernet, gigabit Ethernet, and native ATM. This analysis shows that ATM is clearly differentiated from its LAN peers in at least one area. Switched 100-Mbps Ethernet is the closest contender for all around capability of the group. This is why a number of network managers are using this route to upgrade their existing LAN backbones and high-performance workgroups instead of ATM. Until gigabit Ethernet proves in and collects additional feature support, ATM may still be the best bet for a high-speed LAN backbone. We explore this topic further in the next section.

While Ethernet switching provides large amounts of dedicated bandwidth to single users, switched networks still operate in a peer-to-peer, flat layer 2 bridged architecture. This can be a major disadvantage as the size of the network grows, affecting performance, management, and scalability. Also, Ethernet is distance-limited, whereas ATM networks have no distance limitations. Another major disadvantage of Ethernet technology is its inability to interoperate with dissimilar LAN technologies, such as FDDI, on a single network without translation bridges or routers. ATM's LAN emulation and MPOA protocols achieve interoperability with legacy LAN. And for FDDI, its high price and lack of widespread support and adoption are still major disadvantages. For all of its benefits, moving to 100-Mbps switched Ethernet and gigabit Ethernet solutions still only throw more bandwidth at the problem. Although simple, less costly, and familiar, these solutions don't solve the QoS, bandwidth allocation, and WAN extension issues.

24.1.2 Gigabit Ethernet

Let's take a closer look under the covers of the latest technology developed to serve the need for higher speeds in the LAN backbone and high-performance applications [2, 3, 4]. Basically, gigabit Ethernet is almost identical to its lower-speed cousins, but scaled up in speed. The IEEE 802.3z began defining gigabit Ethernet in November 1996, with the first standards to be published for full-duplex operation over fiber-optic cable and short-haul copper expected in early 1998. Subsequent standards for half-duplex operation over long-haul copper are planned for early 1999. By preserving 802.3 Ethernet's frame structure and management framework, gigabit Ethernet promises to seamlessly upgrade existing LAN backbones while preserving existing investments in hardware and software.

Gigabit Ethernet utilizes the same collision detection and avoidance mechanism as its lower speed ancestors, the Carrier Sense Multiple Access/Collision Detection (CSMA/CD) protocol. The proposed standard used the Fibre Channel signal structure to accelerate product availability. The reach of gigabit Ethernet over fiber extends from 500 meters to over two kilometers with multimode and single-mode fiber, respectively. It can run up 25 to 100 meters over existing twisted pair cabling. More information on gigabit Ethernet can be found on the Web under Gigabit Ethernet Alliance [5].

24.1.3 ATM versus Gigabit Ethernet

We now turn our attention to a comparison of ATM and gigabit Ethernet. While gigabit Ethernet will partner well with IP networks, there are still missing pieces, namely, prioritization, switching, and quality of service support. Gigabit Ethernet has created a lot of hype around solving many of the problems faced by today's IP networks. Table 24.3 provides a comparison of ATM to gigabit Ethernet to confirm or expel these beliefs.

24.1.4 Will Gigabit Ethernet Displace ATM in the LAN?

There are three key driving factors for gigabit Ethernet to replace ATM in the LAN [6, 7]:
- Industry forecasts for the hub and switch market clearly show Ethernet dominance for the next few years.
- Equipment availability and pricing favors Ethernet.
- The requirement for multimedia, in particular voice and video, has not dominated LAN traffic.

Table 24.3 ATM Compared with Gigabit Ethernet

Attribute	ATM	Gigabit Ethernet
LAN support	Yes	Yes
WAN support	Yes	No
Upgrade path	DS1 through OC-48	1 Gbps only
Migration path from lower speeds requires hardware change	Yes	Yes
Learning curve	High	Low (given Ethernet experience)
New NIC required	Yes	Yes
Equipment cost	High	High
QoS support	Built-in	Planned in 802.1p
Installation difficulty	High	Medium
Speed	Ranges from DS1 (1.5 Mbps) up to OC-48 (2.5 Gbps)	1 Gbps
Configuration	Some required	Plug and play
Manageability	More complex	Simpler

Let's look at each of these in more detail. Industry forecasts for the hub and switch market clearly show Ethernet dominance for the next few years. Figure 24.1 shows the results of an August 1996 Dataquest study on switch and hub port revenue forecasts. It clearly shows that the growth of Fast Ethernet (100 Mbps) and gigabit Ethernet (1000 Mbps) far exceeds that of ATM in the LAN, and that the ATM switch market lags the Ethernet switch market. In fact, this survey forecasted that the gigabit Ethernet market would hit $3B by the year 2000.

Equipment availability and pricing favors Ethernet. Gigabit Ethernet switching and routing devices soon promise to be only two to three times the cost of 100-Mbps Ethernet full-duplex devices — yet will achieve nearly a 10 to 1 performance advantage over current 100 Mbps internetworking gear. This results in a three- to fivefold increase in price/performance. ATM switches are still more expensive than conventional LAN Ethernet switches, but the gap is narrowing rapidly. Note that most major equipment vendors are providing both Gigabit Ethernet and ATM products, and are members of both the ATM Forum and the gigabit Ethernet Alliance. But beware: there are many vendors producing gigabit Ethernet products prior to a mature standard, which can create vendor compatibility issues.

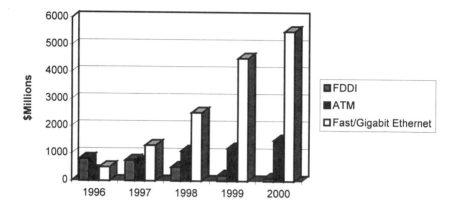

Figure 24.1 Switch and Hub Port Revenue

The requirement for multimedia, in particular voice and video, in the LAN has not materialized in force. One example is MPEG2 full-motion video with a 64-kbps voice quality line and data transfer on every workstation. We believe that this lack of adoption is due to the lack of APIs and applications designed to specifically take advantage of ATM's QoS capabilities. The 802.1p prioritized Ethernet Link Layer Control (LLC) standard could change this for native Ethernets. Also, the recent Microsoft WinSock 2.0 standard could rapidly change this situation.

Thus, gigabit Ethernet stands a strong chance of displacing ATM in most tactical LAN implementations. But users that choose this route will have to rely heavily on early prestandard versions of 802.1p and/or RSVP to assist with IP's shortcomings.

24.1.5 NICs, Switches, Ports

An eight-port Ethernet workgroup switch, which supports a dedicated 10-Mbps connection to the desktop, costs as little as $4,000. This places the price per switch port at $500. An Ethernet adapter for the desktop is priced at under $100. Thus, the cost per Mbps to provide 10-Mbps Ethernet to the desktop is $600/10 Mbps = $60. Ethernet switch and Network Interface Card (NIC) pricing is dropping almost daily, and by the time of publishing the average cost per NIC was $60 and per switch port was around $200, placing the cost of switched 10-Mbps Ethernet at $26 per Mbps. Even 100-Mbps (fast) Ethernet adapters cost less than $100, making them the new point of entry for Ethernet. The cost difference between 10-Mbps and 100-Mbps Ethernet NICs is negligible, and most cards sold will soon be of the 10/100 autosensing variety. With Ethernet switch ports averaging $500 each, the cost per Mbps reaches $6. By comparison, an ATM switch provides a user with 310 Mbps (155 Mbps full duplex) of ATM bandwidth at a cost per Mbps of less than $5. These are list prices — actual street prices could fall much lower if driven by intense competition .

24.1.6 Cost Comparisons of LAN Media

Table 24.4 compares the cost per Mbps of competing Ethernet, ATM, and FDDI technologies. All costs are presented as an average, not the minimum. For example, the average cost of a 10-Mbps Ethernet NIC is around $60, but some can be bought for as low as $35 (or cheaper if you want to buy them out of the back of a truck for cash). These costs also assume that the user can derive the full bandwidth specified, which is rarely the case. For example, most Ethernet networks achieve a maximum of 8 Mbps before excessive collisions limit the throughput. Also note that ATM speeds are full duplex, versus half duplex for the other technologies, thus effectively doubling ATM's available bandwidth. Use the rules defined above to adjust the numbers in this table as required when doing your own cost analysis based upon vendor quotes [8, 9, 10].

From this table it is clear that both gigabit Ethernet and 155/622-Mbps ATM offer the most cost-effective bandwidth. Furthermore, note from the previous analysis that ATM offers the additional key capabilities of offering a seamless LAN/WAN technology, more choices for bandwidths, and mature support for multiple QoS classes.

Obviously, these cost benefits are most relevant when designing a network from scratch. But if an existing network is upgrading to ATM, and has many legacy Ethernet and FDDI LAN NICs and switches in place, moving to an all ATM network may be cost-prohibitive. In closing, we list some real questions to ask. When do I run out of steam (bandwidth) in the LAN? When do I need QoS features? And how do I scale the LAN across the WAN? The answers typically point back to ATM.

Table 24.4 Technology Comparison Cost per Megabit per second (Mbps)

Protocol	Speed (Mbps)	Cost per NIC	Cost per Switch Port	Cost per Mbps
Gigabit Ethernet	1000	$1000	$3000	$ 3
ATM 155	310 (155 FDX)	$500	$1000	$ 4.84
ATM 622	1244 (622 FDX)	$4000	$3000	$ 5.63
Fast Ethernet	100	$100	$500	$ 6
ATM 25	50 (25 FDX)	$200	$200	$ 8
Ethernet	10	$60	$200	$ 26
FDDI	100	$1200	$3000	$ 42
Token Ring	16	$500	$1100	$ 100

24.1.7 25-Mbps ATM

In fact, 25-Mbps ATM was developed for one thing — cost-effective desktop ATM LAN connectivity. ATM 25.6 Mbps offers a full-duplex link, and thus achieves the equivalent of 50 Mbps when compared with unidirectional LAN media. This can be compared to Fast Ethernet, a simplex collision-based scheme, which under light loading achieves 50 Mbps. Also, every feature offered by ATM over 155 Mbps can also be offered over 25 Mbps.

To date, 25-Mbps products have been slow to come to market because the encoding scheme has been difficult for chip vendors to implement. Thus the NIC and switch vendors have shied away from the specification. Despite this handicap, the 25-Mbps ATM switch market was valued at $150M in 1995.

Perhaps the biggest advantage of 25-Mbps ATM is that it can run over existing Category 3 (Cat-3) Unshielded Twisted Pair (UTP) wiring, versus other standards that require installation and upgrade to more expensive Category 5 wiring. The 25-Mbps ATM protocol uses a 4B5B encoding scheme and an NRZI line coding scheme to place the data stream over the UTP 3 cabling. The maximum distance is 100 meters per run. Of course, Category 5 cabling will be required when upgrading to 155 Mbps ATM.

Clearly, 25-Mbps ATM competes with 100BaseT fast Ethernet. Their costs are comparable at about $300 per workstation. The only issue is that if you later decide to upgrade to 155 Mbps, you need to replace the NIC card, and in many cases the switch port. When ATM becomes more prevalent in LAN, this will drive ATM 25 Mbps adoption.

The pros to using 25 Mbps ATM include:

- Cost comparable to switched Ethernet
- Sustained 25-Mbps full duplex per desktop
- Enables true end-to-end user QoS
- Support for emerging multimedia applications

The major cons to using 25-Mbps ATM include:

- New NIC adapters in workstations and switches required
- Upgrade to 155 Mbps ATM requires new NIC, switch port, and wiring

Currently, 25-Mbps ATM switches are available from 3Com Corp., Advanced Telecommunications Modules Ltd. (ATML), Connectware Inc., First Virtual Corp., FORE Systems, IBM, NEC, and Whitetree; 25-Mbps adapters are available from 3Com Corp., Adaptec Inc., Advanced Telecommunications Modules Ltd. (ATML), Connectware Inc., Efficient Networks Corp., First Virtual Corp., FORE Systems, IBM, Interphase Corp., NEC, and Olicom A/S.

Table 24.5 Market Factors for LAN Technologies

Technology	Market Size	Vendor Interoper-ability	Technology Interoperability
10-Mbps switched	Decreasing	Excellent	Poor
100-Mbps Ethernet switched	Rapidly growing	Good	OK
100-Mbps Ethernet shared	Growing	Good	Poor
FDDI	Decreasing	OK	Poor
Gigabit Ethernet	Growing	Poor (so far)	Unknown

24.1.8 What Is the Market Demanding?

Of course, price is not the only consideration. Market size, vendor interoperability, and technology interoperability (with the installed base) play a major role in technology selection. Table 24.5 provides the state of the market for each major LAN technology, the ability for vendors of different equipment types to interoperate over the same technology, and the ability of the technology to interoperate with other technologies.

The market (end user) has clearly demanded 10- and 100-Mbps shared Ethernet to date. Today 10 Mbps has the dominant market share, but most new installations are using shared and switched 100-Mbps Ethernet — driven by the phenomenal growth of the LAN switching market. Switched 10- and 100-Mbps Ethernet have also prospered much more than ATM in the LAN. Furthermore, many reports on gigabit Ethernet position it to also outpace ATM. In fact, 80 percent of all desktops today are Ethernet, which represents a tremendous installed base for Fast Ethernet and gigabit Ethernet. But these requirements for gigabit Ethernet in the LAN drive requirements for Mbps and Gbps WAN transport — placing ATM in a position to become the dominant WAN switching technology to connect tomorrow's high-performance LANs. And those users that rely heavily on multimedia and QoS requirements in the LAN will look to ATM to provide the end-to-end technology of choice. Currently, only IP provides QoS options for Ethernet networks through its Real-Time Protocol (RTP) and Resource Reservation Protocol (RSVP).

24.1.9 User and Application Requirements

The choice of LAN and WAN technology should also be based on the needs of the users and their applications. Table 24.6 shows both the ATM and non-ATM (or legacy) technology solutions for solving the user and application needs. Note that ATM provides the best LAN to WAN single technology migration path (25 Mbps to OC-48) in the industry. Thus, a server can have anywhere from a 25-Mbps connection to a giant 622 Mbps pipe — more than the leading servers can currently use. And ATM is already standardizing OC-48, almost 2.5 Gbps of full-duplex bandwidth, over 5 times that of half-duplex gigabit Ethernet!

Table 24.6 ATM and Non-ATM Solutions to User and Application Requirements

Objective	Non-ATM solution	ATM solution
Increase speed per shared segment	100/1000 Mbps Ethernet, FDDI	155-Mbps ATM
Increase speed per user	Micro-segment 10 Mbps, single-user 10 Mbps	Dedicated 25-Mbps ATM
Dedicate BW per user	Switched Ethernet with microsegmentation	Switched 155-Mbps ATM
Voice and video traffic	Isochronous Ethernet, upgrade to 100M Ethernet	Any ATM (25 to 155 Mbps)
Match technology to workflows — reduce add/move/changes	VLANs	LANE VLANs
Multicast	IP multicast	IP over ATM multicast, LANE
QoS/BW reservation	802.1p, RTP, RSVP	Standard service categories

24.2 WAN TECHNOLOGY COMPARISON

ATM competes with the following technologies in the WAN, but in some cases complements or provides protocol interworking with these potential competitors:

- Legacy protocols over private lines
- High-speed frame relay
- Frames versus cells

In some sense, ATM in the WAN domain is comparable to Microsoft Windows in the computer operating system domain — it works with everything. Let's take a brief look at each of these competing/collaborating technologies in more detail.

24.2.1 ATM versus Private Lines

Private lines offer a single dedicated physical channel between two fixed points, whereas ATM offers each point multiple logical connections to a number of endpoints. Furthermore, private lines offer a small number of bandwidth choices dictated by the rigid Time Division Multiplexing (TDM) hierarchy, while ATM provides fine bandwidth granularity and multiple service categories across logical virtual path and channel connections. Private line networks also require one egress port for every ingress port, as contrasted to a single ATM access port logically connected to all other access ports in a virtual private PVC network.

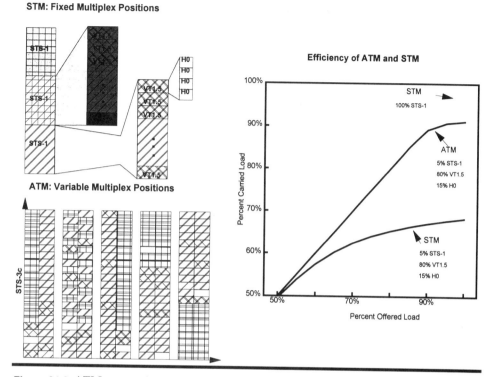

Figure 24.2 ATM versus STM Efficiency

ATM has its overhead, as many other protocols do. This section compares ATM efficiency with TDM. The analysis also considers the flexibility of ATM in contrast to systems optimized for circuit switching. A key advantage of ATM over STM is the ability to flexibly, and efficiently, assign multiple Continuous Bit Rate (CBR) circuit rates on a SONET transmission facility, as illustrated in Figure 24.2.

The upper left-hand corner of the figure illustrates a specific example of STM for the SONET hierarchy carrying STS-1 (51.84 Mbps), VT1.5 (1.792 Mbps), and H0 (0.384 Mbps) within an OC-3 channel. The STS-1 channel must be dedicated. The VT1.5 channels are allocated within an STS-1, and the H0 channels are allocated in another set of VT1.5s, as shown in the figure.

The same OC-3 channel is allocated as an STS-3c ATM channel, as illustrated in the lower left-hand corner of Figure 24.2. There are approximately 42 ATM cells per time slot (125-μs interval), shown as a series of rectangles. The STS-1 channel has 16 cells per time slot. The VT1.5 channels require approximately one cell every other time slot. The H0 channels require approximately one cell every eighth time slot. The cells can be assigned in any position or order, as illustrated in the figure. The inefficiency of the 5 bytes of cell overhead and 4 bytes of AAL overhead results in a maximum utilization of 91 percent for ATM versus the channelized SONET mapping. This is shown by the line labeled STM 100 percent STS-1 and the line labeled ATM.

A graphical representation of a calculation where 5 percent of the traffic is for STS-1, 80 percent for VT1.5, and 15 percent for H0 is shown on the right-hand side of Figure 24.2. The carried load is shown plotted versus the offered load. The carried load is proportional to the offered load, minus any blocked load. SONET and ATM are equivalent at lower levels of offered load, up until the offered load exceeds 50 percent of the trunk capacity. At higher loads, the higher efficiency of ATM becomes evident.

For this particular example, the maximum efficiency of STM is about 65 percent, compared to 91 percent for ATM. This represents about a 25 percent improvement in efficiency. When the mix of circuit rates becomes even more varied, or unpredictable, the advantage of ATM is even greater.

24.2.2 Frame Relay Compared with ATM

Frame relay and ATM share a close family resemblance: Both arose from the narrowband ISDN standards developed in the 1980s, and both use the connection-oriented service paradigm with guaranteed bandwidth. ATM adds several additional dimensions. First, ATM rigorously defines the notion of quality of service, while frame relay defines only prioritization. Also, ATM adds high-performance Segmentation and Reassembly (SAR) and interworking to deliver the QoS required by integrated voice, video, and data. However, recent frame relay implementations encroach upon ATM's claim to the high ground of raw speed in the WAN. Often, frame relay provides access to ATM through service interworking as described in Chapter 21.

Table 24.7 provides a comparison of low-speed frame relay (DS0 through DS1) and high-speed frame relay (nxDS1 through DS3) with ATM.

24.2.3 High-Speed FR Compared with ATM

Frame relay service providers of all types (carriers and RBOCS in the lead) are just beginning to roll out nxDS1 (3 to 12 Mbps) and DS3 (45 Mbps) "multimegabit frame relay" access service. High-speed frame relay provides some competition for DS3 ATM, especially when a customer requires only cost-effective WAN data transport. Users may also turn to high-speed FR if they currently own and operate a DS0, nxDS0, or DS1 FR network. High-speed FR provides a smooth migration for select sites that require additional bandwidth over DS1 speed, such as headquarters sites or the center site of a hub-and-spoke network, or to ATM.

ATM's counterbalancing factor to high-speed FR is the capability to provide FR-to-ATM service interworking. Here, a user can access the network DS1 FR and egress the network at 155 Mbps ATM — and the network provides the protocol translation and interworking between FR and ATM.

Table 24.7 Comparison of Low- and High-Speed Frame Relay with ATM

Attributes	Low-Speed FR	High-Speed FR	ATM
Throughput	56 kbps to 1.544 Mbps duplex	3 to 45 Mbps duplex	25-Mbps to 622 Mbps duplex
Evolution potential	Some	Minimal	Best
WAN risk	Low	Low	Low
Isochronous support	No	No	Yes
Multiple traffic classes	No	No	Yes
Projected costs	Low	Medium	Medium
Ubiquity of public service	Yes	No	Some
Implementation cost	Low	Medium	Medium
Scalable to wide area	Somewhat	No	Yes
New equipment required	Minimal	Yes	Yes
Upgrade type	Software	Software/hardware	Hardware
Investment protection	Minimal	Minimal	High
QoS support	Priorities	Priorities	Yes
Ease of deployment	Simple	Less complex	More complex

Pricing also plays a major factor. While ATM pricing varies, an ATM DS3 can cost you the equivalent of two DS1s, plus usage. DS3 FR rates also claim to break this barrier, making it more cost-effective to purchase a DS3 FR access than three DS1 dedicated circuits, and this does not even include the potential ability to burst to the entire DS3.

But DS3 FR still has the same limitations as DS1 or DS0 FR: the inability to handle multimedia traffic with the QoS capabilities of ATM. Time and pricing will tell the true winner, and both will probably coexist for some time [11].

24.2.4 Frames versus Cells

While overall efficiency isn't so important in the LAN — after all, 40 percent utilization on a shared Ethernet is considered acceptable, high utilization of expensive WAN facilities is a key consideration for many network designers. Hence, a great debate continues regarding the efficiency of ATM versus alternative technologies. Meanwhile, other groups busy themselves extending ATM's premier attributes to legacy LANs and internetworks. One thing that you may want to consider is the tradeoff of efficiency versus features. Increasing the number or quality of features often comes at the expense of decreased efficiency. We compare the efficiency and features of three major data protocols used in private or public networks: frame relay, ATM (using AAL5), and 802.6/SMDS (using AAL3/4). The protocol efficiency is shown in Figure 24.3.

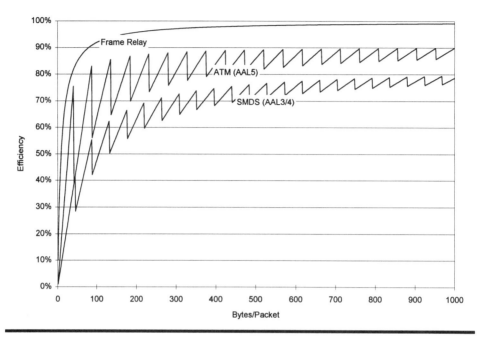

Figure 24.3 Protocol Efficiency versus Packet Size

Frame relay and HDLC support variable-length packets, with an overhead of between 5 and 8 bytes per packet (excluding zero insertion). This is the most efficient protocol with respect to overhead of the three protocols considered here. However, frame relay and HDLC don't readily support multiple QoS classes, especially if some frames are very long. The longest standardized frame size required is 1600 bytes, while the protocol will support frames up to 8192 bytes long. Its efficiency approaches 100 percent for very long user data packets (for example, IP packets), as seen from the figure. For a typical average packet size of 100 to 300 bytes, the difference in efficiency between ATM using AAL5 and FR/HDLC ranges from 15 to 30 percent.

ATM using AAL5 provides functions very similar to frame relay and HDLC, while simultaneously providing the additional flexibility of mixing very long packets with other delay-sensitive traffic. AAL5 also allows support for up to a 64-kbyte packet length, which frame relay, HDLC, and SMDS do not. The 8 bytes in the AAL5 trailer combined with the 5 bytes of ATM cell header overhead reduce the achievable efficiency to approximately 90 percent for very long packets. Because the variable-length packet must be segmented into fixed-length cells, the resultant efficiency decreases markedly when this segmentation results in one or a few bytes of packet data in the last cell.

SMDS currently utilizes the IEEE 802.6 Distributed Queue Dual Bus (DQDB) cell formatting. The per-cell overhead and formatting of the payload field are identical to AAL3/4. AAL3/4 provides an additional level of multiplexing in the MID field and a per-cell CRC, consuming an additional 4 bytes per cell. The first cell in an SMDS packet contains 44 bytes of information, including the source/destination addresses and other fields. Much of the flexibility and many of the features of SMDS derive from this header. Packets may be up to 9188 octets long, slightly longer than the maximum in frame relay. This flexibility reduces efficiency, with the best limited to about 80 percent maximum efficiency for very large packets.

Figure 24.3 plots the resulting efficiency of each protocol versus user packet size. Note how very short packets are handled very inefficiently by AALs 3/4 and 5.

In one further example, in a study performed on current Internet traffic, a calculation showed that the efficiency of offering this traffic over ATM would be approximately 60 percent because of the large proportion of very short packets!

Which protocol is best for your application? If you need a feature that only the less efficient protocols support, then the choice is clear; you can't use a more efficient protocol if it doesn't support a critical feature. If your network will require support for multiple QoS classes for different concurrent applications, then ATM is probably a good choice. If you need to connect to other networks via a public service, or require an additional level of multiplexing, then 802.6/SMDS is probably a good choice, either as a stand-alone service or carried over an ATM-based service. If raw efficiency is key, and support for multimedia applications is not required, then frame relay or basic HDLC is a good choice.

24.3 MULTIMEDIA QOS OPTIONS: RSVP, CIF, OR ATM?

Do you need to be concerned about quality of service? Ask yourself the following three questions; if you answer yes to any one of them, then you probably do.

1. Do you plan to run multimedia applications on the workstation?
2. Do you want to mix voice and/or telephony traffic with data across the WAN?
3. Do you want to consolidate voice and data infrastructures (wiring, equipment, maintenance, support staff, etc.)?

In this section, we compare the following technologies that support multiple QoS classes :

*   Switched Ethernet using RSVP
*   Cells in Frames (CIF)
*   ATM

Table 24.8 RSVP, CIF, and ATM Comparison

Technology	Signaling	Program Interface
Switched Ethernet	RSVP	QoS-aware APIs
Cells in Frames (CIF)	Q.9231	QoS-aware APIs plus CIF edge device
ATM	Q.2931	WinSock2 API

These three networking technologies deliver a consistent QoS to applications that require low delay and jitter, such as real-time voice and video, as shown in Table 24.8.

We will now explore RSVP and CIF and compare it with ATM in the next two sections.

24.4 RSVP VERSUS ATM: THE QOS BATTLE

Legacy LAN routing and switching devices do not have any standard method of guaranteeing user QoS to legacy LANs (i.e., Ethernet) that are non-deterministic in nature (i.e., their performance at any one point in time cannot be predicted with accuracy). Ethernet is still only a MAC layer, collision-based technology, and must rely on higher-layer protocol schemes to assure specific quality of service to users. Thus, QoS planning starts at the workgroup level — because each successive move toward the WAN typically decreases bandwidth. One way to provide QoS management between Ethernet segments is using IP's RSVP, defined by the Internet Engineering Task Force.

24.4.1 RSVP Defined

IP has no native method for specifying QoS class; the seldom-used precedence field in the IPv4 header defines only relative priorities. RSVP, on the other hand, provides application developers the capability to request a specific service quality and bandwidth from a IP network. RSVP is a signaling protocol used by a receiver to request QoS and bandwidth from a multicast sender. RSVP does not guarantee QoS or bandwidth.

The RSVP signaling protocol allows an IP user to specify QoS and bandwidth per application flow (using the IPv6 packet header), without requiring application program modifications. New APIs like Microsoft's WinSock 2.0 specification already specify the QoS to the application, making QoS in the LAN environment critical. This is where ATM has the advantage. RSVP is supported in two ways:

- By most major router vendors in a proprietary way. For example, Cisco Systems supports RSVP capability within its proprietary NetFlow software.
- Using an industry standard API like Microsoft's WinSock 2.0.

Designers must also implement shaping and policing functions to control bandwidth usage to ensure fair QoS allocation among all users. Today, requests for QoS are dynamic and voluntary with WinSock 2.0 and RSVP, creating the same environment as is found on Ethernet networks — users competing on a "first come, first abuse" basis. The main drawback to RSVP is that as the number of flows requiring QoS increases, the routing forwarding tables increase proportionately.

In comparison, ATM controls and enforces traffic contracts starting at the originating edge of the network to manage and guarantee the specified bandwidth and QoS using connection admission control [12]. In contrast, IP cannot deny new RSVP-requested "connections," since its underlying networking paradigm is connectionless.

24.4.2 Internet Service Providers — RSVP vs. ATM

One of the key battlegrounds of RSVP and ATM is in the Internet. The many claims that the Internet will soon resemble the LA turnpike gridlock during rush hour may be exaggerated. But one thing is for sure — businesses increasingly rely on the Internet to disseminate information, advertise, and conduct mainstream activities. This content-focused activity causes bandwidth requirements to skyrocket. And the amount of multimedia traffic on the Internet is also increasing. These drivers leads to a common answer — use ATM in the Internet backbone. This is precisely what many service providers have done. Proponents of ATM in the Internet see ABR service and RSVP competing head on. But ATM has been out for years, and IETF-defined RSVP has yet to hit the street in product form. This is one battle where ATM is the incumbent over IP [13].

24.4.3 The Internet — A Study in Voice over ATM

Most of the large-scale Internet Service Provider (ISP) traffic is switched by ATM. Currently IETF standards development on RTP and RSVP promises high-quality voice support over the Internet. A central issue with placing voice traffic over the Internet with RTP and RSVP is that there is still packetization delay induced by large IP frames to deal with that is not present in the 53 byte ATM cells. The IP delay can easily exceed hundreds of milliseconds and reduce usability. We discuss this subject further in Chapter 25.

24.4.4 Vendor Offerings

Several vendors offer ATM-like QoS and RSVP capabilities today. 3Com's PACE technology allows Ethernet networks to prioritize traffic. Cisco routers running version 11.2 Internetwork Operating System (IOS) allow applications to "reserve" network bandwidth using the RSVP standard. Madge's MadgeOne provides for voice and video over both Ethernet and ATM. Bay Networks and Lucent Technologies support I-PNNI with ATM-like quality of service. But even with these early implementations of RSVP, ATM still provides better QoS support at a lower cost than a next-generation router running RSVP. RSVP also suffers initially from a lack of intercarrier communications standards on implementing RSVP — a must in today's multivendor environments.

24.5 CELLS IN FRAMES

Wouldn't it be nice if you could keep existing legacy Ethernet NIC cards and LAN devices, yet still get much of ATM's capabilities to the desktop? Enter CIF, which uses software to place ATM cells inside LAN frames and forward them to a separate CIF attachment device that interfaces to native ATM networks. An eclectic group of hardware and software vendors, service providers, user organizations, and members of the trade press joined to form the Cells in Frames Alliance in early 1996 [14]. Membership in the alliance is free, as the National Science Foundation funds part of the work. The Cells in Frames Alliance seeks to:

- Ease deployment of ATM-based networks.
- Make migration to ATM economical by reusing existing Ethernet hardware.
- Establish specifications for carrying ATM over existing LAN infrastructure.
- Empower user applications by giving them control over network methods used to provide quality of service.

To accomplish these goals, the CIF Alliance released version 1.0 of a specification in October 1996 detailing how to carry ATM over Ethernet, 802.3, and Token Ring networks. Some believe that CIF may be the great enabling API for ATM; in other words, it is ATM for the rest of us outside of those small workgroups with high-end workstations.

Figure 24.4 illustrates the network context of CIF. A legacy LAN network connects to an ATM network via a CIF Attachment Device (CIF-AD) that supports ATM service, in particular multiple classes of service, over an existing LAN NIC. CIF utilizes existing LAN framing protocols transparent to applications written to an ATM-compliant API.

Critical to the CIF concept is the End System (ES) architecture depicted in Figure 24.5. Functions defined in the CIF specification define how a LAN-attached workstation can implement ATM Header Error Checking (HEC), AAL5 Cyclic Redundancy Check (CRC), priority scheduling, leaky bucket traffic shaping, and end-to-end protocol-independent flow control using the Available Bit Rate (ABR) service — all in software! The specification actually provides source code examples for many of these features.

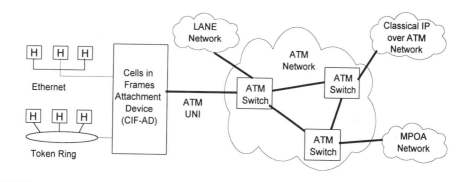

Figure 24.4 Cells in Frames Network Architecture

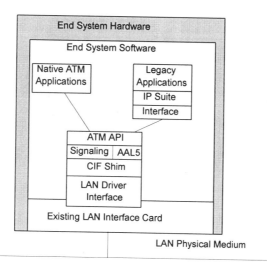

Figure 24.5 Cells in Frames End System Architecture

CIF end systems also implement signaling and ILMI modules as part of an ATM processing layer that works with the existing LAN driver. Legacy applications have access to the AAL layers via LAN Emulation (LANE), Multiprotocol over ATM (MPOA), or classical IP over ATM, enabling direct connection with high-end native ATM end systems.

Some ATM vendors view CIF as a way to rapidly extend ATM's reach to the desktop in order to support real-time interactive traffic [15]. The attachment device does most of the segmentation and reassembly work and hence relieves the PC of a low-level, processor-intensive burden. The PC must implement standard ATM signaling and build ATM PDUs as its part of the implementation. ATM thus uses CIF to bridge the gap between legacy and ATM end systems — without the requirement to change desktop hardware.

This allows ATM vendors to capture market share from legacy LAN system vendors — like routers and LAN switches.

CIF offers one alternative to the purchase of expensive devices like new 25-Mbps or 155-Mbps ATM NICs. CIF is available in switching and concentrator devices. CIF bridges the time gap until more ATM APIs can be written. CIF also directly competes with RSVP signaling. See [15] and [16] for more information on CIF.

24.6 COMPARISON OF RSVP, CIF, AND ATM

Table 24.9 provides a comparison of RSVP, CIF, and ATM features.

Table 24.9 Comparison of RSVP, CIF, and ATM

Feature	ATM	IP/RSVP	CIF
Cost	Expensive	Cheap	Affordable
Use existing NIC cards?	No	Yes	Yes
Use existing wiring?	Maybe	Yes	Yes
Use existing hubs?	Maybe	Yes	No
Migration strategy	Excellent	Poor	Good
Latency	Low	High	Low
Use native ATM applications	Yes	No	Yes
End-to-end managed QoS	Yes	Minimal	Yes
Flow control	ABR	None	ABR
Assures QoS (vs. requesting it)	Yes	No	Yes
Load sharing	Yes	No	No
Auto traffic reroute	Yes	No	No
QoS request originated by	Sender	Receiver	Sender
Predictable application performance	Yes	No	No
Multicast handling	Add-on	Native	Native
Additional workstation software required?	Yes	No	Yes
Cost	Expensive (<$500/port)	Expensive (<$400/port)	Affordable (<$200/port)

The key difference between ATM and RSVP when it comes to QoS is that RSVP only *prioritizes* delivery over fixed bandwidth in a logical broadcast medium, whereas ATM *guarantees* delivery and bandwidth over circuit-switched connections. Connectionless protocols like IP and Ethernet cannot offer guarantees because they operate on a hit-and-miss system of congested traffic, collisions, restarts, and unpredictable delay — and thus cannot guarantee bandwidth or quality. Don't forget that gigabit switches will still need expensive routers to provide connectivity and routing, where both of these functions are less expensively performed within the ATM switch — in software rather than hardware. The distance limitations of Ethernet can also play a factor in large campus environments.

Note that as the price of ATM per port drops, the viability of CIF begins to disappear. In the last analysis, ATM and RSVP will probably coexist for some time. Indeed, the IETF and the ATM Forum are working closely together to ensure that these protocols interoperate. Legacy IP networks are growing, not disappearing, and ATM has yet (if ever) to dominate the LAN. These two trends point to a coexistence of the two technologies. In fact, IETF efforts are under way to map MPOA to RSVP to reconcile RSVP requests to MPOA's virtual routers [17, 18].

24.7 REVIEW

The reader should now understand the key technologies that challenge and complement ATM in both the LAN and the WAN. While ATM is the clear tactical and strategic winner in the WAN, the jury is still out about the LAN. New initiatives like Ethernet switching and gigabit Ethernet have extended the life expectancy of legacy LAN technology and, along with slow deployment of multimedia applications, these factors have postponed the requirement for ATM in the LAN. But ATM remains the clear winner as the best strategic choice for an end-to-end technology. ATM still remains the leader in delivering quality of service and guaranteed bandwidth to applications. The competing proposal of the IETF's RSVP has promise, but it is still immature and cannot overcome limitations inherent in IP's connectionless paradigm. Transition strategies such as CIF offer the potential to allow migration of legacy hosts and servers to ATM sooner via a simple software upgrade.

24.8 REFERENCES

[1]   A. Chiang, "Parallel Paths Emerge for Fast Ethernet and ATM," *Telecommunications*, March 1996.
[2]   3Com, "Gigabit Ethernet on the Horizon: Meeting the Network Challenge," 1997, http://www.3com.com/0files/strategy/600220.html.
[3]   IEEE, "802.3z Standard Drafts, Proposals and Meeting Minutes," ftp://stdsbbs.ieee.org/pub/802_main/802.3/gigabit.
[4]   Gigabit Ethernet Alliance, "White Paper: Gigabit Ethernet — Applications Driving Network Technology," August 1996, http://www.gigabit-ethernet.org/technology/whitepapers/gige/.
[5]   Gigabit Ethernet Alliance, www.gigabit-ethernet.org.
[6]   S. Saunders, "Closing the Price Gap Between Routers and Switches," *Data Communications*, February 1995.

[7] L. Wirbel, "At N Plus I, Unity — and All Hell Breakin' Loose," *Electronic Engineering Times,* September 16, 1996.

[8] Source: Extreme Networks 1997.

[9] Independent news briefs and announcements on vendor products.

[10] J. Cohen, "ATM and Gigabit Ethernet Camps Collide," *Network World,* September 16, 1996.

[11] T. Greene, "FR to Get 28-fold Boost," *Network World,* October 21, 1996.

[12] T. Nolle, "The Great QoS Debate: IP vs. ATM Is Only the Tip of the Iceberg," *Network World,* July 15, 1996.

[13] M. Cooney, "Can ATM Save the Internet?" *Network World,* May 20, 1996.

[14] "Cells in Frame Home Page," http://cif.cornell.edu.

[15] R. Jeffries, "Three Roads to Quality of Service: ATM, RSVP, and CIF," *Telecommunications,* April 1996.

[16] R. Cogger and P. Elmer, "Is CIF a Viable Solution for Delivering ATM to the Desktop?" *Network World,* June 24, 1996.

[17] J. Caruso, "Dynamic Duo: RSVP + ATM," *Communications Week,* June 23, 1997.

[18] IBM, "Whitepaper: Desktop ATM versus Fast Ethernet," 1996.

25

Whither (or Wither) ATM?

The question now is not whether ATM will succeed; rather, the question is, How successful will ATM be? Will ATM dominate the wide area networks? How much voice traffic will ATM carry? Will ATM penetrate the LAN, or will the ever-resurgent spawn of the Ethernet species dominate? Will the Internet continue to adopt ATM's best features [1] and hence reduce the need for ATM in end systems, leaving ATM to wither away in its wake? This final chapter addresses these questions by reporting on opinions expressed by industry experts, as well as reviewing emerging standards and industry activities.

25.1 COMPETITION AND SURVIVAL OF THE FITTEST

Will ATM become a dominant networking technology in the twenty-first century? Or, will it go the way of ISDN? Will gigabit Ethernet encroach upon its claim to high performance? Will RSVP deliver Quality of Service (QoS) more effectively? We cannot say for certain; however, one thing is clear — ATM will continue to compete in an environment of legacy and new competing technologies. The communications industry appears to operate on a Darwinian principle similar to nature's survival of the fittest, where only the strong survive. However, one key difference in this analogy is that in order to survive, the newcomers must coexist (that is, interwork) with those they intend to replace for overextended periods of time. We can safely say that many X.25, SNA, Ethernet, frame relay, and IP networks will exist ten to twenty years from now. ATM is still on the cusp, standing at the brink of the chasm, ready to join the cast of legacy protocols. If ATM continues at its current 100 percent annual growth rate into the twenty first century, then most would concede that ATM succeeded.

As we discovered in Part 4, most of the leading U.S. carriers and traditional Regional Bell Operating Companies (RBOCs) now offer ATM service, and the few who don't plan to offer it soon. Carriers continue to work together to deliver switched ATM services. Furthermore, international ATM service is now becoming available, as we saw in Chapter 20. Despite the competitive pressures in the LAN and WAN covered in the previous chapter, ATM continues to expand into new areas, as well as experience significant growth. Furthermore, ATM technology continues to improve price/performance with respect to other technologies in both the LAN and the WAN.

25.2 ATM'S EXPANSION INTO NEW FRONTIERS

ATM continues to expand into brave new areas of communication networking. As we saw in Chapter 21, even McDonald's is already using ATM — bringing ATM ever closer to the McDonald's-invented benchmark of counting the number of millions of units sold. So you might ask: What frontiers remain? A promising area is the developments occurring in the area of high-performance Digital Subscriber Line (DSL) access networking, as discussed in Chapter 18. ATM over satellite and terrestrial radio networks enables many commercial and military applications never before possible at ATM speeds. We covered the status of trials and an emerging service using ATM over satellite in Chapter 20. One of the latest exciting areas is wireless, where ATM aims to serve mobile users within the office, a metropolitan area, and even the residence. We cover Wireless ATM (WATM) in the next section as further evidence of ATM's continued expansion into new frontiers.

25.3 WIRELESS ATM

With the advent of wireless LANs, wireless ATM looms on the horizon. Surprisingly, quite a few companies are on the verge of announcing products compliant with today's ATM switches. NewBridge Networks, Siemens AG, and Broadband Networks Inc. have teamed to integrate wireless ATM into the MainStreetXpress family of ATM switches. Broadband Networks Inc. makes a 28-GHz broadband ATM system capable of transmitting between two ATM switches. Lucent Technologies also has a wireless ATM LAN product produced by its WaveLAN division. Cascade, now part of Ascend, is providing ATM switches to Bell Atlantic NYNEX Mobile and GTE Wireless. Here ATM switches set up low-latency Virtual Channels (VCs) among voice switches to provide call- and service-type signaling. In this manner, ATM switches provide a front end to the wireless services, eliminating the need to connect every wireless switch to every voice switch and saving lots of money. Northern Telecom ATM switches are used by Sprint's PCS service for this type of signaling and backhaul to wireline services. ATM switching will also play a major role in supporting wireless multimedia services and as Internet gateways for wireless subscribers. Figure 25.1 illustrates these methods of providing broadband wireless subscriber access to wireline services.

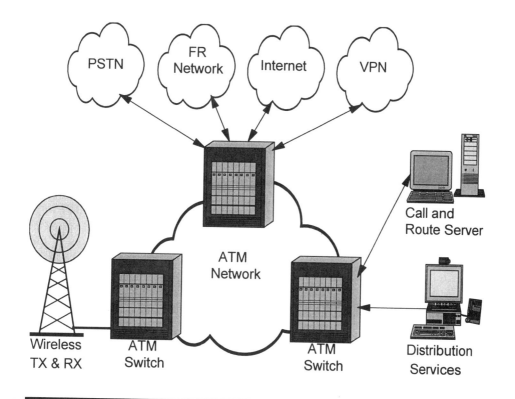

Figure 25.1 Wireless Access to Wireline ATM Switching

Cost-effective wireless ATM could produce a very viable access alternative to ATM service providers, especially in hard-to-reach or congested areas. It would also provide an excellent second source of access to improve reliability and disaster recovery. Many of the benefits of ATM over satellite are also applicable to wireless ATM. But many hurdles remain. High error rates inherent in wireless transmission require special modifications to the protocols riding over ATM. Another hurdle is frequency allocation constraints – closely regulated by government agencies both in the United States and abroad.

The challenges facing wireless ATM include:

- Access schemes — development of access protocols that can overcome high error rates and noise inherent in radio systems.
- Reliability and availability — coverage areas, fading, temporary outages, error detection and correction.
- Service ubiquity — while wireless can reach hard-to-get-to areas, access stations still need to be built.
- QoS mobility — how to ensure consistent QoS and handoff as a user "roams."

- Applications — applications need to be written that understand and overcome the limitations inherent in wireless transmissions.

Most of the major wireless players are active in the ATM Forum's WATM group, having looked at the alternatives and then selected ATM as the technology that best fit their requirements. Mobility is no longer a luxury for ATM; it is a necessity. Responding to this industry consensus, the ATM Forum founded the WATM working group in June 1996 [2] with the charter to develop a set of specifications applying ATM technology across a broad range of wireless network access scenarios, both private and public. This includes extensions for mobility support within ATM networks and specification of a wireless ATM radio access layer. The WATM specifications target compatibility with ATM equipment adhering to current ATM Forum specifications. The group also is establishing liaison arrangements with other relevant wireless standards bodies.

Several companies in the radio industry spearheaded formation of the group in the hope of utilizing ATM to achieve greater efficiencies in the use of scarce radio spectrum. This effort also aimed to avoid proprietary solutions that could result in another Beta versus VHS shoot-out for a de facto industry standard. The group foresees wireless as an extension to existing ATM signaling, traffic management, and network management specifications, even though the WATM specification will be published as a separate document.

WATM will enable users wireless connectivity to anywhere the ATM network serves, and gain all of its advantages. The initial work items include specification in the following areas, as illustrated in Figure 25.2:

- Radio Access Layer protocols, including:

  ⇒ Radio's physical layer
  ⇒ Medium access control designed for wireless channel errors
  ⇒ Data link control for wireless channel errors
  ⇒ Wireless control protocol for radio resource management

- Mobile ATM protocol extensions including:

  ⇒ Hand-off control (signaling/NNI extensions, etc.)
  ⇒ Location management for mobile terminals
  ⇒ Routing considerations for mobile connections
  ⇒ Traffic/QoS control for mobile connections
  ⇒ Wireless network management

The radio access work will define wireless access to an ATM network from laptop computers or hand-held devices inside a building, such as an office, a convention center, a hotel, or even a residence. A key challenge for the radio access specification is handling the multipath fading and time-varying error rate of the high frequencies targeted by wireless ATM.

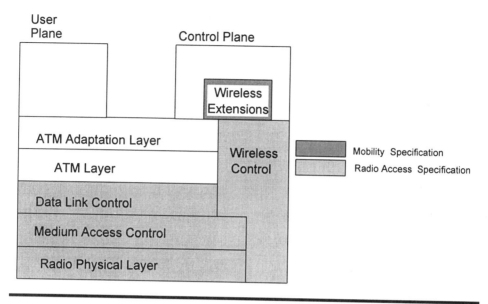

Figure 25.2 Wireless ATM Specification Relationship to Existing Standards

The work on mobility extensions in the control plane targets ATM-based access to intelligent network features, such as authentication, roaming, and assured delivery services.

Figure 25.3 illustrates the elements and context of the wireless ATM specification efforts. The model places the public switching infrastructure and wired private networks at the center of the drawing, surrounded by a number of scenarios envisioned for wireless ATM. These scenarios could be implemented as wireless extensions of the public/private infrastructure, or as mobility-enhanced wireless networks.

Mobile end users communicate directly with the fixed network through wireless access nodes or PCS interworking gateways. Satellite-based switching could support wireless end users in remote areas (e.g., natural resource exploration) and connectivity to military or emergency vehicles. Wireless LANs allow users to move within buildings or between locations. Mobility across locations is a highly valued capability in wireless corporate networks for executives and highly compensated information workers. Wireless ad hoc networks are capable of supporting a group of laptops utilized in a collaborative environment. An attractive feature of wireless ATM is true plug(in)-and-play operation, without having to plug any equipment together! Coupled with Virtual LAN (VLAN) use, this benefit alone can save information technology shops a large portion of their desktop support costs.

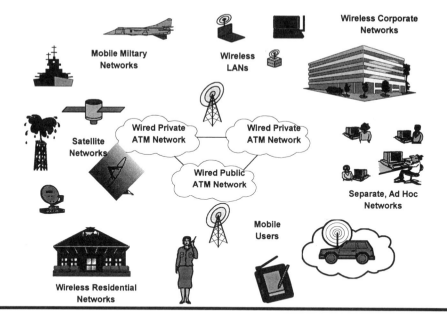

Figure 25.3 Wireless ATM Application Model

There are many competing standards for wireless LANs:

- IEEE 802.11
- HIPERLAN as standardized by ETSI/RES10 in Europe
- IETF Mobile-IP
- ITU AAL class for multiplexed compressed VBR signals for wireless

Each of these standards offer various base station designs and architectures, and the protocols differ markedly. There are also two efforts under way in Europe to standardize 5-Gbps ATM wireless technology to deliver 10- to 20-Mbps service:

- European Community Wireless ATM Network Demonstrator (Magic WAND)
- Advanced Technology Program's (ATP's) Mobile Information Infrastructure project

25.4 SERVING THE LEADING-EDGE USER

Leading-edge applications are an ever-increasing, emerging driver for hybrid public-private ATM networking. Announcements by high-tech, high-content as well as high-dollar enterprises jumping on the ATM broadband wagon continue a systematic increase.

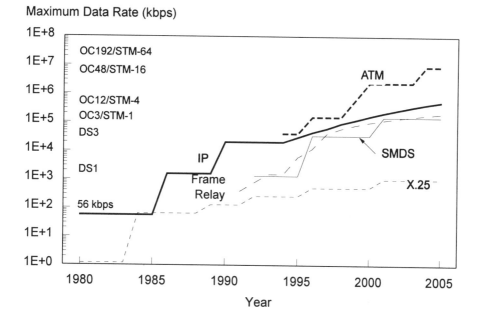

Maximum Data Rate (kbps)

Figure 25.4 Frame-based versus ATM-based Maximum Port Speed

25.4.1 Faster and Faster, Larger and Larger

A major advantage of ATM is high speed. When frame relay and routers were operating at DS1 and Ethernet speeds, ATM was running at DS3 and OC3 speeds. Now that frame relay and routers approach DS3 and even OC3 speeds, ATM is operating at OC12 speeds. OC48 speeds are on the horizon for ATM as the highest-end routers broach the OC12 barrier. Figure 25.4 illustrates these historical trends as well as an extrapolated trend.

25.4.2 Multimedia Now, or When?

Something of a chicken-and-egg syndrome currently exists for multimedia applications. The industry press provides a range of answers to the following dilemma:

Will emerging multimedia applications create demand for networks that support multiple QoS classes?
>   *or*

Will the availability of networks that support multiple QoS classes stimulate the development of multimedia applications?

The arguments for the first stimulus-response model, applications create demand for networks, include the following. Currently, true multimedia-enabled hardware and software is too expensive for use in all but the leading-edge high-tech or executive user communities. The localized, limited need for multiple QoS categories in networks drives enterprises to implement ATM workgroups, or overprovisioned high-speed LANs, to support the limited demand for expensive multimedia applications. Only when PC-class hardware and software supports multimedia applications cost-effectively will there be demand for networks with multiple QoS classes.

Supporters of the contrary view, that networking stimulates application development, see things differently. Only lightly loaded LANs can effectively support multimedia applications involving bandwidth-hungry media, such as full motion high quality video. This lack of an effective networking infra-structure provides a small market for multimedia application developers. Only when networks, their supporting protocols, and APIs capable of supporting multiple data types cost-effectively become available will multimedia applications be developed.

The time when these questions will be resolved is rapidly approaching. As we have seen, Resource Reservation Protocol (RSVP) promises to add the notions of QoS and a connection-oriented service to the Internet.

25.4.3 Future-proofing Investments

A touted benefit of ATM is that investments today in ATM will not become obsolete as soon as investments in other technologies. However, some recent experience with the ATM Forum runs counter to this argument. Many users found that they must replace the User-Network Interface (UNI) 3.1–compatible hardware they purchased with UNI 4.0 hardware to achieve the benefits of closed-loop congestion control. The ATM Forum responded to this problem with the "Anchorage Accord," effectively putting a freeze on any major new specification development for several years so that implementers could catch up to the wave of specifications released by the de facto industry standards body in 1996. The current set of ATM standards promises to be quite stable for many years to come. In fact, the ITU-T I.610 standard defines perform-ance measurement methods that will enable users to accurately measure the QoS their networks actually deliver. No other communications standard has anything remotely like this today.

25.5 TROUBLE IN ACHIEVING QOS WITH FRAMES

A fundamental performance issue with store-and-forward packet switching occurs when a long frame gets ahead of a short one, particularly on a lower-speed WAN circuit. If an application that is sensitive to variations in delay — for example, voice — generated the short packet, then it may not be able to wait until the long packet finishes transmission. Let's consider an example where a user's router is connected to the network via a DS1 link operating at 1.5 Mbps. Alternatively, this could be the high-speed downstream direction on an Asymmetrical Digital Subscriber Line (ADSL) connection to a residential subscriber. Typically, a maximum-length Ethernet packet is 1500 bytes, which takes approximately 8 ms to transmit on a DS1. A long Ethernet packet getting ahead of a short voice over IP packet could delay it by up to 8 ms, even if the router performed nonpreemptive priority queuing so that a higher-priority voice packet is sent immediately after the lower-priority data packet completes transmission. Voice over IP implementations compensate for these large variations in delay by inserting a large playback buffer at the destination. If this effect occurs at several intermediate DS1 (or worse yet, even slower) links, then the voice application will not be interactive and will eventually approach the delay experienced in voice over satellite systems. This effect means that real-time gaming, circuit emulation, or interactive videoconferencing cannot be effectively performed over store-and-forward packet switching systems operating even at modest link speeds.

One solution to this problem requires a preempt-resume protocol, similar to that used in most multitasking operating systems. In essence, the packet switch must stop transmission of the long packet (i.e., preempt it) by reliably communicating this interrupt to the next node, and then transmit the high-priority packet. After completing service of the higher-priority packet, the packet switch can then send the lower-priority packet (i.e., resume). Currently there is no standard for preemptive-resume packet switching, although several vendors have announced proprietary implementations. For example, Cascade breaks larger data frames into shorter segments so that voice frames do not experience excessive delay variation [3]. Of course, IP also provides for segmentation to overcome this delay variation problem, however, it introduces significant additional processor and packet header overhead when doing so.

On the other hand, ATM inherently implements a preempt-resume protocol in a standard fashion on 53-octet boundaries. Hence, for lower link speeds, ATM is the only standard protocol that enables true support for voice, video, and data on the same physical link.

An even simpler solution to this problem in packet networks is to simply increase the link speed and/or decrease the maximum packet size. As we pointed out earlier, the threshold of human perception of delay variations is on the order of 10 ms for auditory and visual stimuli.

Problems occur on some high-speed networks, however, in particular on shared media LANs, even those operating at 100 Mbps. The collisions that still occur on 100BaseT Ethernets can create significant delay variations during periods of relatively high load [4]. The 100VG-AnyLAN technology overcomes this problem by prohibiting shared media and requiring that intelligent hubs use a demand priority scheme to serve high-priority traffic before any low-priority traffic.

Another issue affecting QoS in large internets occurs in response to frequent state changes in routers, their ports, and the links that interconnect them. Whenever a state change occurs, the routing protocol distributes the updated topology information, and the packets may begin following another path. A change in routed path usually results in jittered, lost, missequenced, or, in some cases, duplicated packets. These impairments will likely cause annoying interruptions in the video playback. Customers may not be as tolerant of such poor quality when they are paying for video content over the Internet, instead of watching a free video clip.

25.6 IP AND ATM: HAND IN HAND, OR IN EACH OTHER'S FACE?

Recall that LAN emulation utilizes bridging as its underlying paradigm. Many experts in the internetworking community view bridging as a foul concept — "It won't scale!" their T-shirts cry out in reaction to the proposal of large bridged networks. Instead, they advocate routing solutions. Indeed, a major focus of the IETF is designing for a global Internet. However, to an enterprise network, as long as a LAN can be built on a scale that meets the enterprise's needs, the fact that it won't scale to serve the entire world is not an immediate business concern. Nonetheless, for some of those with a vision of a global Internet, ATM still plays a pivotal role. For example, many Internet Service Providers (ISPs) utilize ATM-based backbones and interconnect at ATM-based Network Access Points (NAPs) .

While some Internet service providers have chosen the IP over ATM path, others pursue high-performance IP over SONET implementations. Beginning in 1995, ATM had an edge over packet switching because it was the only technology capable of operating at 150-Mbps speeds. However, now router manufacturers plan to support IP directly over SONET at 150-Mbps speeds in 1997 and 600-Mbps speeds in 1998.

Another differentiator for ATM is that the relatively simple fixed cell size enables construction of larger-scale switching machines than devices utilizing frame-based protocols do. For example, today's routers struggle to get to the 1 Gbps benchmark [5]; however, this throughput only qualifies as an ATM enterprise switch in the taxonomy used in Part 3. Carrier edge and backbone switches are already 10 to 100 time larger than the upcoming generation of gigarouters! This huge difference in scale is due to the fact that many of the parts in ATM switches are now built from commodity integrated circuits. Also, ATM switching avoids the processor-intensive layer 3 functions implemented in routers.

25.7 THE REAL COST OF DATA NETWORKING

So where is the real cost element in data networking in the next century? There will always be an access switching and transmission cost, regardless of the technology or media. However, their unit costs should decline over time. Information will be the new currency of the next century. The valuable elements in future networks will be sought after information content, knowledgeable network management, competent technical support, and effective maintenance. Since price usually follows value, intelligent networks of the future will focus on these areas instead of the raw costs of switching and transmission.

25.8 ON DEMAND SWITCHING — THE KEY SUCCESS?

As we have seen in Parts 2 and 3, the design of many higher-layer protocols running over ATM requires Switched Virtual Connections (SVCs) to perform optimally. The dynamic bandwidth allocation and resource sharing of SVCs also make them an economical alternative. In contrast to Permanent Virtual Connections (PVCs), where the bandwidth is dedicated 100 percent of the time, SVCs make bandwidth available on demand, returning this resource when a user completes an activity or when the network devices detect a period of inactivity. The key protocols described in Chapter 11 that need SVCs are:

* Classical IP over ATM subnetworks
* LAN emulation (LANE)
* Multiprotocol over ATM (MPOA)
* IP multicast over ATM

These protocols create brighter prospects for ATM than for frame relay [6]. The operation of these protocols in larger networks create a challenge for equipment manufacturers to develop equipment that can process high rates of SVC call attempts. SVCs bridge the gap created by the fundamentally different paradigms employed by IP and LANs when compared with ATM. IP and LANs utilize connectionless packet-by-packet processing, as opposed to ATM's connection-oriented protocol that switches once for an entire stream of packets communicated between endpoints. In essence, the standards defining support for IP and LAN protocols over ATM replace packet-by-packet forwarding with three stages of protocol: flow recognition, address resolution, and connection establishment. Hence, ATM's SVC-based support for higher-layer protocols is efficient only for long-lived traffic flows. In other words, the combined cost required for address resolution and call setup for the more efficient ATM SVC must be less than the cost saved by the less efficient packet-by-packet routing. The IETF concluded that for flows that are too short, the overhead of ATM SVCs is probably not justified [7].

The ATM SVC protocol, as specified in the ITU-T standard Q.2931, is very complex [8]. In addition to signaling similar to that needed to set up telephone calls, ATM must also signal a number of additional parameters. The additional information elements in ATM signaling messages convey requests for different service categories, traffic parameters, information about higher-layer protocols, and topology information, such as point-to-multipoint connections. In essence, the ATM signaling standards carry along with them the evolutionary baggage of interworking with telephony protocols conceived of over a century ago, plus all of these additional information elements. Furthermore, the complexity of emulating connectionless protocols with various forms of registration, address resolution, flow recognition, and fast connection setup will require some time to optimize the price/performance of hardened implementations.

Thus, the key challenge for ATM switching is to achieve high call setup rates and low call setup times cost-effectively. Since ATM signaling is computer- and memory-intensive, it should be able to follow the technology curves for computing and storage to achieve these goals. Another linchpin of success is interoperability. ATM signaling must be as interoperable as telephone signaling if it is to succeed. Furthermore, ATM addressing must be assigned logically and consistently so that carriers will interconnect and customers can call any other ATM user [9]. Finally, ATM signaling must seamlessly interwork with N-ISDN and telephony signaling and addressing to support voice over ATM.

25.9 WILL ATM REPLACE TODAY'S VOICE INFRASTRUCTURE?

A great topic to bring up at a technocrat voice provider's dinner party is whether ATM switching will replace today's voice switch infrastructure. While on first blush this may appear to be a religious more than a technical argument, there are many real reasons why ATM may indeed eventually replace the voice switched network — or at least part of it. Tremendous benefits in support cost aggregation, voice-aware client-server applications, and ATM LAN telephony are already being realized by VPN users that consolidate voice and data traffic on a single corporate network, interconnecting via gateways to the PSTN and public data networks.

One major factor that will heavily influence a service provider's future switching fabric is the projected mix of voice and nonvoice traffic. Nonvoice traffic volumes continue to grow at a more rapid pace than voice traffic; this is more so true of corporate calling patterns than of residential. Nonvoice traffic's longer connection-oriented, bandwidth-intensive traffic patterns are no match for existing voice switches and trunking. One technology that is already pushing this envelope is ISDN. Voice service providers that offer ISDN must carefully plan their trunking requirements, as each ISDN user requires much more bandwidth than the typical phone call (128 kbps versus 64 kbps for voice) and for much longer periods. Data calls are on the average many tens to hundreds of minutes long, whereas voice calls are usually only a few minutes in length. Thus, growing nonvoice traffic requirements place a much greater strain on existing networks than does voice growth. While today it makes sense to keep these two networks separate, network architects must at least consider whether it makes economic and operational sense to merge the two.

The second major issue is voice services. Take a good look at your local service phone bill, and you will see at least a dozen calling options — from call waiting to message services to call blocking security features to automatic redial when a busy number becomes clear. These custom calling and handling features generate huge amounts of revenue for the voice service providers, yet consume expensive resources in large central office (CO) voice switches. These services might be provided more cost-effectively on ATM- or Internet-based network servers, with the added bonus of unlimited options.

The third major issue is mobility. Voice services have been mobile (i.e., cellular phones) for some time. Yet now users want mobile data services — and they definitely don't want to pay for two separate services and access devices. This points to a single access infrastructure. You can already see this today in many cell phones that have small data cards for attaching your laptop for remote dial access to corporate resources. The trend toward Personal Data Assistants (PDAs) adds to the amount of data (voice mail is now joined by E-mail, paging, stock quotes, etc. – you get the idea) on the voice network. Quickly the actual voice traffic is subsumed by the volume of data and eventually video traffic.

ATM takes on this challenge by offering a front-end technology that can accept various access types (POTS, ISDN, xDSL, etc.) and convert them to ATM switching, feeding them to private voice and data networks as required. Calls can originate and be terminated at the edges of the ATM network and then be switched and processed from there.

However, the wholesale replacement of our current PSTN infrastructure is still years away. Efforts like the Advanced Intelligent Network (AIN) are an attempt to bring the PSTN into its next generation of switching and services. AIN is a strategy and framework for the next generation of voice services over legacy voice switches. To compound this movement, the depreciation cost tied up in legacy voice switches alone is enough to make even the more progressive service providers shudder. In many cases, a migration strategy using many of the concepts and technologies defined in this chapter will be a service provider's best bet. This replacement will probably happen much faster in countries that lack an existing infrastructure, where existing voice infrastructure services are expensive and fragmented, and/or in environments where ATM service is particularly attractive for other reasons.

Some champions of the movement to combine traditional voice and ATM switches are some of the largest manufacturers of traditional voice switches: the Siemens Stromberg-Carlson and NewBridge partnership and the AT&T and NorTel partnership [10]. These players offer the benefit of statistical multiplexing of voice calling patterns with data calling patterns, which in many cases are quite complementary. Nortel's Passport switches have the capability to switch and route calls that originate and terminate within the ATM network's domain without PBX intervention — achieving significant cost savings. An ATM approach also allows network managers to pick and chose where they want high-quality voice (extranet) or lower quality voice (intranet). This will change over time, as ATM and public voice network service providers merge their backbone architectures into a single ATM infrastructure, allowing for seamless intercorporate voice and data networking.

The key to ATM service and equipment providers replacing existing TDM networks is the price of the combined equipment and service over the depreciation period, matching the features and functions that are most important to the customer. ATM networks should also support integrated access, particularly in support of voice. In fact, the integration of voice over ATM is very attractive in European and Pacific Rim countries where inter-country voice communications are extremely expensive.

25.10 ATM'S KEY CHALLENGES

ATM equipment sales have been much stronger than ATM service revenue, although ATM service revenues continue to double year over year. ATM services are now proliferating, and the largest providers (the interexchange carriers) have almost 100 ATM customers now [11]. In the most optimistic case, ATM services could outstrip private line and frame relay revenues by the year 2000, even subsuming some of the nation's voice traffic and switching. ATM could also make a strong penetration into the LAN backbone and high-performance workgroups if the vendor implementations of LANE, MPOA, and Private Network-Network Interface (PNNI) become cost-effective. A more pessimistic view would place ATM as the WAN transport technology of choice for only carriers and service providers. Contrarians believe that gigabit Ethernet will succeed over ATM in the LAN backbone, with QoS-aware IP protocols over switched Ethernet to the desktop and workgroup.

25.10.1 Key Challenges for ATM Technology

What are the challenges facing ATM technology in its play for world dominance as the technology of choice for LAN and WAN applications? We have listed the key battlegrounds and deciding factors below:

◊ Support for voice traffic over ATM
◊ Interworking between ATM QoS and IP RSVP
◊ Lower-priced CPE ATM access devices
◊ Lower-priced ATM network interface cards
◊ Further standards for video over ATM
◊ Effective end-to-end network management
◊ Adoption of ATM or QoS-aware application programming interfaces

25.10.2 Key Challenges for ATM Service Providers

The greatest challenge to the service providers is to offer all the features of ATM to the user community in a cost-effective and easy-to-use manner. This means that they must keep their internal capital costs down while simultaneously keeping the pricing competitive with existing legacy services like private lines, frame relay, and telephony services. There are many options open to service providers. One option left to carriers is the large-scale adoption of ATM as a service offering and consolidation of their transport infrastructure. The hurdle they face is a costly depreciation of the existing voice infrastructure, balanced against the cost savings of deploying ATM network-wide. Another option is to offer many access options to users that want to deploy ATM access multiplexers, connect via scalable and flexible nxDS0, DS1, and nxDS1 ATM access methods, or only migrate to ATM for sites that require its benefits and perform interworking (FR-to-ATM interworking between sites) [12].

Carriers must also deliver on the following features in order for ATM to be successful:

◊ Widespread availability of SVC services
◊ Interconnection of carrier SVC networks
◊ ATM SVC interworking with frame relay SVCs
◊ True end-to-end service QoS guarantees over a public network
◊ FR-to-ATM service interworking
◊ Attractive service pricing

Look for each of these capabilities to play a key role in the future success of ATM in the WAN.

25.11 ATM ARCHITECTURES OF TOMORROW

Will the telephony model that brought us ubiquitous voice service across the planet prevail in the twenty-first century, or will the radical concepts of the Internet explosion dominate networking for the upcoming decades? Or, will evolution result, taking the best from both? Have you ever wondered what the architecture of tomorrow's data network will look like? This section takes a glimpse into what network architectures may look like in the twenty-first century, and how ATM will play a key role.

Static, predefined private communications networks are migrating to dynamic, virtual networks — networks with ubiquitous access that can interwork past, present, and future protocols — that provide anyone-to-anyone, anywhere-to-anywhere communications. The flexible, extensible capabilities of ATM, interworking well with LANs and the Internet protocols in both the local and wide area network, position it well to be the key vehicle in the rapidly changing world of networking. Virtual private networks implemented over public ATM infrastructures employ sophisticated switching and routing intelligence, in essence making the network the computer. Major corporations are becoming more and more dependent upon virtual networking to run their day-to-day businesses, increasingly relying on their partitioning and security features. ATM services already are becoming ubiquitous worldwide and are now moving out towards mobile and telecommuting users via wireless ATM and xDSL technologies. ATM enables the user to win the war with technical obsolescence — offering a network infrastructure that will last well into the next century. Will ATM be the Rosetta stone for protocol interworking in both the LAN and WAN, allowing multiple protocols to be deciphered and understood? Will these ATM networks provide ubiquitous, any-to-any access for all users? Only time will tell.

25.12 REVIEW

This final chapter sought to answer various questions regarding the degree of ATM success in the LAN and WAN. This analysis was built on the comparisons with various competing technologies covered in Chapter 24. We also explored one of ATM's latest forays into frontiers of networking, wireless services over ATM. The text also highlighted several critical success factors for ATM, including maintaining its lead as the highest-speed networking solution, continual cost reduction, excellent support for SVCs, and cost-effective support for voice over integrated access lines.

25.13 REFERENCES

[1]   J. McQuillan, "Deconstructing ATM," *Business Communications Review*, March 1997.
[2]   L. Dellaverson, "Reaching for the New Frontier," *ATM Forum 53 Bytes*, 1996.
[3]   Cascade White Paper, "Priority Frame — Absolute Quality of Service in a Frame Relay Environment," January 1997, http://www.casc.com/products/data sheets/008_97.pdf.
[4]   S. Saunders, *The McGraw-Hill High-Speed LANs Handbook*, McGraw-Hill, 1996.
[5]   E. Roberts, "IP on Speed," *Data Communications*, March 1997.
[6]   D. Passmore, "Who Needs SVCs?," *Business Communications Review*, June 1997.
[7]   R. Cole, D. Shur, and C. Villamizar, *RFC 1932: IP over ATM: A Framework Document*, IETF, April 1996
[8]   N. Shelef, "SVC Signaling: Calling All Nodes," *Data Communications*, June 1995.

[9]   Cascade White Paper, "Addressing and Numbering Plans for Public ATM Networks," November 1996, http://www.casc.com/products/data sheets/008_97. pdf.

[10] T. Nolle, "The great QoS debate: IP vs. ATM Is Only the Tip of the Iceberg," *Network World*, July 15, 1996.

[11] ATM Report newsletters, Broadband Publishing Corporation, Rockville, MD 20852, circa 1996.

[12] K. Hodges and J. Hamer, "Carrier Implementation of ATM Services," *Telecommunications*, April 1995.

)

Acronyms and Abbreviations

Comments in parentheses are a clarification or refer to the standard or protocol from which the term is derived. Many acronyms are used by multiple standards, only the most prevalent are mentioned.

AAL	ATM Adaptation Layer
AARP	AppleTalk Address Resolution Protocol
ABM	Asynchronous Balance Mode (HDLC)
ABR	Available Bit Rate
AC	Access Control (IEEE)
ACF	Access Control Field (DQDB)
ACK	Acknowledgment
ADM	Add/Drop Multiplexer
AII	Active Input Interface (used in UNI PMD specs for copper/fiber)
AIS	Alarm Indication Signal (SONET, UNI fault management)
ANS	American National Standard
ANSI	American National Standards Institute
AOI	Active Output Interface (used in UNI PMD specs for copper/ fiber)
API	Application Programming Interface
APS	Automatic Protection Switching
ARM	Asynchronous Response Mode (HDLC)
ARP	Address Resolution Protocol
ASN.1	Abstract Syntax Notation One
Async	Asynchronous
ATE	ATM Terminating Equipment (SONET)
ATM	Asynchronous Transfer Mode
AU	Access Unit (DQDB)
AUI	Attachment Unit Interface (Ethernet 802.3)
AVSSCS	Audio-Visual Service-Specific Convergence Sublayer (ATM Forum)

B8ZS	Bipolar with 8 Zero Substitution
BCC	Block Check Characters
BCD	Binary-Coded Decimal
BECN	Backward Explicit Congestion Notification (FR)
Bellcore	Bell Communications Research
BER	Basic Encoding Rules (ASN.1)
BER	Bit Error Ratio or Rate (link quality specification/testing)
BGP	Border Gateway Protocol
B-HLI	Broadband High-Layer Information
B-ICI	Broadband Intercarrier Interface
BIP	Bit Interleaved Parity (8)
BIPV	Bit Interleaved Parity Violation
BIS	Border Intermediate System (ATM Forum, PNNI SWG)
B-ISDN	Broadband Integrated Services Digital Network
B-ISSI	Broadband Inter-Switching System Interface
B-LLI	Broadband Low-Layer Information
B-NT	Broadband Network Terminator
BO	Bit Oriented (SONET)
BOC	Bell Operating Company
BOM	Beginning of Message (DQDB)
bps	Bits per second or bytes per second
BRI	Basic Rate Interface (ISDN)
BSC	IBM's Binary Synchronous Communications protocol
BSS	Broadband Switching System
B-TA	Broadband Terminal Adapter (ATM)
B-TE	Broadband Terminal Equipment (ATM)
CAC	Connection Admission Control
CAD/CAM	Computer-Aided Design/Computer-Aided Manufacturing
CAN	Customer Access Node (SMDS)
CBDS	Connectionless Broadband Data Service
CBEMA	Computer and Business Equipment Manufacturers Association
CBR	Constant Bit Rate
CCI	Carrier-to-Carrier Interface
CCITT	Consultative Committee, International Telegraph & Telephone
CD	Countdown counter (DQDB)
CDV	Cell Delay Variation
CE	Connection Endpoint
CEI	Connection Endpoint Identifier (UNI 3.0)
CEPT	Conference on European Post & Telegraph
CES	Circuit Emulation Service
CIR	Committed Information Rate (FR)
CL	Connectionless (SONET)
CLLM	Consolidated Link-Layer Management (FR)
CLNP	Connectionless Layer Network Protocol
CLNS	Connectionless Network Service (OSI)

CLP	Cell Loss Priority
CLR	Cell Loss Ratio
CLSF	Connectionless Server Function (ITU-T)
CMIP	Common Management Interface Protocol (ISO)
CMIS	Common Management Information Service (ISO)
CMISE	CMIS Element (ISO)
CMT	Connection Management (FDDI)
CNMS	Customer Network Management System
CNR	Complex Node Representation (ATM Forum, PNNI SWG)
CO	Central Office
COAM	Customer Owned and Maintained
COCF	Connection-Oriented Convergence Function (DQDB)
COM	Continuation of Message (DQDB)
CONS	Connection-Oriented Network Service (ITU-T)
CPCS	Common Part Convergence Sublayer
CPE	Customer Premises Equipment
CPI	Common Part Indicator
C/R	Command/Response Indicator or Bit
CRC	Cyclic Redundancy Check or Test
CRF(VC)	Virtual Channel Connection Related Function (related to UPC/UNI 3.0)
CRF(VP)	Virtual Path Connection Related Function (related to UPC/UNI 3.0)
CRS	Cell Relay Service
CS	Convergence Sublayer (DQDB, CS_PDU)
CSMA/CD	Carrier-Sense Multiple Access with Collision Detection
CSU	Channel Service Unit
CTD	Cell Transfer Delay
DA	Destination Address field
DAL	Dedicated Access Line
DARPA	Defense Advanced Research Projects Agency
DAS	Dual-Attach Station connection (FDDI)
DCE	Data Communications Equipment
DCS	Digital Cross-connect System
DDD	Direct Distance Dialing
DDS	Digital Data Service
DE	Discard Eligibility (FR)
DEC	Digital Equipment Corporation
DH	DMPDU Header (DQDB)
DLCI	Data Link Connection Identifier (FR)
DMPDU	Derived MAC PDU (DQDB)
DoD	Department of Defense
DPG	Dedicated Packet Group (FDDI)
DQDB	Distributed Queue Dual Bus (IEEE)
DS0	Digital Signal Level 0

DS1	Digital Signal Level 1
DS3	Digital Signal Level 3
DSAP	Destination Service Access Point (LLC)
DSG	Default Slot Generator (DQDB)
DSU	Data Service Unit
DSX	Digital Signal Cross-Connect
DT	DMPDU trailer (DQDB)
DTE	Data Terminal Equipment
DTMF	Dual Tone Multifrequency
DXC	Digital Cross-Connect
DXI	Data Exchange Interface (SMDS, ATM)
E1	European Transmission Level 1
E3	European Transmission Level 3
EA	Extended Address
ECN	Explicit Congestion Notification (FR)
ECSA	Exchange Carriers Standards Association
ED	End Delimiter (IEEE 802)
EDFG	Edge Device Functional Group (ATM Forum, MPOA SWG)
EFCI	Explicit Forward Congestion Indication
EGP	Exterior Gateway Protocol
EGRP	Exterior Gateway Routing Protocol
EIA	Electronics Industries Association
EIR	Excess Information Rate
ELAN	Emulated LAN (ATM Forum LANE)
EMA	Enterprise Management Architecture (DEC)
EOM	End of Message
EOT	End of Transmission
EPRCA	Enhanced Proportional Rate Control Algorithm (ATM Forum)
ES	End System (OSI)
ESF	Extended Superframe
ES-IS	End System–to–Intermediate System protocol (OSI)
ETB	End of Transmission Block
ETSI	European Telecommunications Standards Institute
ETX	End of Text
F	Flag
FC	Frame Control field (FDDI)
FCS	Frame Check Sequence (FR)
FCVC	Flow-Controlled Virtual Circuit
FDDI	Fiber Distributed Data Interface (ANSI)
FDDI-II	Fiber Distributed Data Interface Version II
FDM	Frequency-Division Multiplexing
FEA	Functional Entity Action (UNI 3.0, C.3.2.3)
FEBE	Far End Block Error (SONET)
FEC	Forward Error Correction

FECN	Forward Explicit Congestion Notification (FR)
FERF	Far End Reporting Failure
FG	Functional Group (ATM Forum, MPOA SWG)
FM	Frequency Modulation
FOIRL	Fiber Optic Interrepeater Link (Ethernet 802.3)
fps	Frames per second
FR	Frame Relay
FRAD	Frame Relay Assembler/Disassembler, or Access Device
FS	Frame Status field (FDDI)
FT1	Fractional T1
FTP	File Transfer Protocol
FUNI	Frame-based User-to-Network Interface (ATM Forum)
Gbit	Gigabits (billions of bits)
Gbps	Gigabits per second (10^9 bps)
GCRA	Generic Cell Rate Algorithm
GFC	Generic Flow Control
GFI	General Format Identifier (X.25)
GFID	General Format Identifier
GGP	Gateway-Gateway Protocol (DoD)
GOS	Grade of Service
GOSIP	Government Open System Interconnection Profile
GUI	Graphical User Interface
HBFG	Host Behavior Functional Group (ATM Forum, MPOA SWG)
HCS	Header Check Sequence (DQDB)
HDLC	High-Level Data Link Control (ISO)
HDTV	High-Definition Television
HEC	Header Error Control
HOB	Head of Bus (DQDB) A or B
HSSI	High-Speed Serial Interface
Hz	Hertz or cycles per second
IASG	Internetwork Address Subgroup (ATM Forum, MPOA SWG)
IBSG	Internetwork Broadcast Subgroup (ATM Forum, MPOA SWG)
IBUFG	Internetwork Broadcast/Unknown Functional Group (ATM Forum, MPOA SWG)
ICF	Isochronous Convergence Function (DQDB)
ICFG	IASG Coordination Function Group (ATM Forum, MPOA SWG)
ICIP	Intercarrier Interface Protocol (SMDS)
ICMP	Internet Control Message Protocol
IDRP	Interdomain Routing Protocol
IDU	Interface Data Unit (UNI 3.0)
IE	Information Element

IEEE   Institute of Electrical and Electronics Engineers
IETF   Internet Engineering Task Force
IGP   Interior Gateway Protocol
IGRP   Interior Gateway Routing Protocol (Cisco)
IISP   Interim Interswitch Signaling Protocol (PNNI Phase 0)
ILMI   Interim Local Management Interface
I-MAC   Isochronous Media Access Control (FDDI)
IMPDU   Initial MAC Protocol Data Unit (DQDB)
IMSSI   Inter-MAN Switching System Interface (DQDB)
intra-LATA   Intra–Local Access Transport Area
IP   Internet Protocol (DoD)
IPCP   Internet Protocol Control Protocol (DoD)
IPX   Internetwork Packet Exchange protocol (Novell)
IS   Intermediate System (OSI)
ISDN   Integrated Services Digital Network
ISDU   Isochronous Service Data Unit (DQDB)
IS-IS   Intermediate System–to–Intermediate System (OSI)
ISN   Initial Sequence Number (DoD)
ISO   International Standards Organization
ISSI   Interswitching System Interface (SMDS)
ISU   Isochronous Service User (SMDS)
ITU   International Telecommunications Union
ITU-T   ITU Telecommunications standardization sector
IXC   Interexchange Carrier

kbit   Kilobits (thousands of bits)
kbps   Kilobits per second (10^3 bps)
km   Kilometers (10^3 meters)

LAN   Local Area Network
LANE   LAN Emulation (ATM Forum)
LAP-B   Link Access Procedure — Balanced (X.25)
LAP-D   Link Access Procedure — D (ISDN/Frame Relay)
LAP-F   Link Access Procedure — Frame Mode
LAT   Local Area Transport protocol (DEC)
LATA   Local Access Transport Area
LB   Letter Ballot
LCD   Loss of Cell Delineation
LCGN   Logical Channel Group Number
LCP   Link Control Protocol
LCT   Last Compliance Time (used in GCRA definition)
LE   LAN Emulation (also, LANE)
LEC   Local Exchange Carrier
LEC   LAN Emulation Client (ATM Forum LANE)
LES   LAN Emulation Server (ATM Forum LANE)

LGN	Logical Group Node (ATM Forum, PNNI)
LIS	Logical IP Subnet (RFC 1577)
LLC	Logical Link Control (IEEE 802.X)
LME	Layer Management Entity (DQDB)
LMI	Local Management Interface (FR)
LOF	Loss of Frame (UNI fault management)
LOP	Loss of Pointer (UNI fault management)
LOS	Loss of Signal (UNI fault management)
LSB	Least Significant Bit
LT	Line Termination
LTE	Line Terminating Equipment (SONET)
LU	Logical Unit (SNA)
LUNI	LANE UNI (ATM Forum, see LANE)

m	Meter
MAC	Media Access Control (IEEE 802.X)
MAN	Metropolitan Area Network (DQDB, FDDI)
MARS	Multicast Address Resolution Service (Draft IETF — IPATM)
Mbit	Megabits (millions of bits)
Mbps	Megabits per second (10^6 bps)
MBS	Maximum Burst Size
MCF	MAC Convergence Function (DQDB)
MCP	MAC Convergence Protocol (DQDB)
MCR	Minimum Cell Rate
MHz	Megahertz
MIB	Management Information Base (SNMP)
MIC	Media Interface Connector (FDDI)
MID	Message Identifier (DQDB), Multiplexing Identifier (ATM)
MIPS	Millions of Instructions per Second
MMF	Multimode Fiber
MOP	Maintenance and Operation Protocol (DEC)
MPEG	Motion Picture Encoding Group
MPOA	Multiprotocol over ATM (ATM Forum)
ms	Millisecond (one-thousandth of a second, 10^{-3} second)
MSAP	MAC Service Access Point (SMDS)
MSB	Most Significant Bit
MSDU	MAC Service Data Unit (SMDS)
MSS	MAN Switching System (SMDS)
MTU	Maximum Transmission Unit
MUX	Multiplexer

NANP	North American Numbering Plan
NBMA	Nonbroadcast Multiple Access
NBP	Name Binding Protocol
NCP	Network Control Protocol or Point (SNA)

NE	Network Element
NetBIOS	Network Basic Input/Output System protocol
NEXT	Near End Crosstalk
NFS	Network File Server
NHRP	Next-Hop Routing Protocol (IETF)
NIU	Network Interface Unit
NLPID	Network-Layer Protocol Identifier
nm	Nanometer (10^{-9} meter)
NMP	Network Management Process (SMDS)
NMS	Network Management System or Station
NNI	Network-Node Interface (ATM, SONET)
NNI	Network-to-Network Interface (FR)
NOS	Network Operating System
NP	Network Performance
NPA	Numbering Plan Area
NRM	Normalized Response Mode (ISO)
NRZ	Non-return to Zero
NRZI	Non-return to Zero Invert 1s
ns	Nanosecond (10^{-9} second)
NSAP	Network Layer Service Access Point
NTx	Network Termination x (where $x = 1, 2, \ldots$)
OAM	Operations and Maintenance
OCD	Out-of-Cell Delineation (ATM UNI)
OC-N	Optical Carrier Level N (SONET)
OH	Overhead
OID	Object Identifier (SNMP)
OOF	Out of Frame
ONA	Open Network Architecture
OS	Operating System
OSI	Open Systems Interconnection
OSI CLNS	Connectionless Network System (OSI)
OSIRM	OSI Reference Model
OSPF	Open Shortest Path First
OTC	Operating Telephone Company
PA	Prearbitrated segment or slot (DQDB)
PABX	Private Automatic Branch Exchange
PAD	Packet Assembler/Disassembler (X.25)
PAF	Prearbitrated Function (DQDB)
PBX	Private Branch Exchange
PCR	Peak Cell Rate (UNI 3.0)
PDC	Packet Data Channel (FDDI)
PDH	Plesiochronous Digital Hierarchy
PDN	Public Data Network

PDS	Packet Driver Specification for public domain
PDU	Protocol Data Unit (IEEE)
PGL	Peer Group Leader (ATM Forum, PNNI)
Ph-SAP	Physical-layer SAP (DQDB)
PHY	Physical-layer Standard (FDDI)
PID	Protocol Identification
Ping	Packet Internet Groper
PIR	Protocol-Independent Routing
PL	PAD Length (DQDB)
PLCP	Physical-Layer Convergence Protocol (IEEE 802.6)
PL-OU	Physical-Layer Overhead Unit (ATM UNI)
PM	Performance Monitoring
PMD	Physical-Layer Medium-Dependent standard (FDDI)
PMP	Point to Multipoint (UNI 3.0)
PNNI	Private Network-Node Interface or Private Network-to-Network Interface (ATM Forum)
POH	Path Overhead (SONET)
POI	Path Overhead Identifier (DQDB)
PON	Passive Optical Network
PoP	Point of Presence
POTS	Plain Old Telephone Service
PPP	Point-to-Point Protocol (Internet)
Pps	Packets per second
PRI	Primary Rate Interface (ISDN)
PSPDN	Packet-Switched Public Data Network
PT	Payload Type
PTE	Path-Terminating Equipment (SONET)
PTI	Payload Type Identifier
PTSE	PNNI Topology State Element (ATM Forum, PNNI)
PTSP	PNNI Topology State Packet
PTT	Postal, Telegraph & Telephone Ministry/Administration
PU	Physical Unit (SNA)
PVC	Permanent Virtual Circuit or Channel (ATM, FR, X.25)
QA	Queued Arbitrated segment, slot, access function(DQDB)
QAF	Queued Arbitrated Function (DQDB)
QoS	Quality of Service
QPSX	Queued Packet and Synchronous Exchange
RBOC	Regional Bell Operating Company
RCP	Remote Console Protocol (DEC)
RDI	Remote Defect Indication (ATM)
REJ	Reject frame
RFC	Request for Comments
RIP	Routing Information Protocol
RISC	Reduced Instruction Set Computer

RJE	Remote Job Entry
RMT	Ring Management (FDDI)
RNR	Receive Not Ready
RQ	Request Counter (DQDB)
RR	Receive Ready frame
RSFG	Route Server Functional Group (ATM Forum, MPOA SWG)
RTMP	Routing and Management Protocol (Apple)
RTP	Routing Update Protocol
s	Second
SA	Source Address field
SAAL	Signaling ATM Adaptation Layer
SAP	Service Access Point (ISO)
SAPI	Service Access Point Identifier (ISO)
SAR	Segmentation and Reassembly (ATM)
SAS	Single-Attach Station connection (FDDI)
SCR	Sustainable Cell Rate (UNI 3.0)
SD	Start Delimiter
SDH	Synchronous Digital Hierarchy (ITU-T)
SDLC	Synchronous Data Link Control protocol (IBM)
SDU	Service Data Unit (DQDB)
SEAL	Simple and Efficient Adaptation Layer (AAL5)
SECB	Severely Errored Cell Block
SES	Severely Errored Seconds
SF	Superframe
SIG	SMDS Interest Group
SIP	SMDS Interface Protocol (SMDS)
SIR	Sustained Information Rate (ATM, SMDS)
SMDS	Switched Multimegabit Data Service
SMF	Single-Mode Fiber
SMT	System Management protocol (FDDI)
SN	Sequence Number
SNA	Systems Network Architecture (IBM)
SNAP	Subnetwork Access Protocol (SMDS)
SNDCF	Subnetwork-Dependent Convergence Function (ATM Forum)
SNI	Subscriber Network Interface (SMDS)
SNMP	Simple Network Management Protocol (DoD)
SOH	Section Overhead
SONET	Synchronous Optical Network (ANSI)
SPE	Synchronous Payload Envelope (SONET)
SPF	Shortest Path First protocol
SPM	FDDI-to-SONET Physical Layer Mapping standard
SREJ	Select Reject frame
SRT	Source Route Transparent protocol
SRTS	Synchronous Residual Time Stamp
SS	Switching System (SMDS)

SSAP	Source Service Access Point (LLC)
SSCF	Service-Specific Coordination Function
SSCOP	Service-Specific Connection-Oriented Protocol (ATM)
SSCS	Service-Specific Convergence Sublayer (ATM)
STE	Section Terminating Equipment (SONET)
STM	Synchronous Transfer Mode or Station Management (SDH)
STM-n	Synchronous Transport Module Level n (SDH)
STP	Shielded Twisted Pair
STP	Spanning Tree Protocol (IEEE 802.1d)
STS-n	Synchronous Transport Signal Level n (SONET)
STS-Nc	Concatenated Synchronous Transport Signal Level N
SVC	Switched Virtual Circuit or Signaling Virtual Channel
SYN	Synchronous Idle

t	Time
TA	Terminal Adapter
TAT	Theoretical Arrival Time (used in GCRA definition)
TAXI	Transparent Asynchronous Transmitter/Receiver Interface
TC	Transmission Convergence Sublayer of PHY Layer (ATM)
TCP	Transmission Control Protocol (DoD)
TCP/IP	Transmission Control Protocol/Internet Protocol (DoD)
TDM	Time-Division Multiplexing
TDMA	Time-Division Multiple Access
TE	Terminal Equipment
TIG	Topology Information Group (ATM Forum, PNNI)
TP	Transport Protocol (CCITT)
TP4	Transport Protocol Class 4 (ISO)
TR	Technical Report
TUC	Total User Cell Count
TUCD	Total User Cell Difference

UDP	User Datagram Protocol (DoD)
UME	UNI Management Entity (ATM)
UNI	User-to-Network Interface
UNMA	Unified Network Management Architecture (AT&T)
UPC	Usage Parameter Control
UTP	Unshielded Twisted Pair

VBR	Variable Bit Rate
VC	Virtual Channel or Virtual Call
VCC	Virtual Channel Connection
VCI	Virtual Channel or Circuit Identifier (ATM, DQDB)
VCL	Virtual Channel Link (UNI 3.0)
VC-n	Virtual Container n (SDH)
VINCE	Vendor-Independent Network Control Entity
VLSI	Very Large Scale Integration

VP	Virtual Path (ATM)
VPC	Virtual Path Connection
VPCI	Virtual Path Connection Identifier
VPI	Virtual Path Identifier (ATM)
VPL	Virtual Path Link (UNI 3.0)
VPN	Virtual Private Network
VPT	Virtual Path Terminator (UNI 3.0)
VT	Virtual Tributary (SONET)
VTx	VT of size x (currently x = 1.5, 2, 3, 6)
VTx-Nc	Concatenated Virtual Tributary (SONET)
WAN	Wide Area Network
XNS	Xerox Network Systems protocol (Xerox)
ZIP	Routing and Management protocol (Apple)
µs	Microsecond (10^{-6} second)

Standards Sources

Alpha Graphics
  10215 N. 35th Avenue, Suite A&B,
  Phoenix, AZ 85051
  Ph: 602-863-0999
  (IEEE P802 draft standards)

American National Standards Institute (ANSI) Sales Department
  11 W. 42nd Street,
  New York, NY 10036
  Ph: 212-642-4900/Fax: 212-302-1286
  (ANSI and ISO standards)

Association Francaise de Normalisation, Tour Europe — Cedex 7
  92080 Paris La Defense, France
  Ph: 33-1-4-778-13-26; Telex: 611-974-AFNOR-F; Fax: 33-1-774-84-90

ATM Forum
  303 Vintage Park Drive,
  Foster City, CA 94404
  Ph: 415-578-6860; Fax: 415-525-0182; Internet: info@atmforum.com

Bell Communications Research — Bellcore Customer Service
  8 Corporate Place, Piscataway, NJ 08854-4156
  Ph: 908-699-5800 / 800-521-CORE (800-521-2673)
  (Bellcore TAs and TRs)

British Standards Institution
  2 Park St.,
  London, WIA 2BS England
  Ph: 44-1-629-9000; Telex: 266933 BSI G; Fax: 44-1-629-0506

Canadian Standards Association
  178 Rexdale Boulevard,
  Rexdale, ON M9W 1R9 Canada
  Ph: 416-747-4363; Telex: 06-989344; Fax: 416-747-4149

Comité Européen de Normalisation
  Rue Brederode 2 Bte 5,
  1000 Brussels, Belgium
  Ph: 32-2-513-79-30; Telex: 26257 B

Computer and Business Equipment Manufacturers Association (CBEMA)
  311 First Street N.W., Suite 500,
  Washington, DC 20001-2178
  Ph: 202-626-5740; Fax: 202-638-4299, 202-628-2829
  (ANSI X3 secretariat)

Dansk Standardiseringsrad
  Aurehojvej 12, Postboks 77,
  DK-2900 Hellerup, Denmark
  Ph: 45-1-62-32-00; Telex: 15-615 DANSTA DK

DDN Network Information Center — SRI International
  333 Ravenswood Avenue,
  Menlo Park, CA 94025
  Ph: 415-859-3695 / 800-235-3155 / E-mail: NIC@NIC.DDN.MIL
  (Requests for Comments [RFC] documents)

Deutsches Institut für Normung
  Burggrafenstrasse 4-10, Postfach 1107,
  D-1000 Berlin 30, Germany
  Ph: 49-30-26-01-1; Telex: 184-273-DIN D; Fax: 49-30-260-12-31

Electronics Industries Association (EIA)
  Standards Sales, 2001 Eye Street NW,
  Washington, DC 20036
  Ph: 202-457-4966; Telex: 710-822-0148 EIA WSH; Fax: 202-457-4985

European Computer Manufacturers Association (ECMA)
  Rue du Rhone 114,
  CH-1204 Geneva, Switzerland
  Ph: 41-22-735-36-34; Telex: 413237 ECMA CH; Fax: 41-22-786-52-31

European Conference of Postal and Telecommunications Administrations (CEPT)
  CEPT Liaison Office, Seilerstrasse 22,
  CH-3008 Bern, Switzerland
  Ph: 41-31-62-20-78; Telex: 911089 CEPT CH; Fax: 41-31-62-20-78

European SMDS Interest Group (SIG)
  Merlin House, Station Road,
  Chepstow, Gwent, NP6 5PB, UK
  Ph: 44-291-620425; Fax: 44-291-627119

Exchange Carriers Standards Association (ECSA)
  5430 Grosvenor Lane,
  Bethesda, MD 20814-2122
  Ph: 301-564-4505 (ANSI T1 secretariat)

Global Engineering
2805 McGaw Ave.,
Irvine, CA 92714
Ph: 800-854-7179
(ANSI, IEEE, U.S. federal and military standards and drafts)

Information Handling Services
15 Inverness Way East,
Englewood, CO 80112
Ph: 800-854-7179; Fax: 303-397-2599

Institute of Electrical and Electronics Engineers (IEEE) — Computer Society
10662 Los Vaqueros Circle
Los Alamitos, CA 90720
Ph: 800-272-6657; Fax: 714-821-4641; Interop: cs.books@compmail.com

Institute of Electrical and Electronics Engineers (IEEE) — Standards Office/Service
Center
445 Hoes Lane,
Piscataway, NJ 08855-1331
Ph: 800-678-4323; Fax: 908-981-9667
(IEEE standards)

International Organization for Standardization
1 Rue de Varembe, Case Postale 56,
CH-1211 Geneva 20, Switzerland
Ph: 41-22-734-1240; Telex: 23-88-1 ISO CH; Fax: 41-22-733-3430

International Telecommunications Union — General Secretariat — Sales Service
Palais des Nations, CH 1211, Geneva 20, Switzerland
Ph: 41-22-730-5860; Telex: 421000 UIT CH; Fax: 41-22-730-5853
Ph: 41-22-730-5554; Fax: 41-22-730-5337; Internet: helpdesk@itu.ch
(Information Services Department)
(CCITT and other ITU recommendations)

Internet Access to Request for Comments (RFCs)
Internet: logon "anonymous", password "guest"

Japanese Industrial Standards Committee
Standards Department, Agency of Industrial Science & Technology
Ministry of International Trade and Industry
1-3-1, Kasumigaseki, Chiyoda-ku,
Tokyo 100 Japan
Ph: 81-3-501-9295/6; Fax: 81-3-680-1418

National Institute of Standards and Technology
Technology Building 225,
Gaithersburg, MD 20899
Ph: 301-975-2000; Fax: 301-948-1784

National Standards Authority of Ireland
  Ballymun Road,
  Dublin 9, Ireland
  Ph: 353-1-370101; Telex: 32501 IIRS EI; Fax: 353-1-379620

Nederlands Normalisatie-Instituut
  Kalfjeslaan 2, P.O. Box 5059,
  2600 GB Delft, Netherlands
  Ph: 31-15-61-10-61

Omnicom, Inc.
  115 Park St. SE,
  Vienna, VA 22180-4607
  Ph: 703-281-1135; Telex: 79678 OMNI UR; Fax: 703-281-1505

Omnicom International, Ltd.
  1st Floor, Forum Chambers, The Forum,
  Sevenage, Herts, SG1 1EL, UK
  Ph: 44-438-742424; Telex: 826903 OMNICM G; Fax: 44-438-740154

Pacific Rim Frame Relay/ATM/SMDS Interest Group (PR FASIG)
  AT&T Taiwan Inc.
  12th Floor Overseas Trust Building
  249, Sec.1, Tun Hwa South Road
  Taipei, 106, Taiwan, R.O.C.
  Ph: 886-2-775-6398; Fax: 886-2-775-6356; Internet: attitw.attmail.com

Rapidoc, Technical Indices, Ltd.
  Willoughby Rd.,
  Bracknell, Berkshire, RG12 4DW, UK
  Ph: (0344) 861666; Fax: (0344) 714440

Saudi Arabia Standards Organization
  P.O. Box 3437,
  Riyadh 11471, Saudi Arabia
  Ph: 9-661-4793332; Telex: 201610 SASO

SMDS Interest Group (SIG)
  303 Vintage Park Drive,
  Foster City, CA 94404-1138
  Ph: 415-578-6979; Fax: 415-525-0182; E-mail: sig@interop.com

SRI International
  333 Ravenswood Avenue, Room EJ291,
  Menlo Park, CA 94025
  Ph: 800-235-3155
  (Internet Protocol RFCs)

Standardiseringskommissionen i Sverige
 Tegnergatan 11, Box 3 295,
 S-103 66 Stockholm, Sweden
 Ph: 468-230400; Telex: 17453 SIS S

Standards Association of Australia — Standards House
 80-86 Arthur Street,
 North Sydney N.S.W. 2060 Australia
 Ph: 61-2-963-41-11; Telex: 2-65-14 ASTAN AA

Suomen Standardisoimisliitto
 P.O. Box 205,
 SF-00121 Helsinki 12, Finland
 Ph: 358-0-645-601; Telex: 122303 STAND SF

United Nations Bookstore
 United Nations General Assembly Building, Room GA 32B,
 New York, NY 10017
 Ph: 212-963-7680; Internet: itudoc@itu.ch
 (ITU recommendations)

U.S. Department of Commerce — National Technical Information Service
 5285 Port Royal Road,
 Springfield, VA 22161
 Ph: 703-487-4650; Fax: 703-321-8547
 (ITU/CCITT recommendations, U.S. government and military standards)

Glossary

10BASE2 - IEEE 802.3 standard specifying Ethernet over thin coaxial cable.

10BASE5 - IEEE 802.3 standard specifying Ethernet over thick coaxial cable.

10BASET - IEEE 802.3 standard specifying Ethernet over UTP.

10BASEF - IEEE 802.3 standard specifying Ethernet over fiber.

100BASEFX - 100-Mbps standard specifying Ethernet over fiber.

100BASET4 - 100-Mbps standard specifying Ethernet over category 3, 4, or 5 cabling. Compatible with 802.3 MAC sublayer format.

100BASETX - 100-Mbps standard specifying Ethernet over category 5 and Type 1 cabling. Compatible with 802.3 MAC sublayer format.

100VG-AnyLAN - IEEE standard specifying 100 Mbps Ethernet and Token Ring over four-pair UTP.

access unit - In DQDB, the functional unit within a node that performs the DQDB layer functions and controls access to both buses.

address - An identifier of a source or destination in a network. Examples of addresses are IP, E.164, and X.121.

Address Resolution Protocol (ARP) - Protocol used to resolve a destination host MAC address from its known IP address.

address translation - A method of converting a user-protocol address into the standard address format of the network protocol, and vice versa.

agent - Software residing in a managed network device that reports MIB variables through SNMP.

American National Standards Institute (ANSI) - A private, nongovernmental, nonprofit national organization which serves as the primary coordinator of standards within the United States.

analog - Voice or data signals that are continuously variable and possess an infinite number of values (compared to digital, which has discrete variables).

Application Layer (OSI) - Layer 7 of the OSIRM. Provides the management of communications between user applications. Examples include E-mail and file transfer.

Asynchronous Transfer Mode (ATM) - A high-speed connection-oriented multiplexing and switching method specified in international standards utilizing fixed-length cells. to support multiple types of traffic. It is asynchronous in the sense that cells carrying user data need not be periodic.

asynchronous transmission - The transmission of data through start and stop sequences without the use of a common clock.

ATM Adaptation Layer (AAL) - A set of internationally standardized protocols and formats that define support for circuit emulation, packet video and audio, and connection-oriented and connectionless data services.

Available Bit Rate (ABR) - A traffic class of ATM.

Backward Explicit Congestion Notification (BECN) - Convention in frame relay for a network device to notify the user (source) device that network congestion has occurred.

bandwidth - The amount of transport resource available to pass information (passband), measured in hertz for analog and bits per second for digital carriers.

bandwidth balancing - A DQDB scheme in which a node that is queued for access will occasionally *not* seize an empty QA slot. This helps to ensure effective sharing of QA slots.

basic mode - An FDDI mode of ring operation that supports packet-switching services only where MAC PDUs are transmitted directly by the PHY protocol.

Basic Rate Interface (BRI) - An ISDN access interface type composed of two B channels, each at 64 kbps, and one D channel at 16 kbps (2B+D).

B channel - An ISDN bearer service channel that can carry either voice or data at a speed of 64 kbps.

Bell Operating Company (BOC) - One of the 22 local telephone companies formed after the divestiture of AT&T (e.g., Illinois Bell, Ohio Bell).

Bisync (BSC) or Binary Synchronous Communications Protocol - An IBM proprietary bit-oriented protocol.

bridge - A LAN/WAN device operating at layers 1 (physical) and 2 (data link) of the OSIRM.

broadband - While broadband once referred to bandwidths in excess of the voice channel (3 kHz) in basic data communications using analog modulated signals, it now refers to channels supporting rates in excess of DS3 (45 Mbps) or E3 (34 Mbps).

Broadband ISDN (B-ISDN) - A set of services, capabilities, and interfaces supporting an integrated network and user interface at speeds greater than that of ISDN. The ITU-T initially decided to develop B-ISDN using ATM in 1988.

broadcast - A transmission to all addresses on the network or subnetwork.

broadcast address - A predefined network address that indicates all possible receivers on a network.

brouter - A device that combines some elements of both bridging and routing.

busy slot - A DQDB slot which is "in use" and not available for access by the QA access functions.

cell - A fixed-length 53-octet packet, or Protocol Data Unit (PDU), used in ATM. The ATM cell has a 5-octet header and a 48-octet payload.

cell header - A 5-octet header that defines control information used in processing, multiplexing, and switching cells.

Central Office (CO) - A telephone company switching office providing local user access to the local switched telephone network and its services; often the first interface to interexchange carriers.

central office vendors - A reference to vendors who provide switching equipment conforming to central office standards, such as DQDB switch vendors Siemens and Alcatel.

circuit switching - A connection-oriented technique based on either time- or space-division multiplexing and switching providing minimal delay. Bandwidth is dedicated to the connection.

client-server architecture - The distribution of network control across many computing elements within the network. Thus, some elements act as servers, controlling the transfer, and some as clients which transmit and receive the information. Servers can perform all three functions, and are often the workhorse computing elements (multi-MIPS machines), while the clients are typically workstations and terminals.

colocated - Devices near one another at the same site.

Committed Information Rate (CIR) - For frame relay service, a term that defines the average rate at which a user can send frames and be guaranteed delivery by the network. Transmissions exceeding the CIR are subject to lower-priority treatment or discard.

Concatenated Virtual Tributary (VTx-Nc) - A combination of VTs where the VT envelope capacities from N VTx's have been combined to carry a VTx-Nc that must be transported as a single entity (as opposed to transport as separate signals).

concentrator - A device providing a single network access for multiple user devices. In FDDI, a device which has additional ports beyond those required for its own attachment to the ring.

congestion - The condition in which network resources (bandwidth) are exceeded by an accumulation of demand.

Consolidated Link-Layer Management (CLLM) - In frame relay, an ANSI-defined method of sending link-layer management messages over the last DLCI (1023). These messages are used to identify the exact cause of congestion and modify transmissions based on each DLCI.

convergence function - A DQDB protocol layer that provides service-specific interfaces to higher-layer protocol functions.

Countdown Counter (CD) - A queued, arbitrated access method for determining how many empty slots must pass before a node has access to the DQDB bus.

Customer Premises Equipment (CPE) - Equipment that resides and is operated at a customer site.

cycle - The Protocol Data Unit (PDU) used in FDDI-II.

Cyclic Redundancy Check (CRC) - An algorithm that detects bit errors caused in data transmission.

D4 - AT&T-defined framing and synchronization format for T1 transmission facilities.

Data Communications (or Circuit Termination) Equipment (DCE) - As defined by the standards, a modem or network communications interface device.

datagram - A packet mode of transmitting data where there is no guaranteed sequential delivery (connectionless service).

Data Link Connection Identifier (DLCI) - A frame relay address designator for each virtual circuit termination point.

Data Link Layer (OSI) - Layer 2 of the OSIRM. Provides for error-free communication between adjacent network devices over a physical interface. Examples include the LLC and MAC layers, which manage LAN and MAN operation.

Data Terminal Equipment (DTE) - As defined by the standards, data processing equipment interfacing to the communications network (DCE).

D channel - The ISDN out-of-band (16 kbps or 64 kbps, depending on BRI or PRI, respectively) signaling channel which carries the ISDN user signals or can be used to carry packet-mode data.

default slot generator function - In DQDB, the function defining the identity for each bus in the dual bus network. In the looped bus topology, this function also provides the head of bus function for both buses.

delay-insensitive - *See* time- insensitive.

delay-sensitive - *See* time-sensitive.

Derived MAC Protocol Data Unit (MAC-PDU or DMPDU) - In DQDB, a single 44-octet portion of the original IMPDU, composed of 4 overhead octets and a 44-octet segmentation unit.

digital - Signals that have discrete values, such as binary bit streams of 0s and 1s.

Digital Cross-Connect System (DXC) - System that breaks down a T1 into individual DS0s for testing and reconfiguration.

Digital Signal 0 (DS0) - One 56-kbps framed channel out of the 24 contained in a DS1 channel.

Digital Signal 1 (DS1) - The North American standard 1.544-Mbps digital channel.

Digital Signal 3 (DS3) - The North American standard 44.736-Mbps digital channel.

Discard Eligibility (DE) bit - Used in frame relay, this bit signals (when set to 1) that the particular frame is eligible for discard during congestion conditions.

distributed processing - Sharing of applications, data, and tasks among several small or midrange processing devices, as opposed to a single mainframe in centralized processing.

distributed queue - The operation of the DQDB queued arbitration MAC scheme, in which all nodes keep track of the number of stations queued for access in their request counter; when a station queues itself for access, it keeps track of its position in the queue using its countdown counter and counts the number of stations behind it in the queue in the request counter.

Distributed Queue Dual Bus (DQDB) - The IEEE 802.6 MAN architecture standard for providing both circuit-switched (isochronous) and packet-switched services.

DQDB layer - The lower portion of the DQDB link layer which provides the connectionless MAC data service, connection-oriented data service, and an isochronous service with the help of physical-layer services.

dual-attachment station (DAS) - A workstation that attaches to both primary and secondary FDDI MAN rings which enables the capability for network self-healing.

dual bus - Bus A and bus B, in the DQDB bus structure. The dual bus supports both the open dual bus and the looped dual bus.

E1 - The European T1 CEPT standard digital channel operating at 2.048 Mbps.

E1 carrier - Part of the European and Asian (excluding Japan) digital TDM hierarchy: a single multiplexed 2.048-Mbps channel.

E.164 - A CCITT recommendation for defining addresses in a public data international network, varying in size up to 15 digits (carried as 60-bit addresses in DQDB).

empty slot - In DQDB, a queued arbitrated slot not currently in use that may be seized by a node queried for QA access.

enterprise network - A network that spans an entire organization.

entity - In the OSIRM, a service or management element between peers and within a sublayer or layer.

Ethernet - A LAN that uses the CSAM/CD media access method and operates at 10 Mbps, usually over coax medium.

Explicit Congestion Notification (ECN) - In frame relay, the use of either FECN and BECN or CLLM messages to notify the source and destination of network congestion (as opposed to implicit congestion notification).

fast packet - The generic term used for advanced packet technologies such as frame relay, DQDB, and ATM.

FastPacket - StrataCom Corporation's trademark for its proprietary switching technique, which uses 192-bit packets and packetized voice.

FDDI-II - FDDI standard with the additional capability to carry isochronous traffic (voice/video).

FDDI Follow-On (FDDI-FO) - Future ANSI standards for extending the speed of FDDI up to 600 Mbps.

Fiber Distributed Data Interface (FDDI) - Fiber-optic LAN operating at 100 Mbps.

fiber optics - Plastic or glass fibers over which optical signals transmit data at high rates.

filtering - The selection of frames not to remain at the local LAN but to be forwarded to another network by a network device (e.g., router).

flag - Character that signals a beginning or end of a frame.

Forward Explicit Congestion Notification (FECN) - Convention in frame relay for a network device to notify the user (destination) device that network congestion is occurring.

Fractional T1 (FT1) - The transmission of a fraction of a T1 channel, usually based on 64-kbps increments but not less than 64 kbps total.

frame - An OSI Data Link Layer unit of transmission whose length is defined by flags at the beginning and end.

Frame Check Sequence (FCS) - A field in an X.25, SDLC, or HDLC frame which contains the result of a CRC error-checking algorithm.

frame relay - An ANSI and CCITT LAN/WAN networking standard for switching frames in a packet mode similar to X.25, but at higher speeds and with less nodal processing (assuming digital transmission).

Frame Relay Assembler/Disassembler (FRAD) - A device which acts as a concentrator and protocol translator from non-frame relay protocols (e.g., SDLC, SNA) to a standard frame relay transmission.

Frequency Division Multiplexing (FDM) - The method of aggregating multiple simultaneous transmissions (circuits) over a single high-speed channel by using individual frequency passbands for each circuit (for example, RF broadband LANs).

full duplex - The simultaneous bidirectional transmission of information over a common medium.

gateway - A network device that interconnects dissimilar types of network elements through all seven layers of the OSIRM.

global addressing - A frame relay addressing convention in which a single, unique DLCI value is given to each user device on the network.

half duplex - The bidirectional transmission of information over a common medium, but where information may only travel in one direction at any one time.

head of bus (HOB_A and HOB_B) - In DQDB, the node responsible for generating empty slots and management information octets.

host - An end-communicating station in a network; also an IP address.

implicit congestion notification - A congestion indication which is performed by upper-layer protocols (e.g., TCP) rather than network or data link layer protocol conventions.

individual address - The address of a specific network station or node. In IP, the format is XXXX.XXXX.XXXX.XXXX.

Initial MAC Protocol Data Unit (IMPDU) - In DQDB, the PDU formed by the DQDB layer providing a connectionless MAC service to the LLC.

Integrated Services Digital Network (ISDN) - CCITT I-series recommendation defining the digital network standard for integrated voice and data network access and services and user-network messages.

integrated switching - The method of performing multiple switching techniques with one device or within a single hardware architecture, including consolidated configuration and network management.

Interexchange Carrier (IXC) - A provider of long distance (inter-LATA) service in the United States; also the provider of worldwide switched voice and data services.

interface - In OSI, the boundary between two adjacent protocol layers (i.e., network to transport).

Interim Local Management Interface (ILMI) - An SNMP-based management protocol for an ATM UNI defined by the ATM Forum.

internetwork - A master network made up of multiple smaller networks, or the concept of bridging, routing, switching, or gateways between homogeneous network devices, protocols, and standards.

interoperability - The ability of multiple, dissimilar vendor devices and protocols to operate and communicate using a standard set of rules and protocols.

intra-LATA - Within LEC-defined geographic areas (Local Access Transport Areas). An LEC must pass cells to an IXC to go inter-LATA.

isochronous - The circuit-switched transmission service offered in DQDB and FDDI-II. This allows a consistent timed access of network bandwidth for time-sensitive transmission of voice and video traffic.

latency - The minimum amount of time it takes for a token to circulate around the LAN Token Ring or FDDI ring in the absence of a data transmission.

layer management - Network management functions which provide information about the operations of a given OSI protocol layer.

Layer Management Entity (LME) - In DQDB, the entity within the protocol layer responsible for performing local management of the layer.

Layer Management Interface (LMI) - In DQDB, the interface between the LME and network management systems.

Line-Terminating Equipment (LTE) - A device which either originates or terminates an OC-N signal and which may originate, access, modify, and terminate the transport overhead.

Link Access Protocol on the D channel (LAPD) - CCITT Recommendations Q.920 (I.440) and Q.921 (I.441) defining standards for the data link layer operation of ISDN D and frame relay channels.

Local Area Network (LAN) - A MAC-level data and computer communications network confined to short geographic distances.

local bridge - A high-throughput, collocated LAN-to-LAN interconnectivity device.

Local Exchange Carrier (LEC) - In the United States, traditionally a local phone service provider, now can compete in inter-LATA service.

Local Management Interface (LMI) - A set of user device–to–network communications standards used in ATM DXI and frame relay.

Logical Link Control (LLC) - The upper half of the OSIRM Data Link Layer, layer 2, as defined by the IEEE 802.2 standard. This layer provides a common LAN platform for all IEEE 802.X protocols.

logical ring - The circular closed set of point-to-point links among network stations on a Token Ring and FDDI network.

looped dual bus - A DQDB bus configuration in which the head of bus functions for both A and B buses are contained within the same node.

MAN Switching System (SS) - A single metropolitan area network composed of many MAN switches, usually linked by a common DQDB bus.

media - The plural form of medium, or more than one medium (twisted-pair wire, coaxial cable, fiber, etc.).

medium - The single common access platform, such as a copper wire, fiber, or free space.

Medium Access Control (MAC) - IEEE 802 protocol defining medium-specific access control.

Message Identifier (MID) - In DQDB, a value used to identify all DMPDUs that together make up the same IMPDU.

Metropolitan Area Network (MAN) - A MAC-level data and computer communications network which operates over metropolitan or campus areas; the term recently has been expanded to include nationwide and even worldwide connectivity of high-speed data networks. A MAN can carry voice, video, and data, and has been defined as both the DQDB and FDDI standards set.

multicast - A connection type with the capability to broadcast to multiple destinations on the network.

Multimode Fiber (MMF) - 50- to 100-µm core diameter optical fiber with many propagation paths for light, typically used for lower speed or shorter distances (as compared to single-mode optical fiber).

multiplexing - The technique of combining multiple single channels onto a single aggregate channel for sharing facilities and bandwidth.

network - A system of autonomous devices, links, and subsystems which provide a platform for communications.

Network Layer (OSI) - Layer 3 of the OSIRM. Provides the end-to-end routing and switching of data units (packets), as well as managing congestion control.

network management - The process of managing the operation and status of network resources (e.g., devices, protocols).

node - A device that interfaces with the transmission medium through the Physical Layer (and often the Data Link Layer) of the OSIRM. This device is sometimes called an access unit in DQDB.

octet - An 8-bit transmission unit of measure.

open dual bus - In DQDB, a non-fault-tolerant subnetwork configuration where the head of bus functions for bus A and bus B are in different nodes (this can also be the configuration after a failure and subsequent network self-healing).

Open Systems Interconnection Reference Model (OSIRM) - A seven-layer model defining the international protocol standards for data communications in a multiple architecture and vendor environment. Both the OSI and CCITT define standards based on the OSIRM.

Optical Carrier level N (OC-N) - The optical carrier level signal in SONET which results from an STS-N signal conversion. In SONET, the basic transmission speed unit is 58.34 Mbps.

Packet Assembler/Disassembler (PAD) - A concentration and network access device which provides protocol conversion into X.25 packet format.

packet switching - A method of switching that segments the data into fixed or variable units of maximum size called packets. These packets then pass the user information (addressing, sequencing, error control, and user-controlled options) in a store-and-forward manner across the network.

Packet Switch Public Data Network (PSPDN) - A public data network utilizing packet switching technology (X.25, SMDS, ATM).

packet type - Identifies the type of packet and its use, such as for user data, call establishment and termination, and routing information.

Path Overhead (POH) - Overhead transported with the SONET payload and used for payload transport functions.

payload pointer - Indicates the starting point of a SONET synchronous payload envelope.

Permanent Virtual Circuit (PVC) - A logical dedicated circuit between two user ports in a point-to-point configuration.

Physical Layer (OSI) - Layer 1 of the OSIRM. Provides the electrical and mechanical interface and signaling of bits over the communications medium.

Physical Layer Convergence Protocol (PLCP) - The IEEE 802.6 standard defining the physical layer that adapts the actual capabilities of the underlying physical network to provide the services required by the DQDB or ATM layer.

Physical Layer Medium Dependent (PMD) - In FDDI, the medium-specific layer corresponding to the lower sublayer of the OSIRM Physical Layer.

Physical Layer Protocol (PHY) - In FDDI, the medium-independent layer corresponding to the upper sublayer of the OSIRM Physical Layer.

Plastic Optical Fiber (POF) - A low-cost, short-distance plastic alternative to glass fiber.

Presentation Layer (OSI) - Layer 6 of the OSIRM. Identifies the syntax of the user data being transmitted and provides user service functions such as encryption, file-transfer protocols, and terminal emulation.

Primary Rate Interface (PRI) - An ISDN T1 access interface type comprising 23 B channels, each at 64 kbps, and one D channel at 64 kbps (23B+D). The European version will operate at 2.048 Mbps (30B+D).

primary ring - The main ring for PDU transmission in FDDI, and the only attachment for SAS FDDI stations.

private (automatic) branch exchange (PBX/PABX) - An (automatic) customer-site telephone switch, with some capability to integrate data.

private network - A network providing interorganizational connectivity only.

protocol - The rules and guidelines by which information is exchanged and understood between two devices.

Protocol Data Unit (PDU) - The unit of information transferred between communicating peer-layer processes.

Public Data Network (PDN) - A network designed to provide data transmission value-added services to the public.

queued arbitrated access - In DQDB, a scheme by which packet-data users contend for access to the bus by queuing their requests; since all of the nodes know the length of the queue and their position in the queue, the access scheme is referred to as distributed queue.

Regional Bell Operating (or Holding) Company (RBOC or RBHC) - One of the seven U.S. regional holding companies formed after the divestiture of AT&T (e.g., Ameritech, Southwestern Bell). The RBOCs also manage the 22 BOCs.

remote bridge - A high-throughput bridge which provides remote LAN-WAN connectivity.

ring - A closed-loop, common bus network topology.

router - A LAN/WAN device operating at layers 1 (Physical), 2 (Data Link), and 3 (Network) of the OSIRM. Distinguished from a bridge by its capability to switch and route data based upon network protocols such as IP.

secondary ring - In FDDI, the ring that carries data in the opposite direction from the primary ring; primarily used for backup to the primary ring.

section - A transmission facility between a SONET network element and regenerator.

segment - In DQDB, the payload (user data) portion of the slot.

segmentation unit - The 44-octet unit of data transfer in DQDB.

self-healing - The ability for a LAN/MAN to reroute traffic around a failed link or network element to provide uninterrupted service.

service - The relationship between protocol entities in the OSIRM, where the service provider (lower-layer protocol) and the service user (higher-layer protocol) communicate through a *data service*.

Service Access Point (SAP) - The point at a network node or station where the service users access the services offered by the service providers.

Service Data Unit (SDU) - A unit of information transferred across the OSI interface between service provider and service user.

Session Layer (OSI) - Layer 5 of the OSIRM. Provides the establishment and control of user dialogues between adjacent network devices.

Shielded Twisted Pair (STP) - A twisted-pair wire with jacket shielding, used for long distances and less subject to electrical noise and interference than UTP.

simplex - One-way transmission of information on a medium.

Single-Attachment Stations (SAS) - In FDDI, stations which are attached only to a single ring (primary ring).

Single-Mode Fiber (SMF) - 8- to 10-μm core diameter optical fiber with a single propagation path for light; typically used for higher speeds or longer distances (as compared to multimode optical fiber).

slot - The basic unit of transmission on a DQDB bus.

SMDS Interface Protocol (SIP) - The three layers of protocol (similar to the first three layers of the OSIRM) which define the SMDS SNI user information frame structuring, addressing, error control, and overall transport.

SNA - IBM's communications networking architecture.

source routing - A routing scheme in which the routing of packets is determined by the source address and route to the destination in the packet header.

station - An addressable logical or physical network entity, capable of transmitting, receiving, or repeating information.

Station Management (SMT) - FDDI station management entity.

subnetwork - A smaller unit of a LAN (called a LAN segment) which can be more easily managed than the entire LAN/MAN/WAN.

Subscriber-Network Interface (SNI) - A DQDB user access point into the network or MAN switch.

Switched Multimegabit Data Service (SMDS) - A MAN service offered at present over the IEEE DQDB bus.

Switched Virtual Circuit (SVC) - A virtual circuit similar to a PVC, but established on a call-by-call basis.

Synchronous Digital Hierarchy (SDH) - The CCITT original version of a synchronous digital hierarchy based on optical fiber; called SONET in ANSI parlance.

Synchronous Optical Network (SONET) - A U.S. high-speed, fiber-optic transport standard for a fiber-optic digital hierarchy (speeds range from 51.84 Mbps to 2.4 Gbps).

Synchronous Transfer Mode (STM) - The T1 carrier method of assigning time slots as channels within a T1 or E1 circuit.

synchronous transmission - The transmission of frames which are managed through a common clock between transmitter and receiver.

Synchronous Transport Module Level N (STM-N) -The SDH line rate of N STM-1 signals.

Synchronous Transport Signal Level N (STS-N) - SONET transmission signal created with byte interleaving of N STS-1 (51.84 Mbps) signals.

Synchronous Transport Signal Level Nc (STS-Nc) - Concatenated SONET synchronous payload envelope.

T1 - A four-wire repeater system; commonly used to refer to a DS1 signal.

T1 carrier - The TDM digital T1 hierarchy used in North America and Japan, with 24 voice channels constituting a single 1.544-Mbps T1 trunk.

T3 - Commonly used to refer to a DS3 signal.

telecommunications - The transmission of voice, video, data, and images through the use of both computers and a communications medium.

Time-Division Multiplexing (TDM) - The method of aggregating multiple simultaneous transmissions (circuits) over a single high-speed channel by using individual time slots (periods) for each circuit.

time-insensitive - Traffic types whose data is not affected by small delays during transmission. This is also referred to as delay-insensitive.

time-sensitive - Traffic types whose data is affected by small delays during transmission and cannot tolerate this delay (e.g., voice, video, real-time data).

token - A marker indicating the station's right to transmit that can be held by a station on a Token Ring or bus.

Token Ring - A LAN that uses a token-passing access method for bus access and traffic transport between network elements, where bus speeds operate at either 4 or 16 Mbps.

Transmission Control Protocol/Internet Protocol (TCP/IP) - The combination of a network and transport protocol developed by ARPANET for internetworking IP-based networks.

Transport Layer (OSI) - Layer 4 of the OSIRM. Provides for error-free, end-to-end communications between two "host" users across a network.

transport overhead - In SONET, the line and section overhead elements combined.

twisted pair - The basic transmission medium, consisting of 22 to 26 American Wire Gauge (AWG) insulated copper wire. TP can be either shielded (STP) or unshielded (UTP).

Unshielded Twisted Pair (UTP) - A twisted-pair wire without jacket shielding, used for short distances but subject to electrical noise and interference.

user channel - Portion of the SONET channel allocated to the user for maintenance functions.

User-to-Network Interface (UNI) - The point at which the user accesses the network.

user-to-user protocols - Protocols that operate between users and are typically transparent to the network, such as file transfer protocols (e.g., FTP).

Virtual Channel Identifier (VCI) - In DQDB, a field within the segment header which determines whether a node is to read, write, or copy the segment payload. In ATM, a field within the cell header that is used to switch virtual channels.

virtual circuit - A virtual connection established through the network from origination to destination, where packets, frames, or cells are routed over the same path for the duration of the call. These connections seem like dedicated paths to the users, but are actually network resources shared by all users. Bandwidth on a virtual circuit is not allocated until it is used.

Virtual Path Identifier (VPI) - In ATM, a field within the cell header that is used to switch virtual paths, defined as groups of virtual channels.

Virtual Tributary (VT) - An element that transports and switches sub-STS-1 payloads or VTx (VT1.5, VT2, VT3, or VT6).

Wide Area Network (WAN) - A network that operates over a large region and commonly uses carrier facilities and services.

window - The concept of establishing an optimum number of frames or packets that can be outstanding (unacknowledged) before more are transmitted. Window protocols include X.25, LAP, TCP/IP, and SDLC.

X.25 - CCITT recommendation of the interface between packet-switched DTE and DCE equipment.

Index

DS3 64, 616 121, 90

ABOUT THE AUTHORS

DAVID E. MCDYSAN is Director of Strategic Planning of ATM Services at MCI. He has been an active ATM Forum board member and technical committee chairperson. Recognized as a leader in ATM traffic management, McDysan is a frequent speaker and teacher at industry conferences. He lives in Richardson, Texas.

DARREN L. SPOHN is Chief Technology Officer of NetSolve Inc., where he manages the company's engineering, product development, and business development efforts. Previously he worked at MCI, where he held a number of critical engineering, marketing, and management positions in the development of advanced data networks. He lives in Austin, Texas.